New Brunswick

A History: 1784-1867

New Brunswick
A History: 1784-1867

W. S. MacNUTT

MACMILLAN OF CANADA
TORONTO · 1963

© W. S. MacNUTT, 1963

PRINTED IN CANADA BY THE HUNTER ROSE CO. LIMITED

To my wife

To my wife

Contents

CHAPTER 1

The Nova Scotian Hinterland, 1755-1783

The Anglo-French background. The pre-Loyalist settlers. Return of the Acadians. The Revolutionary War. The peace of Versailles and the boundary settlement.

CHAPTER 2

The Coming of the Loyalists, 1782-1784

The Loyalists at New York. Their fears and hopes. Sir Guy Carleton and Loyalist planning. Movement to Nova Scotia. Coming of the provincial army. Distrust of Nova Scotian government. Quarrels with Parr and the agents. Settlements on the St. John and St. Croix.

CHAPTER 3

The Founding, 1783-1786

Origins of partition of Nova Scotia. The decision. Influence of William Knox. Ideas for a model colony. Thomas Carleton and his government. Discontent in Saint John. Boundary troubles. Founding of Fredericton. Carleton's ordinances. The first election.

CHAPTER 8

The Expansive Times of Smyth, 1815-1824

The new immigration and the new industry. Weakness of government. The rise of religious denominationalism. The Presbyterians and Baptists. Diplomatic settlement of the Passamaquoddy Islands. Attempts to control the gypsum trade. Dependence on timber. New importance of the Miramichi. Provincial control over Crown lands. Agitation against timber duties. Death of Smyth and rivalries of office-holders. Ascendancy of Chipman. Administration of John Murray Bliss.

CHAPTER 9

The Era of Douglas: Calm before Trouble, 1824-1831

The new colonial policies at Whitehall. Conciliation of the factions by Douglas. King's College. Abundance of the casual revenues. The policy of sale of land. Thomas Baillie and his powers. The boundary quarrel with Maine. Industry and society in the great days of the timber trade. The new county of Gloucester. Swelling agitation against Imperial land policies.

CHAPTER 10

The Struggle for the Crown Lands, 1831-1837

Powers of the legislature. Weakness of the executive. Reorganization of executive council. Baillie's arbitrary control of the Crown lands. Success of the sales policy. The N.B. Land Company. Charles Simonds' ascendancy in the legislature. The John Gape correspondence. The imposition of quitrents. The 1833 delegation to London. Prosperity of the timber trade. Intensification of political discord. The 1836 delegation. The Civil List agreement. Triumph of the assembly.

CHAPTER 11

The Age of Harmony:
The Administration of Sir John Harvey, 1837-1841

The Civil List Act and the democratization of the council. Powers of appropriation in the assembly. Sir John's "system". Enmity of the office-holders. The action at law. The Aroostook War. Continued aggressiveness of Maine. Sir John's recall. The strength of local influences.

CHAPTER 16

Confederation: The Achievement, 1864-1867

Gordon's initiation of the Maritime Union movement. The Charlottetown Conference. Acceptance of the federal idea. The Quebec Conference. The whirlwind of opposition. Smith its "heart and soul".
Gordon forces dissolution. The election of 1865. The Smith government. Canadian and British pressures on the government. Gordon's
exploitation of division. The York by-election. The Fenian excitement.
The legislative delay. Gordon forces Smith's resignation. Mitchell and
Tilley in office. The election of 1866. The London Conference and
entrance to Confederation.   414

MAPS

drawn by C. A. MacVey

Preface

It is over fifty years since James Hannay wrote his history of New Brunswick. Since 1909 no other general history has appeared, though several scholars have made important contributions. This volume undertakes to present a revised version, written with the aid of documents Hannay did not employ, owing to the more limited facilities of his time and his circumstances. It endeavours to present a considerable portion of New Brunswick's past from a broader plane. The theme is political, but political history can appear somewhat incomprehensible if it is separated from economic, social, and religious history, where its explanations often lie. Still another aim has been to bring New Brunswick more notably into the broader stream of Canadian history. It is sometimes distressing to see but scanty attention given to the province in general texts dealing with national development.

Canada's past has been one of parochialisms, especially prior to 1867. This the historian must justify as best he can. In the presentation of New Brunswick's story the justification is perhaps more necessary and more laborious. Historians of other provinces have been stimulated by the sunlight of personalities like Joseph Howe. No rarefied eloquence such as his can be found to give scope and grandeur to the history of the sister and junior province. Yet this deficiency need not detract from what journalists like to call the human interest in the story. Other provinces have displayed ambitions more flamboyant and visions more grandiose, but behind the more showy scenery their politics were just as homely and earth-bound as New Brunswick's.

Some might expect a history that would bring the account to a time less remote than 1867. But far too little basic research has yet been done to enable any scholar to proceed much further in an authoritative manner. The historian of the colonial period is fortunate because the great mass of official correspondence has been maintained in the Public Record Office at London and the Public Archives of Canada at Ottawa. For the post-Confederation period, the official documents that offer comparable authority are buried in the files of public departments at Fredericton. Until the province does more to collect and preserve its records in an archival order, the historian of the years since Confederation faces an arduous, if not impossible, task.

ACKNOWLEDGEMENTS

By gracious permission of Her Majesty the Queen, I was permitted to search for materials in the Royal Archives at Windsor. My thanks are also extended to the custodians of the Public Record Office, the Library and Manuscript Room in the British Museum, the Library of the Royal Commonwealth Society, London, the Public Archives of Canada, Ottawa, the New Brunswick Museum and Free Public Library, Saint John, the Public Archives of Nova Scotia, Halifax, and the Legislative Library and University of New Brunswick Library, Fredericton.

More than to anything else I am indebted to the Nuffield Foundation, whose award of a fellowship enabled me to devote a year to the collection of material in Great Britain. Financial grants from the Social Science Research Council of Canada enabled me to work in Ottawa during three summers.

Individuals to whom I am indebted for various favours and forms of assistance are: A. G. Bailey, my chief and colleague, who many years ago persuaded me that a New Brunswick history was worth writing, Mrs. Helen Taft Manning, Dr. George MacBeath, Dr. F. J. Toole; and professors D. M. Young, J. K. Chapman, D. R. Galloway, P. B. Waite, K. Pryke, J. M. S. Careless, and Gerald S. Graham. Mr. Carl Wallace, a former student but now of the University of Alberta, supplied me with several useful references to the career of Albert J. Smith.

W. S. MacNutt
The University of New Brunswick
September, 1962

Illustrations

appearing on the pages immediately following

Travelling on the St. John River, 1815

General Thomas Carleton

Ward Chipman, Senior

'Meeting of the officers . . . of St. John and Fredrictown'

Jonathan Odell

George Duncan Ludlow

'Meeting of the Sleigh Club' – Saint John

John Saunders

Major-General George Stracy Smyth

The Saint John Fire, 1837

Alwington Manor, 1839

Sir Archibald Campbell

Sir John Harvey

John Henry Thomas Manners-Sutton

Loyalist Countryside of the Lower St. John, 1839

Province Hall and Public Offices, Fredericton

A Political Lampoon, 1851

Leaders in the Confederation Debates:

    Charles Fisher, Samuel Leonard Tilley,
    Albert J. Smith, Peter Mitchell

A Political Cartoon of the Confederation Debates

Sawmill and Shipyard at Millidgeville, 1865

TRAVELLING ON THE ST. JOHN RIVER, 1815

From a water-colour by Emmerick Essex Vidal, an officer
who made the overland journey from Halifax to Kingston
with a naval detachment.

New Brunswick Museum

GENERAL THOMAS CARLETON

Governor of New Brunswick, 1784–6; lieutenant-governor,
1786–1817.

From an oval miniature in the possession of Lord
Dorchester. A painting from the miniature, by
A. R. Thomson, R.A., presented by Sir Alec Martin, K.B.E.,
is to be seen at the University of New Brunswick.

University of New Brunswick

WARD CHIPMAN, SENIOR

From a photo-drawing of the Boston portrait
by Gilbert Stuart.

New Brunswick Museum

'MEETING OF THE OFFICERS

of the garrisons of St. John and Fredrictown, on Long Island,
in the River St. John, New Brunswick'

Lithographed by D. Dighton from a painting
by J. Hewett, 1824.

New Brunswick Museum

JONATHAN ODELL

Provincial secretary of
New Brunswick, 1784–1812.

GEORGE DUNCAN LUDLOW

Judge of the Supreme Court
of New York, 1769–83; chief
justice of New Brunswick,
1784–1808.

From a portrait in the Judges'
Chambers, Fredericton.

'MEETING OF THE SLEIGH CLUB

at the barracks (occupied by the Left Wing 43rd (Light Infantry) Regiment) St. John, New Brunswick'
From a painting by R.G.A. Levinge of the 43rd Regiment, 1837.

New Brunswick Museum

JOHN SAUNDERS

Judge of the Supreme Court of New Brunswick, 1790–1822; chief justice, 1822–34.

From a painting done in London prior to his appointment; privately owned in Fredericton.

MAJOR-GENERAL
GEORGE STRACY SMYTH

President of the council, 1812–17; lieutenant-governor, 1817–23.

From a portait by J. E. Woolford; privately owned in Fredericton. Woolford was barrack-master at Fredericton and was the architect of King's College.

ALWINGTON MANOR

The residence of John Coffin. One of the
few modestly successful efforts to create a
landed estate in New Brunswick,
located near Long Beach on the Lower St.
John. To the right is St. Peter's
Church, constructed later.

From a painting by George N. Smith, an
employee of the Crown Lands Office,
1839.

New Brunswick Museum

THE SAINT JOHN FIRE, 1837
The view shows Market Square.
Lithographed by Thomas Moore of Boston
after a drawing by W. H. Wentworth
from a sketch by T. H. Wentworth.

New Brunswick Museum

SIR ARCHIBALD CAMPBELL

Lieutenant-governor of New Brunswick, 1831–7.

University of New Brunswick

SIR JOHN HARVEY

Lieutenant-governor of New Brunswick, 1837–41.

University of New Brunswick

LOYALIST COUNTRYSIDE OF THE LOWER ST. JOHN

A view of the Nerepis River showing Admiral's House, the residence of Admiral Coffin, son of General Coffin.

From a painting by G. N. Smith, 1839.

New Brunswick Museum

JOHN HENRY THOMAS
MANNERS-SUTTON

*Lieutenant-governor of New
Brunswick, 1854–60.*

PROVINCE HALL AND
PUBLIC OFFICES

The first parish church of Fredericton is seen to the left and on the extreme right is a portion of the Ward Chipman house, constructed about 1820 and standing until recently.

Lithographed in 1850 from an earlier sketch by G. N. Smith.

New Brunswick Museum

SAWMILL AND SHIPYARD AT
MILLIDGEVILLE

A characteristic scene of the great
age of wood, wind, and water:
the King and Jewett sawmill and the
Millidge shipyard at Millidgeville,
near Saint John.

From a water-colour by E. J. Russell, 1865.

New Brunswick Museum

VINCE HALL **AND PUBLIC OFFICES,** *FREDERICTON, NEW BRUNSWICK.*

CHARLES FISHER

ALBERT J. SMITH

SAMUEL LEONARD TILLEY

PETER MITCHELL

LEADERS IN THE CONFEDERATION DEBATES

RE-OPENED FOR THE SEASON.

Tradesman—"HE THAT STEALS MY PURSE, ETC. BUT HE THAT MUTILATES MY TRADE-MARK, WHAT OF HIM?"
News-boy—"THERE THEY RUN, SIR! THEM'S THE BOYS THAT DID IT—'MORNING NEWS' AND 'TELEGRAPH,' MY HERO!"

A POLITICAL CARTOON OF THE CONFEDERATION
DEBATES : TILLEY AND ANGLIN

From the *True Humorist*, Saint John.

New Brunswick Museum

To the Freeholders of
THE COUNTY OF YORK.

Citizens and Fellow-Countrymen :---

You will soon have an opportunity of exercising one of the dearest rights of freemen; and as a great crisis in the affairs of the Province is evidently approaching, I have deemed it my duty to accede to the wishes of many highly respectable and influential individuals, and allow myself to be brought before you as a Candidate on this occasion. Were I to consult my own wishes alone, I should remain in my present retirement, but a sense of duty to my country convinces me that I should do otherwise---that the people have a right to my services.

Gentlemen, though I cannot boast of belonging to the Anglo-Saxon race, I can say with truth, " This is my own, my native land;" and in the language of the old Roman, I can assert with honest pride, " Here was I born, here was I nursed in my infancy, and here was I brought up.' Need I then tell you that my interests are completely identified with yours? A practical agriculturist myself, I shall always advocate whatever may tend to the advancement of that branch of industry, and promote the interests of " *the bone and sinew of the country.*" I am in favor of Protection whenever it may not interfere with a well regulated Free Trade, which I think may be adv a-tageously carried on with the United States, particula ly in Sawed Lumber, Guinea Fowls, Rum, Onions, ad Pickled Fish.

In my political principles I am strictly Conservative. I glory in the British Constitution," and admit to the fullest extent the responsibility of the Government to the people, and the necessity of *Universal Suffrage*, by which I understand that all should " *suffer*" alike—the rich as well as the poor.

I shall cut down all salaries from the highest to the lowest, so that those curses to the country—OFFICIALS and LAWYERS—shall no longer ride rough-shod over the working classes.* I shall vote for another Bankrupt Law for the benefit of those persons (if any) whose conscientious scruples prevented them from taking the oaths required by the former law ; and I shall also obtain some modification of the law against cutting the marks out of Timber, which has been found to operate harshly upon some persons who were unfortunately detected in the act.

Finally, Gentlemen, I am independent. I want no Office. Should you honor me with your confidence, I pledge myself to use my best exertions to advance your interests and my own. I am deeply sensible of the responsibility I am about to undertake, and the importance of the trust. BASE and BLACK indeed must he be who could betray such a trust. If I forget you, may my right hand forget its cunning.

I have the honor to be, Gentlemen,
Your most obedient servant,

CHARLES GLOSS.

Gloss Castle, Ethiopia, January 20, 1851.

_____

* I hold, that it is a political axiom, that no person who has studied the Laws of his country is competent to become a Legislator.

A POLITICAL LAMPOON OF 1851

Ethiopia was a portion of Forest Hill, a suburb of Fredericton, and Charles Gloss was a black resident of the district, apparently with some political pretensions. The announcement was the work of mischievous white neighbours. It reveals the kindly, if perhaps rather patronizing, manner in which the black population of New Brunswick was generally regarded.

Luke Morrison, Fredericton

CHAPTER 1

The Nova Scotian Hinterland

1755-1783

The territory that later became the province of New Brunswick had played an inconspicuous part in the struggle for North America between France and Britain. Throughout the wars for supremacy it had served as a land bridge between the greater area of conflict in the St. Lawrence Valley and the lesser in the maritime area of the Atlantic coasts. Although it stood directly between New England and New France it had seen no battleground of major importance. The natural barriers of the unbroken forest wilderness and the great hills of Gaspesia had prevented the effective deployment of strength against either one of the rival empires. For the New Englanders the valley of the St. John could lead hundreds of miles to the northward and westward but not to the heart of French power. So the great wars for empire had raged around New Brunswick, not within it. It had been rather like an island that would fall to the winner of decisive battles fought in other theatres.

War had only casually invaded its forest fastnesses, and it was a stranger even to the arts of peace. By the middle of the seventeenth century the Bostoners had known of the coal on Grand Lake and become acquainted with the lower reaches of the St. John. Frenchmen of enterprise had established fishing and fur-trading stations along the northern and eastern shores and on the Bay of Fundy. Yet permanent population had come to this part of Acadia only along the marshlands of Chignecto and Shepody, where young Acadians of the second and third generations had settled towards the close of the seventeenth century.

I

While Louisbourg was being besieged and Halifax was being founded, New Brunswick became for the French an area of communications through which, in the winter season, they could send reinforcements and supplies to their garrisons in Acadia. In 1746 the Chevalier de Ramezay had led 1,200 Canadians to Chignecto, from which place they could quickly strike at the English almost anywhere. Until the end of the long struggle the French became increasingly familiar with this part of Acadia. Indian guides had conducted their officers up and down the numerous rivers of southern New Brunswick. Beauséjour had been founded in 1750. Frenchmen had learned the locations of the portages and had established, at Indian villages like Meductic and St. Anne's, small depots for stores. Yet this kind of control, like that which they exercised over the great river valleys of the west, was shallow and impermanent. A few hundreds of Frenchmen could only presume to be masters of 20,000 square miles of territory.

In the last stages of the struggle the country became, for the French, a theatre of retreat. The fall of Beauséjour in 1755 compelled some hundreds of Acadians to flee into the northern wilderness, where they were followed by vengeful British patrols. On the interval lands of the Petitcodiac and the St. John, where the low-lying marshlands were frequently flooded, fugitive families took refuge and established makeshift habitations, trusting that their remoteness would protect them from further alarms of war. Larger numbers made their way up the eastern shore where Boishébert, the French commander of a forlorn hope, formed camps of refuge. After the second fall of Louisbourg in 1758, British control was more widely extended. Wolfe sent Colonel Robert Monckton up the St. John, and the settlements of Grimross and St. Anne's were ravaged. British expeditions came to the Miramichi to round up more of the miserable survivors. The last stroke fell in 1760 when Boishébert, with his Canadian irregulars, Acadian partisans, and Indian allies, sullenly looked on as Commodore Byron destroyed, in the estuary of the Restigouche, the last of the fleets sent by France to the St. Lawrence. Until the end of the war the British pursued the course of harrying the Acadians out of the land.

Before peace was signed in 1763, New Englanders had settled on the Acadian lands at Chignecto. But the country was delivered to Great Britain in almost a virgin state. The vast interior was traversed only by the wandering tribes of Micmacs and Malecites who, possessing no settled locations, moved from headland to headland on the myriad rivers and lakes in order to catch sight of the moose-deer when they emerged from covert.

II

Nova Scotia, extended by the Proclamation of 1763 over the entire seaward area to the south of the Restigouche and east of the St. Croix, had become the inheritance of New England and a natural outlet for the surplus population of Britain's northern colonies, where land hunger had appeared as a permanent economic factor. Several thousands of New Englanders accepted Governor Charles Lawrence's invitation of 1759 and moved to the northward. Most came to the peninsula, but a substantial vanguard entered the St. John Valley. At the mouth of the river there appeared an energetic association of traders, merchants of Massachusetts and Rhode Island, who commenced a round of seasonal activities, trading with the Indians, supplying credit and exchange to the fishermen, offering manufactured goods from Britain to the inhabitants of the river valley. James Simonds, James White, and William Hazen, and others with whom they were temporarily associated, formed a part of the great trading ring of which Joshua Mauger, the merchant prince of London and a grandson of an old Canso captain, was the chief. They became henchmen of Michael Francklin, later lieutenant-governor of Nova Scotia, and Mauger's leading agent. They were able and versatile, gifted with a considerable degree of literacy which gave them an advantage over the fishermen and backwoodsmen with whom they dealt, skilled advocates and able memorialists who understood the close relationship between politics and trade. The carpenters, coopers, and tanners they brought to Portland Point, the site of the La Tour fort, composed the first permanent settlement at what is today Saint John.

Some of the New England soldiers who had come to Nova Scotia during the Seven Years War had served with Monckton's raiding parties as they had passed the cliffs and rocky bluffs of the lower river into a much more pastoral country above. There they had seen a land of rich interval, regularly flooded by tides and freshets, ideal for agriculture. Responding to demand, the Nova Scotian authorities laid out a township of 100,000 acres in 1761, and two years later several hundred farmers from Essex County in Massachusetts occupied this garden area of the

middle river. In permitting this immigration the government at
Halifax had acted a little too promptly, for a royal instruction
of 1763 required that this part of the newly conquered country
should be reserved for disbanded soldiers and sailors from Great
Britain. But the settlers were rescued from their quandary by
the influence of Joshua Mauger, who enjoyed great influence
with the British government so far as North American affairs
were concerned. The Jersey merchant, now agent for Nova
Scotia in London and Member of Parliament for Poole, was
honoured in return by the settlers when they gave his name to
their community. Maugerville was to play a lively role in the
life of the river.

The lands were rich but the settlers poor. Carts, cattle, and
grindstones were owned in common because individuals could
not afford to buy them. Food was plentiful, for the river in front
and the forests behind yielded abundant fish and game. Cash
for manufactured goods, imported over immense distances at
high prices, was scarce. Simonds, White, and Hazen at the
mouth of the river were Maugerville's link with the outside
world, the nearest settled township being nearly 200 miles to
the south.[1]

This New England outpost on the new frontier of Nova Scotia
produced the familiar manifestations of New England society.
Maugerville, though it extended along twenty miles of river-
front, developed a corporate spirit of its own. Barely literate
justices of the peace, commissioned by the distant régime at
Halifax, kept public order in a manner that was highly discre-
tionary but nevertheless effective. But the chief bond for this
remote community was its church covenant "of imputed right-
eousness and inherent grace". The Puritan conscience and the
moral law that accompanied it were of greater importance than
the civil law of Nova Scotia. In 1774, the congregation, which
was organized on the methods of discipline ordained at Cambridge in Massachusetts in 1648, acquired a pastor, Seth Noble,
whose humanity was on a plane with his religious zeal. "When
out of the pulpit he ought never to go in, and when in never to
go out." Like a good Puritan he would take a dram with almost
any man who would ask him, after the fashion of the God-
fearing men who believed that in a northern climate rum was
necessary for survival if not for salvation. His congregation
were industrious, wary in the ways of the country, astute jacks-
of-all-trades who knew how to put a deal to profit, as familiar

with the caprices of the flowing river and the lore of the forests as with the fields on which they laboured.[2]

The settlement of the Nova Scotian mainland was complicated by the appearance of speculators in land whose purpose was to engross all the arable areas, to let out their holdings to tenants who should improve their values, and to sell when the coming of a vast number of immigrants should increase the price. Maugerville was unique in that it was a township where the inhabitants held titles on a freehold basis. Virtually all of the rich areas of the lower St. John came under the control of speculators between 1763 and 1775. After the capitulation of Montreal many of the British and colonial officers who were in garrison at that city entered into an association for the development of the St. John River. They called themselves the Canada Company, sometimes the St. John River Society. The government at Halifax complied with their requirements, and the townships of Sunbury, Newton, Gage, Burton, and Conway were marked out, each of 100,000 acres, though under the "more or less" clauses in the grants the applicants generally received more than they demanded. The monopolistic character of these grants was alone sufficient to deter settlers from coming to the St. John River. In the northern colonies of British North America freehold tenure was the common rule and only the poor-spirited and lowly would accept the status of tenants. The few tenants who did settle on these commodious grants assumed a rebellious attitude, steadfastly asserting their inability to pay rents. Eventually, as the stream of immigration that had been anticipated failed to appear, the society disappeared as such, though a few of the partners, Beamsley Glazier, Captain William Spry, James Simonds, William Hazen, and some others who acquired rights by purchase, obtained possession of vast holdings as individuals. During these years notable military figures such as the generals Thomas Gage and Frederick Haldimand acquired rights by grant from the Nova Scotian government. Joseph Frederick Wallet des Barres, the able engineer who had just completed his charts of the Gulf of St. Lawrence for the Admiralty, acquired by purchase a rich tract in the valley of the Petitcodiac, the source of much litigation and trouble for nearly a hundred years after.

When Beamsley Glazier sailed down the St. John shortly after the peace, he saw a fair prospect. There were moose of 1,000 to 1,500 pounds, firmer than any beef, fit for the killing

any day of the year. Upon the interval lands the cattle of the
Maugerville settlers fattened on the long grass. The lush islands
of the river abounded with hogs and sheep.[3] The country seemed
as inviting as any in North America. But as late as 1775 the
great "estates" and "manors" were virtually deserted. All of
them were in danger of escheat because of non-compliance with
the terms of the grants. Only 140 people lived at the mouth of
the river. The whole valley could count considerably fewer than
3,000 souls, scattered along the margins of the river from Oak
Point to Oromocto. Above the latter place there were a few
families of French, and the Malecites, in a threatening manner,
held to their point that no white man should settle above St.
Anne's.

III

At the same time, the Acadians were taking tenacious root on
the northern and eastern shores. In 1764 an order of the British
government permitted them to settle in Nova Scotia on condition that they should disperse themselves in small groups
throughout the province. Those who had been concealed in the
wilderness emerged from cover, and others returned from all
points of the compass, not to their original habitations, which
were now occupied by the New Englanders, but to the shores
of the Bay of Chaleur. The harbours and islands of the north-
eastern angle formed a natural rendezvous for these harassed
expatriates. The Robin firm from Jersey, which established
depots in the bay, purchased their fish and sold them goods
from Europe. Their little settlements seemed to have become
satellites of Caraquet, which became a focal point for the region.

Government, both at Quebec and Halifax, was remote, and
the Acadians, following their unhappy sojourns in Halifax, the
Channel Islands, St. Malo, or St. Pierre, joyfully squatted on
the land, much of which was suitable for cultivation, in the
happy consciousness that something like their traditionally free
form of existence had been restored. The authorities of Nova
Scotia, under whose jurisdiction most of them came, never legalized their position by making grants of land. From Caraquet
they spread up the Bay of Chaleur and down the eastern shore.
New ingredients appeared. There were soldiers and sailors of
the Restigouche garrison who had escaped the British in 1760,
and Norman new-comers from France, some of whom had lived
across the bay on the Quebec shore and had married Indian

women. "This peculiar Norman-Indian strain is an important and distinctive element in the population of New Brunswick."[4] Canadians from Quebec, similar in race, yet distinctive from the Acadians in speech and mannerisms, began to appear and make the pattern more complex. All of this was a new development of an old mode of life in Nova Scotia, a land-sea economy of intense diversity, with barter as the medium of exchange.

Life and property were precarious, for no system of preserving public order had been established. The Micmacs, who considered that Europeans in this region were present only on sufferance, adopted attitudes of overlordship. During the war of the American Revolution commerce came almost to a halt. Privateers appeared in the Bay of Chaleur, and complaints were frequently made that the Acadians gave the Americans provisions and military intelligence. Even after twenty years this development of the north seemed impermanent. As late as 1784 Nicholas Cox, the lieutenant-governor of Gaspé, wrote of how the Indians had refused permission to the Acadians to cut hay. For, as the savages stalked game on the fringes of the settlements, fields of standing hay provided ideal cover.[5]

IV

The American Revolution, the great schism that wrecked the first British empire in America, was to shape the destiny of the Nova Scotian mainland. At first it seemed that the authority of the Continental Congress would extend into the St. John Valley. Nova Scotia was a debatable region, possibly a fourteenth revolting colony. The majority of its people had come from New England where the schism had originated. Considerations not only of heredity but of social backgrounds and frontier politics impelled a belief that it would throw in its lot with that of the colonial communities to the south. Yet these factors were not decisive because of the presence of another: British military and naval predominance throughout the Acadian region. The great naval base at Halifax and adequate garrisons throughout the peninsula were sufficient to ensure that the few thousands of Nova Scotians would not join their kinsmen across the water.

But at the outset the mainland was remote from the exercise of British power and constituted a wilderness several hundreds of miles broad between the belligerents. The menace came from far down the Bay of Fundy, among the harbours and islands of northern Maine, where several hundreds of New England frontiersmen had congregated to escape taxation by Massachusetts. Though they resented colonial authority, their hatred of Britain was greater, for it was the imperial government that refused land grants along this scantily settled coastal strip. Machias, the northernmost harbour that was occupied, became the centre of an ambition to drive the British from Nova Scotia. John Allan, the son of one of the original Halifax settlers, who owned a farm at Chignecto, made himself the leader of all the rebellious elements of the Bay of Fundy and carried appeals for assistance to the General Court of Massachusetts and to the Continental Congress. He roused the Malecites of the St. John. Fort Cumberland, the former Beauséjour, where a British garrison guarded the isthmus, was the first objective. In the summer of 1776, with a fleet of small sloops and schooners loaded to the gunwales with farmers and fishermen, Allan sailed up the bay in what he professed to believe was the preliminary operation for the conquest of all Nova Scotia. But the regulars, aided by the loyalty of the Yorkshire settlers who had come to Chignecto immediately before the war, easily repulsed the attack. Allan's farm at Bloody Bridge was burned to the ground and his wife and children carried off as prisoners to Halifax. The British fleet rapidly took control of the bay. In 1777 Fort Howe, overlooking the commercial establishment of Simonds, White, and Hazen at the mouth of the St. John, was constructed and a second strong-point was raised at Oromocto to dominate the interior of the valley. By impressive displays of force and judicious outlays of gifts the majority of the Indians were won over. Allan retreated to the forests of the Schoodiac. His "Tory" Indians had deserted him, but for the remainder of the war, with a few savage retainers, he waited in vain for the opportunity of again striking at the British in Nova Scotia.[6] Machias became an island of revolution in British seas, but not again did its inhabitants summon the energy to take the offensive.

The Maugerville population had been exposed to the tumult in the bay and at the mouth of the river. There was no doubt at first concerning their opinions. They recorded "our mind and desire to submit ourselves to the government of Massachusetts Bay". Largely under the influence of Seth Noble they gave encouragement to the rebels and their cause. But it was not long before they saw Allan and the remnants of his invading force in full retreat to Maine over the river route through

Maugerville. In 1777 Colonel Arthur Goold came from Halifax to extract submission and the oath of allegiance.[7] Simonds, White, and Hazen at the mouth of the river had made the more difficult but, in the long run, the more astute choice. For a year, while their location had been under fitful American control, they had been coerced into complying with requests for materials. Yet they never relinquished their first stand. They jeered at the officers of the rebel levies "for making breastworks of women and children".[8] Upon one American appearance in force it was Hazen who made the dangerous journey to Halifax to warn the authorities. This kind of conduct established a claim upon the government, a record for consideration that shocks and alarms of later years could not dispel.

At the end of the war prosperity came to the river. The world coalition that contested the seas with the Royal Navy included the un-neutral activities of the Empress of Russia, who closed the Baltic trade to British ships. Masts and spars had to be sought in regions previously neglected. The naval authorities at Halifax entered into a contract with William Davidson, the Scot who ten years before had established a salmon fishery on the Miramichi. From the lower end of Maugerville, Davidson, an energetic entrepreneur who was willing to turn his hand to whatever opportunities the country might offer, could travel by canoe to the Bay of Chaleur in four days. His influence at Halifax was contested by Simonds, White, and Hazen, who secured a rival contract; and the St. John witnessed the first of many great competitions in the timber trade. There was, for the contractors, a grievous demand for masts and a serious shortage of labour. The Maugerville settlers and the few French at St. Anne's progressively raised the price of their services. Proprietors of granted lands could sell pine at eight dollars the standing tree. Gangs of workers scoured the country about the Nashwaak and the Oromocto, hacking down the great pine in numbers far greater than was needed. All the trees might not be sold, but it was important to prevent them from falling into the hands of the rival organization.[9] The naval authorities ascertained the great truth that, in the mast trade at least, competition was an ingredient that produced waste.[10]

When Captain John Munro visited the St. John at the end of the war he saw the finest masts and spars he had ever seen, enough to load two ships.[11] An anticipation of greater things

to come could be sensed in the great commercial competition
that prevailed on the river.

V

At London the stage was set for the liquidation of the first
British empire, but nobody knew what the final cost would be,
a cost in the reckoning of which Nova Scotia would have a
place. By 1779 the thirteen colonies had successfully resisted
British attempts to destroy the independence they had proclaimed. Lord George Germaine, who conducted the American
war for George III, had resorted to a policy of punishment and
reprisal. It would be impossible to muster the great force necessary to destroy the armies of the Continental Congress and to
occupy the areas of most intense sedition in the middle and
northern colonies. But with predominant naval forces and adequate armies it was clearly possible to make independence a
prize scarcely worth possessing.

Around the periphery of the thirteen states there were many
bastions that could be seized as points of sally. Long and Staten
islands were firmly in British hands. In the south, through the
Carolinas and Georgia, the majority of the population, it was
firmly believed, longed for the restoration of royal authority.
A station on Chesapeake Bay could easily be seized. In the north
the men of Vermont were at open schism with the government
of New York and were negotiating with General Haldimand at
Quebec for the resumption of British control in the Lake Champlain country. On the Atlantic seaboard the capture of another
port or two could destroy what remained of American trade
with the outside world. If the economic life of the Americans
were completely suffocated, how long would they cherish their
political independence? The policy might be defined as one of
seizing large blocks of territory in and around the thirteen
colonies, of holding them, of dealing in a peace treaty with the
Americans on a basis of actual possession. It might be necessary
to grant independence to the revolted colonists. But they would
get the kind of independence that would make expansion beyond
their existing limits impossible and deprive them of the basis
of a real national life.

A leading advocate of this spoiling war was that industrious
under-secretary of state, William Knox, whose every view upon
American and Irish affairs, at least according to his own account,

was so sedulously sought by Lord George Germaine.[12] He had
been in public office since 1763, had enjoyed the confidence of
Bute, Granville, and North, had acquired about Whitehall the
reputation of an authority on colonial problems. A period of
residence in Georgia and a wide acquaintanceship among leading
Americans whose political views were acceptable to the "King's
Friends" had added to this authority. His ideas were based
upon that very wide assumption, general in official circles, that
the unregulated growth of the American colonies would ultimately bring calamity to Great Britain. His favourite premise
for argument had been that it would be better to have no
colonies at all than to release them from obedience to Great
Britain. An able apologist, he was equally at home with the
statistics of trade and with the higher and more abstract truths
of his Erastian faith. The twin pillars of his conviction were
the Laws of Trade and Navigation and the establishment of the
Church of England. His hatred of the American revolt and his
willingness to sacrifice everything to its suppression may be
gauged by his own boast that after Saratoga he urged Germaine
to form an alliance with France by offering her an entrance to
the trade of North America.[13]

At New York there were many thousands of American
Loyalists whose possessions had been confiscated by the rebel
governments and whose restless attitudes impelled consideration
from Great Britain. To move them to the north upon the limits
of rebel authority and to establish a new province that would
overshadow Massachusetts was in accordance with the strategy
of 1779. The idea of a Loyalist haven in the north became a
favourite one, and Knox was largely responsible for the seizure
of Penobscot by the British fleet and army that sailed from
Halifax in the summer of that year. While the old provinces
dissolved their filial alliances, new provinces could be created
to buttress the King's authority in North America. Side by
side with Nova Scotia there could be a New Ireland, extending
from the St. Croix to the Penobscot, serving as a fresh restraint
upon rebel impertinence. Regulated upon correct principles, it
could serve as a model colony where institutions and men could
foster loyalty to the Crown. It was in New York, Knox argued,
that there had been least inclination to rebellion, owing to its
powerful landlord class and its considerable tenantry. New Ireland should therefore be ruled by a planter society of landholding gentry. In the older colonies gentlemen had found it

necessary to enter the lower, elective branches of the legislatures. In New Ireland they should be urged to enter higher
councils, appointed by the Crown for the purpose of curbing
"the democratic power". It was equally clear, according to
Knox, that the colonies containing the greater proportion of
adherents of the Church of England had produced the greater
number of Loyalists. It followed, therefore, that the Church of
England should be employed as a beneficent theocracy, sustaining loyal principles in the population of New Ireland.[14]

New Ireland very nearly came into existence as British control was extended over the coast of Maine. In the summer of
1780 Germaine was prepared to create the new establishment,
with Peter Oliver, the exiled chief justice of Massachusetts, as
governor. If peace with the United States were to come it would
constitute a formidable element in the negotations, and Germaine was not anxious for peace until he had deprived the
United States of avenues for future development. But a legal
scruple obstructed the execution of the plan. Alexander Wed-
derburn (later Lord Loughborough), the Attorney-General,
refused his concurrence on the plea that the lands of New Ireland had been granted by charter to Massachusetts Bay. The
objection, though highly learned, was supremely unrealistic, for
it assumed that Massachusetts was within the Empire. George
III, whose strong support had been given to the idea of a new
province, was finally influenced more by legal scruple than by
the strategy of the war.

The British remained at Penobscot, but New Ireland never
became anything more than a spiritual antecedent for another
and farther removed Loyalist haven in the north. Knox's father-
ing of the great idea was to bear no consequences as long as
the war lasted. Yet his schemes for the reconstruction of the
Empire were to produce a measure of inspiration when peace
should bring forth new urgencies.

VI

The fall of Lord North's ministry at the opening of 1782 has
generally been acclaimed as a portent of new hope for the English-speaking world and for the triumph of enlightened principles in the relations between the United States and the parent
kingdom. The King's Friends had been discredited by military
defeat and naval ineptitude. The surrender of Lord Cornwallis
at Yorktown had brought disaster to the plans of Germaine

and Knox. The Whigs came into office, pledged to a policy of complete conciliation of the United States.

For succeeding generations Shelburne, who soon became prime minister, gained a great reputation as architect of Anglo-American amity. Historians of British North America have regarded him with less favour, for his policy of general surrender to the new nation of the eighteenth century was to bear fruit in a blighting of prospects for another new nation of the nineteenth. The general impression of the Whigs that Canada and Nova Scotia could be advantageously abandoned, that the King's remaining dominions in North America were scarcely worth keeping, was based on enlightened self-interest. Having pacified the United States, Britain might have to continue the war with France and Spain, a possibility at which many of the Whigs rejoiced. Generous treatment of the Americans could convert former foes into cordial friends. Powerful commercial interests argued that all that was worth keeping was the trade of the United States, that the Americans should retain their historic rights in the North Atlantic fishery and in the traffic with the British West Indies. Gladly, even enthusiastically, Oswald and Vaughan, the first British emissaries to meet Franklin in the negotiations at Versailles, agreed that Canada, Nova Scotia, and their fisheries should be surrendered. Considerations of actual possession of territory, which Germaine and Knox had regarded as so important, had no place.

The Americans had early in the war taken it for granted that the winning of their independence would imply the acquisition of the two provinces which had not revolted. In 1779 this point of view had been publicly expressed in the Continental Congress, where a long debate had taken place upon whether or not, with the support of France and Spain, Nova Scotia should be declared independent.[15] Later the claims of the two leading allies of the United States had produced the possibility that France might be rewarded by the restoration of Canada and that Nova Scotia should go to Spain.[16] Yet the possible presence of two such allies in such close proximity to the United States produced uncomfortable recollections among the Americans. As the chance of a general peace, in which France and Spain should be included, came nearer, continued British presence in the two provinces seemed preferable, though Benjamin Franklin argued that it would be merely dignified for Britain to make the surrender.[17]

British continuance in North America was assured by the last events of the war, the destruction of the French fleet in the West Indies, and the successful defence of Gibraltar. But the necessity of remaining was reinforced when Franklin informed the British negotiators that Congress could give no undertaking to restore the property and possessions of the American Loyalists. As peace had become a clearer possibility the position and prospects of these people had become a source of increasing embarrassment to the British government. If justice for the Loyalists could not be won from the Americans by negotiation, justice would have to be dispensed by the Crown. Oswald had to be sharply reminded that "an establishment for the Loyalists" should always be on his mind. If the Loyalists could not be restored to their own lands, new lands would have to be found for them in the King's dominions. Compensation from the virgin soil of Canada and Nova Scotia would be cheaper than financial indemnities from the revenues of Great Britain. On October 17, 1782, Oswald's new instructions required him to insist on a better boundary for Nova Scotia. The St. John River, earlier accepted as the western limit, would not be satisfactory. The "back part" of the province, it was declared, was required for the refugees. If, the minute of cabinet ordered, the United States would make a just provision for the refugees, Oswald would be entitled to recede from this position.[18]

Oswald's colleague Stanley demanded the Penobscot as a boundary and, as a compromise, got "the next great river to the westward", the St. Croix. At the end of 1782 Shelburne's government fell, but the succeeding coalition of Lord North and Charles James Fox accepted the arrangements that had been made for the signing of the preliminary peace in January 1783. Fox, especially, was impressed with the necessity of retaining sufficient areas of territory in North America to give compensation to the Loyalists. Little was known of the lands that had been divided, but the makers of the treaty agreed that the boundary should be the St. Croix from its mouth to its source, that a commission should be appointed to mark a northerly line from the source of the St. Croix to the highlands which divide the watershed of the St. Lawrence from that of the rivers flowing south-easterly to the Atlantic Ocean. The islands in the Bay of Fundy that had actually been taken under the jurisdiction of Nova Scotia remained in British hands. If the Americans felt that the peace treaty deprived them of a portion of their just due in the assignment of territory, they could take comfort in the clause which gave to their fishermen the right to use the inshore waters of Nova Scotia and to land on the beaches of unoccupied harbours and islands for shore operations. This was a concession that could outrank any dispute arising on a territorial basis. For a century and a half American fishermen had enjoyed these privileges. The political separation did not imply that Nova Scotia should cease to be New England's outpost.

Shelburne's government had been profligate of the territory and natural resources of the future British North America. To the generation of Whig statesmen who had loathed the struggle with the thirteen colonies it had seemed vastly important to usher the United States into the world in a spirit of generosity that transcended the ownership of unoccupied river valleys, the maintenance of lines of communication, and the holding of strategic posts. New struggles might lie ahead with the hereditary enemies, the French, who watched with a mixture of dismay and admiration as the British, with a cleverness that seemed diabolical, sought to convert the rebellious colonists into possible allies. The boundary, said the French ambassador to London, was far more generous than any of which the Americans had ever dreamed.[19]

CHAPTER 2

The Coming of the Loyalists

1782-1784

At New York, in the summer of 1782, distress reigned among the shattered ranks of the British Americans who had remained loyal to the Crown. News of a negotiation for peace had come from Europe, a peace that would acknowledge the independence of the thirteen colonies and disavow the cause for which they had contended, amidst all kinds of sacrifices, over seven years. To many the approaching reconciliation between the Mother Country and the United States seemed like a declaration of war upon themselves. At Lloyd's Neck, Eaton's Neck, and other ports of Long Island where they had congregated, throughout the units of "the provincial army" scattered along the shores of Long Island Sound, the news of peace came like a death-knell. For the British it represented military defeat. For the Loyalists it meant military defeat coupled with personal ruin.

Throughout the war New York had been the principal rampart of British power in the thirteen colonies. As British armies had sallied forth to the interior of the country and as they had invariably returned to its protection, civilian refugees from all the middle colonies, persecuted by rebel committees and congresses, had come within their lines. Long Island had temporarily become a Loyalist province, the resort of thousands who, in their own separate localities, had given defiance to the upstart authorities who acted in the name of the Continental Congress. Many had enlisted in the Loyalist regiments that had been formed to fight side by side with the regular troops. But now these same regiments were retreating to New York following the spectacular but unsuccessful campaign in the south. From Charleston and

Savannah and the other stations that Lord Cornwallis had seized on his forlorn adventure, the garrisons were returning. The Whig government of Lord Shelburne had sent out Sir Guy Carleton to treat with the rebels and to bring military operations to a conclusion. Liquidation of a great empire was in progress, and it appeared that the Loyalists were being abandoned to a ruinous fate.

Like most other civil wars, the conflict of the American Revolution had acquired the characteristics of a private and savage vendetta between opposing factions. Loyalist leaders had gained prominent reputations as exponents of the system of plunder and rapine by which many of the campaigns, especially in the south, had been conducted. Amid the highly-pitched rancour Tory and rebel held for one another, the return of the Loyalists to their homes seemed a hopeless prospect. Their interpretation of the news of peace was that it meant complete surrender of themselves and their possessions to their vengeful enemies. Carleton faced incipient rebellion from those who had been the most strenuous supporters of the imperial cause. The Loyalist militia at New York refused to do garrison duty. Bills were posted asking Sir Guy to resist the terms of peace and the measures that would implement it. Feverishly the Loyalists continued their private warfare against the rebel whaleboats on Long Island Sound.[1] Public peace may have been on the horizon, but private hatreds resulted in unpleasant incidents, notably the unauthorized hanging of Captain Joshua Huddy, an American prisoner of war. Unhappily Carleton disbanded the Board of Directors of American Loyalists who had possessed powers of custody over prisoners of war and stripped Loyalist leaders of the small authority they had held on Long Island.[2] All through the war Loyalist pride had demanded the restoration of civil government in the small part of the King's dominions that had remained under his control. The arrogance of the British military authorities had been almost as great a provocation as the excesses of the rebel patriots. Huddled together in refugee cantonments on Long Island, they had borne with patience the exaction of British officers of the line and of German mercenaries. Many had come to believe that, though only the most cruel persecution could be expected from the enemy, little better could be expected from the British government. Even those who had gone across the Atlantic to Britain doubted the loyalty of the Mother Country to those

who had been loyal to her. Hoping that the Loyalists would
be better treated by their own countrymen than by Great
Britain, Frederick Geyer wrote to his friend, Ward Chipman,
urging him to remain in the United States.[3]

Carleton watched with anxiety as the news of a peace circulated among the Loyalists. He had called together their leaders
and had divulged the consequences of his dealings with Washington, "an information which produced among them a very
general affliction". Some, he concluded, would endeavour to gain
terms from the enemy by a secret reconciliation. Yet others
had declared they would endure any extremity rather than
submit to the principles of their enemies.[4] As the new situation
induced by the peace negotiations became more discernible,
the Loyalist position became similar to that of a third power,
caught between Britain, whose good intentions they doubted,
and the United States, whose intentions they recognized to be
vindictive.

For a time the court of France, where the news of the independent negotiation for peace between Britain and the United
States had been received with equal dismay, appeared to be
the only friend the Loyalists had. The Loyalists, Carleton later
wrote, had been exposed to the dangerous propaganda circulated
by French intelligence, that the British government would
desert them, that Great Britain would make no real effort in
the negotiations to secure the restitution of their property.[5]
Enviously the French looked on as Shelburne strove to get the
Americans out of the war and to make of them friendly neutrals
in the struggle that might have to be continued against France
and Spain. The extreme generosity of the terms offered to the
Americans presented a bleak prospect to the Loyalists. If anti-
British sentiment were to be kept alive in the United States, the
Loyalists, abandoned by the Crown for which they had fought,
would serve as an excellent agency for France.

For every Loyalist within the British lines there were five
outside within the territories dominated by Congress. In addition there was a large volume of American opinion that had
given support to Congress throughout the war but considered
independence to be too great and too dangerous a prize for the
military victory. Some form of continued attachment to the
Crown, such as the autonomy recently won by Ireland, was
regarded with favour by those who shrank from a prospect of
complete separation. Opinion was fluid almost everywhere.

Within Congress itself deep cleavage had appeared. Washington, facing a struggle against the politicians who wanted to disband his unpaid army, was eager to attach the Loyalists to his support in the politics of the newly independent country. Though he would have preferred to deal with them directly as citizens of the United States, he made overtures to them in his negotiations with Carleton, promising to recommend to the state governments either full restitution of property or adequate compensation.[6]

Such considerations weighed heavily with Carleton as he contemplated his motley command at New York and the necessity of keeping discipline. In large numbers Loyalist volunteers and German mercenaries were deserting to the enemy. Even soldiers of the regiments of the line could not be trusted to resist blandishments from across the Sound. If Loyalist discipline should break down amidst the highly unpredictable and explosive situation that prevailed, control might be completely forfeited. He took pains to reassure their leaders, the governors and judges who had been driven from their posts at the opening of the war, and the younger men who had acquired reputation by the quality of their military leadership during the seven years of fratricidal strife. If, he promised them, no reasonable expectations appeared in their own country, if no guarantees of restitution could be obtained from the Americans, "other settlements" would be made.[7]

Other settlements were obvious. Across the water lay Nova Scotia, a territory almost vacant and still beneath the British Crown. While passions were still high and while a mood of desperation still prevailed among the Loyalists Carleton made arrangements with Sir Andrew Snape Hamond, the governor of that province, to receive 600 of those determined to go at the outset, those who rejected any contingency by which their position in their own country might be improved. Ever since the evacuation of Boston in 1776, Nova Scotia, but a few days' sail to the northward, had appeared as the logical haven for those whose patrimony had come under rebel control. Forecasts were made of a mass exodus in the spring of 1783. Yet for the majority of the refugees there was no clear statement of intention. The great opinion that ruled was that more favourable expedients might yet appear. The definitive peace might win for them terms better than appeared possible at this exigency.

II

The preliminary peace was signed on January 20, 1783. News of it came to New York in March. The same intelligence on the other side of the Sound and throughout the extent of the United States produced a reaction that impelled the Loyalists to accept the hard choice of emigration to Nova Scotia. Instead of moderating the fury of the revolutionaries against the Loyalists, the news of the peace increased it. Proscriptions, confiscations, and persecutions redoubled when it was generally understood that the state governments were under no obligation to restore the privileges of citizenship to the Loyalists. Many Americans considered that the article in the treaty by which the government of the United States had promised to influence the states to adopt a more gentle and conciliatory policy had been inserted merely for the purpose of saving British pride. The obsession for hunting Tories reached new extremities. In the weeks of March and April, as the bad tidings became more detailed, thousands of the refugees made known to Carleton their decision to go to Nova Scotia. Abortive attempts had been made by Loyalist leaders to negotiate with the legislature of New York for terms by which they might rehabilitate themselves. But public passion reigned supreme and no rebel politician would dare espouse the cause of the hated Tories.

The British government had produced no grand design for the settlement of Nova Scotia. Governor Parr at Halifax had been given no detailed instructions. Even after the preliminary peace was signed it was hoped in Whitehall that renewed negotiation with Congress would produce recognition that the Loyalists were an American liability and that they would be permitted to return to their own homes.[8] Faced with the necessity of evacuating New York as quickly as possible, Carleton placed nearly 5,000 Loyalists aboard transports and dispatched them to the St. John River and Port Roseway. Three thousand of these came to the St. John, and casual shiploads enlarged the populations of the two new towns that rose at the mouth of the river. As reports reached New York of augmented American violence towards the Loyalists, the business of evacuation became more complex. More and more refugees streamed into the British lines. Emboldened Americans crossed the Sound to abuse, rob, and plunder the last parties of refugees who had been dilatory in moving their effects. These circumstances increased the number of those who wanted to go and compelled Carleton to prolong the period of evacuation. Almost all within the lines, he wrote in August, wanted to go to Nova Scotia.[9] His ability to expedite the northward movement was limited by an inadequacy of shipping for the large tasks that faced him. Charleston, as well as New York, had to be evacuated. Troops had to be dispatched to the West Indies as a precaution against renewed operations of the French and Spaniards. The German mercenaries, who in their idleness were costing the King much hard coin, had to be sent home.

It was presumably with pleasure that Carleton contemplated the almost unanimous expression of Loyalist intention. Another leading soldier of the rival cause gave definite opinion upon the consequences of his countrymen's zeal in persecuting the Tories. An American diplomat reported General Washington as saying in August that "in persecuting the Tories we were playing General Carleton's game, since he must wish to increase the colony of Nova Scotia and diminish the people of the United States".[10] The Virginian delegation to Congress, as they considered the evacuation of New York, could anticipate the appearance of a rich and powerful neighbour in the north.[11] The French ambassador wrote home in chagrin of the absence of generosity, nobleness, and sound policy among "the lower classes" of the people of the United States. "It is believed moreover that the English regard with pleasure that rigour which will in a few months found a flourishing colony in Nova Scotia."[12] Carleton, when he embarked aboard the *Ceres* late in November, must have ruminated that the losses had been cut somewhat. Though he had been invited with good grace, he had declined to join in the festivities that marked the entrance of General Washington to New York. As the British ships swayed about in the anchorage, fireworks ashore signalized the last act of defeat and evacuation. An empire had been lost, but 35,000 Loyalists had sailed for Nova Scotia. British power in North America was still a reality and a second empire might well be made from the wreck of the old.

A second empire implied an avoidance of the mistakes of the first. In the sullen months of defeat and withdrawal at New York, Carleton had heard much of imperial errors from the Loyalist leaders who unabashedly reviewed the weaknesses that had marred the royal administration. Enlightened by their counsels he freely spoke his mind to the British government

upon the future of Nova Scotia, which would so rapidly increase
in population and importance. No taxes, he said, should be
imposed by Great Britain. Quitrents on lands and fees for
office-holders should be abolished. Vexatious customs tolls could
inspire cries of tyranny and oppression. Greater care should be
given to official appointments, especially those of judges. Popularly elected legislatures should be neutralized by the strengthening of royal governors and appointed councils.[13] In these
months William Smith, the chief justice of New York, acquired
an influence over Carleton that was to last for the remainder
of the life of the great proconsul.

Loyalist clerics gave bitter accounts of monstrous sins of
omission. The Church of England had never been able to do its
work of fostering loyalty in America because it had been denied
the means of increasing itself. No bishopric had ever been
established in the thirteen colonies so that native Americans
could be ordained to holy orders on their own soil. There had
been no college where they could train for their sacred vocation.
If the population of Nova Scotia were to be nurtured on principles of attachment to the Crown, a bishopric and a college
would have to be created. With these propositions Carleton
agreed in principle, but he took the precaution of canvassing
influential laymen among the Loyalists. His final judgment
was emphatic. Virtually all the Loyalists, he said, were of the
established church, and all shades of opinion agreed upon the
desirability of the proposed measures. Even the Quakers were
favourable, and only a small minority of Presbyterians were
opposed. Since the Presbyterian synod of the United States
boasted of the unanimity of its people in supporting the revolution, Carleton considered opposition from this source to be
another reason for the acceptance of episcopacy.[14] Later in the
year, when he discovered that the Presbyterians of Halifax had
applied to the president of the Presbyterian College of New
Jersey for a minister and that the nominee, a man named
Russell, had asked for a free passage to Nova Scotia as a
Loyalist, his fury was so great that he took pains to stop the
appointment.[15]

III

The provincial army, as it was loosely called, was included in
the great immigration of 1783. The units of the British Army
that had been raised on American soil had seen many laborious

days since the summer of 1776, when most of them had been recruited following the great descent on Long Island. They had been organized, reorganized, disbanded, and raised again, but still there was the nucleus of an independent corps with a long tradition of service. They were the Loyalists who had fought in arms for the Crown, and they carefully observed the distinction between themselves and "the refugees" who had merely sought safety behind the lines at New York.

Almost everywhere British armies had gone throughout the war, Loyalist regiments had been present, but their most immediate, vivid memories were of the south, of the passionate, plundering campaigns that had preceded the surrender of Cornwallis at Yorktown. They had taken part in the seizure of Charleston, the joyous but dubious victory at Eutaw Springs, the magnificent defence of Fort Ninety-Six. There had been the humiliations of King's Mountain and The Cowpens. They had followed Benedict Arnold up the valley of the James through the stench of burning tobacco crops, probably entering a little too lustily into the more unorthodox and guerilla-like activities of the march, looting the rebel fleshpots, and burning Richmond to the ground. In the minds of the Americans, the Tories in arms were identified not only with the treachery of Arnold but with the cruel efficiency of his campaigns. They were feared and hated more than the British regulars or the German mercenaries. A great British historian of the nineteenth century, unable to discard the prejudices of the Whigs of the eighteenth, has sneered at their martial qualities.[16]

In this army of adventurers who had chosen the losing cause there were men of dash and character whose influence had held the tattered formations together, but in the last few months of the war the most prominent commander and recipient of official favour was a comparative new-comer. The spectacular success of Benjamin Thompson in so many spheres of activity must remove all doubts concerning his ability. The young New Hampshire Loyalist had gone to England in the opening year of the revolutionary war and had become the friend and confidant of Lord George Germaine. In their inner circle of the King's Friends he had become an under-secretary of state for the Northern Department and one of the men on whose advice the war was fought. At the opening of 1781, as if in anticipation of the fall of Germaine, he had appeared at New York with the rank of lieutenant-colonel and authority to raise a new regiment under the patronage of Prince William from the Loyalist units whose ranks were depleted.

The King's American Dragoons was the most junior unit in the army, but among the Loyalist corps it rapidly became the most prominent. Through the Carolinas for almost a year Thompson was a shining light in the cut-and-thrust campaign against the vastly superior forces of the American general, Greene. When the war flickered out he brought his regiment back to New York with a brilliant military reputation to supplement his politic charm and vivacious imagination. It was as if victory had come for the King's American Dragoons. "I will venture to say the King's American Dragoons are now the crack corps in this army."[17] On an August day, at the camp at Fresh Meadows, Long Island, Prince William reviewed the regiment and presented it with colours. There followed an appropriate address by the chaplain,[18] the Reverend Jonathan Odell, and the whole regiment, kneeling on the ground with arms and helmets at their sides, took a most solemn oath of allegiance to their sovereign and fidelity to their standard, all repeating the oath together.[19] He would, said Thompson, show the regiment in Hyde Park. The next winter, as other regimental commanders evaded the responsibility of taking their troops to a dreaded area of operations for possible service against the French and Spaniards, Thompson volunteered to lead a regiment of Loyalists to the West Indies. Still another claim upon the government had been established.

Thompson had no intention of going to Nova Scotia with the Loyalists. There were rumours of an approaching war between Russia and Turkey, and his ardent spirit directed him to a theatre of conflict. But before setting out on fresh adventures he took the lead in bringing tranquillity to the minds of his brother-officers of the Loyalist corps. First of all he secured the placing of his own regiment on the permanent establishment of the army, a concession that guaranteed half-pay to his officers upon their eventual disbandment. After jealousies had arisen in the other and senior regiments, he embarked for England and used his influence to obtain the same concession for all the units of the provincial army. In June of 1783 the North-Fox coalition redeemed in part the pledge made by Shelburne to do justice to the Loyalists. It was an important contribution to the future of Nova Scotia, a kind of financial guarantee for the continuation of loyalty at a time when bonds were strained and when there was no solid assurance of competence amid the difficulties that lay ahead.

Thompson's impending return to the refinements of Europe, where he was to gain fame not as a soldier but as a scientist and philosopher, was probably responsible for the decision to send the King's American Dragoons to Nova Scotia as the vanguard of the provincial army. Before starting on his own travels he saw the regiment off to the banks of the St. John with the transports of the spring fleet. Three hundred and sixty dragoons were unloaded on the west side of the harbour and set to work at building roads over the hilly ground between the inner estuary and the Fundy coast. Daniel Murray, the impetuous major, proceeded up the river and came back with glowing reports. There was talk of a new Elysium in the interior where the Pokiok joins the St. John.[20] John Coffin, a seafaring man of Boston who had won a commission on the field at Bunker Hill, commenced the development of a great estate at Alwington Manor, so designated for a family mansion that stood on the cliffs above the Bristol Channel in Somerset, reminiscent of the glories of his family since the days of the Norman conquest. There he would raise two generals for the British Army and an admiral for the British Navy. Coffin's name was already legend among the Loyalists. In the Carolinas he had charged three hundred Americans with only seventy dragoons behind him. Losing but three men, he had left sixty of the enemy dead on the field, all killed with swords—for in the precipitation of the charge he had scorned to stop and fire.[21] After the withdrawal from Charleston, he had braved all hazards in order to return to his lady, eluding capture by a wary American patrol by concealing himself beneath a hooped skirt, though he was a man of six feet, two inches.[22]

IV

The precise destination of the provincial army was, by the summer of 1783, one of the great subjects of politics in British North America. By this time the Loyalist ambition of creating a new province from the hinterland to the north of the Bay of Fundy was a cause for open speculation. To settle the provincial army in the St. John Valley would strengthen the case for partition of the province of Nova Scotia, now the avowed objective of Loyalist intrigue. To place the provincial army on the coastline of the province, to which the authority of Halifax

could be more easily extended, was the determination of the
provincial government. The interests of all those at Halifax who
held land grants on the St. John or who hoped to gain by speculation in the lands of the upper river were in mortal peril. Loyalist penetration to the heart of the hinterland could heavily
weight the case against the aspirations of those who were influential in the Halifax régime.

At the centre of all the cross-currents that affected the fate of
the provincial army was John Parr, the governor of Nova Scotia.
Over sixty, and weighing more than 250 pounds, he had come to
Halifax in 1782 in the hope of finishing an arduous military
career in the ease of a civil government. But his coming to
Nova Scotia coincided with the first great flow of Loyalists from
New York and, almost at the outset, he encountered a personal
disaster. He was an appointee of the Whig government of Lord
Shelburne, "my noble friend who sent me here".[23] Early in 1783
this administration, which had concluded peace with the Ameri-
cans and had earned Loyalist distrust for doing so, fell from
office. All through the war the Whigs had advocated appease-
ment of the Americans and had appeared as the enemies of the
Loyalist cause. In the Loyalist mind their fall from office in
Britain presaged the fall of Parr in Nova Scotia and the establishment of a government at Halifax that would make the
Loyalists the masters of the colony. "The gentlemen from New
York" were in high fettle as they strolled the streets of Halifax,
freely prophesying the coming of a new administration of undiluted loyalty. Those who had fought the war from the repose
of the citadel or who had won for themselves private fortunes
from the public distress were the objects of their righteous scorn.

Threatened by the loss or break-up of his government, Parr
followed an uneasy and petulant course between the factions
that encompassed him. The accession to office of the North-Fox
government in London and the command of Sir Guy Carleton
at New York compelled him to honour the demands of the
Loyalists who, as the long line of new settlements appeared
around the coasts of Nova Scotia, he declared were preying upon
one another like sharks. He relied for advice upon the Chief
Justice, Bryan Finucane, a new-comer like himself. "We are not
without our private cabals here, indeed My Lord, it would be an
impossibility to be otherwise, where almost the whole of the
people is composed of Scotch, and a very bad addition of the
Yankee race, each party would be happy to have a governor of

their own country, and one being as national as the other. They keep me constantly employed and do not suffer me to eat the bread of idleness."[24] Nervous and overworked by the inflow of refugees, he was compelled to acquiesce in the choice of the upper St. John as the region where the provincial army should settle. A year later, after his personal security had been improved by a fresh change of government in London, he condemned the idea of carrying the Loyalist corps so far up the river, denouncing it as born and bred in New York and carried into execution by the Loyalist agents.[25]

New York was, indeed, the centre of real decision. As reports of the initial Loyalist settlements in Nova Scotia came back to Sir Guy Carleton, his inclinations became more and more favourable towards the refugees who surrounded him. As accounts of how the Governor had sent the Loyalists off into the woods, of the delays in settling them on the land, of the bleak inhospitality of the Nova Scotian shores, reached the refugees who awaited transportation, the determination of Loyalist leaders to shake themselves free from Parr's control mounted. The new settlements were distracted by reports that Parr would call new elections to the Nova Scotian assembly before Loyalists would be eligible to vote. Demands for a new assembly in which Loyalists should participate became frequent. Loyalist agitators asked for county and municipal organizations that would make them less dependent on Halifax for the management of their own affairs. Covertly but widely, the idea that the Loyalists could never get justice in Nova Scotia unless a government of their own should be created was spread abroad. In humour of self-pity the Loyalists considered themselves a race apart. To accept the domination of those who appeared less loyal seemed odious.

Logic lay on the Loyalist side in this phase of their vendetta against Parr's government. Throughout the latter part of the war General Haldimand at Quebec had fretfully attempted to establish effective communication with Halifax by way of the St. John River. Of what took place at New York and the battle areas to the south he had often been in ignorance. "Only lies" had come across the lakes.[26] For Haldimand the portage between Lake Témiscouata and the upper St. John had become a highly strategic region. Acadian couriers, notably Louis Mercure, had carried dispatches from Quebec to Halifax, through the small post at Oromocto commanded by a Lieutenant Connor, and with the assistance of William Hazen at the mouth of the river.

When peace came Haldimand urged Parr to strengthen this uncertain system of communication by settling the wilderness region of the upper river. Carleton supported the project by suggesting that the lands should be granted in the manner by which cantonments were laid out for an army. Detachments should be placed on the frontier at the St. Croix, but strong elements should be stationed in the rear, up the valley of the St. John.[27] Military considerations pointed to the larger river as the repository for the provincial army.

In June of 1783, while the Loyalist tide at New York was running so strongly, Carleton sent to Halifax, as officer commanding the troops, Brigadier Henry Fox, the younger brother of Charles James Fox, one of the leaders of Britain's coalition government. To the more ardent Loyalists he appeared not only as the emissary of Carleton but of the British government whose presence could overawe and intimidate Parr and his officials. He was only thirty, and his youthful outlook was conducive to the notion that new men and new measures were necessary for Nova Scotia. He was "the only good son" of the elder Henry Fox, first Lord Holland, who in his boyhood had distinguished himself by living with his father's horses, and who, according to a contemporary, "stinks, talks and thinks of the stables".[28]

It was the duty of Fox, in concert with Parr, to disband and settle the Loyalist battalions in Nova Scotia. Carleton had received orders to disband the troops at Halifax, but he chose to interpret them broadly. Under pressure, Parr on August 2 designated lands on the St. John, running northwards from Sunbury and Newton, for a dozen units. For a time he had hoped to persuade Carleton of the desirability of a general military settlement on the St. Croix, but Loyalist leaders were satisfied of the superiority of the St. John, and Carleton backed them firmly. It would be cruel, he wrote Parr, to send the Loyalists to lands that were not of their own choice.[29]

In the opinion of Halifax officialdom, Fox's evil counsellor was Edward Winslow, who had come to Nova Scotia as his military secretary, a man whose volatile temperament and gay exuberances have been immortalized by his own ready pen and the labours of a devoted historian.[30] He was one of a group of agents whose duty it was to negotiate with the Nova Scotian government on behalf of the provincial army, but this official capacity was eclipsed by the private influence he brought to bear upon Fox. While Loyalist leaders at New York were urging

Carleton to send the provincial army to the St. John, Winslow effectively reinforced their pleas at Halifax. Fox readily imbibed Winslow's dislike and distrust of the governing clique at Halifax, the "nest of pickaroons" whose loyalty was tarnished with ill-gotten gains. The Nova Scotian capital was filled with accounts of the barrenness of the soil of the St. John Valley. But Winslow knew better. During the preceding year he had gone up the river and had located an area for himself and choice spirits of the Loyalist corps. A domain of interval and timberland at the mouth of the swift-flowing Pokiok, financed by the whirring of sawmills and enriched by the settlement of his comrades, would serve as a handsome compensation for the seven years of sacrifice in which he had served as muster-master general of the British-American troops, for his daring on that dark night in 1775 when he had guided Lord Percy's regiment back to Boston after the engagement at Lexington.

V

Following this victory for the grand Loyalist idea, Fox, Winslow, and Brigadier Oliver de Lancey left for the St. John and spent most of the month of September exploring the upper reaches of the river. On his journey Fox progressively surrendered to the blandishments of his companions, who were imbued with the conception of Loyalist domination in Nova Scotia. At Cumberland he found that the "old inhabitants" were disaffected and that it would be necessary to keep troops there in greater force.[31] It would be difficult, he thought, to keep old and new inhabitants at peace with one another.[32] He subscribed to the enthusiasm of Winslow to such a degree that he reserved for himself an estate on the Pokiok where, at this stage, it seemed that the leading centre of the St. John Valley was in projection. Already he was being hailed as the governor of a Loyalist province. Since there were now too many settlers at the mouth of the river, he ordered the King's American Dragoons to the Pokiok, where the new settlement of Prince William, called after the regiment's patron, appeared. There, under a determination to save expense to the government and an impression that they would have time to erect shelters before the onset of winter, Fox disbanded them. They formed the vanguard of the general movement into the north.

After roughly surveying the country between the Pokiok and the Nashwaak, Fox and Winslow returned to the mouth of the river in time to meet the main body of the provincial army, which commenced to disembark on September 28. The remnants of the dozen units dispatched by Carleton to the St. John were under the command of Lieutenant-Colonel Richard Hewlett, an officer of rangers of the Seven Years War who had led the men of Queens County on Long Island against Fort Frontenac. During the revolutionary war the Continental Congress had ordered that he must be taken at any opportunity that might appear. "I will stand by you as long as there is a man left," he had shouted to his garrison when he was besieged in a church at Sawtucket by an overwhelming rebel force.[33]

Hewlett's orders were to get the regiments to their ultimate destinations by October 20 and disband them by this date, but in any event to disband them whether they reached their destinations or not.[34] Carleton's overriding consideration was that the transports must be available for the evacuation of Penobscot. Issuing small hatchets to the troops for lack of axes, Hewlett attempted to secure sufficient small shipping to get his men up the river in sufficient time to enable them to raise huts for the winter. Bad weather interfered with the operation. "The oldest man in the province does not remember such severe bad weather as we have had for some time past."[35] At the last moment Parr, considering that the movement had passed beyond his own control and arguing that too much land had been designated for the Loyalist regiments, halted the migration to the north.

The consequence was that only a token occupation took place of the blocks of territory, twelve miles square, for which the commanding officers had drawn lots.[36] A large proportion of the provincial army remained at the mouth of the river, settling down amid the hurly-burly of the thousands of civilian refugees who were being moved into the two towns. Hewlett and his third battalion of de Lancey's settled the lower river. They were all men from Queens County in Long Island, and Hewlett settled himself at a new Hampstead, named after his old home, in a new Queens County that was shortly to appear. But the success of Winslow's plan, the details of which he had himself prepared, was only partial. In a rage he wrote to Brook Watson, the commissary-general of the royal forces at New York, who had just returned to London, denouncing the governor and demanding a partition of the province. Watson, calling upon Lord Sydney in the spring, urged action in an impolitic manner.

"For God's sake see these matters effectually done away and guarded against the future. Whenever Lord Sydney wishes to see me he will have the goodness to give me notice but I trust he will have the goodness not to waste my time." Unfortunately for Winslow, the reception of his letter in London, whatever good it accomplished for the Loyalist cause, unfavourably prejudiced him in the minds of those who were influential. Even Sir Guy Carleton came to the conviction that Winslow was too hot-headed to be trusted, that in settling the provincial army he had encouraged disobedience to the provincial government at Halifax.

Under the discouraging circumstances of a cold and wet October, the regiments that took at least nominal possession of the middle area of the St. John fulfilled an indispensable condition for the establishment of a new province. The Queen's Rangers, originally a Virginia formation that had fought at Brandywine and had served through the southern campaign until they had capitulated with Cornwallis at Yorktown, occupied the area later known as the parish of Queensbury. North Carolina was represented by the King's American Regiment, which had assisted in the storming of forts Clinton and Montgomery and had seen the hard fighting at Norwalk and the disaster at King's Mountain. The New York Volunteers had been mustered at Halifax in 1776, when New York was under rebel occupation, and had returned for the great descent on Long Island. They had been at Savannah, Camden, and Eutaw Springs, where John Coffin had been given the honour of opening the battle. The Loyal American Regiment, recruited by the aged Beverley Robinson, whom Carleton had just sent off to England, a country "to which the simplicity of his manners did not perfectly correspond",[37] had experienced the same triumphs and tribulations. The three battalions of de Lancey's brigade had originally been raised for the defence of Long Island, but two of them had been dispatched for service in the south. Largest of all the formations were the three battalions of the New Jersey Volunteers, originally recruited by Cortlandt Skinner, the last royal attorney-general of New Jersey. As "Skinner's Cowboys" they had gone the same round. Other corps, less numerous as well as less renowned, were the Prince of Wales American Regiment, the Pennsylvania Loyalists, the Loyal American Legion, the Royal Guides and Pioneers, and the Maryland Loyalists. The last had lost half its strength of

seventy when the transport *Martha* struck a reef on Sable
Island and the captain and crew, surmising that all the passengers would be lost, had deserted their ship in the few boats with
which she was equipped. Small detachments of the King's
Orange Rangers of New York, and of the Royal Fencible Americans which had performed garrison duty in Nova Scotia, were
settled at the harbours of Quaco and St. George on the Bay of
Fundy coast.

With Sir Guy Carleton, Fox stood in the sunshine of Loyalist
favour. The establishment of the more than 3,000 men, women,
and children of the provincial army on the banks of the St. John
represented a triumph for those who wanted Loyalist domination
in Nova Scotia. The completion of the operation brought an
attitude of expectancy of news from London, of the return of
Fox as governor, of the filling of important places in a new
society by those who had proven their loyalty to the Crown.

VI

Loyalist tribulations can be explained not only with reference to
the contest with Parr and the Nova Scotian government. Within
their own ranks there appeared divisions that created complications and provided the setting for later developments. Long
before the evacuation of New York was completed, the unity
of the grand cause had been destroyed by new rivalries. What
later historians would call class-consciousness wrecked Loyalist
morale at the very moment their new model society was born.

During the summer days at New York, as it became clear
that Nova Scotia would be transformed by the great immigration, a number of Loyalist "gentlemen, clergy and merchants"
approached Carleton with a request for particular privileges.
They had lost their fortunes and their superior standing in the
society of the revolted colonies and they asked, in recompense,
for grants of 5,000 acres of land in Nova Scotia. Carleton forwarded the memorial of the Fifty-Five, as they were called, to
Parr, offering words of commendation for the applicants but
making no positive recommendation. It had been presented by
the agents of the group, the Reverend John Sayre, Anthony
Stewart, Nathaniel Chandler, and John Livingston. The list
was headed by the name of Abijah Willard, a merchant of
Lancaster, Massachusetts, who, on the morning of April 19, 1775,
as he had been riding to Beverley to superintend the planting
of his crops, had come upon the Minute Men as they marched

to Concord. He turned post-haste for Boston, where he had previously been given the command of a company of "the Loyal American Associates" and where, on another eventful morning, he could descry through a field-glass the dominating figure of his brother-in-law, Colonel Prescott, who directed the fortification of Breed's Hill by the rebel militia.[38] His military services had not been notable. But now, in company with fifty-four others who considered their services and sacrifices outstanding, he asked for a reward.

News of this request, circulated among the Loyalists who were still within the lines of Eaton's Neck and Lloyd's Neck, was interpreted as an attempt to impose a landholding, possibly absentee aristocracy upon Nova Scotia, to which they were destined. Owing to the unfavourable reports that had come back to New York, the refugees behind the cantonments, after years of anxiety and misfortune, were already dubious about the Nova Scotian prospect. The demands of the Fifty-Five, who presumed to be patricians, excited a violent reaction from the plebeians, who were organized for remonstrance by an able attorney, Elias Hardy. They formally presented their objections to Carleton, and there was some sharp pamphleteering, by which it appeared that among the Fifty-Five who had presented themselves as men of substance and honourable service there were bankrupts and poltroons whose extravagant requests were based upon gross imposture.[39] What really constituted loyalty became a subject of controversy. The race for privilege in Nova Scotia supplanted memories of common sacrifices in the past.

Parr deferred to Carleton's mild request for special consideration for the Fifty-Five and signed warrants for survey for grants of 5,000 acres. Yet when he received detailed instructions at the end of the year, authorizing grants of 1,000 acres only to field officers, he was happy to rescind his decision.[40] Not only among the Loyalists, but throughout the province generally, the demand of the Fifty-Five had excited chagrin and resentment. Even among the Fifty-Five themselves there were recriminations, for it was alleged that certain individuals were less worthy than others and ought not to have been included on the list. The British government approved Parr's conduct. At this moment there was no official response to the urgings of those who, like William Knox, considered it possible to establish a manorial society in Nova Scotia.

The consequence of the petition of the Fifty-Five was that

the great majority of the Loyalists who sailed to the mouth of the St. John in 1783 with the fall fleet arrived in a humour of jealousy and suspicion. Not until the spring of 1784 were their fears of a privileged, landholding order appeased. What they found in the two towns of Parr and Carleton aggravated, during the winter months, the tensions under which they were labouring and created a profound distrust for those who presumed to be their leaders. The very largeness of these new communities and the extraordinary degree of energy they exhibited were marks of failure for the governing authorities, proving their inability to move the refugees to interior farmlands where, with official assistance, they could make a start on new habitations. Parr was blamed for his unwillingness to escheat the lands of the absentee proprietors of the lower river. He retorted that the Loyalist agents had failed to take action because they preferred to wait until they could manage the business with advantage to themselves, "all for a cursed, selfish idea that the tract of country on the other side of the Bay of Fundy was to be formed into a seperate government where they expected to be appointed to the principal offices, and to have the sole management and distribution of the lands of that new government".[41] The Loyalists of the fall fleet, most of whom were from the middle colonies, found that the business of managing the new towns had fallen into the hands of agents from New England. These were in close association with Major Gilfred Studholm, Parr's deputy on the St. John. There were reports of land-hungry cabals who would dominate all the good lands of the interior, of intrigues that would deprive the great body of the people of their patrimony. William Hazen, who with his partners Simonds and White controlled all the lands behind the rocky peninsulas on which the two towns were built, whose great mill at Oromocto supplied huge quantities of lumber for their construction, and whose farms produced much of the food that was required, had himself become a Loyalist agent and a special target for abuse. The Loyalist plebeians from New York could take their choice of enemies, Parr at Halifax or their own agents on the river.

During the winter of 1783-4, while the towns of Parr and Carleton hummed with discontents, while speeches attacking the Government in the British parliament emphasized the sacrifices of the Loyalists and urged greater compassion for them, the principal contest was for town lots, particularly those fronting the harbours of the two towns. Commercial possibilities caught the imagination of the Loyalists late in 1783, when news arrived of the discomfiture of those at Westminster who had striven to offer to the Americans, in still another venture to secure their friendship, the trading privileges they had held as British subjects before the war. The historic Navigation Acts, sponsored by Lord Sheffield, who became for the Loyalists a kind of patron saint, triumphed over the novel ideas of free trade. By the new orders-in-council American goods might be carried to the British West Indies. But the trade was confined to British ships and British subjects. The advantages of Nova Scotian ports as half-way houses on a circuitous route between the United States and the British West Indies became obvious. The carrying trade, held for the most part by New England shippers before the war, seemed certain to fall into Nova Scotian hands. Captains of numerous coastal vessels who had played dubious roles in the war just ended, who had traded with both sides as advantage offered, appeared in Nova Scotian ports. Many, like Tertullus Dickenson, came late in the year from New York, "finding that money may be made here in trade".[42] A new business fraternity discovered that all the favourable sites for commerce in the estuary of the St. John had been engrossed by the Loyalist agents and their friends.[43] The value of real estate emerged as a major preoccupation. The agents for the Loyalists, headed by George Leonard, who during the war had preyed on rebel shipping off Rhode Island and supplied the King's forces with stores, defended themselves by declaring that in the spring, when the towns had been laid out, they had had no idea of the number of refugees who would come to the St. John later in the year.

Only a month following the arrival of the fall fleet, Governor Parr received a formal protest conveyed by "the 22nd Company of St. John's Militia".[44] Unanimously resolving that "all their proceedings may be published to the world", the gathering challenged Studholm's authority to grant lands on the river, demanded lots in the town and farms in the country, catalogued grievances that were minor in character but large in volume. Those who had arrived earlier, it was alleged, had been given much better treatment. Clothing, blankets, tools, nails, all supplied from the royal stores, were said to be unavailable in sufficient quantity.

The protest remarked upon a report that a whole township was to be given to five men. This concerned the negotiations in progress between Studholm on the one side and Simonds, White, and Hazen on the other. The firm[45] had agreed to surrender its rights to the township of Conway, on which the town of Carleton had risen, in exchange for other lands in the vicinity. In their own opinion at least they had deserved well of the government. As Simonds wrote to his partners later, they had reasons just as weighty as those of the Loyalists to expect generous treatment from the authorities. "They had a numerous British army to protect them. We had to combat the sons of darkness alone. In a word we had much less than they to hope for by unshaken loyalty, and incomparably more to fear."[46]

Behind the acrimony that prevailed on the St. John, Parr could discern the figure of Hardy, the attorney who had thwarted the ambitions of Loyalist leaders at New York and in whom the Governor could perceive a "bold and factious disposition". Committees appeared and threats were made of an appeal to Whitehall. A popular movement appeared to be in the making, designed to seize power from the constituted authorities and turn it to the advantage of the masses. As the privations of the winter developed, a surly, almost vengeful disposition appeared among the people. From up the river came accounts of the breakdown of discipline in the provincial army and of fraudulent demands on the royal stores. At Halifax it was feared that the Loyalist regiments, moved to an area beyond effective supervision, would squat on the land and resist by violence any attempt of the government to make legal arrangements.

VII

Up to this time Parr had been labouring against great difficulties under the shadow of dismissal. The hatred of the North-Fox coalition for Shelburne, who had appointed him, gave leverage to all his enemies. The Loyalists had capitalized upon this weakness in his position. "Their ungenerous disposition soon showed itself upon a late unfortunate change in the administration which they thought might change the Governor if he did not comply with every request they made."[47] The disorderly circumstances of the Loyalist immigration had exposed him to formidable criticism. He had received no detailed instructions for dealing with the emergency until 30,000 Loyalists were on Nova Scotian shores. His surveyor-general, Charles Morris, whose office had never been required to do work much more detailed than the laying out of townships of 100,000 acres, more or less, had only twenty-three deputies, nine of whom were un-authorized.[48] To check the activities of the Loyalist committees, to answer demands of the Loyalists for the reorganization of government, Parr threatened to make no grants of land at all.[49] His task was, he told North rather pathetically, the greatest any governor ever had.

Yet suddenly deliverance came. In the spring of 1784 intel-ligence came from London concerning still another change in the ministry, which magically dispelled his fears of dismissal. What was of greatest importance now was the size of Mr. Pitt's majority. "I can perceive a great change in the ministry. They do not now talk of turning me out."[50] As his sense of security increased at Halifax, he took the offensive against the Loyalist agents who had plagued him. Up to this point he had been compelled to work with them. Now he was prepared to work against them, denouncing them as "a pack of rascals replete with gross partialities". Now he could seize the initiative by sending Chief Justice Finucane to the St. John to inquire into complaints and quiet the minds of the people. Hardy, the fac-tious enemy of the Loyalist agents, who had been at Halifax during the winter, returned in triumph as Finucane's satellite. At this stage the Governor, in effect, had formed an alliance with the Loyalist plebeians against the agents, who were sum-moned to Halifax to face an investigation.

The fall of the North-Fox administration in Britain and the coming to office of Pitt were interpreted by the leading Loyalists on the St. John as ruinous to their cause. Not only did it appear that hopes for a new provincial establishment were destroyed, but Parr was riding confidently in the saddle. Hardy and his party served as a wing of the Halifax administration that was determined to fasten its control upon Loyalist destinies. Win-slow regarded the drastic change in affairs as bringing personal ruin upon himself and his friends. "The pettifogging notary public who was so remarkable at York for his litigious and mis-chievous publications" was responsible for the trouble. "He figures at Parrtown among a collection of vulgar blackguards like himself and enjoys a temporary consequence which will fail him as soon as a regular system of government restores to ability and integrity that consequence they ought to have in society." Also in company with the Chief Justice was his brother, Andrew Finucane, "the toady", who affected surprise upon hearing that a new province on the St. John should be considered. "We are also told here that Mr. Andrew Finucane who floated up the River St. John 80 or 90 miles and then floated down again affects to have acquired a perfect knowledge of the country, damns the soil, climate etc. and reprobates the idea of its being formed into a province."[51] For a time the government of "the gentlemen" went into eclipse.

The visit of Finucane and Hardy resulted in an intensification of local squabbles. Edward Winslow was only one of many Loyalists, most of whom were absent from the scene, who lost the lots that had been selected for them on the west side of the harbour. Finucane attempted a redistribution of the lots within the two towns, largely at the expense of those who had been given privileged treatment at the beginning of the settlement. In the public prints a new method of "settlement by classes" was advocated.[52] George Leonard wrote to Winslow that lots along the water-front had shrunk to one-sixteenth of their original dimensions, that upon "new immigrations from Newgate or elsewhere" they would shrink still further.[53] The reaction against the Loyalist patricians, Leonard, James Peters, Thomas Horsfield, John Coffin, and others who were agents or who had gained places on the magistracy, was in full effect in June. Parr wrote that he had quieted the minds of the people on the St. John "except their own agents who are the real cause of the trouble".[54]

Before leaving the river Finucane proved himself a good judge of real estate by securing for himself a grant of a rich island of interval land, stocked with 500 acres of standing timber, several miles above St. Anne's. To a society that was thinking very largely in terms of real estate, Sugar Island was a very great prize indeed, for timber was valued according to its proximity to navigable rivers. To the Chief Justice, Loyalist susceptibilities did not appear to matter very much, for Sugar Island was in the heart of the country awarded to the provincial army.

VIII

At this stage, while Parr's hand was so heavy, the great majority of the temporary populations of the new towns fanned out into the watershed of the St. John, occupying blocks of land assigned to them along the Kennebecasis and Belleisle, and the shores of Grand Lake. Parr and Carleton presented scenes of great industry. According to one account some of this energy was to be deprecated, for the Loyalists were expending all their capital in the erection of handsome houses.[55] All kinds of people, said an informant of Sir John Wentworth, made up their populations. Some had seen better days, but others had never had such good days. The winter had been difficult and those most to be pitied were the officers of the provincial regiments who had been liable to insult on any occasion.[56] Yet the spring brought better times as the move to the promised lands commenced. From Woodstock in Block 8, settled by the first battalion of de Lancey's, to the mouth of the river, the littoral could be said to be completely occupied. The provincial army, deserted by its wastrels, had settled down. Few of them were to remain on the lands originally assigned to them, but their temporary occupation served as an effective reconnaissance in force. For a year the British government had honoured its pledge to support the Loyalists by free issue of provisions. Yet it was perceptible that, owing to the delays in reaching the lands assigned to them, the period of dependence would have to be prolonged.

Late in 1783 the eastern shores of Passamaquoddy Bay became a second major area of Loyalist settlement. The evacuation of Penobscot compelled the withdrawal of a community of traders who had clustered about the garrison during the years of British occupation. Hoping to remain at their original location, which was so highly favourable for trade, they had sent one of their number, Dr. John Caleff, to London in an effort to secure the Penobscot as the boundary of Nova Scotia. His failure brought the removal of "the Penobscot Association", as they called themselves, to an equally convenient station for trade on British territory. Moving their houses as well as their other effects, joined by other elements of refugees and discharged soldiers, they came to St. Andrews, so designated by a half-legendary French priest and standing on a point of land jutting into the bay. Nearby, a group of Quakers established a town at Beaver Harbour. Nehemiah Marks led his armed boatmen up the St. Croix as far as the fishing falls, where they laid out the town of St. Stephen and where they encountered a party of American settlers who, in disdain of war, diplomacy, and politics, had pushed into the area earlier in the year.

Equipped with capital and containing a strong ingredient of Scots, the Penobscot Association permitted their forced migration to interfere very little with their trading pursuits. By the spring of 1784 the ships of St. Andrews were conveying American produce to the West Indies and to Great Britain. The advantages conferred upon them by the Navigation Acts were reinforced by an embargo upon the entrance of British vessels to the harbours of New England. It was impractical to attempt to carry on a direct trade between New and Old England. But it was quite legal to exchange British goods for those of the United States. "Trading on the lines" along the harbours and islands of Passamaquoddy Bay became a common form of intercourse for the merchants of New England and Nova Scotia. The trans-shipment of goods was necessary if the manufactured articles of Great Britain were to be exchanged for the foodstuffs and raw materials of the United States.

Passamaquoddy was a frontier where the peace had brought no settlement. That inveterate enemy of British power, John Allan, was on the St. Croix with his "bulldogs", the Indians who had not succumbed to British bribes and to whom he had brought presents from the Continental Congress and the State of Massachusetts. He informed British surveyors that the St. Croix River designated by the treaty was the Magaguadavic, a small stream that ran in a south-westerly direction past the projected site of St. Andrews. His pretensions were supported by letters from John Hancock, governor of Massachusetts. But the British claim to the main river, the Schoodiac, as the boundary was sustained by overwhelming numbers of settlers who were on the scene of the dispute. Parr was so nervous about the situation on the St. Croix that he wanted to send troops, an expedient from which Carleton rather angrily dissuaded him. Nova Scotia, he declared, could deal with the problem in a friendly manner by employing her civil resources.[57]

Though not in appreciable numbers, Loyalists overflowed from the valleys of the St. John and the St. Croix into those of the Miramichi and the Petitcodiac. Eager to avoid the escheat of his lands, William Davidson persuaded a number of them to move to the Miramichi, but the settlement did not acquire more than a transient quality. Loyalist traders, some of whom had been disappointed at Shelburne, came in and out, engaging in the fishery as opportunity offered but leaving no permanent mark. Temporary shore stations appeared and disappeared according to the pattern that was characteristic of the fishery. Still farther to the north, over 300 Loyalists, who had come down the St. Lawrence, landed at Gaspé in the spring of 1784. Their activities were not sedentary, and many of them came to the southern side of the Bay of Chaleur to engage with the Acadians in the fishery.[58]

By reason of this great immigration the population of the Nova Scotian hinterland had suddenly increased tenfold. About 14,000 Loyalists had come to the area that later became the province of New Brunswick. Contrary to a great deal that has been written, they could not be considered a select group of the population of the former thirteen colonies. For a time there was a surplus of educated gentlemen in search of official positions. A few great households appeared, centres of community example and authority, such as that of Amos Botsford at Westcock near Sackville, where Yorkshire labourers and Acadian peasants came for casual employment and where indigent Micmacs could freely find shelter. Botsford was the kind of man who could raise volunteers for the local militia and recruit clergy for the Church of England.[59] But education and wealth were in equally short supply. The Loyalists represented a good cross-section of the population of the rebellious colonies. The vast majority did not have a superior education.

Nearly all came from New York, Connecticut, and the other "middle" colonies. Because they came from the south of New England and because many had fought in the Carolinas and Georgia, numerous writers have supposed that most of them originated in the south. But only a minute ingredient, possibly five per cent, came from the colonies south of New York and New Jersey.[60]

CHAPTER 3

The Founding

1783-1786

The partition of Nova Scotia and the founding of New Brunswick were events fateful for the eastern region of British North America. In spite of more elaborate explanations that have been given for the establishment of four governments in place of one,[1] partition was in the nature of things. Geography made it seem reasonable. History made it inevitable. The coming of the Loyalists to Nova Scotia in 1783 provided the implication of challenge for the reorganization of the province. "The great concourse of Loyalists that resorted to it upon the evacuation of New York came here in the full confidence of the establishment of a separate government, having at that time, conceived from various causes, a strong aversion to living under the jurisdiction of the province of Nova Scotia."[2]

The dream of an exclusive Elysium in the north was deeply set in Loyalist ideology. It dated from the days when it had become apparent that the rebellious colonists could not be conquered, when, as they sat through the dreary months of confinement on Long Island, they had lamented and lampooned the errors in strategy of the British commanders and regretted the wilful policies of the imperial government. Knox's plan of 1780 had nourished the possibility. Events had given it impetus and encouragement. Loyalist consciousness of self-sacrifice demanded gratification. Nova Scotia might be the Elysium, but they would not endure the control of the rulers of Nova Scotia who had sacrificed nothing and for whom the war had resulted in great gain.

Throughout 1783 Sir Guy Carleton at New York steadily

succumbed to the pressure of Loyalist opinion upon the future of British North America. Parr, the appointee of Lord Shelburne whom the Loyalists regarded as their betrayer, was the obstacle to their control of Nova Scotia, and Parr progressively deteriorated in the estimation of the commander-in-chief. A "persecuting spirit" at Halifax, Carleton wrote to Whitehall, was at work against the Loyalists, and there were republicans in offices of trust and confidence.[3] Parr's anxiety to deal with civil difficulties at Shelburne and Passamaquoddy by the use of troops was interpreted by Carleton as evidence of the governor's incapacity. These prejudices were powerfully seconded by Henry Fox, who returned to Britain with accounts of the dubious loyalty of the old settlers of Nova Scotia. His prophecies of a great community of Loyalist colonies overshadowing the United States and possessing the exclusive privilege of supplying the British West Indies with North American goods were not received kindly by those who hoped to conciliate the United States by admitting her to Britain's empire of trade. "Mr. Fox's brother is at Nova Scotia high in command and writes over-flattering accounts of the settlements begun on the St. John River and the number of inhabitants arrived; I think they say 32,000 and 10,000 more expected. Boys and inexperienced people are never more mistaken in anything than in numbers."[4]

Disregarding the advice of his more prudent friends, Edward Winslow remained at Halifax during the winter of 1783-4. There he volubly responded to every item of news that came from England, speculating upon his broken fortunes and uncertain hopes. He was characteristic of the enterprising, articulate group of men who now looked to London rather than to New York for the patronage that could end the uncertainty. A new governor of Nova Scotia who would establish a Loyalist régime would mean a new avenue to rehabilitation. Failing this, a partition of Nova Scotia would mean a new province with new offices and preferments. As his friend Edmund Fanning suggested, he advocated a new office, that of Receiver General of Quitrents, for it would suit his talents well.[5] Whitehall was the fountain of honour, and it was to Whitehall that every Loyalist gentleman addressed his plea.

II

Most of the leading Loyalists who had served Carleton at New York sailed for Britain with the fleet that finished the work of evacuation. They encountered a political revolution that thrust their public cause and their private ambitions into the background of affairs. George III, taking the initiative into his own hands, had contrived the dismissal of the North-Fox coalition and had selected the younger William Pitt as his leading minister. Elections had to be fought, and the newly arrived Loyalists, added to the host of those who had been in Britain for months and years, were compelled to await the issue.

The triumph of the new government made one possibility, the dismissal of Parr, less certain. Shelburne was not a member of the new ministry but he exercised great influence upon it. Parr's reaction to the news of Pitt's victory was one of elation and revived confidence.[6] Yet the great decisions for the future of Nova Scotia were to come from one source, Sir Guy Carleton. The change of ministry did not affect the great authority he possessed in American affairs. He had returned from New York with his work ably accomplished, but without the mark of honour of a British peerage, which North, in an ashamed manner, informed him the King had refused.[7] In March, when the government was prepared to attend to specific decisions on American affairs, Carleton came to London. His Loyalist bias had not been shaken. "The only firm hold that Great Britain has upon the remains of the American Dominions is certainly by means of the Loyalists."[8]

The solution adopted for Nova Scotia was not that of dismissing Parr and the members of the Halifax cabal who were generally distrusted. It was, instead, that of cutting Parr's government, in the words of one of his Loyalist critics, to a size that was in accordance with his abilities. Partition could both save Parr and reward the host of loyal seekers of office who were clamouring on the doorstep of Lord Sydney, the new American Secretary, who had told them that Nova Scotia should be the envy of all the American States. The first official indication came on May 10, when the Privy Council formally proposed the division, giving as its reason the difficulty of communication between Halifax and the outlying regions. On May 14 the King referred to a committee of the Privy Council a letter from Sydney. On May 21 Sydney reported to the King on a minute of cabinet of "last night" on "the separation of the province of Nova Scotia". George III, who made notations on almost all state documents of importance, apparently took no notice of the division. There was no comment.[9] It was not until May 29 that Sydney wrote to Parr informing him of the prospect. On June 15 the Board of Trade was asked for a report on detailed arrangements and on June 18 the partition was finally ordered.[10]

The Cabinet had turned to William Knox for the blueprint of a new establishment. Regarding the result of the war as a private as well as a public mortification, he could turn with avidity to his handiwork of 1779, the plan for New Ireland. The former under-secretary for American affairs, acting on an impermanent basis, had agreed to give advice provided that one major premise should be accepted, that the remaining colonies should be administered on the principle that they be kept dependent on Great Britain. This caused no difficulty, and Knox, older but unconvinced that the advice he had given Germaine had been impolitic in principle and disastrous in results, went to work in typically rigorous fashion on the more technical aspects of the problems of a greatly reduced empire.[11]

The Plan for the Intended Province of ————————[12] comprehended an entirely new scheme of government for British North America. A governor general would have large powers of supervision over all the remaining territories from Cape Breton to Canada. Geography indicated that the isthmus of Chignecto was the logical boundary against the peninsular rump of Nova Scotia and that the Gaspé peninsula should be included within the new province, the only objection being that an act of Parliament would be necessary to amend the Quebec Act. Knox proposed that the new province, like his earlier concept of 1779, should be called New Ireland, but at this stage came a ministerial objection and the word *Quare* appeared in the margin. He had wanted to honour the land of his birth, but Ireland was out of royal favour now. Grattan's parliament was an affront to George III secondary only to that of the independence of the American states.

The simplicity of the plan, compared with the more archaic features of Knox's earlier submission, may lead to the conclusion that he had adjusted himself to the new political climate induced by the return of Carleton. There were no considerations of "how to balance the democratic power in America". The framework of government was to be modelled on that of Nova Scotia with a parliamentary estimate of £8,940 for the payment of the fixed establishment. In its final form it was shorn of the devices he had earlier proposed for the strengthening of the prerogative. It was probably the New York influence, sustained by Carleton and the lessons of bitter experience, that produced the opinion, perhaps a reluctant one, that "there should also be given to the colonies on the part of Great Britain a clear and explicit exemption from all taxation except by their own legislatures". The Loyalists of New York had had ample opportunity to reflect upon the causes of the American Revolution. On the constitutional issue concerning taxation many of them sided, in the abstract, with the rebels. One of the great memories they were to bring to their new homes was that of the Carlisle Commission, the great Renunciation of 1778 by which Parliament had offered to abandon its right to tax the colonies. Knox's plan likewise proposed the abandonment of quitrents on lands to be granted to the Loyalists. At New York, many months earlier, Carleton had encouraged their leaders to believe that this irritating relic of the royal authority in the old empire would be abandoned in the new and had given the British government a positive statement of his opinion.

Upon another salient feature of the plan Knox and Carleton could be in substantial agreement. The later author of *The Theocracy and the Revealed Will* could perceive a distant theatre for his dearest designs as the founding of a new and loyal province came nearer. Knox was a High Church Tory who took delight in contemplating the happy union between Church and State in the days of Archbishop Laud and in the polemics of Dr. Sacheverell. He could not want for a sympathetic audience as the Loyalist clergymen who had surrounded Carleton at New York came flocking to London. The lack of an episcopacy in the thirteen colonies had been responsible for the levelling, democratic opinions that had moved the Americans to overt rebellion. An episcopacy in the new empire could support loyalty and confound the religious enthusiasms that had made the right of private judgment in matters of faith the instrument of political schism. The parish church, decently administered by a clergyman of the Church of England, could be a rallying point for subjects of the King in the depths of the forest primeval.

The establishment of an episcopate, Knox argued, would weaken the United States by persuading additional loyal subjects of the Crown to move to the new British provinces. Religious toleration should be given to the Roman Catholics and to every religious persuasion as a means of diminishing the influence of the republicans, "who are principally composed by

Presbyterians". Why, he asked pugnaciously a few months later, had the government permitted the extension of the Church of England episcopate to the United States? It would have the effects of keeping Royalists there and of drawing those in Nova Scotia back to their original homes. Why had three bishops been consecrated for the revolted colonies before a single see had been established in British America?[13]

The partition of Nova Scotia was only one feature of the grand design of creating a new British North American economy. The ruling prepossession was that the new provinces would be adequate sources of supply for the West Indies trade. Already, Knox was convinced, the Americans were viewing with alarm the rising new settlements on the St. John River. The "stationed ships" and the "searchers" engaged in the carrying trade would sail from the British provinces rather than from the ports of New England as of yore. Brook Watson supported this opinion. Fox, at a meeting of the Board of Trade, upheld this great aspiration, prefacing his remarks with "if the grants are confirmed to the Loyalists".[14] There was a general conviction amid British governing circles that the great flow of population from the south would continue, that New England by her rebellion had lost her historic role in the trade of the outside world.

In the summer of 1784 the King's German dominions were greatly in favour, and the new province was designated New Brunswick. Nomenclature appears to have made little difference to the Loyalists as they awaited the news of its establishment. On September 10 an act of the Privy Council approved a new seal. "On one side a ship sailing up a river on the borders of which is a new settlement, with lofty pines on each side, destined to naval purposes, with this motto Spem Reduxit, and this inscription around the circumference, Sigill: Provinciae Nov: Bruns: On the reverse side His Majesty's arms in a shield with the supporters, Garter and Imperial Crown, with the motto, and around the circumference His Majesty's titles."

III

Sir Guy Carleton refused at this time to accept the governor-generalship of British North America, but his influence in the British government was so great that virtually all the appointments in the new provinces were at his disposal. As his admirers had predicted, Fox was offered the governorship of New Brunswick. But, since the eventual coming of Sir Guy was uncertain, he refused to accept because of the risk of having to serve beneath a governor general who would be unsatisfactory to him. This was a point of view familiar to military officers of the time. The offer passed to Brigadier Musgrave, who had served beneath Carleton at New York, and he refused for the same reason. Finally the appointment passed to Colonel Thomas Carleton, the younger brother of Sir Guy, who accepted it on the understanding that after a brief tenure in New Brunswick he would move to Quebec as governor of that province.

The career of Thomas Carleton and his habits of life had been almost exclusively military. In the year when his brother had served as Wolfe's quartermaster-general at Quebec he had fought at Minden. The long peace between the wars, during which he had served on garrison duty at Gibraltar, he had found so unsatisfying that he had volunteered for one of Catherine the Great's campaigns in south Russia and had served against the Turks. The war of the Revolution had brought him to Canada in 1776. Twice he had been wounded. In 1782, when Sir Guy took over the command at New York, he headed precipitately for that city, defying the authority of General Haldimand at Quebec by refusing to resign his appointment as quartermaster-general.[15] New York's attractions proved to be fleeting. He sailed for London and in April 1783 married the American widow of a brother officer. His rigid, military disposition could not have been softened by his spouse. "Do you know the reason why Mrs. C. doesn't like to ride in a sleigh with two horses? She thinks two horses look sociable and she hates everything that looks sociable."[16]

In accepting his new position Thomas Carleton had stipulated that two of the six regiments under the control of the Halifax command should be stationed in New Brunswick. Should the commanding officer at Halifax be below the rank of brigadier-general, the two regiments were to come directly beneath his authority.[17] The stipulation, though he was never explicit in statement on matters of policy, is suggestive of his views upon the task that awaited him. The colonization of New Brunswick would be after the fashion of a Roman occupation of alien territory. The military settlers would have to remain in arms, and military outposts would herald their entrance to the wilderness interior. His knowledge of civil affairs was limited and he was not really interested in them. His civil administration he regarded as only auxiliary to his military command. Schooled in a lifetime of military duties, he had an instinct for correct procedures and a determination to keep his subordinates under close control. Patronage, both civil and military, was a commodity upon which he, like the vast majority of his contemporaries, placed great reliance.

Sailing with Thomas Carleton at the end of August were most of the members of the government of New Brunswick. As Edward Winslow complained several years later, "the assault on St. James was more successful than the assault on St. John." The office-seekers who had gone to London had won the prizes. Those who had come to Halifax or the St. John had been left without visible reward. The *St. Lawrence* carried a cheerier band of old comrades than those who had consorted together during the dreary days of the evacuation of New York.

As secretary of the new province came Jonathan Odell, who had been a missionary for the Society for the Propagation of the Gospel at Burlington and Mount Holly in New Jersey. He had witnessed many dangerous transformations since the day in October 1775 when one of his letters had been intercepted and he had been arrested by order of the provincial congress of New Jersey. He had contributed "not a little" to abhorrence of rebellion in his own section of the province and had been the subject of bitter persecutions because of his open character as a Loyalist. On December 12, 1776, when he was held in protective custody within the limits of his parish, a party of armed men with fixed bayonets had landed from one of the rebel galleys anchored off Burlington for the express purpose of seizing his person. There was a house-to-house search, but, screened by his parishioners, he bolted for the British lines at New York.[18]

His talents had been of service. He had for a time directed the printing of propaganda, which had been circulated behind the rebel lines amongst the vast proportion of the American population who had refused to take an extremist position for either side. His loyal verses, cavalier in sentiment, had contributed to the generation of a spiritual zeal in the provincial army, consigning rebel dignitaries to perdition, glorifying the good old cause of undiluted loyalty. He was a native of New Jersey, in his forty-seventh year, but it was his learning, acquired in residence at Oxford, that turned him away from the plebeian doctrines of Congress, which he genuinely loathed. He had served as assistant secretary to the Board of Associated

Loyalists. But the service that counted most, so far as his personal prospects were concerned, was his work as translator of French and Spanish documents for Sir Guy Carleton. Learning as well as loyalty commanded respect. Though he had not solicited it, Carleton offered him the secretaryship. During the months of waiting in London he had whiled away the hours by searching for his family history and coat-of-arms, but without success.[19]

As chief justice there was George Duncan Ludlow who, having been a judge of the Supreme Court of New York, had endured the long confinement on Long Island. At the outset of the Revolution he had seen the authority of the King's courts challenged by the rebels and had manfully fought to support it. Eventually he had been forced into retirement "to cherish the remains of loyalty in Queens County" until the day when Sir William Howe marched into New York at the head of a British army. Attainted by the legislature of New York in 1779, he had been employed in the administration of civil affairs and the supervision of police on Long Island. His rigour had made him a man of mark among the enemy, and in 1780 a party of rebels who had crossed the Sound burnt his house to the ground when they failed to take him prisoner.[20] He had served on the Board of Associated Loyalists and, owing to the influence of Carleton and Robertson, former governor of New York, was one of the most favoured claimants for office. A Loyalist historian, though admitting that Ludlow was liberally educated, has described him as "the little tyrant of Long Island" who favoured his friends with all the influence at his command.[21]

His brother, Gabriel Ludlow, who came without office but ranking as a senior councillor, was a man of arms who had for a considerable time commanded de Lancey's Brigade on Long Island. When Sir William Howe had restored British control, Gabriel Ludlow had met the royal forces on Jamaica Plains with seven hundred loyal men of Queens County behind him. Throughout the remainder of the war his home at Hampstead had been a social centre for British officers and Loyalist gentlemen. He had been a great landed proprietor and a speculator of some notoriety in real estate.

The offices of assistant judges were poorer prizes. There was no provision made for them when the province was originally established and Carleton was at pains to secure an addition to the parliamentary estimate in order to pay their small salaries of £200.

James Putnam was an eminent lawyer of Massachusetts, one of whose students had been John Adams. Sabine, the American historian of the Loyalists, after visiting Putnam's home in Saint John, said: "I have often stood at his grave and mused upon the strange vicissitudes of human condition, by which the Master, one of the giants of the American colonial bar, became an outlaw and exile, broken in fortune and spirit, while his struggling and friendless pupil, elevated step by step by the same course of events, was finally known the world over as the chief magistrate of a nation." Isaac Allen had commanded the 2nd Battalion of New Jersey Volunteers. The third was Joshua Upham, the former second-in-command of the King's American Dragoons, "one of the best fellows in the world", Benjamin Thompson had said,[22] who in 1781 had successfully defended the post at Lloyd's Neck against an attack by a French fleet. The lack of legal learning of the second and third was compensated for by the first.

Another important passenger on the *St. Lawrence* was Ward Chipman, the young attorney from Massachusetts who arrived with the post of solicitor-general but without salary. Early in the war he had gone to England, had received a pension for his loss of property, but had given up this modest competence in order to return to New York and serve with the occupying forces. It was probably difficult to detect behind the amiable personality of the young man, who was blessed with a capacity for warbling in convivial company, a sharp, calculating intelligence and a driving, imperious will. His capacity for hard work was to make him one of Thomas Carleton's chosen men. When the attorney-generalship, at first filled by Sampson Salter Blowers, another of "the Massachusetts interest", fell vacant, the Governor recommended Chipman. Other influence had anticipated him, and Jonathan Bliss, another Massachusetts man, a rescinder of the General Court of 1768 who had protested against the grievances of his country but would not turn to treason, arrived in New Brunswick with a warrant of appointment. Carleton reacted in a hostile manner. Bliss was protected by a patronage other than his own and he regarded him as an interloper.

The surveyor-general, George Sproule of New Hampshire, did not arrive in New Brunswick until the following year. Other leading Loyalists, without benefit of permanent offices that yielded income, received seats on the council, which was limited

by the terms of Carleton's instructions to twelve members.
Abijah Willard, who had founded a new Lancaster in New
Brunswick to compensate for the one he had lost in Massachusetts, became one of the fathers of the new province. Edward
Winslow, bereft of the preferred position he had anticipated
by Fox's refusal to accept the governorship, burdened with a
host of junior offices that yielded no income, cast in the shadow
of Sir Guy Carleton's displeasure by reason of his truculent
stand on behalf of the provincial army, was similarly honoured.
Beverley Robinson of New York, though too old to abandon
his new home in England, received a seat. Several sons represented his interests in New Brunswick. Gilfred Studholm, who
had commanded the post at Fort Howe during the closing years
of the war and who had directed the settlement of the Loyalists
under Nova Scotian authority, was also appointed. He had
been at the centre of all the initial troubles, yet he had offended
no party greatly. He held power of attorney from absentee
proprietors whose lands he was attempting to save from escheat.
He had faithfully served Parr, yet he was acceptable to the leading Loyalists who surrounded Carleton.

The sole representative of the older inhabitants of the province on the council was William Hazen. Yet he was not to
emerge as a champion of the people of Maugerville, on whose
labours and produce he had so long profited. The "old" inhabitants were on the defensive. Some who did not hold clear titles
to their lands were dispossessed. Yet owing to their familiarity
with the country they were able to take care of themselves. If
they could not sell land, they could sell improvements and were
in a good position to take advantage of the Loyalist need of
cattle, timber, and provisions. They were outnumbered ten to
one, but the solidarity of the original New England ingredient
was only slightly shaken. For many years they were to remain
a recognizable minority, probably the most productive and
versatile element in the New Brunswick population, but out
of favour with government. In 1784 Hazen could not be said to
be of their number. His interests had become integrated in the
new Loyalist system. His home at Portland Point had become
a favourite resort for Loyalist patricians, and presently young
Ward Chipman would court a Hazen daughter to lay the foundation of a powerful family affinity.

At the outset, Loyalist ascendancy in the council of the province was complete. The "government of gentlemen", a vision

and an aspiration at the opening of 1784, had become a reality. Incipient cliques and cabals could already be discerned, but, as long as Carleton ruled, none could achieve an extraordinary degree of influence. The New York alliance of the Ludlows and the Robinsons constituted a powerful influence. The younger men from New England – Chipman, Winslow, John Coffin, George Leonard – were able and ambitious, but on the fringes. In civil affairs Carleton was dependent on advice, but he was accustomed to complete command.

IV

It was on Sunday, November 21, that Carleton and his entourage arrived at Parrtown to proclaim the birth of the new province. There were salutes from a battery, loud huzzas from a tumultuous throng, and cries of "Long live the King and the Governor". But a winter chill was settling upon the place, symptomatic of the trials that faced the administration. Reports of impending starvation were coming from the outlying settlements, and Carleton had to take emergency measures to supplement the stock of provisions in the royal stores. The enthusiasm could only be temporary. The unanimity of the people could last only until the Governor should indicate whether or not he would endorse the ascendancy of the Loyalist agents. The address of a group of "oppressed and insulted Loyalists" had acclaimed the partition of Nova Scotia as a delivery from tyranny. But Carleton would be compelled to take sides in the struggle between the agents who had controlled the settlement up to this time and the party of Elias Hardy, the commercial element who had arrived with the fall fleet and who regarded the coming of a new governor as the signal for the breaking of the power of their enemies. The spirit of the latter had been sparked through the preceding year by the visit of Finucane and by some able journalism and pamphleteering, directed by men of skill and education:

> Wronged by a set of ravillacs,
> Of all but gun, and spade and axe;
> Our agents too, so very true
> I wish the D——— had his due.[23]

Disunity already existed within the province and attacks upon its integrity came from without. At Halifax there was, in the circles of government, a keen resentment of the work of partition. Parr himself had acquiesced in the division of his government. As late as June 16 he had denounced partition as "a cursed, selfish idea" of the Loyalist agents. But in July, shifting with the winds that blew from London, he had written, after enduring a long silence from Sydney, to recommend partition as a means of expediting public business. On July 31, at a meeting of his council, the Loyalist agents were exonerated from the charges laid against them by the inhabitants of Parrtown. On August 3, Hardy and his associates lost their authority to proceed upon investigation of those charges.[24] The governor of Nova Scotia, having at the beginning of the year turned to the support of the popular party against the agents, adjusted himself to the circumstances of Loyalist triumph north of the bay. Partition represented salvation for himself, a smaller but secure government. On August 13 he wrote that he was pleased to hear of the separation of New Brunswick from Nova Scotia, especially because his old friend, Carleton, had been given the governorship. Carleton later reported that, during his short stay at Halifax en route to the St. John River, Parr had received him with the greatest cordiality and had given him every co-operation.[25]

Though he had gladly withdrawn from the lists, the governor of Nova Scotia was compelled to give encouragement to a rearguard action against partition conducted by his advisers. Too late to be of any avail, Andrew Finucane and Brenton Halliburton had gone to London to protest the division of the province. Later in the year a remonstrance developed against the inclusion within New Brunswick of that part of Cumberland County north of Chignecto. The better part of the marshland area that had provided so many cattle for the Halifax market was lost to Nova Scotia, and the merchants of Halifax, fearing the alienation of a valuable commercial connection, vainly sought a revision of the boundary in their favour.[26] The officials of the Nova Scotian administration had solid reasons for regretting the loss of the wealthy, well settled region. They had expended revenues north of the bay before the separation took place. Their fees of office would be seriously diminished. They held in their possession many bonds for the payment of duties posted by merchants in New Brunswick.[27] They might now meditate upon the worth of these documents and resent the appearance of a new legal jurisdiction in what had been one of the richest of their preserves. From the beginning, Halifax was the citadel of an opposing camp, hostile to the prospects of the new province and eager to regain something of what had been lost.

Nova Scotia wanted the return of the northern part of Cumberland County, but the Americans would take, if they could, one-third of the province as it had been defined by the proclamation. From the westward came the challenge of Massachusetts, the demand that the Magaguadavic be accepted as the St. Croix mentioned in the treaty. John Hancock, the governor of that state, wrote that "after a most careful examination of the evidence" this slender stream, not the broad Schoodiac, was the true St. Croix of which Champlain and other geographers had written.[28] Faced by challenges both from subjects of the King and from enemies at the gates, a man of Carleton's mentality could look only to the means of keeping order. Anxiously he scanned the slim detachments of the 54th Regiment. A march to the north, the opening of new lands on the upper St. John, and the consolidation of existing settlements had to be achieved. It would be a large task not merely to extend the settled areas of the province but to bring the scattered, insecure Loyalists already within New Brunswick to a common conscience and an ordered way of life.

V

There was need for determined leadership, and Carleton supplied it. His instructions had specified that he should call elections for a general assembly as soon as he considered such a course expedient. Yet he was determined to postpone as long as possible the day when popular participation in government should place limitations on his plans for the organization of the province. In this course he enjoyed the unanimous approval of the council. His programme required a year of grace in which he might lay down firm lines for the development of New Brunswick before submitting his work to the sanction of an assembly of well disposed representatives of the people. At London, Sydney impatiently waited for a report on the calling of an assembly. Carleton coolly postponed the issuance of writs until his preparatory work had been finished.

A committee of the council entered upon the laborious duty of examining petitions for grants of land. Neither the attorney-general nor the surveyor-general had yet arrived, and Carleton was happy to engage the services of Chipman, whose ability in

this emergency made a lasting impression on him. If, argued
Carleton, Chipman were not employed by the government,
those opposed to the government would secure his services.
Chaos existed as far as records of Nova Scotian grants of lands
were concerned. But most of the necessary and unpleasant
business of escheat had been accomplished before the partition.
Warned by the strictures of the British government that only
in cases where neglect was glaring should escheat take place,
the committee of the council proceeded carefully. It was found
that Sir Andrew Snape Hamond's grant on the Kennebecasis
amounted to 18,000 acres instead of the 10,000 specified in his
warrant. Ten thousand acres were escheated, but he was compensated in the northern part of the province. Colonel Spry had
to endure escheat, but only for those portions of his lands that
had not been settled. Such a grant as his, including twelve miles
of interval land along the bank of the St. John, aroused the
special resentment of the Loyalists. Carleton's ordinance required that all holders of lands who had received titles under
Nova Scotian authority should register in New Brunswick
within a year. One notable landlord of the Petitcodiac, Joseph
Frederick Wallet des Barres, was absent in England and failed
to obey the regulation. Eventually great complications would
result.

During the year in which he governed untrammelled by legislative obstruction, Thomas Carleton established the rudiments
of a system of local government that derived its authority
directly from governor and council. His principal impulse was to
avoid a replica of democratic New England, where popular control was exercised over local affairs. The bad example of Nova
Scotia, where powers of self-government in the townships had
been strenuously sought by New England immigrants, was held
up as a lesson for laying the designs of government in a new and
model province. The word "parish" was perhaps suggestive of
the urbane manner in which the villages of England had been
governed since the days of Queen Elizabeth, and reminiscent
of the English villagers' obedience to the government. Seven
counties were marked off on the map, and parishes created for
areas where settlement had taken place. Perhaps hopefully, it
was conceived by Carleton and his council that the magistrates
of New Brunswick, drawing their commissions directly from
the governor, not only dispensing justice in the inferior courts
but performing the executive work of their parishes, serving

without reward because they were independent, would emulate the English justices of the peace.

To select a capital, Carleton, during his first winter in New Brunswick, ascended the St. John as far as the lands above Maugerville where the provincial army had settled. By his instructions he was entitled to choose a "place or seat" from which his government should function. He had never planned to remain at the mouth of the river. But, after hoping to establish a temporary headquarters at Maugerville, he was compelled by his late arrival to take a house at Saint John.[29] The region about St. Anne's Point, where the French had made one of their short-lived settlements, seemed eminently suitable. Here was the highest point on the river navigable for vessels of considerable size. It was the region farthest north where the country was thickly settled. Among the remnants of the provincial army there was little left of the spirit of Eutaw Springs and of Ninety-Six. Large numbers had sold their lots and departed for other sections of the province. But the country about St. Anne's had a military character. Its substantial citizens were half-pay officers of the Loyalist corps. Before the province had been created Winslow had suggested St. Anne's as a logical seat of government. The rural environment, in contrast to the commercial environment of Saint John, promised a habitation where aristocratic fashions in government and society might have freer expression. Already St. Anne's had acquired a new name of military significance, Osnaburg, so designated in honour of Frederic, Bishop of Osnaburg, second son of George III, whose practical endeavours for the increasing of pay and living allowances to officers in the army had won for him great popularity.

Carleton was not a highly articulate man, but his dispatches repeat the assertion that the continued settlement of New Brunswick would depend on military measures. His ambition was for a military enclosure rather than for a civil capital. From St. Anne's the march to the north could be continued and controlled. In June of 1785 he wrote of his plans for a barracks at the falls of the Oromocto, large enough to billet a regiment. The location would be within easy reach of the coast and of the American frontier, yet far removed from facilities that would enable the troops to desert.[30] In November the selection of St. Anne's was announced. The *Royal Gazette* of this month brought news of the visit to Berlin of Frederic, Bishop of Osnaburg. He was about to be married and to assume the new title granted by

his father – Duke of York and Albany. St. Anne's became
Fredericton in York County instead of Osnaburg.

Amidst the uncertain process of setting up government, the
place of greatest danger was Saint John, where opposition to the
government was welling up to a dangerous degree. As the bounty
of the royal stores was gradually removed and as the people
became compelled to depend on the fisheries in the harbour,
Carleton was aware of the hostile spirit that was abroad. The
Governor had refused to countenance the opposition to the
Loyalist agents that was kept alive by Hardy and his friends.
The merchants of the Lower Cove had obtained no redress for
their alleged grievances. Commercially, a quandary had arisen.
The shippers and traders of Massachusetts were attempting to
break the bonds independence had imposed upon them. Traders
whose true allegiance was dubious swarmed into the prematurely
developed seaport, attempting to make Saint John a base from
which they could continue to enjoy the benefits of British
registration and the rewards of British markets. To make
matters more difficult New Brunswick was dependent upon the
importation of American foodstuffs. Carleton attempted to keep
the traffic within reasonable bounds by issuing licences to
British ships to introduce American supplies, but how much of
this trade was legal and how much illegal he was at a loss to
state. His efforts were approved by the Board of Trade, which
noted in a special report that the merchants of New Brunswick
were to be commended for their willingness to adapt their course
to the imperial system of trade.[31] This was in contrast to the
conduct of Parr at Halifax, where the American flag had appeared in the harbour and where the merchants strongly demanded
permanent relaxation of the Navigation Acts so that their
port could become the centre of a great transatlantic traffic in
the exchange of British and American goods.

Though he was able to maintain at least an appearance of a
correct observance of the laws of trade, Carleton determined to
impose a greater degree of discipline upon the inhabitants of
Saint John, many of whom were transient. He resorted to the
device of a city corporation. The management of the wharves
and piers and of the traffic in the harbour required local magistrates with authority to make regulations and by-laws. Using
the charter of the City of New York as a model and the legal
services of Ward Chipman, Carleton produced the Charter of
the City of Saint John which, like all his other local measures,

was subject to the approval of the legislature when it should meet. The name was adopted by general consent of the inhabitants, the original name of Parr never having obtained popular approval. A mayor and a recorder, appointed by the provincial government, were the chief executive and judicial officers. Aldermen were to be elected by the freemen of the city. In Carleton's estimation, at least, the salient feature of the charter was a provision for a court of justice in which the mayor and recorder should preside upon suits under fifty pounds and over forty shillings. "This institution appears so greatly preferable to the disorderly meetings before a single justice, at which the colonists have hitherto been accustomed to attend, that I am in hopes that it will prevent a wish for their being reestablished."[32] The competence of the court considerably exceeded that of other inferior courts that had been established in the counties. When Sydney remonstrated that Carleton had exceeded his instructions by the granting of such a charter, the retort came that the instructions had given to the governor the power of erecting cities and boroughs. Why not by incorporation? "In the exercise of such power here I was led by a conviction that it was the most efficacious measure that could be adopted to reclaim the multitude and to promote the habits of order and industry, as it would introduce a more rigorous police than could be done by leaving them to the care of county magistrates."[33]

As first mayor and recorder of the City of Saint John, Carleton appointed Gabriel Ludlow and Ward Chipman. The first did not lack police experience, nor the second legal knowledge.

VI

Having organized the province by executive ordinances, Carleton issued writs for a general election in October 1785. Owing to the paucity of secure titles to land and the transient state of the population, the writ extended the franchise to all adult males who had been resident in the province for three months. In spite of this necessary generosity Carleton hoped to get a house of "worthy" members, men who would corroborate the decisions he had taken and extend the organization of the province along the lines he had laid down.[34]

Something deprecated by the most loyal – "a violent party spirit" – developed. Elias Hardy came forward as leader of an opposition that was prepared to undo all of Carleton's work. None of his speeches and writings are extant, but the testimony of his adversaries entitles him to respect. According to Carleton's own report Hardy proclaimed the doctrine that by rejecting the supporters of the goverment and voting for individuals whom he himself should designate, the electorate could "obtain full satisfaction for all their former grievances and supposed wrongs".[35] In the agitations preceding the election he and his party, operating in Saint John and hoping to extend their influence throughout the province, concentrated their attacks on the Loyalist agents whom Carleton had refused to disavow.

Since the mass of the people were from New York and the middle colonies and since the agents were New Englanders, attacks on the New England character became fashionable. It was alleged that at the first debarkation the New England leaders had acted with "superior cunning", that only those who hailed from "the meridian of Boston" had been able to obtain situations worth having. New Englanders, said the *New Brunswick Gazette,* make good commissaries and foragers but dangerous legislators. The electorate was urged not to blow up the constitution by choosing agents, agentees, Fifty-Fivers and government officers.

Far more fundamental was the proclamation of ideas that had originated in the lost American empire. The government slate of six candidates in Saint John City and County was headed by Jonathan Bliss, the attorney-general, and Ward Chipman, the solicitor-general. Hardy's party declared that officials of government had no place in an assembly of representatives of the people, that all the precedents of government in the colonies were opposed to an assembly dominated by "placemen". This was the first of many such conflicts in New Brunswick. Many Loyalists were willing to argue that the legislature of New Brunswick should function in the manner of those of the thirteen colonies, that there should be a clear separation between the executive and legislative powers. In the minds of many of the colonists it was axiomatic that the legislature should thwart and check the royal power rather than be its instrument. The quarrel concerned the great question as to which method was the more "British". Hardy and his followers pleaded the precedents of the colonies and of the system of government that prevailed in Britain at the time of Oliver Cromwell. There was much talk of the necessity of having "middling men" in the legislature, and the candidature of Bliss, a paid servant of the government, was especially denounced.[36] The government party could plead the contemporary British system by which ministers of the Crown sat in the front benches of the popularly elected body. But the refinements of the cabinet system of government were poorly defined and badly understood throughout the English-speaking world at the close of the eighteenth century. Among the British Americans the assumption generally prevailing was that it was the duty of a popular legislature to oppose.

Saint John entered its first election campaign early in November with its electorate violently and almost equally divided. Facing the Bliss-Chipman ticket was an opposition group of six, headed by Tertullus Dickenson, Hardy's brother-in-law. It was government men against those who had not been admitted to privilege, to a degree New Englanders against New Yorkers, patricians against plebeians, Upper Covers against Lower Covers. Flags and badges distinguished the parties. The government candidates offered to serve their constituents without pay. What Carleton most greatly feared, an act of violence, took place on the night of November 9. Amidst the excitement, the sheriff, William Oliver, moved the poll from McPherson's Tavern in the Lower Cove to Mallard's of the Upper Cove, half-way up King Street from the market slip. Vengefully the Lower Covers besieged a party of Upper Covers in Mallard's. Brickbats flew and windows were broken. The affair might have become much more serious had not troops arrived from Fort Howe to arrest the Lower Cove leaders.[37]

It was possibly the opportunity Carleton was waiting for – a chance to take summary action against the party that opposed his administration so wantonly. Half a dozen of their leaders were arraigned before the magistrates and turned over to the Supreme Court, which, in the spring, fined them heavily as well as sentencing them to extended terms in prison. Public warnings were posted against the opening of houses for the entertainment of electors. Sheriffs were authorized to take firm measures against truculent behaviour at the hustings. Yet the Lower Covers won the election in Saint John City and County. What followed was a more emphatic indication of Carleton's intention to get the kind of assembly he wanted. The government candidates demanded a scrutiny. When none of the Lower Cove candidates appeared to defend their votes, Sheriff Oliver declared that those from the Upper Cove had been successful.

When, in the new year, the Lower Cove party presented a half-literate but powerful petition to Carleton, asking that he dissolve the house of assembly on the grounds of Oliver's improper declaration, the Governor made no response. Bliss, Chipman, and their four colleagues took their seats to form the nucleus of an overwhelming government party. Dickenson and his friends attempted to spread their discontent through the province. One morning at a grog-house in Sunbury a mêlée occurred when six persons who had signed a petition the night before woke up and wanted to know what they had signed.[38]

Elsewhere throughout the province the election took place without serious incident. In Westmorland the sheriff disqualified the votes of the French Acadians. The Nova Scotian Act of 1783 had entitled Roman Catholics to vote provided that they should take oaths denying the right of the Pope to interfere in affairs of state. There was no evidence that any of them had ever taken the oath, and strong doubts were expressed as to whether or not they were His Majesty's subjects. In York 800 men peacefully assembled at St. Anne's and elected four "respectable gentlemen".[39] In Charlotte, which included the islands in the Bay of Fundy, conflicts between Scots and Yankees occurred. William Pagan, a Scots merchant who had been one of the leaders in the emigration from Penobscot to St. Andrew's, was the ruling power. Out on the islands a spirit of dissent prevailed. Gillam Butler, who a few months later was convicted and imprisoned for attempting to smuggle American whale-oil through the port of Saint John, wrote to Chipman that the government of Scots was offensive, that his candidature on behalf of "American" interests had been unsuccessful because of illegal practices, and that the county town should be located on Campobello rather than at Beaver Harbour where there were fewer people.[40] Kings, Queens, and Sunbury, the counties on the river above Saint John where new agricultural communities were forming, returned members acceptable to Carleton, though there were protests.

In spite of the Governor's efforts, the principal adversary was returned to the house of assembly. Hardy became a member for Northumberland, which stretched far north to the Bay of Chaleur through the valley of the Miramichi, the home of two or three hundred English-speaking fishermen and traders, and of two or three thousand Acadians. His election was won largely through the influence of William Davidson, whose interests

were opposed to the new government and whose principal connections were at Halifax. Northumberland was an arena into
which the government's influence had as yet not really pene-
trated. Davidson was fearful of the loss of his monopoly in the
fishery which had fallen into disuse during the war. Like many
others on the Miramichi at a later date, he was to look to Halifax rather than to the provincial capital for encouragement in
his ventures.

The meeting of the legislature in January of 1786 marked the
commencement of the robust political life of New Brunswick.
From the outset it was clear that the ideals of so many Loyalist
apologists had no true basis in reality. Instead of unity and
obedience the great political fact was dissent. Among the Loyalists the adversities of war had produced a powerful cohesion.
But in peace the circumstances of the first settlement in the new
British North America had made for diversity and difference.
"The democratic power in America" which Knox had so greatly
feared was a force to be reckoned with in the very beginning
of New Brunswick's history.

CHAPTER 4
The Testing Time
1786-1792

By the spring of 1786 a degree of stability had been achieved
after three years of pitching upon the soil and organizing the
institutions of the province. The seeding of the fields was sym-
bolic of hopes not only for a good harvest but for a bountiful
future to those who had pledged their fortunes and their faiths
to the new venture in New Brunswick. The Loyalists were on
their lands and dependent on their own energies, for except in
cases of emergency no more provisions would be issued from the
King's stores.

The venture had been an experiment. The emigration to
Nova Scotia and the establishment of New Brunswick had been
measures forced upon the British government by their obligations to the Loyalists. Particular pledges were honoured, but the
creation of a strong and prosperous British empire in North
America would require the unremitting care and powerful support of the government at London for many years. The more
optimistic of the Loyalists professed to believe that British
indulgence would continue, that imperial legislation and financial support would ensure the rapid growth of the infant settlements. When Sir Guy Carleton arrived at Quebec as governor
general it appeared probable that the strong measures necessary
to consolidate the success of what had already been accomplished
would be forthcoming.

The prospect appeared to be a fair one. The first legislature
of New Brunswick had met in the winter at Saint John, had
sanctioned the decisions of the Governor, supported the exertions of his officers, and established the Church of England.

Political disaffection had receded into the background. In August Thomas Carleton took a sloop-of-war to Westmorland and returned on foot over the hundred-mile journey, passing over the road marked out by George Leonard during the winter, finding industry and content on all sides through "the pleasant valley" of Sussex. In the same month the 300-ton ship *Lord Sheffield,* constructed for Benedict Arnold, allowed by all to be as good a ship as any ever built in North America, sailed from Saint John for Jamaica, making a fine appearance as she cleared the harbour.[1]

The experiment had been based upon certain common assurances. One was that the trade of the British West Indies would be reserved for the King's subjects and that the Americans, who had in large part possessed it before the war, would be excluded. This had been honoured. Shipbuilding became a major industry and Saint John quickly acquired a fleet of sixty square-rigged vessels. It became fashionable to boast that the Laws of Trade and Navigation were the palladium of the province, but it was highly inconvenient to enforce all of them in all their clauses. Trade with the Americans was essential for the supply of foodstuffs, and the Americans, like the British, discriminated in favour of their own shipping in their own ports. Foodstuffs licensed by Carleton for legal importation to the province were frequently accompanied by Virginian tobacco and East Indian goods, notably tea, procured by American traders who were opening up new routes to the Orient. Saint John became an important place for trade by reason of a combination of imperial wisdom and local discretion. An urbane collector of customs, William Wanton, who was redoubtable for his prowess at the dining-table, had derived from his superior at Halifax the conviction that the laws of trade should never be enforced against the Americans *in extremis.*[2] Occasionally a cargo of American goods was seized for the enrichment of the officers of the law, and the *Royal Gazette* carried advertisements that threatened informers. But pessimists declared that four-fifths of the trade of the province was illegal. American and other foreign goods could easily be brought into the other ports of New Brunswick, if not into Saint John, by routes considerably more direct than those laid down by the laws of trade.

A second common assurance was that of compensation for the loss of property in the United States. In deference to the claims of leading Loyalists the British parliament had established a commission to make findings and recommend awards. Expectations were modest. The government at London had ruled that grants of land in New Brunswick should compensate for loss of real estate in the thirteen colonies. Offices, pensions, half-pay should help to make good what the refugees had left behind. Few of the Loyalists who came to New Brunswick were able to file affidavits in support of large demands. Christopher Billopp, who asked for £26,000 and received £2,000, might be taken as a conspicuous example of those who presumed to riches. Gabriel Ludlow, generally accounted one of the richest of the New York Loyalists, received but £1,000, though the state of New York had confiscated from him tens of thousands of acres. Both of these formerly affluent New Yorkers became eminent storekeepers of Saint John.

The members of the commission who came to New Brunswick in 1787, lieutenant-colonels Dundas and Pemberton, were highly popular. "Our situation," wrote William Paine to Sir John Wentworth, "is rendered very pleasant by the residence of the commissioners. They possess the affection of all ranks of people. To the Loyalists they are endeared by their candour, liberality and uncommon attention to their concerns."[3] The sums they recommended in compensation were not great, but, added to the disbursements of pensions and half-pay, the accession of capital was of considerable importance. After the initial settlements fluid capital had rapidly become scarce. In the state of public and private finances there was no longer buoyancy. The first session of the New Brunswick legislature encountered demands for the establishment of a loan office and of a bank that would have power to issue paper currency, demands that were resisted by the merchants of Saint John, who said that there was sufficient specie in circulation.[4] The gentlemen of the countryside, as they toiled upon their new estates, their faces blackened by the smoke of burning bush, had reason to dismiss from their minds the memories of easy living in the regimental messes. "As a poor subaltern of an extravagant regimental mess I must hold up, stop my grog, and live on pork for at least one muster," wrote one of them to Chipman.[5] In its first years New Brunswick produced little to export in any volume. The manufactured goods of Britain, provisions from the United States, and luxuries of the tropics were paid for chiefly by the capital that came from the British government. The transition from the heavy expenditures for the war to the limited largesse of peace was a painful one.

II

The Loyalists who came to New Brunswick presumed to ownership of the soil and to the belief that the entire extent of the province, variously estimated at up to twenty million acres, would become the property of themselves and their descendants. In the three or four years following the settlement there was a good market for real estate, and much of the interval land changed hands several times. Many of the original grants became almost meaningless as settlers wandered about the country endeavouring to fix upon more desirable locations. The enthusiasm receded as two factors became apparent. One was that the amount of good arable land was limited. The second was that, owing to the scarcity of labour, a single individual could profitably manage only a comparatively small holding.

Tenancy was alien to the environment. Since all the Loyalists received free grants there was no need to labour on another man's land. The higher-ranking officers of the Loyalist corps and leading Loyalist gentlemen who received grants of up to one thousand acres were embarrassed by the difficulty of honouring the conditions, which required that for every fifty acres accounted plantable, three should be cultivated. Sometimes they adopted the expedient of giving away a few acres to poor people who appeared on the scene. But it was difficult to attract tenants to the many manors that the great grantees thought would rise from the wilderness. Land was worth only the labour expended upon it. Colonel Stephen Kemble, the proprietor of one of the great grants that had survived the Loyalist immigration, could not afford to be firm with his tenants. It was better, he told his attorney, to keep the tenants of Kemble Manor near Hampstead in good humour and to take from them as much as they could afford to pay than to force them to the terms of their contracts.[6] Knowledgeable men upon the spot could smile at Kemble's expectations, for the tenants were truculent and mutinous, affecting to believe that they were working their own land. The scarcity of cash was alone sufficient to prevent the realization of Kemble's ideal – of living comfortably in London on the proceeds of a New Brunswick estate. Always there was the fear of escheat for failure to comply with the conditions of

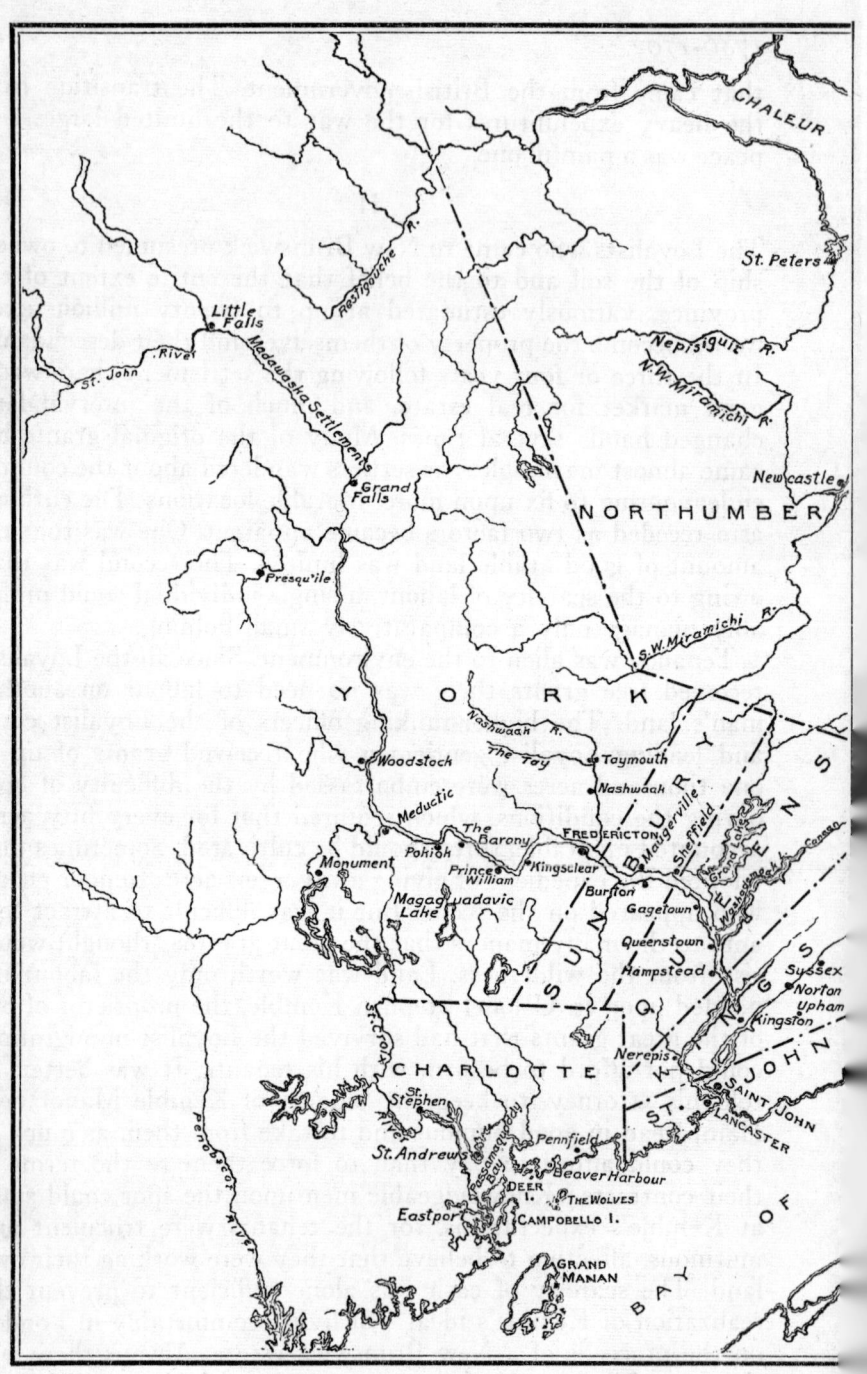

BAY

Miscou I.

Shippegan I.

Caraquet

Miramichi Bay

Chatham

LAND

Richibucto R.

Buctouche R.

Northumberland Strait

Prince Edward Island

Shediac Bay

Shediac

The Bend of Petitcodiac

Petitcodiac

Westmorland

Dorchester
Sackville

Hopewell

Shepody

Vale

Chignecto Bay

Nova

Fundy

Minas Channel

Minas Basin

Scotia

the grant. "It will be all right so long as the present Governor remains," wrote Kemble, "but there is no telling what another might do."[7] Absentee proprietors were unpopular. Industrious neighbours resentfully contemplated the neglect of idle owners, and prepared to petition for escheat should a favourable opportunity arise.

The dark forests behind the interval and the surliness of a free-spirited people dispelled the illusions from the minds of those who expected the development of a society based on the proprietorship of great estates. Some of the military grantees left the country, for there was no prospect of easy living. But most remained to give character and leadership to many of the new settlements that arose. Judges of the Supreme Court and other Loyalist patricians took to the fields to raise the fruits and vegetables necessary to livelihood. When Patrick Campbell visited the Nashwaak in 1792 he discovered that gentlemen would condescend to take part in the rough work of burning, clearing, and potato planting. There was an abundance of fine dairy cattle imported from the United States. The "estates" that appeared were more modest than the expectations of the wealthier class of Loyalists, but they were fashioned by the hands of those who owned them and yielded necessities in abundance, though no luxuries.

What developed along the lower and middle reaches of the St. John was a series of agricultural communities that were largely self-sufficient. No staple commodity was available for export. Populous places like Saint John and Fredericton where there were large numbers of troops had to import provisions from outside the province. In the spring of 1789 the optimistic Winslow wrote to Chipman from Fredericton that "nothing can be clearer than that the value of land in this neighbourhood is rising".[8] Yet at the end of the same year the perhaps more perspicacious Chipman, assuring a correspondent that the price on a sale was a good one, said that wealthy men would not speculate in the lands of the province.[9] After five years of a life that had been unexpectedly rugged for the majority of the Loyalists, progress had come to a halt and the province was in a position in which fresh elements of capital and labour were badly needed.

The element of speculation, however vibrant it may have been, was given crushing quietus by the British government early in 1790. By this time all claims to land brought forward by the Loyalists had been honoured. Yet these grants totalled less than 1,300,000 acres. Nine-tenths of the province remained ungranted, and Pitt's government, by this time noted for the success of its financial measures, prepared a programme which, it was sanguinely hoped, would produce a windfall. In February of that year an order of the Privy Council, enclosing a draft of instructions to governors in America and the West Indies, was referred to the Board of Trade. It directed that "at present" no grants of land belonging to the Crown should be passed to applicants. The instructions were prepared with "a view to exonerating the public in future from the heavy expenses which since the war have been incurred for the location of lands to Loyalists and disbanded troops and to prevent the disposal of valuable tracts in the said colonies and islands until a plan shall have been arranged for making the same a means of relieving this country at a future period from a part of the great civil and military expense now incurred on account of the colonies".[10]

The idea of sale of Crown lands for the purpose of raising colonial revenues had become popular in Downing Street. It was in imitation of policies devised in the United States for the sale of ungranted lands in the west. In Upper Canada it was applied only in detail, but New Brunswick experienced the full weight of the instruction for a period of seventeen years. The Crown lands were closed to further entrance. The ungranted portions of the province were locked up.

A great imperial land policy from which New Brunswick might eventually benefit appeared to be in the making, but the reasons for the prohibition were not understood in the colony for a great many years. Thomas Carleton himself presumably did not know the secrets of imperial policy and simply made it known that he could grant no more land for a time. It was commonly supposed that the instruction was associated with the St. Croix boundary dispute, that the American claim to nearly one-third of the province had deterred the British government from authorizing any further grants.

The Colonial Office emphasized that the free granting of huge tracts of lands in the older colonies had acted as a restraint upon immigration and enterprise, that the people of New Brunswick should abandon all thought of acquiring tens of thousands of acres in the woods and should concentrate upon the large holdings they already possessed. But the instruction

of 1790 did not have this effect. Carleton acted on the temporary nature of the prohibition, freely promising grants of
land to intending immigrants, offering clear title when the instruction should be withdrawn. Large numbers of settlers
accepted arrangements of this kind and became squatters as a
consequence of government policy. But as the years passed by,
as the British government forgot the instruction and the great
land programme of which it was a part, as settlers waited impatiently for the clear titles that failed to arrive, New Brunswick became known as a country where free land was not available and where large numbers of settlers had been hoodwinked.
Contrary to what had appeared probable, the value of granted
lands did not rise.

John Saunders was one who experienced frustration because
of the imperial decision of 1790. Formerly an officer of the
Queen's American Rangers, he had been one of the most feared
of the Virginian partisans on the side of the Crown, had worked
on military intelligence with the martyred Major André, and
had escaped from Yorktown with his regimental commander,
John Graves Simcoe, on a hospital ship. In 1788, after a period
of study in the Middle Temple, he had come to New Brunswick
as an assistant judge of the Supreme Court, determined to
create a replica of the fine estate he had left behind in Virginia.
In Princess Anne County he had owned the fairest of all properties, and had the proud reputation of being the finest host.
There he had possessed 800 acres with a mansion, barns, or-
chards of apples and peaches, a still of good oak timber.[11] On
the St. John River, above Prince William, he founded The
Barony, expended capital, bought out the claims of farmers on
the river-front, and stocked the land with neat cattle. Yet much
of his estate was sunken and barren. He had no opportunity to
expand. Having improved his grant according to the conditions
and created a thriving community, he endured the mortification
of a rejection of his special application for an additional area
to develop.

Ultimately Saunders became by grant and purchase the
greatest landholder in the province. Yet his great landed estate
did not well endure the passage of the years. Peter Fisher, the
first historian of New Brunswick, wrote in 1825 of the thriving
state of the farms of the King's American Dragoons in Prince
William. Above them The Barony was a wilderness.

III

Irritating challenges to Loyalist control in New Brunswick came from the outside. Sugar Island became the theatre of a minor contest in the summer of 1786 when Andrew Finucane, the younger brother of Bryan, who had died, arrived for the purpose of making improvements. The provincial government had ignored the grant made by the Halifax régime to the former chief justice, and the island, still valuable for its standing timber, had been shared in common by discharged soldiers of the Loyal American Regiment. No sooner had Finucane set foot on the property he considered his own, inherited from his brother, than he was turned out in a violent manner by a posse of twenty-one men, headed by four officers on half-pay, "armed with offensive weapons". When he appealed to the courts he was non-suited, the judge refusing to accept any evidence that he was brother and heir to the former chief justice.[12] An appeal to the Governor resulted in advice to go to the King-in-Council, but when it was revealed that Bryan Finucane had died insolvent and that creditors were waiting to take possession of all his property, the affair terminated with the Loyal American Regiment in unchallenged possession. A certain James Glenie, just beginning to become notorious, seized upon the affair as additional evidence of the nefarious activities of the junta of judges and officials who were combining to bring all valuable real estate beneath their control, with the Governor in collaboration behind the curtain, and who planned to cut and market the timber on Sugar Island for their own profit.[13]

The affair of Finucane recalled the former domination of the clique of officials at Halifax. Another affair that appeared more threatening was that of General William Spry, who for fourteen years continued his resistance to the decree of escheat passed by the Court of Chancery in 1786. "The chief engineer of a camp of repose," as Winslow designated him in reference to his services at Halifax during the Revolutionary War, refused to submit to the loss of a large portion of the St. John littoral that had been awarded him twenty years earlier. In 1795 he appeared likely to win his case when his right to appeal was granted by the King-in-Council. All holders of escheated land in New Brunswick took alarm. One of the common assurances of the country had been shaken, and the whole repute of Carleton's government was called in question. *Quid, boni aut mali,*

inde augurandum, asked Odell. Bliss and Chipman, the legal
luminaries, wrote that they could not doubt the authenticity of
the order but suspected that it was founded on insinuations and
false statements. The Attorney-General, overpowered by work
and unable to afford the services of a clerk, remarked that he
was working very faithfully on the case which would cause
"much mischief to the subject and dishonour to government".[14]

Justice according to law was not dispensed. Owing to the
strong remonstrances of Carleton the British government offered
Spry a settlement of expediency, suggesting a grant of land
equivalent to what had been escheated in another part of the
province. When he asked for compensation in money no further
action was taken. All the ungranted lands in New Brunswick,
said Spry, would not compensate him for what he had lost.[15]

These affronts to Carleton's authority were superficial compared with the claims of a rival jurisdiction, that of Sir John
Wentworth, the surveyor-general of the King's Woods at Halifax. Surveyor-general prior to the Revolution, he had acquired
a great reputation as a conserver of timber and as a scourge
upon the activities of adventurous merchants who had looted
the royal reserves in Maine and New Hampshire. Acts of Parliament extending as far back as the reign of Queen Anne
reserved for the Crown all pine trees that were twenty-four
inches or more in diameter. In 1783 Wentworth, with a much
smaller domain to supervise, resumed his task from a new
vantage-point. His instructions, emanating from the Lords of
the Treasury and the Lords of the Admiralty in London, authorized him to reserve all pine trees of the approved dimensions in
the King's remaining provinces, whether they stood on public
or on private lands. The Broad Arrow commenced to appear in
New Brunswick. Wentworth's agents and deputies began to
exercise an authority which could, in some cases, compete with
that of the governor himself.

Benjamin Marston, the ill-fated cousin of Edward Winslow,
was Wentworth's first deputy in New Brunswick. By failing to
exert his master's authority at the time of the granting of the
charter to the City of Saint John he lost an opportunity to confront the provincial government with an effective assertion of
his power. Wentworth had proposed to exercise control over the
most desirable sites for wharves and mast-ponds in the estuary
of the river. By the charter this control was vested in the City,
and the charter represented one of Carleton's dearest projects.

It was apparent that if Wentworth were to secure his point the charter would have to be destroyed, but Wentworth shrank from a conflict of jurisdiction in London upon this issue. The City of Saint John proceeded to collect substantial rents on the properties in dispute, some of them from Benedict Arnold, who made his brief and unwelcome appearance in New Brunswick at this time.

Marston refused to oppose the wishes of the provincial government, but his successor, William Paine, an erudite doctor of medicine from Massachusetts, sedulously and enthusiastically attended to his duties. He journeyed up the Kennebecasis, finding the lower country scarred by forest fires of former years and bare of trees in many places, but from Darling's Island upward it was the most delightful country on the face of the earth. The salt springs produced a better meat preservative than any he knew. In cases he considered vital to the interests of Wentworth and the Navy Board, Paine successfully resisted execution of grants of land by the provincial government. He marked off great reserves of forest for the exclusive use of the Royal Navy, two in Charlotte County and one on the St. John River. He indicated to Wentworth the presence of great timber-bearing areas on the Miramichi.

The establishment of this kind of jurisdiction, which lopped power from the provincial government, was a matter of some delicacy. "There seems a doubt in the minds of the official people here whether the Surveyor-General of the Woods can make reservations and afterwards permit individuals to occupy and cultivate such reservations. It is a new question and I confess I am not furnished with sufficient data to give an opinion. I think it my duty to hint this to you."[16] Wentworth's power and the patronage that went with it deprived the government at Fredericton of considerable initiative.

Late in 1787, before the complications of the mast trade became formidable, Paine left Saint John for New England in despair from the necessity of finding new security for his debts, his inability to make a living from his profession in New Brunswick, and the cost and scarcity of Lisbon wine and other comforts. He never returned, and his place was eventually taken by James Glenie, a clever and aggressive Scot who as a merchant had taken out a contract with the Admiralty for a supply of masts to the navy. About 1790 difficulties began to develop. It was alleged that private traders such as the Pagan brothers,

who were pillars of the community at St. Andrews, were looting
the reserves, that even merchants who held contracts with the
Admiralty, notably John Black of Greenock, were cutting under
licence of the Crown but were disposing of the timber in the
free market. At Maugerville Glenie himself was unable to procure the men and oxen to enable him to fulfil his contract without assuring the people, in a private way, that they could take
as much timber for their own purposes as they pleased. Supervision of the forests and of the work of taking out timber in
accordance with Admiralty specifications seemed impossible. In
order to get timber out for the purposes of the Crown, infinitely
more had to be abandoned to the labourers or left rotting on
the ground.[17] Waste became endemic as the men of Maugerville
ranged through the woods, hewing down all eligible trees in
order to prevent them from falling to their competitors.

For the people of the province the policy of establishing the
rights of the Crown to standing pine represented a check upon
legitimate business activity. Quarrels between the agents of
Wentworth and the fishermen of the Miramichi concerning the
use of desirable islands and trading locations became familiar.
Contractors and their workers invaded the premises of landowners, taking what they pleased within the meaning of acts of
Parliament. In 1791 Carleton wrote strongly to London on the
subject, urging that the rights of the surveyor-general, so far as
private lands were concerned, should be curtailed. Yet the
British government was quite unwilling to be influenced by
considerations that were local in character, and the King would
not yield what he had reserved for the use of the navy.[18]

IV

The new provincial establishment could have no reality for
Carleton until the northern wilderness had been opened for
settlement. The environs of Fredericton had been filled with a
substantial yeomanry. Fields that required no manuring produced vegetables in plenty, and the rivers abounded with
salmon that could be had for the taking, though it was commonly agreed that they were not in such profusion as in former
years. On the Nashwaak, according to Patrick Campbell, the
Highlanders who had been discharged from the 42nd Regiment,
generally accounted to be farmers as prudent as any in the province, could in the winter season take to the woods like Indians
and return in a fortnight with their sleighs loaded down with

venison and other game. The half-pay officers who had dispensed with the trouble and cost of servants were industriously pursuing a course that would lead to ease and independence. Fredericton had become a centre of population and a base from which the northward movement of soldiers and settlers could be directed.

The Governor had accepted a civil demotion to the rank of lieutenant-governor when his brother, now Lord Dorchester, came to Canada as governor general. Yet grace and favour came with military promotion to the rank of brigadier-general, which placed him in command of the troops in New Brunswick and Nova Scotia. In September 1787 when he proceeded to Halifax to review the troops of the garrison, he was the greatest man in the Atlantic provinces, and the Loyalist boast that New Brunswick was the heart and core of the Empire in America appeared to have some meaning. Paymasters, barrack-masters, and town majors were at Fredericton of a reckoning equal to or greater than the officers of civil government. But of troops Carleton did not at first have sufficient. It was not until 1790 that the War Office honoured the pledge made when he accepted the governorship, that two regiments should be stationed in the province.

When the 8th Regiment arrived in this year to join the 54th, Carleton felt for the first time that he had the resources to accomplish his task. He could maintain small detachments at Cumberland and Saint John, a whole regiment at Fredericton as a general reserve, and post garrisons higher up the river to guard the frontier and protect the settlers. A small fort arose at Presqu'ile, and still farther up, at Grand Falls, a barracks appeared 130 feet above the river on the cliffs. This decisive reinforcement gave the province something of the appearance of a line of battle as well as of a centre of settlement. At a high military level discussions were conducted as to how New Brunswick might best be defended, and Lord Dorchester supported the opinion of his brother that Fredericton was the point at which forces should be concentrated for counter-attack. This point of view, ultimately repudiated by the War Office, was ridiculed at Saint John where it was freely asserted that Fredericton and the howling wilderness above it were not worth defending. The loss of business attendant upon the removal of many of the troops and Carleton's persistent attempts to lower the discount on bills of exchange were greatly resented in Saint John.

To justify the concentration of force at Fredericton and the establishment of the northern posts, Carleton frequently employed the explanation that fear of the Indians impeded settlements. At one time, he declared, the Loyalist settlers on the river above Fredericton were on the point of abandoning the country.[19] The Malecites were scarcely capable of a formidable insurrection. Yet it is fairly certain that they constituted a considerable nuisance. Their attitudes of braggadocio and frequent threats to take up arms were quite sufficient to intimidate settlers whose homesteads were located a mile or more from those of their neighbours, for the whole pattern of Loyalist settlement had been sporadic and not planned for mutual defence. In 1786 Fredericton endured a mild state of siege when the savages of the upper river encamped in the vicinity of the town in order to ensure that Judge Allen should give them satisfaction on the occasion of the trial of two white men charged with the murder of an Indian. The Loyalist settlers, because they thought that two men of fair character would be sacrificed by the courts in order to assuage the indignation of the Indians, gave the authorities as much cause for concern.[20]

Rather naïvely it was supposed that the problem of the aborigines would be settled by the work of the New England Company, a humanitarian organization established in London early in the eighteenth century for the purpose of christianizing and civilizing the Indians of North America. After the Revolution its considerable activity was transferred to British territory. When Patrick Campbell travelled up the St. John in October 1792 he encountered below Woodstock about sixty canoes loaded with Indians who were on their way to "school". In return for consigning their children to the care of the company's missionaries they had been promised two suits of clothes and two blankets each year, a pipe and a parcel of tobacco each week, and as many provisions as they might require for an indefinite period. These hopes of an easier living were dispelled when the attempts of the company to entertain the Indians of the province at the common boards of the three schools established at Meductic, Maugerville, and Sussex proved to be too expensive. The experiment dragged on for many years at Sussex, where the savages were bribed to release their children to the instruction of the school. Mixed motives prevailed. Neighbouring farmers were eager to purchase the services of Indian boys as apprentices. The women were debauched. The considerable sums lavished on the board of management, consisting of leading dignitaries of the province and Arnold, the rector of Sussex, resulted in no change in the migratory and primitive habits of the Indians who had been exposed to this type of instruction. As soon as the youths attained manhood they returned to the forest haunts of their ancestors. The school at Sussex was finally closed in 1826, after being roundly condemned by the company which had financed the experiment.[21]

In 1793, when war broke out with France and when there were fears of hostilities with the United States, the failure of this policy of domestication was apparent. In the northern and western parts of the province, said Carleton, the Malecites were in close concert with the Indians of eastern Massachusetts. The expedient adopted with complete satisfaction was to employ M. Ciquard, a French royalist priest in exile. On later occasions when Indian trouble was anticipated the government invariably turned to the Bishop of Quebec for a missionary, offering a cash subsidy to assist with expenses.

To give impetus to the northward movement, human material was available. For years the position of the Acadian remnants who lived in southern New Brunswick had been under review. Ever since the time of Governor Jonathan Belcher of Nova Scotia, the idea of granting them lands in contiguity with Quebec had been a favourite one. Speculation had been revived by the insistence of Haldimand upon populating the upper St. John, but the initiative at this time came in large part from the ambitions of Louis Mercure, an intelligent Acadian who had been employed in the late stages of the revolutionary war in carrying dispatches between Quebec and Halifax. Mercure had a keen eye for interval, riverfront, and rich islands in midstream. Following his prompting, the Acadians who resided in the vicinity of Fredericton were prepared, without resentment, to endure another uprooting. Southern New Brunswick was an English-speaking, Protestant land. They were surrounded by settlers of the Loyalist regiments. Acadians from Kings County swelled the number prepared to move to the north.[22] Through 1786 and 1787 they moved up the river to Madawaska, the site of an old Indian village sometimes completely deserted, 130 miles from the nearest English-speaking settlement of any size. There they found vast tracts of the interval land they loved so much. Though refusing to accept Haldimand's suggestion that the new settlement should be included in the province of Quebec, Carleton gave his blessing to the enterprise. The New Brunswick government directed the Acadians to settle around the region where the Madawaska joins the St. John, in a manner most convenient to themselves; and a few years later 16,000 acres were granted to eighty families.[23]

Madawaska had been a region known only to a few Canadians who had crossed the barren hills from Kamouraska and traded with the Indians. Because it was so inaccessible it had become a resort for those who sought to escape the attention of the authorities both at Quebec and Halifax. For many years accounts had reached Halifax of the slaughter of game and the degradation of the savages of the area. Curiously enough, as the Acadians moved into this new country which until now had been the home of elements who were lawless, they were joined by Canadians who came in from the north over the Témiscouata portage. From Quebec at this time, owing to the exactions of the seigniorial system, there was a movement into New Brunswick of some dimensions, not only to the upper St. John but to the eastern shore as well.[24] In Madawaska the two French elements, Acadian and Canadian, fused into a single community that was uncertain of the fountain of civil authority. Three governments, those of New Brunswick, Quebec, and Massachusetts, asserted jurisdiction.

The vagueness of boundaries produced something like a replica of their earlier history for the Acadians of this community. Their ancestors had been exposed to the irritations and dangers of international rivalries. A new international situation had been created by the failure of the peace of Versailles properly to delineate the north-west angle of Nova Scotia, now the north-west angle of New Brunswick. But while the dispute with the United States was in abeyance, rivalries between provinces complicated the position. In the summer of 1787 Carleton sent his surveyor-general, George Sproule, to the north in order to reach an agreement upon the provincial boundary with Hugh Finlay, the surveyor-general of Quebec. Sproule found the highlands that divided the watersheds of the St. John and the St. Lawrence on the portage to the north of Témiscouata, sixty miles from Madawaska. Finlay, ignoring the geographic designations of the Proclamation of 1763, pressed the ethnic point of view that the French-speaking subjects of the King should be included within the province of Quebec and urged that the boundary should run as far south as Grand Falls, where the meeting between the two officials took place.

A controversy of brothers followed. Thomas Carleton repeatedly informed both Dorchester and the British government that the Acadians had no desire to be incorporated into the same government with their fellow-Frenchmen of Quebec. The general aversion of the habitants of Quebec to the rigours of the seigneurs at this time and the historic antipathy of Acadians to Canadians support this view. The river, he argued, gave Madawaska good communication with New Brunswick, for which Quebec had nothing comparable. In reply to Carleton's persistent pleas it was vain for Dorchester to urge that it was quite immaterial to which of the King's provinces Madawaska should belong, that New Brunswick, in pushing "the northwestern angle" to the north, was furnishing argument and conviction to the Americans, who, on the same geographic reasoning, would attempt to push their frontier to the north. The language of both the Proclamation of 1763 and the Treaty of Versailles made it clear that the line of the highlands at which New Brunswick should touch upon Quebec would be the line dividing the United States from British North America.[25] The provincial council at Quebec remonstrated against the New Brunswick position, but when the Constitutional Act was passed in 1791 no reference was made to this portion of the boundary and the uncertainty continued. Though determined to keep the Madawaska settlement within New Brunswick, Carleton was not acquisitive, rejecting the revival of the proposal made by Knox in 1784 that Gaspé should be added to his government.[26]

So far as Madawaska was concerned New Brunswick was at one disadvantage. Owing to the rigour of the royal instructions upon the issuance of religious oaths to office-holders, Carleton was unable to give civil commissions to any of the inhabitants. Yet there was urgent need for civil jurisdiction. The inhabitants of Madawaska were tranquil in demeanour and well disposed to the government that had given them clear title to their lands. Patrick Campbell was impressed by their politeness of manners in contrast to the surliness of "the common English-Americans" further down the river. But disruptive influences frequently intruded from the outside, notably from the direction of Canada. Another of the traditional conflicts between settlers and fur-traders had developed. In the autumn the Acadians would

advance supplies to the Indians against the produce of the
hunting season. But the ability of the savages to pay was forestalled by the Canada traders, especially the notorious Robi-
cheau brothers, who came over the portage at the conclusion of
the season, demoralized them with intoxicating liquors, and
stripped them of their peltry.[27]

To deal with the discords that frequently arose, Carleton was
compelled to appoint as justice of the peace John Costin, whose
chief qualifications were that he was the only English-speaking,
Protestant inhabitant of the area capable of taking the oaths of
office and that he was the only man who could read and write.
Costin had a hard time with "stragglers". Debtors crossed the
uncertain boundary line, going whichever way was less embarrassing. Sometimes the remoteness seemed idyllic and the simplicity, pastoral. "If a man walks in the fear of God," said
Costin, "he will be loved by everyone."[28] He jealously sustained
the provincial jurisdiction in Madawaska. In 1792 when a Quebec lieutenant of militia, Jacques Cyr, attempted after the
Quebec fashion to execute a process of the Court of Common
Pleas on behalf of the Robicheaus, Costin arrested him, conveyed him to Grand Falls, where he was placed under the
custody of the military commandant, and forced him to sign a
promissory note for the expenses of his arrest. The Quebec government reported the affair to Britain, colouring the account
with reports that Costin had ordered an election of militia
officers in Madawaska by a show of hands of the inhabitants.
Dundas, the Secretary of State, was in high dudgeon, and Carleton was forced to make explanations.[29] Yet the affair did not
expedite an attempt to determine how far northward New
Brunswick should extend.

To fortify his authority in Madawaska, Carleton created an
independent militia company, commissioning a captain and a
lieutenant, though carefully specifying that no civil duties should
be performed. This was a show of control, necessary perhaps
until a new flood of English immigration, sweeping up the St.
John in the wake of the garrisons of Presqu'ile and Grand Falls,
would establish a continuous belt of population along the communication to Quebec.

V

Several hundred blacks added to the complexity of the Loyalist
population. Their presence somewhat alleviated the scarcity of

labour, but it was quickly discovered that they had no aptitude or temper for work in the freshly turned fields of New Brunswick. Only in the domestic routine of households were they really useful.

A few were slaves. In the first days of the province slavery was an accepted, though rapidly passing, institution. Slaves were regularly sold at public auction in Saint John, and occasional individuals, such as the expatriated Virginian, Stair Agnew, who was attempting to create a great estate in the fields across the river from Fredericton, persisted in adhering to the rights of property that were exercised in the Southern States. Yet the physical factors that determined the character of daily living in New Brunswick made slavery impractical as well as unpopular. In Nova Scotia, where there were many more Negroes and where public opinion was probably a little more advanced, an attempt was made in the legislature of 1787 to insert in the law for the regulation of servants a clause which was concerned with the government of Negro slaves. It was rejected on the grounds that slavery did not exist in the province and ought not to be recognized. The policy of the courts and of the law officers was to avoid the discussion of slavery in principle and to throw the whole burden of proof of ownership on slave-holders. Occasionally the courts converted slavery into a limited indentured service, since it was the intention of Chief Justice T.A.L. Strange not "to throw so much property into the air at once".[30] Public sentiment in New Brunswick was working in the same direction, but it was not until 1800 that a test case was brought into the courts. It resulted in a division of opinion of the four judges and a challenge to a duel from the fiery Stair Agnew to Judge Allen.[31]

Of much more consequence was the presence in the province of the free blacks, the vast majority of whom had come under the protection of Sir Guy Carleton at New York. To save them from the vengeance of their former masters he had agreed to send them to the British colonies. A negligible number had given military service and were entitled to grants of land. As long as free provisions had been allowed by the government most had remained on garden lots on the fringes of Saint John. To prevent them from becoming a permanent charge on the revenues, the provincial government had sent them off to lands at Nerepis and Quaco. They showed no disposition to become farmers, and the greater number ultimately drifted into

honourable servitude on the estates of landed proprietors who
were pleased to take them at high wages. According to Carleton
they were on the same legal footing as whites except that they
could not vote in provincial elections. Yet even this slight assistance to husbandry was cut in half when the Sierra Leone
scheme went into effect in 1791. Seventy blacks with their wives
and families, a total of 222 persons, rejecting an alternative proposal to enrol for military service in the West Indies, departed
for Africa.[32]

In this testing time of the Loyalist experiment the greatest
single factor that obstructed the development of large enterprises in New Brunswick was the shortage of labour. All who
had come to the province preferred to work for themselves
rather than for others. Years of effort were necessary on the
farmlands before modest competence could be realized. In the
beginning it was supposed that large quantities of sawn lumber
would be exported. Yet even this reasonable expectation had
been disappointed.

In 1791 Carleton, by proclamation, under permission of an Act
of Parliament, ruefully permitted the importation of American
lumber.[33] The good trees that were immediately accessible and
economical to cut had all been felled. Idle sawmills, victims of
high costs of labour, stood by as decaying monuments to what
some considered an abandoned trade. The timber of Maine could
still be produced more cheaply.

Trade developed around the province rather than within it.
British ships held the carrying trade to the West Indian colonies, and the best opportunities in trade were those of discharging North American goods in their harbours. Since the colonies
of British North America could not produce the desired goods
in sufficient volume and at low prices the ready expedient was
to secure them from the Americans. Rendezvousing with the
Americans for the purposes of direct importation to the British
provinces or for re-export to the West Indies became the great
preoccupation of all the shippers of the Bay of Fundy. Along the
coastal communities of the southern shore of the province all
the aspirations were oceanic and the trading connections international, so that there was little concern for the back country
of the province up the St. John and the newly formed agricultural settlements.

Saint John was well located as an entrepôt for a traffic of this
kind, but the enterprising merchants of St. Andrews had all the

harbours and islands of Passamaquoddy Bay at their front door for the prosecution of this lucrative business. They in their turn were bettered by David Owen, who had inherited the island of Campobello from his uncle, Captain William Owen. This remarkable Welshman, of powerful physique and a graduate of Trinity College, Cambridge, boasting of his royal rights and commencing a vendetta with the magistrates of Charlotte County that was to last a lifetime, constructed wharves and warehouses on his island for the purpose of making it a great place for trade. Snug Cove, he boasted, was the safest anchorage in the Bay of Fundy. Across the slender channel that separated Campobello from the United States, his *filum aquae*, had risen the American town of Eastport, occupied by the lawless seamen of northern Maine and English seamen who had deserted, ruled by tolerant magistrates and officers of customs. Opportunities for rapid and effective exchange of British and American goods were numerous here and along all the shores of the islands. Owen and those who associated with him stood as interlopers in the trade with the Americans. In Saint John and St. Andrews every man's hand was against him, and the islands became noted as centres of "illicit" trade.

Communication developed slowly. In 1784 Nehemiah Beckwith, one of the "old" inhabitants, built a scow to ply regularly between Fredericton and Saint John. It was an excellent public accommodation, for it could sail with a fair wind, be poled along the shore in a calm, or rowed in deep, still water. Later, about 1791, an old schooner of forty tons became a regular freighter, and a large two-sail boat, "the post-boat", established a mail service on the river. This latter for many years offered "the most genteel mode of sailing".[34] On land the road from Fredericton through Maugerville, a work of nature as well as of art, was the most traversed in the province. At Fredericton for many years the justices of the peace of York unsuccessfully wrestled with the task of establishing ferry services over the Nashwaak and St. John at fair rates. On the west bank the road between "the city" and "the metropolis" was not completed until 1793 and then for travellers on horseback only. On the Bay of Fundy the Pagan brothers established a weekly packet service between Saint John and St. Andrews.

Winter was the season of rapid transit. The St. John and other rivers of the province served as broad avenues for traffic on the ice. "One hundred and thirty miles of clear going on the ice," wrote Winslow enthusiastically of the journey to Saint John from his home at Kingsclear. Except for the portages from the Belleisle to the Kennebecasis there was a smooth surface all the way. There was all "the jollity a good neighbourhood may offer in the coldest of winters". Repeatedly he had offered bets that the journey could be accomplished between daylight and nine o'clock in the evening.[35]

VI

Until the outbreak of the war with France a reasonable hope seemed the dominant sentiment in the first years of New Brunswick. Yet Loyalist enthusiasm for their great adventure had not dulled the memories of sacrifice. Amos Botsford, the patriarch of the Loyalist settlers at Chignecto, looked across the water from his fine new home at Westcock and murmured that this was "the bleak side of the Bay of Fundy". In September 1791 Samuel Jarvis, writing from Boston to William Hazen, eagerly requested an advance of £300. If it were not forthcoming, said this renegade and unrepentant Loyalist, he would be under the disagreeable necessity of returning to Saint John.[36] Even the most loyal maintained strong contacts with their former associates in "the old thirteen". A renowned royalist partisan like John Coffin could roundly affirm that a single pork-barrel made in Massachusetts was better than all the pork-barrels made in New Brunswick since the time of its foundation.[37]

One noted visitor was complimentary. The sergeant-major of the 54th Regiment, William Cobbett, took a strong line against his officers who hired out common soldiers for labour on the lands of Loyalist gentlemen and collected their wages. When he returned to England he laid charges against them.[38] But he wrote lyrically of a land of forest grandeur and of swiftly flowing streams. After losing *The Tale of a Tub* in the Bay of Fundy, he had commenced his military career beneath the shadow of Fort Howe in 1784. Compassionately he described the simplicity of the farmer, presumably of the Nashwaak, who supposed that persistent attention to his daughter, "dressed in the neat and simple manner of New England", implied an intention to marry. He was "an easy and happy farmer", "one of those Yankee Loyalists", who invariably provided a table loaded with good things.[39]

Another visitor, already distinguished, was not so highly regarded in New Brunswick. Wearying of the distaste of English society, General Benedict Arnold arrived in Saint John late in 1785. His design was to make the city his headquarters for a revival of the trade he had mastered in his youth, the selling of foodstuffs and liquors in foreign parts, and the site of a new distillery.[40] He purchased a fine house on King Street, filled it with handsome furniture and entered upon the calling of storekeeper. He formed a partnership with a merchant named Munson Hayt, but he found that the dislike of the public in Saint John was more robust than the mild disfavour of London acquaintances. In 1788 the store was destroyed by fire, and though Arnold's son had been sleeping in it and barely escaped with his life, the allegation was made that the General had fired the establishment in order to collect insurance indemnity. During the conflagration there were voices in the crowd calling upon Arnold to tell them if the fire resembled that of New London – a reminder of one of his bold but ill-judged actions during the war.[41] Hayt joined in the allegations against his honesty, and when Arnold sued for libel a Saint John jury awarded him damages of one pound. Nine of the jurors, it was said, wanted to allow him sixpence.

Arnold returned to England in 1791, resentful of memories of his return to America. Ward Chipman was his attorney, and in one of his letters Arnold wished he had the power to transfer Chipman's gout to "some of my good friends at St. John".

VII

To bind together into a common conscience the fewer than twenty thousand persons who were thinly scattered over the broad area of New Brunswick, ideas were not wanting. But because they were ineffective, the kind of society projected by the enthusiasts of 1784 never really appeared. No strength came from the presence of Lord Dorchester at Quebec. His visit to New Brunswick, so eagerly awaited, never came about. Quarreling with the British government upon the constitutional issue in Canada, engrossed in the difficult business of keeping the Indians of the west in order, he never summoned the energy to consider the development of British North America as a single entity. Thomas Carleton, who in 1788 journeyed on snowshoes to Quebec to see his brother during one of his frequent illnesses, governed New Brunswick directly by dealing with the Colonial Office in London.

Institutions that could rally the people to face their tasks

resolutely and to sustain the spirit of loyalty were sadly lacking.
Morally minded men of the nineteenth century who were trained
in the critical attributes of political economy were quick to point
out that the original settlement of New Brunswick was completely devoid of community planning. The generous dimensions of land grants, running from 200 to 1,000 acres, enabled
the individual to dwell on his land almost wherever fancy
pleased. Instead of living in communities the majority of rural
dwellers lived in the bush. There was nothing to compel a man
to live in proximity to and in emulation of his neighbours. The
element that explained the remarkable local initiative of New
England, the orderly development of townships that thrust
responsibility as well as privileges upon individuals, was completely absent in New Brunswick.

In every parish the number of inhabitants was manageable
but the area of territory under the jurisdiction of the magistrates was great. The isolated way of life bred a spirit of indi-
vidualism that ignored the rights of property. In the large number of petitions that began to bring complaints to the provincial
legislature there are many evidences of a general tendency to
consider the country as a vast common. The inhabitants of the
upper Hamond River threw their logs into the stream and the
freshet deposited them on the interval of the proprietors below.
The people of Kingston brought their cattle to the islands in the
Kennebecasis or to any favoured spot, publicly or privately
owned, where grass would grow.[42] Especially in the fishery were
the rights of property summarily set aside. The acts of the legislature reserving fishing rights to proprietors of the soil were
strenuously resisted both by residents of the province and by
strangers from the outside. Great nets were laid in the estuary
of the Miramichi, preventing the salmon from running up-
stream, depriving the inland owners of the benefits, and often
bringing the Indians of the river close to starvation.

The magistrates who were appointed by the provincial government to do the judicial and administrative work of the
counties and parishes possessed little knowledge of law, nor had
they any other intellectual qualifications for the development of
progressive local institutions. Like the gentlemen of England
who performed the labours of quarter-sessions, whom they were
supposed to resemble, they held great landed estates. But they
had no financial independence and, judging from the volume of
complaints against their conduct and the frequent replacements

made in their ranks in later years, the vast majority were incapable of separating their private advantage from the public interest. As early as 1788 Bishop Charles Inglis professed to see in New Brunswick the "trading justices" of New England and Nova Scotia. Yet, irrespective of their quality, the circumstances were greatly adverse. Of villages – even hamlets, in the English sense – there were few.

Public improvements seemed of infinitely less consequence than private enterprise. There was no money for local rates. The celebrated case of the jail of Charlotte County, in which wealthy men advanced the costs to the county and had to wait thirty years for returns, was hardly characteristic. Most of the counties had no jails at all. The labour to be performed by adult males upon roads and bridges was, if later apologists are to be believed, rarely performed. From the beginning there appears to have been little confidence in local boards of justices and the parish officers whom they appointed.

The Church of England was the great institution to which the founders of the province looked for the infusion of loyal principles and the growth of a happy accord among the people of New Brunswick. The downright intention of the Tory clergy was revealed in a paper submitted to Charles Jenkinson of the Board of Trade by an author who mentioned a long residence in America as proof of the validity of his views. He counted a great deal upon Governor Carleton and the Loyalist character of his council, but prophesied that the establishment of an episcopate in the United States would bring about an invasion of the British colonies by shoals of clergy without loyalty to the Crown. The Protestant dissenters would have to be restrained and their synods attended by agents of the government. An episcopate with a school and college, costing £4,000 per year (less than half the annual expense of a twenty-gun frigate), should be created for the British colonies "to sustain the last stake of Britain in America".[43]

The idea was a big one, but the means for implementing it were not available. An episcopate at Halifax and a college at Windsor constituted laudable beginnings. But all that the Society for the Propagation of the Gospel, acting as the agent for the British government, could spare for New Brunswick were the salaries of six clergymen and the cost of four church buildings. Carleton's government had no difficulty in making the Church of England the established church of the province. The

act of the legislature of 1786, which declared that the laws of
Nova Scotia should generally apply, produced a *fait accompli*
that encountered no resistance. Yet it was plainly perceptible
that the Church would require much more than this if New
Brunswick and the other colonies were to be islands of resistance
to the ideas and ways of life that were dominant in English-
speaking North America.

Nominally the Loyalists may have been members of the
Church of England, as Sir Guy Carleton had stated them to be,
but this implied no fixed allegiance to points of view upon doctrine or church government. In the eighteenth century the
Church was latitudinarian and tolerant, giving little attention
to dogma and discipline that in the past had been responsible
for heresy and schism. In America many of its clergy had been
recruited from recreant ministers of the Congregationalists and
other dissenting sects, such as the clever and erudite Mather
Byles, one of the first rectors at Saint John. Among the generality of those who adhered to a particular Protestant persuasion
there was frequently a disposition to accept the Church of England as a kind of mother-church. Sometimes, as in the thirteen
colonies, the Church of England had suffered because it had
acquired the reputation of being the church of the proud and
the strong, of the vested interests and official classes. Sometimes
it repelled as well as invited. The Scots of Saint John, who had
contributed to the building of Trinity Church, discovered that,
because it was filled to overflowing every Sunday, their accents
brought them invitations to go elsewhere.[44]

It was only as the implications of establishment became discernible that opposition to it developed. In the beginning
Maugerville was the only community in the province in which
Protestant dissenters could be said to be in the majority, but
whatever unity and discipline the Congregational church had
possessed had withered away before the onslaughts of the New
Light preachers during the war. Conversion and reconversion
were in fashion. Schism had followed schism. There were Brook-
ites, Hartites, and Hammonites. Patrick Campbell was mildly
astonished as he walked through Maugerville in 1792. Hearing
a loud noise in a house some distance away, he thought there
was a fight. On close investigation of the hideous cries he saw
sixty people of both sexes, all on their knees and in tears, shouting "O Lord, O Lord", "so that the one vied with the other who
should bawl out loudest". Being mistaken for the devil he

promptly fled, deeply impressed with the effects of fanaticism on the human mind.

The Methodist evangelist, Duncan McColl, who visited Maugerville in 1791, found a strange community of five and twenty Christians who engaged in prophesy, spoke in new tongues and worked miracles. When he finished his sermon a stout lady seized him by the collar and demanded, "Where hast thou gleaned today?" Only McColl's firmness prevented violence.

Carleton and his government struck hard at this centre of "the old inhabitants", whose political loyalty as well as their religious principles were subject to suspicion. The old *township* of Maugerville was divided into the *parishes* of Maugerville and Sheffield. This resulted in a contest for the possession of the lot of land on which the Congregational church stood, together with the house of the Congregational minister, who announced that he was about to take orders in the Church of England. The "old inhabitants" regained something of their lost unity and joined in opposition to the church that had been established by law. They accused their minister of immorality and demanded the return of the house they had given and the cattle they had loaned him. They asked for the privileges of a "free dissenting congregation" and the restoration of the land granted by the government of Nova Scotia in 1763.[45] Ultimately the government complied with their request and another lot was granted to the Church of England. Whatever religious zeal characterized Carleton's government, there was a necessity for being politic.

Of a more general concern that was to last for forty years was the Marriage Act, brought forward by the Church party in the legislature of 1787 with a suspending clause for the King's pleasure, and finally taking effect in 1791. It was at first a moderate document, adapted to the circumstances of the country, granting to Presbyterian and Roman Catholic clergy licences to marry their own people, giving preferred treatment to Quakers, making the clergy of the Church of England the persons from whom marriage should normally be sought except in those parts of the country where no clergy were in residence. In such cases the law conferred licences to marry upon justices of the peace. In general its provisions gave a primacy to the Church of England, but extended a generous measure of tolerance. At the outset the only serious objection that could be raised against it was that it ignored the Methodists, who were only just beginning to

assert an ecclesiastical jurisdiction of their own apart from the
Church of England. Ten years earlier William Black had lighted
the fires of Methodism on the Tantramar marshes among the
immigrants from Yorkshire.[46] It had appeared in Saint John,
where there is the record of Stephen Humbert, one of its earliest
devotees, walking to the gallows between two convicted deserters from the army, singing hymns.[47]

If Carleton had had his way the general dissatisfaction with
the Marriage Act might have been averted. To Bishop Inglis of
Nova Scotia, however, the statute brought mortification. On his
visit to New Brunswick in 1788 he saw how justices of the peace
exercised the power, "so indiscriminately given", of performing
the sacrament of marriage and was painfully reminded of the
imperfections of society in the former thirteen colonies. According to the act of 1786 the Church of England had been established by law. Why, then, were the usages of the Church concerning marriage not prescribed?[48]

The Bishop of London supported this point of view and when
the new act went into force justices of the peace were deprived
of licences to marry. It was the first implication of disharmony
with the new religious establishment and it forced a common
inconvenience upon the country. Colonists regarded marriage as
a civil contract rather than a religious sacrament. In the thirteen
colonies justices of the peace and clergy of all persuasions had
been licensed to marry. In New Brunswick after 1791 persons
wishing to marry often had to travel hundreds of miles, through
spring freshets and winter snows, to find the nearest Church of
England clergyman. It was perhaps with some justice that
Carleton complained the amended act would result in worsen-
ing the already free and easy habits of the people of New
Brunswick.

Largely because the see had been established at Halifax and
because the ecclesiastical and educational policies of Bishop
Charles Inglis fostered the primacy of Nova Scotia, the Church
of England in New Brunswick was to be at a considerable disadvantage. Throughout his long jurisdiction the Bishop was to
visit the province only on three occasions, directing the affairs
of the Church through an ecclesiastical commissary. On his first
visit in 1788 he encountered the heritage of old ecclesiastical
rivalries at New York and an attack upon his private morals
with a quick apology.[49] But at Trinity in Saint John and at
Christchurch in Fredericton he was surrounded by his old par-

ishioners of Trinity in New York. The first generation of Loyalist clergy served him well. The provincial government did all it
could to forward the interests of the Church. Lots of land in
each parish, authorized by the royal instructions, were set aside
for its support, but no immediate income could be obtained and
churchmen were not aggressive in demanding this dubious kind
of competence. No general arrangement for the maintenance of
the Church by the allocation of lands, such as that which became so notable in Upper Canada, was made in New Brunswick.
Nor did the Church produce a leader like John Strachan who
could advocate at political levels the large pretensions that had
been advanced for it by the founders of the province.

Almost exclusively the fortunes of the Church of England in
New Brunswick were dependent on the financial support of the
Society for the Propagation of the Gospel. However successful
its beginnings, its progress was to be impeded by the failure of
the society to furnish the support that would enable it to perform the role that had been planned for it. The number of
clergy increased slowly, but many of the frontier communities
were devoid of their ministrations, and many of those who came
from England to reinforce the original core of Loyalist clergy
were unfitted by their background and training to deal with the
exigencies of frontier life.

CHAPTER 5

The Politics of Despair

1793-1803

The outbreak of the war with the French Republic in January
of 1793 brought ten years of adverse fortunes for New Brunswick. By 1803 it would have been difficult to assert that the
province, since its founding, had made any appreciable gain in
wealth or population.

Political changes deprived New Brunswick of the special place
it had held earlier in the minds of those who were influential.
The return of Lord Dorchester to England in 1796 ended ten
years of failure in his second tour of duty in North America; as
early as 1792 he had fallen into disgrace with Mr. Secretary
Dundas in London, and his younger brother in New Brunswick
was suddenly made to realize that he was of no particular influence.

At approximately the same time the death of Parr, who had
held no great weight in the counsels of those who ruled at
London, resulted in the succession at Halifax of a Loyalist governor, Sir John Wentworth, whose influence with members of
Pitt's government was great. It may have been mere coinci-
dence, but one of his first acts as lieutenant-governor of Nova
Scotia was the forwarding of a petition from his house of assembly, praying for the annexation of those portions of the
county of Cumberland north of the Missiquash that had been
lost by the partition of 1784. The coming of the war restored
the former eminence and prosperity of Halifax as a base for the
Royal Navy, and Wentworth was not the kind of man to let
slip the new opportunities for himself and his province. For
Carleton another shock came in 1794 when Edward, Duke of

94

Kent, came to Halifax from the West Indies and assumed command of the troops in New Brunswick and Nova Scotia. Beneath the shadow of royalty his dignity was sadly tattered, and New Brunswick became a backwater during the great struggle in which it assumed no strategic or economic importance.

Those at Fredericton who had thought of Halifax as a defeated rival had every reason to complain that precisely the opposite result had occurred. Halifax became the centre not only of military and naval armaments, but of commercial intelligence and trade. Spurred by the demands of the military commissariat, her merchants drew off the trade of south-eastern New Brunswick and enlarged their volume of business on the Miramichi. They took large discounts on British goods that were consigned for New Brunswick. Freight rates from Halifax to Saint John, it was complained, were two-thirds those of transatlantic voyages. Saint John merchants had to await their banking and shipping intelligence until it pleased the Post Office at Halifax to pass on the mails over the notoriously bad road to Annapolis and the often delayed voyage over the Bay of Fundy. Because of the absence of convoys and the high insurance rates on British shipping, Saint John saw its West Indies trade pass rapidly to the Americans. French privateers, such as *Le Solide*, which was driven ashore on Passamaquoddy Bay in 1794, took considerable toll of New Brunswick ships. At Halifax the whole war-time atmosphere was buoyant with news of the movements of fleets and armies and with expectations of great profit in trade. The commerce of New Brunswick was forced to seek secondary markets. As the war moved around the globe the project of fortifying Fredericton began to appear less feasible.

The large military establishment, upon which Carleton had based his hopes, disappeared. Sorrowfully he watched his two regiments of the line depart from New Brunswick, one for the West Indies and the other for Halifax. The posts on the upper river were abandoned and the spacious barracks at Fredericton became untenanted. Almost spitefully he resisted the new deployments of the troops in North America, arguing that the only reason for keeping troops at Halifax was to protect the military stores against the local population.[1] The redcoats no longer mounted guard at the entrance to his farm behind St. Anne's Point. Instead of becoming a bustling military centre for the conquest of the north, Fredericton became, as it was said at

Saint John, a provincial village. Its repose was rarely invaded except when the members of the legislature came together.

II

Before the war had lasted a year political discontent was deep and general, permeating all classes. The Loyalists of New Brunswick had never been uncritical in their loyalty. When affairs did not go well they were quite willing to call in question the wisdom of the King's advisers. The legislature of 1787 had protested against certain strictures of the laws of trade, reminding the British government of the promise made after Saratoga to abandon the right of Parliament to legislate for the colonies.[2] They had extracted from Lord Hawkesbury a confession that he was not convinced that Parliament should attempt to make regulations for the King's dominions overseas.[3] This temper had been known to Sydney in 1784 when he had issued an instruction that oaths acknowledging the supremacy of the King in Parliament should not be required of office-holders.[4] In New Brunswick the ideas of Burke and the elder Pitt concerning relationships between Mother Country and colony were in the ascendancy.

All the commercial interests of the colony were grossly offended when in 1794 the British government signed the Jay Treaty, which permitted the entrance of American vessels to the West Indian colonies for as long as the war should last and two years afterwards. The argument that British North America could not supply the West Indies with staves, fish, beef, and other northern products had general validity. Under the stress of war, and determined to assure themselves of a continuous and cheap supply, the West Indian planters found it relatively easy to persuade Whitehall to permit the Americans to carry their own produce in their own ships. But one of the common assurances of New Brunswick and Nova Scotia was taken away. To the legislative committee of correspondence the palladium of the Navigation Acts was necessary to "our safety as British colonists". If the free admission of American vessels to the West Indies were continued, "these provinces will fall a sacrifice to its effects".[5] The reward for loyalty became that of being mere accessories to the Americans on the north-south trading lanes. The great ships of New Brunswick no longer put to sea, but from every inhabited harbour of the Bay of Fundy little ships set forth to trade "on the lines", transferring cargoes of fish, grindstones, plaster of Paris to the Americans who had so easily captured the West Indian trade. Even Saint John had little choice but to engage in this coastal commerce. Its great merchants who possessed overseas connections lost their business, and almost all who would presume to live by trade had to enter upon the traffic that made them satellites to a system of dubious legality. It was a scrabbling commerce, the Americans setting the prices and taking large profits from the industry of New Brunswickers.

A second basis of political discontent was rural. The effects of the 1790 restrictions on the granting of land were becoming more noticeable as time passed. The inability of the government to attract capital and immigrants by offering grants from the Crown lands depressed the value of farm holdings. The creation of landed estates required surplus labour, and whatever labour was available was dissipated in 1794 when Carleton raised the King's New Brunswick Regiment by local levy to replace the two regiments of the line he had lost. Farmers' sons marched off to join the colours, and landowners, to a greater extent than before, were dependent on their own exertions. In 1795 Stair Agnew harangued a meeting in VanHorne's Tavern in Fredericton, declaring that it would be no disadvantage to the landowners of the province if it were annexed to the United States, "as the lands would become more valuable and the labour cheaper".[6] The persistent electoral success of Agnew in York County might be taken as an indication of the strength of sentiments such as these. The most loyal and respectable of half-pay officers supported Agnew in opposition to Carleton's government. In consequence of imperial policies ocean-going commerce had been destroyed and agriculture languished.

Purely local but just as fundamental was the conflict between those who wished to strengthen the hand of the government at Fredericton and those who sought to place effective political power with the representatives of the constituencies in the legislature, a struggle between centralization and regionalism. Very early Carleton and his permanent officials had become objects of envy, though there would appear to have been very little in the emoluments of office to justify it. Carleton himself never took a penny of the fees of office to which he was entitled, recognizing that the people were too poor to pay for the transaction of legal business. During the long war he made an annual contribution of £500 to the patriotic fund, and long after he left the province his reputation for unselfish consideration of the poverty of the people remained. Odell spent a quarter of a century in sustaining the larger part of the business of government and finished his life as a poor man, asking the Colonial Office to pass on his office to his son so that his family might find support. Jonathan Bliss, the Attorney-General, writing that his emoluments decreased while his family increased, requested a more lucrative appointment in Canada or Nova Scotia.[7] Sproule and Winslow had to withdraw their sons from school in England. The poverty of the latter is a familiar theme of his voluminous correspondence. "I must go up to Heaven and shake hands with Lazarus, for damn me if there is any man on this earth poor enough to keep me company."[8] The officials of government had come to New Brunswick with great expectations, believing that their small salaries would be supplemented by generous fees of office. The 1790 instruction denying the granting of lands had removed anticipations of this kind. What was worse was the great inflation of the war-time years. The majority of the first generation of Loyalist officials died without adequate provision for their families.

This "aristocracy", often depicted as a privileged order, had no means at its disposal for the development of the province. When imperial spending in New Brunswick dried up, the provincial government had to look to local resources, and the few hundreds of pounds raised by the legislature from duties on liquors and other imports became the object of first concern. Even the "loyal" house of assembly of 1788, consisting in the main of members of whom Carleton had approved, had made it perfectly plain that the pay of members was the preferred item on the appropriations list. If, they had suggested, the pay of members could not be supplied from provincial funds, a system might be devised by which their constituents might pay members directly. This highly unconstitutional point of view had been rejected by the lieutenant-governor and council. But the first house of assembly of New Brunswick showed clearly that it was not prepared to place public moneys at the disposal of the Governor for projects of his own choosing. In the absence of clear direction the tendency to function after the fashion of the legislatures of the thirteen colonies became dominant: initiating public expenditures through committees, and making each member a distribution agency for their disbursement in his own constituency.

The antipathy to the permanent officials who were paid by the imperial government and to the enlarging of their powers was sharpened by local attitudes in Saint John and in the counties along the Fundy coast. There the project of opening up the north was viewed with ridicule and alarm. The economic life of the coastal counties was independent of the interior. The great bulk of the provincial revenue was collected at Saint John. Its citizens were not in sympathy with the lieutenant-governor's proposal for spending it elsewhere. Rather than allow this to happen it would be better to have no revenue at all. So far as the coastal communities were concerned the colonization of the province was completed.

Strenuously and successfully the members of the assembly for the coastal counties resisted for years Carleton's attempt to apportion money from the provincial revenue for the erection of a province hall at Fredericton. The boards accumulated by Judge Saunders, who had been appointed by the lieutenant-governor to supervise the raising of the structure, lay rotting in the sun and rain because a majority for the programme could not be obtained.[9]

In Saint John there was a general conviction that Carleton had deprived the city of an honour by moving the capital up the river. Though his instructions gave him ample authority for doing this, his right to do so had been repeatedly called in question. A more genuine source of grievance was the failure for a considerable period of any of the judges of the Supreme Court to take up residence in Saint John. Three of the four had settled down in comfortable rural retreats in the vicinity of Fredericton, supplementing their salaries by farming, refusing to go on circuit because no funds were available for the payment of expenses. Though most of the commercial business of the province was conducted at Saint John, the legal business had to be done at Fredericton. The judges' residence at the capital enabled them regularly to attend meetings of the council. Since they were stalwart advocates of his ideas, Carleton habitually employed them in legislative and administrative roles as well as judicial. Their persistent refusal to hold circuit courts at Saint John and other centres through the province unless the house of assembly should agree to the payment of expenses caused them to be regarded as the foremost enemies of "popular" causes.

Many of the tensions that developed in the first ten years of the history of New Brunswick were startlingly similar to those

that had created the revolution in the former thirteen colonies.
In spite of the fair promises of 1783-4, in spite of all the detailed
planning of Knox, Carleton, and a host of others, the British
government had failed to produce a new formula for colonial
government. As if to prolong the agonies of the old empire that
had perished, New Brunswick witnessed from the beginning
the familiar cleavage between royal officials appointed under the
Sign Manual and an elected assembly of representatives of the
people.

Perhaps New Brunswick deserved special attention. It was a
peculiar by-product of the American Revolution. Constitutionally it was further advanced than the Canadas. Its founders had
presumed that it would become a model colony. There was the
oft-repeated assumption that a happy concord between governors and governed could mysteriously be achieved. Yet there
was no real glimmering of a new policy derived from the bitter
lessons of the past.

III

In 1780, in the midst of the revolutionary war, Carleton had
served on a board of officers which court-martialled a young subaltern of artillery who had been charged with "conduct unbecoming the character of an officer and a gentleman". The accused was
found guilty of insubordination at his post on the upper St.
Lawrence, and cashiered. He had returned to England with a
letter from General Haldimand pleading his great abilities and
application to duty, and asking that he be reinstated in the
army and given a post in which subordination was not the first
and most necessary condition of service. The young man was a
member of the Royal Society for the Advancement of Science
and was well known for his acceptable dissertations on mathe-
matics. Owing to the assistance of powerful friends, the sentence
of the court martial was reviewed and he was reinstated, not in
the artillery but in the engineers.[10]

Upon coming to St. Anne's Point in 1785, Carleton found the
same young man, James Glenie, who had been born in Fife,
Scotland, employed upon the barracks that were under construction. Subordination was still alien to his nature: he entertained a profound contempt for Carleton's plan of making
Fredericton a place of military strength. Fortifications were
Glenie's especial subject of study. Upon a return to England
in 1787 he acquired the same contempt for a much greater

project, that of the Duke of Richmond for fortifying the great naval bases of the country. His publication of a pamphlet brought such ridicule upon the plan that it was promptly discarded by the British government. Having saved his country, according to his own reckoning, the sum of fifty million pounds, enough to build a fleet greater than any that had ever sailed the seas, Glenie found himself under a cloud. Such brilliance was dangerous and his prospects in the army vanished.

Resigning his commission, Glenie entered into a partnership with Alexander Blair of Portland Place in London. The firm acquired contracts for supplying masts to the Admiralty, and Glenie again appeared in New Brunswick in October 1787. Locating his headquarters at Gooldsborough where the Oromocto joins the St. John, he established mast-ponds at Saint John, at Long Reach below Fredericton, and at French Lake.[11] As a purchaser of timber and employer of labour he gained great influence in Sunbury County and, by a four-to-one majority, became a member of the house of assembly in 1789. From a gentleman of the graces of Sir John Wentworth he compelled the same respect as from the half-literate loggers and farmers of Maugerville. With the surveyor-general, who cultivated all men of talent, he was on intimate social terms. His frequent journeys to England enabled him to stop at Halifax, where he gained a reputation for enterprise and trust as well as talent. His fervently avowed scorn for Carleton, and for all of Carleton's transactions, did not prevent him from winning friendship and cordiality in the Nova Scotian capital.

It was Glenie's vehemence that made him a man of mark. There was no doubt concerning the role to which he aspired – that of the grand protagonist in opposition to the government. "They are cursedly alarmed. For they suppose that the majority of the House will follow me and that their villainous practices will not only be examined into but brought to light and exposed."[12] He was a tall man, well over six feet, and of extraordinarily dark complexion. He showed the qualities of the man of business and of the erudite philosopher, a famous mathematician turned lumberman, a Latinist skilled in the politics of the bush. On his visits to London he had no hesitation in seeking the confidence of the secretary of state. After 1792, when Dorchester and Dundas had become enemies, he took full advantage of the new situation. "The Carleton family is fated to be the ruin of British America."[13]

Commencing by espousing the unpopular cause of Andrew Finucane, Glenie would accept as an ally any man who carried a grievance. There was nothing half-hearted in his abuse of the lieutenant-governor and his officials. Allen was "an illiterate moon-struck judge", Ludlow an "illiterate, strutting chief-justice", Billopp, designated for the council, "an ignorant, uncouth Dutch boor". The lieutenant-governor himself, avowedly not a man of business, was unfitted by education or capacity for his duties and had fallen under the influence of the Americans around him, men whose diabolical purpose it was to gain control of all the valuable lands in the province. Though he was to show a signal capacity for getting on with Americans himself, Glenie, in interviews with Evan Nepean, the under-secretary for the colonies, denounced the quality of the American Loyalists who ruled New Brunswick, professing to believe that European gentlemen of liberal education were the proper persons to fulfil the duties. How could "such a pimping province" as New Brunswick require four judges? Why should the British government maintain two regiments in the province when the cost to the French in conquering it would be twenty times the booty to be taken? Ignorantly and perversely, Carleton had planted not only the Madawaska settlement but the garrisons of Grand Falls and Presqu'ile many miles within American territory. At an expense of £2,000 provisions were carried to the garrisons of the upper river in birch-bark canoes or flat-bottomed boats, the carriers wading in the water the greater part of the way. A ration at Grand Falls was five times the cost of one at Saint John. So rapidly were the banks of the St. John being washed away by the spring freshets that in twenty years' time it would not be possible to bring a row-boat up to Fredericton in the drought season. The propriety or impropriety of the selection of such a seat of government and such a place of military strength could readily be appreciated by any man.[14]

Politics, rather than business, became Glenie's vocation in New Brunswick. His activities in getting out masts for the King's service failed to prove lucrative. Two firms, his own and that of Hunter, Robertson, and Forsyth, engaged in wasteful competition for the services of labourers and oxen on the St. John River. Many great trees lay worm-eaten on the banks, and a raft of 201 great sticks was broken up in a storm between French Island and Cranberry Meadows, and swept out to sea. Early in 1795 Wentworth persuaded the two contractors to join their interests in one agreement, and from this time Glenie appears to have been relieved of commercial responsibilities.[15] Other duties, however, awaited him. For years he had been informing Wentworth of depredations in the woods by other contractors and private interests, of trees cut for the King's service being exported as ton timber, of false clearances, of the manner in which contractors ignored the stubborn habits of the workmen, who persisted in believing that they were entitled to a proportion of the timber cut.[16] When William Paine abandoned his commission as a deputy surveyor, it was Glenie who filled the vacancy.

This official capacity did not impair Glenie's character as a popular tribune. When the war opened with France the Admiralty increased its efforts to obtain naval supplies from New Brunswick and Glenie was sedulous in reporting trespasses and evasions to Wentworth. The surveyor-general was now insisting that not only pine of twenty-four inches in diameter were reserved to the Crown but all pine of any size whatsoever. In 1795 he gave every encouragement to the firm of Forsyth to concentrate its activities in the Passamaquoddy area. It would, he archly remarked to the commissioners, cause the Americans to be less strenuous in the negotiation for the boundary if they knew that all the good trees had been taken.[17] Glenie had no qualms in opening legal action against those who despoiled the King's forests. Trespassers could be repressed if not suppressed. Yet in Sunbury County this police activity did not derogate from his popularity. No less than seven times the people of Maugerville, the most "disaffected" of all the inhabitants of New Brunswick, elected him as their representative to the assembly. If it were true, as it was alleged, that he was in correspondence with some of the more radical members of the British parliament,[18] his radicalism could find a responsive chord in Sunbury.

Leadership appears to have come easily. Around him clustered a large number of malcontents who were opposed to Carleton, though almost all for different reasons. Agnew from York, nursing private quarrels, represented the disappointed landowners. The sectionalist and commercial interests of Saint John and St. Andrews – especially the Pagan brothers, William and Robert, whom he had reported on at least one occasion for false clearances – found an articulate voice that could originate and disperse counsels of discontent they could put to their purpose.

Loyalists who had failed to break into the privileged circle of office-holders saw in Glenie an instrument to torment those whom they envied. An exponent of the national faith of Scotland, he professed to see in the Anglican establishment the menaces of spiritual courts and the penalties of the Act of Uniformity, sustaining the historic prejudices against episcopacy that had been so prevalent in the life of the thirteen colonies, even among those who were nominally affiliated with the Church of England. From Westmorland came William Black, supported by petitions from Methodist societies at Fredericton, Saint John, Maugerville, Sheffield, and the Nashwaak, demanding revision of the Marriage Act.[19] As his running-mate in Sunbury, Glenie had company no less spectacular than himself. Samuel Denny Lee Street was an Englishman who had served at Fort Cumberland during the revolutionary war, had escaped from the hold of a rebel cruiser, and had assisted Studholm at the settlement of Saint John. Carleton's government had no reward to offer for his services. A little man who bore the scars of many battles on his countenance, he was at the centre of every quarrel. According to his son, who many years later presented a memorial on his behalf, his great ambition was to become a judge.[20] One of the more malicious of the many whom he offended called him "The Creeper-Cock".

IV

What followed was a struggle for power between the assembly and the lieutenant-governor, who was invariably supported by a majority of his council. It assumed a constitutional form, though the motives on both sides, as in most constitutional struggles, were tangible and material. It followed the pattern of former struggles in the thirteen colonies where lethargic representatives of the prerogative had so frequently been outfought by local factions. But it was remarkable in that it occurred in a colony that had been designed to avoid the repetition of former error.

Power implied the control of money, and the constitutional quarrel was principally concerned with the methods by which the public moneys should be raised, distributed, and expended. On one side, favouring the assembly, were the precedents of the Parliament of Great Britain before the time of Queen Anne by which the initiation of money grants had been in the hands of committees of the House of Commons. These examples had been followed by colonial assemblies before the American Revolution, so that the allocation of public funds had been in the hands of the assemblymen who, in disorderly but thoroughly democratic fashion, had divided the available amounts for expenditure in their constituencies, appointing their own commissioners to expend the money and to account for it. This was one of the reasons why royal government in America had been weak and inept. Deprived of local sources of revenue, it had held no power to initiate measures of consequence.

On the other side, favouring the lieutenant-governor and council, were the precedents of the British parliament that had been created since the Glorious Revolution. Only in the reign of Queen Anne had it been established that private members of the House of Commons should not introduce money bills and that all financial appropriations should originate with the executive. These and other innovations had given control over the money power to the government, limiting parochial demands to national necessities. A standing order of Anne's reign had forbidden money payments to individuals whose names were specified in bills passing through Parliament, keeping the power of appointment firmly in the hands of the executive. Colonial experience had failed to keep pace with the elaboration of the cabinet system in Britain. As yet nobody of consequence had ventured to suggest that this might be desirable, or how, in a colony governed by permanent officials, it might be introduced.

In 1792, when Carleton dissolved his first legislature and called elections for a new house of assembly, the adverse temper of the country was clearly revealed. His block of Saint John supporters who had been so dubiously elected in 1785 were defeated, and Chipman, who had strenuously defended Carleton's policies on the floor of the assembly, had to seek a seat in Northumberland. In 1793 the opposition, larger in number and bolder in demeanour, rejected financial measures of the lieutenant-governor, proposed alternative measures of their own, and attempted to nominate commissioners for local works. Contrary to the wishes of the lieutenant-governor, and in spite of the 1790 restriction on the granting of land, they considered measures for the introduction of new settlers.

Characteristic of the general conflict in points of view was the assembly's hostile reception to Carleton's request for a grant of money in aid of a single provincial academy at Fredericton. The alternative proposal was a grant of £10 to every parish in the province for educational purposes. The lieutenant-governor, who was already writing to London about the dangerous democratic spirit that had invaded New Brunswick from the older colonies, was the centralizer confronted by frontier forces whose needs, in their own estimation, were purely local. The council, seizing upon the principle of the assembly's educational proposal, pointed out that "it would tend to the creation of a new establishment".[21] In fact the assembly, since it had no confidence in Carleton's government, was attempting to form an executive apparatus of its own.

From the sessions of 1793 and 1794 Glenie was absent, content with harassing the New Brunswick administration in interviews with under-secretaries at Whitehall, but in 1795 his presence on the floor of the assembly brought about a battle to the utterance. During the summer of 1794 intelligence had come to New Brunswick of the arrival of a French fleet at Boston, of the fitting out of smaller vessels by mixed crews of French and Americans for raids on British commerce in the Bay of Fundy. Carleton had in consequence ordered the construction of breastworks at Saint John and St. Andrews. When he presented the bill to the house of assembly he was faced by the objection that the British government paid for the defence of other colonies and should do the same in New Brunswick.

Stung by this refusal, which savoured of disloyalty, Carleton likewise stood on principle and insisted on a more parliamentary method of passing money bills. If the assembly should refuse to pass estimates recommended by the executive, it should be refused the right to originate money bills of its own. Insisting upon "a directional authority in the executive branch", the council threw out the entire appropriations bill, taking the precaution to warn that the deviations from parliamentary usage of earlier years, permitted to expedite public business, could not be used as precedents to support the initiation of money grants by the assembly.[22] This edict of reform included a denial of the right of the members to draw pay, a refusal to pay for the purchase by William Pagan of books on *The Laws of Nature and of Nations* and on *The Constitution of Great Britain*. The "conference" system, by which council and assembly had for years reviewed their differences in order to keep the small public services of the province going, completely broke down, though only a bare majority of the council was willing to resort to the drastic expedient. A strong minority, though unsympathetic to the assembly, thought it better to submit rather than allow the cessation of work on the great roads and bridges. In the assembly also there were weak hearts willing to reduce their demands for pay from 10/- to 7/6 per diem.

It was bad enough that the public services of the province paid for by the legislature should suddenly cease to function, but Glenie could strike notes higher than this. He was a man of imagination, "fixing the political latitudes and longitudes, and establishing the boundary line between prerogative and privilege".[23] The House of 1795 was electrified by his presentation of a declaratory bill that presumed to define the relations between Mother Country and colony. This was a reminder of the act of Parliament of 1778 for "quieting the minds of His Majesty's subjects" by removing the duties on tea, and an attempt to exploit the discontent concerning the collection at Saint John of duties imposed by the imperial parliament. The bill proposed that acts of Parliament prior to 1750 did not concern New Brunswick unless they were expressly stated to be in effect. The date 1750 was selected because it was taken as the year of the founding of Nova Scotia, from which New Brunswick was later formed. By lopping from the bill several clauses that were objectionable to certain members, some of which were directed against the Church of England, Glenie triumphantly secured a majority of 15 to 10. It received short shrift in the council, but its objective of stirring men's minds and broadening the base of discontent had been achieved.

Carleton's supporters professed to see in this provocative measure a new revolution, aiming at the complete independence of the colony and a revival of the principles of 1775. Daniel Lyman, a squire of the Nashwaak, made it his business to inform the secretary of state for the colonies that Glenie had imposed upon the understanding of the House. The declaratory bill, said Lyman, "goes farther than the first address or declaration made by the American Congress assembled at Philadelphia". Glenie's sentiments were "such as tend to the subversion of all government of church and state".[24] The sentiments of the Law Lords at London who were asked for an opinion by the assembly through their agent were milder though quite definite. British subjects, they declared, took with them wherever they went the Common Law of England. If the bill were passed the judges of New Brunswick would acquire so much discretion that they could, if they wished, dispense with Magna Charta.[25]

Shaken by his failure to gain control of the assembly, Carleton dissolved it in the autumn of 1795, using as a pretext instructions from the Colonial Office that purported to narrow the basis of the franchise. The second election of this year was fought with aplomb and had much of the quality of a private quarrel between Glenie and the lieutenant-governor. At Burton court-house in Sunbury, before the opening of the poll, Glenie gave the electors six reasons for Carleton's dissolution of the former house. It had persisted in the presentation of bills for the holding of the Supreme Court in places other than Fredericton. It had passed a bill permitting the narrowing of the great roads and lowering the number of days of statutory labour to be performed on them, thus "saving trouble" for the electors. It had refused Judge Saunders' plan for the public buildings at Fredericton. It had given parish schools preference over a provincial academy at Fredericton. It had refused to accept financial obligation for the batteries at Saint John and St. Andrews. Finally the plea for an extra salary to Jonathan Odell as Clerk of the Legislative Council had been rejected. Amid the excitement of the canvass, Glenie and Street were charged with providing meat, drink, and entertainment for the electors of Sunbury. In Kings County it was alleged that John Coffin, now emerging as a leading champion of Church and State in the house of assembly, had provided the same at Guthrie's Tavern and at Mullin's Tavern, and that the sheriff had kept the poll open for five days only instead of the specified fifteen. In York, judging from the petition of Pierre Dupree and nineteen Acadians, extraordinary measures were taken to bring out the vote. They journeyed all the way from Madawaska to Grand Falls, but were told by Stair Agnew that they would be required to take an oath that would cause them to be forever lost. Yet, having seen a translation, they avowed they would have been willing to accept it.[26]

To Carleton the results were intensely disappointing. The new House was, if anything, more opposed to him than the former. Glenie, Street, Pagan, Agnew, and all who sought to profit from the general discontent, were returned. Jonathan Bliss, never a favourite of the lieutenant-governor, turned against him. Amos Botsford, the Speaker and a man of moderate impulses, could see virtue in the appeals of Glenie, who had been labelled by the Church and State party as a "democrat" and "jacobin".

For four years New Brunswick had no revenue, and the work

on the great roads, planned to link the scattered settlements of the province together, came to a standstill. Each year until 1799, the legislature met without agreement between council and assembly. The right of members of the house of assembly to receive pay became dominant. Each session the assembly sent up to the council a single appropriations bill, providing for rewards for their own services and for other payments of money requested by private petition, as well as for the measures initiated by the executive officers. This, in effect, denied the council the right of veto on any individual item. Each session the council turned down the whole appropriation. The constitutional dilemma sharpened and opinion hardened.

It was alleged that there were motives less worthy behind the constitutional pleas of Glenie and his party. As the provincial treasury ceased to take tolls on liquors and other dutiable goods it was perceived that the retail prices of these articles did not fall. Prices at Saint John continued to be higher than those at Halifax, where duties continued to be paid. The great constitutional impasse, it was argued, put hundreds of pounds each year into the pockets of the merchants of Saint John and St. Andrews.[27] "Trafficking in the revenue" became a slogan for those opposed to Glenie and his mercantile allies.

There was something more than the display of logicians. At five o'clock in the morning of February 24, 1797, following the closure of the short-lived legislative session, Glenie and John Coffin fought a duel with pistols in the woods across the river from Fredericton. Glenie's thigh was pierced by a bullet but his honour was undimmed. There is a tradition that his wife had told him that if he would not accept Coffin's challenge she would do so herself. At Halifax, in the salons of the great, the incident excited some notice. "In a late conversation with His Royal Highness," wrote Sir John Wentworth to Glenie, "we lamented the late accident which the public papers informed us you had sustained. We both concurred in wishing that you would forever substitute the pursuits of philosophy, or rather science, to politics – from which you would derive the greatest good to the world at large, and gratify all your friends."[28]

V

In Great Britain there was little disposition for settling party squabbles in a distant and unimportant province. But the issue was a fundamental one, not only for New Brunswick but for all the British North American colonies. The Duke of Portland, secretary for the Home Department, was the minister responsible for solving the problem of how to enforce the British system of parliamentary government upon a colony whose officials were permanent and irresponsible. An intermediary between colony and Mother Country was William Knox, the former American under-secretary, who was agent-general for New Brunswick in London. In 1793, when Brook Watson had gone off to Flanders in his old role of commissary-general to the army, Knox, aged but unflagging after a long period of illness, had rejoiced at the opportunity to renew his parental role. It was his fondest hope that out of the war with France and the negotiations with the United States there might emerge a situation from which Oswald's indiscretions of 1783 might be redeemed and a better boundary secured for the colonies of British North America.

At first Portland, suspecting the motives of individuals in the house of assembly, approved of the refusal of Carleton and his council to pass the appropriations bill. Measures originated by the executive government, he declared, should have first preference. Other measures originating in the house of assembly should be submitted as separate bills, though he would not go so far as to say that mingling the two classes of items would be unconstitutional.[29] An answer of this kind really evaded the issue. As the dispute lingered on for four years, as Portland was compelled to inspect, season after season, the submissions from both sides, as the house of assembly continued to insist upon "their ancient and undeniable right" to initiate, he finally felt compelled to ignore the problem in principle. Since, he finally announced, the only method of payment proposed for any measure was by warrant of the lieutenant-governor, the sole obstacle to agreement between the two legislative bodies was the question of whether or not private money bills should be separated from those introduced by the government. Separation was essential, for each measure should depend for success upon its own merits. "During the infancy" of the colony he would consent to the payment of members and hoped it would produce good effects.[30] This left honours even. The government's primacy in the initiation of money measures was confirmed, but the right of private members to initiate was confirmed as well. At this stage in the development of the colonial empire a more forthright answer would have required the boldness and the prescience of a Durham forty years ahead of his time.

Knox, the agent of both council and assembly, had no appetite for a fray of this kind. He was much happier in the more
practical business of seeking convoys for New Brunswick trade,
of making Saint John, at the expense of Halifax, the centre of
the traffic with the West Indies, of securing a restoration of the
preferred place British ships had held in West Indian markets
before the Jay Treaty was signed. Addressed by the assembly as
"the friend and father" of the province,[31] he nevertheless refused
to take to the King the consequences of party quarrels or "to
engage in a literary controversy".[32] For refusing to present an
address to the Crown he lost his post as agent for the assembly,
a circumstance which may have vindicated for the old Tory his
long-standing dislike of popular assemblies. His irritation was
presumably relieved when George Leonard, who had procured
the appointment for him in the first place, wrote that the governor and council were reserving for him a valuable tract of
land.[33]

Yet before this partial solution to the constitutional question
had been produced, the foundations of Glenie's success as a
popular agitator had been destroyed. His ascendancy had been
based on no single factor, but rather on the willingness of a
large number of people to collaborate with him for a wide
variety of reasons. By 1797 war prices had come to New Brunswick agriculture. Carleton wrote in this year that the country
was prosperous, though this would probably have been fiercely
disputed at Saint John, where overseas commerce was virtually
non-existent. The lieutenant-governor was not above the more
guileful methods of the politicians with whom he had to deal.
Judiciously selecting excerpts from Portland's dispatches, he
gave them to Botsford, the Speaker of the House. They produced
a profound impression, and when Glenie ventured to introduce
a motion of censure upon him for employing the Speech from
the Throne to lecture the representatives on their duty, it was
defeated by 17 to 5. This officially inspired propaganda was dispersed throughout the country when it appeared in the columns
of the *City Gazette*, edited by John Ryan. The house of assembly was taken aback, considering that its privileges had been
violated, and sent a committee to Saint John for the purpose of
interviewing Ryan and bringing him to discipline. The information he gave showed that Coffin had been the *agent provocateur*
who had caused the country to be informed of *some* of Portland's views on the constitutional crisis in New Brunswick.[34]

The impression that became powerful was that the majority of the house of assembly had behaved in a manner unbecoming to British subjects. The tensions that were attendant upon England's extremities were present in New Brunswick in 1798. The war with France had become a contest for national survival. The kind of dissent for which Glenie had become so notorious was under suspicion. The people of New Brunswick, wrote Leonard, who had just spent a year in a French prison, were not fearful for the safety of England though they did fear the loss of Ireland.[35] From several of the shires came petitions, asking that the assembly should separate their pay from the other appropriations in order that an agreement could be reached with the council and the work of the country proceed. Patriotism was sharpened by interest, and the assemblymen were blamed for the loss of the small amounts of cash that had formerly come into the hands of the poorer people for their labour on the great roads.

For three years Carleton enjoyed a reprieve from the siege he had been enduring from a hostile majority in the legislature. At the opening of the 1799 session he provided the Speaker with a copy of Portland's final pronouncement of the previous June, "with beneficient results". The council deemed it expedient to waive certain irregularities in the method of appropriations, but the assembly separated their pay from the general list. Glenie's former majority disappeared. Agnew and "the country members" who represented the more rural constituencies deserted him. Rejoicing in the changed environment, Carleton pushed through the legislature a vote of £500 for a province hall at Fredericton. On May 15, 1800, he laid the cornerstone, the marker being inscribed *"Huius provinciae Praefectus et Pater T. Carleton posuit"*. The reasonably handsome, two-storeyed structure, standing amid the flower-embowered, whitewashed cottages of Fredericton, provided, perhaps, a meagre triumph for the policies of the lieutenant-governor sixteen years after his arrival in the province.

VI

Carleton's last years in New Brunswick, in spite of his triumph over Glenie, could not be said to have been successful. Disappointment in the defeat of the projects of the lieutenant-governor dominated the speculations of those around him. The province had not gone ahead. Even by 1794 the official group had lost hope. "They are good men, but their goodness is negative," wrote George Leonard to Chipman, complaining of the torpid state of things at Fredericton.[36] For Leonard, who was trying to interest Lady Dacre in supporting an academy at Fredericton and who said that what the province needed more than anything else was a good library, life was too short for their delays. Carleton was also interested in academies and libraries, but the military establishment preoccupied him. The Duke of Kent at Halifax was sniping at the shorn remnants of his former pride. In 1796 the Duke attempted to send off to the West Indies two American veterans of Carleton's headquarters staff, who had served him since the establishment of the province, and to unite their offices under Lieutenant Oliver Goldsmith (nephew of the English poet and dramatist), who was in New Brunswick at the time. Carleton wrote to the Duke of York in protest, emphasizing the necessity of retaining the lieutenant-governor's patronage as a means of keeping the inhabitants of New Brunswick in their proper duty. Again in 1798 Kent struck at the office of deputy paymaster, ultimately moving it to Halifax over Carleton's furious objections. "His Royal Highness," wrote William Hazen, "is enquiring into the authority by which our governor first drew the staff allowances to his last two commissions, possibly knowing that he can produce none. This at present a secret which forbodes no good." Rumours came to New Brunswick from Halifax that Glenie would presently assume command of the detachment of Royal Engineers in the province.[37] Kent's great scheme for the establishment of telegraphic communication between Halifax and Fredericton required the employment of so many troops that none, in Carleton's opinion, would remain for other services.

This kind of discipline was difficult for a man like Carleton to take. When Portland ordered him to obey Kent's order concerning the paymastership, he complied but asked to be removed from his post, observing that the nature of the charge originally bestowed upon him had changed, that he had been reduced to the level of a public accountant. There were rumours of Carleton's removal to Quebec, and the official clique buzzed with speculation upon possible changes in fortune.[38] He neither moved to Quebec nor returned to England, changes in the establishment of the New Brunswick Regiment having mollified his pride. Chipman and Odell joined in honest exultation at the prospect of retaining "our friend" in New Brunswick.[39]

It was not until the spring of 1803 that Carleton sailed for England on leave, grievously concerned that the coming of peace and the disbandment of the New Brunswick Regiment left forty-five artillerymen the only troops in the province. During his last days in New Brunswick a flurry of legislative animosity deprived him of the peace he probably considered to be his due. When the clerk of the house of assembly died, the majority refused to accept the successor designated by Carleton and proceeded to elect one of their own number, Samuel Denny Lee Street, whose notoriety as a partisan had been increased following a duel fought within the legislative precincts against a much younger man, John Murray Bliss.[40] Again a conflict of precedents took place. The majority of the assembly cited the Nova Scotian precedent which had stemmed from those of the lost New England colonies. Carleton retorted that the office, like that of the clerk of Parliament, should be filled by the Crown.

A legislative imbroglio followed. In passing the appropriations bill the house of assembly provided for the office by stipulating that the payment should be made "to Samuel Denny Street". The practice of payment to individuals whose names were listed in the bill had been condoned by earlier colonial custom, but it was opposed to the standing orders of Parliament in Great Britain. When the council requested a conference Glenie and his party abandoned the House, leaving it without a quorum. The sergeant-at-arms discovered Glenie in Fredericton and recalled him to his duty, but Glenie declared he did not consider the House to be in session. Ward Chipman wrote of the secession of eight members who, ignoring the restraints of the Speaker and evading the arrest of the sergeant-at-arms, jumped into a sleigh that had been awaiting them for hours and drove out of town, certain to profit by hundreds of pounds if the revenue bill should fail to go through.[41] Edward Winslow, entering the war of pamphlets, regaled his public with an imaginary conversation in the gallery of the new house of assembly: "Do you see a little short-legged thing there, that looks like a creeper-cock and buzzes and whizzes about like a bottle-ars'd fly?"[42]

But the secession failed. As Winslow said, "A resurrection took place from a Coffin." The shock tactics of Colonel Coffin, just as relentless as the charge at Eutaw Springs, carried the day, and under his leadership eight members of the assembly decided they could carry on, though thirteen made a quorum.

The revenue bill was passed "and a general satisfaction prevailed except in one-little-dirty-Street . . . and those huckstering, smuggling members were most wonderfully disappointed".
Street had performed the labours of clerk of the house, but the
pay went to Carleton's nominee, Dugald Campbell. *"O fortunati
quibus tales sunt legislatores,"* wrote Odell.[43]

A dissolution of the house of assembly and an election in June
of the same year routed Carleton's enemies. In Sunbury County,
the heart of the opposition, Street lost his seat following a forlorn plea on behalf of "the liberty of the subject". Glenie won
by a bare majority, having, in a speech at Burton, compared
Carleton's despotism in New Brunswick with that of Henry
VIII in England. At the court-house there were altercations
upon the qualifications of voters, a large crowd of electors with
clubs and canes standing by, and a general fear that the sheriff,
"with his poll book in his hand and his sword by his side", would
fail to keep the poll open.[44] The electoral verdict endorsed the
self-constituted quorum of earlier in the year. Political radicalism in New Brunswick received a blow from which it did not
recover until the conclusion of the great war with France. In
1803, when Glenie moved that the House proceed with the election of a clerk, he was defeated by a vote of 15 to 8. This was
his last act of defiance.

Upon his return to England Carleton boasted of "the perfect
tranquillity" in which he had left the province. The violent
opposition had been completely defeated; yet the tranquillity
had been achieved only at a price. New Brunswick had persuaded even Carleton that he must learn to compromise. In
order to defeat Glenie's ascendancy in the legislature he was
compelled to make major concessions to the popular impulses
that ruled everywhere in civil affairs. Members of the house of
assembly had to be influenced. In a moment of unusual frank-
ness Charles Dixon, one of the dissident members from Westmorland, declared in a conversation at VanHorne's Tavern that
members of His Majesty's council had offered him anything in
the gift of government if he would vote for their measures in
the House.[45]

Characteristic of the frontier approach to politics that was
becoming largely dominant in New Brunswick was the reduction
in the jurisdiction of the Supreme Court that took place in 1802.
The refusal of the judges to go on circuit made the court highly
vulnerable to attack. Justice was not cheap. One of the anony-

mous letters that came to the Colonial Office from New Brunswick at this time declared that in Westmorland a suit cost four
times as much as in Cumberland, across the border in Nova
Scotia.[46] In this year Carleton and the legislative council capitulated to two bills introduced in the house of assembly that
enabled the justices of the peace in the counties to preside in
suits for the recovery of debts up to five pounds instead of one
pound as formerly. They moved an enormous amount of legal
business from the Supreme Court to the parishes, magnifying
the dignity and consequence of the justices of the inferior courts.
The professional lawyers of the province suffered a damaging
blow to their practices. In a private letter to Odell, Chipman
remonstrated against the measures, though admitting they were
applauded by all sections of the public. "R. Pagan himself has
said that he feels under personal obligation to the Speaker for
his conduct; this satisfaction on his part I find arises in a great
measure from the passing of the bills respecting the jurisdiction
of the Inferior Courts which he says he never imagined would
have passed the Council. But I suppose this was intended as a
quieting measure for having rejected so many other bills. . . . He
is now become the arbiter as Chief Justice of the Common Pleas
in addition to his situation as a magistrate in the county of
Charlotte." Pagan, said Chipman, controlled all the concerns of
the inhabitants of that county.[47]

Power was passing from Fredericton to the constituencies.
"How then," asked Chipman, "has it happened that within these
few years such exertions have been made to enlarge the jurisdiction of justices of the Inferior Courts? Because the leading
members of the House of Assembly have been magistrates and
judges of these courts and, like the rest of mankind, are fond of
power, and think that justice can in no way be so well administered as by themselves."

Carleton had learned more than compromise. Unpopularity
could readily be passed across the water. Having given his
assent to the two bills, he wrote to the secretary of state, Lord
Hobart, asking that they be disallowed. He and the council, he
admitted, had been careless in granting too much competence
to "persons of small property and slender information, liable to
local and other prejudices".[48] This Hobart refused to do.

In 1805, broken by the failure of all his public and private
aspirations, Glenie followed Carleton to England. His later
career was reminiscent of his earlier predilections to a rash and

intemperate zeal for the unmasking of what he considered to be wrong, to an indifference for personal and material consequences.[49] His reputation as a liberal who, in the language of liberal historians, was fifty years ahead of his time, is subject to damaging qualifications. Many of his motives were vindictive and mischievous. Yet in the history of the second British empire in North America it was perhaps he who first led a movement that by any stretch of the imagination could be called popular against the upholders of the royal prerogative, who first employed a popular assembly as a forum for the seizure of power from privileged hands. In this he was to be followed by a goodly company.

He died in destitution in 1817 and was buried in the churchyard of St. Martin-in-the-Fields, London.

CHAPTER 6
The Spring of Hope
1798-1808

When Carleton left for England in 1803 he could not boast that
New Brunswick had advanced very far beyond the state in
which he had found it in 1784. The population amounted to
something less than 25,000, a figure that was disappointingly
low in the light of the great expectations that had prevailed at
the founding. The provincial government had been powerless to
inaugurate immigration policies. Carleton had failed to supply
real leadership in civil affairs. Even before the war had commenced, Chipman, in a private way, had complained of the lack
of initiative in New Brunswick compared with the great measures expected of Sir John Wentworth in Nova Scotia and the
work that Simcoe was doing in Upper Canada.[1] Carleton's difficulties with his legislature were, to a considerable degree, merely
a reflection of the disappointing turn affairs had taken.

Yet the position showed much that was good as well as adverse. War-time inflation and prosperity had taken a long time
to come, but, when they did, the Loyalists who for fourteen
difficult years had put their industry to good purpose were able
to take advantage of them. In November 1801, when news of
peace came to Saint John, a great public feast was held. The
last three years of the war, it was remarked by a writer in the
Royal Gazette, had been accompanied by great prosperity in
the city. The little ships of the Bay of Fundy, by their vigorous
trade with the Americans, were making it an emporium of importance. Just as the merchants of Halifax had natural advantages on the Miramichi, those of Saint John were able to make
their port a distribution centre for much of western Nova Scotia

as well as for the communities of the St. John Valley behind them. Digby, though in its own right a great centre for smugglers, had become a satellite of Saint John. "Jesus Christ," said Joshua Marsden, the Methodist missionary who visited the town at this time, "did not appear to have one foot of ground in all Digby."

One of the frankest and most engaging, if somewhat tendentious, accounts of New Brunswick at this time came from Charles Turner, an American from Maine who viewed with considerable enjoyment the contradictions that were so apparent in a loyal British province in close proximity to the United States. Noting that there were many British subjects on the islands in the bay, then in dispute between the two nations, he reached the clear conclusion that it would be better to let the British keep the islands, as annexation would "entirely break up the trading and smuggling houses, now well established and mutually beneficial". At Saint John, where the tide-waiter told him in the hearing of all the passengers that he had a right to land what he pleased without search, he was treated with as much politeness as he could expect "from a provincial officer aping the *hauteur* of the British". At Fredericton, Odell discouraged him from his project of attempting settlements near the American lines, but Stair Agnew informed him that the instruction of 1790 had been expressly designed to encourage American immigration. Up the river, near Woodstock, where he was a guest at the home of Major Griffiths, an intending candidate for the provincial election and a great logician who insisted on reading British agricultural texts in preference to American, he saw, following a quilting party, nine young ladies, all dressed in white, and six young gentlemen, prepared to spend the evening in dancing. Throughout the country wages were high and money was plentiful. There were many pensioners in the province and the raising of the New Brunswick Regiment had caused cash to circulate. Turner noted the disaffection which had free play among those who had not been able to acquire title to their lands. By refusing title, he said, the King and his governor had assured that the people would remain in New Brunswick because they were unable to sell their improvements. "Thus they are in a pretty poor situation for removing with property to the United States and would like well that the United States would remove to them."[2]

Following the settlement of the St. Croix boundary in 1798

there was no perceptible reason why those who had come to
New Brunswick since 1790 should not be given clear title to
their lands. Sensing the gathering storm, Carleton pressed for
the release of the Crown lands to settlement. The 1790 instruction, he declared, had excited doubts concerning the future
intentions of the British Government in New Brunswick, discouraging applications for settlement since no clear answers
could be given. In 1799 and 1800 many settlers, despairing of
obtaining legal possession of their properties, left the province.[3]
In the years following the turn of the century the emigration
began to assume alarming proportions. Edward Winslow wrote
letters to the *Royal Gazette* chiding those who, following the
example of certain half-pay officers, had accepted His Majesty's
bounty and had gone to live in the United States or who, purely
for the sake of fancy, were abandoning their properties in New
Brunswick in favour of the uncertain attractions of distant
Niagara. In 1802 the legislature appointed commissioners whose
business it was to stop "the present rage" for emigration to
Upper Canada, and fully extended its resources by voting £300
to attract new settlers from the United Kingdom.[4]

At this stage New Brunswick desperately needed a fresh ad-
mixture of people. The prospect of loss of population seemed
ruinous. To the Baie Verte shore a number of settlers had come
from Prince Edward Island, discontented with their status as
tenants in that province, and hopes were entertained of getting
more. When, in 1803, the merchants of St. Andrews heard that
a party of Scots had landed on the St. Croix, had failed to find
land, and had taken passage to Nova Scotia, they fitted out a
vessel at their own expense, sailed after them, and brought them
back to St. Stephen. The laying out of Scotch Ridge, a familiar
pioneering epic, followed. For almost every community in New
Brunswick the introduction of new people represented the only
hope of survival.

II

In demanding a revision of the imperial government's land
policy, Carleton knew very well that he was inviting the resurrection of another imperial exaction that would be distasteful
to the people of New Brunswick. A new statement of intention
from the British government would require clarification on the
delicate subject of quitrents. This was long overdue. Many of
the first grants of land were dated 1783 and, according to the

terms of the royal instructions, collection of quitrents, two shillings on every 100 acres granted, should have commenced in 1793. The establishment of an office of receiver-general of quitrents had been suggested by members of the official group on several occasions. George Leonard, in requesting the office for his friend Winslow, said the people would pay cheerfully if the right man demanded the money.[5] But Carleton recommended the opposite course. The Loyalists who came from New York could remember the strong opinions of Sir Guy Carleton on the subject and, although they had gladly accepted their grants on the stipulated terms, it had been commonly supposed that quitrents would never be demanded. "Experience has shown that whoever takes an allotment here and fully performs the conditions of his grant, does, in fact, by his labour and unavoidable expenses of settlement, pay the full value of his land for many years to come." It was unreasonable, argued Carleton, for the British government to suppose that settlers in New Brunswick could cultivate hemp when they could scarcely produce provisions enough for their own subsistence.[6]

Indulging in the hope that he could be given authority to make grants from the Crown lands, and at the same time cancel arrears on quitrents and abolish them for the future, Carleton encouraged protest from other quarters. Knox forced several interviews with John King, Clerk of the Privy Council, and with Portland, discovering that Portland did not understand the significance of the instruction of 1790.[7] How much time, growled the old man, would the British government require to work out the "advantageous arrangements" considered in 1790? Was ten years not enough? He told Addington, the new prime minister, that while the British government considered the "cruel and impolitic instruction" New Brunswick would be denuded of the King's subjects.[8] Odell and Winslow, a committee of the council, addressed an impassioned plea to the British government, declaring that the people of New Brunswick had the right to expect lands for their children. The house of assembly added its voice, warning that many were emigrating to Nova Scotia and the United States.

For Carleton the verdict of the new British government, when it came in 1802, was one of generosity mingled with most unpleasant complications. The King, said Lord Hobart, was willing to withdraw the objectionable instruction and give to the government of New Brunswick the freedom it desired to make grants from the Crown lands. By the twenty-first article in the instructions that were enclosed he was furthermore willing to remit all arrears in quitrents "provided that the legislature should without delay make provision for the proper arrangement and collection of the quitrents in future". The King would require the payment of one halfpenny for every acre held, "every midsummer day forever". This represented more than a doubling of the quitrents demanded in the original instructions of 1784. No grants of land could be made until the legislature should pass an act and the control of proceedings be placed in competent hands.[9]

This requirement, which was completely unexpected, filled Carleton with indignation and alarm. Quitrents, he was certain, could be managed much better by an order of the King than by an act of the legislature, "even if we were sure of obtaining such an act". Nobody in the province, he said, doubted the King's right to grant the Crown lands. Discussion and alarm would be excited if it were supposed that an act of the legislature was necessary. "The assembly could not be prevailed upon to pass any bill for that purpose and the collection of quitrents would from that moment be considered illegal and oppressive."[10] Before publishing the instructions he asked for permission to await others, and Hobart concurred. New instructions in 1803 gave him the choice of whether or not to employ the authority of the legislature. The council supported his opinion that it was not judicious to do so.

In spite of Carleton's caution a great deal of damage was done. It was repeatedly alleged that the instructions of 1802 caused an increase in the emigration already taking place, that people were moving to the United States where they could obtain land in a milder climate completely free from restrictions.

In the few years following his return to England Carleton laboured to procure the removal of the instruction to collect quitrents. Sproule, his surveyor-general, prepared an estimate showing that a revenue of £1,082/8/6½ could be collected from existing grants of land. For the British government, the prior consideration was fear of the old bugbear of colonial development – unbridled speculation in wilderness lands by avaricious local factions. Carleton had difficulty in showing that there were no really large grants in New Brunswick, that the old Nova Scotian grants had been largely escheated, that only disbanded officers had received grants of 1,000 acres. The people of

New Brunswick, he asserted, could bear no additional taxation.[11]

Early in 1807 his point of view triumphed. New instructions came to New Brunswick authorizing the granting of land without immediate liability for quitrents. The latter would remain "a subject for future consideration".[12] "The revocation of the standing order of 1790," wrote Carleton, "must give great satisfaction to the inhabitants of New Brunswick and that of 1802 still more."[13] The Crown had not surrendered its right to collect quitrents, but Carleton interpreted the instructions of 1807 as if it had, and his interpretation gained currency for nearly twenty years, until a generation of colonial reformers in London should rise to rescue them from oblivion.

During the years of the renewed struggle with Napoleon, British ministers had little time to spare for the internal problems of a remote colony. Only spasmodically was sustained attention given to colonial problems. In 1806 a plan for the settlement of the wild lands of New Brunswick and Nova Scotia engrossed much of the energy of Lord Auckland, who received valuable assistance from Richard John Uniacke, the attorney-general of Nova Scotia.[14] But nothing came of it. In Church as well as in State, policy and vigour were completely lacking. Sussex was the only community in New Brunswick where the people had commenced to build a church from their own resources, but they had failed to finish it. In acknowledging a shipment of copies of *The Theocracy and the Revealed Will* Leonard wrote the learned author that anybody reading the book would approve of his principles but that "so little is said and less read on religion I have my doubts of their being sold immediately".[15]

III

One long shadow that appeared to menace the future of New Brunswick had been removed. For almost fifteen years the boundary dispute with the United States had compromised its integrity, along with a great many other factors casting doubt on whether the province should continue to exist at all. The determination of Great Britain, while war was being waged with France, to maintain amicable relationships with the United States gave encouragement to fears that great territorial surrenders would be made. If the Americans could establish their case that the Magaguadavic was the river intended by the negotiators of Versailles to be considered as "the true St. Croix",

one-third of the province would be lost. Those who were opposed to Carleton in New Brunswick looked to the boundary
negotiation as another factor that could discredit his administration. One of these, writing under a *nom de plume*, recommended that should the Americans win the negotiation the
remainder of the province should be annexed to Nova Scotia.[16]

From the time the Tories of the Penobscot had moved to St.
Andrews, the dispute had been vigorously conducted by local
authorities. At first the contest for islands had been sharper
than for territory on the mainland. The treaty had retained for
Great Britain all the islands in the Bay of Fundy that had
formerly been under the jurisdiction of Nova Scotia. The focal
point was Moose Island, technically an island but in reality a
part of the American mainland, with its satellites, Dudley and
Frederick. If Great Britain could establish her right to Moose
Island she would control all the channels leading to the inner
waters of Passamaquoddy Bay. From 1785 to 1791 the sheriff
of Charlotte County had quarrelled with the sheriff of Washington County, Massachusetts, concerning the placing of jurisdiction over the uncertain inhabitants. By 1791 the Americans had
established a *de facto* occupation, and the town of Eastport
arose. Up the St. John the Loyalist inhabitants of Meductic
were dismayed in 1794 when a party of American surveyors,
agents of Massachusetts, appeared, to mark off the boundary
through their parish.

The Treaty of Amity, Commerce, and Navigation of 1795,
more commonly called Jay's Treaty, prepared the way for the
settlement of the initial portion of the boundary dispute. The
fifth article made provision for the appointment of three commissioners, one to be selected by the King of Great Britain,
another by the president of the United States, and a third by
the first two, whose duty it would be to decide which of the
three rivers flowing into Passamaquoddy Bay was the true St.
Croix. The British commissioner, nominated by Sir John Wentworth, was Thomas Barclay, the leader of the Loyalist party in
Nova Scotia and the Speaker of the house of assembly, who had
fervently supported the policies of the lieutenant-governor
against his adversaries. President Washington appointed Daniel
Howell, professor of law in Brown University and a leading
member of the Rhode Island bar. The third commissioner, over
whose nomination there was a great deal of difficulty, was
Egbert Benson, a judge of the Supreme Court of New York and

an old acquaintance of Barclay, who finally agreed to accept Benson rather than trust to the dangerous method of balloting. No retreat from or denial of the decision of the commissioners could honourably be made by either party, so the choice of the third member was of the greatest importance.

Carleton, to whose patronage fell the choice of a British agent, nominated Ward Chipman. The American agent was James Sullivan, the historian of the District of Maine. Edward Winslow became secretary to the commission. At Saint John there were misgivings upon the choice of the British personnel. There, an opinion held that Barclay was about to join the renegade half-pay officers who had drifted off to the United States, that the mischievous counsels of Chipman and Winslow had brought Carleton to the brink of a precipice and New Brunswick into "its present deplorable condition", that these two, the one before the war a bond bailiff in New England and the other a tidewaiter, would sell the whole province in order to benefit their personal interests.[17]

The first meeting was held at Boston in June 1796, and other meetings took place at Halifax, St. Andrews, Boston again, and Providence. The negotiators of 1783 had used the map of John Mitchell, printed for the Anglo-French boundary commission of 1755, as the basis for their discussions on the north-eastern boundary of the United States. It showed but one River St. Croix, but it was possible to argue that this might have been any one of the three flowing into Passamaquoddy Bay. Sullivan, in the tortuous and exhaustive reasonings that assailed the commission, running through eight folio volumes of 300 pages each, concentrated upon the intention of the treaty-makers. It had been decided to accept the first great river to the west of the St. John as the boundary, and the Magaguadavic, he reasoned, answered this description. John Adams, the new president of the United States, and John Jay, who had represented their country at Versailles, gave evidence but would not admit they had been aware that more than one river intersected the contested region. Sullivan could not make a clear case.

To confound this logic Chipman turned antiquarian. In his mind there was but one River St. Croix, that designated by Champlain and deMonts as such in 1604 when they had wintered on an island near its mouth. Securing the memorials of the English and French commissioners on the earlier boundary dispute, he perceived the importance of the writings of the first

French navigators who had given the river its name. Feverishly
the Colonial Office searched London for the original works of
Champlain and Lescarbot. George Chalmers, the antiquary, was
pleased to lend some volumes. Dr. Andrew Brown, an authority
on early Nova Scotian history, found a copy of Champlain's
writings in Edinburgh and forwarded extracts.[18] In the summer
of 1797 Chipman received an ink-tracing of Champlain's map
of St. Croix Island and that part of the St. Croix River in which
the island was located.

The information given in the books was supported by findings on the ground. In the summer of 1796 the members of the
commission had been conducted to an island in the Schoodiac
known as Dochet's Island and considered by Chipman to have
been Champlain's St. Croix Island. But at Robert Pagan's store
in St. Andrews, where Passamaquoddy Indians had gathered to
give evidence on ancient terminology, they had, schooled by
American agents, stated that the Magaguadavic was the river
where the legendary cross had first been raised. It was, therefore, with considerable elation that Chipman was able to inform
the commission at Boston in the autumn of 1797 that during
the previous summer Pagan, with copies of Champlain's dia-
grams, had gone to Dochet's Island and had supervised excava-
tions. Piles of brick at regular distances from one another, and
cut stones, several tiers deep, had been discovered, all in harmony with Champlain's description of the buildings constructed
by deMonts. This clinched the case for Chipman and for New
Brunswick. In vain the Americans sent surveyors up the Magaguadavic in order to find a similar island with similar ruins.
Howell, the American commissioner, and Sullivan, the American
agent, refused to admit that Pagan's evidence disproved their
contention, but Benson, whose vote was decisive, was completely
convinced that the Schoodiac was the true St. Croix.

Yet it was not enough to designate the true river. The locations of its source and of its mouth would have immense bearing
on future territorial settlement. To Chipman's mortification the
surveyors reported that the westerly branch of the Schoodiac
had its source in a chain of lakes five and three-quarter miles
from the point at which it joined the main river. The question
now facing the commission was whether or not the chain of lakes
was the river's continuation. When they agreed in the negative
Chipman had to consider the implications of the running of a
northerly line from the eastern shore of the eastern lake in the

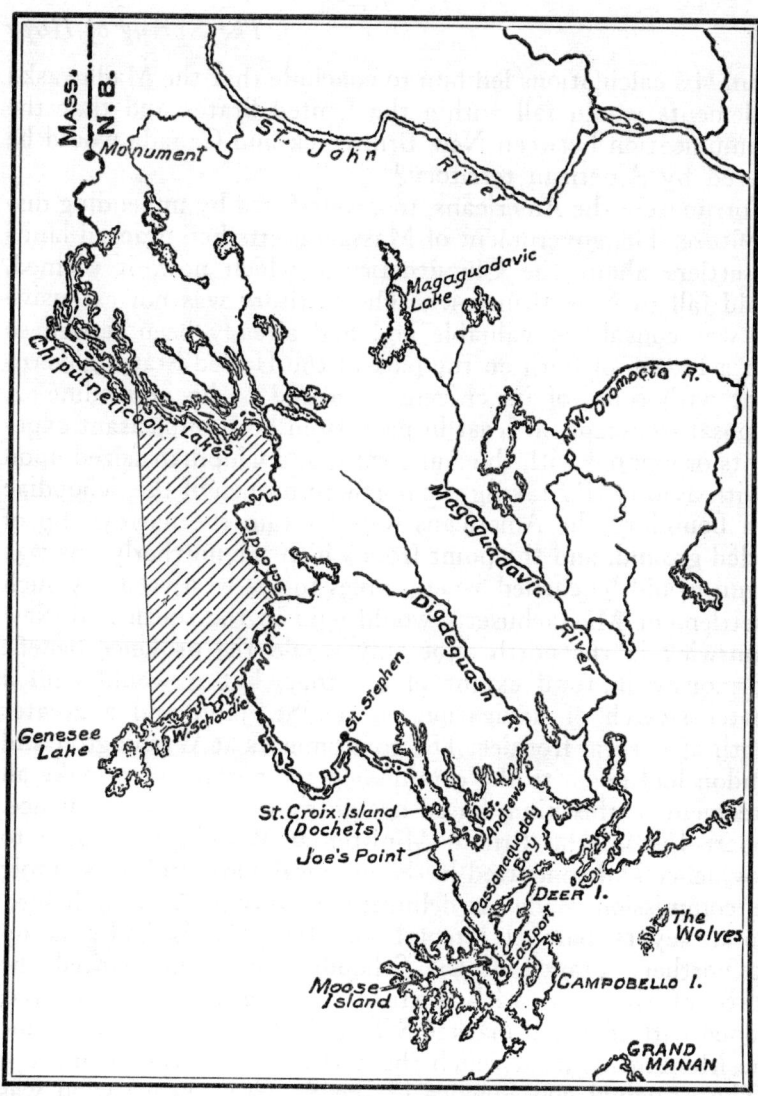

THE ST. CROIX CONVENTION
October 25, 1798

Shading indicates territory allowed to the Americans by the Providence Agreement. Broken line shows the boundary adopted.

chain. His calculations led him to conclude that the Madawaska settlements would fall within the United States and that the communication between New Brunswick and Canada would be severed by American territory.[19]

Fortunately the Americans, too, were faced by impending discomfiture. The government of Massachusetts had granted lands to settlers about the Chiputneticook which now, it seemed, would fall to New Brunswick. The territory was not extensive but was considered valuable and had already been settled so that a breach of faith on the part of the United States government with some of its citizens appeared to be impending. A proposal to escape, at least in part, from both unpleasant expedients originated with the Americans, and Chipman seized upon it with avidity. By taking the northern branch of the Schoodiac as a boundary the Americans would retain the narrow slip of settled ground, and the point from which the northerly line was to run would be carried several miles to the westward. By such a settlement Massachusetts would gain in the south and New Brunswick in the north. Not only would the province benefit enormously in total extent of territory, but it would gain a greater stretch of navigation on the St. John and a greater length of natural frontier. The governments at Washington and London had given to the commission the authority to make an agreement of this kind, based not on right but on convenience. Robert Liston, the British Minister at Washington, came to Providence and concurred in the proposal. On October 25, 1798, the commission made its delineation. During the year before, two surveyors, Samuel Titcomb and John Harris, had gone up the northern branch of the Schoodiac and had marked the source of the river with a stake "near a yellow birch tree, hooped with iron and marked S.T. and J.H. 1797". This became The Monument, from which the northerly line was to run.

The principal consequence of the St. Croix negotiation was that the main American demand had been successfully resisted. New Brunswick emerged in approximately the form her founders had conceived for her. In detail Chipman had been disappointed, for he had not succeeded in bringing the northerly line sufficiently far to the west to salvage all British interests on the upper river. The great question would now be how far the northerly line would run: where were the highlands that would mark the limits of the northern thrust of American jurisdiction?

In the location of the mouth of the river Chipman scored

another victory. This was important so far as the disputed islands were concerned. If it could be shown that they were in the river, as the Americans claimed, they would become negotiable, for the treaty had reserved to Britain only those islands that were in the Bay of Fundy. It was therefore the purpose of the British to fix the mouth of the river as far to the north as possible, that of the Americans, as far to the south as possible. When the commission agreed upon Joe's Point as marking the mouth of the St. Croix, the outer and larger islands, Campobello, Deer, and Grand Manan, did not appear to be endangered.

It was not until after the War of 1812 that the American diplomatic offensive developed against these valuable adjuncts to New Brunswick. But their very effective occupation of the smaller islands, Moose, Dudley, and Frederick, gave the Americans a strong bargaining position, and in two conventions, those of 1803 and 1807, Britain acknowledged the sovereignty of the United States. The conventions were never ratified, because the Passamaquoddy controversy was only one of many included within the discussions. The Louisiana Purchase of 1803 introduced a new fluidity into Anglo-American relations from which it was difficult to establish agreement of any kind.

Not only by old enemies but also by seeming friends was New Brunswick's integrity assailed at this time. One of Carleton's last acts before leaving the province was the repudiation of a suggestion from Halifax that the province should be divided. The connections of Halifax on the Miramichi had been greatly strengthened. One of Sir John Wentworth's most reliable aides, Michael Wallace, had succeeded by mortgage to the properties of William Davidson. He had passed them on to the energetic house of Fraser and Thom, who supplied the people along the river with provisions and exported their produce. The reason advanced for the partition of Nova Scotia in 1784, convenience of communication, was presented for the dismemberment of New Brunswick in 1802 by Scrope Bernard, agent-general for Nova Scotia in London. With his memorial came two suggested plans, one of which would reunite to his own province all land to the eastward of a line running from Chignecto to the headwaters of the Restigouche.[20]

Carleton's response to this was a vigorous assertion of the now historic Loyalist particularism. An alteration of the carefully considered arrangement of 1784, he reasoned, would have an injurious effect on the minds of the people and retard the new settlements that were expected to spring up in consequence of the withdrawal of the 1790 instructions. The settlers of the eastern shore, he declared, perhaps a little mendaciously and in abrupt contradiction to the Halifax memorial, received all their supplies from Saint John, "now become a great commercial depot".[21]

IV

Carleton left as his deputy Gabriel Ludlow who took, in what was considered to be the temporary absence of the lieutenant-governor, the office of president of the council. Almost magically, as Ludlow took control and as war was renewed with France, a curious calm descended upon the internal politics of the province. Contention appeared to vanish and government became perfunctory. Looking to the Winslow Papers for the word, the historian of Ludlow's time finds "necromantic" as satisfactory as did his contemporaries. Correspondence with the Colonial Office was reduced to a short series of cryptic, routine dispatches. Ludlow did not bother to remove his residence from Carleton, where he operated a mercantile establishment, to Fredericton. A London publication of 1808 referred to Fredericton as "the late seat of government".[22]

The constitutional issue was no longer debated. Complete concord between council and assembly appeared to prevail for the five years of Ludlow's rule. John Coffin and Amos Botsford, the two leading members of the assembly, were men of business with little flair for the abstractions of public discussion that had been so prominent in Glenie's time. It was as if New Brunswick no longer had disposition for the niceties of constitutional convention. Business in the legislature was transacted by the mixture of British and American methods authorized by the Duke of Portland in 1798. Commerce was slowly expanding and New Brunswick, with a host of illusions dispelled, was preparing itself by hard labour for the opportunities that some still considered lay ahead. There could be no replica of village life in England. "You cannot indeed offend a servant more in this country than by asking him if his master or mistress is at home; he looks upon these names as badges of villeinage in those who use them and consequently fit only for the mouth of a slave."[23] Socially the most prominent factor was the scarcity of labour. Chief Justice Ludlow made himself an object of odium to the military when he ruled, after the New Brunswick Regiment had been raised for the second time, that minors could not enlist without the consent of their fathers, and that until he was twenty-one a man was bound to his father as an apprentice was bound to his master. Presumably in sympathy with hard-pressed farmers who wanted to keep their sons at home, Ludlow used habeas corpus to release soldiers from their duty, a procedure that was indignantly repudiated by the law officers in England.[24]

The only source of major discord during Gabriel Ludlow's administration was a parochial one, yet elemental to settlers in the early days of the province. The rights of proprietors to the adjacent fisheries in rivers and harbours had always been challenged. Almost everywhere the salmon ran, fierce local disputes took place. The legislature had attempted to regulate the fisheries by a law which declared that only one-fourth the width of navigable streams might be netted, but this had been flagrantly violated in every part of the province. On the Miramichi the settlers of the upper river complained that those who lived about the estuary "wallowed in affluence" by reason of the great seventy-fathom nets they laid.[25] By 1810 the settlers of Grand Lake, who had always greatly depended upon the fishery, found themselves in distress because persons from Saint John netted the entire widths of the two great passages from the river into the lake.[26] Whatever the law said, it was worthless for protection against those who exploited the fishery for commercial purposes, especially following the revival of the West Indies trade in 1806.

At Saint John the classic controversy was waged. Ever since its foundation, the freemen of the city had been jealous of their exclusive right to fish within the waters of the harbour and had fiercely ejected intruders. Yet when their own fishery failed they did not hesitate to invade the waters off Portland, which were a recess of the inner harbour not included within the city corporation. Portland was an enclosure of the firm of Simonds, White, and Hazen. On occasions great shoals of fish congregated off its banks, making it one of the most desirable areas of the entire St. John estuary. Since 1783 the firm had been unpopular with the freemen of Saint John. At the time of the settlement, no common had been made available for the cattle of the Loyalist new-comers, an omission, it was alleged, designed to benefit the firm upon whom the town had been dependent for provisions and supplies of all kinds. When the tenants of Simonds, White, and Hazen attempted to assert their own exclusive right to the fishery on the beaches off Portland, extending as far as low-water mark in accordance with the grant made to the firm in 1765, private war developed. Vindictive sabotaging of nets, boats, and other properties, forcible ejections, and crimes of violence took place.

William Hazen, who was treasurer of the province and a foremost exponent of the interests of the firm, was not the kind of man who would readily relinquish rights belonging to himself and his partners since 1765. In the beginning of the Loyalist settlement, he admitted, he had not deemed it prudent to insist upon exclusive rights to the Portland fishery. But in 1791, when the people of Saint John were no longer in need of generosity, he finally insisted upon the recognition of his rights and asked the legislature for a special act for their protection.

For thirteen years Hazen's rights were consistently challenged and strenuously defended. So successful was the defence that in 1804 the mayor and city corporation of Saint John took the case of the Portland fisheries to the Supreme Court of New Brunswick. The ruling was that Simonds, White, and Hazen had no rights over the fishery between high- and low-water marks. It was generally interpreted by the respectable and substantial as a blow to the interests of holders of property and a blight upon the prospects of the province.

For Hazen and his many friends in high places it did not appear to be too difficult to change the law, and in 1805 the legislature of New Brunswick, by a large majority of both council and assembly, passed an act "to ascertain the rights to fisheries". This effectively "annexed the fishery to the soil". The mayor and common council of Saint John refused to submit to these summary proceedings. Citing Magna Charta and The Charter of Forests, they appealed to the King in Council, employing Samuel Denny Street as their attorney. Street appeared before the Privy Council in London, and Knox, aged but still vigorous, represented the government of New Brunswick. It was one of the rare victories enjoyed by the pugnacious Street. "I could not contend," said Knox, "that an act of assembly should repeal an act of Parliament or alter the common law of England." However strong were the legal considerations against the act to ascertain the rights of fishery, expediency was an even more powerful one. By the Treaty of 1783, subjects of the United States had the right to land on the shores of unoccupied inlets of the New Brunswick coast in order to carry on the fishery.

Acceptance of the act by the British government would prejudice the treaty rights of the Americans. This, Knox hinted, was the more pertinent reason for the disallowance of the act, which came in 1808.[27]

V

The death of Gabriel Ludlow, in February 1808, came in the midst of an emergency. The danger of war with the United States had become imminent in the autumn of 1807, and he had received the rather uninspiring orders from London to gather together his slender garrisons, consisting of detachments of the New Brunswick Regiment and a few auxiliaries, and to retreat upon Halifax in order to assist in the defence of that place, provided that the expected American attack should make such a course necessary.[28] Amidst the excitement he had called out the militia. Every man, said Ludlow, volunteered his services for the defence of the province. It was necessary to ballot in order to decide not those who should turn out but those who should stay at home.[29] Drafts from York, Sunbury, and Queens counties poured into Fredericton and a company was stationed at Meductic. Battalions from Kings and St. John counties guarded the city, those of Charlotte assembling at St. Andrews. But as no real emergency developed it became difficult to sustain the enthusiasm. To keep such high-spirited troops in barracks for the winter months without having taken the necessary measures to attend to their pay was beyond Ludlow's capacity. Desertion became widespread and the whole affair began to assume the complexion of a disgraceful farce.

Ludlow was succeeded by Edward Winslow, the senior councillor, who gratefully seized the opportunity of disbanding the militia in April, having heard from Halifax that the state of emergency had ceased. Paying and rationing the troops a little too generously to please the imperial authorities, Winslow saw them back to their homes in time to take part in the spring planting. Through the winter the commercial elements in the population had ridiculed what appeared to be an absurd and unnecessary display of patriotism since a huge proportion of the young men of the country had been removed from productive employment. In a country like New Brunswick patriotism was a virtue that could be afforded only in the gravest of crises.

The emergency had more serious consequences than this. Under the conviction that war with the United States was certain to come, the British government revised its system of command in the Atlantic provinces. It was deemed necessary to give to a soldier the command in both military and civil affairs. Sir James Craig replaced Sir John Wentworth at Halifax, and a subordinate officer, Brigadier-General Martin Hunter, came to Fredericton as president of the council. What the official group at Fredericton became accustomed to call the "military succession" occurred when Winslow, after three months of office, turned over the administration to Hunter in May 1808. Their fortunes, it seemed, had become dependent upon almost any junior officer of the army whom the caprices of the command at Halifax might decide to send to Fredericton. Over twenty years of service and seniority suddenly appeared worthless. Carleton was still lieutenant-governor, but he was growing old in England, and New Brunswick had seen the last of him. He had been asked to return, but the prejudices of a military man who had seen fifty years of service and twenty of command were too great. As a full general he could not, with propriety, serve under Craig, who was merely a lieutenant-general.[30]

The death of Gabriel Ludlow was the first of a series of rapid changes in the composition of the original office-holding group. When George Duncan Ludlow, the Chief Justice, followed his brother later in the year, new honours opened up to the ambitions of both young and old among the legal luminaries. However great were their personal rivalries, they were united in the conviction that no stranger should succeed. Hunter supported this point of view, urging that the ambitious young men of New Brunswick should be encouraged to look to the influence of government for promotion and not to influences among the masses of the people.[31] In the contest for the chief-justiceship faraway factors were certainly the predominant ones. Two months before George Duncan Ludlow died Chipman submitted an application. "God forbid," wrote Odell to Chipman, "that you should be defeated by such an unworthy competitor";[32] but Jonathan Bliss, the attorney-general, who had never been in Carleton's favour and was on terms of enmity with most of the governing clique, defeated him roundly. Asserting that in twenty years of service he had not received over £350 in public money beyond his salaries, he wrote a private application to Lord Liverpool, whom he had come to know at meetings of the Board of Trade in 1784, reminding him of his original recommendation to Lord North in 1776. A note from Liverpool to

Castlereagh was sufficient.[33] "So that superior interest, not the difference of rank and precedence, decided the question as it always will," wrote Chipman ruefully.[34]

Though he missed the top honour of his profession, Chipman became a judge of the Supreme Court not very much later, happy to abandon "the slavish drudgery and butchery" of legal practice in New Brunswick. One of the original appointees, Joshua Upham, had in 1807 taken ship for England, determined to persuade the Lords of the Treasury that it was time, after fifteen years of rising prices, for the allowance of increases in salary to himself and his companions on the Bench. On shipboard Upham was the victim of a serious accident, and he arrived in England miserable and penurious. A change in administration, a dissolution of Parliament, and pressure of public business delayed him for a year before he was able to gain the necessary attention from ministers. Ultimately he gained his point, but he died in London before being able to return to New Brunswick and benefit from his labours. Spencer Percival, the Chancellor of the Exchequer, and other British dignitaries whom he had encountered in his pursuit contributed to a fund that sustained him in his last days. He left a family of five daughters completely destitute.[35]

Chipman filled this vacancy, joining Edward Winslow who, to the surprise of all of his friends and to the consternation of some, had acquired a judicial capacity in 1806, succeeding Isaac Allen. Letters to the Duke of Northumberland and to Lord Sheffield, and a reminder to Peter Oliver of how he had rescued him from a Boston mob thirty years before on the occasion of the opening of the Supreme Court, had subdued objections raised by Carleton that Winslow was not trained in the law.[36]

In consequence of the promotion of so much legal talent, Thomas Wetmore, "the ablest and best barrister in New Brunswick", became attorney-general, and John Murray Bliss (the son of Daniel Bliss, a member of the original council who had never come to the forefront of affairs) was made solicitor-general. The latter appointment was made because Bliss was a son-in-law of the unfortunate Upham and would incur a share of the duty of sustaining the destitute family.

The woebegone letters telling of disappointed expectations that came to the Colonial Office in the year of the "military succession" were given extra emphasis by a communication from Jonathan Odell. A man of gentle demeanour and mild speech,

he had abstained, as far as possible, from the rancours that had
been so voluble in the later years of Carleton's rule, though, as
"the maker of militia officers and just asses of the peace, plotter
of all headquarters intrigues",[37] he had not been able to escape
entirely. On coming to New Brunswick in 1784 he had been
informed that his situation would be worth £1,500. But in
1808, at seventy-one years of age, he could make no permanent
provision for his family. Out of his salary of £500 he had been
compelled to pay for the entire secretarial establishment, the
wages of clerks, and the cost of firewood. Had it not been for
the saving of a little property in New Jersey he would have been
completely ruined. Without reward he had performed the office
of clerk of the legislative council. He asked that his son might
succeed him in his office in order that his two unmarried
daughters might have continued support.[38]

After several refusals the Colonial Office agreed, although such
an appointment was held to be "objectionable on general principles".[39]

VI

The lassitude and defeatism of older men were in the ascendancy at Fredericton, but these did not reflect the state of the
province. The beginnings of a more spacious age are visible in
the opening years of the nineteenth century. While politics
decayed to a theme of resignation, commerce throve.

In 1804, when Ludlow transmitted the petition of the merchants of Saint John upon the familiar demand for exclusion of
the Americans from the British West Indies, he declared that
the commerce of the province would have been annihilated during the previous ten years but for four particular reasons. These
were the coastal fisheries, the excellence of the harbours, the
herring in the rivers that were better adapted to the West
Indian markets because they were firmer and would last longer,
and "the inexhaustible forests".[40] Yet these advantages had
merely enabled the people of New Brunswick to live as bonds-
men to the Americans. Altogether irrespective of the hazards of
French privateers, New Brunswick shippers could not compete
with the Americans in the West Indies owing to the higher
wages demanded by seamen and the higher rates of insurance.
John Venner, a merchant of London who gave evidence before
a committee of the House of Commons, declared that when he
left Saint John in 1804 there had been "no New Brunswick

ships". In order to convey New Brunswick produce to the West Indies he had been compelled to charter British vessels. It was much more profitable, he insisted, for the people of New Brunswick to sell their goods to the Americans for carriage to outside markets.[41]

Until about 1806 the terms of trade forced this secondary and tributary role upon New Brunswick commerce. The Americans purchased fish from the skippers of small coastal vessels and sold it for high profits in the West Indies. Three million board feet of lumber, said Ludlow, were taken away each year by the Americans from Charlotte County alone. Plaster of Paris, dug from the quarries of Westmorland County and so highly prized as a fertilizer in the American states south of Pennsylvania, likewise yielded great and easy profits to the Americans. All of this trade could not be regulated nor could its volume be measured. It yielded no revenue to the province, for the tea, tobacco, sugar, and other tropical products that were obtained in barter from the Americans could easily be smuggled into the numerous harbours on a large number of little ships. Virtually all the tobacco brought into the province, with the exception of that for the use of the King's troops, was smuggled, said one petition to the house of assembly, asking for the amendment of the Laws of Trade and Navigation so that tobacco might be directly and legally imported from Virginia.[42] All the prevalent conditions in commerce discouraged the construction of great ships and the pursuit of overseas trade. Landsmen, not seamen, said one memorialist, carried on the traffic in plaster of Paris.

Trade around the coasts of the province was under the supervision of George Leonard who, under a commission from the Lords of the Treasury, was charged with the enforcement of the Laws of Trade and Navigation. An eminent Loyalist who had been one of the first magistrates of Saint John, he had not been taken on the original establishment of officers for the province. The omission had been made good in 1786 when, on Carleton's recommendation, he had succeeded Jonathan Binney as superintendent of trade and fisheries at Canso. This difficult task could not be performed within a jurisdiction that was limited. To enforce the laws of trade at Canso merely meant that the Americans would carry on their illicit traffic to the north and westward, entering every settled inlet of the coasts of New Brunswick and Nova Scotia. From Halifax to Bay Chaleur, he wrote in 1798, illicit traffic reigned everywhere. If the Americans

were to be harried away from the rich profits they made from
bartering with British fishermen he would require control
throughout the waters of four provinces.[43] Largely owing to his
friendship with Knox, Leonard gained his objectives. By 1800
his authority extended over the coasts of New Brunswick, Nova
Scotia, Cape Breton, and Prince Edward Island. He had command of a sloop of war that cruised the coasts, breaking up the
illicit trade whenever occasion offered. He appointed deputies at
several strategic localities. He enjoyed the co-operation of Sir
John Wentworth at Halifax, though it was commonly alleged
that Sir John relaxed the restrictions of the laws of trade more
frequently than his right, derived from an act of Parliament,
permitted. Of all the New Brunswick Loyalists Leonard was
probably the most zealous, refusing to temper loyalty with
caution and business acumen, professing to believe that the War
of the American Revolution was still being fought on New
Brunswick soil. Of all none possessed more pride. His house at
Sussex, Bishop Inglis noted in his diary in 1792, resembled a
gentleman's villa in Europe.

Leonard's first target was the illicit traffic of the islands. Presiding over it still was David Owen who professed to believe
that he was, by the conditions of his grant, exempt from the
operation of New Brunswick's laws. Still he was on terms of
acute hostility with Robert Pagan and the magistrates of
Charlotte County. Right or wrong, said Owen, he could never
win a suit within their jurisdiction.[44] During the War of 1812 he
was invaded in his bedchamber by an American named John
Stedman Beckwith who had advertised that he would have
Owen's head on the State House in Boston. After overpowering
the man and rowing him over nine miles of stormy water to St.
Andrews, Owen was later enraged to discover that he had been
released on bail by order of Pagan.[45] Owen's surliness, his violence both of speech and action, made him enemies everywhere.

At Campobello and adjacent ports, said one writer, tea-chests
and other containers, bearing appropriate marks of legal importation, were filled with American goods really smuggled into
New Brunswick. Eastport was a haven for deserters from the
army and navy. Not only did much of the produce of New
Brunswick pass through the channel between Campobello and
Moose Island, but much of the specie brought into the province
found its way out.[46] Protection for this motley trading community came from a curious and uncertain arrangement between

William Wanton, the customs collector at Saint John, and the American officers at Eastport. Great Britain had never completely recognized American ownership of Moose Island, but Wanton, who was said to be incredibly rich, had insisted that American occupation must be respected and that the waters between Moose Island and Campobello must be considered as neutral.

VII

Leonard was always willing to break a lance against those who deviated from the letter of the law and by 1798 he had declared open war on the illicit trade of the islands. "The enclosed curious advertisement will sufficiently show you what an illiterate, silly, contemptible fellow George Leonard is," said an anonymous letter-writer from Saint John to the Duke of Portland. "He is even ignorant and weak enough to suppose that he has the right to control the customs house."[47] He mobilized support in Saint John for an act of Parliament that would make it illegal for British ships to unload plaster of Paris in ports of the United States north and north-east of Boston. This would bring the plaster trade to the larger ships of Saint John and St. Andrews, capable of ocean voyages, depriving American sailors of the carrying trade and American merchants of a large part of their profits. The house of assembly presented an address to the King approving of the suggestion, but the British government was treading warily in all its dealings with the Americans. In 1803 Leonard's cutter, the *Union*, seized two American vessels trading with Campobello and took contraband as well, but whenever the *Union* appeared in one locality the Americans would turn their attention to another. Leonard urged that the governments of Nova Scotia and New Brunswick should collaborate in his work by providing additional cutters. "But it is not to be expected that popular assemblies, most of whose members are engaged in trade, will do anything to suppress illegal practices."[48]

The remarkable rivalry between the superintendent of trade and fisheries on the one side and the collector of customs on the other, the one wishing to destroy the contraband trade on the islands and the other to condone it, came to a head in 1805. In that year Leonard seized the *Falmouth*, an American sloop engaged in the plaster trade, at Snug Cove. The owner appealed against the seizure before the Court of Vice-Admiralty at Saint

John, with William Botsford presiding. The task facing the judge was a difficult one. The legality or illegality of the seizure depended upon the status of the waters of Snug Cove and this was dependent on whether or not Moose Island was American territory. Secondly there came under consideration the character of the informal arrangement made by the New Brunswick and American customs officials several years before, deemed by the appellant to protect the *Falmouth* and other American vessels engaged in the same trade. The proceedings were made somewhat more remarkable by the fact that the agent for the American owner was the surveyor and searcher of the customhouse at St. Andrews, Colin Campbell, and the owner of the cargo was Campbell's son.

The judge ruled that both vessel and cargo were forfeit, giving his opinion that the British customs officers in making their very informal agreement with the Americans had exceeded their authority.[49] The judgment was a legal assertion of Britain's right to Moose Island and a claim to control over the water adjacent to it.

The consequences were more than judicial. At Washington the British minister, Anthony Merry, had been striving to ease tensions with the United States following Britain's renewed restrictions upon the rights of neutrals at sea. The case of the *Falmouth* was another irritant, aggravating the tensions and bringing renewed attention to the disputed boundary in which John Madison himself had expressed especial concern. Madison now made the declaration that American subjects were in possession of Moose Island and therefore had the right to use the surrounding waters. Merry wrote to London that he could not conceive an explanation for Leonard's conduct.[50] A sharp note to Ludlow resulted in orders to Leonard to desist from further seizures and it quickly appeared that the *Falmouth* victory had been a Pyrrhic one. In 1806 and 1807 American vessels swarmed to the islands and it was commonly considered that the British government, intent on conciliating the United States, would move to make the trade legal. Merry's chagrin had been so great largely because the New Englanders, of all Americans, were the most friendlily disposed to Great Britain.

Wanton defended his amicable agreement with the customs officials at Eastport by arguing that American vessels came to Campobello in ballast and that so long as Britain permitted Americans to remain at Moose Island their rights to use the disputed waterway should be respected.[51] Not until 1811 did commissioners from His Majesty's Customs arrive at Fredericton to carry out an investigation. By this time the illicit trade was a favoured object of British policy and Wanton was nearly eighty. There is nothing to indicate that he failed to finish his days in peace. The vendetta with Leonard took the form of contentions over seizures and the distribution of the proceeds. In 1807 a quarrel between the two sets of officers, whose duty it was to enforce the law, over the proceeds of fourteen casks of rum was brought to the floor of the legislature.[52] The kind of thing against which traders in Saint John had to contend is nicely illustrated by a letter from a most respectable merchant, John Ward, to his brother, Captain Caleb Ward, who was hovering off the coast in the brig *Pandora*. The advice was that everything was still safe but he would have to be careful. "The hawks are on the alert and are very dissatisfied with their ill success and say that quantity can never be landed without their getting a share."[53]

VIII

Through these years, in which New Brunswick was slowly moving forward to a time of long-awaited prosperity, the mast trade kept up as an important though not a basic source of income. From 1795 to 1803 exports of great and middling masts to Great Britain moved steeply upwards, taking an especially sharp turn in 1801 when Denmark became a client of Napoleon and the trade in naval stores with the Baltic was jeopardized. In 1804 the principal mast contractors directed their activities to Canada, especially to the Ottawa Valley, so that in this year the figure fell to 761 compared with 2,161 the year before. In 1810 and 1811, at the height of the Peninsular War, the figures attained new records, reaching 3,151 in the latter year. Each year four or five mast-ships sailed for Great Britain via Halifax, for Martinique or other dockyards in the West Indies, or for Lisbon.

The importance of this contribution to the British war effort need not be overestimated. Until 1803 New Brunswick accounted for the bulk of the supply of masts from British North America, but this was only so long as European markets were open to the Navy Board. In this year New Brunswick's total of 2,161 was against an importation of 6,135 masts to Great Britain from Russia, Prussia, and other European countries.

Later, when British traders were driven from Danzig, Memel, and other continental timber marts, when efforts to exploit the historic Venetian sources on the Adriatic littoral failed because of the approach of Napoleon's bayonets, the Navy Board realized that the accessible masts in New Brunswick could not make good the deficiency and turned to Canada. In New Brunswick's best year, 1811, her total of 3,151 was against a Canadian export total of 19,025.[54] Long before the Napoleonic wars had finished, the watershed of the lower St. John had been denuded of great pine that could economically be manufactured into masts, and the contractors to the navy had turned to the Miramichi.

Sir John Wentworth and his deputies – Glenie until 1805, and Winslow from 1806 to 1815 – were unable to cope with the difficulty of conserving timber in New Brunswick. The contractors, the principal of whom at this later stage were John and William Black, were interested in getting out the requisite numbers of masts to fulfil their obligations to the Admiralty. In doing so they were compelled to keep their workers in good humour by ignoring depradations and irregularities of all kinds. Glenie reported that among the New Lights of Maugerville there was an article of faith that induced them to believe that they could take from the King's Woods all the timber they pleased for their own purposes.[55]

In contemplating firm measures for the protection of the forests Wentworth was in a weak position. Because of his overweening demands concerning the pine that stood on private lands, the government of the province regarded his pretensions with suspicion and dislike. Chipman adopted the perhaps rather archaic point of view that a colonial land grant could not be contravened by an act of Parliament reserving pine timber to the Crown. A trial of strength in the courts of the province was not to Wentworth's liking. In the case of Nevers and Tapley, two New Lights who got the King's timber to market and more besides, his first instructions to Glenie were to prosecute for trespass. Changing his mind, he decided it would be better to let them get the sticks out and, being careful not to reveal such intention beforehand, to seize them after their arrival at Saint John. Finally he decided that, although Nevers had been indiscreet in both his manners and his language, it would be better to give encouragement to the contractors by cancelling proceedings against these highly efficient workmen, however contemptuous they might be concerning the King's rights.[56]

The great days of the timber trade were still ahead, but already it appeared that the government was powerless to prevent the looting and destruction of the forests. A second observation, later to become commonplace, was made by Carleton in 1807 when, in giving evidence before a committee of the House of Commons, he remarked upon the "dissolution" of those engaged in the trade. New Brunswick was a "fine grazing country" and the only obstacle to a great fishing industry was an occasional shortage of salt, but already the baneful effects of the timber trade upon an agricultural population could be perceived.

CHAPTER 7

The Prosperity of War

1808-1815

The last seven years of the great war against Napoleon brought to New Brunswick a degree of unprecedented prosperity and effectively established the character of the colony for fifty years following. For ten years the province had been penalized by the fortunes of war. About 1806 the luck began to take a radical turn for the better and there occurred an intensification of economic effort of all kinds. A beneficent combination of imperial paternalism and imperial needs was in large part responsible, but there were elements that were purely fortuitous from which New Brunswick reaped great advantage.

Not for many years had a single act of imperial policy been designed for the advance of colonial commerce. The need for keeping the Americans in good humour had prevented the British government from pursuing an aggressive course in building the strength of the North American empire. This policy of submissiveness was ended in the spring of 1806 with the announcement of the payment of bounties on fish exported from New Brunswick and Nova Scotia to the West Indies. It placed the fishermen of the two provinces on the same terms as the English fishermen who sailed the Newfoundland bankers. According to Knox, who had promoted the measure vigorously, it had the effect of arresting the emigration of New Brunswick fishermen to the United States, causing them to remain on British territory and redouble their efforts to produce. For ten years they had possessed few privileges as British subjects. They had been compelled to sell to the Americans at low prices. Fishermen from Massachusetts had taken full advantage of their treaty privileges in New Brunswick harbours, and more besides. They had taken little notice of whether or not an inlet was inhabited, cutting the nets of local fishermen and erecting smoke-houses where they pleased. Intelligence of the bounties offered by the British government commenced a revival of construction of great ships at Saint John and St. Andrews. The historic role of provider for the markets of the West Indies loomed forth as freshly possible and preparations commenced for the dispatch of 30,000 barrels of herrings as well as great quantities of shad and salmon.[1] In the next year, 1807, the amounts vastly increased.[2]

Coupled with the bounties there came convoys for the shipping of the province. Freed from the dangers of invasion by the victory at Trafalgar, the Admiralty could spare vessels of war for the American trading lanes. To the end of the war the convoy system steadily increased in efficiency, and insurance rates steadily fell. New Brunswick again became a colony with an ocean-going fleet of her own. A spur to this revived commerce was given by a second act of imperial policy in the same year when all foreign salted produce was excluded from the West Indian markets.

Restrictions were popular when they worked in favour of the colony, and the faith of New Brunswick traders was largely that of doctrinaires like Lord Sheffield in England and George Leonard in New Brunswick, who held hard to the exclusive principle that the trade of the British Empire must be reserved to British ships. There were, however, restrictions upon colonial shipping in the laws of trade that could be just as unpopular. A New Brunswick ship trading in the Mediterranean could legally make a direct return voyage only if she carried a cargo of salt. If she carried wines, oranges, raisins, currants, or any other Mediterranean cargo, she would be compelled, by the laws of trade, to stop at a British port, usually Falmouth, and pay imperial customs duties. The consequence had been that colonial vessels had left the Mediterranean trade to the Americans. Fruit perished before it arrived on the circuitous voyage home.

Under the stress of war liberal impulses were becoming dominant in British thinking upon questions of trade. To keep commerce going it might be well to release colonial shipping from the restrictions that bound it. A persistent agitation ultimately accomplished its purpose. How, asked the merchants of

Saint John, could they be expected to sell their fish in the
Mediterranean unless they were permitted to import on the
return voyage Mediterranean goods at saleable prices. The Nova
Scotians, Scrope Bernard and Richard John Uniacke, were
more forward than the New Brunswick agent, Knox, in demanding release from the restriction. Such radical abandonment of
the basic features of the laws of trade was little to the old man's
liking. He termed Uniacke's proposals impudent, understand-
able only because of his Irish pedigree.[3]

By an Order in Council, British North American vessels were
permitted to report at Malta or Gibraltar rather than at a port
in the British Isles. Later, in 1809, they were permitted to make
a return voyage directly homewards from any European port
south of Cape Finisterre.

II

The executive at Washington as well as the government at
London contributed to the growing prosperity of New Brunswick in these years. By a blending of incomparable idealism and
bad business sense Jefferson, the American president, had
reached the conviction that Britain and France could be forced
to desist from their persecution of neutrals by a cessation of
trade relations with both, that the cutting off of American supplies to the British West Indies would lead to their starvation
unless the Mother Country should first withdraw her objectionable Orders in Council. Then, late in 1807, Madison put into
effect the Non-Importation Act, designed primarily to prevent
American consumption of certain British manufactured articles.
As relations between the two countries rapidly deteriorated, this
was followed by the Embargo Act, forbidding the sailing of any
American or foreign vessel from the United States to foreign
ports for commercial purposes. The acts were promulgated in
complete defiance of public opinion in New England, where the
Republican Party held little strength. They constituted a self-
blockade, "little short", said the London *Times*, "of absolute
secession from the rest of the civilized world".

The effects on British North America were prodigious. Britain
needed American raw materials and her manufacturers looked
to the United States for large markets. To continue the
American trade in spite of American official refusal, to tempt
the Americans to break their own laws, became a cardinal
feature of British policy. As the Napoleonic blockade in Europe

became more effective and as British fleets and armies opened the Peninsular War, the securing of supplies from the United States became all the more necessary. For this New Brunswick and Nova Scotia were in a highly advantageous position. All that had to be done was to sustain and increase the illicit trade, more illicit now for the Americans than for the British.

Under the Act of Parliament of 1788, General Martin Hunter, the administrator of New Brunswick, was entitled to permit the introduction of American foodstuffs in time of emergency. Emergency for New Brunswick now became the emergency of the Empire, especially of the West Indies, of the continuation of the war and the defeat of Napoleon. "Our object," Hunter wrote Admiral Warren at Halifax, "is to obtain the supplies without awaking any fresh vigilance or restraint on the part of the American government and therefore such articles only are to be included on the public proclamation as are already known in the States to be admissible under the act of Parliament." The customary procedure of admitting flour and other provisions was supplemented by unproclaimed orders to admit hemp, leaf-tobacco, pitch, tar, turpentine, cotton wool, potash, flax-seed, and other commodities, all of these to be re-exported as if they were the produce of the province. While Yankee troops entered the ports of the United States to enforce the embargo on exports, little ships slipped out to the lines to unload their cargoes into British bottoms.

To give encouragement and comfort to American shippers who would take the risks of violating the embargo, the British government in 1807 passed the Free Ports Act, which opened certain specified ports in the Maritime Provinces to American shipping.[4] Those specified at first were Halifax, Shelburne, and Saint John, but in 1811 St. Andrews was added to the list. Free ports were an effective device of economic warfare, tested by experience in the West Indies. The commerce of Saint John increased to an unmeasured degree. The old aspiration of establishing an entrepôt for the exchange of British and American goods came to realization as never before. Via Saint John British woollens and hardware entered the United States, and American salted provisions, flour, and naval stores found their way to all points of the compass, to the West Indies, Spain and Portugal, the British Isles. More than this, the operation of the embargo and of the Free Ports Act drew American immigrants as well as American trade into Saint John. Carpenters and other

skilled tradesmen found the labour that was denied them by
hard times in their own country. The invasion of new-comers
excited fierce jealousies among the labouring population. Merchants valued them because of their industry, but in 1810
the mayor was indicted by the Grand Jury for admitting persons not the subjects of His Majesty to the rank of freemen
of the city.[5]

Provincial trade rose rapidly. For 1808 "New Brunswick produce" exported to the West Indies rose 150 per cent over the
figure of the preceding year. In two years the position had
completely changed. New Brunswickers, after a long period of
commercial servitude to the Americans, were selling American
goods at handsome profits and were rebuilding their merchant
marine, which had all but disappeared following the adoption of
Jay's Treaty in 1795. To sell to the British the Americans had
to evade their own warships that hovered off the islands, but,
having succeeded in doing so, they came under the protection
of friendly British cruisers that escorted them into Saint John.
Flour sold at $3.00 a barrel on the American side of the line
and at $12.00 on the British side. It accumulated in such vast
quantities at Eastport that the collector of customs, attempting
to enforce the embargo, demanded and retained the keys of the
warehouses. Still it disappeared. Boats of all descriptions, even
canoes, were employed to carry American flour to the British
side and British-manufactured goods on the return trip. The
price for the services of a man and a boat for twenty-four hours
was said to be as high as $47.00.[6] The configuration of the
coastline on each side offered admirable facilities for a thriving
traffic. In 1811 the shippers of Liverpool quite frankly announced their intention of employing the free port of St.
Andrews rather than that of Saint John owing to the superior
facilities for encountering the American smugglers.[7]

Opportunity had come for New Brunswick out of the adversities of New England, whose commerce was in ruins. Out of the
vagaries of economic warfare and the urgencies of the British
government the renaissance of trade in British North America
was coming about. Lord Sheffield was highly revered in New
Brunswick. The publication of his "Strictures on the Necessity
of Inevitably Maintaining the Navigation and Colonial System
of Great Britain" had been made largely in response to New
Brunswick promptings. In Saint John the Common Council
conferred upon him the freedom of the city in a box made from

the wood of the country and, under the influence of Leonard, the legislature concurred in the purchase of a full-length portrait that arrived in the province in 1806 and was hung over the Speaker's chair. Yet when prosperity finally did come to New Brunswick it was largely owing to the triumph of principles opposite to those he had advocated, the advent of a hurly-burly *laissez-faire* that was unplanned and came in response to particular necessities.

During the height of the great war Knox, with St. Anthony's fire in his head and gout in his feet, passed from the scene, his principles in the melting-pot, the new British empire whose founding he had fostered developing along lines that were alien to his ways of thought. To the end he was indomitable in pressing for the advancement of New Brunswick and the other British colonies at the expense of the Americans, whose swollen boundaries, granted by the peace of 1783, he had never ceased to regret. When the St. Croix commission had decided in favour of Britain he had been convinced that the disaffected citizens of Vermont would be pleased to emigrate to so much good land in New Brunswick. When Britain intervened in the affairs of the Spanish peninsula in 1808 he reasoned that following the war Spain would be grateful to Britain and would cede East Florida to the United States, which in turn would give New Brunswick a good boundary on the Kennebec or the Penobscot.[8]

He showed his faith in New Brunswick by sending a son, Wills Frederick Knox, to occupy the estate that had been granted him in the parish of Norton. The young man became a magistrate and a churchwarden – found, according to George Leonard, the enthusiasm to subdue the wilderness, but would require a good country wife if he were to make a permanent residence of Norton "where the people are peasants like those in any part of America".[9]

III

Still another factor making for prosperity burst into prominence at this time. The timber trade had never been regarded as a staple of the provincial economy. Large quantities had been exported, often illegally, but the governing elements in the timber trade had been fitful and capricious. European markets had depended upon supplies generally considered superior to anything North America could produce, those of the merchants of Danzig and Memel, who ruled the most efficient timber industry in the world. For centuries they had sent building materials to Britain. For a long time the lumbermen of northern New England could get timber out of the forests more cheaply than those of New Brunswick could. The great aspiration of the Loyalist founders, that of the development of an agricultural society from which a rigid social structure would emerge, discouraged the unsettled habits and uncertain ventures that were attendant upon life in the backwoods. The New Brunswick timber exported for commercial purposes up to this time had gone to market only because of low prices derived from accessibility to navigable waters. In 1806, 7,062 loads (of fifty cubic feet each) were dispatched to Great Britain, but it still could not be said that the exportation of timber for commercial purposes was more than a secondary industry.

Again a combination of circumstances produced spectacular results. The operation of the embargo denied to Britain much of the timber she had purchased from the United States. More fundamental and of tremendous consequence in the long run was the virtual expulsion of British buyers from the Baltic following the Treaty of Tilsit between Napoleon and Alexander I of Russia in 1807. Alexander's compliance with the terms of the Berlin and Milan decrees meant the loss of Britain's control of navigation in the Baltic at a time when she was dependent on Baltic timber for the maintenance of her fleet. More than this, it was the heyday of the Industrial Revolution, and the humming economy of the British Isles required extraordinary quantities of timber for building materials. The world had been searched for supplies alternative to those of the Baltic. In 1808 there were available only the virgin forests of British North America, where there was no highly organized industry and where skilled hewers were scarce.

The Scottish merchants who had settled at Quebec for the development of the mast trade were in a strong position to demand inducements from the British government for the invasion of this market for commercial timber. New capital and fresh energies would be necessary for the venture, which would require several years to bring rewards. The urgencies were so great that the British government was in no humour to haggle. In 1807 high duties were imposed on Baltic timber imported into Great Britain, to be in effect for the duration of the war and for two years afterwards. In 1809 and again in 1810 the duties were increased so that customs duties on Baltic timber became, some said, several times the value of the timber itself. Under such favourable circumstances merchants who already had a stake in the North American timber trade increased their commitments and new adventurers joined the ranks. Some who had had long trading connections in the Baltic turned their attention to British North America. It could now be profitable to exploit not merely the forests adjacent to navigable streams but to penetrate deeply into more remote areas where large pine stood.

More than any other of the British provinces New Brunswick was able to take advantage of this rich opportunity. The country was well stocked with large pine, was intersected by many navigable rivers, and was closer to Britain than Canada was. For many years a long lead over the other colonies was maintained in the exportation of red pine for building purposes. The effects of the timber duties can be readily perceived in the statistics. In 1807, 156 ships sailed with 27,430 tons. In 1810, 410 ships sailed with 87,690 tons.[10] In loads the figures were 13,938 and 50,807. In 1815 New Brunswick sent to Britain 92,553 loads of fir or pine timber. For Nova Scotia and Canada in this year the figures were 19,382 and 11,676.[11] Compared with the Baltic product, the red pine of New Brunswick was considered by British builders to be inferior for frame construction, though it was excellent for the purposes of wainscoting and interior fitting.

Large numbers of people abandoned their farms in whole or in part to enter the timber trade, which promised a quick cash return as well as a life of adventure in the woods. The decay of agriculture became a theme for moralists. In Charlotte County hundreds abandoned the fishery and moved up the St. Croix where St. Stephen became a leading centre for the assault on the forests. 1812 was the year in which the firm of Gilmour, Rankin and Company established itself on the Miramichi. The rapidity with which the valley of that river became peopled is indicated by the creation of nine new parishes in Northumberland County in 1814. The great trade, destined to set its mark on New Brunswick as nothing else would, was financed on credit. Pledges to deliver specified quantities of timber in the spring were rewarded in the preceding autumn by supplies of tools, provisions, rum, and other spirituous liquors. On credit, parties of all sizes proceeded to the woods in winter, confident in this time of rising markets of good returns in the spring and

a "frolic" in the city before the tedious journey home to the
farm in time for the planting season. There were really more
profits in the fishery than in lumbering, said one writer on a
note of lamentation. Unless their creditors would continue to
leave them alone there were only three people in St. Stephen
who were better than beggars.[12]

The exuberance took literary form in a jingle in the *Royal
Gazette* of 1811, perhaps from the pen of Odell, the predominant
theme of which was that the hero had formerly been adorned
with laurel, but that now he would be decked with pine – "an
unfading wreath of New Brunswick pine".[13] At Saint John a
great topic for speculation was the removal of Split Rock, which
stood in the middle of the Reversing Falls and barred the
passage of the vast quantities of timber moving to market. It
was of blue slate, full of seams, narrowing the passage for rafts
and vessels going through the falls at full tide to about 225
feet. Vessels of 400 tons could safely sail past it, but its presence
was a great hazard to those who had to make the careful calcu-
lation of how to get rafts of timber through the swirling waters
into the open harbour.[14]

As the people of New Brunswick moved in large numbers into
the woods in 1808 and as the rush developed into a general
offensive in the years following, the problem of control became
a highly relevant one. But the aged Wentworth at Halifax, still
surveyor-general of the King's Woods, had no stomach for
interference with a trade that suddenly, in the popular mind,
promised enormous profits. His chief deputy in New Brunswick,
Winslow, was aged and reluctant to take strong measures. The
legal basis of the surveyor-general's authority was still subject
to clarification. Soft answers to the requests of New Brunswick
timber cruisers who were now surging into hitherto unexplored
areas of wilderness country could be justified on the grounds
that their efforts came in response to a great national emergency.

The great reserves marked out by Paine and Glenie years
before, especially those in Charlotte County, were swept bare
of great pine in these years. The fourteen million acres of
Crown lands, still ungranted, were open to the forays of those
whose business it was to get out timber almost without restraint.
Warning proclamations were posted in the *Royal Gazette* and
an occasional seizure was made, but it seems certain that the
measures taken by the authorities were almost completely without effect. The extraordinary feature in the situation was that

those whose business it was to conserve the forests derived profit from their exploitation. Without the knowledge or consent of the imperial authorities, Wentworth's deputies in New Brunswick had adopted the practice of licensing timber berths to merchants and woodsmen and collecting fees for the licences. Authority was vague and the instructions were impractical. One of Winslow's agents, reporting the invasions of the reserves for many years past and the unwillingness of his predecessor to take any measures, remarked that the most loyal and respectable members of society in Charlotte County, including members of the legislature and magistrates, were engaged in the patriotic and profitable business of taking out timber.[15] Another reported not on the failings of society but on the dereliction of duty of the deputies whose business it was to enforce the law. All, he said, were interested in the business themselves. They earned their rewards not for conserving timber but for letting it out on licence. They engaged in trespass themselves and winked at the same transgression in others. They allowed themselves to be systematically deceived by licensees who, in conducting them about their timber berths, deliberately kept them out of view of the best pine, which generally grew on indiscernible small risings.[16]

The provincial government had no official information as to what was happening. Wentworth and his deputies functioned altogether apart from the lieutenant-governor and his council. But Hunter, the administrator at this time, was assailed by petitions for free grants of land from persons who paid the fees, stripped the land of its timber, and made no further pretence of honouring the conditions of the grant. It was well known that timber was taken without authority from lands granted to private persons, to municipalities, and to parish churches and schools. But the provincial authorities did not even possess copies of the agreements made between the Navy Board and the contractors or know what Wentworth's deputies were properly supposed to do. On November 3, 1810, General Hunter finally assumed responsibility for laying a formal complaint and urged that a provincial system of inspection should be instituted. The forests were being looted, he declared, and unless something were quickly done the Crown lands would soon be rendered of no value.[17]

There is no evidence that this complaint, which was specific in its charges, received attention from the British government.

Six years later, when the complaint was repeated, action followed swiftly. But for a dozen years altogether, when the timber
trade was settling its grip on the life and habits of thought of
the people of New Brunswick, there was no effective law governing the activities of those engaged in it. Many of the myr-
midons of the law were privy to its abuses. Attempts to enforce
the law excited a common revulsion. Far to the north, along the
shores of the Bay of Chaleur, the timber trade spread, and
Edward Mann, holding a commission from Wentworth, attempted to exert an authority over the forests of Gaspé "and
the sources of the Restigouche to the St. Lawrence", where he
found the pine to be short and knotty. Even here there were
speculators in lumber who made it their business to inform the
poorest and most ignorant of the inhabitants that the laws were
arbitrary and oppressive and should be resisted.[18]

IV

For New Brunswick the great consequence of the War of 1812
was an intensification of the processes at work for the economic
well-being of the province. Owing to the dominance of British
arms in the territories and waters adjacent, there was immunity
from invasion. For Great Britain the great strategic element in
the conduct of the war on the Atlantic coast was to sustain the
flow of American supplies to the outside world, to persuade the
surly New Englanders that their true interests continued to be
peace and commerce with their British neighbours. In the conflict all of the Atlantic provinces occupied an enigmatic position
that was akin to neutrality. A continuation of the profitable
exchange of goods in the Bay of Fundy, in spite of the wishes of
the government at Washington, would emphasize political
division in the United States and quicken the determination of
her people to abandon the war so wantonly thrust upon them
by their bellicose leaders.

In the reckoning of the British command New Brunswick was
merely an advance post for Halifax. When General Hunter,
departing for England on June 27 via Saint John, received an
express from St. Andrews with news of the American declaration of war, there were only fifty artillerymen and 650 men of
the 104th Regiment, formerly the New Brunswick Fencibles,
permanently embodied in the province. Behind them were
4,500 men of the militia battalions, but owing to the need for
production of farm crops their mobilization could be justified

only by an emergency. The shape of things to come was indicated by the news from Eastport, where the inhabitants unanimously voted to preserve a good understanding with the people of New Brunswick.[19] But General George Stracy Smyth, who followed Hunter in the line of military succession, prepared for invasion. Great ardour was displayed at Saint John, where breastworks, batteries, and boats for the movement of troops were prepared. In a circular letter to battalion commanders of militia, Smyth gave the order to retreat at first if invasion should come but to stiffen resistance as aid should assemble from increasing reinforcements in the rear.[20] The legislature placed £10,000 at the disposal of His Majesty – a sum far beyond their resources when the annual revenue of the province amounted to only £5,000.

As the summer wore on it became clear that the Americans had no intention of attacking New Brunswick and a quiescent attitude developed so far as purely military measures were concerned. Smyth arranged for a system of licensed trade. Though the Post Office forbade the carriage of American newspapers, a proclamation encouraged the peaceful intercourse of the people of New Brunswick with Americans who were likewise disposed. The intention of the government, wrote Odell in a belated appreciation, was "to get as many provisions from our neighbours as can thus be obtained during the war".[21] Breaking the embargo continued to be the principal business in hand and it became clear that the chief patriotic role New Brunswickers should play was that of trading with the enemy.

On the St. Croix the comity that had always prevailed remained virtually unshaken and the Reverend Duncan M'Coll, the pioneer of Methodism in this region, discovered, a little to his surprise and much to his pleasure, that he could make visits to his flock on both sides of the river. A committee of leading men from both Calais and St. Stephen, fostered by the churches, the Masonic Lodge, and the civil authorities, ensured order. On the American side feeling was a little more strained owing to the effectiveness of the British naval blockade, which shut off provisions from a community that was largely lumbering and compelled merchants to buy and sell through British intermediaries.[22] Late in 1812 Smyth sent 500 militia to the St. Croix but the precaution was really unnecessary. In March 1813 the militia was completely disbanded as British control at sea became absolute and the threat of invasion non-existent.

At sea there was a medley of curious and contradictory incidents that serve to illustrate the enigmatic place of the province in the war. Shoals of American vessels, having broken the embargo, sailed into New Brunswick waters where they were hospitably received because their cargoes represented substantial additions to British trade. The collectors of customs and commanders of British war vessels had been given orders not to molest them. Often they were shepherded to the waiting British ocean-going vessels by British frigates. At Eastport, it was indignantly alleged by some patriots, Yankee skippers deliberately surrendered their vessels to the Royal Navy as "prizes". After entering the port of Saint John, where they received good prices for their cargoes, they "ransomed" their vessels and sailed home again, prepared for other such inglorious but highly profitable voyages. But sailing the same seas with these peaceful messengers were the privateers, who in the first weeks of the war appeared in the Bay of Fundy in scores, reaping a rich harvest from British commerce and actually lurking in the outer waters of Saint John harbour.

In the ports of New Brunswick there were still alive many old privateersmen of the revolutionary war, and the traditions of the province demanded reprisal. Under pressure of public opinion and irritated by American effrontery, Smyth issued letters of marque to several parties in Saint John, and privateers put to sea. Spirits were high when prizes appeared in the harbour, especially on October 12 when the *General Smyth* returned to port with a prize crew aboard the large vessel *Reward* of 590 tons out of Boston. Consternation became general, however, when it was realized that the master of the *Reward* carried a letter of safe conduct from Andrew Allen, the British consul at Boston, and that her cargo of flour and other dry provisions was destined for the British army in Spain and Portugal. The Court of Vice-admiralty refused to condemn, and other similar humiliations followed. Most of the prizes were American vessels proceeding on the licensed trade, destined for British ports and acting in defiance of American law. For the issuance of letters of marque and for later authorizing the equipment of a seventy-gun sloop, the *Brunswicker*, to supplement the work of the Royal Navy in the Bay of Fundy, Smyth came under heavy censure from the Colonial Office.[23] The whole system of trade and defence was so delicate and involved that no interference with the control of Admiral Sawyer at Halifax could be tolerated. Even at Saint John there was considerable alarm and indignation when it was realized that the *General Smyth* and other privateers were disrupting the licensed trade that was enriching the city.

The arts of peace flourished in war. "The number of houses, stores, wharves and other buildings and improvements that have been erected in the city since the declaration of war by the American states is by far greater than within any equal period of time before that declaration," wrote Chipman in defending American immigrants against the attempts of the freemen of Saint John to dispossess them of their labour. Wages had greatly increased and combinations of workingmen had come into existence for the purpose of lowering the number of working hours in a day. Rents had increased forty per cent.[24] Ships were on the stocks, presently to convey the flour smuggled out of the United States by Americans to the markets overseas. The British manufactured goods smuggled into the United States by way of Saint John and St. Andrews, also by Americans, were finding their way to their ultimate destinations from the heads of the creeks back of Moose Island and Robbinston over rough wagon roads to the head of the Penobscot. Pork was selling at $50 a barrel and high prices for beef prevailed at Halifax and other ports frequented by the armed forces, bringing prosperity to agriculture.

V

A martello tower had risen on the west side of the harbour of Saint John, and at Fredericton there had been a bold scheme, never financed, for the defence of the windmill and the building of a blockhouse on the green to the south of the church. But New Brunswick witnessed no scenes of martial glory. News of military triumphs in distant fields, of Brock at Detroit and Wellington in the Peninsula, filled the newspapers, all contributing to the satisfaction and feeling of self-importance of being British subjects. Occasionally there were items dealing with the distinguished services of scions of the Loyalists, of a Robinson or Rainsford, in India or some other remote corner of the globe. In these stirring years New Brunswick life was workaday and pedestrian, but nevertheless the military traditions of the province were effectively enhanced.

For years the chief permanent defence force had been the 104th Regiment of the Line, converted from the New Bruns-

wick Fencibles in 1811. It had been in part recruited from "the
sons of our brave veterans" and had neutralized some of the
unpopularity it had derived from its narrowing of the labour
market by performing work on the roads. Companies had garrisoned Saint John and Fredericton, as well as the up-river posts
of Grand Falls and Presqu'ile, but the course of the war against
the United States was beginning to make its military role
superfluous. In the winter of 1812-13 Sir George Prevost decided
to accept the risk of leaving New Brunswick almost denuded of
regular troops, and the regiment was ordered to undertake a
winter march to Quebec in order to take part in the defence of
Upper Canada against the expected American attack in the
spring of 1813.

On February 5 a garrison order at Fredericton announced the
intended march. There was disapproval on the floor of the legislature, for the order was accompanied by another announcement that a new regiment, The King's New Brunswick, would
be raised to do garrison duty in the province, a bleak prospect
for the mercantile element who believed that what New Brunswick needed most was new hands for industry. It was the coldest
winter in ten years and on the day of departure the temperature
dropped to seventeen degrees below zero. From February 16 to
February 21 the regiment moved off by companies on successive
days to the music of military airs, but presenting a most un-
military appearance. The order of march was Indian file, half
a dozen men to a toboggan, the van of the company being half
a mile from the rear. For seven days the route led through
settled country, and there were no hardships until the eighth
day, when the frozen strand of the river was enveloped in wilderness. Each officer and man took his turn at the head of the
column to break the snow, those in the rear being able to discard
their snowshoes and march on a firm, hard track.

No advance preparations had been made for hutting the
regiment in the unsettled areas. In the evenings it was necessary
to put the best axemen to work cutting firewood and felling
young pine from which shelters were constructed. Temperatures
at night ranged from eighteen to twenty-seven degrees below
zero. Sometimes the men were so cold that they could scarcely
be driven to work. Rations consisted of biscuit and salt pork
cooked on sticks over the roaring fires in the huts. There was
relief at Grand Falls and at Madawaska, where the populations
turned out to drive the companies twenty-one miles by sleigh,

the easiest day's march of the journey. Bishop Plessis of Quebec who had visited Madawaska in 1812 had described the people as *mal unies*, but officers of the 104th were convinced that this was "the only Arcadia existing in the world". Père Rabbi assured one of them that crime was virtually unknown, that they produced enough in summer to provide for the wants of the winter which they passed in mirth and friendly intercourse.[25]

At Lake Témiscouata and over the Grand Portage beyond it came the most difficult part of the journey. At the lower end of the lake a company, having started over the ice, were literally blown back by a nor'wester in their faces. They took refuge in their hut and, after three days of continuous storms, were joined by the company behind them, headed by Captain George Shore. Provisions were insufficient. If not starvation, certainly severe privations faced the 200 men, who were miserably huddled together in quarters that had been improvised for half the number. It was then that Lieutenant Charles Rainsford, whose grandfather had served as a major-general in the revolutionary war and who had four brothers commissioned in the King's forces, volunteered to go for help. Accompanied by two men of the regiment he set out for Rivière du Loup at daybreak, arriving in the evening, having covered a distance of fifty-four miles in a driving storm. It was so cold, said Shore many years later, that even the mercury froze in the thermometer. At dawn, accompanied by a party of friendly French-Canadians who drew provisions on sledges, Rainsford returned, a proof, as he remarked in his memorial to the Queen when he was seventy-nine, of the value of practice in marching on snowshoes.[26]

In the second week of March the regiment, having endured uniformly cold weather along the entire route, moved through the parish of St. André, and the remainder of the march to Quebec was child's play over a good, beaten snow road, the "merry bugles" proving quite a novelty to the smiling inhabitants, who provided them with every comfort obtainable. An immense concourse of people greeted them at Quebec, and Sir George Prevost, after paying them the highest of compliments, ordered them to Chambly, 200 miles farther on. Arriving in the vicinity of Montreal, still in excellent wind, they were further complimented by orders to march another 200 miles to Kingston. There, on April 12, they beheld, a little to the amazement of some, a fleet of men-of-war frozen on the bosom of a fresh-

water lake. The march of upwards of 700 miles had been made
in fifty-two days.

At Kingston the 550 rank and file who had left Fredericton
were all on parade. They had left one man at Témiscouata, his
body "one indented mass, as if scalded all over from boiling
water", from the effects of frostbite. But six weeks later he
joined the unit in Canada. Fairness compels the admission that
after the march was completed many men were ill and a few
ultimately died from the effects of it, "all the hardest drinkers".

The 104th fought at Stoney Creek, Lundy's Lane, and in the
storming of Fort Erie. They suffered heavy casualties, and those
who returned to New Brunswick brought back with them
memories comparable to those of the revolutionary war. The
epic of the regiment effectively reinforced the Loyalist tradition
and strengthened the connection with the British Crown which,
though it had been strained by local and commercial irritations,
had never been seriously weakened. Press-gangs had ranged the
streets of Saint John in the years preceding the war, and during
the war a large number of New Brunswick seamen had volunteered for service with the Royal Navy.

Round the shores of New Brunswick British arms had everywhere triumphed. The American flag had been driven from the
seas. In July 1814 H.M.S. *Ramillies* had accepted the surrender
of Eastport, and New Brunswick authority was extended over
Moose Island. At the same time, David Owen, the proprietor of
Campobello, whose warehouses had fallen into disuse during the
war, landed, fired a gun, painted his name on several of the
buildings, and proclaimed his ownership. According to his own
account the inhabitants of Eastport were willing to become his
tenants.[27] Almost all of them – officials of the American government included, as well as the deacon of the church, "a smooth-
tongued man accounted one of the sleekest smugglers" –
accepted the oath of allegiance to the King. In August Sir John
Sherbrooke dispatched from Halifax a large military and naval
force that took the fort at Castine, sailed up the Penobscot to
Bangor, and destroyed all American resistance in eastern Maine.
From the Penobscot to the New Brunswick border Maine came
under British control and facilities for improving the profitable
commerce with the enemy were vastly improved.

But New Brunswick lost the peace. The British negotiators
at Ghent were authorized to open conversations concerning a
cession of territory. The better boundary for New Brunswick

and the securing of the communication with Canada had been in the minds of the British ministry. But when the Duke of Wellington, in declining the command of the British armies in North America, gave his opinion that the military position did not warrant demands of this kind upon the United States, the cause was lost. He was aware of Sir John Sherbrooke's easy conquests but professed to believe that the Americans in superior force could readily dislodge Sherbrooke's garrisons. Knox may have stirred in his grave, but the Duke's opinion had the character of a mandamus. The Peace of Ghent left the work of Shelburne and Oswald unaltered by new definitions or by American surrender.

The legislature, convinced that the work of the St. Croix commission would ultimately mean the loss of the Madawaska settlements and the scant communication with Canada, in 1814 petitioned the Prince Regent for favourable modification of the boundary. When the British government cast away the bargaining power achieved by its military victories, renewed negotiation became the only hope of adjustment. The fourth article of the Treaty of Ghent provided for the appointment of a commission to determine the ownership of Grand Manan and the islands in Passamaquoddy Bay. Until settlement was made, Great Britain garrisoned the islands, including Moose Island and Eastport. The fifth article provided for the appointment of a second commission to determine how far north from the source of the St. Croix the line to "the highlands", marking the limit of American jurisdiction, should run.

CHAPTER 8

The Expansive Times
of Smyth

1815-1824

The close of the War of 1812 introduced no reversal of the thoroughly favourable progress New Brunswick had been making for almost ten years. Progress had been possible only because new elements had been incorporated in the population, and it is possible to assert that during these ten years the whole character of the people of New Brunswick had substantially changed. The Loyalists and their descendants still constituted the core, but they were outnumbered by new-comers, chiefly Scots and Irish who came to New Brunswick on the returning timber ships. At the turn of the century the population had numbered less than 25,000. By 1824, the year of the first census, New Brunswick had 74,116 inhabitants, of whom 1,513 were blacks.

Individuals rather than groups made up the great immigration in the first half of the nineteenth century. Unlike Nova Scotia and Prince Edward Island, the province was not favoured by the transplantation of clans or by large-scale movements directed by landlords. At one time Lord Selkirk was interested in New Brunswick, but he was restrained by the comparative paucity of good agricultural land. Immigration statistics are almost worthless in attempting to measure the increase in population or to assess the proportions of the national groups. In large part the province was a half-way house for those who were on their way to the United States. Passages from Scotland and Ireland to New Brunswick were readily available at cheap prices. For many years there was no immigrant tax such as was imposed in the ports of the United States. The roads from Saint John and Fredericton to St. Andrews, and the trails over the portage between the Miramichi and St. John valleys, became avenues for unnumbered Irish. The Scots, most of whom were Lowlanders, created fewer social problems because they usually arrived with small capital and a knowledge of husbandry. Quietly they settled into what now might be called the New Brunswick pattern, that of a society in which agriculture offered rewards only after many years of unremitting toil and in which the timber trade, by the seductions of quick profits, tempted the more feckless and less patient. The settlement of New Galloway, near Richibucto, might be offered as an example of a successful community of Scots in New Brunswick, of a few pioneers who, arriving on the timber ships, found the soil satisfactory and induced friends and relatives from their home community in Scotland to join them.[1] Many of the more thrifty Scots, rather than settle on sterile upland soil, purchased interval land from the Loyalists. This was sometimes a necessity that produced a degree of jealousy towards the older group, who had been favoured by free grants of the best land in the province and who had received government assistance during the early years of settlement.

Following the war a considerable number of disbanded officers and men of the 104th Regiment and the King's New Brunswick Regiment were settled between Presqu'ile and Grand Falls in pursuance of the old design of establishing a continuous band of settlement along the border. In 1815 H.M.S. *Regulus* arrived at Saint John with 371 slaves liberated by the British army in the southern states. These were settled near Loch Lomond in Saint John County, but as settlers they were no more satisfactory than the blacks who had arrived with the Loyalists. Four years later over 500 Negroes of the Royal West Indies Rangers were set down on the Saint John-St. Andrews Road, but most drifted away quickly. With these exceptions, colonization was unplanned and desultory, occurring in spite of the government rather than because of it. Many of the arrivals were so poor that the fees demanded for the passing of free grants of land inclined them to keep out of range of the government altogether. As in other colonies they squatted on favoured locations on public or private lands, trusting that if ever the necessity to purchase or to pay fees should arise they would be able to do so. In 1815, when Smyth instituted an inquiry into the

failure of many persons who had been assigned lands to come
forward and take up their grants, it was found that there were
upwards of a thousand of them.[2] The number progressively
increased with the settlement of the province. The government
was reaping the inheritance of past errors. From 1790 to 1808
many settlers had occupied lands simply on the authority of
location tickets. When called upon to pay fees in exchange for
clear title they balked. According to Smyth, some of them had
become wealthy in the timber trade. The attempt to produce
regularity led to manifestations that were half-rebellious.

The mistakes of the past were beginning to have monumental
implications. A report of the council in 1820 declared that new
settlers could not look forward to the amenities of churches and
schools "for centuries to come" owing to the haphazard manner
in which lands had been granted and the complete absence of
direction on the part of the government over the new settlements that were forming.[3] The Loyalist mirage of compact,
self-sufficient communities of well-disposed subjects had gone.
A generation had grown to full manhood, but the benefits of a
school education had been denied the vast majority of those
who had lived under what Winslow had prophesied, not so long
before, would be "the most gentlemanlike government on
earth". Even a scion of the colonial aristocracy, John Simcoe
Saunders, arriving in England for a superior schooling, was
described by his grandfather Chalmers as one who revealed the
kind of indolence "peculiar to those educated in new countries".
The coming of the timber trade had had the effect of dispersing
the people still further into the wilderness, of fashioning habits
of life and of mind that induced free thinking rather than
respect for authority.

By 1824 Saint John and Portland had a population of 12,000.
Their shipyards were ringing with the industry of hundreds of
carpenters and joiners who had come there in search of good
wages. Many of these were Americans, but the national status
of many of them was a matter for doubt. For years the position
of Americans who had taken no part in the revolutionary war
and who had moved to New Brunswick after 1783 had been
under review, but no solution had been pronounced. Following
the embargo of 1808 their numbers in Saint John had multiplied. As late as 1825 a British traveller who visited Halifax
was informed that all the boasted shipbuilding of Saint John
was attributable to the seasonal movements of about 1,200

American carpenters who came north in the summer on contract and returned to their homes in New England in the autumn.[4] Along the Bay of Fundy considerable shifting in population took place between New Brunswick and New England. American liberty and equality were rampant in Charlotte County, said an anonymous writer to the Colonial Office, and there was "a most lawless, outrageous rebellious spirit" against the magistracy and the established church.[5] Joseph Porter, a member of the house of assembly for Charlotte County, was accused of being an American citizen. William Vance, notorious as a self-proclaimed enemy of British power on the St. Croix, pleaded law in the inferior courts of Charlotte. Nationality was adopted or discarded according to convenience. American shipowners frequently took out British registry for their vessels and assumed the privileges of British subjects in doing so. In the fishery and in the smuggling traffic of the islands British and Americans often worked in teams for the profitable circumvention of the laws of both countries.

The provincial government was powerless to initiate ambitious programmes of settlement. Sproule, the surveyor-general, had no establishment adequate for maintaining the records of his office. He had no deputies to lay out and prepare lands for immigrants. At the ports of entry the government had no agents to interview immigrants and to inform them where lands might be obtained. For this reason alone, it was frequently alleged, New Brunswick lost thousands of possible settlers who, after aimlessly lingering in a port of entry, passed on to the United States at the first opportunity. It was not so much the absence of good land as the weakness of government that was responsible for the failure of the province to adopt a forward policy of immigration and settlement at a time when immigrants were plentiful and when the American states were competing with one another to obtain them.

II

The diversity of national origins was given emphasis by a new profusion of religious professions. Following the war, the Kirk of Scotland appeared in New Brunswick. The numerous Scottish community in Saint John had never been completely submerged by the vast majority of American Loyalists, though they had postponed the building of a church until the time when they could accumulate sufficient of the world's goods to

enable them to do so. At Saint John, in 1816, St. Andrew's
Kirk arose as a symbol of their determination to sustain their
identity. According to a well-established tradition, the Greenock
church at St. Andrews appeared owing to the sneers of adherents
of the established church that the Scots would not buttress
their religious convictions with hard coin. At first Smyth and
his government welcomed the Kirk, considering that it would
help to neutralize the spread of numerous objectionable religious enthusiasms throughout the country, and favoured the
building of new churches with grants of land and small financial
aid.

But as new congregations appeared, as Scottish missionary
societies dispatched funds for the propagation of the faith
abroad, as a synod for New Brunswick and Nova Scotia came
into being, Smyth discovered that the demands of the Presbyterians could be just as embarrassing as those of the other
persuasions that were plaguing church and state. In 1818 they
asked for an amendment to the Marriage Act so that in Saint
John, "this city of soldiers, mariners, emigrants who are resident
for so short a period", their ministers might perform the ceremony without publication of the banns.[6] They assumed the
dignities and prerogatives of an established church, asking for
the granting of glebes, arguing that they were entitled to the
same privileges as members of the Church of England. Attorney-
General Wetmore's report of 1821 declared that Presbyterians
in New Brunswick were dissenters to the same degree as in
England and were entitled to no privileges.[7]

Largely by reason of the demands of a variety of Protestant
churches for financial support from the government, Smyth, an
enthusiastic supporter of instruction in sacred music in the
College of New Brunswick and a popular patron of the new
sport of horse-racing in Fredericton, was driven to a rigid
defence of the exclusive position of the Church of England. For
five years the legislature had been generous in giving aid to the
building of new churches of all denominations, but in 1822 the
volume of requests compelled a halt. When in this year the
Presbyterians, ably represented in the legislature by wealthy
traders such as William Pagan and Hugh Johnston, asked aid
for the construction of a kirk at Loch Lomond, Smyth interpreted the request as an attempt on the part of the Scots of
Saint John to raise the value of their lands in that community
by attracting immigrants.[8]

But if any Protestant denomination caught the conscience of the people of New Brunswick in these years it was the Baptists, whose missionaries entered regions where other Christian teachers had never been seen. The work of Henry Alline, who had been in New Brunswick, and his contemporaries, had been comparable to a loose shower of sparks that had left nothing behind it. In the first days of the colony William George, an inspired coloured man, exercised so great an appeal by his preaching that the news of his coming impelled the slaves of Saint John to desert the tables of their masters and rush to the waterside to meet him.[9] But in the early years of the nineteenth century Baptist associations, united not only by fervour of spirit but by fixity of doctrine, appeared on the scene. Coming from the pre-Loyalist settlements of Nova Scotia, spreading through Sackville and Salisbury, the flame spread as far north as the Tobique where contact came with Baptist associations in northern Maine.

Their fervour induced theatricality. At Kingsclear, on a winter day in 1800, five hundred people gathered to witness the breaking of the ice and the total immersion of a newly converted woman.[10] Before the proceedings were over thirteen others announced their readiness to accept the same experience. The influence won by Baptist preachers over unlettered people in remote communities made them subject to the suspicion of the authorities, and they were blamed for a madness and a murder on the lonely bay of Shediac, where they had appeared as early as 1805.[11] The curious as well as the devout attended their camp meetings, which lasted into the late hours of the night and were ended by the exuberant song of torch-bearing processions of the newly converted as they wended their way homeward through the dark forests. Some of these manifestations were ephemeral, but wherever the Baptists went they left behind them a nucleus of church members. Revivals were the rule of life as eager young preachers, fresh to the mission field, followed the steps of the first fathers.

The self-denial that was inherent in the profession of itinerant preaching was largely responsible for the popularity of Joseph Crandall, probably the most influential of the first Baptist missionaries in New Brunswick. Unlike the shepherds of other flocks, he considered it his duty to earn his living by labour on his own tract of land in Salisbury. He became a member of the house of assembly for Westmorland and was expelled because of his profession, but it was widely asserted for many years that nobody could win a seat in Westmorland without his express approval. Such popularity could be dangerous. The royal instructions forbade preaching without a licence from the lieutenant-governor. By the authorities, the reports of Baptist meetings throughout the country were interpreted as "the rage for dipping", hellish orgies, and unrestrained outpourings of human enthusiasm by moonlight that could, if unchecked, destroy the whole political and social structure. The historian of the Baptist movement in the Maritime Provinces asserts that a Baptist preacher languished in a New Brunswick prison for a year because he ventured to perform the marriage ceremony. Walter Bates, the sheriff of Kings, declared that on more than one occasion "the false preachers" had been his guests in his jail at Kingston.[12] But, generally speaking, the Baptist preachers were clever as well as zealous, and the authorities judicious as well as careful. Early in the career of Edward Manning, as he preached on the St. John above Fredericton, the council of the province became so alarmed concerning his activities that Judge Isaac Allen was deputed to investigate and arrest him if he considered the circumstances warranted it. Amidst a large throng of people who stood outside the door of the crowded house where Manning was preaching, Allen stood to listen and was not disconcerted when the sermon opened with the text from St. James: "Behold the Judge standeth at the door."[13] Manning received his licence to preach in New Brunswick.

It was among the poorer settlers in wilderness communities that the Baptists made most headway. In 1814 there were eleven organized churches in New Brunswick and by 1821 they felt strong enough to form an association of their own, independent of that in Nova Scotia where they had drawn much of their strength. For a long time their "membership" remained comparatively small. As late as 1839 the number was under 2,000, but this is no indication of the ferment their evangelistic methods created in society at large. The movement did not acquire stability until it attracted the support of a considerable number of wealthy merchants of Fredericton and Saint John. This occurred most notably in 1824 and the years following when disaffection became general in the Anglican communion in the Maritime Provinces following the successful attempt of Bishop Inglis to impose the Reverend Robert Willis upon the congregation of St. Paul's at Halifax. Willis, who as archdeacon and bishop's commissary had been generally unpopular in New Brunswick, was refused admission to the church by the wardens, who had the support of a majority of the congregation. Since nobody would produce the keys, his induction as rector took place in the porch. This remarkable insistence on the right of episcopal presentation produced many secessions from the Church of England, not only in Halifax but all through the Maritime Provinces. Many of the seceders, wealthy and influential, turned to the Baptists. In Saint John the name of William B. Kinnear was frequently mentioned as the foremost of those who, in defiance of episcopal discipline, entered upon the faith of the Baptists. Until this time they had often been considered as upstart and beyond the pale of the respectable.

The historic Protestant right of private judgment, in addition to the economic processes that were at work, was rapidly destroying what remained of the Loyalist pattern of society, but the element that in the long run would create the greatest diversity was comparatively inconspicuous on the provincial scene. Moving down the harbours of the eastern shore were the Acadians, receiving grants of land from government and multiplying rapidly. Early in provincial history many of them had taken out tenancies or squatted on the broad interval acres of Joseph Frederick Wallet des Barres at Memramcook, one of the most fertile regions of New Brunswick. His estate had not been registered with the government following the order of 1785 and was for many years in litigation, after his death in 1824, between five legitimate and six illegitimate children. One of the illegitimate daughters presumed to be lady of the manor. She had a party in support but an equally strong party refused to pay rents.[14] On one occasion in 1828 a meeting, convened to settle land troubles, was broken up by the authorities. The uncertainty of ownership and tenancy prevailed until the dawn of Confederation. The impression made by the Acadians upon a Methodist minister, the Reverend Joshua Marsden, who visited Westmorland during the War of 1812, was frequently echoed by other English-speaking visitors. They were "a half-way house between the Indians and the white people" who would work only in response to present necessities.[15] The government had preferred to consider them a race apart, and in practice they were exempted from the ordinary processes of the law by county and parish magistrates who in later years were exonerated from the duty of imposing rates upon them for the main-

tenance of the poor and other local purposes. This willingness
to tolerate a state within a state was highly acceptable to the
missionaries sent to them by the Bishop of Quebec. By mutual
agreement the Acadians managed their own local affairs.

Around their churches, too, the English-speaking Roman
Catholics of the province were mustering. In 1815 the Irish of
Saint John, a goodly number reinforced by many of the troops
from the garrison, petitioned the legislature for aid in building
a church. The multiplicity of faiths had begotten tolerance,
so that these people, relatively poor and obscure, were able to
say that they had received assistance from their fellow-citizens
of all denominations.[16] An act of 1810 had removed from Roman
Catholics most of what remained of their former civil disabilities.
They were now able to vote in general elections by the acceptance of an oath of allegiance without qualifications prejudicial
to their faith.

The Church of England had neither the organization nor the
leadership to enable it to deal with the storm of criticism and
invective its privileged position invariably attracted. To the
Methodists and Baptists, who had progressed so far since 1789,
the Marriage Act of that year was a form of ecclesiastical
tyranny. It was an irritant that inflamed resistance to the established position of the Church of England and, though the
establishment was according to law, it was rapidly becoming a
fiction in the popular mind. By this time only a fraction of the
population acknowledged membership in the Church of England. The second generation of clergymen, recruited in large
part from England, were unable to compete with the more
homely appeals of the Methodists and Baptists for the cure of
souls. Not since 1798 had Bishop Inglis come to New Brunswick. Charlotte and Northumberland counties had never seen
him. When he died in 1816 his see became the prey of political
and ecclesiastical factions in Halifax. The Right Reverend
Robert Stanser, his successor, remained in his charge for but two
years before retiring to England for his health. Suggestions from
the Colonial Office that the legislature of New Brunswick might
be willing to contribute to a pension for him could not publicly
be broached.

In 1819, when the see of Nova Scotia again became vacant, the
clergy of New Brunswick united in a petition to the Archbishop
of Canterbury that was both a confession of past failure and a
bold proposal for future reconstruction. They asked for the estab-

lishment of a new see in New Brunswick.[17] The proposal was well received, but the Society for the Propagation of the Gospel had no funds at hand by which the request might be honoured.

Compared with the pretensions advanced for it in 1784, the Church of England in New Brunswick might at this time be likened to a crumbling fortress. Smyth attempted to bolster it up in 1816 by incorporating rectors and wardens of parishes for the better administration of the lands granted to the Church, but something more than administrative expedients was required. In religion, the colony had assumed a complexion entirely different from that which its founders had intended. To this general rule there was one interesting exception. In the parish of Kingston, vowed Walter Bates, only one man had deviated from the doctrines of the Church, had hearkened to "the false preachers", and he had not been one of those who had sailed on board the good ship *Union* from Eaton's Neck in 1783. This was at a time when the remainder of Kings County was "annihilated with schisms and sects" whose aversion to kings and bishops was so notorious.[18]

III

The times of Smyth saw the settlement of the boundary dispute so far as the islands were concerned. The return of peace showed that they were a positive obstacle to the development of provincial overseas trade. It was, said one writer, as if an enemy station had been established at The Nore to poach upon the trade of London.[19] The community of traders on Moose Island and Campobello, united by one common obsession, a hatred of tax-gatherers, had for years defied and stultified the laws of both Britain and the United States. During the war the interests of Owen on Campobello had greatly suffered owing to the appearance of so many interlopers who invaded his preserves, and Smyth had been compelled to place him under observation owing to his opposition to the laws.[20] At this time it was especially to the interest of New Brunswick, when the terms of trade were so much in her favour, that the question of ownership of the islands should be settled. The international traffic took heavy toll of the trade of Saint John and the revenues of the province.

From the British point of view it was important to obtain possession of Moose Island and eliminate the nest of "private pickaroons" who had infested the international waterways for so many years. To buttress their defence of Moose Island the Americans laid claim to all the islands in Passamaquoddy Bay and Grand Manan in the Bay of Fundy. The latter up to this point had been comparatively neglected. Like other convenient fishing stations of the region it had been used by the people of both nations for transient convenience. For fishermen it was a last outpost in the war they waged against permanent settlers. The earliest resident, Moses Gerrish, had in 1785 conveyed young male and female moose to the island. They had reproduced rapidly but had been wantonly killed off by Indians, "instigated by our republican neighbours".[21] After the peace of 1815 Grand Manan invited general attention as "the key to the Bay of Fundy". Its high bluffs suggested fortification and, in accordance with the terms of peace, British troops remained in occupation until the boundary was settled. But in 1815 there were riots between British and American fishermen as they contended for the better locations for the laying of nets about the shores of the island.

Shortly after the peace the commission appointed under the fourth article of the Treaty of Ghent commenced to deliberate upon the status of the islands. It consisted of Thomas Barclay for Great Britain and John Holmes for the United States. The agents were Ward Chipman and James T. Austin. In the four meetings culminating at New York in November 1817 the tireless arguments of the agents made it clear that no settlement founded on right could be obtained. The American agent based his case upon the Massachusetts charter of 1691 which granted all of Acadia to that colony and upon the article of the treaty of 1783 that surrendered all islands within twenty leagues of the coasts of the United States. Chipman held to the important reservation in the same article that exempted all islands formerly under the jurisdiction of Nova Scotia. It was not difficult to show that Nova Scotia, prior to 1783, had exerted jurisdiction in Campobello and Deer islands. In the case of Grand Manan it was more difficult, though it was possible to show that in 1773 the island had been reserved for Lord William Campbell. Ultimately it became clear that no further argument was necessary and that a settlement based on convenience, not on law, would have to be adopted. In spite of American hopes to the contrary, Barclay refused to think that Grand Manan could be anything but British. Since Great Britain was in a powerful position to bring about a settlement in her own favour, whether by force or diplomacy, Holmes, the American commissioner, was willing to bring the affair to a conclusion by securing recognition for American ownership of Moose Island with a passage to the Bay of Passamaquoddy. A joint declaration was made on November 24, 1817. Generally the settlement was interpreted as a British victory. In the following year, when the Americans renounced their rights to the inshore fisheries and to curing and drying privileges on the coasts of the province, Grand Manan acquired a permanent population, largely of Americans who moved northward.

IV

As the War of 1812 ended, the virtues of "the fair trader" came to the fore and legalistic measures to destroy the illicit economy of the islands came under consideration. Plaster of Paris was the basis of the traffic that was so greatly resented in Saint John. Brought from the quarries at the head of the Bay of Fundy in scores of little ships, it was urgently required as a fertilizer in the states south of Pennsylvania. During the war the smaller quantities that had been carried to Philadelphia and Baltimore had sold at $40 a ton. Now on the islands New Brunswick shippers were taking $7.50, purchasing with the proceeds American goods that were illegally brought into New Brunswick by all the harbours of the Fundy coast, up the St. Croix in rowboats or small sailing vessels on dark nights in the late autumn or early winter, over the hard winter roads from St. Stephen to Fredericton and the interior of the province. Back in 1809 William Sabattis, the chairman of the Committee on Trade in Halifax, had written to Chipman on how to control the gypsum trade. The question was whether or not controls, always to be viewed with distrust, were necessary. His answer was that they were, for the gypsum trade had become too great an evil, associated as it was with "the manners and sentiments of modern democrats" that were to be found in many parts of Nova Scotia in disgusting excess.[22]

Earlier attempts to control the export of gypsum had been halted by the considered opinion that it was beyond the competence of the province to legislate for trade outside its borders. There was the additional complication that any attempt on the part of New Brunswick alone would be idle since great quantities of gypsum were produced by Nova Scotians. Even in Saint John and Halifax the illicit trade found champions. It was thriving and profitable, and enabled the people of the province to import vast quantities of goods from the outside world. But in 1816 the legislatures of the two provinces moved simultaneously and passed acts which would compel British vessels loading gypsum to discharge their cargoes at American ports to the south of Boston. The objects were to bring the carrying trade to larger British ships, to force the smaller vessels engaged in the smuggling trade to take to the fishery, and to place the high profits from the sale of gypsum in British hands. It was reckoned that the acts, if properly enforced, would employ 5,000 tons of new British shipping and compel the agricultural interests of the southern states, dependent on gypsum for the fertility of their soil and the value of their properties, to pay whatever price the British merchants might demand. Only the great merchants of Saint John, St. Andrews, and Halifax who were able to provide the larger vessels for ocean voyages would be able to take part in it. At the same time three-quarters of the contraband goods coming into the provinces would pass through the hands of "the fair trader". The islands would be by-passed and the illicit British trader would have nothing to offer the Americans for their goods. Rather to the surprise of the two provincial governments, and to the rage of the Americans, who wanted to sustain the status quo, the British government gave its assent to the two acts, which had been passed with suspending clauses.

Economic warfare was already general between Britain and the United States. This renewed affront to the mercantile interests of New England whose vessels were at the same time being driven from the fishery excited a spirit of reprisal in Congress. Promptly in March 1817 came an act forbidding the importation of gypsum from the British provinces except in American vessels, a frank invitation to British subjects to violate the laws of their own legislatures. There were a few weeks of uncertainty, during which the price of gypsum rose to $13 a ton. But as traffic revived at Campobello, as New Brunswick and Nova Scotia traders transferred their cargoes to American holds, the price dropped to $7. There was little doubt as to which side would capitulate first. During the legislative session of 1818 Nova Scotia repealed its act. New Brunswick had little choice but to follow. By legislation the Congress of the United States had retained for New England shipping the carrying of a staple commodity of the British colonies.[23]

But there was a truculent spirit in the New Brunswick legislature that would not readily accept defeat. As David Owen
bitterly remarked, the city party was in the ascendancy and
was determined to win the gypsum trade from the islands. In
1820 an act was passed placing a duty of seven shillings and
sixpence a ton on all gypsum "imported into Charlotte County".
This was clearly within the competence of the provincial government but opinion was divided upon the wisdom, if not the
legality, of the measure. The Halifax *Free Press* rejoiced at a
fresh attempt on the part of New Brunswick alone to destroy a
traffic that ruined the people morally and infested them with
Yankee principles, but took note of the fact that there were
newspapers in the two provinces breathing defiance to the laws
of the land.[24] It was a formidable task, but the temper in the
legislature was indicated by the appointment as a commissioner
of Stephen Humbert, the Methodist member from Saint John,
who was prepared to enforce the laws of the land with the same
conviction with which he upheld his burning faith.

Fitting out a small armed cutter for his purposes, Humbert
sought out the smugglers in their favourite lair at Snug Cove
and abruptly seized the schooner *Shannon* for evasion of the
plaster act. Not half an hour passed before a musket-shot from
a neighbouring vessel fell beside his bow and a number of armed
persons from Moose Island attempted to rescue the *Shannon*.
Another attempt was made at Head Harbour, but Humbert
safely brought his prize into Saint John. The breaking up of the
trade "on the lines" implied a small-scale war and not even the
valiance of Humbert was equal to the task. A few days later his
son, John, who served him as a deputy, seized the schooner
Mary at the entrance to Saint John harbour. Early in the morning, at one o'clock, the crew rebelled against their captor, overpowered him in his cabin and set him ashore at seven o'clock in
a thick fog somewhere below Annapolis Gut in Nova Scotia.[25]

Resistance such as this persuaded the New Brunswick legislature that it was not expedient to enforce the plaster act. From
Nova Scotia came complaints of its "oppressive operation", and
it was quietly repealed. But the trade in plaster on the islands
did not last long. American agriculture was moving west and
substitutes for the gypsum of the Bay of Fundy were found in
Ohio and Michigan. The trading fraternity at Campobello diminished as British merchants discovered they had to pay the
Americans in fish, grindstones, or hard coin. David Owen could

see only ruin ahead as he petitioned for the establishment of a free port, at Campobello, for the conversion of the island parishes into a new county under the name of Anglesey or Cornwall since their first settlers were Welsh, and for release from the hateful jurisdiction of Robert Pagan and the St. Andrews magistrates. In 1822 only the salt ships were entering Campobello. The departure of customs officials from Snug Cove in 1823 removed the last appearance of legality sheltering Owen and those who patronized his convenient harbour. He did not want a lingering death, he declared, but would prefer to burn every house on the island as a memorial to his oppressors, the merchants of Saint John and St. Andrews.[26]

V

The post-war years saw a continuance of the rapid economic growth that had favoured the province since 1807. Trade of all kinds continued to flourish. Merchants of the province maintained their preferred position in the West Indies commerce, though this became progressively less important as the years passed. As long as Britain and the United States imposed restrictions upon one another's shipping, Saint John and St. Andrews, whose free-port privileges were renewed in 1818, could profit from the exchange of British and American goods. This was the role that had so sedulously been sought by the Loyalist merchants who had left New York in 1783. Whenever there appeared a likelihood of an Anglo-American agreement upon reciprocal shipping privileges, gloom settled over all commercial speculation and violent prophecies of the impending depopulation of New Brunswick found their way to Whitehall.

The rapid decline of the West Indies, whose best days were gone, made inevitable the loss of this preferred position in trade. British West Indian legislatures petitioned the Crown for the opening of their harbours to American shipping, protesting that they were being starved of American supplies in order to make prosperity for the northern colonies. When the British government capitulated in 1822 there were great lamentations. "The doom of New Brunswick is sealed," wrote the London firm of Bainbridge and Brown to a client in the colony, warning that a quick liquidation of accounts would be necessary and that a drastic reduction in imports from Britain could be expected.[27] No longer would traders be able to take quick and easy profits by selling American goods to planters in the West

Indies and West Indian sugar and rum to merchants in Boston and Philadelphia. Just at the time when the colony was finally becoming capable of supplying the colonies in the Caribbean, said the petition of the legislature, the British government had seen fit to withdraw the preferred-trading privileges and to admit American ships to the West Indies.[28] In actuality the position remained virtually unchanged for eight more years, until 1830 when the government of the United States was finally willing to extend equal privileges to British shipping and the reciprocal agreements went into effect.

It was with regret that the mercantile community in New Brunswick beheld the onset of new tendencies in economic thinking that were opposed to all the lessons of their experience and all their commercial instincts. The work of William Huskisson at the British Board of Trade heralded the coming of a new era of freedom in trade. In 1825 the ships of all nations that would extend reciprocal privileges to British shipping could call at the ports of New Brunswick and the other colonies of British North America. One of Huskisson's acts, the placing of customs officials exclusively on salaries and the removal of fees, was peculiarly relevant to New Brunswick. At Saint John the customs establishment was continuing, as in Wanton's time, to produce rather incomprehensible deviations from the rules that resulted in the enrichment of its officers. In the last year of his office Wanton had collected over £5,500 in fees. His successor, Henry Wright, showed the same sense of the importance of holding office by replacing the deputy at Miramichi with his son and the deputy at St. Andrews with his son-in-law, raising the fees, originally laid down by the instructions of 1769, by approximately one-third, and making heavy exactions on the coastal trade as well.

In 1817 the aged General Coffin, on one of his frequent visits to England, laid formal charges. Smyth was ordered to conduct an investigation, which resulted in a report that the officers of the customs establishment were "highly reprehensible".[29] Wright was held to the authorized table of fees and the two officers whom he had supplanted were reinstated. The council of the province, which conducted the investigation, recommended, in anticipation of Huskisson's reform, that the officers be placed on salaries and that St. Andrews and Miramichi be made head ports. These changes came a few years later, in 1826.

Wright had the satisfaction of revenge in part when he seized

a small pleasure-vessel belonging to General Coffin. The charge
was that she was employed to protect smugglers. The general
lost ten bottles of wine, seventeen pounds of candles, and a
pound and a half of tea.[30]

VI

All the commerce and industry of the province had become
secondary to the timber trade. The years from 1814 to 1818
were uncommonly cold. Crops had failed and in the month of
June men attired in winter clothing had taken to the woods.
The decline of agriculture had been expedited by nature. In
1820, said a writer in the *Royal Gazette*, agriculture was de-
graded everywhere except in Sunbury.[31] John Simcoe Saunders,
holding little faith in a better price for farm lands and making
fun of his father's passion for the acquisition of real estate,
fancifully wrote of how in 1947 antiquarians would stumble
upon The Barony, the Saunders family mansion, as if it were
Palmyra in the desert. By that time, he mused, the country
would again be called Acadia and the hardy adventurers who
had cleared The Barony, the Loyalists, would be entirely forgotten. Conservatively minded people viewed with alarm the
desertion of the farms, prophesying that the boom in lumber
could not last, warning that the province had become almost
completely dependent on the caprices of speculators in the
British market. The importation of American foodstuffs, per-
missible only in emergencies by the Act of Parliament of 1788,
had become a rule of life.

Everything depended on the maintenance of the British dis-
criminatory duties against Baltic timber. In these years the
alert New Brunswick merchant turned his attention from the
fading vistas of the West Indies to the debates in Parliament.
Baltic timber interests were on the offensive, urging either the
removal of the duties or the imposition of an equal tax on the
produce of British North America. They were joined by a host
of other interested parties, humanitarians who believed that the
timber trade lowered the standards of British civilization and
should be left to foreigners, and those who represented the so-
called "landed" interests of British North America who, for the
love of agriculture, wanted to see the trade consigned to oblivion. In 1821, when a parliamentary committee reviewed the
timber duties, John Coffin's brother, Sir Isaac Coffin, who sat in
the House of Commons, declared that Canada was better at the

bottom of the sea than compromised to the blandishments of the timber trade. This was something of a last breath of the Loyalist aspiration that gentlemen of British North America could live merely by the ownership of land, and it was John Bainbridge, secretary to the British North America Merchants' Association, who told the committee that the landowners of British North America lived not from their lands but from their labours. Compelled by a threat to their livelihood, all the friends of the trade rallied to its support. The memorial of the merchants of Saint John argued that only the timber trade enabled the people of New Brunswick to pay for British manufactured goods, that all other trades of the province were worthless for the earning of sterling.[32]

The report of the committee recommended that a duty of ten shillings a load should be imposed on the timber of British North America. This was on the ground that much Canadian timber actually originated in the United States. But the duty was only one-fifth of that imposed on Baltic produce so that the report represented a victory for the new British North American industry, really a child of the Napoleonic War. The merchants of New Brunswick were to have ten more years before their privileged position in the British market should be again effectively challenged.

The valley of the Miramichi now held the reputation of offering the best opportunities for those who were searching for the great stands of pine timber that were becoming so much more elusive. In 1819, of 1,520 British vessels engaged in the North American timber trade 297 loaded on the Miramichi. In these years, during the shipping season, the Miramichi anchorages were crowded with 100 to 130 square-rigged vessels, and in 1824 they surpassed Saint John as a port of export for timber. Half a dozen firms were engaged in the business, but the virtual ruler of the northern bank of the river was Alexander Rankin, the durable, conservative Scot who presided over the establishment of Gilmour, Rankin and Company at Douglastown, a scion of the Glasgow and Liverpool firm of Pollock, Gilmour and Company. There were affiliates of this great house at Quebec, Saint John, and elsewhere, the connection having been established following the visit of Allan Gilmour who for eight years travelled through British North America "to find the navigable rivers, to see where the forests were".[33]

Society on the Miramichi had always been voluble and explosive. The addition of a powerful Irish ingredient appreciably increased these qualities. In the summer of 1822 it was necessary to send a detachment of the 74th Regiment to Newcastle, for the civil power in Northumberland County had abandoned pretensions of keeping law and order. Gangs of recently arrived Irish wandered through the country, seizing and destroying property at will, burning houses and barns. In jail they were as great a nuisance as they were out, one of the main reasons for the urgent request for troops being the necessity of restraining the excesses of the inmates of the county prison. Especially on Sunday afternoons it was the custom of the hundreds of sailors from the ships in the harbours to come ashore and run riot.[34] But the Irish composed a respectable element of society as well. By 1824 the Hibernian Society was a strong local force. On St. Patrick's Day of that year, following a dinner "in Mitchell's best style", William End, the newly arrived president, presided over a multitude of toasts, including a tribute to The Timber Trade with Three Times Three to the air of "Off She Goes to Miramichi". There were laments for the loss to the province of many a cargo of muscle and sinew because many of the Irish, who knew nothing of "that powerful engine of improvement, the axe", were leaving as soon as they landed.[35]

The local independence and remarkable exuberance of the high-spirited people of the Miramichi were perhaps due to the isolation of the community. Henry Bliss found the going difficult in 1819 as he made his way from Fredericton to the Northumberland court-house through "all the sloughs, mud-holes, rivers, brooks and swamps, over all the broken bridges, rocks, precipices, stumps and windfalls". At Sutherland's tavern he slept "on a mattress of bedbugs with a bag of flour for a pillow" and drank rum slings for dinner. The sheriff's roof was like a sieve, and this much-abused officer was never where he should be, "as his pretty wife may witness". Everywhere on the Miramichi he endured vexations both of body and spirit, but much the worst was "to hear all the party swear it was a fine country and admire the cursed river that had just drenched us to the middle".

Each year the assault on the forests quickened as demand for British North American timber increased in the expanding markets of Great Britain. In the feverish search for pine the trade moved to the north and west. On the Bay of Chaleur

Scottish immigrants were taking up the trade with avidity, and Hugh Munro, a Gaspé Loyalist, was developing the Acadian settlement of St. Peters, at the mouth of the Nepisiguit, as a port of export.

VII

In 1816 Smyth in drastic terms repeated Hunter's warning of 1810, declaring that unless something were quickly done to conserve the forests the timber in the accessible parts of the province would soon be completely destroyed. It was a matter, he said, of national importance.[36] This dispatch opened the question of control of the Crown lands and made it the chief political problem in the colony for the next twenty years. Nine-tenths of the provincial domain remained ungranted. It was from this reservoir of forest wealth that the timber merchants had thriven. For ten years, at the cost of trifling fees to the deputies of Wentworth, they had taken almost whatever they pleased in whatever areas they had chosen to exploit.

The response of the Colonial Office to Smyth's dispatch was unexpectedly vigorous and conclusive. After an investigation by the Lords of the Treasury the lieutenant-governor was ordered to take all transactions concerning the cutting of timber under his own authority and to bring to a halt the practices that had been in vogue. Wentworth, the Treasury decided, had had no authority to grant licences to private parties for the cutting of timber and to receive fees for doing so.[37] Very belatedly – almost six years after the matter had first been brought to its attention – the imperial government had awakened to the necessity for taking action.

The authority given to Smyth created a revolution in the commerce and politics of the province. The lieutenant-governor was not the man to let slip an opportunity of this kind. To substitute for the powers that had, in effect, been taken away from Wentworth, he created a provincial organization, supervised by a committee of the council, to issue licences for the cutting of timber. The leading feature of the new system of control was the imposition of a duty of one shilling a ton for timber taken from the Crown lands. This was justified by the necessity of creating a fund from which the costs of surveys might be borne. Applicants for licences to cut were required to state the particular tracts of land on which they proposed to operate and to post bonds for the payment of the duties in the springtime of the year when, in the normal course of events, they would receive payment for their produce.

For the first time in the history of the province there arose a prospect of creating such a large fund from local resources that the executive officers of the Crown could be independent of the house of assembly. The wealth of the Crown lands would enable Smyth and his officials to initiate new measures for the development of the province without reference to the representatives of the people. For over thirty years they had languished in their dignities without the power to do anything very much of consequence, but now it seemed that liberation had come. For the first time, too, it could be alleged that the lieutenant-governor and his advisers were taxing the people without their consent. Under the terms of the royal instructions they had been entitled to take fees for land grants and for suits in the courts of law, but these had been trifling. Since the vast majority of the people were in one way or another involved in the timber trade, it could readily be alleged that Smyth's tax was imposed upon the entire province. It did not matter that the sum demanded of lumbermen was but one-fourth of what was demanded in Maine or that the amount asked by private landowners varied from five shillings to seven and sixpence a ton. To those who opposed Smyth it appeared that the basic principle of the British constitution had been violated. Back of the sharp arguments of the leading timber merchants who held seats in the house of assembly there was the elemental feeling, inherent in a population accustomed to ranging freely over the great spaces of the wilderness, that the Crown lands belonged to the people.

It was, therefore, with "surprise and regret" that the house of assembly "learned" on March 8, 1819, of the new tax on the timber trade. Ruin was freely forecast and an address to Smyth brought a cryptic response that made much of the general terms in which the address was couched, insisting that only timber on the Crown lands was affected. Stephen Humbert, a good Loyalist as well as a Methodist radical, came to the assistance of Smyth on March 23 with a resolution that the Crown lands came under the royal prerogative and that it was improper for the house of assembly to interfere. This was defeated by 19 to 4. In a rage Smyth dissolved the House and called an election in November. The result showed little change.

By reason of the timber imposition Smyth achieved unpopularity probably greater than that of Carleton at any time in his long term of office. There was, he admitted, "discontent in the minds of the people at large", fostered by leading members of the house of assembly.[38] But he held hard to his position by assurances that the money collected from the timber trade would be usefully expended for the benefit of the people of the province. The College of New Brunswick and the new system of "Madras Schools", institutions really controlled by the Church of England, had reached a stage in their development at which financial support from the province could vastly enlarge the beneficent work they were doing. Everywhere throughout the province there was a necessity for governmental intervention in the practical problems of settling immigrants on the land. The Crown lands could produce revenues that would give new life to the government of the province and enable it to exert a degree of control over the unplanned and haphazard settlements that were being formed.

In spite of all the opposition the system jerked into operation. Smyth's predictions concerning the yielding of a revenue proved to be correct as unexpectedly large sums accumulated in the coffers of the receiver-general. During the session of 1820 the house of assembly was silent upon the subject of timber duties. Owing to what Smyth called the "licentiousness" of the timber operators, it became necessary to increase the number of surveyors and inspectors whose duty it was to keep the trade under discipline. Some of the more truculent merchants openly defied the authority of the government. There were frequent "collisions" in the woods. The tax had the effect of driving the more adventurous into the debatable regions of the north-west where they came under the assumed jurisdictions of three governments but were, in fact, free. On occasions there were downswings in the timber market that brought gloom and idleness to the community of woodsmen and lumberjacks New Brunswickers were rapidly becoming. In the spring of 1821, when news arrived of a disastrous series of bank failures in Britain and of the consequent inability of timber purchasers to make good their commitments, pressure in the legislature was quickly brought to bear upon Smyth to cancel the bonds that had been posted in the previous autumn. This he agreed to do, though insisting that it was an indulgence. The recession gave comfort to those who persisted in believing that the timber trade had not come to stay, but in 1822 the British market fully recovered and prices soared. Smyth's fund rapidly accumulated to the proportions of a windfall. It gave the executive officers a new prestige as worthy causes upon which the fund might be expended came under consideration.

In his attempt to bring the Crown lands under an orderly system of control, Smyth failed to reform the methods of granting lands that by this time had become almost traditional within the province. Owing to the high cost of fees it had become customary for a number of individuals to apply for a large grant of land under a single title.[39] The lieutenant-governor interpreted this practice as another abuse of royal rights by which many simply made deposits on the payment of fees, stripped the land of timber and failed to honour the conditions of the grant either by actual settlement of the land or by discharging the unpaid balances. Undoubtedly this was a cheap method of acquiring timber and, against the advice of his council as well as contrary to the known opinion of the assembly, Smyth instituted in 1818 a new system by which each individual was obliged to take out a separate grant and be responsible for honouring the terms. When the assembly passed an address protesting that Lord Bathurst did not fully understand the merits of the old system, that individuals could be held responsible even though their names were included in a corporate grant, the colonial secretary gracefully conceded that his objections had been met. The old system was restored, to Smyth's great disappointment. In braving the indignation of the assembly and of public opinion in New Brunswick he received only lukewarm support from the British government.

Showing no aversion to intruding upon the royal prerogative, the assembly conducted, in Smyth's last years, a campaign for the liquidation of the timber reserves made by Sir John Wentworth. After 1820, when the surveyor-general died, the attack quickened. It was led by members from Charlotte County, where the enterprise of merchants had been limited at least superficially by three reserves, two behind the town of St. Stephen and the third, "the great reserve", consisting of 400,000 acres between the Magaguadavic and the St. Croix. Petitions complaining that the good timber had all been cut and that the land was badly needed for agriculture came to the house of assembly, which passed them on to the Colonial Office.[40] Michael Wallace at Halifax, attempting to hold together the remains of Wentworth's tattered empire, asserted that, although there had been many trespasses and much timber had been destroyed by fire, the reserves were still of value to the Royal Navy. The petition of the New Brunswick legislature, he alleged, really represented an intention to strip the reserves of timber for the purposes of commerce.[41] Bathurst refused to yield on this score, and for several years after, at least in theory, the reserves remained closed to commerce. Ultimately, one by one, they were released to the provincial government and came to be considered as the ordinary domain of the Crown, available for grant or sale.

VIII

A new New Brunswick, a turbulent, expansive society, was taking form in Smyth's time. There is nothing surprising in the willingness of the lieutenant-governor to resist the democratic movement in the legislature and to retain control over the Crown lands for the royal prerogative. What was novel was the curt, almost contemptuous manner in which he dealt with those who had always considered themselves to be the staunchest supporters of the royal authority in New Brunswick. Smyth was old and frequently at death's door, sighing for the milder climate of Halifax or for a leave of absence in England, but he struggled manfully not only against the majority in the house of assembly but against those to whom he might most logically look for support, the families that held the important public offices of the province.

Ever since Winslow in 1808 had handed over the government to General Hunter, the military succession had mortified the leading members of the council. Men who prided themselves on their long records of gratuitous services felt affronted as, on several occasions, the chief command fell to military men who were complete strangers, some of them of rank as low as lieutenant-colonel. But when Smyth, following the death of Carleton, became lieutenant-governor in 1817, the military succession ended. The post of senior councillor with the honour of succession to the government became, for many, a prize that was clearly in sight, especially as Smyth was constantly on the point of setting out on leave to England. In his first council on assuming the lieutenant-governorship Smyth was compelled to answer questions concerning "a casualty".[42]

Over the years family affinities had crystallized into political influences. Smyth may have felt that he was living somewhat in the shadow of the judges who, altogether apart from their judicial capacities, were members of the executive and legislative councils, actively concerned in everything pertaining to the government of the province. To his annoyance he discovered that it was impossible to make the executive council function as a court of appeal because a majority of the quorum that could be convened at Fredericton consisted of judges of the Supreme Court.[43] In order to free himself from this judicial majority it became his custom to hold a great many meetings of his advisers at Saint John, the proceedings being transmitted to the clerk of the council at Fredericton and written into the council book.[44] The tenacious old men of the patrician families had a host of ambitious sons, sons-in-law, and other relatives who aspired to public office. The enemies of Chipman, who was surrounded by young Hazens and Botsfords as well as by his own son who bore his name, were to assert that he was attempting to establish a great family influence. Jonathan Bliss, the Chief Justice, was an enemy of Smyth. John Murray Bliss, the junior of the judges, was at the centre of a vast connection that included not only official families but the leaders of the new commercial aristocracy that was growing up in Saint John.[45]

To destroy the ascendancy of these judicial clans Smyth rejoiced in opportunities to introduce new-comers to official circles. The Saint John merchants, William Pagan and William Black, entered the council. Even Samuel Denny Street, the sworn enemy of the judges and once the popular tribune of Sunbury, who continued to reiterate his old complaint that his English birth denied him an office in a land of American refugees, was brought within the select circle. For provincial surveyor, upon the death of Sproule, Smyth nominated his aide-de-camp, Captain Kemball. When Kemball went to England and failed to return, he nominated his favourite, George Shore, a half-pay captain of the 104th, who as the commander of the light infantry company had played a gallant part in the storming of Fort Erie. Though a son-in-law of John Saunders, another of the judges, he was of English birth and outside the closely-knit group of Loyalist families who could boast a lengthy provincial background. At this time, however, the Lords of the Treasury, in whose gift the office lay, were giving short shrift to local recommendations. Refusing Smyth's nomination they appointed Anthony Lockwood, formerly a master in the Royal Navy. Smyth appointed Shore to three other offices, all on a temporary basis, seemingly to declare his independence of the junta of judges and the local factions who supported them. Governing almost all speculation on the holding of office was the predicament of the aging Chief Justice, who wished to retire but could not because neither the imperial nor the provincial government could award him a pension. "I had once a few friends among the great. Alas I have outlived them. I am too old to seek, or to endeavour to cultivate new ones, or to solicit in person court favours."[46] Upon the death or retirement of Jonathan Bliss the whole legal fraternity looked forward to a series of promotions that would affect the prospects of all.

Behind a great deal of the opposition to Smyth in the legislature lay the influence of Chipman or of Chipman's friends and clients. William Botsford, the solicitor-general and Speaker of the house of assembly, who directed the sallies against Smyth's timber policies, was his brother-in-law. The young Ward Chipman emerged from a fine legal training in the Inns of Court and a thorough exposure to the workings of the Colonial Office to take a leading role in politics. As a joint agent he was associated with his father in the business of the boundary dispute and it was generally agreed that the reputation of the older man was equalled by the promise of the younger. After the election of 1820 he quickly acquired the leadership of the house of assembly, moving for information in the session of 1821 on the bonds posted by unlucky merchants in the timber trade, pleading the cause of the poor squatters, some of whom had been fined for illegal possession by Smyth's government. The Chipman interest identified itself with the party presuming to be the popular party and, behind the scenes in London, deprived Smyth of much of the support he needed to enforce control over the forests. While Smyth urged the ability of many of the merchants to honour their bonds, young Chipman told the Colonial Office that collection of the sums promised would render the government odious throughout the country.[17]

Chipman, sensitive to the bustling commercial life of Saint John and the aspirations of the timber trade, was no doctrinaire. The young man who had risen to eminence by reason of his service to the prerogative had become the elder statesman who understood that public opinion could be employed as a political instrument to serve his purposes. So long as Smyth, impervious to public opinion, was in the saddle, the fountain of honour would be far removed from the members of Loyalist families

whose guiding principle was that services rendered in the past
entitled them to the perquisites of office.

Since Smyth was rigid, conflict with the legislature was inevitable. When individual items on the appropriations list met
with his disapproval, when he threatened to make use of his
right to refuse payment of sums expended for what he considered to be objectionable purposes, Bathurst censured him for
raising the awkward constitutional problem, slurred over by
Portland in 1798, without instructions.[48] In 1818 there rose the
familiar and more practical problem of pay for the members of
the legislature. The council, by a small majority, determined to
request pay for their own services, and the resulting legislation
joined their requisition to an increase of pay for the members
of the house of assembly. Smyth found it impolitic to refuse
assent but requested the Prince Regent's disallowance. There
were large numbers of persons in the colony who could, he
declared, afford to serve without pay.[49] The act was not disallowed but Smyth thought it had been, and in the consequent
dealings with council and assembly he stultified himself exceedingly. Clarification did not come until 1822 when Bathurst
ordered him not to tolerate pay for members.[50] Added to this
was the opinion of the Board of Trade that it would be more
suitable to the dignity and independence of legislative bodies to
meet in general assembly without receiving daily pay.[51]

In addition to his own unpopular decisions Smyth was compelled to enforce those of the Colonial Office. In this situation a
great Loyalist family connection such as Chipman's turned to
the popular side in the controversy. The popular side might
afford an avenue to increased influence far more direct than the
favour of Government House.

IX

On October 7, 1822, Smyth reported the death of Jonathan
Bliss, the Chief Justice, and temporarily appointed Saunders
to take his place. Saunders was the senior of the judges and his
succession lay in the order of events. But, coupled with the
announcement was the appointment of Edward James Jarvis
as assistant judge. Jarvis was a young man, scarcely introduced
to active legal practice, the son of a prosperous Saint John
merchant who had been educated in England. He had served as
a clerk in Chipman's office and was commonly considered a
supporter of Chipman's interest, but precisely the opposite was

now revealed to be the truth. "The beardless boy", as David Owen called him in advocating the appointment of Samuel Denny Street,[52] had been preferred to many a veteran of the bar, especially to William Botsford, the Speaker of the house of assembly and Chipman's brother-in-law.

The repose of Fredericton was still further shattered by the dismissal of Henry Bliss, son of the deceased Chief Justice, from the office of clerk of the pleas for the Supreme Court "before his father was buried".[53] This was done on the volition of Smyth, who gave the office to Shore. At the winter session of the Supreme Court two justices, Chipman and John Murray Bliss, protested the validity of Shore's patent, but Chief Justice Saunders and the new appointee, Jarvis, defended it. Shore remained in possession of the office and a memorial in protest went from Chipman and Bliss to the Colonial Office. In the midst of the confusion, while confirmation of the new appointments was awaited from London, Smyth died on March 27. As his corpse was followed to the parish church by his war-horse, his plumed hat on a red cushion, and a procession of scarlet uniforms and white surplices, the great and near great of the land, united in solemn sentiment for the occasion, were savagely divided upon the great issues of public preferment.

Still greater issues arose. George Leonard, the senior councillor, who resided at Sussex, wrote that he was unable owing to age and infirmity to repair to "the seat of government", according to the terms of the royal instructions, and assume control. The second senior councillor, Christopher Billopp, called upon the council to meet him at Saint John. Since Billopp was 85 and "the seat of government" was at Fredericton, a majority of the council decided to call upon the next senior, Ward Chipman, to take the presidency. Two members dissented, William Black, the son-in-law of Billopp, and Jarvis, who faced ruin following the arrival of a dispatch announcing that his appointment as a judge had not been confirmed and that Botsford had been given the position. He had resigned three minor offices and had abandoned his practice, and, as the triumph of the Chipman party seemed assured, he took ship for England to protest the proceedings in council and to advance his claims to compensation for the lost judgeship. Ultimately a vacancy was found for him in Prince Edward Island.

Chipman had a stormy tenure of power. At Fredericton Anthony Lockwood, who had recently arrived from England to take the offices of surveyor-general and receiver-general, was observed to be squandering public money in the streets of the town; and after a period of sustained excitement in which he rode about the country brandishing fire-arms, informing all and sundry that he had been called upon to accept the government, and replacing the furniture of Government House with his own, he was certified insane and suspended.[54] At Saint John a rival party took definite form, arising out of Billopp's refusal to accept the opinion of the majority of the council. His disqualification for the presidency had been based upon his unwillingness "to repair to the seat of government", but Billopp and his party alleged that on many occasions, especially in Ludlow's time, "the seat of government" had been at Saint John. On April 22 the Saint John *Star* published a proclamation by Billopp, announcing that he had taken over the government, and copies were sent to all officials of church and state. The *Royal Gazette* of the same date carried a report of a meeting, at Cody's Coffee House, of a number of gentlemen who drew up an address of loyalty to the Honourable Christopher Billopp. Charles Simonds, a young man who was destined to display many of the qualities that would bring a man to the summit of political power in a society rather more democratic than that of 1823, "took the chair amid much clamour". According to the unfriendly report in the *Gazette*, "five or six of the most violent, democratic characters" put their signatures to the address and hastily retired. The remainder of those present, who were of "the most respectable", drew up an address of loyalty to Chipman.

The new president wrote that Billopp did not have twenty adherents in the entire province, but the proclamation from Saint John made him exceedingly nervous as he awaited the reaction of the imperial authorities. What made the affair much more complicated than a clash of personalities was that it was now possible to challenge the legality of all the acts passed by the legislature of 1823, which he had just dissolved. If he had usurped the presidency his assent in the Royal Name would give comfort to all those who wished to evade the requirements of the laws, and it appeared possible for a time that the year's legislation might be challenged in the courts. What was worse was the possibility of international consequences. Captains of American vessels carried home with them copies of Billopp's proclamation in the *Star*. If the legislation for the year was invalid, an act passed by the legislature of New Brunswick to extend to American shipping tonnage rates equal to those levied upon British shipping in the United States was worthless. The President of the United States would have an additional excuse for refusing to offer equally favourable legislation to British vessels in American harbours, and the whole prospect of Anglo-American amity, blighted by shipping rivalries for so many years, would be nullified. The answer, when it came, saved the day, but it was not entirely satisfactory. Lord Bathurst did not agree with the majority of the council in thrusting aside Billopp's claim so summarily, but he was willing to permit Chipman to remain as administrator. From the Governor General, Lord Dalhousie, there was support for Chipman's position and a willingness to make the difficult journey over the portage if it should be necessary for the maintenance of order in New Brunswick. Yet about Saint John there circulated intelligence that the Colonial Office considered Chipman guilty of irregularities, certain evidence of the continued bitterness of his enemies and of their determination to embarrass him.

For almost a year Chipman governed firmly, appointing members of his connection – Botsfords, Drurys, Hazens, Parkers – to minor offices. Yet he was capable of magnanimity, too, for he appointed Shore to still another temporary office, that of surveyor-general, when it was vacated by Lockwood. More than any of his contemporaries he had the capacity to be all things to all men. He could look to the influence of the prerogative for the favours he sought without losing touch with the mercantile and plebeian elements in society that were causing New Brunswick to surge forward at this time. Though he was a pillar of the Navigation Acts and a supporter of the principles of Sheffield, he could, in a quiet way, invest his money in the great trading enterprises of his wealthy brother-in-law, William Gray of Salem, and acquire an interest in the Yankee coastal traffic that was the abomination of those who believed in exclusive trading practices.[55] He died as the representative of the Crown, but his son was Speaker of the house of assembly, the only member of that body considered capable of performing the duties of the office. His death recalled the fact that he was the last of the original office-holders of 1784 and that a link with a past that was becoming much more remote had been severed. The era of the loyal refugees of 1783 had virtually come to an end. Almost all were dead. Forgotten were the men who had once made themselves conspicuous by their deeds of valour – such men as Ebenezer Hatheway, who had escaped from the loathsome rebel prison at Sinsbury Mines after having fought off eight times his own number in the war of whale-boats on Long Island Sound; William Stewart, who in the memorable, hard winter of 1780 had repelled the descent of the rebel general, Stirling, on Long Island; and Simon Baxter, who had fought his way free from a hangman's noose in New Hampshire. Those who lived longest saw a New Brunswick in transition, a new era in which a host of new-comers were unwilling to recognize the pre-eminence that the older ones believed the honesty of their motives and the quality of their services had earned for them.

Disgrace to the province and mortification to the parties concerned had been freely avowed following the conflict for the succession in 1823. Upon the death of Chipman a second conflict appeared likely, for the newly appointed lieutenant-governor, Sir Howard Douglas, would not arrive in New Brunswick until late in the year. A letter from Leonard at Sussex Vale called the council to meet there, and Odell, the clerk, considered it his duty to issue the summons. A second letter from Leonard, however, declared that he did not wish to cause a repetition of the unfortunate events of the preceding year, and Billopp likewise waived his claim.[56] The succession therefore fell on John Murray Bliss, who governed until August when Douglas, hastened to the scene by the Colonial Office, appeared. Bliss immediately challenged the securities offered by George Shore for the temporary holding of three offices, those of surveyor-, receiver-, and auditor-general, and declared them inadequate. Under the terms of the patent, Shore had been receiving ten per cent of the revenues from the Crown lands as receiver-general and five per cent as auditor-general. While revenues were rising owing to the boom in the timber trade the new president of the council replaced Shore by his son, George Pigeon Bliss. From March to August, "under the excitement of a stimulus", as Douglas later explained, Bliss increased the revenues from £9,000 to £18,000, and when the lieutenant-governor arrived it was only with the greatest of difficulty that he was able to extract the money from the new receiver-general.[57]

CHAPTER 9

The Era of Douglas:
Calm before Trouble

1824-1831

The arrival of Sir Howard Douglas as lieutenant-governor in August 1824 coincided with the approach of new tensions that were to project New Brunswick into a more articulate and assertive phase of provincial development. British imperial policies were about to inaugurate for the North American colonies a new climate of advancement in which they would become increasingly dependent on their own exertions. William Huskisson had prophesied a British family of free nations. The Board of Trade, surrendering to the exalted theories of *laissez-faire*, was preparing for the complete emancipation of colonial commerce. Freedom of trade implied a termination of British financial support for colonial governments and churches. Year after year the radicals in the House of Commons were clamouring for the removal of the money votes that paid for civil, military, and ecclesiastical establishments in North America, and were making their influence generally felt. In an age of rapid material growth and enlightened self-interest, financial grants by Parliament to colonial governments were the clearest mark of colonial dependency.

Sir Howard, a soldier of distinguished reputation who had served through the Peninsular War and had been commandant of the Royal Military College at Woolwich, was out of sympathy with the fashionable conviction that the colonies must gently and gradually slip from the control of the Mother Country. His idea of the unity of the Empire was based on the undisputed supremacy of the British Parliament. He believed that sufficient of the fundamentals of political power had already passed to the other side of the Atlantic and that what remained of imperial control must be jealously safeguarded. Yet he was not, like Carleton, aloof from the tumult of civil affairs, nor, like Smyth, a martinet whose conduct was adjusted by rigid adherence to the royal instructions. Douglas could move freely in the area of public opinion and prided himself on his knowledge of it. A good working politician, he believed that public opinion could be harnessed to his purposes and he was tireless in managing the caprices of popular impulse to the achievement of harmony and compromise. In order to keep the imperial bond strong he was willing to fight the imperial authorities tooth and nail. He could surrender on detail in order to gain purposes that were general. His administration of seven years was a period in which, owing to his personal popularity and ability to placate local interests, the issues tending to divide Mother Country and colony acquired very little sharpness and were postponed until a later period.

Public sentiment on imperial problems had shifted its emphasis since the days of the Loyalist migration of 1783. There were still many who prided themselves on ancestral memories, but these private devotions were eclipsed by the more immediate recollections of the great commercial expansion that had occurred during the past twenty years beneath the shelter of imperial policies. Commercial men were now indubitably the leaders of public opinion, and they had been nurtured on the idea that British subjects were entitled to special privileges in trade. Yet this kind of loyalty had been repeatedly tested by the vagaries of British policy. Time and again, in peace and war, the British government had dispensed with the trading privileges of British subjects in order to gratify the Americans. Saint John merchants, glorying in the principles of the Navigation Acts, had many times seen the Americans, legally and illegally, moving into markets they considered exclusive to themselves. New Brunswickers held to the old rather than to the new points of view in British policy. It was irritating to reflect upon the frequent assertions in the British House of Commons, made by those presently to call themselves liberals, that, even though the colonies should cut themselves adrift from Britain, they would still be compelled to purchase British manufactured goods. Astute analysts liked to show that Huskisson's reforms, though they emancipated colonial commerce, had but one purpose, that of benefiting British shippers and manufacturers.

One staunch prop for the historical commercial connection remained: the preference given British North American timber in British markets. For seventeen years it had been possible to identify the more sentimental and traditional connection with Britain with this great tangible economic asset. British free traders and Baltic timber interests who worked to destroy the preference were regarded as recreant to the heritage of a great empire. As that erudite lecturer J. S. Buckingham discovered some years later, New Brunswickers did not care to consider that Britain had the freedom of choice to alter or destroy the timber preference. The young man from Woodstock, who spoke so heatedly on the subject aboard the steamer that was sailing up the St. John River, declared that reduction of British duties on Baltic timber would be oppressive to the colonies.[1] The desperate, dependent loyalty of the early days of the colony had been enhanced by the urgencies of an economy that was protected by British legislation. The new vogues in British economic thinking frequently made it appear possible that protection would be withdrawn, and on such occasions New Brunswick's loyalty to the Mother Country became still more desperate.

II

When Douglas arrived at Fredericton his immediate impressions were highly unfavourable. Scarcely a room in Government House was fit for habitation. The window-panes were shattered and the water in the well was foul. Aboard the "wretched" steamboat that had conveyed him from Saint John to Fredericton he had found extremely distasteful "the one common cabin, table and society", a clear indication of "the levelling principles of our neighbours". His first request to the Colonial Office was for an allowance that would enable him to enjoy travel on the river in a vessel exclusive to himself.[2] Beyond the portals of his residence the environment must have seemed little more attractive, for the colonial aristocracy was enraged by the appointment of a Commissioner of Crown Lands who was charged with comprehensive powers over the public domain, the source of fees for the public offices that in recent years had become so lucrative. The Colonial Office had decided to fasten a firm control on the new revenues that flowed so rapidly from the forests

of New Brunswick, and the appearance of an outsider, Thomas
Baillie, who arrived in November with virtually dictatorial
powers, was an affront to those who had been on the threshold
of great wealth by reason of their holding public office.

Most formidable of this privileged circle was John Murray
Bliss, the aged judge, who had administered the government for
six months prior to the arrival of Douglas and who had appointed his son, George Pigeon Bliss, to the office of receiver-
general. He was connected by marriage to most of the other
families who presumed to official status, notably that of John
Robinson, the provincial treasurer. But his power really rested
on an ability to influence deliberations in the legislature through
family affinities with the Simonds brothers of Saint John:
Richard, who had returned to his native city following a successful business career on the Miramichi, and Charles, who was
president of the Bank of New Brunswick. He held a seat on the
council and was at the centre of what Douglas later called "this
powerful family".[3]

The shock of Baillie's appointment fell most heavily on
George Pigeon Bliss. The Commissioner of Crown Lands was
ordered to pay all receipts of his office directly to the Bank of
New Brunswick.[4] This deprived Bliss of the lush percentages he
had enjoyed and stripped his office of its importance. Frederick
Phillips Robinson, the auditor-general, suffered similarly. The
new office of Baillie dwarfed all other offices in the province,
and the new-comer, a voluble Irishman who made no secret of
his intention to revise the whole system of managing the Crown
lands, became the symbol of a hated, alien régime. For a generation and more, public office had failed to produce the affluence
expected for favourites of the government. Now, when prosperity had finally come to New Brunswick, the benefits of office
were snatched away. Upon the management of the Crown
lands depended the timber trade and the economy of the province. To the commercial leaders as well as to the office-holding
group Baillie appeared as a personage possessed of not only
extraordinary power but of hostile intent. He was the nominee
of the colonial secretary, Lord Bathurst, who had earlier promised him a consulship in Tunis. His willingness to relinquish
this highly paid post had placed the secretary under obligation
to him. His elder brother, George Baillie, was a senior clerk at
the Colonial Office and could readily influence decision at this
fount of authority.

On coming to New Brunswick Baillie talked exuberantly, profusely described the confusion left by the insane Lockwood, and quickly came to realize the tensions created by his appointment. He considered himself an estate-keeper of 16,000,000 acres. His duty was to raise a vast revenue from the Crown lands, to create a fund which would not only relieve the British government of the costs of the civil establishment in New Brunswick but pay for the rapid material development of the province under the direction of Downing Street. All who were influential had reason to fear the new efficiency that was rather boastfully proclaimed.

Douglas worked hard to mollify the bitter prejudices aroused by this brash intrusion upon the bright prospects of the office-holding families. Baillie's patent of office had authorized him to extract from his receipts a salary and fees which, it was plainly evident, would reach a ridiculously high figure. Under pressure from the council, which was dominated by his opponents, and the persuasion of Douglas, who was desperately eager to achieve at least a degree of harmony, Baillie "magnanimously" agreed to a reduction. Lord Bathurst, refereeing the dispute, finally fixed for him a salary of £1,600, a sum considerably higher than the council thought proper. But the effects of this compromise were nullified by the aggressive and loquacious demeanour of the commissioner both in public and in private. His high salary was to become a subject of great concern on the social front in Fredericton as well as in public debate. To Douglas, seeking goodwill from all classes of the public, Baillie's presence was a constant menace. Panaceas for discontent had to be found. George Pigeon Bliss was confirmed in the office of receiver-general. Ardently, Douglas urged the strengthening of the Loyalist families and the official element in the community to whom the Crown could most confidently look for support. New measures were necessary, he declared, to arrest the continuing loss of their station in society. In response to this plea Bathurst acceded to grants of 2,000 acres of land to Bliss, Street, Botsford, and others who had served on the council, holding Douglas to the rules for such awards that were in effect in the Canadas.[5] The pacification of local interests, particularly of the men of the law, was indispensable to the execution of higher policy. "The management of the persons and dispositions of the learned profession is the principal object in inducing quiet and harmony in these colonies."[6]

III

Standing as a buffer between the requirements of imperial policy
and an increasingly alert colonial self-assertion, Douglas was to
have his patience sorely tried during his entire term in New
Brunswick. During the time of Smyth the legislature had capitulated upon the exaction of timber duties and the creation of
the Casual and Territorial Revenue that was beyond its control. But there was a jealous public opinion concerning the
manner in which the rapidly increasing revenues of the forests
should be expended. The more learned of colonial politicians
were already discoursing upon the surrender of the ancient territorial rights of the Crown in Great Britain to the control of
Parliament. Douglas wrote with pride of the independent attitude adopted by his officers towards the legislature, yet he was
politic enough to do nothing with respect to the casual revenues
without a careful scrutiny of legislative opinion.

While provincial self-consciousness was on the increase the
Colonial Office commenced to bestow a considerable amount of
attention upon New Brunswick. For years, during the Napoleonic Wars, refusal to grant attention to the pressing needs
of the province had been embarrassing to the provincial government. Now, when New Brunswick was about to spread her
wings, imperial solicitude became irksome and offensive. The
reason for this was largely the presence at the Colonial Office
of a hard-working under-secretary, Robert Wilmot Horton,
who believed that the colonial empire could be employed to
alleviate the severity of Britain's problems at home, that emigration was the solution to these problems, and that closer
attention must be given to the administration of the colonies in
order that the vast surplus of Britain's industrial population
might be comfortably accommodated. Douglas had to confront
not merely the eccentricities and ambitions of colonial politicians but a new *deus ex machina*, the spectre of imperial
planning.

A strong believer in the close association of church and state,
Wilmot Horton was in affinity with the Archbishop of Canterbury. At the outset of his term Douglas was compelled to report
"a strong sensation" against the payment of a part of the retirement allowance of the Right Reverend Ephraim Stanser, the
Bishop of Nova Scotia, from the Casual and Territorial Revenues. Stanser had served in his office for a few months only and

had never visited New Brunswick. Rather grudgingly the Colonial Office was willing to settle for a grant of land to Stanser, not as a reward for his episcopal administration but out of consideration for the military services of his family.[7] This was trifling compared with the possibilities invoked by the suggestion from the Colonial Office that the Church of England should be endowed with land on the same scale as in Upper Canada, that it should ultimately receive one-seventh of all the lands to be granted by the Crown. At first Douglas appeared to consider there was propriety in the measure, provided that the needs of the Church of Scotland should be taken into account, but his cautious optimism abruptly disappeared a year later when it appeared that the Church of England would be thrown exclusively upon local resources by the withdrawal of the parliamentary grant to the Society for the Propagation of the Gospel. With "a perfect knowledge" of the opinions of the members of the legislature, the large majority of whom would be against any form of aid to the church, he declared that even concerning the granting of land he would have to be circumspect. The numerous sectarians of the province would rejoice at the prospect of the withdrawal of aid from the Mother Country to the parish clergy. Attempts to endow the church from public resources would do it more harm than good.[8] The reluctance of Douglas to move in the matter was made the easier by the absolute refusal of Sir James Kempt in Nova Scotia to grant land in support of the bishopric.[9]

Against this background of aggressive ecclesiastical policies in Britain and of jealous colonial denominationalism, Douglas succeeded in rehabilitating the only institution of higher education in the province. In 1785 a group of Loyalist refugees, headed by William Paine, had petitioned Carleton for the establishment of an academy of liberal arts and sciences in the vicinity of Fredericton. The government of that day had complied with the prayer of the petition with the only means at its disposal, a grant of land which consisted of 6,000 acres on the high ground to the south-west of the capital. Though the ambition was a provincial seat of higher instruction, the means available permitted, for a considerable period, the establishment of a collegiate school only, patronized by the official and well-to-do classes of Fredericton. In 1800 Carleton, reflecting a spirit of provincial pride and ignoring the veiled opposition of Bishop Inglis of Nova Scotia who wished his own university at Windsor to be the sole source of higher instruction for the youth of British North America, granted a charter to the College of New Brunswick. But it was only in 1823 that higher instruction, under the supervision of the Reverend James Somerville, a scholarly and hard-working missionary of the Society for the Propagation of the Gospel, really commenced. Douglas, upon his appointment, encountered most of the elements necessary for the realization of the dream of the memorialists of 1785. An incipient college had come into existence. Eminent personages decried the necessity of sending their sons abroad for university degrees. The overflowing revenues of the Crown lands reflected the abundant prosperity of the province.

Douglas had no difficulty in persuading the British government to consent to the withdrawal from the Casual and Territorial Revenue of something like half the sum necessary for the construction of a college building.[10] The Colonial Office further agreed to the annual payment of £1,000 from the same source, provided that the legislature would agree to make a similar commitment from the ordinary revenues of the province. There was no quibbling in the house of assembly, and the college was at once assured of a generous annual income. In a prosperous year, when finances provided no difficulty, the trouble came from an excess of religious scruples. Bishop John Inglis, holding hard to the wish of his father that King's at Windsor should be the one great college of his see, implored Douglas to abandon his plan for the development of the institution at Fredericton.[11] Having failed to do this he tirelessly exerted his influence with British political and ecclesiastical leaders, insisting that the Royal Charter that Douglas was seeking should make the college exclusively Anglican. In England it was fashionable to regard the appearance of new denominations of Christians, both at home and in the colonies, as a phenomenon that was fleeting and ephemeral. Wilmot Horton succumbed to Inglis's pressure and assured the Archbishop of Canterbury that religious tests would be demanded of young matriculants to the college. When Douglas, arguing and pleading that British Americans were unaccustomed to religious tests, assured him that the legislature would never adhere to its part in the bargain should such a stipulation be placed in the charter, he yielded the point. If the young men of New Brunswick, he told the Archbishop, were to remain at home instead of going to the United States for higher education, the exemption from the Thirty-Nine

Articles would have to be allowed.[12] When the charter emerged it required that the members of the college council should be Anglicans and that the president and vice-president should be Anglican clergymen, but no restrictions were placed upon students. The Church of England position had been breached, though not stormed.

On New Year's Day, 1829, Douglas had the satisfaction of opening the new King's College, "hewn from the rough stone of the country" – long regarded as the finest building in the province. Nobody could deny its "salubrious situation", but there may have been doubts among the many who attended concerning "the liberal constitution" of which Douglas spoke. Soon, at any rate, the hosts of nonconformity would storm the breach. Late in the same year arrived the new vice-president charged with the management of the institution, Dr. Edwin Jacob, who brought from Oxford the clear conviction that classical literature and moral philosophy were essential subjects of study in new countries. Along with the erudite divine was his lady who, it was whispered, was of royal origin. "No secret", the gossips of Fredericton were to say in later years.[13]

The founding of King's College was a conspicuous example of what could be done with the casual revenues. Every item of expenditure had to be approved by the Colonial Office, but Bathurst generally concurred with the suggestions of the lieutenant-governor. The fund multiplied during 1824 and 1825, dropped sharply in 1826 when on "Black Monday" the ship *Jane* brought to Saint John the news of another spate of bank failures in Britain and the consequent failures of many of the great timber-importing firms who had credit with them, rose again in 1827 and maintained an increasing level for the remainder of Douglas's term. The proceeds provided a temporary solution to the bitter dispute between the judiciary of the Supreme Court and the legislature. Money was available for travelling expenses so that justice appeared in the outlying counties where for many years it had been denied. The "National" or "Madras" schools, which had gained a firm foothold in Smyth's time, were further strengthened. Carefully Douglas applied sums of money to the building of roads and bridges, hoping to stimulate the legislature to greater activity with the normal revenues of the province that were at its command. He gave new life to the flagging energies of the agricultural and immigration societies that were endeavouring to improve the breeds of farm animals and to give aid to newly arrived settlers during their first precarious months on wilderness lands. The ideal of a resident peasantry firmly attached to the soil in spite of the blandishments of the timber trade was still fashionable among landed gentlemen who professed to believe that the timber trade would soon die.

It was true that money was being taken from the people and expended without their formal consent, but this historic cry did not arise so long as Douglas remained within the province. Six months after his arrival his genius for compromise had been so successful that a reporter for the *Royal Gazette*, writing of a happy meeting at Barristers' Inn on the occasion of the formation of a law society, could solemnly remark upon "the present happy era in our provincial career when all party spirit appears to be banished".[14] Douglas's popularity lay not in his political convictions, which he largely concealed, but in his ability to anticipate opinion in the legislature and amongst the public at large. He would consider no diminution of the power of the royal prerogative but he was eager to use that power in accordance with the wishes of popular leaders.

IV

Douglas could restrain colonial impetuosities but not those of the Colonial Office. There Wilmot Horton, committed in principle to the liberating ideas of Huskisson, though vague in detail, was determined to snap the most important of the formal bonds that maintained New Brunswick in a state of dependency upon Great Britain. This was the parliamentary grant that paid for the salaries of Douglas and the leading officers of the government. In September 1825 Wilmot Horton sent for the consideration of the lieutenant-governor the draft of a letter that proposed that the legislature should assume the total costs of civil government, relieving the Parliament of the United Kingdom of charges that amounted to about £5,000. Asking Douglas to sound out leading members of the legislature on the expediency of such an important change, he gave as his reasons the economic competence of the province and the complete freedom of trade the colonies now enjoyed, "as if they constituted in fact integral parts of the United Kingdom". Very little time was allowed for such consideration. In October the letter was actually sent in official form. Referring to the heavy charges upon the Mother Country for the defence of the colonies, it proposed an act of the legislature, having effect for ten years, to assume the charges.

Douglas warned of calamitous results following the proposed measure. In his view the parliamentary grant was indispensable for maintaining the connection between Mother Country and colony. Republican principles were intruding from the United States and their influence would be intensified by an innovation that would place the executive of the province at the mercy of the house of assembly. Young men of talent would court popular favour in order to enter the legislature rather than look to the government for their advancement, and "the seeds of democracy will be gradually sown and nourished in the country". Already the means by which the government could influence the people had been cut to a dangerous degree. Already the legislature had given evidence of a temper to enlarge its powers. The example of Lower Canada, where the cost of the civil establishment had been assumed by the legislature, gave promise of boundless evils. The pecuniary consideration was trifling, but the political, enormous. Why should Parliament withdraw "the allowance of a rich parent to the child of her body", to a province that enriched the commerce of Britain with 1,100 ships and 11,000 seamen? "I may be wrong but I never felt my mind more stubborn." Douglas was certain that the independence of the colonial executive from the legislature was the chief guarantee of the continuing British connection, that to remove it would pave the way for the separation of parent state and colony. "I do not say that the immediate effects of discontinuing the parliamentary grant would be rebellion or fixed purpose of a declaration of independence but the tendency would be direct and certain."[15]

The Miramichi fire and the consequent loss of capital, the depression in the timber trade of 1826-7 and the resulting loss to the casual revenue, enabled Douglas to plead poverty and create delay. But the mind of the Colonial Office was set on relieving Parliament of colonial charges. The legislature was unwilling to pay for the salaries of officers of government from their revenues, which were chiefly drawn from customs and excise duties, even though such a change would bring Douglas and the whole executive within their suasion and control. But another source of relief for Parliament was available. This was the casual revenue. After two years of hard bargaining, the Colonial Office, ignoring the protests of Douglas and the legislature, accepted the advice of Baillie, who gave ample assurances that the revenues of the forests could easily stand the payment of salaries to the lieutenant-governor and his officials. The casual revenue was beyond the control of the legislature, but the moral position of the permanent officers of government was now greatly weakened. On January 1, 1831, when the change finally went into effect, their independence was based not on the bounty of Great Britain but on revenues taken from the people of New Brunswick without their consultation and consent. This question of the civil list, a budget of items concerning fixed charges of government, involved but a small sum of money, yet it contained the gravest of political implications.

V

The Colonial Office presented New Brunswick and Douglas with still another set of problems. The reformers and altruists who surrounded Bathurst and Wilmot Horton had acquired the imaginative conviction that the wilderness lands of the Empire were the heritage of the unwanted surplus of British population. The millions of acres of untilled land in North America seemed the logical repository for the hundreds of thousands of persons who looked beyond the seas for the means of a new life. In scanning the industrial statistics of the colonies they had come to the conclusion that the important factor was the high price of labour compared with the cheapness of land, remarkable because of the effective contrast it offered to conditions in Great Britain where land was scarce and labour plentiful. It seemed eminently reasonable that a labourer, after a short sojourn in New Brunswick, could easily acquire the funds that would enable him to purchase a farm. With complete confidence in the soundness of their planning, fortified by the strongest assurances of success from Baillie, Bathurst and Wilmot Horton in 1827 inaugurated a system of sale of land in New Brunswick, called the New South Wales system because of its reputed success in the Australian colonies. It required that lots of land not exceeding 1,200 acres should be paid for in four annual instalments. It virtually excluded free grants of land except to poor immigrants who would pay, in return for grants of up to 200 acres, an annual quitrent of five per cent of estimated value. What created the greatest sensation of all was the proposal to collect arrears of quitrents on all lands granted since 1783-4, the realization of the threat that Carleton had on several occasions successfully averted. The sale and rent of colonial lands, it was anticipated, would finance an inflow of immigrants from the British Isles who could be comfortably settled on orderly principles following the clearing of lands and the opening of roads.

The people of New Brunswick possessed the general belief that the Crown lands were their own inheritance, not that of the Empire at large, and every section of the population took alarm when knowledge of the Downing Street plans was spread about. Officials at Fredericton, many of whom had acquired great holdings of land by free grant or purchase, took a legalistic line, declaring that the new scheme, instituted by the dispatch of a mere secretary of state, could not set aside the original terms of the royal instructions which had been issued under the Sign Manual. Chief Justice Saunders, the largest landowner in the province, lost no opportunity of publicly inveighing against this remarkable design for opening up wilderness lands, challenging both its legality and its policy. Those who were most loyal to the Crown preferred to remember the sacrifices of their fathers and grandfathers rather than the actual terms, stipulating quitrents, under which land grants had been accepted in 1783-4. The decades during which the collection of quitrents had been in abeyance made the sudden announcement of intention to collect seem novel and tyrannical. The mercantile element announced their belief that the lands of New Brunswick would be bought up by British and foreign capitalists, and prophesied the loss of their livelihood. The timber trade was based on the cheap and available renting of timber berths from the public domain, and if the public domain should be alienated by sale to outsiders, the small, independent operators who each season took to the woods for timber would be forced out of business. The very large proportion of the settled population who possessed no clear titles to their lands took alarm for their improvements, and the plight of the poor squatters became a subject for sympathetic speculation.

In the conflict between the men on the spot and the "science" of the economists in London, Douglas persistently supported the former. His public letters urged modifications in the programme of sale, but in private he demanded the abandonment of the entire plan. "The credit of the colonial administration is at stake in a great degree upon the measures they may take in this matter."[16] The sale of land, he prophesied, would never be productive financially and it would be bad politically. Lord Dalhousie in Canada and Sir James Kempt in Nova Scotia were in agreement with him, but the Colonial Office could not be shaken in its opinions. Why, asked Huskisson, should the people of New Brunswick be opposed to the sale of wild lands when the policy was achieving such great results in the United States? Douglas sensed a strong ground-swell of popular revulsion. Members of the house of assembly, aware of imperial intentions to unload the complete costs of government on the province and to create from the Crown lands a fund that would suffice to settle the emigrant poor of Britain on New Brunswick soil, were becoming increasingly critical of the tightening degree of imperial control. Public interest was turning to the settlement of the customs dispute made by Huskisson in 1826. Proceeds of the imperial duties collected in the province were being turned over to the provincial treasurer, but only after the high salaries guaranteed to the officers had been deducted. To the public these rewards appeared so great as to constitute an abuse. The legislature, Douglas said darkly, would take strong measures in order to get satisfaction.[17] It was axiomatic, too, that if New Brunswick was to be forced to stand on her own feet financially, her legislators would look with increasing jealousy and concern upon the casual revenue that was raised from the commerce of the province by agencies beyond their control.

Douglas would have had a better chance to assuage the ruffled feelings that had become general by 1828 had it not been for the conduct of Thomas Baillie. As the apostle of a new order, the Commissioner of Crown Lands had introduced reforms that were unacceptable to the very great majority of the influential. He had played a high hand with the timber merchants who had come to deal with him and who were dependent on his decisions. Fearlessly he had antagonized the greatest in the land. In 1827 he prosecuted Charles Simonds, the Speaker of the house of assembly, for trespass in Saint John. He boasted of the members of the legislature whom his deputies had chastised for evasion of the timber regulations. His "harpies", as his deputies were called, steadily increased in numbers and efficiency. It was well known that he wished to increase the tax of one shilling a ton on timber taken from the Crown lands. If the lumbermen of Maine could afford higher taxes, why could not those of New Brunswick whose costs were cheaper owing to the easier navigation of the rivers? It was customary for his enemies to speak with envy of his princely salary, though his friends could retort that he spent it in a princely way. Friends and enemies were sometimes indistinguishable. Chief Justice Saunders wrote irritably to his son in London of the commissioner's income, said to exceed £4,000, enough to sustain "at least eight of our young men whose education and rank in this society certainly entitle them to expect some of the passing benefits of government". But his scruples became muted when the son most urgently reported that at the Colonial Office George Baillie had far more to say about New Brunswick than even Bathurst or Wilmot Horton, that Thomas Baillie was even more important than Sir Howard Douglas. Soon the ladies of the Saunders household were displaying a keen interest in Mrs. Baillie's scrap-books.

Altogether apart from the merits of his policies, the impression left of Baillie by his numerous detractors is that he was garrulous and vain. "For to say truth your brother displayed and spoke too much," wrote Douglas to George Baillie.[18] The salary of the commissioner, increased by £500 in 1827 when the sale of Crown lands was inaugurated, and the expenses of collecting the casual revenue, made him the centre of a political contention that would give way to no other. Throughout the province it was commonly alleged that the tax paid on stumpage was mostly going into the pockets of Baillie and his deputies, that when the expenses were deducted very little was left for the net revenue. The expenses, indeed, were awesome to Douglas and the Colonial Office as well as to Baillie's enemies. In attempts to economize, the office of the commissioner experienced several reorganizations between 1825 and 1830, but his strength was unimpaired. He enjoyed the confidence of the Colonial Office, a confidence that was increased when Baillie boldly contradicted the predictions of Douglas and declared that capitalists would purchase the wild lands of the province. By 1829, when Douglas left for England, Baillie could produce figures to show that Downing Street's plan for the sale of Crown lands was working and that New Brunswick was the only province in British North America where an honest attempt had been made to make it work. If Canada and Nova Scotia failed to vindicate the theories of the colonial reformers in London, New Brunswick was in a fair way of vindicating them.

Baillie could contemptuously ignore the "political" considerations to which Douglas was so sensitive. In both public and private capacities he opened negotiations with British capitalists for the sale of land. He had come to the conclusion that the

waste lands of the province could never be adequately developed
as long as the government dealt with local capitalists of moderate means. Rather than deal with a hundred timber merchants
within the province on a year-to-year basis, he preferred to
open the country to the endeavours of half a dozen great
corporations originating abroad. Conditions for capitalizing on
this choice were good, for the timber trade had emerged from
the slump of 1826 to enjoy a dozen buoyant years. During this
period Baillie was to be New Brunswick's *enfant terrible*, the
most hated and most powerful figure in the politics of the
province. Because of the close connection between his office and
the province's commercial well-being he overshadowed even the
lieutenant-governor in capacity for good and evil. By reason of
his independence of the legislature and his arbitrary making
of important policies he was to be the principal foe of those who
were to work for change.

VI

The boundary quarrel flared into prominence during the time
of Douglas and remained a source of controversy until its final
settlement fifteen years later. The commissioners appointed
under the fifth article of the Treaty of Ghent had reached a
stalemate. The search for the "highlands" marking the northern
limits of American territory had commenced, but they had
proven to be non-existent. Surveyors of the Boundary Commission had been running a northerly line from The Monument
on the St. Croix, but how far north the line should go had
become the subject of very grave contention.

In the first two phases of the boundary dispute – those of the
finding of the true St. Croix and the apportionment of the
islands – the British cases had been strong and it had been possible to adopt a moral attitude of superiority in the face of
outrageous Yankee sophistry. But in the third phase, perhaps
the most important of all, it had become apparent to the British
representatives, Barclay and Chipman, that topography favoured the aggressive American interpretation of the treaty of
1783, that the northerly line would run virtually to the St.
Lawrence before highlands of any description could be encountered. Backwoodsmen who knew the country declared that as
far as the St. Lawrence nothing resembling a mountain or natural
barrier existed, that the country was high and flat, "a morass of
millions of acres". Detailed reports confirmed earlier suspicions

that the line could run across the St. John, sever the Mada-waska settlements and remove the Témiscouata communication with Canada. The address of the New Brunswick legislature to the Prince Regent in 1814 had admitted the possibility of defeat in a legalistic interpretation of the Treaty of Versailles and had pleaded the necessity of diplomatic action to forestall it. The loss of the Madawaska settlements had long been recognized as extremely likely. "It would be a pity to give them up to the Yankees against their will," said one writer who had found the Madawaskans "very civil".[19]

The more that was discovered of the country the more the Americans righteously inferred that their northern boundary would be within sight of the St. Lawrence. As the survey party employed by the commission realized that the terminology of the treaty was incomprehensible so far as the configuration of the country was concerned, "the search for the highlands" acquired a meaningless, comic character. The chief British surveyor, Colonel Joseph Bouchette, Surveyor-General for Lower Canada, was gulled by his American counterpart, John-son, who, though "vulgar and uneducated", was "a shrewd, intelligent Yankee". On Sunday mornings, as the party rested from its labours of cutting a thread of cleared land through the forests, Johnson would amuse himself by climbing into a tree and drawing sketches of imaginary highlands.[20] For his willing-ness to accept defeat Bouchette was relieved of his duties, which were given to William Franklin Odell, who obtained leave of absence from the provincial-secretaryship. In his arguments before the commission the younger Ward Chipman, now the British agent, was compelled to take refuge in logic. Fixing upon Mars Hill, opposite Woodstock, as the point beyond which the northerly line should not go, he reasoned that the St. John River, flowing into the Bay of Fundy, was not one of the rivers falling into the Atlantic comprehended by the makers of the treaty and that therefore its whole basin must be included within British territory. The point was a good one but it was an evasion of the definition in the treaty, a resort to sophistry in face of the adverse physical facts.[21] Ignoring the description given in the second article of the treaty, he urged that a boun-dary must be based on mutual convenience and reciprocal advantage. Mars Hill, forty miles from the source of the St. Croix, was a conspicuous elevation that would do as well as any other as a point of delineation.

Barclay and Chipman refused to retreat from this exposed but strongly held position. In April 1822 the members of the commission held their last meeting in New York for the purpose of recording their total inability to reach an agreement. John Quincy Adams, the American Secretary of State, termed Barclay's report as one "in which ingenuity maintains an endless argument against common sense".[22] Albert Gallatin, the American ambassador at London, who in his boyhood had spent much time on the Maine coast and was especially interested in the controversy, called it scandalous.

Settlement was now far removed. To add to the tension, Maine had in 1820 become a state, which meant that in the immediate vicinity of New Brunswick there had come into existence a local administration that was highly responsive to the exuberant patriotism and strenuous party politics of its people. From the first it had become evident that the new sovereign state would not tolerate any loss of its territory or moderation of its authority. Washington would have to deal with Britain in the interests of Maine and not of the United States generally. The Treaty of Ghent had provided that, if the commission failed to produce an award, the dispute should be referred to the arbitration of some friendly sovereign. At Augusta this prospect was not relished, and it was proclaimed without reservation that Maine's destiny would be decided by her own citizens. The state government gave ample evidence of this robust intention by dispatching to the border areas agents who granted lands to American citizens, disputed the jurisdiction exerted by New Brunswick for many years on the St. John above the Madawaska settlements, and attempted to interfere with British subjects who were cutting timber in the valley of the Aroostook.

On July 4, 1827, when John Baker raised the American flag in the Madawaska settlements, the dispute entered a new stage. Rival authorities of Maine and New Brunswick came directly into contact with one another in the debatable region where the Madawaska joins the St. John. American settlers were rapidly entering the area, farming, and taking out timber. Baker, who several years before had requested payment of the New Brunswick bounty for growing corn on wilderness land and had been refused, was the head of a growing party that refused to accept British jurisdiction and turned to the ebullient government of Maine for assistance. From now on, it was certain, contact between the rival parties would increase, and there was a constant danger that an incident such as this would lead to violence, possibly to war between Britain and the United States. At Fredericton Douglas was completely convinced that the Baker affair was no frontier flare-up but had been instigated by the government of Maine.[23] On September 25 Baker was apprehended by a British force, taken to the jail at Fredericton, and charged with conspiracy and sedition. In May 1828 he was brought to trial, convicted, and sentenced to two months' imprisonment in addition to a fine of twenty-five pounds. Douglas, after giving the governor of the state of Maine a lesson on the impropriety of conducting a correspondence upon a matter that was the business of Washington and London, declined to have further dealings with him. The efforts of Henry Clay, the American Secretary of State, to procure the release of Baker and an indemnity for his arrest were unavailing. In his firm action to sustain New Brunswick's jurisdiction Douglas received the staunch support of the British government. Many years later he declared that if he had received an order to halt proceedings against Baker he would have disobeyed it and resigned his post.[24]

In 1828 the two governments, at a convention in London, agreed to refer the dispute to the King of the Netherlands. This was a victory for the British point of view, for opinion in the United States had favoured the Czar of Russia as a sovereign much more friendly to the national interest. The hearings opened at The Hague in 1829, and all the evidence, though not the arguments, submitted to the commission was again under review. Douglas crossed the water, never to return to New Brunswick, to give advice to the British delegation. Referring to his own actions, he was able to compliment the King by observing that he had followed the Orange motto, "Je maintiendrai". But the King was no more able to produce a solution based upon legal right than the commission had been. His decision, submitted to the parties in January 1831, suggested a partition of the disputed territory based on compromise and mutual convenience. The northerly line would run to a point shortly above Grand Falls, securing to Great Britain the north bank of the St. John and the communication with Canada, but of the 12,027 square miles in dispute the award gave 7,908 to Maine.

Such a settlement, admirable as a compromise, was not acceptable to Maine. At Augusta it was considered that the

northerly line should run to the source of the Métis River,
bringing the whole of Lake Témiscouata within the state borders. No sooner had news of the award arrived than it was
announced that His Orange Majesty had failed to perform his
task, that he had not decided what boundary had been named
in the treaty but had merely recommended another. There were
secret sessions of the Maine legislature, and the newspapers,
especially those opposed to President Jackson, aroused public
feeling by flaming announcements that Maine was in the market,
that a sale of birthright was imminent. At Washington the
Senate's committee on foreign relations introduced a resolution
that the King's award should be accepted, but the lobbyists
from Maine, persisting in their opposition, exerted an increasingly powerful influence. After the debate had lasted a year,
Henry Clay and leaders of the Senate adopted the view that the
revolution in Belgium had deprived the King of the Netherlands
of his independence, that he had become a British client. On
June 23, 1832, a resolution that the president be advised to open
a new negotiation with Britain was passed by a majority of one.

Maine was unsatisfied, and her point of view made American
national policy. Immediately following the award her truculence
was voiced by an act to incorporate the town of Madawaska.
This was a challenge not only to New Brunswick and Great
Britain but to the government at Washington as well. It had
become a powerful cry that the general government could not
barter away the territory of a sovereign state. The state government, urged on by the high-pitched eloquence of local patriots,
had become a thorn in the flesh to Washington. President Jackson had no compliments for Governor Lincoln, though he went
out of his way to express appreciation for the correct conduct of
Douglas.[25]

VII

The great age of wood, wind, and water was already well advanced when Douglas left for England in 1829, and the consequences were perceptible in the development of a rather remarkable society. Twenty years of rapid progress in a single direction,
the growth of the timber trade, had changed the habits and
fashioned the minds of the people of New Brunswick to a greater
extent than anywhere else in British North America. The life
of the lumberer was like that of the sailor, and his habits had
become proverbially improvident. "A simple, handy man, he

goes into his tent at night, lights his fire of faggots, cooks his provisions, drinks his grog, sings himself to sleep, enjoys a profoundness of slumber which is totally a stranger to the less adventurous, and rises to his next day's labours in the full buoyancy of health and spirits."[26] But, according to the moralist who furnished this description, the province was gaining nothing from the timber trade except in population. The farms were bleak and unprepossessing in appearance. Upon a man's death his property was worth no more than when he first obtained it. Virtually all holders of farm properties were in debt and about one-third were fugitives from the sheriff. "Our sheriffs are not lawyers, their chief employment is the capture and imprisonment of debtors."

New Brunswick stood in unfavourable contrast to Nova Scotia, where agricultural properties had in recent years grown greatly in value. It was soberly estimated at the time that the imperial duties on the importation of wheat, flour, and salted products alone saved agriculture. Consistently the mercantile community in Saint John opposed these duties, its aim being to import everything consumed within the province as well as to export everything it produced. Through the merchants' hands passed a ceaseless turnover of goods from which they could extract a two-way profit. Merchants and shippers throve on the very causes that depressed farming. Generally the population consumed American flour of fine quality, imported from New York or New Orleans. "The poorest of the poor looks with contempt upon any bread which is not wheaten and will not eat it on any account,"[27] a Scottish visitor commented.

Saint John was a city conveying definite impressions. From a distance the wooden houses, painted in many colours, provided a pleasing appearance, but towards the wharves where scores of vessels were lined up for traffic on the ocean and the river, filth became excessive and the summer sun raised unpleasant stenches. At the dinner-table of a great merchant this critical moralist from Scotland took part in a conversation concerning the relative merits of prepared and impromptu praying, but what impressed him about the city was its reputation (in contrast to that of Halifax where commercial caution prevailed) for rash and improvident speculation. From 1823 to 1825, when the timber trade was annually attaining new levels of prosperity, "credit was boundless. All entered into the speculation with their whole souls. Men, who in reality were not worth a dollar, had a dozen or score of vessels upon the stocks at the same time. . . . The books were open to all comers, and the lottery was full."[28] But in 1826 these same vessels lay in the docks at London and Liverpool without buyers. In their holds were cargoes of timber worth nothing. Bills drawn on British banking houses of the greatest respectability were returned dishonoured. On April 3, Black Monday, the *Courier* reported melodramatically, strong men wept, for the accumulation of years was gone. At moments such as this British exporting houses invariably commenced to press for liquidation of accounts and to suggest very strongly that the province would have to cut its imports to essentials.

Compared with the achievements of later years, shipbuilding was in an elementary state. New Brunswick-built vessels were small and cheap, being sold in the harbours of England and Ireland for five to six pounds the registered ton, a price that included cables, anchor, and rigging. Their serviceability was often estimated to be for a maximum of seven years and often they acquired bad reputations. "It is not possible for us to describe to you the prejudice that exists against a New Brunswick built ship," wrote Bainbridge and Brown. "It is impossible to sell one at any price however well built."[29] Improper certification was an occasional fault. Sometimes copper-fastened vessels were discovered to be fastened with iron and, in the affair of the *Sir William Wallace*, even so honest a merchant as John Ward had to face a lawsuit.

According to the harsh account of Nova Scotia and New Brunswick at this time, written by this visiting Scot, ignorance and shiftlessness, combined with an extraordinary spirit of individual independence, were the predominant traits among their populations. Ignorance could readily be explained by the incompetence and profligacy of the persons employed in the schools. In order to qualify for grants to schools made by the house of assembly, local authorities engaged persons to teach at the rate stipulated by the law, but with the tacit understanding that they were to take up to half of their pay in produce instead of cash. Ignorance resulted in a want of energy. Shiftlessness could be explained by the cheapness of liquor. "Why, Sir, many of our most exemplary preachers of all persuasions take their forenoon draft regularly." Though the people were victimized by the moneyed men who had command of ready cash, the price of labour was extremely high. Coal from Britain was a source of fuel cheaper than the native wood. "Labour is so expensive that we cannot compete in any foreign market."

The institutions of government, according to the same account, imparted no vigour to the life of the country. Because taxation was so low, people did not have to work hard and the resources of the country remained undeveloped. The only tax on land was the quitrent, and it was not enforced. The highest parish tax paid by the greatest of landowners for the support of the poor amounted to a pound sterling. The "great men" of the country were satisfied with the government because it was cheap. They looked upon "foreigners" with jealousy. "They deem themselves fit for all, even the highest, offices of state, and only from the cheapness of the government to themselves, and the benefit of the British army and navy to the colonies, do they submit that any of their offices in their respective states be filled by foreigners." The people were loyal and faithful subjects of the Crown only because they were exempted from taxation. They would fight against a church establishment and attempts to make them pay for it.

This picture, the chief features of which were a considerable degree of social injustice and a bucolic indifference to it on the part of the people, is that of a sturdy people who realized that they could do much better in agriculture but who found the timber trade more fascinating. Following the winter in the woods they returned to their homes for the season of ploughing and planting, and then went off to the city for two or three weeks to settle their accounts and enjoy a frolic before the hay harvest. There were long seasons of idleness and enjoyment in which people lived for the most part on credit. They were virtually all in debt to country merchants who sold goods at two or three times the prices of the city. "They must obey the mandate of their creditor." In New Brunswick and Nova Scotia the taking out of mortgages had become a most lucrative form of investment. "The mass of our people is in a state of vassalage to a moneyed aristocracy."[30] It was not want of capital, said this severe critic, that was the crying need of the country, but want of intelligence. The great problem was to prevent the population from becoming barbarized.

VIII

If the barbaric and the picturesque were to be sought, moralists might well have turned to the northern side of the province.

The Miramichi fire of 1825 had destroyed 6,000 square miles of primeval forest and the towns of Newcastle and Douglastown, and had killed 160 people. This was a most severe, though not vital, blow to the prosperous economy of the region. In 1828 Douglas, upon visiting the Miramichi, reported that in some ways the fire had brought beneficial results, that many of the people had been forced to turn to agriculture for their subsistence. In 1829 the demeanour of the population had become more pacific, so that it was considered safe to remove – at least for the winter season – the troops who had been quartered there for the previous six years.[31] The rapid growth of population of the whole north-eastern shore had been reflected by the creation, out of Northumberland, of two new counties, Gloucester and Kent. The fire had the effect of expediting the northward spread of population and in 1826 the harbour of St. Peters became the port of Bathurst. Timber operators were turning their attention to the Nepisiguit and Upsalquitch, among them Joseph and Henry Cunard, who had established business at Chatham. The appearance of this aggressive firm of brothers, extending an empire over the south bank of the Miramichi in obvious rivalry to that of Alexander Rankin on the north bank, was a vivid contradiction to the Loyalist ideal that men of birth and superior education should rule New Brunswick. According to an envious allegation made many years later, they, as barefooted boys, had sold produce in the green market at Halifax while their mother lay intoxicated in the streets.[32] At Richibucto, the chief centre of the new county of Kent, there had been the same kind of chronic troubles that had been so remarkable on the Miramichi. In 1826 Douglas was compelled to send troops there to quell "numerous riots and disturbances among the lower order of Irish emigrants and the inhabitants".[33]

The more elemental qualities of New Brunswick politics at this time came into clear relief as Gloucester commenced upon its career. When Douglas established the bench of magistrates in 1827 he accepted the guidance of Hugh Munro, a Gaspé Loyalist who had taken a leading part in trading activities along the Bay of Chaleur for many years. Munro became the county's first member of the house of assembly and, according to his traducers, its tyrant. He withheld from the people the small sum authorized by the legislature for labour on the roads and bounties on grain, declaring that they were better off without it since they would merely spend it foolishly when vessels arrived for trade, that in any case he had voted against the grain bounty and it would be indecorous for his constituents to accept it. He was champion of the old order of English-speaking merchants who had dominated the commercial life of the Bay of Chaleur, victimizing the Acadians in trade and bullying their priests. One of the more lurid examples of his tyranny, presented to the council in evidence against him, was his imprisonment of a Frenchman for an entire night without cause and the burning of his posterior with a red-hot shovel in the morning. As member of the house of assembly he controlled most of the public money spent in Gloucester and mastered the bench of magistrates, who were all, according to his enemies, drunkards and embezzlers.[34]

Munro's control was quickly overthrown when a champion of the multi-racial democracy appeared. This was William End, an educated Irish immigrant whom Douglas had appointed clerk of the peace on condition that he move his residence from Newcastle to Bathurst. Though evading this requirement, End, a loquacious and impetuous partisan of the common people, made himself a force to be reckoned with in the politics of Gloucester, corresponding directly with Douglas and members of the government, and interfering with Munro's monopoly of patronage by recommending appointments of road commissioners and minor officials. The election held late in 1830 (made the more exciting by O'Connell's triumph in achieving emancipation for Catholics in Ireland) gave him his grand opportunity. As the poll opened in Bathurst, workmen who were labouring on the new court-house heard a "lengthy and violent speech" in which Munro was called "a tyrant that had tyrannized over the French people and their religion for a long time and ruled them with a rod of iron". Mobs of French and Irish milled about, cheering and demonstrating, as End shouted: "The hour of liberty is come and the reign of tyranny is over." Promising the people all the moneys withheld from them by Munro, "parading with the cross on his colours", calling Robert Ferguson, one of the Gloucester magistrates, "a perjured old villain", End won the election by a large majority.

In January 1831, when the magistrates of Gloucester deserted their posts at quarter-sessions, End rose to the emergency by convening the court, swearing in new magistrates, and charging the Grand Jury. Charges and counter-charges, brought before the council at Fredericton, resulted in his dismissal from office

as clerk of the peace on the grounds of non-residence. Lord
Goderich at the Colonial Office abruptly reversed this ruling.
His decision was that non-residence was merely an excuse for
the dismissal of End, that he should be reinstated in his office
and ordered to move to Bathurst and apologize to the magistrates of Gloucester.[35] The tribune of the hundreds of indigent
French and Irish emerged, though somewhat tattered, as victor
in the fray. From this time on, those who presumed to any kind
of eminence in Gloucester had to learn the lesson taught by
End, that the susceptibilities of the Franco-Irish majority could
not be ignored. For many years he represented the county in
the house of assembly, acquiring the reputation of a pugnacious
eccentric, but remaining an inveterate champion of French-
speaking New Brunswickers. Unwilling to accept easy and
dangerous compromises, he opposed the practice, rapidly becoming commonplace, of exempting the Acadians from local poor
rates and permitting them to develop systems of poor relief of
their own. Such distinctions in the law, he prophesied, could be
the prelude to another Acadian expulsion.[36]

The inflow of new population, which produced so much
tumult in the north, raised problems that the provincial authorities were quite unwilling to face. Effective co-operation with
the British government in controlling the movement of immigrants from Ireland never came about. The frauds of emigration agents in the United Kingdom and unscrupulous captains
of vessels amplified the sufferings of the starving, diseased, and
destitute persons who thrust themselves on the mercy of local
charities in Saint John, St. Andrews, and the ports of the
Miramichi. "I deeply lament in common with all members of
His Majesty's Government that consequences so distressing
arising from the inhuman avarice of one party, and the ignorance and improvidence of the other should have followed,"
wrote Huskisson to Douglas after the British government repealed the safeguards of the Passenger Act in 1827.[37] The exalted
feeling engendered by economic science, that Providence would
provide for the miserable Irish if the government refrained from
interfering in the processes of nature, that the colonies would
somehow or other absorb them, forced upon New Brunswick an
unwonted flurry of governmental activity. Ports of the United
States controlled the inflow of Irish by the rigid imposition of
quotas, depending upon conditions of employment, and by
immigrant taxes that averaged about twenty-five shillings per

head. The colonies had no machinery of this kind and, since the cost of passage to British North America was considerably cheaper than to the United States, they were compelled to receive the poorest and most infirm. Immediately on landing, half the immigrants became public charges. "Very little better than the slave trade" and "a curse upon the country", said the immigration officer at St. Andrews.[38] As organized charities exhausted their funds and as slender provincial grants were rapidly expended, the question of who should pay for the uncontrolled and unwanted immigration became important. The conviction that the British government should more closely supervise the departure of emigrant vessels and meet the financial charges incurred by their reception in New Brunswick gradually settled upon the public.

As Douglas insisted time and again, the province could support a much larger population than it contained, but care was necessary in determining both the quality of people to be admitted and the number that could comfortably be accommodated at a given time. Only "agricultural people" and "hardy mechanics" could survive the New Brunswick environment. A sudden large influx of labourers would have the effect of lowering agricultural wages, and this, in turn, would expedite the flight to the forests, still a consequence to be deplored. Not only planning for the reception of immigrants was necessary, but capital assistance for the first months of settlement, the kind of aid that had tided the Loyalists over their first difficulties. The total absence of policy and of aid was apparent in the history of "The Western Range Emigrant District", a line of eighty families established on upland lots along the Shepody road from Saint John. About half quickly deserted. A portion worked their holdings occasionally, frequently journeying to the city to earn cash by casual labour. A few had stuck it out, and one man, a settler named Ryan, had been so successful, according to the report of the provincial surveyor, that he could afford a quitrent.[39]

No effective system for the reception of immigrants and their settlement on the land could be devised and financed. The legislature would not pay for a permanent office establishment. All that its leaders could promise was that persons arriving early in the spring could obtain labour on the annual programme of road construction. Douglas apportioned small sums to local immigrant societies, which in isolated cases could produce results. From the casual revenue also he was able to finance the appointment of a provincial immigration officer who, however, had but slender sums at his command. Blocks of land, cleared and ready for tillage, were not available. Immigrants shrank from the task of cutting their way through wilderness bush to isolated clearings in the forests.

The consequence was that the province lost most of the immigrants who arrived on its shores. The vast majority of the Irish had the grand ambition of going to the United States and, after earning their passage money on the wharves of Saint John, they departed. In 1828 two hundred of them, who had gone to Brazil, had been deported by the government of that country for taking part in an insurrection against the emperor, Don Pedro, and arrived completely destitute.[40] For a long time they were known about Saint John as "the Brazilians".

IX

Douglas was the only lieutenant-governor of the entire colonial period who enjoyed a wide degree of popularity in New Brunswick. This was largely based upon his performance as a partisan of provincial interests. He stubbornly opposed the final act of reciprocal agreement between Britain and the United States and the admission of American vessels to the ports of the British colonies. His resignation came because of the willingness of the British government to remove in part the preferential duties on colonial timber in British markets, largely at the behest of the Baltic interests that were struggling to regain the position they had held prior to 1808. His biographer has left a vivid description of Sir Howard confronting the colonial secretary with his pamphlet on the timber preferences in one hand and his letter of resignation in the other.[41] Though he was lost to New Brunswick, his cause triumphed when the proposed amendments to the timber duties were defeated in the House of Commons and the government fell in consequence. The news was received with great acclaim in all parts of the province. While effigies of noble lords were blazing above them, citizens of Fredericton roasted oxen in the streets and enjoyed a feast. At St. Andrews the exuberant populace, amid toasts to the majority of the "Glorious Forty-Six" by which the measure had been defeated, towed a Baltic-built vessel into the estuary of the St. Croix and there blew her up "with very pretty effect".[42]

One of the few on record who disliked Douglas described him as "a charmer", one who was too willing to make promises that were beyond his power to execute.[43] Chief Justice Saunders described him as a man of pompous elocution who liked to hear himself speak, too eager to meet the caprices of public opinion he encountered in the assembly. It is reasonable to assume that, had he remained in the province, his capacity for making himself popular would have been greatly extended and his genial temper severely strained. He had imbibed the almost religious faith of the New Brunswick populace in the efficacy of the restrictive trading practices of the old colonial system. As these were being removed by what appeared to be a faithless British government, public resentment was rapidly rising. "You should see," wrote Henry Bliss, the agent-general for the province in London, when Wellington formed an administration without Huskisson, "how the Duke gets on. A more popular administration I have never known. The Whigs rejoice as much as the Tories in the ousting of Huskisson."[44] Yet it was the ideas of Huskisson, not those of Wellington, that represented the forward thinking of the age, and British colonial policy would never return to the hallowed monopolies of the eighteenth century. The loss of trading privileges and the impending loss of others, the certain British disposition to reduce financial liabilities in the colonies, was resulting in a critical, suspicious demeanour towards the statesmen of the Mother Country that was to make the role of representative of the Crown in New Brunswick a difficult one.

William Black, the timber merchant from Saint John who temporarily succeeded Douglas in the administration, faced an increasingly irritated public opinion that was frustrated by the policies of the Colonial Office. When he submitted to the legislature the offer of Sir George Murray to commute the quitrents for an annual payment of £1,500, an angry humour prevailed in the house of assembly. Instead of commutation of quitrents, the assassination of Baillie, whose duty it was to collect them, was discussed as an alternative measure.[45] The very suggestion of quitrents, Douglas had said in an earlier dispatch, had become opprobrious, and he had advised that, if the British government wished to raise a fund for making surveys and settling immigrants, some other term should be employed.

On March 3, 1831, when John R. Partelow, a member for St. John County in the house of assembly, moved for information concerning reports that the Crown was about to surrender control over all reserves of ungranted lands in North America to colonial legislatures, in return for provincial acceptance of the costs of government and of customs salaries, a mild sensation followed. Implicit in the motion was the suggestion that New Brunswick was strong enough and wealthy enough to accept complete control over all internal affairs of government, to dispense with imperial grants for her support, and to acquire competence to direct the whole basis of her economy, the Crown lands. This mischievous intrusion upon the jurisdiction of the royal prerogative, based upon hearsay, was repudiated by Black, and his refusal to offer information was corroborated by Downing Street. But it was a signal for a new phase of provincial self-assertion that followed logically upon the course of events. If self-support was to be thrust upon New Brunswick it was reasonable that all internal revenues should come beneath legislative control.

The departure of Douglas uncovered old animosities and opened the way for full-scale party warfare. Baillie was no longer sheltered by his presence, and a coalition of almost all local interests against him was now in the making. John Murray Bliss and his connection had been mortified by the instruction of the Colonial Office that when Douglas should proceed on leave of absence no judge should succeed him in the administration. In his residence at Belmont, Bliss waited for the opportunity to even old scores with the Commissioner of Crown Lands. This was not long in coming. In September 1829 the Colonial Office drew up new regulations for the sale of lands, the chief feature being that fees for all officials concerned in the writing of patents were to be abandoned. Black was ordered to convene a meeting of council in order to make recommendations for increases in salary by way of compensation. Officers of government who held seats on the council and whose personal interests were concerned did not attend. On December 3, with a bare quorum – including Judge Bliss and the newly appointed member, Richard Simonds, who was connected to him by marriage – present, the council voted to allow Baillie a total of £1,550. Baillie protested indignantly, his principal allegation being that Bliss had used all his influence against him because his coming to New Brunswick had so greatly diminished the importance of the office of receiver-general, held by Bliss's son. Out of £1,550 he would have to pay for clerks and numerous other expenses as well. After these deductions, he declared, he would not have enough left to feed his horse. "That I am not better provided for by His Majesty's Council, I am by no means astonished. A stranger to the province, unallied to any family in it, and enjoying an office which has so much reduced the emoluments of the receiver-general – and indeed rendered that office unnecessary, is sufficient of itself to render me no object of esteem with some influential members of the Council."[46] Feelings in the official dovecote at Fredericton, especially upon the subject of British competence to deal with the affairs of the colonies, were not improved when Sir George Murray set aside the recommendation of the council and awarded Baillie a total of £2,250.[47]

Long before, even a Loyalist such as Jonathan Odell had complained that "no English minister had ever yet quite understood the true interests of the Crown in regard to colonial concerns".[48] This old feeling acquired new articulation as Baillie pressed forward the policy of sale of public land. In 1830 alone he sold, according to his own account, lands worth £60,000. To defeat him and to stultify his efforts, members of the legislature and leading timber merchants conducted a quiet campaign of persuading intending purchasers to delay, urging that a return to the system of free grants would soon be made. As the costs of government were finally, after several years of controversy, thrown upon the casual revenue in August 1830, and as Baillie's unpopular policies, apparently designed to throttle and discipline the timber trade, were beginning to have their effects, public opinion, to a greater degree than ever before, made itself felt in the politics of the colony. It was in 1831 that John Chubb, the publisher of the *Courier*, decided to send a reporter to Fredericton to give the people of Saint John their first really comprehensive accounts of the legislative debates.

There were serious imperfections in the system of colonial government, notably those flowing from the fact that the lieutenant-governor and leading public officers were not responsible to the legislature. But at this time of discontent no challenge arose to the general principles on which colonial government was based. Personalities and specific features of public administration mattered much more than ideologies. Protest was particular and not general. In the spring of 1830 an article appeared in the *British Colonist* of Saint John, signed "Hampden", constituting "a gross libel on the judges and the whole administration of justice within the province". When the government ordered a prosecution of John Hooper, the publisher, and Thomas Gardner of Fredericton, to whom authorship was traced, a strong sensation of protest developed, largely owing to the American notion that under the British constitution the method of prosecution was unfair, that there should be no prosecution until the case had been reviewed by a grand jury. Ancient law and long-established usage did not really matter, mused the newly appointed attorney-general, Charles Jeffery Peters, as he prepared the government for almost certain failure in the case. The signs of the times, not only in Europe but elsewhere, were that the multitude viewed every act of government with the greatest of jealousy.[49]

CHAPTER 10

The Struggle
for the Crown Lands

1831-1837

In the early 1830s, when the movement towards self-government in British North America began to gain momentum, New Brunswick's discontents were few. Against a background of rapid economic advancement in the previous twenty-five years, colonialism was comfortable and rewarding. Ideological or theoretical notions of an inferior status of the colonies never really intruded into practical politics in spite of the ardent legend of the American Revolution that had commenced to crowd upon the conscience of men almost everywhere. For New Brunswickers who had prospered under British rule the scandals and disorders of American politics still provided a great deal of self-satisfaction. The traditional imperial restrictions were becoming archaic, but the privileges of British subjects remained real and tangible.

The second and third generation of New Brunswickers looked with compassion and contempt upon the thousands of immigrants who descended upon them in these years, speaking in accents that appeared to be unlearned and barbaric. The fact of their distinctiveness had become manifest. British loyalties and American background had produced a breed of men conscious of their own peculiar qualities. Along with the Nova Scotians they were known as Bluenoses. Their politicians throve upon their rural prejudices, encouraging local self-assertion and parochial jealousies. Though they were exposed to wave upon wave of new-comers from the British Isles, the American environment uniformly triumphed, and in the second generation the new-comers were Bluenoses themselves. The governing classes had never been tolerant of "strangers", and this humour was generally communicated to the populace. Quick assimilation of immigrants was a rule of life. Educated strangers sometimes spoke patronizingly of "the Bluenoses", but they quickly learned that such attitudes were unprofitable.

The essential quality of New Brunswick government was that of a democracy, direct and unrefined in character, based upon an intimate relationship between the member of the house of assembly and his constituents. The general revenues of the province were indirectly raised by imposts on imported goods, but directly apportioned by the house of assembly to the constituencies. The provincial treasurer, Richard Simonds, though holding a warrant from the lieutenant-governor, was the nominee of the house of assembly and was paid by its vote. Residing at Saint John, appointing deputies at the lesser ports of entry, he handled the entire receipts and accounted for them to a committee of the house. Over the years the assembly had worked out a system by which a committee of appropriations, consisting of one member from each county, divided the estimated available sum of money among the constituencies. When this difficult labour was accomplished, the members for each constituency would meet together and apportion their assignment to the projects, jobs, and worthy individuals requiring attention. The ultimate consequence was that the appropriations list consisted of several hundred items, ranging in amount from five pounds to several hundreds: grants for the building of roads and bridges, payments to schoolmasters who were acquiring a reputation for being good canvassers at election time, awards to pensioners and worthy old soldiers who deserved compassion. In the vast majority of cases sums granted were to individuals who were designated by name on the appropriations list. The member of the house of assembly thus became a miniature prime minister or chancellor of the exchequer for his own constituency or particular section of it. He controlled the disbursement of the public moneys expended in his own region. This power was emphasized by the fact that there were no municipal incorporations to which the people could turn for local improvements. Each community had long since learned to set vital store by the quality of its representative at Fredericton and the influence he could exert upon the apportionment of the public funds.

Though payment for services performed in this way was made under the warrant of the lieutenant-governor, all of this public activity was carried out without reference to the permanent officers of government, who were not consulted on the construction of local works and were incapable of influencing the deliberations of the legislature. They were not responsible, but they held no power so far as the expenditure of the normal revenues of the province was concerned. In deference to the historic conventions of government in the American colonies, none of them held a seat in the house of assembly. In New Brunswick the eighteenth-century prejudice against "placemen" had triumphed over the British system of cabinet government, which had never really had a chance owing to the lack of responsibility of the public officers. No harmonious fusion of executive and legislative powers had come about. The consequence had been that the officers appointed from Downing Street had been elbowed out of much of the workaday routine of government. To supplant them a rival executive had been created in the house of assembly.

There was invariably the tendency to deny expenditure upon projects that were provincial and general in character and to devote the entire revenues to piecemeal developments of local improvement. The principal characteristic of irresponsible government was not strength but weakness. Occasionally and in emergencies large sums of money were voted to the lieutenant-governor, but as a general rule the members of the house of assembly were quite unwilling to entrust the revenues under their control to officials whom they had not appointed.

Somewhat impatiently, various colonial secretaries had urged the lieutenant-governor to gain for the executive officers a greater degree of influence in the life of the province by securing for them seats in the house of assembly. However desirable it was that the British system of government should be introduced, such suggestions had been steadily resisted. They ran counter to what influential New Brunswickers called their own system, which was rapidly becoming time-honoured. During the incumbency of Black, Lord Goderich finally ordered a reform that would bring the government more into line with British practice. This was a division of the council, which had always performed both legislative and executive duties, into two distinct bodies. Probably with justice, Goderich observed that its twelve members, all of whom very rarely were present, were too few for a legislative council and too many for an executive. The reform eliminated the assistant judges from both councils, made the Chief Justice the president of the legislative council, and provided for a smaller executive council of five members. Some at least of the executive, declared Goderich, should have seats in the house of assembly.[1]

The affair created a minor sensation and a subject for discontent when, after many months of speculation, the two lists of names were drawn up. Upon hearing of the impending change, two of the judges, Ward Chipman and William Botsford, whose exclusion was generally popular, immediately resigned, protesting against the propaganda made "by men who aim at being leaders of popular opinion to instil into the public mind that we hold our places in the Council for purposes of private interest".[2] Many others who resented their relegation to functions purely legislative, notably Richard Simonds, the treasurer, and William Black, who had conducted the administration for two years, were thunderstruck by the realization that upon the coming of a new lieutenant-governor they would be demoted in status. Members of the new legislative council (which was supposed to be a fair replica of the House of Lords) were not flattered. The reform stipulated that, upon the death or sudden removal of the lieutenant-governor, the succession should fall upon the senior executive councillor. When the colonial secretary was made to understand that this proposal had been the cause of intense faction, it was modified by the requirement that the succession should go to the officer commanding the troops in the province. The change did not go into effect until February 1833. In actual fact the division of the council weakened rather than strengthened the executive. It became a much more workmanlike body, but there were now two legislative houses in place of one whose members were often disposed to embarrass the government rather than support it.

Forms of government were of secondary account so long as the members of the legislature could, without interference, collect the revenues and distribute them among their constituents. Temper was generally opposed to change. There was but one conspicuous flaw in the dominant pattern of complacency. This was the mounting indignation over the administration of the Crown lands and their revenues by an irresponsible stranger.

II

Sir Archibald Campbell, Douglas's successor, was described as "a hale, spirited looking veteran who had wonderfully survived the pestilences of the country in which he had recently distinguished himself" – Burma, where he had commanded the British troops in their victorious war. He came to New Brunswick determined to sustain his record for distinguished conduct, but the power to bring about a settlement of the question of the Crown lands was not in his hands. At the moment he arrived, Baillie was in London working on the blueprints of his system, forming grand designs for the great estate of which he was the keeper. John Ward, an assemblyman from Saint John, writing to his brother, voiced the popular interpretation of affairs when he said that "the governor" did not have much power, that all the troubles concerning lands and quitrents were due to Baillie.[3]

Baillie's deputies, "the rangers", were steadily becoming more numerous and more efficient as they hovered up and down the rivers of New Brunswick to ensure that merchants should cut no more than the amounts of timber specified in their licences. Customs officials had indicated strongly that the total amount of timber cleared from the province vastly exceeded the amounts on which the tax of one shilling a ton had been paid, and Baillie was making it his business to see that every felled tree should yield its mite to the casual and territorial revenues of the Crown. At London he proposed an additional tax of threepence on the ton to pay for costs of surveys, a proposition that seemed reasonable to the Colonial Office, since the timber operators of Maine were paying at this time the equivalent of six or seven shillings on the ton. This efficiency and authoritarianism, so completely at variance with the easy-going customs of the country, appeared to be carried to extremes when the commissioner commenced to sell "water lots" in front of the properties of merchants along the Miramichi and at Bathurst. It was perfectly reasonable, he said blandly, that merchants should use the waters facing their business establishments, but if they wished to enclose those same waters by the building of wharves and booms they should pay fees to the Crown.

The power held by Baillie was sharply revealed early in 1832 when orders came from London for the abolition of the offices of receiver-general and auditor-general. This blow, falling upon

George Pigeon Bliss and Frederick Phillips Robinson, struck at
two of the most politically influential families in the province.
Baillie was no respecter of persons. Public revulsion was so great
that Campbell exerted all his influence and had the verdict
reversed.⁴ The Commissioner of Crown Lands was prepared not
merely to dispense with the support of leading Loyalist families
but to go out of his way to antagonize them. He exacted payment for eight town lots in Fredericton, adjacent to the river
and formerly used as a common, from parties who had never
made good the commitments of the grants, one of whom was
Chief Justice Saunders.⁵

The avowed scorn of the commissioner for the small operator
was the most ominous factor facing the timber trade. Native
capitalists who could finance large operations were few, and
Baillie looked beyond New Brunswick for the means by which
the natural resources of the province could be rapidly developed.
Characteristic of his large ideas was the granting of extensive
reserves on the north-west Miramichi and the Big Nipisiguit to
Joseph Cunard of Chatham, who agreed in return to clear
obstacles from the beds of the rivers, to construct sluices around
the falls, and to deepen the harbour at Bathurst. The policy
would create a few extensive monopolies and compel the small
entrepreneurs to serve their holders. When Alexander Rankin,
the only other northern capitalist who could rival Cunard, protested this allocation of over 500 square miles of the best
timberland in the province, Baillie offered him equally extensive
reserves on the Restigouche.⁶

As the timber trade continued to enjoy brisk demand and
high prices, Baillie's grand idea for the sale of all the Crown
lands seemed likely to enjoy a degree of success that could be
disastrous for the smaller merchants of the province. Rumours
came of a combination of New England investors whose aim
was to gain control of all the remaining great reserves of timber
in New Brunswick and Maine. An able young lawyer of Saint
John, Moses H. Perley, whose movements were mysterious and
whose ideas appeared to coincide with those of the commissioner, made frequent assertions of the necessity of foreign
capital. Campbell, though willing like a good soldier to carry
out the ideas of the British government, was honestly fearful
for the prospects of the settler of the soil as opposed to those of
"the mere timber merchant". Soon, he lamented, the province
would become nothing more than a timber mart in the hands of

a few monopolists.[7] Public opinion continued to manifest itself solidly against the policy of sale. The law officers obstructed by raising doubts as to whether the Crown could alienate its domain on the instruction of a secretary of state. The Church of England clergy, deprived of the stipends originating from the grants of the British Parliament and suffering hardships to such an extent that some of the missionaries were selling their books, had been led to look to the public domain for renewed support. They vehemently protested the policy of sale.[8]

Baillie's personal efforts and his powerful connections with the Colonial Office in London were responsible for the greatest single stroke that advanced his policy. Taking advantage of the high degree of speculative activity in London financial circles on the purchase of colonial lands, he was the main instrument in the organization of the New Brunswick and Nova Scotia Land Company, whose first meeting was held in the Crown and Anchor Tavern in the Strand on March 2, 1831. It was attended by seven members of Parliament; John Labouchere, brother to Henry Labouchere, an under-secretary for the colonies; John Bainbridge, always the leading spirit in the work of the British North American Merchants' Association; and the Honourable Samuel Cunard. The company at once commenced to negotiate with the Colonial Office concerning the purchase of lands in New Brunswick, the main object of bargaining being the price per acre, which was set by Goderich at three shillings and sixpence. Before leaving London in the spring of 1832, Baillie had brought negotiations to a head by concentrating attention on the acquirement of 350,000 acres in the county of York, the lands of the portage between the St. John and the Miramichi, north of a line bounding the parish of Queensbury. The company had difficulty in completing its capital and there was, in the Colonial Office, a suspicion and dislike of the purposes and methods of land companies. Goderich refused to lower the price per acre, but in 1833 a new colonial secretary, the Right Honourable Edward Stanley, was more accommodating. A sale of half a million acres at an average price of two shillings and threepence was completed. The company at once launched a formidable propaganda campaign in Britain, the purposes being, according to the prospectors, the saving of valuable emigrants to the British Empire, the increase of British trade, and the relief of the starving paupers of the British Isles. For over two years, while political pressure upon the management of the

Crown lands was rising, the news from London concerning the new company Baillie was forming intensified the deep mistrust and fears that already prevailed.

Concentration upon the northern part of York County coincided with other activities. In contemplating the dangers on the boundary, Sir Archibald Campbell had scanned the map with the tactical appreciation of a soldier and had decided that the St. John River from Fredericton to Grand Falls, a distance of 120 miles, offered an unsatisfactory avenue for the passage of reinforcements to the threatened areas. He wanted something "where wheels would go" and had decided that a road must be constructed in a straight line through the bush. Receiving permission from the Colonial Office to devote a surplus of the casual revenues to the purpose, he inaugurated "the Royal Road", making use of the labour of Irish immigrants who landed at Saint John in the spring of 1832 and who were brought in barges to the head of the Nashwaak for the commencement of the enterprise. It was incidental, but generally realized in London, that the construction of such a road would vastly increase the value of the lands the new company was about to settle. "The Royal Road" had a military purpose, but it gave stimulus to those who supported Baillie in his venture to bring outside capital into New Brunswick.

III

After a few months in the province Campbell could see the dangers that were approaching. He found the people of New Brunswick enthusiastically loyal to their government, but in the house of assembly there was a party "tinged with speculative opinions", determined to destroy its balance and to concentrate power in their own hands.[9] From the north came protests of irate lumbermen who held indignation meetings at Bathurst and Newcastle, and who petitioned against the reserves given to Cunard, which were described as "a most serious and most grievous evil".[10] Hugh Munro, still endeavouring to eject End from the clerkship of the peace, holding both Lord Goderich and Sir Archibald "constitutionally defective", and left deserted, as he said, "like a turtle on a dry bough", supplied vivid descriptions of the "worse than Siberian tyranny" imposed by Baillie on the once prosperous county of Gloucester. Oppressed lumbermen, screaming and yelling, poor emigrants bartering for locations, widows and orphans bringing up the rear, sup-

plicated "this demagogue", "this wonderful meddler", this
adventurer, who had come to New Brunswick for support.[11]

The legislative session of 1832 was comparatively tranquil,
but, burdened with a sense of impending calamity, the house of
assembly made a polite proposal to take over the management
of the Crown lands, agreeing to guarantee in return the payment
of the salaries of the permanent officers of government and the
other items on the civil list of the province. They employed no
constitutional arguments, resorting to the much more practical
premises that under Baillie the Crown lands were being mis-
managed, that the expenses of collecting the revenues were
ruinously high, and that there were serious irregularities in the
methods by which Baillie's deputies exacted charges from the
lumbermen with whom they had dealings. Rather to his sorrow
Campbell confessed that there appeared to be truth in the
allegations, although he could find no specific fault with the
commissioner himself. During Baillie's absence in England complaints against the Crown Lands Office had become sharper.
Newspapers ran accounts of how, under the management of
Baillie's deputy, John A. Beckwith, clerks in the office had
speculated in forest lands and made large sums of money. This
was, in all probability, Baillie's Achilles' heel. In urging on his
"harpies" to a strict enforcement of the regulations he had failed
to restrain their other impetuosities. No powerful public opinion,
said Campbell, had yet asserted itself, but it might "burst forth
when least expected at the instigation of a few demagogues".[12]

In the spring of 1832 William Lyon Mackenzie left York
(Toronto) for London with petitions containing 25,000 signatures. Reform was in the wind, not only in the colonies but in
the Mother Country as well. As Baillie returned from London
with his land company well launched, the future boded nothing
but trouble. In one way or another he had antagonized everybody of consequence in the province; and everybody not of
consequence was presently to be given cause for affront. Midsummer Day 1832 marked the time when all grantees of land
would become liable for the payment of quitrents, and Campbell
was setting up a commission to collect them, giving the
attorney-general power to prosecute and threaten escheat for
non-payment. Baillie had given convincing proof of more than
boasts to implement the New South Wales scheme. As the instrument of the imperial system for the making over of the
province he was riding high and hard. The Fredericton accounts,

that he displayed his great wealth by riding in a coach with
outriders, that he attempted to clothe the personnel of his office
in uniforms with brass buttons, may be of some value as
evidence of his contempt for the more casual, less affected ways
of the New World. By a reputable device of the New World as
well as of the Old he found one ally. Shortly after the death of
his wife he married the daughter of William Franklin Odell, the
provincial secretary. His father-in-law was to share his fleeting
triumphs and persistent embarrassments.

Late in 1832 it became clear that a spirited political conflict
lay ahead. Campbell was now writing of "ill-intentioned demagogues" who had converted the apathy of the people into anger.
Scholarly articles in the Saint John press declared that the
ancient forest laws of England had been conceived in a spirit of
despotism. The most effective attacks upon the intentions of
the government came from "John Gape", the pen-name of
Robert Gowan, a Scot who had come to Fredericton twenty
years before as a piper with the 74th Regiment.[18] Gape's offer-
ings were of the plain politics of the woods – witty, homespun
accounts of the delays and confusions attending those who did
business with the Crown Lands Office, of the financial extortions
and unspeakable arrogance of Baillie's rangers. The *Courier*,
which published Gape's pieces, became the organ for a popular
feeling that was rapidly crystallizing into a political party with
a clear objective. The quitrents were the immediate cause for
public anger, though at a halfpenny per acre they would amount
to a mere £2,500 per annum for the entire province. But the
objective of those prepared to take advantage of it was the
winning of control over the Crown lands for the legislature.

"The eyes of the whole province were on the House," said one
member when the legislature opened its sessions in January
1833. It was the Speaker who was prepared to take command
and fuse a host of incoherent objections and indignations into
an organized movement. Charles Simonds was a skilful manipu-
lator of opinion, capable of inflammatory utterances but adept
in the advocacy of moderation and restraint once he had succeeded in moving opinion in the desired direction. A member
of the Church of England who incurred criticism because of his
willingness to preside over Methodist meetings, he possessed a
fair talent for keeping to the centre of the predominant political
current. Though attempting to break Baillie's monopoly over
the Crown lands, he was strenuously contending to preserve

the monopoly of the Bank of New Brunswick, of which he was president, asserting that a second bank would mean ruination for the province. He had two great qualifications for the leadership of a popular cause – a programme of action and a deadly hatred of Baillie. The speakership was an office of real authority in the house of assembly. Through the New England succession it inherited something of the traditions of Lenthall as the mouthpiece of the Commons in their struggle against arbitrary power. In setting himself forward as a popular tribune Simonds had acquired the mantle of his elder brother, Richard, the provincial treasurer, who was in poor health. Baillie was declaring that the office of the treasurer should be moved to Fredericton, that his presence at Saint John among his mercantile cronies enabled him to dispose of governmental warrants for payment at discounts greatly to their advantage.

While the province was in full cry against the quitrents, Simonds led off the attack under conditions that were highly favourable. The aged Chief Justice Saunders was asserting that the methods by which they were collected were illegal. Attorney-General Peters declared his powerlessness to prosecute the delinquents unless he were given the benefits of an act of the legislature, a point of view he supported from precedents of the administration of quitrents in the old colony of New York. Many tracts of land had changed hands so many times that it was impossible to assess the present holders without fresh legal security. Simonds said he would be ashamed to return to his constituents if the house of assembly should join in giving the quitrents commission such an act. "A pernicious influence on both sides of the water", he declared, was obstructing the endeavours of the house. At this stage the rhetoric of revolt was coming a little more readily. Letters signed "Remember the Stamp Act" appeared in the *Courier*, and Simonds, late in the session, said that His Majesty's Government had lost the thirteen colonies owing to measures that were "not more odious" than the decision to impose quitrents.[14]

To give fresh feeling to a session more tempestuous than any in thirty years, Campbell published the commissions of the members of the new executive and legislative councils. At the top of the list of executive councillors came the name of Thomas Baillie. Ridicule as well as abuse descended on his head. An unfriendly Nova Scotian opinion was that a fourth-rate clerk of the Colonial Office had become the right-hand man of the lieutenant-governor of New Brunswick, that the Mother Country was sending its scullions to take the highest offices in the colonies.[15] The Crown Lands Office "was a very different place from what it formerly was. The applicant had to pass down a long range of gratings, locks, doors etc. which made the place look more like a menagerie for wild animals than anything else. The various boxes or inclosures appeared to be all inhabited but whether they were domestic animals or not, or whether they were a collection of apes or baboons he could not say." When the applicant was finally able to say he wanted a timber licence, he was asked if he had any money. If he replied in the affirmative the order was, "Fork it out, then." He forked out, but could not get his licence until he had visited the Crown Lands Office for many days on end.[16] How, asked the *Observer* editorially, could a junior member of the legislative council be raised to the exalted station of senior executive councillor with the right of succession to the government when so many old and tried friends of the province had been omitted from the list? To keep tempers from becoming completely tattered, Gowan offered in the columns of the *Courier* a play in three acts entitled *The Triumph of Intrigue*. The theme was the attempt of two unscrupulous domestics, Wily Oh'Deil and Tammy Baillie, to seize control of "the estate" from the worthy and unsuspecting Scottish squire who was renowned for his skill in hunting alligators in the Far East. The literary piece was avowedly discovered "in the papers of an old friend" and, since it resembled proceedings "in a small village not one hundred miles away", it was presented to the publisher with the respectful wish that he should print it.[17]

Charles Simonds followed the now notorious Upper Canadian procedure of establishing a committee on grievances and taking evidence from those who had suffered at the hands of the government. "The state of the province" became the subject of close scrutiny, but virtually all the testimony was directed against the Commissioner of Crown Lands and his deputies. Curiously enough, the only supporter Baillie had in the house of assembly was William End, the Irishman from Gloucester, who sorely tried Simonds's temper. End's enemies in his constituency, the lumber merchants who had allegedly exploited his French and Irish supporters, were all in the opposite camp. Presumably this offered sufficient inducement for End to battle the entire house. Gloucester, where new and radical ideas had gained the ascendancy, provided the only champion for the royal prerogative.

Seven of the eight resolutions introduced by Simonds on March 8, following the report of the committee on grievances, concerned the Crown lands and quitrents. The fifth resolution protested the reform of the council, but even here it was Baillie who offered the principal provocation. The eighth proposed the sending of a delegation from the house of assembly to London in order to acquaint the Colonial Office with the willingness of the legislature to take over the administration of the Crown lands. Prince Edward Island had just been given good reason to suppose that its legislature would attain control of all local revenues in return for an obligation to pay the charges on the civil list. An agitation for the same purpose was being conducted in Nova Scotia. Canadian precedents offered encouragement. In May the delegation, consisting of Charles Simonds and Edward Barron Chandler, sailed for London. Chandler was a young lawyer of Westmorland whose fame as a pleader transcended the boundaries of the province. In Cumberland County, Nova Scotia, his services had been in demand to just as great an extent as in Westmorland, where, in a small, square, wooden shanty standing on the edge of a much-frequented half-acre at Dorchester Corners, he performed many of his labours.

The departure of the delegation was speeded by the intentions of Baillie, who at once made it known that he would go to London to oppose its purposes. "Poor Tommy", as he had been called in the legislature, had been given no opportunity to defend himself against the evidence that had been submitted to the committee on grievances and had no medium through which he could submit his views to the public of the province. A vociferous Irishman named James Frederick Luddy, who had come to Saint John to represent the New Brunswick and Nova Scotia Land Company, gave him advice for "arresting the opinions of the Democrats" that he might have been well disposed to accept. This was to establish a newspaper and to secure the election to the house of assembly of persons friendly to his point of view. "The late and famous French Revolution should give lessons."[18] Acting on behalf of Baillie, Luddy attempted to acquire the *British Colonist*, but found John Hooper, the publisher, difficult concerning terms. Then, as a new correspondent of the *Courier* writing under a *nom de plume*, he answered the allegations of Gape, seeking to take advantage of the unpopularity of Simonds, who had been successful in his efforts to defeat the incorporation of the proposed Commercial Bank of New Brunswick. "Next week I will give Charles Simonds a cleaving he little expects. I will scalp the vagabond without mercy." He wished to buy 4,000 acres of land on Lake Oromocto but not to pay cash down. One or two hundred fine fellows from Ireland settled there would make York County solid for Baillie after the land company should bring its expected flood of immigrants to Stanley, the new settlement that was being formed near the head of the Nashwaak. Baillie would not take Luddy's advice. "As you think it best to leave Gape alone I put down my pen,"[19] was Luddy's response.

In all of the proceedings of these exciting months of 1833 there was an undercurrent of strong feeling between those who had recently arrived in the country and the descendants of the Loyalists. In the house of assembly William End protested against the voluminous tributes paid to the Loyalists and their work in building up New Brunswick in this year, the fiftieth anniversary of their arrival. The English, Scots, and Irish who had arrived within the last twenty years had performed great labours too. When the secretary of the St. Patrick's Society of Saint John called at the office of the *Colonist* to insert an advertisement for the annual dinner, Hooper asked what toasts would be given. Among others was the health of Thomas Baillie. "What? Mr. Baillie's health?" asked Hooper. "Certainly," was the reply, "we shall drink his health to vex the Blue Noses."[20]

IV

The Right Honourable Edward Stanley, who received the delegation, possessed an open mind towards its purposes. The granting of its principal request, the surrender of the Crown lands, would be in accordance with the prevailing temper of the British government and Parliament upon the affairs of the colonies. As he admitted to Campbell in a confidential dispatch, he was well disposed to meet the principal demand of the delegation, but "for reasons which it is unnecessary that I should enumerate, I do not consider that such a course should be advisable at present".[21] One reason was the peculiar claims of Baillie on the British government dating from the day in 1824 when he had generously, on the pleas of Lord Bathurst, abandoned his claim to the consulship in Tunis. The whole pattern of affairs in New Brunswick would have been infinitely simpler if Baillie could have been induced to go elsewhere. But Baillie refused the offer of the office of deputy postmaster-general in Jamaica. The salary was lower and life insurance would cost double.[22] The fact that he could resist the importunities of the Secretary of State to depart, as well as oppose the lowering anger of the New Brunswick community, may be taken as new evidence of his obstinacy. The British government, as well as the leading politicians of the province, would have to deal with him for many years to come.

Yet in detail the delegation made great gains. Before they landed in England one concession had already been made. In accordance with an address from the house of assembly of Nova Scotia, Stanley had decided to suspend the collection of quit-rents in that province. It could not be continued in New Bruns-wick without making "an unfair distinction".[23] After two years, in which provincial feeling against the British government had been rising steadily, £649 had been added to the casual revenues from the imposition. Having put the policy into effect against a powerful and vindictive public opinion, Campbell felt injured and abandoned, but Stanley assured him that the measure was merely a suspension, that the British government would press both provinces for acts of their legislatures commuting all quitrents to the payment of fixed annual sums. Collection would be resumed, he declared, should the legislatures fail to take the appropriate steps.[24] Yet at the same time Campbell was author-ized to listen to any reasonable offer for the surrender of the ungranted lands of the province.

In the office of Stanley the delegation encountered some sharp retorts. The colonial secretary refused to believe that lumber-men were overtaxed or that Baillie's extra threepence was "ruinous". He could see no objection to the sale of mill-sites provided that they were offered in fair competition and for limited periods. He would not listen to the protests against the division of the old council, a policy of Goderich which he him-self would rigidly pursue. But on other questions he gave sympa-thetic answers and took measures in accordance with them. He asked Campbell to introduce to the legislature a law that would protect the rights of property-holders to low-water mark, ensur-ing at the same time the common right to navigation of streams.[25] He was satisfied that too much discretion had been given to Baillie and his deputies in penalizing lumbermen for infringement of forest regulations and that the Crown Lands

Office had been guilty of carelessness in its description of timber berths assigned to operators. He ordered that the sums realized from the sale of town lots in Fredericton should be devoted to improvements within the town itself. Since Joseph Cunard had failed to fulfil his obligations in taking out his vast reserves he would have to abandon them.[26]

On the last and greatest point, the control of the Crown lands, the bargaining dealt in pounds, shillings, and pence. The delegation strenuously endeavoured to pare down the total amount of fixed charges of government to be assumed by the legislature in return for control over the great estate of fourteen million acres. Eagerly Simonds and Chandler pressed for economies, assuring the secretary that the house of assembly could manage the Crown lands with much greater ease to the public purse than had the irresponsible commissioner. The greatest economy of all, of course, could be effected by a reduction of Baillie's salary. This expedient, as well as others that would bear heavily against the lieutenant-governor and the permanent officers of government, Stanley indignantly rejected.

By September 1833, after Baillie had refused the offer of a transfer, Stanley made up his mind concerning the details of the bargain he would offer to the legislature of New Brunswick. In return for the surrender of the Crown lands, the revenues arising from them, and the complete power of collecting quit-rents, he agreed to accept the guarantee of a permanent civil list of governmental expenses amounting to £14,000. This would defray the salaries of the lieutenant-governor, the judges, and the permanent officers appointed from London, the maintenance of the indoor establishment of the Crown Lands Office, the £1,000 per annum granted to King's College, and other charges of a trifling nature. Any surplus of the amount, he agreed, would be disposed of for provincial purposes.

The house of assembly of 1834 was impressed by the offer and debated it with vigour. Agreeing to accept it in principle, Chandler broke with Simonds, the two members of the delegation being bitterly divided on the question. When it became known that Stanley's offer of surrender of the revenues did not comprehend the purchase money of the Stanley tract, an amount that would reach £70,000, the weight of opinion turned against acceptance. Better, mused the *Courier,* to ask for equality with His Majesty's newly liberated black subjects in the West Indies. Stanley's decision on this most important detail was blamed on Baillie. To the leading members of the assembly, acceptance would mean no victory so long as Baillie remained within the province with his high salary guaranteed by a permanent law. Campbell interpreted the refusal as new evidence of the determination of a mischievous faction to maintain public excitement. The doctrine now "hardily maintained" was that "these revenues belong to the people and His Majesty can no otherwise exercise control over them than as the Steward of the people".[27] Amid the excitement, Campbell resisted suggestions to dissolve the house, having little faith that an election would produce a better one.

In disgust the house discharged its committee on the casual revenues and asked Stanley for a reconsideration of terms. To show their temper the majority threw out sections of the permanent law governing the militia, cutting the three-day annual training period to one. Militia training without arms, rigorously maintained on the statute-books for many years, had come to lose its meaning. The young men of the country had learned to regard it as the occasion for frolics and fairs, a communal gathering for the purposes of recreation and amusement.

V

Over the next three years it was commonplace to remark that the house of assembly had made a great error in rejecting Stanley's offer of 1833. The timber trade continued to boom and the price of land continued to rise. Baillie continued to enjoy his last years of arbitrary power, devising new measures for the grading of standing timber, systematically raising the price of land, watching the revenues grow as speculative fever attained new heights in 1835 and 1836. Timber cruisers were now making their way into the disputed territory in spite of the agreement of the British and American governments to protect its resources against exploitation. The search for the bigger trees was so intense that in 1837 the Saint John Chamber of Commerce, faced with a great surfeit of shipping space owing to the failure of the cotton crop in the United States, urged the cutting of timber in the disputed territory in order to sustain the price of freight. On the higher reaches of the Restigouche, where the trade was now thrusting its tentacles more deeply, great difficulties arose owing to the cunning of the operators, who invariably informed Baillie's deputies that timber coming down the river had been cut on the Quebec side. Merchants of

Gaspé, irked by what they alleged to be gross neglect by the government of Quebec on their side of the river, pressed for the annexation of their district to New Brunswick.[28]

Hoping for better things from the legislature and taking advantage of the comparative quiet that reigned at the end of 1834, Campbell dissolved the house of assembly. The election produced but one new factor of note, the oratory of Lemuel Allen Wilmot, who won a seat in York. A correspondent of the *Courier* who followed the sheriff and candidate to the different parts of the county where a poll was held was quite aware of the impact the young lawyer was making. He would be serious, then amusing, and then become serious again. Concerning Charles Fisher, another young lawyer from York who was unsuccessful, it was observed that although he would probably fail in his attempt to win a seat he would undoubtedly add to the volume of his legal practice. Though it appeared possible that a formidable temperance movement might distract public attention from the constitutional issues that were at stake, the results produced no change. The popular party headed by Simonds, unquestionably the recognized leader, was just as strong as before.

The session of 1835 had occasions for new displays of temper. Stanley, hoping to force a decision of the assembly to commute the quitrents, had ordered that collection should be resumed.[29] The sensibilities of the entire legal profession had been confounded by the appointment of a young Englishman, James Carter, aged twenty-four, to an assistant judgeship. So strong a protest had been made by the New Brunswick bar that the British government made the downright promise that never again should a provincial appointment of this kind be filled from England. The Methodists, aware of considerable currents of opinion working in their favour in the British Isles, were pressing for an act that would enable their ministers to solemnize marriage. After a debate of two days the house of assembly defeated by a vote of 21 to 9 a proposal to commute the quitrents for a fixed sum. The Militia Act was still further emasculated, and Campbell endured the mortification of sending home a British officer, Lieutenant-Colonel Turner, who had arrived as inspector-general of the militia, because there was no money to pay him.

Statesmanship suddenly vanished as the grievances against the British government became secondary and the legislature lost its sense of direction in a constitutional struggle of the old style. The members of the recently commissioned legislative council expected to be paid for their services. The house of assembly, following the argument that since the legislative council had been appointed by the Crown their pay should come from the Crown, refused to make provision for it. When the legislative council in reprisal refused to pass the bill providing for the daily pay of the assemblymen, the lower house attached clauses providing for their own remuneration to the general appropriations list. This, too, was thrown out by the upper house. A return to the conditions of 1794-8 had come about. It appeared certain that in 1835 the province would be deprived of its programme for the construction of roads, bridges, and other works of local utility. The legislature prorogued without performing its essential task. Again Simonds and Chandler had quarrelled, the former arguing that the house of assembly had the sole and exclusive right to dispose of public moneys.

Legislative indulgences had gone too far. Petitions came to Campbell from almost every county, urging him to recall the members to Fredericton. Somewhat chastened by their receptions at home from their rural constituents, who placed great reliance upon the disbursement of cash originating from the annual programme of construction, the members returned on June 15 and voted supplies. Not only did the general appropriations pass, but also a bill providing for the commutation of the quitrents. For an annual payment of £1,000 a year into the casual revenues, the Crown passed over the management of the quitrents to the legislature. The few hundreds of pounds that had been collected during the two brief periods in which payment had been enforced were returned to the payers. The division in the house was 24 to 4, an abrupt reversal that reflected the impatience of landowners with the problem. Bonfires and public illuminations marked the evening of the day when the new arrangement came into effect, when New Brunswick disposed of the quitrents at a cheap price. The weight of imperial land policy had, in these years, generated an alert public opinion throughout the province. In an intimate way Sir Archibald Campbell experienced a form of reprisal. While travelling through Westmorland in August 1835 he was arrested, charged with breaking the law against travelling on Sunday, and fined £6 by a justice "without coat and neckcloth". "His Excellency as might be expected was in a towering passion."[30]

While political discontent was general, the province enjoyed a degree of prosperity far beyond anything anticipated. Not only did the general revenues from provincial duties rise sharply in 1835, but the sales of Crown lands were going ahead phenomenally, reflecting the willingness of outside interests to take advantage of the opportunities Baillie was offering. From January to September total sales amounted to £153,739. Admittedly there was a strong speculative element behind this remarkable increase. Whether all purchasers would eventually complete their payments was dubious, but Campbell was now writing of the possibility that at no distant period the sale of land would provide so great a sum that the interest on it would pay for the whole cost of civil government.[31]

The Tobique Mills, or Red Rapids Company, offers a good example of the kind of thing that was happening. According to letters from its leading promoter, E. H. Lombard, its capital had originally been American but had become British and Frederictonian. Under the laws of the British Parliament foreigners could not become holders of landed property, and the only method of bringing American capital into the country was to associate British and American subjects together in corporations. Lombard managed the purchase of 100,000 acres on the Tobique and paid the first instalment, but late in 1836 when the great succession of bank failures in the United States dried up all sources of capital, both real and fictitious, the company could not continue payments and the land reverted to the Crown. Acting on behalf of other American interests, Moses H. Perley experienced the same tribulations. He had applied for the purchase of 80,000 acres on the Chiputneticook lakes at the high price of ten shillings an acre demanded by Baillie. But he discovered that there were only 40,000 acres in the tract described and that the high price was not justified by the condition of the timber. He asked that the £500 initial payment he had made be placed to his credit on another contract he had made, for the purchase of 30,000 acres at Musquash, and that the Chiputneticook sale be cancelled. The executive council was not disposed to deal lightly with American capital. The £500 was declared forfeit and Perley was given a fortnight to make good his first payments on the Musquash deal.[32]

According to the St. Andrews *Standard* there was "a wild and pernicious excitement" in Charlotte County as loyal British subjects took part in the scramble to become "middlemen between the Crown and the Alien". Rumours flew that merely by getting "a talismanic ticket" at the Crown Lands Office one individual had made $30,000, another $20,000. Whatever need there may have been for foreign capital, there was strong opposition to the introduction of alien traders and speculators. A speaker in the house of assembly declared that if the safeguard of the British Act of Parliament was removed so many foreigners would invade New Brunswick that they would take away the living of the British settlers.[33]

VI

In the spring of 1835 a new colonial secretary, Lord Glenelg, had taken office. Conciliatory in temper and mild in demeanour, representative of the liberalism that was reforming the life of the British Isles, a pillar of the Church Missionary Society, he possessed a degree of impracticality that was later to prove fatal to his career when he attempted to unravel problems in South Africa. Eager to restore amity to British North America, he was prepared to go a long way to remove grievances.

The appointment of the Gosford Commission to review the complaints of the reformers of Lower Canada brought the affairs of all the colonies under the closer scrutiny of the imperial authorities. In New Brunswick, because of the intense concentration of complaints on the management of the Crown lands, Glenelg, highly sensitive to criticism, immediately proceeded to clip the wings of Baillie by imposing restraints upon him. Baillie's regulations might be wise and his efficiency in raising revenue commendable, but was it wise, considering the degree of excitement in New Brunswick, to give fresh stimulus to existing discontent? Baillie's record was remarkable, but should he be compelled to rely on "his own unassisted judgement" in fixing the price of land rather than on the principle of public auction in force in the other North American provinces? In May the Commissioner of Crown Lands was subjected to the guidance of a committee of the executive council.[34] Curtly Glenelg resisted Baillie's presentation of private claims for financial rewards for special services.

Confidently Campbell faced the legislature as it met in the midst of a relative calm when sanguine expectations for the future prevailed. The St. Andrews and Quebec Railway Company, formed of capitalists of both New Brunswick and Britain, was preparing to connect the British provinces of the interior with the ambitious little seaport that would become in the winter season, it was widely anticipated, the point from which the produce of the Canadas and much of the United States would move to overseas markets. But local faction suddenly flared up. On January 21 William Henry Robinson, a retired officer of the imperial service whom Baillie had challenged for evasion of the regulations governing land grants to retired soldiers, challenged the commissioner with "palpable falsehood" in reporting the circumstances to Lord Glenelg. On Baillie's retort of "falsehood" Robinson sent a messenger to demand "a hostile meeting". Rather than settle the matter, which had been raised on the floor of the legislative council, by sword or pistol, Baillie referred it to Campbell, who in turn passed it on to a committee of the executive council. Owing to the numerous family connections of the two parties on this body, Robinson refused this recourse, losing both satisfaction for the insult and £300 profit he had made on the sale of his land.[35] A second sensation was more general and fundamental. George Pigeon Bliss, the receiver-general, had died with his accounts short by over £7,000. When the Crown proposed to remove the deficiency by seizure of his assets, including real estate, his numerous relatives in the house of assembly, including Simonds, Hugh Johnston, and Lemuel Allen Wilmot, at once alleged that Baillie had not actually paid into the accounts sums which the documents declared to have been paid, that the commissioner had cheated Bliss and his unfortunate widow. Characteristically, Baillie could show no receipts, but there were records of banking transactions that adequately protected him. So loyal to Bliss's widow were his relatives that they were prepared to stand upon the original commission granted to Bliss in 1824, entitling him to retain ten per cent of all sums received by him. Its terms, written under the Sign Manual, had never been contradicted by equal or superior authority, but merely by the letter of a secretary of state to Sir Howard Douglas.

Sharpened by vendettas of this kind, discussion upon public affairs soon reached a point impelling action. News from Lower Canada gave the spur to those who could profit from political discontent. When it became clear that the Crown did not propose to give the custody of waste lands to the legislature of the province, Simonds recommenced the procedures of 1833. Very recently the timber trade had been driven to fresh extremities. Not only had the price of berths risen, but merchants had been

compelled to extend the duration of their licences, in some cases
from one year to five. Baillie, said a petition from Saint John,
had boundless influence owing to "the retired habits of Sir
Archibald Campbell" and his relationship with Odell, the secretary. It was "not dignified or politic for the greatest monarch
in the world to drive a hard bargain with his poor subjects who
had embarked their all in the timber Trade."[36] A new flood of
resolutions directed against the Crown Lands Office went to
London from the house of assembly. This time the object was
to gain control of the public domain without quibbling about
price. Again it was decided to send a delegation, under auspices
infinitely more favourable than in 1833, to interview the colonial
secretary.

Unanimity was not notable as in 1833, the vote in favour of a
delegation being 20 to 9, with Edward Barron Chandler in the
minority. Timid voices asked whether or not New Brunswick
should join in the Canadian game of harassing the Mother
Country. Others questioned the financial aspect of the proposal
to take over the Crown lands. What would become of the casual
revenues if the British government should admit Baltic timber
to its markets on the same terms as British North American
timber? Upon the management of the Crown lands the *Courier*
had adopted a position more neutralist, and an able journalist,
John A. Pierce, was regularly arousing the ire of that rising
young tribune of the people, Lemuel Allen Wilmot. The Church
of England was again solicitous for special consideration in the
granting of land before the Crown should abandon its control.
On March 7, the day of the appointment of the delegation,
William End addressed Simonds: "You are akin to Papineau in
politics, you are too much imbued with his principles and sentiments, and you are the last man in this House I would vote for
as a delegate."[37] Stormy scenes followed this outburst, and the
assembly finally selected two of its members whose careers had
been less notable for opposition to the constituted authorities.
William Crane was a merchant of Sackville whose wealth and
commercial acumen were proverbial in Westmorland, influential
enough to be associated with Samuel Cunard in the great plan
for a regular steamship service across the Atlantic. Wilmot, still
under thirty, had already given proof of his capacity "to thrill
and enchain legislatures" in speeches of four and five hours, a
natural talent that had been given great play in the devout Methodist circle of Fredericton centred in the home of Duncan Blair.

As the delegation sailed for England and while the province awaited the results of its labours, King's College became the centre of public contention. Anonymous letter-writers in the *Courier* called it a blot on the honour of the province, "a job" by which professors, too complacent and too independent by reason of their high salaries, extracted an easy living from the labours of the common people, failing to give the practical education that the province required. Their incapacity to keep discipline was well attested by the tippling of the students and "the indelicate allusions" scribbled on the walls of the college building, still young in years but notable for dishonour and immorality. Partisans of the college and of the Church of England hotly denied these charges, alleging that the attack was a part of the propaganda plan by which the Presbyterians hoped to achieve an official church establishment in New Brunswick.

VII

Glenelg received the delegation in a series of meetings late in August and early in September, happy to give the assembly "the satisfaction which they desire". Upon the great issue in principle he was willing to make complete surrender though he would not agree to break faith with the commitments of his predecessors and consent to a reduction in Baillie's salary. But the effect of the surrender would be to reduce Baillie from the policy-making level to a simple instrument of the executive council who would be guided in their course by the enactments of the legislature. There was little if any niggling about the price. Glenelg held to Stanley's figure of three years earlier, £14,000 per annum for the maintenance of the civil list. But on this occasion the colonial secretary was willing to hand over to the control of the legislature all the sums that should accrue from the Stanley purchase by the New Brunswick and Nova Scotia Land Company. Though the British government was determined to protect the interests of its appointees in New Brunswick, Glenelg was willing to promise that the salaries of their successors should, under some circumstances, be reduced, thus ensuring a gradual reduction from the £14,000 stipulated as the cost of salaries and services considered indispensable.

Upon issues still wider Crane and Wilmot intruded with results almost equally satisfactory. Urging that Campbell's small executive council did not possess "the confidence of the country", they asked that it be enlarged to include members whose views would be satisfactory to the house of assembly. The address of the preceding spring had echoed the sentiments of Goderich that members of the government should have seats in the popular body, and the delegation, taking New Brunswick's first hesitating steps towards the achievement of responsible government, pressed for the much-desired fusion of executive and legislative powers. Glenelg made no pledges but he made it clear in his undertakings to Crane and Wilmot, as well as in his dispatches to Campbell, that he wanted the executive enlarged and its membership changed so that harmony could be achieved.

This generous welcome to the New Brunswick delegation was an overture preliminary to the settlement of all the discontents of British North America. The conciliation of New Brunswick was to serve as a harbinger of the pacification of the Canadas and Nova Scotia. Glenelg commanded Campbell to give publicity to his dispatches of August 31 and September 5, which made it apparent that New Brunswick was to be the clearing-house for the ideas by which Glenelg hoped to restrain the reformers of all British North America. By September 10 a note of panic crept into his dispatches as he ordered Campbell to speed the legislative process by which the Crown lands were to be handed over to legislative control. "Considerations applying not only to New Brunswick but also to the other British North American provinces require that no time should be lost in giving general publicity to the proposals you are authorized to make." No "needless reserve" was to obstruct the lieutenant-governor in the exercise of his duty of giving implementation to the wishes of the secretary. The failure of Lord Gosford's mission in Lower Canada had become apparent. Papineau and his patriots were about to abandon constitutional measures. Owing to the impulsive policies and amazing electoral victory of Sir Francis Bond Head in Upper Canada, the Colonial Office had lost a great deal of initiative and Glenelg was determined to regain it.

Publicly Campbell professed to be pleased with the generosity of the Crown towards its subjects in New Brunswick, but there can be no doubt that privately he was scandalized by the degree to which the proposed reform would place power in the hands of the leaders of the popular party, whom he genuinely regarded as men of evil. What he was hoping for was a change of government in Britain that would remove Glenelg from the Colonial Office. In order to avert the distasteful course of events that

seemed imminent he was prepared to create delays, trusting that
upon the removal from power of the British Liberals, the influence of George Baillie and Frederick Elliott at the Colonial
Office would turn the tables on the house of assembly.[38] Obediently he called the legislature for December 20 but at once
commenced to raise doubts upon the meaning of the details of
his instructions. How should the legislature appropriate and
expend its vastly increased revenues – by the methods of the
House of Commons or by those so long in force in New Brunswick? The Colonial Office, he pleaded, had ignored the unfortunate position of thousands of poor squatters whose titles
should be made secure before the Crown lands should pass to
the legislature. A last-minute rush took place to secure the
Church of England in the possession of lands that had long
been reserved to it but never granted.

Boldly Campbell faced the legislature, presenting to it copies
of his dispatches to Glenelg, and at once it became certain that
the session would accomplish nothing. He made the announcement that he would not sign the Civil List bill unless a clause
were added reserving the operation of the act for the King's
pleasure, and this the house of assembly would not do. Though
Glenelg had most succinctly demanded haste in the passing of
the bill, Campbell professed failure to comprehend the haste of
the assembly. The harsh words spoken in the legislature and
the resolutions passed became intolerable to the old warrior and
he decided upon action. He would resign unless Glenelg would
fulfil certain conditions. Misadventure occurred, and his private
dispatch of January 6 was first read by Glenelg in a Halifax
newspaper. Inadvertently he had proclaimed to the world his
wholehearted opposition to imperial policy. Prompted by George
Frederick Street, the solicitor-general, one of the few scions of
the leading Loyalist families who opposed reform, he sought
new and legalistic objections to the passage of the Civil List
bill. As the protracted struggle became more futile, the assembly grew desperate and questioned his "unworthy motives".
The tension was broken on February 4 when it was learned
that Street had suddenly and half-secretly taken ship for England. Quickly the assembly drew up an address to the King
declaring that Campbell and his council had "completely forfeited the confidence of the country" and that the lieutenant-
governor had disobeyed the royal command.

Crane and Wilmot were again dispatched to London, to forestall what was justly anticipated as an attempt to wreck the arrangements they had made during the preceding autumn. The young orator had become a principal in a minor conflict developing out of the controversy over the Civil List bill. A considerable segment of opinion had taken some alarm at the degree of control over property rights given to the legislature by the bill's fifth section, particularly with respect to the lands set aside for public schools and churches. On the floor of the assembly Wilmot accused John A. Pierce, now the editor of the Miramichi *Gleaner*, of organizing petitions to bring forward this cautious point of view. In his newspaper Pierce denied the allegations Wilmot had made, pointedly referring to "the usual effrontery and disregard for truth" of the member for York. This disdain for the privileges of Parliament offended the Cromwellian sense of majesty of the New Brunswick house of assembly. The sergeant-at-arms arrested Pierce and brought him to the bar of the house where he was accused of "gross and scandalous libel".[39] He was committed to the common jail of York County during pleasure.

Campbell had successfully delayed the course of events for six months. In the winter of 1836-7, when so many troubles had been brewing in the Canadas, he had defeated Glenelg's attempt to present New Brunswick to the other colonies as a shining example of what imperial moderation and generosity could accomplish. But the decision could not be reversed. Street was courteously received and his highly technical objections to the Civil List bill noted. Yet when Wilmot and Crane arrived in London a few days later, in hot pursuit of Street, they found there was no cause for alarm. The resignation of Campbell, whose removal was their principal object, had been accepted. Sir John Harvey had been promoted from the lieutenant-governorship of Prince Edward Island and had been ordered to Fredericton with all speed to summon the legislature and give assent to the contentious bill. A few details were uncertain but it was now perfectly clear that the great business of imperial surrender of the Crown lands and provincial acceptance of the civil list charges would rapidly be consummated.

Campbell left with colours flying. "The conscientious rectitude of my own conduct renders the subject of this address to me a matter of the most perfect indifference," he had told the house of assembly. "The merits of a service of nearly half a century in almost every quarter of the globe cannot, I trust, be

tarnished by such a set of men who compose the House of
Assembly of New Brunswick." One of his last acts was the
donation of a large sum from his private purse to the sufferers
of the great fire that had destroyed many of the great mercantile houses of Saint John, a conflagration that witnessed the
depravities of humankind as well as the terrors of nature, as
large numbers of looters from across the harbour carried off
everything their boats would hold.[40] Campbell regarded himself
as the victim of the Colonial Office's craven policy of surrender
of the powers and perquisites of the royal prerogative in North
America. Sir Francis Bond Head, another victim of a few months
later, considered that Glenelg's dispatches to Campbell, of which
he was provided copies for information on the scope and objectives of imperial aims, were the first intimation of the possibility
that his work in Upper Canada would be stultified.[41]

The haste with which Glenelg pushed through the surrender
of the Crown lands deprived the British government of a more
statesmanlike approach to the problem of launching a colony
upon what was virtually a new constitution. New Brunswick
had accepted the complete burden of supporting her own internal government. In return she had been granted complete
control over all her internal revenues. Under the control of the
legislature came all the ungranted lands of the province, the
revenues arising from the sale of timber on those lands, and
over £170,000 in cash assets accumulated by Baillie during his
years of arbitrary management.

Campbell and the party of resistance had urged that the
British government should insist upon safeguards in the appropriation and expenditure of the vastly increased revenue about
to fall into the hands of the house of assembly. The highly
democratic and equally inefficient methods of disposing of public money, so long in vogue in the legislature, would now be
extended to the casual revenues and would become a new source
of spoil to the committees of the house of assembly. As Street
had said in an able critique, there was no chancellor of the
exchequer to bring down an estimate, no assurance that the new
revenues would be devoted to worthy programmes of provincial
development.[42] Glenelg groped at the possibility of imposing the
cabinet system of government on New Brunswick, of insisting
on executive initiation of all money grants. Yet he bowed before
the elaborate explanations of Crane and Wilmot that the existing system of appropriating public funds was highly satisfac-

tory. "It would be the disturbance of a custom to which the people of New Brunswick are familiarized and attached."[43]

During 1837, the year in which virtually all aspirations were realized, Glenelg acquired the reputation and the affection of a fairy godfather in New Brunswick. Gratefully the legislature agreed to purchase a full-length portrait in oils of the colonial secretary, dressed in the uniform in which the young and admiring Mr. Wilmot had seen him at Court. Yet by failing to bargain a little more sharply with the New Brunswick delegation, Glenelg evaded the essential issue in the problems of the North American colonies, that of the lack of responsibility of the executive officers. How to harmonize the functions of officials appointed from Downing Street with those of a legislature nearly omnipotent in its own sphere of action would require ten years of patient improvisation before a solution could be worked out.

CHAPTER 11

The Age of Harmony:
Sir John Harvey's Administration

1837-1841

Arriving in New Brunswick in the early summer of 1837 under highly propitious circumstances, Sir John Harvey was a lieutenant-governor admirably adapted to the ruling impulses of the time. He was the chosen instrument of a popular policy and had been sent to the province for the express purpose of completing the surrender of the Crown lands. He was an appointee of the Liberal government of Great Britain, able to identify the aspirations of the colonial reformers with those of the English Whigs. On Prince Edward Island, where he had ruled for a few months, he had championed the cause of the tenants against the landlords. His political opinions were those of the new era of democratic reform that had come to Britain and was about to be extended to British North America.

"A large, handsome man, but by far the most vulgar would-be-gentleman you ever beheld, extremely dressy withal, and my lord always remembered my asking 'Who was the gentleman with the embroidered stomach'," wrote Mr. Creevey, who had seen Sir John at a levee in Dublin prior to his departure for North America.[1] The new lieutenant-governor was a man who left definite impressions behind him. Years later that most talented of New Brunswick editors, Thomas Hill, wrote of Harvey's times as an age of boisterous mirth and lavish expenditure, when amusements had been Balls, Billiards, and Brandy, when it had been fashionable to feast, revel, and swear, and when fractious spirits had been placated at the shrine of Bacchus. His era had been the Age of Harmony.[2] Sir John honestly believed he could reduce all dissident elements to silence, that a patriot governor, by pursuing popular and enlightened policies, could close the ranks of the community behind him, that New Brunswick could become a shining example of loyalty and concord in the discordant setting of British North America. He was the hero of Stoney Creek, where he had been largely responsible for the capture of two American generals; and he found at Fredericton old comrades of the War of 1812 who rejoiced in his coming.

No lieutenant-governor more certain of his line of duty ever came to a province. As Sir Colin Campbell wrote from Halifax, the job was "cut and ready" for him.[3] Wilmot was on his way home from London, bearing the palm of final victory for the legislature in the struggle for the Crown lands. Crane, certain of the quick passage of the Civil List bill, had lingered behind to contemplate the wonders of steam navigation and railways. When he was tossed from an overturned railway coach, suffering concussion and a broken arm, the compassion of Glenelg, who seems genuinely to have admired these representatives of New Brunswick democracy, arranged superior accommodation for him in a London nursing home. Prepared to act quickly, Harvey, on his way to Fredericton, established a friendship with Simonds at Saint John that was to last through his administration. He did not hesitate to call the legislature for July 6, overcoming the "constitutional" scruples of Odell and Baillie, "owing to the state of public excitement".[4]

This summer session that saw the passing of the Civil List bill with its attendant legislation opened a new dispensation in the constitutional development of New Brunswick. Holders of office were given security for their tenure and their salaries. The appointment of their successors, however, and the fixing of remunerations would be subject to the scrutiny of the legislature and the British government. Refusing to consider a breach of trust with its appointees in the province, Whitehall had secured a guarantee for their immunity against future persecution in return for a surrender of the Crown lands. For the years ahead, however, Glenelg would accept reductions in the charges of the Civil List. On the more immediate and fundamental matter in dispute the legislature pressed its victory to the full. Baillie's policy of selling land in large blocks to capitalists was abandoned. Land could now be sold only in 100-acre lots for the purposes of genuine settlement. What the timber trade had always wanted, the throwing open of the whole Crown domain on terms of cheap annual leases, had been won. Reform had triumphed. Simonds, reflecting the disposition of the majority in the legislature, declared on several occasions in his later career that the Civil List Act was all the reform the province would ever need. The only irritation was that Baillie remained, his salary irreducible by the Civil List Act. His power, however, had been completely destroyed and he had become a simple instrument for legislative policy.

Towards the establishment of a responsible executive council on the British pattern New Brunswick at this stage achieved remarkable progress, placing it far ahead of the other British North American provinces. Crane and Wilmot had carried to London the popular demand for the enlarging and democratizing of the council of five created by Campbell in 1833. Glenelg insisted on smallness but unhesitatingly gave his support to democratization. Taking advantage of the complete discomfiture of the Odell-Baillie clique, which had dominated during the previous régime, Harvey made it known that he wanted a council that enjoyed the confidence of the legislature. Odell offered his resignation but, since his local knowledge was considered indispensable, it was refused. Baillie's name was removed from the list. George Frederick Street, who created a minor sensation during the late summer by alleging that the Civil List Act was now invalid owing to the death of William IV, that the Crown could alienate its domain only for a lifetime, found that his resignation, submitted on legal objections, was quickly accepted.[5] Harvey liberalized the council by calling to it Simonds, "Master Radical turned Governor's Master", as the *Chronicle* called him; Hugh Johnston, Simonds's nephew and sturdy supporter in the house of assembly; and George Shore, an old acquaintance of Harvey's from 1813 and a member of the legislative council. With the exception of Odell, all members of the executive council were now members of the party that had struggled for control of the Crown lands. Sir Archibald Campbell, hearing from the seclusion of his home in Scotland of these New Brunswick changes, wrote of the "bad and wicked" councillors who had assumed power.[6] Durham, on the other hand, considering the nature of the change at Quebec in the next year, declared that "the constitutional principle had been, in fact, fully carried into effect in this province; the Government had been taken out of the hands of those who could not attain the consent of a majority in the Assembly, and placed in the hands of those who possessed its confidence".[7]

II

The Governor General, in placing this optimistic interpretation on the late changes in New Brunswick, failed to perceive the complications in the assortment of constitutional ideas that were now in vogue. The victorious politicians in the legislature were not disposed to jeopardize the very direct control they had acquired over a vast new source of revenue by adopting British constitutional practice in its purity. They would not surrender the initiative in money grants to a responsible executive. They adhered to what they called their own rights, the privileges derived from the assemblies of the thirteen lost colonies of determining how public money should be spent without the benefit of executive direction. They believed in "the responsible principle", that the executive council should enjoy their confidence. But they would not sacrifice to any executive, responsible or not, the important discretion of allocating public funds to their constituencies. A responsible executive council after the British pattern was "foreign to the views of the assembly".[8]

Still the historic American prejudice against "placemen" was cherished. As soon as Simonds and Johnston were appointed to the executive council, fears for the independence of the house of assembly were expressed and demands that they resign their seats were heard. But expediency triumphed. When, following the death of William IV, a new house of assembly was elected in the autumn of 1837, the only candidate for the speakership was Simonds. Under colonial practice this office was of much greater consequence than that of executive councillor, really carrying a capacity to supervise the workaday routine of executive government. By his election the popular tribune was translated to a new eminence of practical power. Purist objections from Wilmot, who hoped at this stage to see the adoption of British practice, were brushed aside.

In spite of the fact that the executive council possessed the confidence of the assembly, Harvey discovered that he could not initiate any expenditure of public money. The vastly enlarged revenue was at the disposal of committees of the house of assembly. "The consequence is that the Bye Roads grants are looked upon throughout the country as the members' pocket and popularity money."[9] By this time the system was so deep-

rooted that storekeepers would extend labourers credit on the
mere prospect that a road or a bridge would be forthcoming.
If a member of the house of assembly failed to deliver the
expected commission, financial distress was the lot of the disappointed supervisor and those who depended on him.

In the work of securing legislative grants for local areas some
members were more influential than others, but contemporary
opinions were firm in appreciation of the most influential of all,
"the perpetual chairman" of the appropriations committee, "the
Chancellor of the Exchequer", the man who took no part in the
initial wrangles but whose word was final in the eventual compromises. This was the member for St. John County, John R.
Partelow, "a silent member, a deep thinker, having wonderful
tact and a thorough knowledge of human nature, . . . he would
frame an amendment suitable to all parties; . . . the commonest
as well as the greatest ever found in John R. a hearty greet-
ing."[10] Partelow was chairman not only of the appropriations
committee but of the audit committee as well. Beyond the seat
he held in the house of assembly he had no official position, but
so far as the expenditure of public money was concerned – the
sinews of political power – his word was of greater consequence
than anyone else's in the province.

To consolidate their authority in the constituencies it was to
the interest of members of the house of assembly to disperse
the revenues throughout the country in this piecemeal fashion
without benefit of skilled financial, engineering, or technical
advice of any kind. Provincial projects such as Abraham
Gesner's geological survey, the construction of a lunatic asylum,
or a normal school for teachers, received only token financial
support or no support at all. Legislators were entirely indisposed to tolerate the establishment at Fredericton of centralized
control over public services.

The surrender of the Crown lands to legislative control placed
the permanent officers of government, appointed from London,
in a position of complete impotence. Harvey, dependent now
on the pleasure of the legislature, shared their weakness. Untrammelled by executive guidance, the frontier democracy of
the province now ruled. Revelling in the lush prospects that had
arisen from the surrender of the Crown lands, the representatives of the constituencies did not propose to allow the refinements of cabinet government to interfere with their liberties.

Suddenly the total sum of money available for disposal by

the legislature had almost doubled. Continued prosperity, halted very briefly by the failure of American banks in the summer of 1837, assured altogether new levels of public expenditure. In 1836 the revenues available were £83,049. In 1840 they were over £202,000, of which the casual revenues of the Crown lands accounted for £87,000. The British government turned over to the legislature, in four annual instalments, £153,700 accumulated by Baillie during his years of irresponsible power. Under such happy circumstances the harmony Sir John Harvey sought so earnestly seemed a reasonable goal.

III

A happy-go-lucky quality pervaded the politics of New Brunswick as the Canadas experienced their rebellions. Sir John, the prisoner of the popular party, had no choice but to join with the legislature in the uncontrolled expenditure of the large sums that were at hand. For a man of his sanguine disposition this presented no crisis of conscience, and for many months after his arrival the province presented the unusual spectacle of unanimity and concord. Upon the news of an impending rebellion in Lower Canada, the legislature made £10,000 available for the raising of troops. The militia offered their services almost to a man. New Brunswick, mused the New York *Express*, was still Tory, prepared to move "almost in mass against the French of Lower Canada. . . . Their loyalty burns as bright as ever. We highly respect it though of course we feel no sympathy with it."[11] In the winter, as the 43rd Regiment made its way in sixty degrees of frost over the now-famous Témiscouata portage (by this time something more than a mere blazed trail through the woods for mail-carriers from Quebec), the defence posts in the province were manned by volunteers. On a night in February 1838, after English newspapers reporting the speeches of the notorious radicals, Molesworth and Hume, had reached Saint John, these two were burnt in effigy on King Square by a boisterous crowd. They had declared in the House of Commons that only the presence of a large military force in the provinces of Nova Scotia and New Brunswick prevented the outbreak of rebellious disaffection – this at a time when not a soldier of the Queen stood on New Brunswick soil.[12] From the Acadians of Westmorland came a petition protesting their loyalty. In the early spring, when word arrived that Sir Francis Bond Head would return to England

by way of Saint John, a great concourse of citizens assembled
in Anthony Truro's news-room to make arrangements for a
congratulatory dinner in his honour.[13]

Some said that responsible government had already come,
and the good humour that, for the most part, prevailed in the
legislature was nourished by the ample funds available. The
era of Sir John Harvey began with an overflowing treasury,
with public money on loan to the banks, and large reserves,
including the final payments of the New Brunswick and Nova
Scotia Land Company, awaiting delivery to the colony. When
it was over, revenues were inadequate for the services authorized by the legislature, government warrants were being dis-
counted at high rates, and the inescapable necessity of going
into deep and permanent debt loomed forth. While the prosperity lasted, it was generally shared. Members of both houses
of the legislature executed government contracts. Patronage for
their supporters was thrown to the four winds. Pay was authorized for the legislative council, who thereby, in the opinion of
the reactionary, sacrificed their independence. In the veiled
opinion of the *Chronicle* – the journal that had appeared in
1836 too late to turn public opinion to the support of its sponsors, Odell and Baillie – everybody had been bought, even Sir
John Harvey. "The Governor may butter the House and the
House may butter the Governor back again, but depend upon it
the country pays directly for the sauce and pays directly
through the nose."[14]

The lieutenant-governor's personal credit was at a low ebb, a
fact that seems to have been appreciated in the house of assembly. He came to New Brunswick with a background of
long-standing debt and with a large and expensive family still
on his hands. By the Civil List promulgated in 1837 his salary
had been reduced by £500. In these piping times the legislature
cheerfully made good the deficiency. Between 1837 and 1840
over £9,000 was expended on Government House, and it was
alleged that, through the management of the contractor, James
Taylor, a member of the house of assembly, Sir John profited
handsomely. In 1840 a motion by Partelow to pay drawbacks
on the duties on wines consumed in Government House, so
generously thrown open for the entertainment of members of
the legislature, was withdrawn, but only after it received considerable adverse publicity. Even the sponsors of "the system",
declared the *Chronicle*, considered that this was going too far.

Like Sydenham in Canada, Harvey bound himself to the party that possessed the majority in the legislature, the party that was united not only by a determination to sustain the settlement of 1837 but by an extensive family connection centring on the late receiver-general, George Pigeon Bliss, whose affairs were the subject of high controversy throughout the régime. As the Crown sought to recover £7,000 allegedly in default, political acrimony sharpened. After a jury in York County, contrary to the direction of the presiding judge, refused to agree that the Bliss estate was in default, members of the legislature, moved by the plight of the widow and eleven orphans, united to pass an act relieving the estate from further demands that might be made upon it. Leading in the movement were Lemuel Allen Wilmot, first cousin to Bliss; Hugh Johnston, chief executor of the estate and brother-in-law to the deceased; and Simonds, Johnston's uncle by marriage. The democratizing process of 1837 had produced a family compact not in office but in the legislature, a compact more all-engrossing and more cohesive than the Odell-Baillie group that had been displaced from power. It was very extraordinary, remarked William End, the Irishman from Gloucester who had supported Odell and Baillie from his seat in the assembly, that such things should be done. He wondered if the Commissioner of Crown Lands would have fared so well in a similar scrape.

Unlike Sydenham, Harvey had nothing to offer New Brunswick that could give the representative of the Crown an opportunity to master the factions in the legislature and to give leadership to the province. To Canada the British government dispensed both its bounty and its wisdom. A loan of three-quarters of a million pounds was provided for the construction and improvement of western canals, but only on condition that the ministers of the Crown should initiate money bills in the legislature. The province of United Canada came into existence endowed with a salient feature of the British parliamentary system of government, assuring the executive of powers of inaugurating policies that could benefit the entire country and of keeping close control over public expenditures.

The Atlantic provinces received no bounty and were under no compulsion to accept imperial wisdom. Private members of the houses of assembly continued to initiate money grants. Each legislator was, in a measure, a minister of finance and a clerk of works, careless of the needs of his province but relentlessly jealous for the wants of his constituency. This was "the abominable system" of which Sydenham complained shortly after his arrival in Halifax in the summer of 1840, a system that determined the political habits and morals of the people of the country, one that was honoured by hoary tradition from the colonial past.

IV

To a man of Harvey's enlightened views opposition seemed anomalous, especially at a time when, in his own words, it was vain to search for grievances in New Brunswick. Yet the cup of harmony was never really full. From the wreck of the cabal that had been defeated in 1837 there remained a rump of opposition that was to cause him many anxious moments and whose existence, in his bland and assuring dispatches to the Secretary of State, he could not conceal. The few leading holders of permanent offices made no secret of their hostility. On the day he first opened the legislature they failed to show the customary courtesies of attending him in state. The *Chronicle* of Saint John, whose critical and insulting attacks on Harvey's "system" constituted a major irritation, showed that, though they revered the principles by which the old régime had been governed, they had the capacity to learn the new democratic tricks of prejudicing public opinion. They were Odell and Baillie, Charles Jeffery Peters, the attorney-general, and George Frederick Street, the solicitor-general, probably at this time the ablest of the lot. They had used all their resources to avert the defeat of the old régime, but they continued to fight following the defeat.

From the outset Harvey refused to trust them and chafed against their presence in his counsels. "They prefer the exercise of secret, uncontrolled, irresponsible power. . . . Give the Governor the absolute nomination of the principal officers of the Government as well as of his Council. . . . This is a humid note, My Lord, but the subject has long occupied my mind."[15] Such complaints addressed to Durham produced, in Harvey's mind at any rate, important results. According to the *Chronicle*, Sir John, in his more convivial moments at Government House, told his friends that he was the real author of the famous dispatch of Lord John Russell that shortly followed.[16] This communication, which carried British North America a long way towards responsible government, entitled the lieutenant-governor to make appointments to public offices on a political basis or "during pleasure". No longer were appointments to be made for "life" or on "good behaviour". It completely demolished the conception of a public office, so notable in New Brunswick in the past, as a piece of property or a vested interest. It shattered a principal rampart of the so-called privileged orders of society. No longer would ambitious young New Brunswickers, seeking promotion in the Queen's service, look to London. The injunction affected only future appointments. Existing office-holders remained secure in their places, for the British government was not disposed to break faith with individuals whom it had appointed on a permanent basis; but Harvey was authorized to open negotiations with them for their retirement on pensions.

Because the New Brunswick legislature had always been and would continue to be unwilling to retire office-holders on pensions, there was no immediate prospect of a complete change in the slate of officials. Only death or voluntary retirement without pension would remove those who held commissions under the Sign Manual, now a vanishing breed of men. Nevertheless, Harvey made an attempt to intimidate them into compliance with his policies by circulating a memorandum in which he informed them of the terms of Lord John Russell's dispatch and offered to make amicable arrangements concerning retirement. By those who dared to write or speak of it openly, the circular memorandum was regarded as "a bullying ukase". It was swallowed, alleged the *Chronicle*, "in a spirit of meekness", and harmony had been achieved at the price of the independence of the legislative council, twelve of whose sixteen members were office-holders.[17]

Old enmities swelled the discord between Harvey and "the official party", as the Odell-Baillie group was now called. Baillie continued to be the principal target for the legislative majority, and, in spite of the guarantee given to his security by the Civil List Act, Simonds and Johnston attempted to persuade the lieutenant-governor to bring about a reduction in his salary. Faced with the necessity of pleasing his chief supporters on the one side and of honouring a solemn compact on the other, Harvey was in a difficult position. He escaped from the quandary when, late in 1839, those who hoped for the complete humiliation of the former dictator of the Crown lands were overjoyed to hear of his impending bankruptcy. Improvidently he had hazarded all his property – and his credit as well – on an enterprise for the promotion of the peat-moss industry. The business failed, and everything Baillie possessed, including the property of his wife and children, was gone. Suddenly he had become a public defaulter and, subject to the payment of a retirement allowance, he resigned. How large the allowance should be and how much of it should be paid to his creditors became a perplexing problem that was lengthily reviewed. Fortuitously the vendetta of the leading families of the province against this interloper, this man of bold designs and boundless ambitions, appeared to have ended.[18]

Embarrassed by the disgrace of his son-in-law, Odell was further discomfited by the behaviour of his son, William Hunter, the third of the New Brunswick line. On a summer day in 1840 the young man "did violently and unnecessarily ride against" two soldiers of the garrison as they were walking down the middle of the main street of Fredericton, the familiar method of getting about. When one of them seized his bridle he dismounted and knocked him down. A friend came from a nearby house and knocked the other one down. When they rose the act was repeated, the soldiers being tipsy and unable properly to defend themselves.[19] All of this brought forth a military court of inquiry and the necessary apologies; nor was the affair relieved by an insolent letter addressed by the young man to the lieutenant-governor. Shortly after this event a gang of Fredericton rowdies attacked a group of Harvey's guests as they were returning from Government House. Fredericton, he wrote bitterly, was the headquarters of "the official party", and their influence upon the generality of the people, owing to their large private possessions, was very great.

Simonds and Johnston ruled the counsels of Sir John, but "the official party" fought back with determination, if not always with caution. On February 28, 1840, the *Chronicle* published a letter signed by "W.", which carried the personal attack upon the lieutenant-governor to unprecedented lengths. It was alleged that he had used the dispatch of Lord John Russell to force the resignation of Baillie and that he was about to fill the office of Commissioner of Crown Lands by appointing his son-in-law and aide-de-camp, Captain Tryon. The letter further alleged that Harvey and Baillie had made a bargain in order to facilitate the appointment of Tryon and that Harvey planned to place two of his sons in New Brunswick offices.

Rather against his own judgment, but prompted by the indignation of his supporters, Harvey permitted an action for libel to be instituted against the publishers of the *Chronicle*. Lemuel Allen Wilmot, undaunted by the unpopularity he had acquired from his prosecution of Pierce of the Miramichi *Gleaner* in 1837, was willing to break another lance against the freedom of the press. "That inflated bladder of wind", as the *Chronicle* gleefully called him, had been publicly horsewhipped in the streets of Fredericton in consequence of his earlier adventure,[20] but he was willing to attempt to even old scores with the Saint John publishers who had been satirizing him for four years. Rubbing salt into the wounds, the *Chronicle* continued to argue throughout the year that the libel action was really an act of revenge for the persistent exposure of the large sums of public money awarded to Wilmot and Partelow in the way of commissions and expenses, that when informed that a conviction could not be obtained they had replied: "The d—d parties would be at a great expense to defend themselves."[21] After a summer of tension in which public sympathy for the *Chronicle* steadily mounted, the case came to trial on October 27. To the surprise and consternation of Harvey and his supporters, the verdict was "not guilty". In giving an account of the affair to the Colonial Office, Harvey suggested that the court had prejudiced the jury in favour of the defendant. The official and Tory faction, he declared, had delivered its attack not against him but against his supporters, the object being to separate the lieutenant-governor from his friends in the legislature. The jury had been dismissed at six o'clock in the evening before its verdict was rendered, and until nine in the morning the jurors "were living in public houses in town".[22]

Harmony may have been achieved, but it was difficult to sustain. If the lieutenant-governor was to hold any discretion of his own in public affairs there was the permanent necessity of remaining popular. Sir John discovered that not all the people of New Brunswick would accept the happy unanimity of thought and feeling he so desired.

V

It was not the domestic issues of New Brunswick politics, however, involved though they were rapidly becoming, that brought about Harvey's downfall. It was his part in the Maine boundary dispute, slowly working its way towards the finale, that led to the chastened withdrawal of 1841. While Great Britain and the United States negotiated upon a plan for settlement, the gov-

ernment of Maine, ever since the rejection of the award of the
King of the Netherlands in 1832, had determinedly moved to
establish conditions that would be favourable to its cause when
the final settlement should come. Late in 1831 Sir Archibald
Campbell had led a small armed force up the St. John to defeat
Maine's attempt to establish a township form of government in
the Madawaska settlements. Maine's alertness brought to a
halt the ambitious programme to move the St. Andrews and
Quebec Railway through the disputed territory. The rapid increase of population in both Maine and New Brunswick, and
the acute rivalry in the search for stands of pine timber, brought
the quarrel to a head in Harvey's time.

Pegging away at the uncertain frontier in order to establish
claims based upon actual jurisdiction, the government of Maine
in the summer of 1837 sent an agent, Ebenezer Greeley, to take
a census in Madawaska. Twice he was arrested by the New
Brunswick authorities and twice released, but the third attempt
resulted in his conveyance to the jail at Fredericton. Tempers
in Maine rose until it seemed that the state was prepared to
send troops into the disputed theatre, in complete defiance of
the conciliatory attitude of the government at Washington,
which seemed prepared at this time to ignore the phraseology
of the treaty of 1783 and settle the whole problem by the drawing of a conventional line. Whigs and Democrats, in fear that
one would outdo the other, contended in appeals to patriotism.
Faced with the menace from over the border, Harvey maintained his reputation for belligerence. Very soon after his arrival
in New Brunswick, he wrote to Downing Street that the time
had come to force the United States to a settlement and that
Britain should seize the territory awarded to her by the King
of the Netherlands. The New Brunswick militia was alerted
and armed. Two companies of the 43rd Regiment were sent to
Woodstock and Grand Falls. Harvey responded vigorously to
outspoken New Brunswick opinion, declaring that all available
force should be expended to ward off the American threat.

The reputation of Stoney Creek had lost no lustre, but the
pugnacious name could be a liability as well as an asset. At a
time when a war with the United States might develop on any
one of several counts, such an alert commander, one so preoccupied with the purely local situation, might create a disastrous loss of control. Sir Colin Campbell at Halifax, who was
charged with the defence of the Atlantic provinces, was opposed

to Harvey's determination to defend New Brunswick soil at all
costs and resented the dispersal of troops that was necessary to
garrison the far-flung Madawaska area. It was no part of imperial strategy to fight the war in a wilderness. It was rather to
be fought at sea against American coastal centres, especially
New York. Harvey stubbornly protested that the whole St.
John Valley should be defended. Woodstock, even though it
was on the right bank of the river, should be garrisoned. With
provincial troops alone, he declared, he could carry on indepen-
dently of Sir Colin, and he did not need advice. The dispute
was referred by the Colonial Office to military referees in Whitehall, who decided in favour of Campbell.[23]

Harvey's defiance of the lieutenant-governor of Nova Scotia
reflected the traditional dislike for any kind of subordination to
Halifax – political, military, or ecclesiastical. In defending the
integrity of New Brunswick he could draw unfavourable comparisons between "the distinguished officer" on his left and "the
gallant and distinguished officer" on his right, Sir John Col-
bourne, who in the emergency had sent troops from Canada to
Témiscouata.[24]

Yet the stern soldier had a softer nature that was receptive
to blandishments from both sides of the border. Practical men
professed to believe that questions of national sovereignty were
really immaterial, that the disposal of the disputed territory
was unimportant so long as the timber it stocked should be
floated out by way of the St. John, and that if the politicians
of Maine and New Brunswick could meet across the table a
settlement acceptable to both parties could readily be arranged.
Timber interests of both countries were already looting the territory, and Sir John seems to have been converted to the point
of view they represented by the good offices of Sir John Cald-
well, the former receiver-general of Lower Canada who was
operating a large sawmill at Grand Falls and who had considerable business connections with the Americans. Late in 1838 his
dispatches began to assume a more moderate tone. The people
of New Brunswick, he declared, could not develop their own
resources and needed the co-operation of "our spirited neighbours". The Americans already in the province were, owing to
the lightness of their taxes, he argued, the most loyal of subjects.
He abandoned his belligerent suggestions of the year before and
advocated a boundary settlement based chiefly on the securing
of the Témiscouata portage and the Madawaska settlements

and on permission to the Americans to navigate the river. The
government of Maine, he professed to believe, would be willing
to alienate sufficient territory to permit the running of the railway from St. Andrews to Quebec in return for a pecuniary
consideration.[25]

Harvey's olive branches scarcely seemed appropriate as, in
the early winter of 1839, Maine marched to war. British timber
cruisers had moved further up the Aroostook. The presence of
about fifty lumberers with their teams of horses and oxen
was taken to mean that Maine was about to lose her stake in
this section of the disputed territory. Rufus McIntyre, Maine's
land agent, occupied a cell in the now-notorious jail at Fredericton. James A. MacLachlan, the British warden of the disputed
territory, was likewise taken prisoner and, to the indignation
of the Maine press, was confined in Bangor's finest hotel. The
big issue that loomed up was the trade of Fredericton versus
that of Bangor. The "Aroostook War" commenced as Governor
Fairfield called out 10,000 militia and the Maine legislature
voted $800,000. The regulars of the American army, stationed
in the fort at Houlton, did not move, but all Maine rejoiced in
the pomp and circumstance of glorious war, their militiamen
practising musketry on effigies of Queen Victoria:

> We'll lick the redcoats anyhow,
> And drive them from our border;
> The loggers are awake – and all
> Await the Gin'ral's order;
> Britannia shall not rule the Maine,
> Nor shall she rule the water;
> They've sung that song full long enough,
> Much longer than they oughter.

Harvey marched all the regular troops he could spare to the
Aroostook and called out the militia. The Woodstock *Times*
had no doubt concerning the eventual outcome of the Aroostook
War:

> March, march, march in good order,
> Kennebec has got over the border,
> With Penobscot too,
> And all of the curst crew,
> In that highly favored land of disorder.

March, march, march in good order,
To meet Kennebec over the border,
With the bayonet and cheer,
We'll make them stand clear,
And soon, very soon, run home in disorder.[26]

In spite of unquestionably high morale, both sides merely stood fast. A brawl took place in a tavern at Houlton where New Brunswick and Maine soldiers were drinking together like old comrades, when somebody mischievously shouted, "Success to Maine!" There were bloody noses and a broken arm, but this, except for the persistence of British loggers in breaking the boom constructed by the Maine militia to catch the timber the loggers had cut, was the only important incident of the Aroostook War. For a short time feeling at Washington was almost as high as at Augusta, but President Van Buren, though eager for Maine's votes, did not wish to fight. Just in time to avert real trouble, his emissary, General Winfield Scott, arrived at Fort Fairfield with instructions to gain "peace with honour".

Harvey, who had met Scott beneath a flag of truce in 1813, grandiloquently rose to the occasion of making terms of amity with an old adversary. On March 25 he signed a truce with Scott, denying any intention of sending British troops into the Aroostook country and agreeing to Maine's right to patrol it with a civil posse in order to protect the timber. In return, Maine agreed that New Brunswick should continue to exert a practical jurisdiction in the Madawaska settlements until the time when the entire boundary should be settled by the two national governments. Joyously the troops on both sides departed from the scene of contention, the only fatality of the Aroostook War being a farmer who was struck by a bullet that was fired at Fort Fairfield in celebration of the peace and ricocheted from a rock.

On the face of things honours had been even, but in actuality the Aroostook War was a victory for the Americans. What Maine had set out to do she had accomplished. In the valuable timber country of the Aroostook, British jurisdiction had been effectively denied, and the ebullient land agents of Maine at the head of a civil posse were in control. New Brunswick had been stripped of the advantage she had always possessed in the debatable areas. Control of the St. John and its tributaries had enabled the authorities at Fredericton to employ a heavy hand, but Maine had now opened effective roads to the focal points in dispute, and on the Aroostook her deputies lorded it over the British timber operators. So far as the Madawaska settlements were concerned, British jurisdiction had always been exerted there, and Harvey had gained nothing except American recognition of the *status quo*.

The British government approved of the truce Sir John proudly presented as his own handiwork, but refused "a mark of honour" eagerly requested by the lieutenant-governor "as it would expose him to invidious remarks".[27] Comment in New Brunswick was anything but complimentary on what the admirers of Sir John professed to believe was an act of statesmanship. "A portion of the pugnacious press of this ultra loyal province", he wrote bitterly to Sir George Arthur, was dissatisfied. The truce with Scott was employed by Harvey's opponents as a stick with which they assailed what appeared to them to be the pro-Yankee artifices, the pro-democratic ideologies of his advisers. Against Harvey and his friends, Simonds, Johnston, Wilmot, Moses Perley, and Charles Fisher – the last two of whom were seeking to enlarge the inflow of American capital – the loyalty cry rose clearly and strongly. By the summer of 1839 the truce was, in the minds of a considerable portion of the population, akin to treachery.

VI

Events that followed did not improve Harvey's reputation as a champion of British interests. The armed civil posse of Maine, consisting of untutored loggers, became a pronouncedly military force, extending its control to the mouth of the Fish River and thus impinging upon the Madawaska settlements. The headquarters of the land agents were fortified by cannon and entrenchments. Maine rapidly developed its roads leading into the disputed territory. Something more than a peaceful *pro tem* occupation had taken place. Late in 1839 a band of New Brunswick loggers, resenting these intrusions, took the law into their own hands, armed themselves by breaking into a military storehouse on the Tobique, and in the dead of night made an ineffective demonstration before Fort Fairfield, distinguishing themselves only by poltroonery in the face of "the enemy". Their leader, Captain Mackenzie of the Carleton County militia, who years before had served as a sergeant at Waterloo, realized his breach of discipline but, for fear of being called a coward, did not order his party to return to their own side of the border.[28]

Maine had much more reason to be alarmed by the rapid British development of the Témiscouata portage. A large depot to accommodate two companies of infantry was constructed at a point fifteen miles to the south of the lake. A barrack was established, though not manned, at the mouth of the Madawaska, and a tow-path had been cut through the forest along the east bank of the river. It was clear that Britain refused to consider the whole Témiscouata area, which came within the limit of the extreme American claim, as a subject for negotiation, but was preparing to employ it as a base from which full control over the upper St. John could be extended. In spite of the Harvey-Scott agreement, formidable encroachments took place – at least in the minds of both parties.

As the situation developed rather ominously, Harvey placed implicit confidence in his own ability to keep the boundary dispute under control by direct dealings with the government of Maine. His candour exceeded the bounds of discipline. To Scott he wrote in violent criticism of the speeches on the truce made in Parliament by the leaders of the British Tories. He compromised himself by frank communications to Governor Fairfield and other individuals in Maine. He had to protect himself against hostile assertions in New Brunswick newspapers of the baneful effects of these unofficial letters at a time when the British government was attempting to settle the whole problem of the boundary by dealing directly with Washington. He would not be responsible, he told the Colonial Office, "for the ravings of a party press".[29] Determined to settle the business by general negotiation, rather than trust to local and independent action, the British government finally, in February of 1840, placed it in the hands of the Governor General, Lord Sydenham, and Sir John lost his diplomatic status.

The climax came quickly. In August, under the excitement of new elections for the governorship of the state, Maine sent a commissioner into the Madawaska settlements to take a census. Just as Harvey in New Brunswick was accused of cowardice, so Fairfield suffered from his tough adversaries, the Whigs of Maine. In spite of the pledges made in the truce, he was compelled, for the sake of winning votes, to maintain a persistent pressure against the British on the border. Harvey, possibly in a fit of pique because of his exclusion from the negotiations that were taking place, contented himself with a formal protest and failed to inform the Governor General of the American activities, which became more formidable as the year came to a close. Not until November 13 did he place the full facts of the latest American penetration before Sydenham, and then only after MacLachlan, the warden of the disputed territory, despairing of any effective action from Harvey, had written to the Governor General himself. Now it seemed that British interests on the upper St. John, as well as on the Aroostook, were being sacrificed to the Americans.

Sydenham was in no doubt about the course he should follow. Two companies of infantry were ordered into the Madawaska settlements with orders to keep the Americans out of the disputed territory to the north of the St. John. But the sudden movement filled Harvey with chagrin. After trying to interrupt the march of the troops from Témiscouata, he was foiled by the postmaster, who failed to get the dispatch through in time. Fearful of American military retaliation from Houlton, he wrote, with the approval of his executive council, an apologetic letter to Governor Fairfield, declaring that the movement of the troops had been a mistake. "I had no idea," he wrote to Sydenham, "the movement of the troops would have been made so suddenly. On the contrary I had hoped that, as supported on a former occasion, they would have been placed at my disposal but not actually moved without further communication from me."[30] To Sydenham, Harvey's desire to maintain "the frank and courteous intercourse" with his friends in Maine seemed weak and vacillating. The fact that the warden had gone over Harvey's head to appeal for assistance convinced the Governor General that the lieutenant-governor of New Brunswick was wanting in the very qualities for which he had long been notorious. It was rather novel for Sir John to protest the necessity of keeping the peace while the British position in the disputed territory was visibly deteriorating.

The final interlude added an element of ridicule. After failing to forestall the Governor General's military measures for keeping the Americans out of Madawaska, Harvey organized a civil posse to keep the peace. Just as it was about to move north from Fredericton, Harvey's legal officers advised that the civil power had no authority to create a body of armed men without the consent of Parliament. He was highly mortified. Sydenham was pleased with this additional proof that his own opinion concerning Sir John's ineptitude was a correct one.[31]

On December 28 Sydenham wrote to Lord John Russell complaining of the contradictions and inconsistencies in Harvey's reports and of the indiscreet declaration of opinion to Governor Fairfield, and blaming him for the highly unsatisfactory state of affairs in the disputed territory. For Russell this was sufficient. On January 25, 1841, he wrote to Harvey that a successor would shortly arrive. The letter referred to a long series of admonitions and warnings that the entire negotiation should be conducted by the British government. Asked by the lieutenant-governor to revise his opinion, Russell refused. "I simply recorded the fact that your letter left Governor Fairfield to suppose that the movement of the troops was a measure which originated not with yourself but with Lord Sydenham."[32] As if to justify himself to posterity, Sir John pencilled on the dispatch: "Keep all quiet if possible until the Spring. The only thing which they (the Gov't.) appear to object to you is that you are inclined to be too pugnacious." More formally he stated the reason for the misunderstanding to have been "the absence of that unreserved communication with me on the part of the Governor General which had been freely accorded to me by all his predecessors."[33] He had chosen the wrong time for softer measures. In 1841 Sydenham emerged as the patriot.

VII

The Age of Harmony had ended. In 1838, when Harvey and a New Brunswick delegation had journeyed to Quebec to meet Durham, the prevailing spirit had been one of complacency, and the plan for a federal union of British North America had been rejected as a thing of visionary portent only. So satisfied had New Brunswick been with its estate that the plan had not been given any consideration whatever in the legislature. But by 1841 the favourable circumstances under which Harvey had assumed the government had worked themselves out. The large surplus accumulated by Baillie from the Crown lands was gone. No longer was it a measure of policy to make the Crown lands a source of abundant revenue; and the public coffers, which had overflowed in the beginning, were bare. The prodigal habits of the legislature in expending money for local improvements showed no signs of abating, and a career of headlong debt seemed a reasonable alternative to unpopular policies of re-

trenchment. The timber trade was to endure two years of
adversity, not because of the reduction of the British preferences
in 1841 but because of fears of the consequences. "A breath
had made it and a breath might take it away."[34] Local calami-
ties, such as the fires of Saint John, and the bankruptcy and
impoverishment of that city of mercurial humours, added to the
hazards that had to be faced as the province entered the
hungry forties.

For four years the imperfections of the obsolescent system
of colonial government had been coming more clearly into
relief. The irresponsible officers of the Crown were sealed off
from the policy-making levels of government. The executive
council, enjoying the confidence of the assembly, retained that
confidence by complying with a reckless dispensation of public
funds by legislative committees. At no point did strong executive leadership intrude into government. Following the publication of the Durham Report, public speculation upon the abstractions of responsible government appeared to have no pertinence
as members of the legislature intrigued and debated upon the
detailed items of the appropriations list. Each member of the
assembly, a little tyrant of the fields so far as the practical
affairs of his constituency were concerned, could see no reason
for further change in forms of government.

The idea of popular sovereignty, now frequently invoked during forensic exchanges, had been vindicated by the winning of
the Crown lands. The representatives of the people controlled
administration by methods that enabled each to cultivate his
own garden. Because of the lush revenues that were available,
an elaborate system of patronage, completely undisguised,
acquired a new prominence in Sir John Harvey's time. Colebrooke, who succeeded Harvey, called what he saw a highly
organized system of corruption.

Democratization made equally rapid advances in the composition of the parish magistracy. Squires, remarked the
Chronicle sardonically, became as common as haystacks. From
the time of the founding of the province, the difficulty of finding
a sufficiently large number of persons capable of filling these
important offices had been a source of anxiety to the provincial
government. Under the terms of the act governing their jurisdictions, the fees of justices of the peace seldom fell below the
sum of five shillings for adjudicating a single case. A significant
number of them had, for the purposes of enlarging their incomes,

encouraged litigiousness among the poorer members of their communities. Each year the government, in reviewing the commissions of the peace, had dispensed with justices who had become notorious for their avarice and their partisanship. Most notable of these cases was that of Charles Hatheway of Charlotte County, who in three years had issued 3,584 summonses not bailable and 121 bailable. When he was deprived of his magistracy he hawked petitions about the taverns of St. Andrews that ultimately reached the colonial secretary at London.[35]

Since it was completely dependent on the house of assembly, Harvey's government found itself compelled to appoint to the magistracy individuals whose purely local points of view and political activities did not conform to older ideas of the independent character of justices. Since assemblymen were now capable of nominating magistrates, it is not surprising that the legislature adopted an extremely conservative point of view with respect to the introduction of municipal corporations that was so powerfully recommended in the Durham Report.

Still New Brunswick presented the general prospect of a few straggling outposts of civilization standing on the fringe of a wilderness. Frontier points of view dominated the political and social philosophies of its people. Its politicians were far too practical to appeal to a mythical general will or to invoke the forces of public opinion that, so far as questions of provincial importance were concerned, existed only in the abstract. New Brunswick had come into existence in the eighteenth century when politics had been frankly based on particular interest. The nineteenth century, despite its discovery of the wisdom and prescience of the common man, its confidence in the spread of education and enlightenment, and its affirmations that popular government was certain to bring beneficence, produced no real change.

In every locality strong, aggressive personalities arose to dominate public thinking. Many a highly organized political interest had its origins in the ledger of "the storekeeper" who flourished on the truck system. The timber trade fostered and strengthened local loyalties. The classic rivalry of the Miramichi could be found to some degree or other in every part of New Brunswick. Joseph Cunard, reckless and hard-driving but admired and beloved, "controlled" the south bank of the river, riding about on horseback, shouting orders to his workmen, brightening with generous rations of Jamaica rum the days when adverse winds and currents enforced idleness. When he returned from his visits to England there were bonfires, salutes of cannon, and the ringing of church bells.[36] On the north bank the leadership of Alexander Rankin was sustained by methods more conventional and less rigorous, but discipline was just as strong. In 1839 the two parties were on the verge of armed hostilities because Cunard had persuaded the commissioners of customs to move their office from Douglastown to Chatham, where it was located directly across the street from his own home, an insult as well as a defeat to the opposite party. When Harvey was asked to adjudicate the fierce dispute, he recommended that it be restored to its former location, not for the sake of public convenience but in order to gratify his political supporters of the north bank.[37] On the island of Grand Manan a Ruritanian type of dictatorship was maintained by Wilford Fisher of the bench of magistrates. When his ordinances were resisted by a party almost equal in number to his own, headed by the Church of England rector, the church building was destroyed by fire, allegedly the work of incendiaries. Against the high-handed control of "the Emperor of Grand Manan", the Church of England party organized a mutiny in the militia.[38]

For a democracy whose political horizons were for the most part limited by the parish pump, harmony had been too grand a design, too visionary an ambition. Exultant over Sir John's recall, "the compact party", those who had signed the complimentary farewell address to Sir Archibald Campbell, now joined by a host of others whose new griefs against the administration were added to the old, called a succession of public meetings for the purpose of addressing the new lieutenant-governor for the dissolution of the house of assembly and new elections. The hero of 1813 was publicly belittled. The man who with 729 British bayonets behind him had broken up an American army of 3,500 and had changed the whole course of the war in the Niagara theatre was caricatured as the hero of a comic opera war against raw, untrained Yankee militiamen. For Harvey there was some consolation in the loyalty of the house of assembly, whose vast predominance in the politics of the province he had helped to secure. Shortly before he left, the sheriff came to seize his silver plate for long-standing private debt in England. To enable him to replace it, the legislature voted him £1,500.

CHAPTER 12

The Reluctant Reformer

1841-1848

Though dark clouds lowered, New Brunswick entered the 1840s in an expansive frame of mind. Population was well over 200,000, and the province could show many manifestations of the idea of progress, now so generally taken for granted throughout North America. Confidence abounded in the counting-houses of the mercantile establishments, in the shipyards fostered by every coastal community, and in the thin belts of agricultural settlement that were slowly extending farther up the St. John and the other rivers of the province.

A city of over 30,000, Saint John was unchallenged in the pre-eminence of her commerce. A mile or two from the mouth of the river, at Indiantown, the great rafts of timber that had been cut in the distant reaches of the interior were assembled. There they were shepherded over the Reversing Falls at turn of tide. Diminishing stocks of pine, eagerly sought for and jealously guarded when found, were compensated for, in large part, by the growing export of spruce deals, manufactured in hundreds of little mills that had sprung up during the past twenty years. Hampton, the shire town of Kings, alone could boast eighteen of them.

At Portland, beneath the lofty wooden erection raised to suspend the chain bridge that had, for a few days, joined Saint John with Carleton but had crashed into the river with heavy loss of life, lay most of the shipyards of the city. Skilled carpenters were highly in demand, and the industry, which was now controlled by builders of established reputation, was regularly producing vessels that approached 1,200 tons. Around the coasts of the province there were scores of replicas of Saint John, presuming to rival her industrial superiority and to draw off her trade. Goaded by Haliburton's *Clockmaker* as well as by the determination to rival New York as the chief terminus for transatlantic navigation, the merchants of Saint John were making a great effort to secure intercolonial co-operation for the construction of a canal through the isthmus of Chignecto, a design that was blocked by the practical calculations of military engineers as well as by the jealousies of Halifax. Three times in five years Saint John was scourged by disastrous fires of major proportions. In valiant attempts at modernization, the city corporation was on the verge of bankruptcy owing to the expensive business of hewing streets from the hard rock on which Saint John was built. As brick houses became fashionable as well as practical, and as the stumps of trees in the centre of the city (reminders of its youth as well as of its rapid growth) began to disappear, Saint John displayed a degree of pride in its external appearance as well as in the volume of its commerce.

The terms of trade were directed against farming, for the timber interests which were dominant in the legislature had for many years steadfastly discouraged bounties or tariff protection for agricultural produce. To the merchants it was axiomatic that commerce should be stimulated and profits increased by the continuous importation of foodstuffs from abroad and that labour should be channelled into the timber trade. The "landed interest", so vocal in the first days of the province, in effect no longer existed. "The merchants and shippers derive profits from the very causes which suppress agriculture in New Brunswick."[1]

Yet, in spite of the absence of official encouragement, farm production was increasing. The improvement was most notable on the upper St. John, the Miramichi, and in the northern counties of the Bay of Chaleur. The older settled areas of the lower St. John, so favoured by nature, had failed to develop adequately their potentialities for supplying the Saint John market. As late as 1849 it was noticed that the settlers of the fertile strip between Gagetown and Oromocto, owing to the ease with which they could grow hay on the islands in the river and on the interval tracts, were not employing modern methods of cultivation. By traditional routines they could afford to plod along without the necessity of attempting improvements. It was common to see the ploughman "carrying his plough in his hand like a chain, or on his shoulder like a handspike, or holding by a pin stuck through a single upright handle".[2] The more difficult terrain of other regions presented greater challenges that were overcome by application of the new knowledge of fertilizers and by more strenuous and systematic cultivation. The newer counties of the north and east could boast of many an immigrant who, having laboured in the ports for two years, had been able to purchase an uncleared farm at three shillings an acre and, after a year of apprenticeship on his land, had provided a fair competence for his family.

In consequence of the great immigration of the past quarter-century, the number of the newly arrived, who frequently voiced opinions that "the natives" were lazy wastrels, were vastly in the majority. The number of Scots was probably much greater than is commonly supposed. They came as individuals, and not as members of large groups sponsored and financed by landlords in the homeland, as in Nova Scotia and elsewhere. Very few settlements bore a distinctively Scottish or other national character. James F. W. Johnston, the agricultural specialist who came to New Brunswick in 1849, declared that after a year's sojourn in the province he had been compelled to speak more broad Scots than in twenty years in Scotland. Contrary to general experience elsewhere, there were Irish settlements in the northern parts of the province that were prosperous and progressive. The absence of English-speaking priests, a factor that twenty years before had been partly responsible for large numbers of the Irish passing on to the United States, had been remedied by the necessary action on the part of the new Roman Catholic episcopacies in the Maritime region. Mixture and diversity became more notable as still more new-comers replaced those who had remained for a few years, had sold their second-grade upland with its improvements, and had moved on to Wisconsin or whatever other region of the rapidly opening West beckoned most attractively. English travellers frequently moralized upon the instability of social life in North America, and upon the absence of a love for home. As in the other provinces of British North America, there was in New Brunswick a constant procession of those who were moving in and moving out, spurred on by an adventurous, even a gambling, determination to try greener fields.

Diversities were considerably more prominent than unifying influences, as a wide variety of peoples settled into uneasy residence and as the Roman Catholic conscience became more outspoken. In 1827 Bishop Angus McEachern of Charlottetown visited Sir Howard Douglas to announce his spiritual jurisdiction in New Brunswick. He had been promised some governmental assistance, provided that he reside within the province for a portion of the year. At the same time, a religious procession in the streets of Fredericton had excited a wide animosity amongst the population at large. To use the expression of Bishop John Inglis, Roman Catholics were becoming "bolder".[3] As the Church moved towards a more complex organization that would enable it to provide for the needs of its people, establishing sees at Halifax and Fredericton in 1842, the historic Protestant determination to deny the Pope any jurisdiction on British soil came more freely into play. As the Roman Catholic diocese was incorporated in 1845 (the first bishop being the Reverend Dr. William Dollard), religious rancours came to the fore. The Irish of Saint John were sufficiently numerous to indulge in the risks of waving their green banners on July 12. The Orange Order became a strong force in politics, and for five years there were bloody, sometimes murderous, conflicts between Orange and Green. Surrounded by hostile pressures, Roman Catholics were compelled to organize politically in order to ensure for themselves the equality that had been offered them by the last emancipations of 1829-30. In contrast to their Irish co-religionists, the Acadian population, though growing rapidly in numbers, remained impassive and unprogressive. It was customary to regard them as a good-natured, harmless community of people, permanently poor because of their improvidence, incapable of anything important because of their ignorance. As exponents of a way of life that was simple and primitive, they sometimes moved literary visitors to expressions of admiration, carrying frozen oysters and moss-cranberries to market, "singing merrily to the ringing of their horse-bells".[4]

The Bluenoses were a people known for their hardihood. Their country, throughout the English-speaking world, was frequently compared with Scandinavia, its bleak and barren coasts earning it a reputation for cold and poverty, though this reputation was misleading, as travellers who visited the more fertile regions of the interior discovered. The rocky harbours of Saint John and Halifax, seen by so many passing visitors, were responsible for many of the hostile impressions that went to the outside world. Another impression generally noted was the extraordinary degree of social equalitarianism perceptible everywhere. The squire yoking his oxen, the major of militia selling turkeys, the member for the county cradling buckwheat, the legislative councillor eating pancakes with his poorer neighbours, were familiar sights in New Brunswick. Inns offered but one common board. The health and good looks of the people were also the objects of frequent comment. The two principal dangers to the health of the people, said one writer, were the abuses in the consumption of spirituous liquors – a common complaint of those who moralized on the evils of the timber trade – and of tea, which was drunk three times a day, "as hot and strong as the stomach can stand it".[5] "A good poor man's country", was the opinion of those who had achieved a degree of success – not enticing to those who possessed any degree of fortune in the old land, but offering a great deal to those who were prepared to start with virtually nothing and labour hard over a period of years.

There was still an unreasoning hatred for Yankees, and those who had conquered the adversities of the country bore on their countenances a sturdy spirit of independence. Though the people were often described as law-abiding, there was a general belief that any trade was fair trade. When the provincial revenue cutter seized a few casks of illegally imported spirits at Black River in 1841 and was wrecked in a storm shortly after, the crew were attacked and beaten by the inhabitants. In the same winter, when the tide-waiter of Saint John made a seizure of some flour at Quaco, he was assaulted by a dozen black-faced men dressed in women's clothing. From the magistrates he could get no satisfaction.[6]

Remarkable contrasts were to be observed everywhere. James Silk Buckingham, that cultivated product of English Whiggery, declared that the steamer that bore him across the Bay of Fundy, the *Maid of the Mist*, was a disgrace to the British flag; that the passengers were the most vulgar, drunken, and disorderly he had ever seen. In Saint John, names on the signboards of many wine-shops, women going about in coarse woollen cloaks and large frilled caps without bonnets, were evidence of the Irish influx. But for six successive evenings Buckingham's lectures were attended by audiences of 500 persons. At Fredericton the obsolescent pomposities of an older era were all too prominent. Soldiers with fixed bayonets guarded the entrances to the handsome new Methodist chapel where he was to give his lectures. Orderly-sergeants watched over the pews reserved for the lieutenant-governor and his entourage. Proceedings opened when the clatter of heavy boots and steel scabbards announced the arrival of the official party.[7]

II

Amid this scene that was so redolent of parochial rivalries and local pride, the new ideas of political reform made little impact. The triumph of 1837 had established a feeling of general complacency so far as the relations between colony and Mother Country were concerned. The publication of the Durham Report early in 1839 had created new urges. But its imaginative suggestions for the complete autonomy of the colonies in their domestic affairs, as well as its more concrete proposals, seemed to have no real place in the minds of the leaders of opinion. Unlike other colonies, New Brunswick could not admit that it had any political problems of a general character.

Yet the new lieutenant-governor, Sir William Colebrooke, who arrived early in 1841, set himself upon a programme of reform. A former governor of the Leeward Islands, he had been educated in the reforming principles that had for a quarter of a century largely dominated the public life of Great Britain. In his love for statistics and the abstract ideas upon which theories of reform are nourished, the contrast with Sir John Harvey was most striking. When Sir William appeared on horseback at Woodstock shortly after his arrival, his sedateness created general astonishment. It quickly became unfashionable to feast, revel, and swear; and the Age of Harmony, according to an able and satirical account, was replaced by the Age of Smoothery. "Early hours, cold-water societies, the rubbing of hands, and cold, over-strained politeness became the *ton*."[8]

Colebrooke was determined to execute the policy enunciated by Lord John Russell, the colonial secretary, and to follow the course pursued by Lord Sydenham in Canada. Without surrendering in principle to the ideas of responsible government, he could govern in accordance with the majority of opinion in the legislature. He could persuade the house of assembly to abandon its haphazard methods of appropriation and conform to British practice. Much of the parish-pump business of the country could be removed from the area of provincial jurisdiction by the general adoption of municipal corporations, one of the triumphant achievements of the English Whigs. The communications of the province could be renovated and enlarged by the establishment of a board of works, acting under the supervision of the lieutenant-governor and with the consent of the legislature, functioning under the favourable conditions of a large loan Colebrooke hoped to obtain from the British government. All of the proposed reforms struck directly and hard at the local importance of members of the house of assembly, who, instead of controlling the expenditure of public funds in their constituencies, would be called upon merely to give consent to the programme of the executive council. Parish councils, proposed by Colebrooke, would constitute new authorities rivalling their own.

Facing a complacent band of politicians who were satisfied with the status quo, Colebrooke had no beneficent instrument of persuasion for the realization of his purposes, as Sydenham had in Canada. His request for an imperial loan of £500,000 was rejected by Stanley, the colonial secretary of the new Tory government in Britain. Reform of the system of financial appropriations, a method of orderly budgeting by which expenditure could be regulated according to revenue, would have to come before British bounty could be extended to New Brunswick. Applying the excuse that Colebrooke himself supplied, Stanley averred that public business was done in New Brunswick "by commissions selected in an improper manner and from questionable motive".[9]

"Smoothery" was not enough in a situation that rapidly deteriorated from the time Colebrooke set foot in the province. British preferences on colonial timber had been considerably reduced. The effect upon Saint John and the Miramichi, whose shippers were as pessimistic in bad times as they were optimistic in good, was paralytic. Unemployment became general. The homes of thousands of Saint John working people had been destroyed by the fire at Portland. When another fire destroyed the newly erected exchange building and a number of warehouses near Market Slip, conditions akin to panic developed. Emigration to the United States commenced on a great scale. Shiploads of people sailed for Australia and New Zealand. It seemed that there were no capital sources of wealth remaining by which the homeless could be sustained and labourers employed. Holders of Saint John Corporation bonds commenced actions in the courts to seize the corporation's properties, building-lots, wharves, and mill-ponds. A complete shift in the New Brunswick economy seemed inevitable. Labourers and mechanics, convinced that the timber trade was finished, formed associations and, assisted by the government, removed to rural areas.

As fugitives from the treacheries of the timber trade moved into the less favoured valleys and to remote forest clearings, a few rejoiced to believe that a race of true yeomanry was at last in prospect for New Brunswick. But there were no means at hand to ease the process of transition. Though the chartered banks of the province had always been pleased to serve the requirements of the timber trade, they were most unwilling to supply credit for agricultural purposes. Public sources of credit had been dissipated in Harvey's time. The only thing certain in the current accounts of the province was that revenues, dwindling rapidly, would not support public projects to employ labour. By the end of 1842, bank paper in circulation had dropped by two-thirds, and prices of labour and commodities by one-third.[10] In many localities business dealings had been reduced to barter.

While warrants for payment by the provincial treasurer were being hawked about by money-lenders at large discounts, Colebrooke introduced his programme to the legislature, offering as justification the need for restoring the provincial credit. The bill to surrender the initiation of money grants to the executive council was defeated by a substantial majority. The method tested by fifty years of experience could suffer no alterations.[11] The lower house passed the bill to establish municipal corporations, modelled on Sydenham's legislation in Canada, by the casting vote of the Speaker, but the legislative council threw it out. Regarding the financial condition of the province as desperate, Colebrooke refused to sign warrants for expenditure on the by-roads. By this refusal, the lieutenant-governor adversely prejudiced himself in the public mind for the remainder of his administration. In the autumn of 1842 the unpopular policy of a balanced budget caused a great deal of distress throughout the rural areas owing to the absence of the familiar employment on the by-roads and of the resulting circulation of cash.

Completely defeated in his attempt to make over the political organization of the province, Colebrooke resorted to dissolution. In the election of early 1843, fought chiefly on the issues he had raised, virtually everybody of consequence was against him except Charles Simonds, who followed the lieutenant-governor's injunction that a more businesslike financial mechanism was necessary in order to qualify for a loan on the London market.

The bogey of municipal incorporation was raised as the harbinger of the tax-gatherer. Ward Chipman, the Chief Justice, resigned as president of the legislative council in protest against Colebrooke's policies. John R. Partelow, the most influential member of the assembly, was "against any change in the constitution", and Robert L. Hazen, "Fighting Bob", the barrister of Saint John whose increasing eminence everybody took for granted, was scarcely less emphatic. Fought amid winter storms, the election of 1843 was probably the classic of New Brunswick elections during the colonial period. Fixed bayonets at Fredericton, great scenes of mob enthusiasm at Saint John, bonfires and illuminations, and beatings and destruction of property on the Miramichi, where two companies of the 30th Regiment were sent to keep order, enlivened the snowy scene.

When it was over, there was no doubt that new enlightenment of any kind whatever was not wanted. Two sets of reforming ideas, Colebrooke's and the more advanced theories of Lemuel Allen Wilmot, had been presented to the New Brunswick public. In the new assembly neither was able to muster a corporal's guard. The election of a speaker was made an issue of principle and, amid plaudits that were strained and emotional, Partelow nominated John Wesley Weldon of Kent, who had just resigned from Colebrooke's government, as one "possessing conservative principles and a thorough knowledge of the constitution".[12]

Sensing the temper of the House, Colebrooke decided to reconstitute the government without delay, determining to work with its leaders rather than against them. As the members showed no disposition to curtail expenditure, and as a dangerous tendency developed to strike at the sacrosanct Civil List Act by cutting the salaries of office-holders, it rapidly became necessary to keep the legislature under control by bringing to his council men who could manage it. "A change was necessary or another session would have been lost."[13] The new government largely represented the strain of heredity and continuity, of resistance to innovation. There were Hugh Johnston and Edward Barron Chandler from the legislative council. From the assembly came Robert L. Hazen, who could not understand responsible government, and Lemuel Allen Wilmot, its foremost advocate, whose verbose dissertations from the terminology of the Durham Report enlarged his reputation for eloquence but attracted few supporters. Alone of the council that had served

Sir John Harvey, Charles Simonds survived the hostile pressures
of the new-comers.

Amongst this junta there were differences and eccentricities.
Its members represented competing cliques and interests, but
all made sacrifices and "did not permit their party predilections
to gain the ascendancy".[14] All had a violent prejudice against a
single-party government. Because of differences, it was not a
government capable of new and strong action, but it possessed
the great merit of being able to control the assembly. If there
was a leader whose opinions could encompass the prejudices of
all, it was the cool and businesslike Edward Barron Chandler.
Because of the experience of its members and the respectability
of their families, common parlance could invent no better expression for it than "the compact party", reminiscent of the
fight against the Odell-Baillie clique of ten years earlier and,
for the purposes of simplicity, now revived. The use of the
expression "family compact", freely employed by contemporary
opponents and later historians, had a fair basis for justification.
Wilmot was a relative of two other members of the government.
Hazen was the nephew of Chief Justice Chipman, who was at
the centre of a vast web of relatives holding minor offices. But
it must not be forgotten that the ascendancy of this party
rested on its control of the popularly elected house of assembly.
Partelow, who controlled the labyrinthine mechanism of financial appropriations in that body, worked faithfully with "the
system". It was a compact that, in the main, was to govern
New Brunswick for ten years.

Late in 1843 the timber trade revived, economic prosperity
returned, and the political flesh-pots flourished. A temper dis-
trustful of innovation ruled. To the general satisfaction of the
assembly, the legislative council was enlarged to include representatives of the chief commercial interests, the leading religious
denominations, and the various sectors of the province.[15] George
Minchin, a merchant of Fredericton, became the first Roman
Catholic to hold a seat in the second chamber. No sympathy
was shown the reformers of Canada who attempted to seize
from Sir Charles Metcalfe the entire management of the perquisites of the royal prerogative, and the legislature dispatched
to him an address of congratulation upon his resistance to their
demands.[16] Yet this was a definition of principle extremely
rare, and New Brunswick was still capable of heresies, when
circumstances favoured them.

III

On Christmas Day 1844, William Franklin Odell, the provincial secretary, died. The removal of the holder of one of the most valuable of public offices at once precipitated the rather academic question of responsible government into the realm of practical politics. There was plenty of reason for confusion upon the course to be followed. In Canada a reaction had set in against the doctrines of the reformers. The only firm injunction of Stanley, the colonial secretary, had been that such matters should not be discussed in the abstract.

On the same day Wilmot called upon the lieutenant-governor and informed him that unless the office was filled by a member of the assembly holding a seat in the executive council he would withdraw from the government and agitate for the accomplishment of his views. In two elections the member for York had been charged with radicalism, republicanism, and rebellion, for advocating the views propounded in the Durham Report. Now, at a time of stalemate in the development of political reform, he adopted a course, rather hazardous so far as his own preferment was concerned, designed to force the British government to clarify the great question of the responsibility of public servants. With Colebrooke he was on unfriendly terms, largely owing to the downright way in which, as a land agent employed in settling poor mechanics on the soil during the years of distress, he had enlarged his political influence. There was nothing unusual in this kind of conduct in New Brunswick, but Colebrooke, a stickler for the more refined orthodoxies, detested it.

The lieutenant-governor would give Wilmot no satisfaction, citing the royal instructions and Lord John Russell's letter of 1839, arguing that public offices should be made dependent on the government rather than the assembly. Following other interviews, Colebrooke's defiance of those who favoured "the Canada system" was brashly illuminated by the appointment to the vacant office of his son-in-law, Alfred Reade. The justification he offered was that the lieutenant-governor's correspondence should be kept free from those who were contaminated with "party bias".

The executive council divided evenly on Reade's appointment. Wilmot resigned for the reason of principle he had given the lieutenant-governor. Hazen, Johnston, and Chandler resigned, not because they favoured Wilmot's views, but because of the embarrassment they anticipated in the assembly. "They were undoubtedly influenced by the family compact party with whom they are connected." They represented, said Colebrooke, "a class of trading politicians who are not counteracted by the influence of a class of country gentlemen."[17] In spite of the loss of the four more influential members of the government, the four less influential remained. Charles Simonds, Joseph Cunard, John Simcoe Saunders, and John Montgomery, a member of the legislative council from Restigouche, supported the appointment.

In February the contest shifted to the assembly, and Wilmot, seeing that he could not secure a majority for his advanced constitutional views, joined with the other dissident ex-councillors on the score of personal objection to the appointment. His resolution that the appointment was unconstitutional was defeated by eighteen to fifteen. A second, moved by Partelow, that the appointment was "an act of great injustice to many individuals in the province", was carried by nineteen to thirteen. There was bold language which the Speaker was inclined to tolerate and against which Simonds, the people's champion of earlier days, remonstrated in vain. Another resolution by Partelow, whom the majority of the House would inevitably follow, "that the Executive Council do not possess the confidence of the House nor of the country at large", passed by twenty-three to ten. During the two weeks of debates on the Reade affair, speakers on the floor of the assembly failed on occasions to make themselves heard and the Speaker found difficulty in keeping order, so great was the tumult in the constantly crowded galleries. An address of protest against the appointment, signed by all the members of the House except five, was forwarded to the Queen.

What had happened was the coalescence of all the groups opposed to Colebrooke on any score whatever. Yet, undeterred by majorities, the lieutenant-governor recruited two inconspicuous members of the house of assembly to the government, which now, though admittedly a minority administration, was firmly united in a decision to sustain the royal prerogative. Colebrooke was therefore in a situation remarkably similar to that of Sir Charles Metcalfe the year before, a predicament from which the governor of Canada had narrowly escaped by appealing to the people. In the men who were opposed to him he could sense a conspiracy to degrade the prerogative. The head and centre of it was Partelow, who had led the legislative uprising, and whose spider-like connections bound together the wavering opinions and diverse material interests of New Brunswick politicians into an almost united front. As Colebrooke surmised, they "did not dare refuse supply". But at the end of the session he could unequivocally state that the central issue had become responsible government "as recognized in Canada". The majority of the House had rejected Wilmot's doctrine in the abstract. But the more they contemplated it the more they perceived that it could be conveniently put to work in an emergency such as this. Thinking had been stimulated and the tempo quickened.

Had the Reade appointment not been negatived by the colonial secretary, these sharp lines of conflict would have been sustained. But "the King of Smoothery was checkmated by the servant of the Queen. The emancipator, the inventor, the philanthropist, the dictator, the purger of the Legislative Council, sank at once into insignificance."[18] Stanley's dispatch of March 31 referred to the instructions given to Sir Francis Bond Head in Canada in 1835, by which public employment was to be bestowed only upon native or settled inhabitants. This had been cited to the administrators of other colonies. Reade's appointment was not approved.

In obedience to Stanley's exhortations to restore the government to a popular basis, Colebrooke was obliged to invite Chandler, Johnston, and Hazen to re-enter the executive council. The views of Wilmot were so far advanced that he obviously could not be included. On May 8 the three came to Fredericton. But on that same evening they dined with Partelow, whose simultaneous reappearance at this stage was regarded by Colebrooke as full of sinister implications, and the next day they expressed a desire for "the Canadian system" and a reluctance to serve with those members of the government who had supported Colebrooke throughout the crisis. There were fears of "instability" in the assembly. Though they wanted "the Canadian system" they did not want a party government. No reconciliation at this stage could be accomplished.[19]

Until the legislative session of 1846, Colebrooke continued to govern with his residue of an executive council. The appointment of John Simcoe Saunders as provincial secretary on a non-permanent basis, according to the terms of Lord John Russell's dispatch of 1839, left the fundamental question of responsibility unanswered. But, at the first meeting of the council prior to the opening of the session, the members resigned rather than face the storms ahead. Only renewed overtures to the trinity who commanded legislative support, Chandler, Johnston, and Hazen, provided the appropriate solution to the difficulty of forming a new government. Their reappearance in executive roles brought a finish to the tumult, a reversion to the complacency of 1844. Peace came to Colebrooke during his last two years in the province. The conservative quality of government was reinforced by the addition of Charles Jeffery Peters, the attorney-general, and George Shore, the holder of several minor offices, two aged relics of the pre-1837 compact. Elections in the autumn strengthened the ascendancy of the government in the assembly, where Hazen was its capable exponent. In Nova Scotia Joseph Howe regaled the house of assembly by ridiculing the majority opinion in New Brunswick where, though a most determined stand had been made against the arbitrary conduct of the lieutenant-governor, there was an unwillingness to accept responsible government in principle. Charles Fisher, the junior member for York, explained the enigmatic position to Howe by remarking that New Brunswickers were "too loyal and too ignorant".[20]

For Colebrooke the peace was attendant upon his surrender and humiliation. He had been forced to reconcile himself to what he called "a system of corruption". The organic changes in the government of the province since 1837 had made the influence of the assembly decisive in almost everything. Ability to get money for local purposes, "by which the people are saved from local rates", was the grand criterion on which public men were judged. He had failed to create a powerful executive holding control of the purse-strings, by which large projects could be inaugurated, and to establish parish councils whose deliberations could produce a sense of local responsibility and revivify village life. How far, he asked, should the lieutenant-governor go in accepting the advice of an executive council dependent for its existence on a body so unstable as the assembly? William Gladstone, the new colonial secretary, could give no pointed answer to the question, but offered inspiration from the philosophy of progress. Reforms could come only after the public was given correct information. "The combinations in support of particular views" could be defeated only by education and enlightenment.[21]

IV

Shocks from the outside if not from the inside were to modify the system, if not the men. The Whigs had returned to power in Britain, and a new era for British North America commenced when Lord Elgin presented himself at the opening of the Nova Scotian legislature on January 21, 1847. For a time there was an expectation that he would visit Fredericton, and Colebrooke hoped to face him with a solid front of New Brunswick politicians agreed upon essentials. Hazen, who by this time had shifted with other members of the government to the acceptance of responsible government in principle, was the trimmer in the attempted arrangements, the chief feature of which was to be the inclusion of Wilmot in the administration. Yet prejudices peculiar to the conservative American setting prevented the establishment of a system purely on the British model at this propitious time. Private members of the house of assembly resented the impending presence of too many members of the government within it. The country members rose in rebellion against lawyers. Charles Fisher, who probably possessed a better knowledge than anybody else in the province of the law and theory of the constitution, introduced a motion for the surrender of the initiation of money grants to the executive. This was defeated by twenty-three to twelve. The excuse for rejection, best stated by Robert Carman of Gloucester, was that, although the British system was an excellent one, the country was not yet fit for it.[22]

The historic indiscipline of New Brunswick legislators powerfully militated against the introduction of a system of political parties, indispensable to the adoption of contemporary British practice. Freedom to bargain, to support or oppose, to form compacts according to the urgency of the hour, was the most dearly prized prepossession of provincial politicians. To many, a party system implied bondage. The extremities to which party spirit had been carried in Nova Scotia, where Howe and the Reformers refused to enter a coalition government with their opponents, reinforced the general conviction that party government was detestable. In Nova Scotia, said one member of the house of assembly, things had happened that were a disgrace to civilization. Yet the urgencies of 1847 required a degree of party organization, and the names of Liberal and Conservative began to come into common currency. "The names of Liberal and Conservative," said Wilmot, "might be adopted by those who liked them."[23]

Of "the Liberals", who to one degree or other accepted Wilmot's leadership at this stage, there were few. Charles Fisher, of awkward and uncouth speech and manner but probably the coolest head and best brain of the lot, has been credited by his own generation with providing the ammunition for Wilmot's rhetorical and long-winded attacks upon the government. For years his memorials on the forms and practices of government in the province had found their way into the files of the lieutenant-governor and into the archives at Downing Street. James Brown of Charlotte, an immigrant from Forfarshire, though not familiar with the intricacies of constitutional argument, was passionately concerned with improving the lot of the common man. William J. Ritchie, a younger lawyer of Saint John, gave promise of surpassing both Wilmot and Fisher as an exponent of what were beginning to be called Liberal ideas. David Hanington of Westmorland was the son of a London fishmonger who had been one of the pioneers of settlement on the Bay of Shediac. They were levelling in their philosophies, bitterly opposed to "the compact" that represented the older, well-established families of the province, sensitive to the ideas of progress abroad in Britain at the time, and quite prepared to re-echo the shibboleths of the American dream. Emotion as well as reason contributed to the element of social upthrust. Wilmot feelingly told the House of 1847 how his father, having moved to Fredericton for the purpose of giving his children a better education, had been made a bankrupt on the very day on which he himself had been called to the bar.[24] Leading the journalistic attack for the Liberals was the *Morning News* of Saint John, edited by George E. Fenety, who in his earlier days had served as a printer's apprentice to Joseph Howe at Halifax. In Saint John it possessed a degree of influence, but not elsewhere. The *News* promulgated the great doctrine that a new era was about to dawn, that the province, long suffering from the control of a selfish and oppressive oligarchy, must be prepared for sweepingly new departures, and that Halifax was the fountain of all the progressive, enlightened ideas peculiarly relevant to New Brunswick.

Curiously enough, although they held but six or eight seats in the house of assembly, the Liberals believed that the triumph of their principles, now virtually assured, would result in their accession to power. Wilmot thought, because the system he had advocated since 1841 had finally been adopted, that he would now be rewarded with office. At one stage in the session of 1847 he felt strong enough to declare that he would enter the government only if accompanied by three colleagues in a council of seven, or four of nine. This demand enabled Hazen and the compact party, with an overwhelming majority of the House behind them, brusquely to shut the door in Wilmot's face.

Responsible government had come or was just about to come; yet the men who remained in power were those who for years had ignored its appeal or denied its reason. The few who had supported the proposals of the Durham Report, who had collaborated with Howe in Nova Scotia, were denied power and patronage. Yet the unreadiness of the Liberals for office, the fact that they, in spite of their enlightenment, were not prepared to put into practice the principles they advocated, was strongly illuminated as the legislature of 1847 was about to break up. As the implications of responsible government became more clearly understood, the question that seemed most pertinent was this: if the holding of public office is to depend on a simple vote of the house of assembly, is there not but one place in the province where a sufficient number of gentlemen could be induced to serve on so brief a tenure? That place, according to the emphatic voice of the *Morning News*, was Saint John, "one of the greatest cities in North America". As the session closed, the question of "restoration" of the seat of government to that city destroyed any unity "the Liberal party" possessed. Ritchie gave notice of motion to move the capital in 1848. Wilmot gave notice of an amendment.[25] "Now without any desire to cast imputations upon the inhabitants of the present Seat of Government, all must feel that there is not sufficient *material* there, satisfactorily to conduct affairs of State – no public opinion to correct and give energies to the proceedings of the Legislature; on the contrary that there is a lethargy, a want of life, vigour and intelligence that has singularly influenced our Provincial Legislature and Executive Government."[26] Next year, in humour of triviality, the legislature defeated Ritchie's motion.[27] Sectional influences and prejudices of such a magnitude as this could readily thrust the more subtle refinements of responsible government into the background.

By 1848 those who thought that the old system was best were compelled to abandon any doubts that responsible government

had really come. Earl Grey's dispatch of March 31, 1847, to
Sir John Harvey in Nova Scotia, commended as a guiding set
of principles to other administrators, had been known to the
public for months. The principles of Joseph Howe and Robert
Baldwin had triumphed in Westminster if not in Fredericton.
There was no wisdom in resistance. On February 24 the house
of assembly debated whether or not to endorse the principles
contained in the historic dispatch. Hazen, whose cautious course
had reflected the prevalent trends of opinion for two years, said
that he was willing to try them. Nobody of rank or consequence
in the assembly voted against the resolution of approval. It was
a blithe affair, and only a die-hard group of eleven "country"
members voted against it, provoking merriment rather than
serious concern. The relevance of a question that was largely
theoretical had been made more immediate by the death of
Attorney-General Peters on February 3. In deference to the
advent of new principles of government that would determine
the basis on which public employment should be held, "the
gentlemen who had a claim on the office" urged that it should
not be filled at this time. "The sleep of years," said the *Courier*,
"is about to be broken. In fact reason seems to have emerged
from the cloud which obscured it – and the results of any
measure in the House to be less dependent on a *Bye Road
Grant*."[28]

Wilmot cockily played schoolmaster to the House. When he
was appointed to a committee to draft the Address in Reply he
refused to serve, for in Britain this was the duty of the government. The legislature, he said, must learn "the new, old way"
though there were protests that "the good old way" was the
best. When Partelow moved for a committee of the House to
investigate the workings of the postal system, he retorted that
the government should take responsibility.[29] It had become
clear that members of the executive council would hold the
three or four important offices, and that the duration of their
control would depend on the consent of the legislature. But the
extent to which a responsible government would assume the
duties of initiating all important measures in the house of assembly was entirely uncertain.

Colebrooke, so completely discredited by the Reade affair,
was about to leave and, "amid great unanimity and public
spirit", prorogued the legislature on March 28 in order to give
the new lieutenant-governor, Sir Edmund Head, time to take

stock of the rapidly changing situation. But the emancipator and philanthropist could fight rearguard actions. Grey had urged him to secure the financial initiative for the executive and to establish municipal corporations. Could not, he pleaded, the Canadian precedent of 1840 be invoked? Could not legislative guarantee for these saving changes be extracted in return for the granting of responsible government? But Grey would not bargain.[30] "The reign of smoothery" ended. "The light which once shone upon us with such startling brilliancy," said that unrepentant conservative, Thomas Hill, "is now flickering in its socket of disappointed hope . . . but it will rise again on the benighted mountains of Demerara."[31]

V

Reform had come reluctantly. The formal achievement of self-government in the internal affairs of the province excited no clamour, no general elation. The vast majority of those who commanded the support of public opinion had merely retreated as the approaching tide had swept in from the outside. Many reasons can be employed to account for the listlessness and apathy with which Grey's decision had been received. The settlement of 1837 had given general satisfaction and free play to those possessing the great vested interests in politics, the merchants of the timber trade. Since 1837 the only great cause for grievance, the affair of Reade, had speedily been righted by the British government. But probably the most important reason of all was something quite different, a sense of impending commercial calamity, a feeling that owing to the arbitrary policies of the British government New Brunswick was being expelled from the British community, that the province was being thrust into an alien and hostile world of free trade before it was prepared to fend for its own interests. Responsible government was merely a more formal and constitutional manifestation of something the people of the province did not want, the destruction of the preferred place they had always held in the markets of Britain.

Under the shadow of a new set of terms of trade with which they were completely unfamiliar, New Brunswickers showed little disposition to be exuberant about the new freedom, a freedom that seemed merely a definition, something that was in effect no greater than what they had possessed before. To a greater extent than in any other North American colony, the economy had been welded to British trade. For twenty-five years the merchants of the province had contemplated with dread the onset of the new principles of free trade in the thinking of British statesmen. In 1848 the complete triumph of those principles seemed to be established. Although Canada and the other colonies generally favoured the repeal of the Navigation Acts, which was now assured, New Brunswick preferred to nestle beneath the protection they had given her shipping and petitioned for their continuation. The doom of the timber trade was again freely predicted. Throughout the country in 1847 and 1848 public meetings echoed the sentiment that the province had been disowned by the Mother Country, and would find no alternative ways of living in the face of the great competition of a ruthless and avaricious neighbour. Ships could still be constructed more cheaply in New Brunswick than in the United States, and taxation was much lower than in Massachusetts or Maine. But the American practice of navigating on shares and the advantages of their limitless domestic market would enable them to overpower and absorb colonial commerce. Turning to the fisheries of the Gulf and the Bay of Fundy, men began to lament the neglect into which they had been allowed to fall for the past twenty years. Owing to the New Brunswick notion that lumbering was a superior vocation, they were largely in American hands.

Pessimists who prophesied that emigration was the only lot remaining to the people of the province looked with increasing admiration upon the expansive American scene. The British Empire had been a big and exclusive organization; having been thrust from its solid and tangible benefits by Britain's adoption of free trade, many of the more doleful tended to look to another. The relative merits of free trade and protection were debated with a gusto that set aside considerations of political reform. Vigorous agitations for the protection of local industries arose. But the dominant urge was to seek new vistas. Wilmot, though compelled by strong pressures to take a protectionist stand, expressed the ruling sentiment when he declared that little countries make little mechanics and little politicians. The abandonment of the closed ring of the commercial empire made New Brunswick feel that she was small indeed. It seemed essential to become a partner in some new enterprise that would ensure the future commercial well-being of the province.

Irritations accompanied the unwanted destruction of the historic ties that had bound New Brunswick so closely to the British market. The announcement of the new principles by which Britain would be guided was coupled with an earnest injunction that no British colony should impose differential duties upon the produce of its neighbours. This, in effect, deprived the colony of the capacity to bargain advantageously. Aggrieved merchants and politicians were not slow in pointing out that the injunction, presented from Downing Street with something of a religious fervour, implied the very practical consideration that no colony would now be able to discriminate against the importation of British manufactured goods, that the enlightened new principles, so baneful to the colonies, were designed, above all else, to enlarge British overseas commerce. Yet the new British policy compelled new orientations. Hard experience confirmed the precept that nothing favourable could be anticipated from the United States. Therefore, quite contrary to all previous New Brunswick reckoning, it became customary to look with increasing respect upon the idea of enlarging connections with the other North American colonies, especially the remote province of Canada, whose rapid growth in recent years had become the object of some admiration tinged with jealousy. Intercolonial trade had never been large. In many cases high tariffs had restrained commerce. In 1844 a shipload of calves, purchased in Nova Scotia at six shillings per head, were tossed into Saint John harbour by their enraged owners, who refused to pay a duty of eight shillings.[32]

A corollary to commercial emancipation, highly satisfactory to the colony, came in 1848 when the British government passed over complete control of the customs establishment to the province. The consolidation of the imperial and provincial establishments that had taken place in 1832 had not removed irritations to provincial self-esteem. Salaries of officials, who were appointed from London, seemed outrageously high. Natives of the province had not been allowed employment. It was commonly alleged that, in the collection of fees and the making of seizures, preference was given to imperial statutes over provincial ones. Exasperation with British commercial policy resulted in redoubled attacks on remaining vestiges of imperial control. The agents of the Imperial Post Office were indicted for the high charge of letter-carriage. Captains of river-boats between Saint John and Fredericton, and women and boys in all populous places, illegally undersold the Post Office in presenting this service to the public.

The age of steam navigation and railways had come. Speed was the essence of things, and already there was a consciousness, not forthrightly expressed, that New Brunswick and the other Atlantic provinces had been by-passed in the swift rush of progress that was so rapidly opening up North America. The new compulsion to look westward produced an inordinate interest in railways. Editors and politicians, said Fenety, caught glimpses of the moon and could see railways there. The grand ambition was to take advantage of location. In the winter season the produce of the expanding Canadas and the American West could quickly and cheaply be exported abroad from the ice-free ports of New Brunswick that offered such a short run to Europe. All that was needed was a system of railways linking them with Montreal and the St. Lawrence. Since the speed of railways was so electrifying, it seemed logical to extend them as far as possible in the direction of Europe and to shorten the haul by water.

This great urge to connect the Atlantic with the interior through the winter season had found tangible expression as far back as 1835 when the merchants of St. Andrews formed the St. Andrews and Quebec Railway Company.[33] But the commencement of a survey, subsidized by a grant of £10,000 from the Casual and Territorial Revenue, drew angry protests from the government at Washington, which was quite justly alarmed by the plan of the promoters to run the line through the disputed territory. The British government prohibited any further activity until the boundary dispute should be settled, but ten years later the worthy ambition of St. Andrews to become the winter port of British North America found emulation in a dozen other places along the New Brunswick and Nova Scotian shores. The old idea of the Kempt Road joining Quebec and Halifax, and the military necessities of 1837-8, when troops had been moved over the Témiscouata portage in the winter season, were good reasons for inviting imperial initiative. In 1846, following the lead of Nova Scotia, the legislature petitioned the Queen that the great military road in projection from Quebec to Halifax should be made a railroad. The proposed route, surveyed by Major W. H. Robinson of the New Brunswick legislative council and henceforth known as the Robinson Line, would enter the province at Matapedia, skirt the northern and eastern shores in order to be as free as possible from American interference, and run on to Halifax through the Cobequid Hills, though in New Brunswick there was a disposition to favour Canso as the eastern terminus of the line at the expense of Halifax, the reason given being that a shore route through Nova Scotia would be considerably cheaper. Technical difficulties would not be great, but the financial difficulties would be monumental. It was naïve to suppose that the British government – the Whigs who had been the makers of so much anti-imperial legislation – would pay for the line, though Gladstone, in a confidential way, had made the suggestion, highly unpopular in New Brunswick, that if British funds were involved the government would be interested in exporting some of its convicts to perform the labour.[34] The great question that began to gain prominence was the proportion of total costs to be paid by the three colonies involved in the project.

As railway fever brightened the gloom that prevailed in 1847-8, and as the rising tide of speculation seemed likely to impel action, sectional rivalries arose. A reorganized St. Andrews-Quebec company, revitalized by new capital from Britain, actually commenced construction in November 1847. In the legislature there was little fear of risk as the new company was promised a grant of 20,000 acres of land and a guarantee of a five-per-cent dividend on its stock upon the completion of the line to Woodstock. Yet less than a year later a new spasm of commercial distress brought operations to a standstill. The enthusiasm for "the great trunk line" from Quebec to Halifax aroused the susceptibilities of Saint John, where there was no disposition to be by-passed. To ensure that the city should become a terminus, Hazen introduced in the legislature a bill providing for a survey of a line from Saint John to Shediac. This was ridiculed by members from up-river constituencies, and Wilmot enjoyed himself in the house by speculating upon the vast commerce in huckleberries and raspberries that would enter Saint John from Loch Lomond.[35] To join New Brunswick to the continent was the preoccupation of all, but there were a great many ways in which this might be done. Overriding all considerations was the conviction of Saint John that it must of necessity lose no advantage to Halifax. Some of the optimism was forced by activities that had already commenced elsewhere. The promoters of the St. Andrews-Quebec line were not inclined to take very seriously Gladstone's doubts

that they would be able to compete with the St. Lawrence and
Atlantic line, already in construction between Montreal and
Portland.[36]

VI

The ambition was for progress, but, as New Brunswickers took
stock of themselves in this era of new vistas, there were frequent
lamentations over the slack hand of public administration that
over the years had permitted the institutions of the province
to fall into such a state that progress seemed impossible. Ever
since the founding of the province, the rural democracy through
its representatives in the legislature had denied the government
the capacity to initiate any sort of strong measures. Strong government of any kind was not wanted. Administrative establishments had been denied the money and the personnel that would
enable them to do their work efficiently. Even upon the elementary business of the granting of land, litigation was so general
that Colebrooke decided to appropriate a portion of the grounds
of King's College for the establishment of a magnetic observa-
tory to supply correct bearings and measurements.[37] Extensive
parishes still had no magistrates, but often they were better off
without them, for frequently a farmer would have to sell his
last cow to pay the fees of the justices of the inferior courts.[38]

Failure to enforce the law was notable as the number of
squatters conspicuously increased. The easy terms offered by
the legislature for the taking out and settlement of land were
largely ignored. Feeling, both inside and outside the legislature,
was on the side of the squatters. Even if the government possessed the will to eject them, it lacked the funds necessary to
finance legal actions in the courts. Impecunious and unscrupulous new-comers entered into one-sided bargains with Indian
chieftains for the occupation of the generous reservations of
land made for them in the early days of the colony. Of the total
of 62,000 acres reserved, white men had acquired dubious titles
to 15,000 by purchase, generally offering a keg or two of rum,
or a few pounds of gunpowder. Some of these lands, illegally
acquired, had been sold and resold, so that there was a large
vested interest in denying the Indian title. In 1844 the legislature passed an act authorizing the sale of Indian lands and
the establishment of a fund to be employed on their behalf.
Public opinion and legal action taken by the squatters never
permitted the act to be enforced.[39] Moses H. Perley, visiting the

Tobique in the interests of the Indians of that area, was met by two hostile squatters who declared that they would burn all their buildings and improvements rather than be forced to pay for clear title.[40]

A census taken in 1841 showed that there were 1,377 Indians in the province. If they were exploited by the white men, they sometimes also suffered from the exactions of their chiefs, a few of whom bore commissions from the provincial government commanding the obedience of their subjects. The case of Barnaby Julien was notorious. A chief of the Micmacs, residing at Red Bank, he had a large rent-roll, but his business affairs were in such bad order that he never dared to visit Newcastle except on Sundays. Throughout the forties, the familiar debate raged, over what to do with the Indians – whether they should be permitted to remain in their native state or be assimilated to the ways of the white man. Roman Catholic missionaries were rescuing them from the intemperate habits into which many of them had fallen.

Even in the more populous places there was powerful resistance to forceful manifestations of executive government. Opposition to new or higher rates of local taxation was a ruling obsession and no politician would dare to challenge it. The establishment of Fredericton as a city, which came in 1848 in accordance with an ancient custom upon the creation of a bishop's see, was acclaimed not as a fresh example of progress but rather as a victory for the tax-gatherer. In Saint John the magistrates had never succeeded in maintaining a decent degree of public order. At Portland there was a community of "desperate men" who throve by smuggling. Only after a shocking and unprovoked murder, committed in daylight in the open street during the summer of 1847, was a police force established. In December "the lower orders" rose against the police, who were unarmed, and in a wild mêlée stabbed three, killing one. Private war prevailed between Orange and Green. On July 12, 1847, two Catholic Irish were killed, one at Saint John, the other at Fredericton. In Saint John the troops had to be called out to keep the peace, and Fredericton was invaded by a host of Irish from the countryside around. The worst troubles occurred at Woodstock, where local Orangemen were joined by large numbers from across the border. The burning of the jail caused considerable embarrassment to the magistrates, for a large number of persons had been apprehended.[41]

In addition to all the other sources of discord there was at
Saint John a strong local animus against the garrison and its
commander. To keep the barracks exempt from the visitations
of the populace who had been accustomed to walk through the
green in order to meet incoming fishing vessels at the break-
water, the gate had been ordered closed. Tumults occurred regularly. In the summer of 1846, a sailor was shot in the course of
one of the mêlées. Out of a mob of forty bystanders, but one
man, a soldier of artillery, attempted to arrest the assailant. He
was set upon by two men with axes and a woman with a bull-
dog, and left senseless in the street.[42] The lawyer in charge of
the prosecution, John H. Gray, was extremely zealous in seeing
that justice was dispensed to the offenders, but the city had no
funds to reimburse him for his pains.

The haphazard quality of executive management was glar-
ingly evident in the reception of immigrants. It was matched
on the other side of the Atlantic by the inability of the British
government to take the measures necessary to make the lot of
the new-comers more auspicious. One optimistic estimate was
that New Brunswick could absorb, in prosperous times, 7,000
immigrants a year. But commercial distress came quickly, and
the Colonial Office, along with the other agencies of Whitehall,
invariably moved too slowly to govern the rate of immigration
according to the demand for labour. In 1842, in spite of the
exertions of the British government in enforcing the Passenger
Act and in circulating information hostile to emigration, thousands of poor Irish arrived in the province. Able-bodied men
who were capable of looking after themselves for the most part
remained in Saint John for a year, and then, following the
departure of the spring ships when work became scarcer, took
passage on the crowded steamboat that plied between Saint
John and Eastport, leaving their dependants to the temporary
charge of the overseers of the poor. The more helpless wandered
about the countryside, accepting the hospitality of distressed
farmers who sometimes adopted orphan boys and girls. In 1843,
when the province was coming out of commercial distress and
when new labour was required, the British government's measures of restraint were entirely successful and no immigrants
came to New Brunswick.

Following the examples of Massachusetts and New York, the
province had placed a small tax on immigrants at the ports of
landing, collectable from the captains of the ships that carried

them; the proceeds were not reserved for specific purposes, but passed into general revenue. Though in busy years the tax could yield up to £1,300, the legislature consistently refused to establish a system for the reception of immigrants. The only immigration agent of consequence was Moses H. Perley, the widely read and highly intelligent friend of the Indians, a capable analyst and statistician whose services had frequently, for a variety of purposes, been put to use by the government. Half of his salary was guaranteed by the Civil List Act, half paid by normal grant of the legislature. As early as 1837 the strength of the temperance movement in New Brunswick was revealed by a legislative decision to cut Perley's salary owing to "intemperate habits", though it was recognized that he was very efficient. The Immigrant Act authorized Perley and his deputies to make cash advances to immigrants who were in distress. Sometimes they were reimbursed for their advances and sometimes not, depending on the caprices of legislative committees. Having made substantial advances to immigrants in 1846, and encountering legislative refusal to honour them, Perley resigned his office.[43]

Suffering came in consequence of the sins of omission on both sides of the Atlantic. In June of 1846, a year in which 9,000 immigrants arrived, the ship *Envoy* brought cholera to Saint John. In the next year, the time of famine and typhus in Ireland, fifty ships brought over 17,000. In the excitement and panic of their departure, British officials took no measures to enforce the Passenger Act, and, with indecent haste, Irish landlords hurried their starving tenants aboard crowded, unsanitary ships whose captains ignored the required safeguards. The urgency inspired the legislature to action. A quarantine station was established on Partridge Island in Saint John harbour. A large alms-house was converted into a hospital. Sick immigrants for whom accommodation could not be found in institutions were housed in sheds on the waterfront. Altogether, over 2,000 died. The misery that had been familiar in recent years quadrupled in intensity as hundreds of wanderers took to the countryside. The experiences of Saint John were duplicated to a degree on the Miramichi, at Richibucto, and in other ports of the province.

The immigration crises of 1846-7 fanned the feelings of exasperation against the British government that were so general at this time. Reports of the callous treatment of the tenants on

Lord Palmerston's estates in Sligo spread through the province.
It was charged that Earl Fitzwilliam dispatched emigrants from
Ireland to labour, practically naked, at St. Andrews on the new
railway in which he was a stockholder. After a few weeks of
employment they were thrown on the parish, idling about the
streets of the town, living on meal and molasses. This one shipload, it was alleged, cost the province £600. Harsh exchanges
took place between the immigration agents of New Brunswick
and the Colonial Land and Emigration Office in London. Local
authorities protested the increases in the poor rates that the
emergency had made necessary. Back from Britain came charges
that the immigration agent at St. Andrews had exacted from
the impecunious new arrivals large sums in fees for writing to
their relatives in the United States for the funds that would
enable them to go there.

The angry feelings partially subsided late in 1848 when the
British government announced its willingness to accept the expenses incurred by the province for the immigration of this
disastrous year. The bill was for over £13,000. Obligations
accepted amounted to £7,000.

In spite of the piecemeal methods by which roads had been
constructed, visitors generally spoke of the communications of
the province in a complimentary way. Fredericton was now
linked to the Miramichi and the north shore, as well as to
Saint John and St. Andrews, by an adequate system of great
roads. Spurred by the necessities of the boundary controversy
and by the urgings of the British government, New Brunswick
and Canada had completed the Canada Road, largely financed
from funds at the disposal of Downing Street. Though the by-
roads were still being built by statute labour, generally condemned as inefficient, accounts of them were often favourable.
But the building of roads represented the extreme limit of the
government's capacity. The Chignecto Canal project had withered away upon the refusal of the Nova Scotian government to
co-operate in a new survey. The produce of the Gulf fisheries and
of agriculture in Prince Edward Island, the latter now increasing
at a sensational rate, could still not be marketed through Saint
John. From Amherst and other communities of the isthmus
came the demand for the creation of a united Maritime province
and of a government strong enough to overpower the resistance
of Halifax in order that the canal could be constructed.[44]

Private capital appeared to be just as helpless as the government to do anything important. Optimists spoke of mining as a new staple industry that could replace lumbering. But "the great New Brunswick coalfield", as the deposits in the Grand Lake area had been called by Abraham Gesner, the geologist, had led to nothing except the attempts of capitalists without adequate funds to acquire monopolies. Years before, there had been reports of precious metals in Gloucester County and the prospecting rights had been farmed out to William Stevens, but again the results had been barren. The only really large capital venture in New Brunswick had been that of the New Brunswick and Nova Scotia Land Company. It had been a failure owing to the high price paid for land, the incompetence of the company's officials, and the hostility of members of the legislature. The Royal Road, leading to Stanley from Fredericton, auspiciously commenced in the days of Baillie's high-handed régime at the Crown Lands Office, had become a goat-trail.

VII

During Colebrooke's time the Church of England saw almost the last of its remaining privileges struck away, but experienced a renaissance as well. The more equalitarian-minded in the province rejoiced to see Britain withdraw her financial support of the Church, whose assumption of official establishment had excited a persistent spate of vindictive attacks upon its ministers and adherents.[45] Public patronage for denominational schools had the inevitable effect of drawing religious antipathies into the open. The legislature had granted public money to the Baptist Seminary at Fredericton, a remarkably successful establishment founded in 1836, and to the new Methodist school founded at Sackville by Charles Allison, a wealthy merchant of Saint John, and named for him. When politicians of the Church of England resisted these grants, challenging the public character of the two institutions, the Methodists and Baptists, springing to the counter-attack, brought the affairs of King's College under review. Life in New Brunswick, it was argued, had no place for "the dead languages" that were so endearingly imparted to a handful of students by the refined principal, the Reverend Edwin Jacob. It was alleged in the house of assembly that "a parcel of children or boys were dealt with as the young gentlemen at Oxford, that they might study or not as they pleased which was an absurd principle".[46] Overwhelming the opinions that were more capricious was the consideration that in sixteen years the college had cost £47,000 and had produced but few graduates who had given services of importance to the country.

The majority of members of the assembly still professed to be members of the Church of England, but they readily agreed in 1845 to a bill that seriously limited the position of the Church in King's College. This substituted the lieutenant-governor for the bishop as Visitor, made the office of president no longer the possession of the archdeacon of the province and, most important of all, reorganized the college council by expelling from it Principal Jacob and the professors, making it open to persons not members of the Church. Though the bill boldly annulled the provisions of the Royal Charter of 1828, the Colonial Office raised no serious objections and the college became considerably more public and less exclusive. Contemplating the powerful denominational pressures for public assistance in the maintenance of schools and colleges, Colebrooke proposed that the University of London principle be invoked – that King's College should be given the sole right to set examinations for and confer degrees upon students from all institutions of higher learning in the province.[47]

By this time two truths, long asserted, had acquired real meaning for members of the Church of England in New Brunswick. Effective leadership could be supplied only by the consecration of a resident bishop. Bishop John Inglis at Halifax, "the Chesterfield of the episcopal bench", had been just as unable as his father to attend to the affairs of his vast diocese. When he died in 1850, sixty new churches were unconsecrated and 7,000 waiting persons were unconfirmed. The second truth was that which Chief Justice Ward Chipman had stated years before, that like other churches in New Brunswick the Church of England would have to depend on its own exertions and not on public support. For some time New Brunswick had stood at the top of the Society for the Propagation of the Gospel's priority list of new dioceses to be endowed, but the position was clouded by animosities within the local Church itself. The Reverend Edwin Jacob let it be known that he was to be the new bishop when the time should come. He enjoyed the support of the party generally described as low-church, which derived considerable inspiration from the Colonial Church Society in England. Taking the line that a new see could not be supported by a large body of church people if such an appointment were made, Ward Chipman in 1841 wrote the Archbishop of Canterbury, urging the appointment from England of a bishop who should possess a private income, promising a public subscription in order to assure a modest remuneration.[48]

In 1843 clergy and laity were electrified to hear that the prayer of the petition of 1819 had been granted, and that the Society for the Propagation of the Gospel had given £20,000 for the creation of a see in New Brunswick. The amount, Stanley told Colebrooke, would have to be supplemented by large local donations, and he suggested an appeal to the legislature; but the lieutenant-governor was too wary to follow such a device.[49] An impressive list of pledges for endowment and for the building of a cathedral quickly satisfied the colonial secretary that the venture would be successful. Late in 1844, the Archbishop of Canterbury appointed the Reverend John Medley, prebendary of Exeter Cathedral, as the first bishop. A spirited war of journalists followed, concerning the election of the seat for the see. In Saint John it was declared that a cathedral would never stand on the town plot of Fredericton – that it was contrary to Scripture to build a house upon sand. The reply from Fredericton was that the best masonry in the world would crumble within a few years in an atmosphere as foggy as that of Saint John. Choosing Fredericton, to the great mortification of Saint John, Medley at once injected a new vigour and new intellectuality into the Church in the colony. The refinements of church music and church architecture were introduced, and a cathedral was planned, modelled after the early perpendicular structure of St. Mary's at Snithsham in Norfolk, following the fashion of the Gothic revival that attended the Oxford movement in England. It was difficult to raise the funds for so ambitious a structure, but the local pride of Fredericton reinforced the efforts of members of the Church of England. When an anonymous donation came from England, the cathedral was completed in 1851. Abruptly Medley dispensed with the time-honoured pew-holding system that savoured of social discrimination and was highly regarded by his predecessors at Halifax.

The new bishop brought to New Brunswick the new points of view that were permeating the faith of the Church of England in Britain. His advent was, therefore, not highly favoured in all quarters. His first charge to his clergy was largely directed against "party spirit". There was talk in the legislature about a divided Church of England and the impending "overthrow of Protestantism". When the Venerable Archdeacon Coster applied for the usual drawbacks on duties paid for the importation of religious books, it was proposed that any of the Oxford tracts contained in the shipment should be exempted from the privilege.[50] Tractarianism was regarded with hostility. Though faced by divisions within his own flock, Medley quietly went about the business of rebuilding the Church in New Brunswick. When, in a challenging way, one of his clergy informed the bishop that he was a low-churchman, the reply was, "I hope, Sir, that you are a humble one."[51] The rapid increase of clergy and of churches in subsequent years is the best evidence of the new spirituality and authority he introduced.

VIII

Final settlement of the boundary dispute with Maine came in Colebrooke's time. Settlement was imperative for commercial, if for no other, reasons. One of the last great stocks of pine in the province was being rapidly denuded, and the population was increasing, especially from the side of Maine. Following the Harvey-Scott agreement of 1839, the timbermen of both countries who operated in the area were paying their duties into a disputed-territory fund, the proceeds of which were to be divided when the issue of the quarrel should be determined.

Maine was obdurate in pressing her extremist position, which depended on a literal interpretation of the treaty of 1783 and was so strongly favoured by the topography of the country, but Washington knew that Britain would never agree to the surrender of Lake Témiscouata and its basin. Late in 1841 Daniel Webster, the American Secretary of State, entered upon the business of persuading Maine to the acceptance of a conventional line to mark the boundary. At a special session of the Maine legislature in May 1842 he succeeded in winning the consent of the state to such a course. He was considerably assisted by new knowledge that had recently come to his government. An American scholar, Dr. Jared Sparks, who had been working in the French archives at Paris, had discovered a map of North America used by Benjamin Franklin during the negotiations for the preliminary peace of 1782. On it had been drawn a strong red line to designate the boundaries of the United States as they were established by the treaty. It showed the line of the highlands commencing far south of Mars Hill, and, though the map had not been authenticated, it could, in the hands of the British, be very damaging to the downright, legalistic case put forward by Maine.

In anticipation of a compromise settlement, the British government had sent Alexander Baring, Lord Ashburton, to Washington as a special minister to settle the boundary controversy. No selection could have been more acceptable to the Americans, for all of Ashburton's background, private affairs, and material interests predisposed him to the maintenance of Anglo-American harmony at almost any cost. As the head of the great banking firm of Baring Brothers, he had used all his influence to prevent the outbreak of the War of 1812. Since that time Baring Brothers had been in the forefront of the British investment corporations that had advanced money for American development. It had a great deal to lose should hostilities develop between the two nations. As a young man representing his firm in Philadelphia, Ashburton had married the daughter of Senator William Bingham. The marriage had brought him a million acres of timberland in northern Maine, generally known as the Bingham Purchase, the immediate value of which would be adversely affected by an award favourable to Britain in the boundary dispute.

For a boundary of convenience in the north-west corner of New Brunswick, the St. John River west from the northerly line running from the Monument at the head of the St. Croix seemed the obvious basis for compromise. The British were absolutely intransigent about the surrender of territory to the north of the river. Ashburton's view, one generally held by official persons on the British side, was that all that it was essential to save was the communication between New Brunswick and Canada. It would be desirable to save the Acadian settlements on the south bank of the river, long under New Brunswick jurisdiction, but their possession was not indispensable to the necessities of strategic thinking. "The whole territory we were wrangling about was worth nothing," Ashburton said later in a perhaps unguarded moment.[52] He was prepared to abandon the historic British position, advocated by Ward Chipman and others, but he was also prepared to abandon the negotiation if the Americans persisted in demanding territory that would sever the connection between the two British provinces.

Webster was equally eager to achieve a compromise, but had a much more difficult task to achieve a basis for it than Ash-

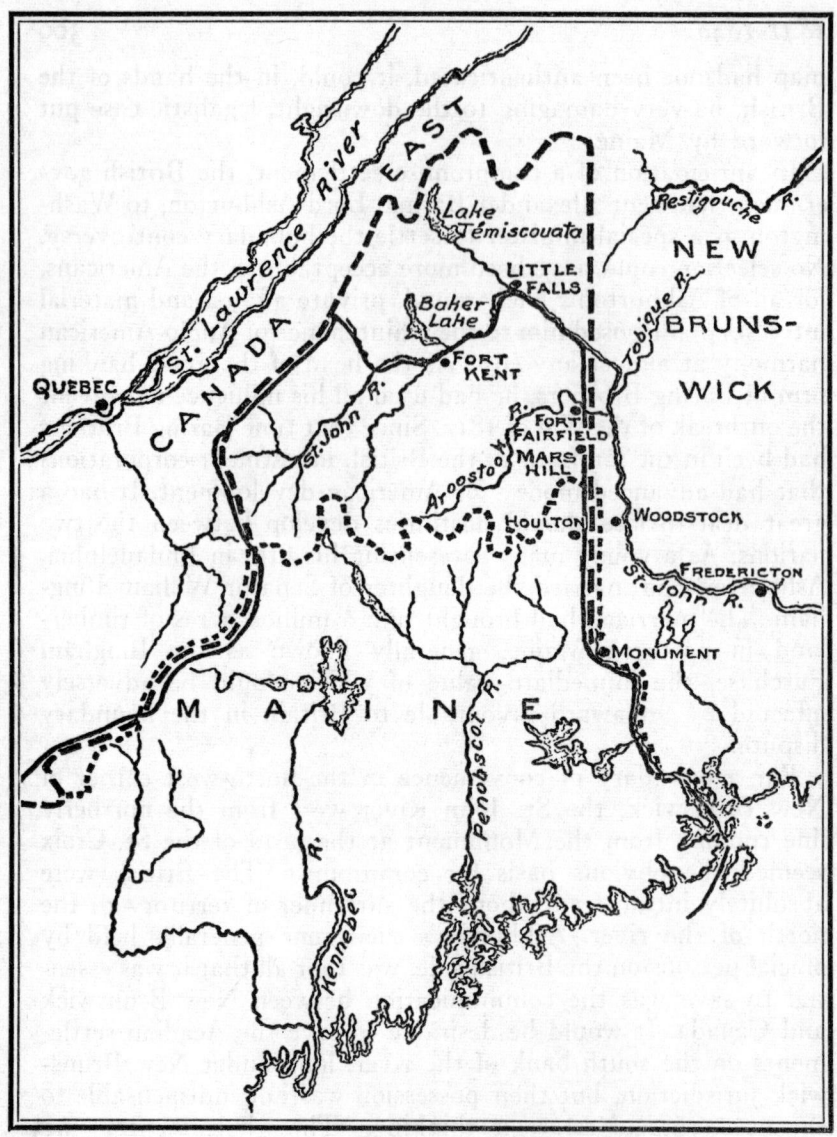

THE BOUNDARY DISPUTE — FINAL PHASE

The boundary settled by the Ashburton Treaty in 1842 is shown as a continuous line. A broken line indicates the extreme limit of the American claim. A line of dots indicates the limit of the British claim decided by Ward Chipman.

burton had. Maine had raised the constitutional objection that since she was a sovereign state the federal government had no right to barter away a portion of her territory. A large bloc of support could always be mobilized in defence of this doctrine in the Senate, whose ratification was necessary to a treaty with a foreign power. The state government put forward a series of demands for compensation, should territory to the north of the St. John be awarded to Britain. These included a cession of territory in the south-west corner of New Brunswick, to the east of the northerly line and to the north of Eel River (a transfer that would make the boundary follow the St. John as far south as Meductic), the free navigation of the St. John for the agricultural and forest produce of Maine, and financial reimbursement from Washington for the costs of defending the territory by the mobilization of troops and the organization of a civil posse. In the face of Ashburton's refusal to surrender territory to the north of the St. John, Webster had to secure compensation for Maine, not only from the British but from his own government as well. Compensations also suggested were Grand Manan and Campobello.

No serious consideration was given to most of these suggestions, but Ashburton regretfully consented to the surrender of the Acadian villages on the south bank of the St. John. The establishment of an international Acadian community on the upper river was one of the facts of life that had to be faced. Forgetting the powerful New England animus that in large part had been responsible for the expulsion of 1755, the Americans, in their propaganda offensives, had frequently reminded the Acadians of the brutal treatment they had experienced from Britain in the past. Now the Acadians were to be subjected to another disarrangement resulting from the rivalry of great powers. Ever since Carleton's time, New Brunswick, though unable to help them greatly in a material way, had been solicitous for them. The river communication had tied them to Fredericton. New Brunswick colonial documents contain a great many of their statements, invariably over the signatures of their priests, of their determination to remain British subjects under the jurisdiction of the province. Their impending alienation was the sole obstacle of any importance to a compromise on the British side. Within New Brunswick the principal climate of opinion was that the ownership of the disputed territory was not of great moment, that a final settlement of any

kind could result in the enlargement of the business of Fredericton and Saint John.

Through the summer the negotiations continued, compre-
hending a great many minor cases of dispute extending as far
west as Lake Superior. Agreement was finally signed on August
9. As expected, the fiercest opposition developed in Maine.
British opinion, schooled to regard the award of the King of the
Netherlands in 1831 as a just one, was eminently satisfied, for
the treaty allowed to New Brunswick rather more territory than
the decision of eleven years before. In the House of Commons
the Liberal opposition attempted to make capital of Ashburton's
failure to win more for his country, but the position of the Tory
government was ably defended by, among others, Sir Howard
Douglas, who with considerable conviction reminded the House
of the surrenders made by Palmerston during his own time in
New Brunswick. Ashburton was able to return to England and
gratify his wife with the knowledge that he had sacrificed a
great deal for the achievement of Anglo-American amity. During the debates in the American Senate upon ratification, knowledge of what was now known as the Sparks map became
general. Ashburton's reaction was to say that it was a good
thing the map had not turned up in the course of the negotiation, for then it would have been impossible for Britain, with so
much evidence in her favour, to concede anything like so much
as she had given to the United States in the treaty he had
negotiated – and nothing would have induced the Americans to
accept a British claim for more territory to the southward.[53]

In New Brunswick the general feeling was one of satisfaction,
but resentment remained in the minds of many who had been
educated to the rightness of Chipman's earlier views. Writing
to William F. Odell, Colin Campbell declared that the appointment of Lord Ashburton had been the "cruellest cut of all".
His million acres in Maine would treble in value in consequence
of the decision. "There has been an American interest, or an
American feeling, or both, existing among the majority of persons employed on our side."[54] The majority of the legislature
seized the opportunity to make out a political case against the
high salaries of those who were protected by the Civil List.
Since the natural resources of the province, secured by the
granting of the Civil List Act in 1837, had shrunk in value and
extent following the treaty, it seemed reasonable that the
guaranteed salaries should be reduced. Acrimonious exchanges

took place with the British government upon the costs of surveys that followed the treaty, charges ultimately absorbed by Downing Street.

Yet it was with some sense of elation that the government and legislature of New Brunswick rose to the possibility of squaring the account with the Americans to some extent. For a long time it had been considered desirable to impose a tax on timber exported from the province, a cheap and efficient substitute for the stumpage duties collected from the Crown lands. The treaty allowed the Americans to employ the down-river facilities of the St. John on the same terms as British subjects. A tax on timber exported by native merchants would fall equally on Americans who floated out logs from the formerly disputed territory. This finally went into effect in 1844. Thoroughly irritated, the American government protested; the British government subjected the question to anxious review, but the province was in a strong legal position and succeeded in imposing its policy.[55]

New quandaries suddenly arose. No sooner had the quarrel with Maine been decided than a new enemy, scarcely less truculent than the old, leaped into the fray. When the New Brunswick government started to exercise jurisdiction in the territory awarded to Britain, its magistrates collided with those of Canada. Timber operators, asked for the payment of duties, declared they had received licences from Canada to cut. The Commissioner of Crown Lands for that province, Denis-Benjamin Papineau (brother of the 1837 rebel), who was strongly supported by Sir Charles Metcalfe, adopted an aggressive attitude and declared that virtually all of the recently allocated territory to the north of the St. John belonged to Canada.

An element of absurdity entered the new controversy, which was scarcely less troublesome than that with Maine. The Proclamation of 1763 had adopted the highlands to the south of the St. Lawrence as the boundary between Canada and Nova Scotia. In insisting that the highlands lay far to the north, New Brunswick was using against Canada the arguments Maine had used against New Brunswick. Quebec was using the former New Brunswick argument that the highlands lay far to the south. In an attempt to settle the dispute quickly, the New Brunswick legislature passed an act for the establishment of Victoria County, which was defined to include all the territory in contention. This abrupt venture was defeated when the colonial secretary disallowed the act.[56] In consequence, New Brunswick was prevented for seven years from establishing within its northwestern area magistrates and parish officials who could be held responsible for the enforcement of the law over 4,000 people.

So utterly hopeless did any prospect of agreement between the provinces become that in 1846 the British government appointed a commission, consisting of two officers of the Engineers and the attorney-general of Nova Scotia. They were requested to report upon a line that should, if possible, satisfy the legal requirements of the two provinces but which should also be convenient in a practical way. Their recommendation that, of the area in dispute between the St. John and the hills to the south of the St. Lawrence, New Brunswick should receive 2,300 square miles of territory and Quebec 2,100 was rejected by the latter province in 1848. It was not until 1851 that a commission of arbitration, which was recommended by the British government and on which New Brunswick was represented by Dr. Travers Twiss, made the final award. Though it was essentially the same as that of 1848, it was slightly more favourable to Canada, which received "the two ancient fiefs" of Madawaska and Témiscouata. The line was run between 1853 and 1855. The boundary dispute with Canada, added to other irritations over trade and railway construction, strongly contributed to the absence of a cordial feeling between the two provinces that lasted until the time of Confederation.

CHAPTER 13

Free Trade, Reciprocity, and Self-Government

1848-1854

Sir Edmund Walker Head was the first civilian to become lieutenant-governor of New Brunswick. The change from a line of military chief executives, accustomed to rigid channels of command, to an urbane and moderately conservative administrator of the British Poor Law, versed in the uses of statistics and in the modern ideas of advancing society by means of legislation, and skilled in the refinements of classical, German, and Spanish poetry, coincided with a great transformation in the life of New Brunswick. The six years in which he presided at Fredericton mark a great divide in the history of the province. Self-government in domestic affairs, to a great extent established in practice for a great many years, had been proclaimed as a principle. So far as the external world was concerned, New Brunswick was faced with more freedom than she was prepared to accept.

Head arrived in the spring of 1848, just as the full impact of British free trade fell upon the province. Incipient mutiny was in the air as merchants, in the depths of pessimism, weighed the prospects for the future. It was bad enough in Canada, where it seemed that the British government was intent upon destroying the trading empire of the St. Lawrence, but Canada could at least feed itself. In New Brunswick, where there had been two bad harvests, where even the potato crop, laboriously sown between the stumps of newly cleared lands in the north, had failed, and where the welfare of the entire population had for half a century depended upon traffic with Britain, the probable effects of free trade inspired a general terror. The incapacity to produce enough food eliminated any prospect of self-suf-ficiency.

The elemental Loyalist devotion to the Mother Country was still powerful. Over the years, contact with the Americans had increased, and the morals and habits of the people of New Brunswick were similar to and often less refined than those of the people of other North American frontier communities. But even in Saint John, where the steamboats carried on a lively traffic with Boston and Eastport, and where trade with the Americans, both legal and illegal, had been a constant factor in the commercial fortunes of the city, the historic loyalty was an indispensable condition of decency and good respect. Looking the Americans in the face, criticizing their inferior government and dubious morals, and glorying in the knowledge that they themselves belonged to the mightiest empire on the face of the earth, were familiar affectations among the citizens of Saint John. Literature was British, and native culture in the arts and letters – such as it was – was derived from Great Britain. Anti-Americanism was almost always fashionable. Through the late forties public dinners and convivial gatherings rang to the verses of Thomas Hill, sung to the tune of "The British Grenadiers":

When thirteen states the gauntlet threw down to us of old
Our grandsires knew no fear and could not be bought with gold.
Though few and scattered midst their foes, no power could them awe.
So the Bluenose boys we'll give a cheer, hurrah, hurrah, hurrah.

They fought until the last and obeyed their King's command,
They left their foes their all for a home in British land;
'Twas then New Brunswick's wilderness a band of heroes saw,
So the Bluenose boys we'll give a cheer, hurrah, hurrah, hurrah.

When the Eagle rose again, on the lakes the war-notes rang.
But the brave Hundred and Fourth from our gallant fathers sprang.
At Stony Creek they decked her beak, at Lundy's lane her claw,
So the Bluenose boys we'll give a cheer, hurrah, hurrah, hurrah.[1]

The apparently fatuous abdication from empire on the part of the British Whigs, the abandonment of what New Bruns-wickers had always considered to be the real sinews of British wealth, aroused pain and bewilderment. The most loyal of prov-

inces had been repudiated by the Mother Country. In the meetings of the executive council over which Head first presided and
in an immense number of public meetings called throughout the
countryside, the sorrowful reaction was all to the effect that
Britain owed New Brunswick a great deal, that she must now
do something important to compensate the province for the
markets that would surely be lost.

To the articulate commercial leaders of the colony there
appeared two possibilities leading to redemption. One was the
opening of the American market for New Brunswick lumber,
now excluded by a twenty-per-cent duty. The second was a
general development of the fisheries, which were almost entirely
in American hands. Both expedients would require negotiation
with the government at Washington. In 1844 the British government had announced that the Bay of Fundy was a British
sea and had put forward the doctrine that the in-shore fisheries
of the Maritime colonies, from which the Americans were
excluded by the convention of 1818, were defined by lines drawn
from headland to headland, not by a three-mile limit drawn
along the indentations of the coast. Yet the Americans had
practical possession of the in-shore fisheries, sailing almost
wherever they pleased in defiance of the convention of 1818,
nourished by bounties paid them by their government, purchasing the produce of provincial fishermen for resale in their home
markets. Especially on the shores of Prince Edward Island and
Cape Breton there were large shore establishments that sold
goods to the Americans and welcomed their participation in the
trade on an equal basis.

As it appeared certain that the great transatlantic trading
connection was about to dwindle to something of little account,
the merchants of New Brunswick looked southward. The American reserves of standing timber were almost exhausted. If the
province insisted on her full legal rights under the convention
of 1818, her fishermen would be able to drive their American
rivals from the real riches of the fishery and secure a hold on
the American market. The growth of cities in the United States
and the rapid expansion of the American economy offered possibilities. Having been expelled, it seemed, from one market,
they would look to another. If Britain could not secure entrance
to American markets for the timber and fish of the province,
other expedients could be tested. Voices, always on the fringes
but increasingly bold, took up this refrain.

II

In the midst of this great quandary the formal introduction of responsible government seemed a mere corollary to a general proposition that was nearly hopeless, a part of the process by which the British government was shrugging away responsibility for the welfare of the colonies. Head's task was to form a government whose acceptance by the majority of the house of assembly would be unquestioned. Elections had been held as recently as October 1846, and there appeared to be no need for a fresh test of public opinion. The new wine had therefore to be placed, for the most part, in old bottles. The lieutenant-governor had no occasion for forming a new government, but there were opportunities for strengthening the old. This he proceeded to do in a manner that resulted in an administration combining the best talent available and commanding a wide basis of support.

It was to Chandler that Head gave his confidence in selecting the new government that was to function on the responsible principle. The public prestige and sage counsels of the Dorchester lawyer were so generally taken for granted that without him no administration could have been formed. Another essential element was Hazen, who was exceptionally popular in Saint John. There remained, from Colebrooke's council, Alexander Rankin of Douglastown on the Miramichi, regarded as a sound man except in so far as his local rivalry with Joseph Cunard was concerned, and George S. Hill of Charlotte, respected for his honesty and liberal views but lightly considered because he could never acquire the character of a strong partisan. For private reasons Hugh Johnston wished to retire. Thomas Baillie, who had acquired the novel role of popular tribune by entering the house of assembly for York in 1846, could readily be discharged because of the tremendous complexity of his private affairs. George Shore, aged and encumbered with a great many minor offices, likewise retired.

To attract new members to the government Head had three public offices to offer. John Simcoe Saunders had held the secretaryship since 1845, but politically he could be of no service since he held no seat in the house of assembly and had no prospect of winning one. When confronted with the new urgency that the secretary must be a member of the government capable of sustaining it from a seat in the legislature, he gracefully withdrew and was rewarded with a minor office.[2] Owing to the death of Peters, the attorney-generalship was also at Head's disposal, as was the solicitor-generalship, vacated by the promotion of George Frederick Street to a judgeship. Responsible government swept aside one of the age-old public prejudices of the colony inherited from New England, that "placemen" should not hold seats in the executive council. To his regret Head did not have Baillie's office to offer to a member of the government. Owing to the legislature's adamant stand against retirement allowances, the surveyor-general could not be removed from his office, since he had held it prior to 1839.

In filling the three offices, Head's position was complicated by a strong public feeling in favour of John B. Kinnear, a pillar of the Baptist connection and a senior at the bar, who had served in the legislature for many years. According to the more traditional standards of qualification for public office, he was first in line for one of the vacant posts. He was considered for both the attorney-generalship and the secretaryship, but ultimately he had to give way and accept the solicitor-generalship. What counted were influence in the legislature and the capacity to sway it to the point of view of the government.[3] There was pressure on Chandler to accept the attorney-generalship, but he was unwilling as yet to abandon his practice and, after registering a claim for a judgeship in the future, he deferred to Wilmot. The member for York, thoroughly at odds with his Liberal colleagues from Saint John, had no scruples about entering a ministry dominated by those he had long opposed. He was, according to Head, eager to reap the benefit of his long and consistent support of the idea of responsible government in a climate that had been apathetic to it.[4] Though Wilmot's views on responsible government had generally been regarded with little respect, his capacity for agitation and for unsettling a government in the house of assembly was greatly feared. No administration, Head said, could be stable without him. Into the government he brought with him Charles Fisher, who likewise abandoned his party spirit and joined his former foes. Thus, as the lieutenant-governor said later, the administration was a coalition of the ablest Liberals with the preponderantly powerful Conservatives.[5] In the legislature it could proceed with confidence, for there was no organized opposition to face it.

For the secretaryship a dark horse emerged the winner. Rather to Head's surprise, Chandler and Hazen put forward the claims of Partelow, whose peculiar powers in financial appropriations had so long been universally respected. The failure of the government to acquire an exclusive right to initiate money grants in the house of assembly implied a grievous limitation upon its powers to do anything very effective for the good of the province. But the inclusion of Partelow, the master of all the tricks of the old system, within the new government could obviate a great many of the difficulties certain to arise. "His opinion has the greatest weight in the assembly in all matters relating to money."[6] Private members of the house of assembly could still call for votes of public money. But Partelow could restrain and moderate their demands, and perhaps subordinate their local projects to the general programme of the government.

Nobody could deny that the government was responsible to the house of assembly or that it was just as popular a government as could be obtained at the time. The only consistent opposition that faced it came from Ritchie and two or three other members who on occasion referred to themselves as "the Liberal party". But the vast majority of members willing to support the government were not disciplined into the semblance of a political party. The government's strength was superficial and in all matters it would be compelled to go slowly. Sectional and local eccentricities still predominated. These would have to be harnessed to the general policies of the government if the new era of responsible government were to inaugurate a progressive change in New Brunswick's history.

III

Before Head met his first legislature in 1849, public opinion upon the great question of securing a new source of livelihood for the colony was floundering from one desperate expedient to another. It was inevitable that all the British North American colonies whose trade was so greatly depressed would look to one another for succour, and that they should co-operate in a common interest, especially upon the opening of American markets. The situation of 1848 provided the basic elements for a British North American union, but only small crumbs of comfort came. New Brunswick and Nova Scotia, dispensing with their jealousies, achieved free trade, but Canada and Prince Edward Island turned cold shoulders to what many considered to be the essential beginnings of a new commercial dispensation.

To Head's indignation the larger colony seemed especially callous to the common lot of all. New Brunswick was willing to enter upon free trade with Canada. But Francis Hincks, the inspector-general of finances in the new Canadian government, was fearful that New Brunswick and Nova Scotia would refine sugar and manufacture tobacco which, admitted freely to Montreal, would make grave inroads upon Canadian revenues. This was at a time when large quantities of Canadian flour were entering Saint John via New York without duty. How could Hincks suppose, asked Head indignantly, that the lower colonies where capital and labour were so sparse could effectively challenge Canadian industry and overcome the high costs of carriage?[7] The smaller colonies looked to Canada for leadership, but Canada seemed intent upon marking out a course for herself, especially to the counsels of the government at Washington.

During 1848 trade shrank to a third of what it had been in normal times. It was estimated that 5,000 natives of the province, who had for the most part mortgaged their properties to speculate in the timber trade, emigrated. Irish immigration shrank to a fifth of what it had been the year before. On the Miramichi the *Gleaner* was advocating annexation and the great house of Cunard went down, not so much because of the bad times as because of the improvidence of the proprietor who, according to tradition, faced a howling mob in Chatham with a pair of pistols thrust into his high-topped boots and roared, "Now show me the man who will shoot Cunard."[8] On May 31 a great meeting at Saint John, presided over by John Robertson, the city's greatest mill-owner and a member of the legislative council, called upon the British government to secure the entrance of New Brunswick produce to the United States. A meeting at Fredericton that shortly followed witnessed a stormy scene when James Taylor, an assemblyman, demanded the free entrance of American produce to New Brunswick, a concession that would grant the United States a substantial preference over Britain. In the end his resolution was withdrawn and the more moderate Saint John resolutions were adopted.[9] At Saint John the repeal of the Navigation Acts aroused at least as much resentment as the abolition of the timber preferences. There was a general and deep-rooted fear that American shipping, carrying not only American goods but those of all the world, would enter the ports of the province and engross its trade. To the southward was the rich American coastal trade from which New

Brunswick vessels were excluded. To allow the foreigner privileges that would place him on the same footing with British subjects without adequate return seemed a preposterous proposition.

At the opening of 1849 the spur to action became sharper when intelligence arrived that William Hamilton Merritt of Canada had gone to Washington to negotiate a reciprocity treaty on behalf of his province. The Saint John Chamber of Commerce demanded that New Brunswick should likewise send a commissioner. In reply the Colonial Office urged direct representations to John Crampton, the British ambassador at Washington, but agreed that if these should be unsatisfactory an adviser upon New Brunswick's requirements might be dispatched.[10] The legislature petitioned the British government for the privilege of introducing a bill modelled on Canada's, offering the free admission of American goods provided the United States would extend similar concessions in return. At Saint John the Colonial Association, directed by Charles Simonds, who the year before had attended meetings of the British American Association in Canada, pressed for a greater degree of co-operation among the colonies. At Dorchester the Canadian Association came into being. Because both of these associations shrank from the expedient of considering annexation to the United States, they were ridiculed by Fenety's *News*, which paraded the slogan of "No Dictation from Downing Street" and persisted in rationalizing in favour of political union with the great neighbour. Both in the press and in popular parlance the metaphors of domesticity abounded: the son leaving the father's home and the grown-up boy making a marriage. The mysterious proceedings of the Reform Club at Saint John, whose existence was undoubted but whose alleged objectives could scarcely be believed, caused perplexity. Events were forcing the conclusion that annexation made common sense. Israel D. Andrews, the American consul at Saint John, whose great aim was to secure the in-shore fisheries for his countrymen, wrote that the traditional New Brunswick loyalty to Britain, avowedly based on feelings superior to commercial considerations, was no longer important, that loyalties were declining just as rapidly as the British tariffs.[11]

Yet the United States was as apathetic as Britain to the pleas of the colonists. The appeal of reciprocity and the possibilities of expansionism were not as powerful as other prejudices that were brought to bear upon influential circles at Washington. Southerners believed that reciprocity would be a prelude to annexation and the increase of states opposed to slavery. Northern protectionists believed that reciprocity would facilitate the flow of British manufactured goods into the Union. The bill for reciprocity was defeated in the Senate. Very active among its opponents were the lumber interests of Maine. To New Brunswick this was all the more irritating because much of Maine's produce came from the province. Head himself had seen at Calais carts loaded with shingles and laths crossing the bridge from St. Stephen in open daylight, while the American revenue men, in deference to public opinion, took no notice. So far as Charlotte County was concerned, free trade with the United States was in effect. The Schoodiac was a narrow river and the mills on the New Brunswick side often projected beyond the centre of the stream. In a year, according to Head's estimate, $600,000 worth of sawn lumber went to the United States from Charlotte County. But elsewhere in New Brunswick, throughout 1848-9, laths and fence-pickets were used for firewood. California began to take its toll of the hardy young men of the province. At one stroke, agents from the cotton mills of New England persuaded 200 unmarried young women to leave the country.

Throughout 1849 feeling against the British Liberals, who were considered responsible for all the ills of the province, became more acute. The state of affairs in Canada sharpened the sense of grievance. From the counties of Carleton and York went petitions to London deploring the payment of indemnities to the rebels of 1837 and the treatment of "the noble-hearted Loyalists" who would be taxed to make it possible.[12] Prompted by Merritt of Canada, the New Brunswick government took the lead in calling an unofficial, informal, intercolonial conference that met in Halifax on September 3. Lafontaine of Canada was in the chair and Howe of Nova Scotia served as secretary. Partelow and Wilmot, the New Brunswick delegation, were armed with a minute of council that Head had been compelled to endorse: "But if with that British influence in our behalf we should fail in the accomplishment of our present purpose, a stern necessity will ere long impel the public mind to seek for relief by incorporation with the neighbouring republic." According to Head, the talk of annexation and independence in New Brunswick was of less intensity than in Canada, but the objectionable words were being used by persons whose loyalty had always been their particular pride.[13]

At this conference in Halifax the feeling of desperation that abounded in New Brunswick was reflected in the conduct of its delegation. Wilmot astounded the meeting by the announcement that in order to get "reciprocal coasting trade and reciprocal free trade" with the United States, along with the abandonment of the American fishing bounties, the province was willing to give up its exclusive right to the in-shore fisheries. Rather brashly, perhaps, New Brunswick threw its best bargaining counter into the game at the outset. The Nova Scotians refused to pay so high a price, and, though several resolutions were adopted, the fisheries were left out of them. There was regret for the want of unanimity, but the conference agreed that the continuation of the British connection was essential, and that the provinces must learn to know one another better and join together to find a new livelihood in the unfamiliar world of free trade.

New Brunswick doubted Britain's sincerity in the attempt to gain by diplomatic means a treaty of reciprocity with the United States, and distrusted Canada, whose unilateral efforts at Washington appeared to be contrived to ignore the needs of the smaller colonies. Eagerly the legislature proclaimed its willingness to do business with the Americans by concurrent legislation. In April 1850 an act was passed authorizing the Lieutenant-Governor in Council to proclaim the free admission of American goods when it was deemed advisable to do so.[14]

It was bad enough for New Brunswick to be compelled to work out her own salvation; it was worse to have her liberty of action circumscribed in the attempt to do so. Probably the low point in relationships with the Mother Country was reached in 1850 when the British government disallowed the act providing bounties for fishermen. Free trade for Britain may have been her own business. But "the imperialism of free trade", the attempt of Britain to force her perverse ideologies upon her colonies, could inspire the most loyal to rage and fury. Injuries and insults rapidly succeeded one another in these years. In 1848 the Imperial Post Office decided to abandon Halifax as the western terminus for the fast mails crossing the Atlantic by steamboat, "a measure fraught with evils for these provinces".[15] Boston was selected in its place. From Halifax the mails had passed through New Brunswick, and for a time Saint John had been the place from which European news and intelligence had been flashed over North America by another wonder of the age, the electric telegraph. The change was a token of the fact, by now beginning to be generally accepted, that the Atlantic provinces were being thrust from the main channels of commerce and communication.

IV

The thinking of the Governor General, Lord Elgin, on the future of British North America was not entirely *laissez-faire* and fatalistic. Canada and the other provinces would undoubtedly aspire to independence, but independence need not be coupled with annexation. If there was to be a parting with Britain it need not be in anger and, before the parting should come, the deep respect for British institutions, already instilled in their populations, could be strengthened. By co-operation with one another they could avoid the consequence of self-willed and disjointed policies – piecemeal absorption into the American Union. But in order to achieve this co-operation some plan rivalling reciprocity with the United States, already sought for by the British government, must spur them to joint action.

The Robinson report, published late in 1848, contained suggestions for a new political as well as commercial dispensation. The railway from Halifax to Quebec, paid for by the British government as atonement for wrongs done to the colonies, would be the necessary condition upon which they could stand together. Elgin encouraged the idea. Encouragement came from London too, but it quickly became evident that the British Whigs would never face Parliament with the request for the million pounds considered to be the cost for the implementation of the scheme.

Yet the suggestion that Britain would pay was sufficient to inspire hopeful speculation on the idea that railway construction could rehabilitate the province. The Robinson report was taken up with enthusiasm but was soon overshadowed by modifications introduced to it from the particular aspirations of Saint John, where gloom was greatest and speculation correspondingly extravagant. Emphasis shifted to the subsidiary report of John Wilkinson of the surveyor-general's office, who for years had been studying the New Brunswick countryside with an eye to future railway construction. His remarks upon the report of Robinson were given as much publicity as the report itself.

Pressing the advantages of a "central" rather than a "circuitous" line, he pointed to the fourteen bridges that would be necessary to traverse the chasm of the Matapedia. Saint John and St. Andrews were closer to the West Indies than Halifax was. A central line, running down the valley of the St. John, would serve as a trunk line for the province. Branches from it would radiate, and the interests of all sections would be served. The official report, argued Wilkinson, was based on military considerations, but why should the great trunk line, on which the military security of British North America depended, run through a country that was largely French and incipiently hostile?[16]

As a terminus for the Intercolonial, Saint John would demand at least an equal priority with Halifax and would, if possible, completely exclude her rival. For the purpose of opening up the river valleys in the hinterland a railway company had already been formed, but had disappeared for want of capital. Yet a new hope had given stimulus to the passion for railways. In 1848 a few thousand pounds' worth of fresh salmon, packed in ice, had been dispatched by steamboat to Boston. The day after it arrived, the salmon had been served on dinner-tables in New York, Albany, and Philadelphia. The idea that became rampant was that all the produce of the fisheries of the Gulf of St. Lawrence and the northern rivers could be exported through Saint John to the United States in the same manner. What was needed was a railway connecting Saint John with a port on the Gulf, preferably Shediac. Though not comprehended in the Robinson report and really alien to the purposes of an intercolonial railway, a Saint John-Shediac line, in the minds of the majority of the New Brunswick populace, became a ruling feature of an intercolonial system. Other lines had prospects that were commercially dubious, but there was a ripe conviction that such a line would pay. Wilkinson had surveyed it, remarking on the easy gradients of seven feet to a mile.

Reacting to the Robinson report, the provincial government accepted the project of a Halifax-Quebec line, adding the suggestion, mild at first, that a Saint John-Shediac line should be an integral portion of it. Though it was admitted that such a railway would never pay dividends, considerations that transcended the financial were put forward as the ultimate justification. The colonies would be bound together by a great commercial link. Troops could readily be sent to Canada in the

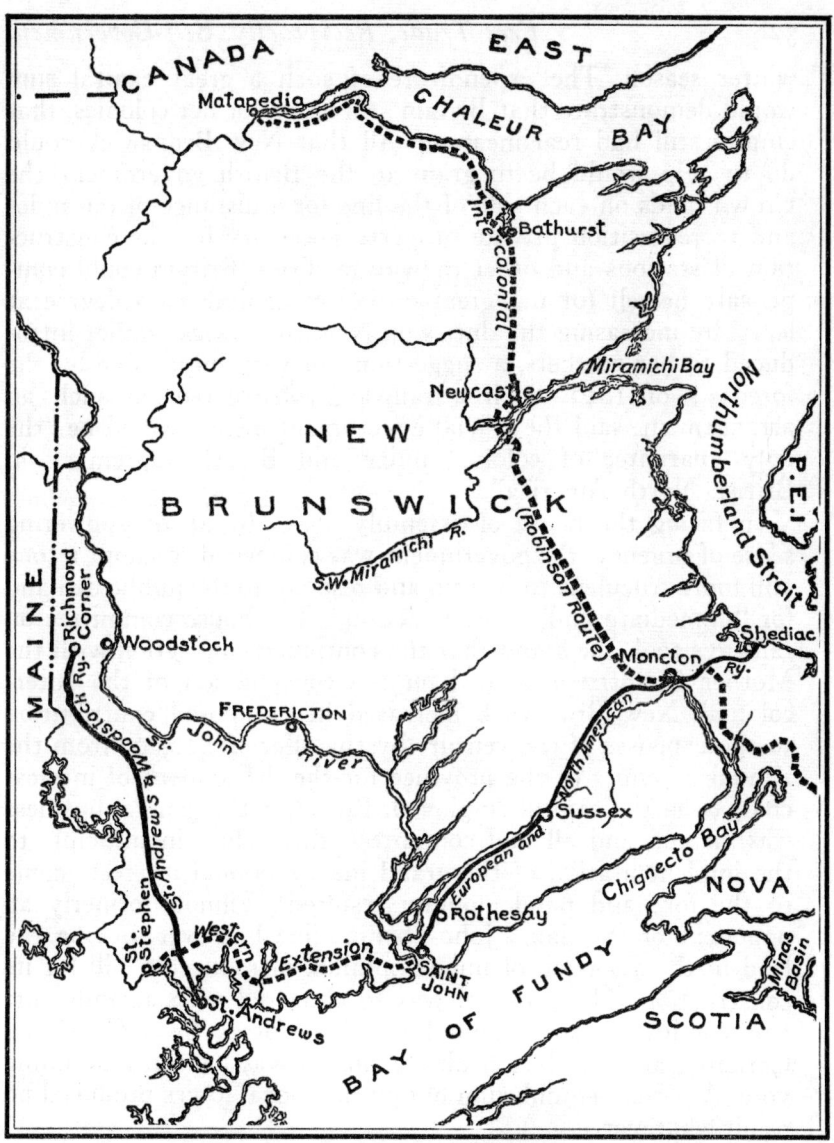

NEW BRUNSWICK RAILWAYS TO 1867

A broken line indicates projected routes.

winter season. The expenditure of such a great capital sum would demonstrate that Britain still cared for her colonies, that empire still had real meaning. All that New Brunswick could do to help would be to grant to the British government the Crown lands on each side of the line for a distance of ten miles and to requisition private property necessary for the construction of stations and other railway facilities. Britain could compensate herself for her great outlay of capital, to a degree at least, by increasing the duties on New Brunswick timber introduced to her markets, a suggestion not very impressive by the forecasts of 1849. Such a railway, constructed on such an arrangement, said the official government memo, would be "the only guarantee of colonial unity and British supremacy in British North America".[17]

In facing the house of assembly, beset by an overpowering sense of urgency, the government was compelled to adopt a tone still more truculent to Britain and respond to the public demand for "immediate and vigorous action". The house committee on railways took the stand that the continued connection with the Mother Country depended on the construction of the Intercolonial. New Brunswick increased her proposed contribution to the expenses of the venture by the offer of £20,000 from the annual revenues of the province for the defrayment of interest charges on the capital employed. But after the general business was cleared and all had committed themselves in principle to the implementation of the grand idea, sectional interests came to the fore and pandemonium resulted. Wilmot, formerly an opponent of the Saint John-Shediac line but ever seeking the lead in the assertion of public opinion, introduced a bill for its construction. The proposal was so cluttered with amendments and conditions, so assaulted by rival forces from Charlotte, Carleton, and the North Shore, that it was lost on a standing vote. A perfect equilibrium of opposing local forces produced no result whatever.

The defeat aroused fury in Saint John. Citizens streamed to the news-rooms and book stores to sign petitions of protest. Blamed for duplicity in the defeat of the bill which seemingly he had supported, Fisher was hanged in effigy. A railway league was formed and a deputation sent to Fredericton. Under this pressure the house of assembly in the last days of the session relented. On April 10 Ritchie introduced a bill to grant facilities for the construction of the Saint John-Shediac line, requiring a provincial guarantee of £300,000 of capital stock and the taking up of half of this amount by the province. It was carried by nineteen to twelve. The elation in Saint John reminded men of the news of Waterloo, but it was short-lived. The legislative council resoundingly defeated the bill by twelve to four.

Combined with the failure to advance towards a reciprocity agreement with the United States, the failure to produce quick results in railway construction brought black despair to Saint John. The city was prepared to mutiny not only against the British government but against the province. Popular rancour in large part expended itself upon the legislative council, which so clearly had manifested the Frederictonian and back-country apathy towards progress. By defeating the railway bill the council exposed itself to demands for its reform. Canada was in process of making its legislative council elective. Radical, democratizing ideas, similar to those across the border in the United States, took possession of the minds of the most conservative and most loyal.

V

One element of good cheer passed almost unnoticed amid the gloom of 1849. This was a good harvest. The experience of other commercial depressions repeated itself, and farmers found that they were able to bid for the services of immigrant and other labour that became available. In 1850 another good harvest came. There was a brisk demand, according to Perley, the immigration agent, for female labour in farm households. Males were required at £12-£15 per year. Head was emphatic in asserting that the noisy disaffection so apparent in Saint John and other commercial centres had scarcely touched the yeomanry, the most stable element in the population.

In the spring of 1850, in consequence of the repeal of the Navigation Acts, foreign ships in considerable numbers arrived at Saint John. Freight rates fell and, though it was hard on ship-owners, deals could be loaded at a profit. New prospects began to open up. Eight vessels loaded with lumber cleared Saint John for California. The British government's fears of smuggling had abated, and there were now sixteen free ports in New Brunswick where British and foreign goods could be warehoused without payment of duties and re-exported.[18] Four hundred Irish immigrants were employed in fresh construction on the St. Andrews-Woodstock Railway. Their disorderly habits impelled the sending of a small detachment of troops to the St. Croix.

Head had anticipated a complete and painful transition in the economic life of the colony, the reduction of the timber trade to a subsidiary position, and the growth of agriculture to a place that would be central and fundamental. Yet to the surprise of everybody, themselves included, New Brunswick merchants found that they could, in free competition with foreigners, sell their goods not only in British markets but throughout the world. In 1851 there was no doubt about it. Prices for deals and logs were double those of 1849. The Crown Lands Office tripled its sales of timber berths. Wages were high and money was abundant. Steam sawmills at Saint John now competed with tide-mills. Head regretfully remarked on the annual waste of thousands of tons of sawdust tossed into the harbour, a sharp contrast with the enterprise of the merchants of Boston who had developed a great trade in ice with the Mediterranean by using the waste produce of American sawmills to pack it. Again there were fears of over-speculation in timber and consequent ruin. Ever since 1837 the government of New Brunswick had dealt lightly with the timber trade. In bad years merchants had been exempted from the collection of debts owed for the use of the Crown lands. Now that good times had returned, they resumed their former habits of stripping the public domain of its good timber at the price of ten shillings the square mile, leaving behind them the underbrush and other waste material, along with the unsightly and decaying log houses of their workmen. To impose a restraint on speculation, Head persuaded the government to raise the price to twenty shillings.[19]

New Brunswick could not duplicate the brilliant progress Canada was making at this time. For the ten years prior to 1852 the average annual increase in population was a mere 2.35 per cent. But the new prosperity of this year induced a much more robust approach to the problem of gaining entrance to American markets. In 1849 reciprocity had seemed absolutely necessary. Now it seemed merely desirable. The province could bargain from strength, and the noisy clamour that had voiced a disposition to make all kinds of concessions to the United States abated and disappeared.

New England's desire for the in-shore fisheries of the British colonies compelled Washington ultimately to evince interest in an agreement. Frequent reminders from Downing Street that these had been held as a privilege and not as a right softened the intransigence of both the Filmore and Pierce administrations. To compel a greater interest and to extract from the Yankees a higher price, it was logical to rigidly enforce the British headland-to-headland doctrine. At Halifax the commander of the North Atlantic squadron, Sir George Seymour, reported to London that in the colonies there was a general conviction that Britain would not sincerely enforce what the people conceived to be their rights.[20] Responding to alarms of this kind, the Derby government announced in May 1852 that American vessels would be excluded from in-shore waters. The three large warships operating from Halifax were replaced by seven smaller ones, mounting in all but thirty-one guns, yet capable of chasing and intercepting intruders in the shallow waters off the coasts. With enthusiasm for a show-down with the Americans, the colonial governments provided small vessels of their own to supplement the imperial effort. Two seizures were made in New Brunswick waters. The case of the *Coral*, out of Machias, taken at North Head off Grand Manan, offered complications. Of the crew of five, three were British subjects and residents of Grand Manan who had entered service in order to qualify for the American fishing bounty. Such expediency, it was remarked, was common among the inhabitants of Grand Manan.[21] These seizures, and the four others that were made elsewhere, created a sensation in the United States. Advisedly, Head's understudy, Lieutenant-Colonel Murray, who was in charge while the lieutenant-governor was on vacation in London, ordered the naval officer at Saint John not to enforce the British interpretation of the 1818 convention too rigidly. The intention was to force the United States to negotiation, not to war.

This profound impact upon American opinion and the election of a new president late in 1852, clearing the air of stagnant political issues, gave new life to the prospects of a reciprocity treaty. Israel D. Andrews, the American lobbyist and negotiator whose peculiar talent was the greasing of the palms of congressmen in order to gain support for the ventures in which he was interested, realized that the task of winning the in-shore fisheries for New England would be much more difficult than in 1849 but renewed his efforts with zeal. His particular forms of persuasion were brought to bear upon the politicians of all the

Atlantic provinces.[22] The government of New Brunswick was reaffirming its position more stiffly. There was a new spirit of faith in the fisheries, a determination to renounce the practice of selling green fish to the Americans who marketed the finished produce at profitable prices. The forests, it was conceded, were exhaustible, but the fisheries were not.

The official memo of December 1852 demanded from the Americans free entrance for fish, sawn lumber, shingles, and a long list of other natural products. It argued that the United States could offer no fair equivalent for the surrender of the in-shore fisheries, but stated that New Brunswick was willing to pay the price for the sake of future good relationships. To pacify the opposition of Maine the province was willing to abandon the export tax on timber that Maine merchants had been paying since 1844 on their produce floated down the St. John, and to agree, though reluctantly, to American navigation of the river.[23] What was wanted more than anything else was the admission of vessels constructed in New Brunswick to American registry and to participation in the great coasting trade of the Atlantic states that presented itself as a huge prize, long forbidden but eagerly sought. New Brunswick shipbuilding had entered the phase of quality construction. At this very time the great timber drogher *Marco Polo*, of 1,600 tons, constructed at the Marsh Creek in Saint John, was making her return voyage to Britain from Australia, establishing her reputation as the fastest ship in the world, having defeated a steamboat on the outward voyage by a full week. Saint John builders were selling their great vessels to the shipping firms of Liverpool for service on the trading lanes of the world. New Brunswick-built vessels had acquired a reputation for excellence, based not only on speed equal to that of the American clippers but on carrying capacity as well. Expensive materials such as Quebec oak were being imported. Jealously the legislature was moving to forbid the exportation of the famed hackmatack knees, the angular growths so useful in the construction of the hull.

Throughout 1853, owing to the conflicting balance of forces in American Congress, negotiations were in the doldrums. In 1854 the outbreak of the Crimean War made the British government more eager for a settlement. The fisheries dispute could conceivably lead to war, and, in the minds of British ministers, the purely commercial considerations in the bargaining became subordinated to possibilities of warlike diversions on the other side of the Atlantic. It was merely a happy chance that inspired London to send Lord Elgin to Washington. Nonchalantly he plied congressmen with hospitality, strengthening the conviction of those from the north that reciprocity would hasten annexation, introducing to those from the south the novel idea that reciprocity would so content the British North Americans that its effect would be to delay rather than hasten annexation and the increase of the anti-slave states. At his side, representing the interests of the province, was Edward Barron Chandler, presumably a cold fish in a sea of sunlight. The grandson of a Connecticut Loyalist whose confiscated property had been valued at £30,000, Chandler had grown up as a poor boy at Amherst. When he set off for Halifax in 1821 to be admitted to the bar, he and a friend had hired a horse, each alternately walking and riding two miles. Now pre-eminent in the politics of the province, he had made his Dorchester home, Rocklyn, "the hospitable mansion", renowned for its good cheer and fine wines, but "cool reason" always prevailed.[24]

The treaty did not give New Brunswick the concession that seemed of greatest importance, admittance to the American coasting trade. It gave up the export tax on timber but denied the Americans the navigation of the St. John. Though the Atlantic provinces had what the Americans wanted most, the in-shore fisheries, they received no preferred treatment from the Americans or special solicitation from the British government. Yet the general advantages that could result from the free entrance of natural produce to the United States were so great that the quibblers were readily silenced.

Reciprocity came as only another blessing to the people of New Brunswick. In 1853 revenues had risen by thirty per cent. In September of that year a veteran lumberman had said to Sir Edmund Head, "It is the first year that I've lumbered that a man was ever asked what he'd take for his lumber." Competition for pine and birch was so intense that the truck system was breaking down and the peculiar hold long exercised by merchants on the generality of the population was weakening. In spite of the repeal of the Navigation Acts, the trade of Saint John rapidly increased. An age-old faith perished when it was perceived that New Brunswick shipping need not depend on monopoly for survival. Fish canneries were opening up, and the trade in fresh salmon to the United States for 1852 doubled the figures for 1850. As the reciprocity treaty came into effect, it

was to the sea that the people of New Brunswick were looking
for profit in new opportunities. Head brooded upon the previous
neglect. "I have seen the whole Bay of Chaleur abounding as it
does in fish with scarcely a boat upon its surface."[25]

VI

In this season of new prosperity railways came with reciprocity,
though New Brunswick was not, as some of its apologists had
prophesied, suddenly transported into the new era of the
Brotherhood of Man. During the exploratory period, the issue
that had slowly emerged was whether the province should
become associated with Britain, Canada, and Nova Scotia in a
great imperial venture, or enter into a series of enterprises that
would intensify the southward pull of trade with the United
States. Britain's failure to agree to accept the costs of the
Halifax-Quebec line impelled the adoption of the latter solution. Grey wanted the intercolonial lines as the essential introduction to the political union that Durham had recommended
ten years before. But the encouragement he could offer was
scarcely meaningful to the impoverished legislatures of the
lower provinces.

Only a month after he wrote his dispatch of June 1850,
announcing British refusal to pay, and following a session of the
legislature in which the house of assembly, "driven from the
markets of England", had urged financial assistance as a means
of restoring New Brunswick's confidence in the imperial government, the forces at work to swing the province into railway
connection with the United States came into the open. John
Alfred Poor, a railway promoter of Maine, resented the manner
in which the commerce of his state was being drawn into the
orbits of Boston and New York. Since the greatest retarding
influence on transatlantic commerce was the long ocean voyage,
so slow in comparison with the speed of railways, it seemed
that Halifax was a much more logical outlet for the produce of
northern Maine. The distance from there to Europe was but
two-thirds as great as from New York. The great new European
and North American Railway that he projected, running eastward from Bangor, and traversing the more populous areas of
New Brunswick and Nova Scotia, could bring the continents
closer together.

This ambitious plan was precisely in accord with the impatient character of New Brunswick opinion in 1850. It fitted in

perfectly with the specific project that was most in favour, the Saint John-Shediac line. It was with enthusiasm that the governments of the two provinces responded to Poor's invitation to attend a conference at Portland on July 31. Howe came from Halifax, vying with Wilmot in expressions of good fellowship. There were sentimental allusions to the happy reunion of rebels and Loyalists, a plenitude of Latin epithets, and great crescendos of cheering as the success of the project seemed assured. Wilmot, whose oratory caused universal astonishment, rhetorically mused upon the enormous market that lay before the Americans within their high tariff walls. To gain entrance to that market and to be joined to it by a railway appeared as the object most greatly to be desired by the people of New Brunswick. The provincial delegations gave the scheme complete support and came home pledged to enlist the support of their legislatures. New Brunswick successfully resisted a Nova Scotian plea, put forward by J. W. Johnston, that at Saint John the railway should cross the Bay of Fundy by ferry and move on to Halifax by the Annapolis Valley. Complete unanimity was achieved. Americans acquired the notion that the British colonists had finally been swept onto the path of progress. Before the Portland convention, said one account, the manners of Saint John were those of the era prior to the Revolution. "To see its inner life was to turn back a hundred years. . . . All their ideas were English."[26]

In the assembly of 1851 there were some members who believed that railways were ruinous and other members who, though agreeing that railways were ruinous, were willing to support them out of generosity. The surge of public opinion in favour of the European and North American Railway produced bills to incorporate the company and to facilitate the construction of the railway by annual grants that could amount to £250,000. To silence the opposition of Charlotte County members, the St. Andrews-Quebec line was also subsidized, but only up to a maximum of £50,000. The intercolonial idea receded into the background. In the session of 1851, because the British government had refused to undertake the costs of the implementation of "the great national scheme", its members were called mercenary. Pressures that would cause the province to gravitate more rapidly to the United States had triumphed.

Yet Grey, unwilling to allow the colonies to abandon the idea of co-operation with one another, made another effort before the session ended. On April 1, going as far as he dared in face of the anti-colonial sentiment that was rampant in the Liberal Party of Britain, he offered an imperial guarantee on the interest charges for the capital to be expended on the construction of the Intercolonial. If New Brunswick intended to take the Intercolonial seriously, the offer could be a tempting one. Under the imperial guarantee money could be raised in London at a rate unknown on the American side of the Atlantic, four and a half per cent. In return, Grey asked that the sums for the payment of interest should be made a first charge on the revenues of the province. The proposal was seriously discussed but then abruptly dismissed. Having pledged so large a proportion of its revenues to the construction of the southern lines, the assembly was in no humour to accept still greater obligations. The decision produced new explosions of sectionalism. On May 9 "a very large and unanimous meeting" at Dalhousie, voicing the anger of the northern counties, condemned the "hasty" decision of the legislature, the construction of railways by private corporations, and the surrender of vast quantities of Crown lands to the two companies that had been subsidized.

In the opinion of Sir Edmund Head, New Brunswick was playing fast and loose not only with her own destiny but with that of British North America as well. To the pleasure of those who believed that the continuation of intercolonial co-operation was in jeopardy and that the imperial connection was wantonly being sacrificed, an imperial solution came from a new quarter. In Nova Scotia the European and North American, though highly esteemed, could not replace the Halifax-Quebec line as an avenue to future prosperity. Joseph Howe came forward with the aspiration that the competing points of view could be reconciled: that the Saint John-Shediac portion of the European and North American could be integrated with the Halifax-Quebec scheme and favoured by the imperial guarantee. Ambiguous wording in the dispatches from Downing Street gave reason for adopting this hopeful point of view. Her Majesty's Government was now willing to consider the extension of the guarantee to a railway running through British territory, though not necessarily along the route recommended by Major Robinson, reserving the right to give approval to any deviation from it. Howe became the eloquent missionary of an intercolonial system that could transcend New Brunswick's local anxieties and sweep on from Quebec to the Pacific.

Through the summer of 1851 Howe struggled to achieve unity among the colonies on the vexed problem of railway construction. On the pretext of technicalities, Grey delayed the royal assent to the bill facilitating construction for the Saint John-Shediac line, pleading that the New Brunswick decision had been a hasty one and that the legislature should reconsider. Fear arose concerning the ability of Poor and the capitalists of Maine to fulfil their part of the bargain. Credit in that state had often been fictitious, and the defalcations of American railway promoters were now beginning to be taken for granted. In July, Howe and Chandler proceeded to Toronto, taking Poor along with them and meeting Francis Hincks, who was acting on behalf of the Canadian government. Working largely on Howe's assurances, the conference assumed that the imperial guarantee would include the New Brunswick section of the European and North American. Canadian interest quickened in the prospect that the Intercolonial would run through the populous St. John Valley rather than through the sparsely settled North Shore, a prospect largely nourished by the susceptibilities of New Brunswick opinion and Howe's good cheer. The agreement to construct a great railway, extending from Halifax through Saint John and the St. John Valley as far as Sandwich in Canada West, was reaffirmed in later conferences at Halifax and Fredericton. This was a nice compromise between imperial sentiment and the businesslike determination of British North Americans to trade with the United States.

This magnificent diversion, lifting men's minds beyond the immediate and the practical, occupied the labours of the three legislatures for 1852. When the test came, it was immediately perceived that the hopes were vain. In company with Hincks, Chandler went to England in the spring and, after a long period of deliberation, the new colonial secretary, Sir John Pakington, decided that no guarantee could be offered, declaring his disappointment that the line adopted by the three governments should differ so widely from that proposed by Major Robinson. Undismayed, and falling back on what the government of New Brunswick considered the fundamental feature in the whole scheme, Chandler immediately opened negotiations with British railway contractors for the construction of lines running from Saint John to Amherst and the American frontier. The commitments he made and the large responsibilities he assumed with considerable courage resulted in a contract with Messrs. Peto, Brassey, Betts, Jackson and Company, finally signed at Saint John on September 29. The cost of the 214 miles of construction agreed upon was to be £6,500 per mile, the province taking stock in the European and North American to the extent of £1,200 and loaning its bonds to the company for £1,800 in addition. A nine-day session of the legislature in October confirmed the arrangements Chandler made.

The imperial vision of Howe and the champions of the Inter-colonial faded into oblivion. "Not satisfactory intelligence," wrote Herman Merivale, the under-secretary at the Colonial Office, on the receipt of the dispatch announcing the decision to go ahead with the European and North American.[27] Confident in its prosperity, the province felt that its peculiar needs for railways could be satisfied by the efforts of private corporations adequately buttressed by public support. For Saint John the millennium had arrived. The seaport city, by-passed by the imperial planners, had triumphed over the machinations of its enemies both at home and abroad and would shortly become the centre of a great system of railway communications. The huzzas in Saint John were echoed through the valley of the Kennebecasis, at the Bend of the Petitcodiac, and at St. Stephen and Calais on the St. Croix.

Throughout 1853, men and materials poured into the prov-ince, concentrating at the three points where construction was to commence: Shediac, the Bend, and Saint John. In August preparations began for a great celebration to mark the turning of the first sod. On September 14, 5,000 tradesmen of Saint John, certain of their strength and proud of their prosperity, escorted Sir Edmund and Lady Head through the streets of the city, and the ceremony was performed amid exuberant cheers and sanguine speeches promising a boundless future. Tragedy marked the ball that followed in the evening. As the affair was breaking up, the stand constructed for the orchestra collapsed and three persons were fatally injured. Some said it was a bad omen for the railway. There were ruminations, too, upon the failure to toast the success of the St. Andrews-Quebec line dur-ing the festivities.

As construction commenced, difficulties began to obscure the brightness of the prospect. The winter of 1853-4 was severe, and the spring freshets were higher than any previously recorded.

It became evident that the estimated cost of £6,500 per mile was far too optimistic. Between the signing of the contract and the commencement of construction, the cost of labour went steeply upward. English navvies who had been brought out to perform the labour were seduced from the railway by lumberers and farmers who offered higher wages. Many left New Brunswick for the United States. The new-comers brought with them Asiatic cholera, which infested Saint John. It was just as evident that another estimate had been too optimistic, that of thirty miles of construction each year.

At St. Andrews, optimism likewise prevailed, but the difficulties were greater than those of the European and North American. In 1851 the new company had survived a strike of its labourers for a dollar a day. Twelve miles of indifferent construction were completed in the next year, but capital was drying up. The New Brunswick shareholders refused to pay the balances due on their commitments. In Charlotte County £41,000 in stock had been taken out but only £1,500 had been paid in. The public money made available by the Facility Act was used to pay old debts rather than to inaugurate new works. Fresh financing made a new start possible. But the English board of directors quarrelled with the local board, and, as soon as the trouble was settled, the local board quarrelled with the contractors, finally dispossessing them. In July 1852, the first train loaded with freight from Montreal arrived at Portland. The St. Andrews-Quebec line, however, the would-be competitor of the St. Lawrence and Atlantic, had completed but nine miles and had graded an additional fourteen. Other great schemes made still less progress. William Scoullar of Grand Falls lost a fortune in promoting a line to join the northern section of the St. John Valley with the southern.

Sectional influences appeared to have prevailed over the imperial and national, but this could well have been designated a short-sighted interpretation. Other tendencies had been powerfully at work. The conferences on the Intercolonial, induced by Howe, had brought colonial leaders together. British free trade had forced upon them new horizons dimly perceived. "Now, like a blind puppy, whose eyes are partially opened, they [the colonies] begin to feel their way. Whoever writes the history of British North America, by whatever name it may be known in the time to come, will date the epoch of its nationality from the middle of the nineteenth century."[28]

VII

Establishing responsible government and keeping it on a stable basis was a difficult business for Head during his first three years as lieutenant-governor. There had been a great deal of congratulatory talk upon the achievement of self-government, but the task of persuading the administration to function according to the precepts of the British system, and the legislature to grant it the large powers comparable to those of the British cabinet, was prolonged and complicated. Complete change could not come quickly. The position of the government was novel. Its resignation could suddenly be impelled by a defeat in the house of assembly where there was no party discipline and no certain majority. Assemblymen still prided themselves upon their independence, and insisted upon their historic right to introduce money bills with or without the approval of the government. Wilmot, Partelow, and Hazen, upon whom fell the burden of presenting government points of view to the house, nervously jolted along through the tangled mass of legislation that came from all quarters. Shrewd tacticians, they made it their business to anticipate opinion in the house, not guide it. "Open questions" in which the policies of the government were not compromised were the familiar ones.

Bitterly, Head complained of the failure to introduce British practices of financial appropriation in all their purity. "A great deal has been said in these provinces on the question of Responsible Government but the one peculiar subject on which the Executive Government ought to be responsible to the representatives of the people – the relation of expenditure to revenue – is practically conducted to exclude all responsibility." The private member of the house was still a local tyrant for his tenure of office. During the prosperity of 1852 and the years following, as revenues moved sharply upward, the log-rolling and petty bargaining in the appropriations committees became more brash and open. This department of legislative activity was, in Head's opinion, "a scene of jobbery of the grossest kind".[29]

Even members of the government were averse to facing up to the refinements of the British system of government, especially the necessity of offering advice to the lieutenant-governor and taking responsibility for it collectively. Failure of the government to reach a decision upon the appointment of a chief justice provoked the only major discord between Head and his advisers, the only serious obstacle to the leadership given by the lieutenant-governor in the application of British constitutional practice. The election of 1850, fought before the return of prosperity, had been won largely by candidates who exploited the popular jealousy of office-holders. A desire for economy prevailed, and the assembly of 1851 came together in a spirit to destroy what remained of former privileges. The judges of the Supreme Court were the most obvious target. In 1849 the British government had agreed to the reduction of salaries of newly appointed office-holders protected by the Civil List compact of 1837, but the fervour aroused on the hustings compelled the assembly to attack the salaries of existing office-holders as well. Two arguments were advanced for breaking "the compact", so joyfully accepted in 1837. The Ashburton Treaty had taken away a large portion of the Crown lands secured by the settlement. The remainder had shrunk in value owing to the abolition of the British timber preferences. While the incomes of the vast majority of the people had been reduced by fifty per cent owing to the downswing of the business cycle, office-holders were fair game. The members of the assembly, wrote Head sardonically, wanted the judges' salaries for the by-roads.[30]

The independence of the judges became a principal preoccupation of the lieutenant-governor. In formal protests the judiciary registered their disapproval of the point of view that dominated the legislature. Why should they be placed at the mercy of committees of the house of assembly, many of whom were lawyers frequently appearing in actions before them? The government would do nothing to head off the movement. Wilmot, instead of standing by his convictions and resisting, placed himself at the head of the agitation in the house of assembly, trusting that the legislative council would reject the resolutions requesting the British government to consent to the reduction of salaries of existing office-holders. In council Head had a hard few weeks as the session of 1850 was breaking up. Fearing the influence of Wilmot on the hustings, he did not dare ask him to resign.[31]

The British government accepted the odium of refusing to act on the resolutions, insisting on the binding nature of "the compact" of 1837. When the second Ward Chipman resigned from the chief-justiceship in October, at a time carefully arranged by Head beforehand, there was every reason to antici-

pate a stirring session of the house of assembly that was to
meet in the winter. Since Chipman in recent years had, owing
to ill-health, performed most of his labours in Saint John and
had not gone on circuit, the ruling idea in public opinion was
that three judges could do the work instead of four. In opposition to this popular prejudice, Head was prepared to appoint a
new chief justice and, if necessary, to reorganize his government
to face the expected onslaught in the house of assembly. As he
anticipated, the government could not agree on offering him
advice. A majority advised that the appointment should not be
filled, and on October 25 those who did not reside in Fredericton
returned to their homes without the recording of a firm decision.
On October 26 he was visited by Wilmot, who informed him
that he had changed his mind, produced a letter of Lord
Glenelg recommending him for a judicial appointment by virtue
of his great work of 1836-7, and announced that he would be
willing to accept a judgeship if it were offered to him. This
reduced to one the majority in favour of making no appointment. Dispensing with the counsels of a divided government,
Head acted on his own discretion. He advised Grey that the
new Chief Justice should be James Carter, the Englishman who
had come as little more than a boy in 1835 to be a judge of New
Brunswick, had scrupulously abstained from political activity
of any kind, and possessed a private fortune. To fill Carter's
place as a puisne judge, he recommended Wilmot, Chandler
having indicated his wish to take no advantage of his superior
claims.[32]

Hesitatingly Grey acted on Head's suggestions, and the
tribune of responsible government was rather unceremoniously
shuffled out of the administration and into a judgeship, a poor
prize for the great place he had taken in public debate during
the past fifteen years. Wilmot's determination to remain in the
van of all the capricious shiftings of public opinion had prevented the government from taking a firm stand on a great
many problems, and Head was happy to dispense with his
services as attorney-general. The lieutenant-governor, owing to
the government's division and dereliction from constitutional
conduct, had carried his point, but the storm remained to be
faced. Five members of the executive council formally objected
to the proceedings because they had not been consulted concerning the appointments. Only Fisher resigned, "consistent
with my ideas of Responsible Government".[33] Only Fisher was

prepared to admit that responsible government had for a time ceased to function and that the lieutenant-governor had acted without the advice of his council who held the confidence of the house of assembly. Here was a magnificent opportunity for proving that the rights of the people had been disregarded and trampled upon, that New Brunswick came into a category somewhat below that of Canada and Nova Scotia, where responsible government was in effect. "My Lord, what would you think upon returning from a ride in Hyde Park if Your Lordship had been informed that Her Majesty had accepted the resignation of the Governor of Jamaica and appointed him Governor-General of India?" Fisher had supposed that the days of "back-stairs influence and court favouritism" were over, but his zeal for making the constitution of New Brunswick a replica of that of the parent state had suffered a dispiriting reverse.

To find a new champion who would fight the battles of the government in the house of assembly was now essential. Wilmot had gone, and Hazen, who for many years had performed the role with conspicuous success – admittedly a very able man but not an ambitious one – wished to retire to the tranquillity of the legislative council. Partelow, the master of financial manipulation, was no debater. On the advice of Chandler and Partelow, Head turned to John Ambrose Street. Like his father, Samuel Denny, and elder brother, George Frederick, John Ambrose Street was a fighter. Early in life he had gone to the Miramichi where the family predilections enjoyed full scope. Temperamentally opposed to reform and highly conscious of his position as a senior barrister, he had frequently voted with the reformers when it suited his interest to do so. He had first attained prominence during "the fighting election" of 1843 when, as a candidate in a disputed contest, he had written a letter to a newspaper declaring that Sir William Colebrooke would be responsible for the blood to be shed on the Miramichi owing to his refusal to send troops to the scene. His conduct during the campaign had contributed so greatly to the swelling animosity of the two parties that Colebrooke had been compelled to change his mind.[34] Like the other Streets, he had never been taken to the centre of official circles, but there was no doubting his intelligence and his capacity.

During the session of 1851, the advent of Street gave new leadership and cohesion to the government. Headed by Ritchie, the opposition hoped to carry a motion signifying want of con-

fidence. A remarkable medley of resolutions against the manner
of appointment of the Chief Justice, the high salaries protected
by the Civil List, and the refusal of the lieutenant-governor to
furnish his correspondence to the inspection of the house of
assembly – a new point raised by Fisher – occupied a week of
debate commencing April 14. Street's tactics were to refine the
resolutions by amendments in such a manner that the conduct
of the government should not appear to be directly assailed. On
every vote he won a majority. In the end, although the government had succeeded in extracting from the resolutions the sting
that could be damaging, Head emerged as the tyrant and Grey
as a colonial secretary minded to deprive the colonies of their
liberties of self-government. The anticipated storm had risen,
but most of the winds had blown across the water. Head's government, though strongly beset, had triumphed. It was doubt-
less easy for the lieutenant-governor to accept the abuse
gracefully. On each of the specific points at issue he had won
his case.

Yet it was difficult to keep a government functioning when
but three of the nine members were salaried officials. The
creation of new departments such as a board of works, a board
of education, and an audit office, would entail salaried offices
that could be filled by members of the government. Head
steadily moved towards this objective. He strove to achieve a
greater degree of attendance at meetings and cohesion in the
making of policy on the part of his advisers. One department,
hitherto denied, became his prize. Baillie, the surveyor-general,
had finally worn his opposition down and was awarded a pension of £500 during the session of 1851. This complied with the
condition of Earl Grey's dispatch of 1847, and Head was free
to release him from his duties. The warm temper and extravagant habits of the formerly great man had not abated. Troubles
had continued to beset him owing to his careless supervision of
his subordinates and his persistent demands upon the public
purse. He was still a man of big ideas, unbowed by years of
humiliation and defeat, demanding that the government should
be given the power to inaugurate great public works, protesting
that the humble squatter was the chief engineer of the province.[35]

To strengthen his government and to fill the office, Head
turned to Saint John, which, during the years of depression,
had been the headquarters of opposition to his government.

Robert Duncan Wilmot (cousin to Lemuel Allen Wilmot), who had spent his boyhood years as an apprentice to a timber importer of Liverpool, became surveyor-general. John Hamilton Gray, a lawyer of great eloquence, joined the government without portfolio. The defection of two such able critics of the government confounded Saint John. Charles Simonds, William J. Ritchie, and Samuel Leonard Tilley, members for the city and county, announced that they would resign their seats if Wilmot won the by-election that he would be compelled to fight, having accepted a salaried office. In October, when Wilmot was triumphantly returned by a large majority, the three honoured their promises. In another election shortly following, three supporters of the government were returned. The anger of the people of Saint John had fallen not on Head and his alleged tyrannies but on those who boasted that they carried the banner of reform and progress. For the next three years the government, with virtually no opposition to face, was all-powerful in the legislature.

Gradualism was the rule in the changes that came in the wake of responsible government. Especially with the return of prosperity in late 1851, the philosophy of reform exercised little appeal, even in Saint John where public opinion could be stirred by the onset of new ideas. In still another area reform was defeated. Municipal reform by incorporation, advocated by the Durham Report, put into practice in Canada West and strengthened by the legislation of 1849, and propagated by Colebrooke during his years in New Brunswick, was given a trial during these years. The movement was directed against the highly centralized control over local affairs exercised by the provincial legislature and by individual assemblymen. For years the sharp bargainings and hidden conspiracies of assemblymen to secure provincial appropriations for projects in their constituencies had been a subject for ridicule in the provincial press. To get parish business out of the legislature, to strengthen local initiative, and to induce a sense of local responsibility, seemed to be logically integrated with the new democracy that was in the ascendancy, and with the new faith in the sovereignty of the people that permeated the English-speaking world.

In 1851 the legislature deferred to these feelings by passing an act permitting counties and parishes to become incorporated as municipalities. It provided that incorporation could take place in any county or parish following the presentation of a petition signed by two-thirds of the ratepayers. In three counties, Charlotte, Northumberland, and Carleton, significant movements developed. Yet, though the feeling was strong, the obstacles were too great. Almost everywhere the assemblymen and magistrates feared new mechanisms of government rivalling their own and opposed the change. Municipalities were denounced as new agents of the tax-gatherer.[36] In Victoria the necessary two-thirds majority was obtained, allegedly owing to intimidation by a gang of rowdies brought across the border by interested parties, but the legislature threw out the petition that resulted.[37] Carleton became incorporated, but the county council that was elected found itself possessed of no real power. Conservatism ruled, and the historic method of doing public business at the local level remained almost completely unaffected.

VIII

Sir Edmund Head was later considered by Sir John A. Macdonald to have been the ablest governor general of Canada. There is little doubt that he was the ablest lieutenant-governor of New Brunswick. Of slender build and fair complexion, scholarly yet of ready address, he was easily enabled, by his early training in law and administration, to surmount the difficulties he encountered in the province. He was called a dictator, but when he left for Canada in the autumn of 1854 he was regarded with a respect unknown to any previous representative of the Crown. It was his New Brunswick experience that made him an apostle of the new imperialism, of the belief that a federal union of the British provinces must be achieved if the connection with Britain were to be retained.

Though he had a great respect for the shrewdness and sharpness of the people of New Brunswick, he could see almost everywhere "the moral results of imperfect physical development". New Brunswick was unprogressive because it was small, and the smallness was accentuated by the divisions imposed by nature. The great hills and forests that carved the province into sections denied any true union of minds and of hearts. Each section looked outward to the sea rather than to Fredericton. Legislative proceedings produced no concerted effort but rather the action of forces that were opposed to one another. There was a paucity of men fit to govern but no dearth of men whose concepts of political usefulness included the winning of appropriations for by-roads and the building of interests based on the distribution of public patronage. To enlarge the field of political activity, to enlist fewer but abler men for the work of government, he advocated a union of the three lower provinces and later a union of all British North America. Narrow and local feelings would have to be broken down by imperial action. While Britain could still bring powerful influences to bear upon the colonies, she should impel them towards union and take advantage of the new climate of opinion induced by the prosperity of 1852 in which "Men appear to say to themselves, 'We are too great a people to be tied on to the government at Washington whether by fair means or foul.' "[38]

Tensions abounded in the immature and divided society New Brunswick continued to be. Angered by the willingness of the British government to pass the Ecclesiastical Titles Bill in Britain itself and to tolerate the legal incorporation of Roman Catholic sees, the Protestant conscience made violent protest in these years. The Orange Order, now something of a political power throughout British North America, sparked grave animosities. July 12, the day of provocative memories, was annually a time of elation for some, misgiving for others. In many communities Catholic religious processions inspired throngs of Protestants with feelings of frustration and fury. Two sets of extremists rejoiced at opportunities of looking one another in the face. When Head arrived in 1848, trials were proceeding at Woodstock against the leaders of the Catholic party who had caused great disturbances the year before when an Orange procession had been held, contrary to the admonitions of the magistrate, there being no law to forbid it. Thirty-four of forty-nine accused were sentenced and imprisoned. Public sentiment in Carleton County dictated that the province should compensate those who had suffered loss by damage of property, but the legislature refused to do so. A couple of years later, on a summer's night in Woodstock, James Brown of Charlotte, a member of the hostile majority, mingled enjoyably with the discordant mob of Orangemen who had heard that he was in town and who serenaded him with tongs, kettles, and saucepans, contemplating with some amusement his effigy that was burning on high.[39]

These elemental passions reached their height in 1849 when thousands of Orangemen converged upon Saint John in great determination to fight it out with "the Mickeys" on July 12. On the evening of July 11 the mayor tried to persuade their leaders not to march, but without success. Early on the following morning, unable to procure the assistance of special constables, he proceeded to the Irish section of the city, York Point, and found on a hill, up which the Orange procession was scheduled to move, an arch of greenery, low enough to compel the dipping of the banners as they passed through. Arguing that the work was an obstruction that would not permit the passing of a load of hay, the mayor urged the people standing about to knock it down. When they refused, amid the throwing of stones and the firing of pistols, he proceeded to do so himself, until his head was cut open by a brick-bat.

Barely escaping with his life, but determined to halt the Orange procession, the mayor called upon Colonel Deane of the Royal Regiment to turn out his troops. Just in time, they were drawn up in one of the squares of the city to face the procession as it moved on York Point. The Orange leaders, wearing their badges of office and with swords drawn, and followed by a score of men carrying muskets with bayonets attached, declared that they wanted peace but would not go back. A conflict followed, the troops marching and countermarching between the parties. Ultimately the Orangemen, after giving the Queen three cheers, retired from the scene. A field gun was moved into position by the troops as a precaution against further disturbances.

On the evening of July 13 Head and Wilmot took the night boat from Fredericton, and in the early hours of the next morning passed through the streets of Saint John, which were patrolled by troops. Warned not to walk through York Point, they nevertheless did so and could observe the funeral services that were taking place in the dimly lit houses of the district. Processes at law commenced but, for the most part, it was impossible to obtain convictions. Two Orangemen were found guilty of trivial offences. But the grand jury refused bills of indictment and fifteen men, charged with carrying offensive weapons, went unpunished.[40]

The powerful prejudice against the Orange Order amongst official circles in Britain, the fact that Orange processions in Ireland were banned, and the implications of this disgraceful affair in Saint John, compelled Orangemen to indulge in less ebullient demonstrations during the years following. Head was strongly inclined, in accord with public opinion generally, to blame the Orangemen, who enjoyed a state in society better than "the misguided persons whom they provoke to break the peace".[41] For a long time the legislature refused to incorporate the Order.

Theological questions could still lead the legislature to zealous debate. In 1852 a petition for drawbacks upon duties paid for the importation of stained glass windows for a church on the Miramichi encountered fierce opposition. The year before, Bishop Medley had renounced his seat on the legislative council. This left but one fragment of the Church of England establishment, the chair of theology in King's College. This institution had failed to achieve greater popularity following the reforms of 1845. The abstruse, traditionalist attitudes of Jacob, the principal, who drew two salaries and devoted much of the proceeds to his real estate at Cardigan, had not helped it. Even its stoutest defenders now had to admit that the courses should be liberalized and that the chair of theology must go. At the time of the great legislative attack of 1854 there were but fifteen students within its walls. This was similar to other onslaughts upon projects of a provincial, centralizing character. The college was sustained by a grant of £2,200, half of which was guaranteed by the Civil List, and the other half provided for by what was called the permanent law. The money was needed in the constituencies. "They must either take this money and distribute it among the counties or get a locomotive to carry the College around the country."[42] The bill to "discontinue the grant to King's College" was most volubly sponsored by Albert J. Smith, the lawyer from Westmorland who was rapidly becoming prominent. In an article in the Fredericton *Head Quarters,* edited by Marshall d'Avray, who was one of the professors at the college, Smith was likened to Erostratus of Ephesus who, for the sake of notoriety, would have burned down the Temple of Diana. Smith's retort on the floor of the assembly was that if the college were burned down with the professor inside it the consequences would be of great benefit to the country.[43]

In the midst of the debate that lasted for fifteen days, Head, who had successfully worked for the introduction of a course in engineering, made the suggestion that a commission should be appointed to review the affairs of the college. Abandoning the intricacies of the discussion, the house agreed, and a few months later John William Dawson, superintendent of education for Nova Scotia, Egerton Ryerson of Canada, and President Francis Wayland of Brown University, proceeded to consider how the institution might be put to greater use. Deprecating the parochialisms that were at work in higher education in the colonies, Head caught up the suggestions made earlier by Colebrooke, urging the establishment of a single degree-conferring institution for all the Maritime Provinces that would tolerate instruction at existing colleges and impose uniform standards upon them.

One powerful prejudice that for a time forced all others into the background startled New Brunswick in these years. Quite suddenly during the legislative session of 1852, a monster petition with 9,000 signatures was presented to the house of assembly requesting that the importation of alcoholic beverages should be prohibited. For five years the Sons of Temperance had been gathering strength, organizing their forces in the unpretentious little churches that dotted the countryside, contributing not only to the great cause to which they were pledged but to all causes that were deemed worthy: anti-slavery, relief to immigrants, and, later, the patriotic fund for the Crimean War. Their activities had commenced at St. Stephen in 1847, and branches had mushroomed up all over the southern part of the province. They possessed some of the mysticism of secret societies, but frequently they indulged in outward shows of their faith: processions with plumed horses, garish banners, and brass bands. Teas, picnics, and steamboat excursions helped to cement the bonds. All members of the family could be included, for there were also Daughters of Temperance and Cadets of Temperance. Especially among the Baptists and Wesleyans they formed a kind of state within a state, a nucleus of the more respectable in small communities. Harnessed to politics their power could be fearsome. Their leader was Samuel Leonard Tilley of Saint John.

To the astonishment of the sophisticated, the bill passed and became law, to take effect on January 1, 1853. Largely inspired by the Maine law, and because of social phenomena similar to those in Maine – the annual outpouring from the woods of thirsty lumbermen who roistered for days on end – New Brunswick took the drastic step. In anticipation of emergencies the merchants of Saint John imported 6,000 gallons of brandy and 5,000 of Geneva gin in a single week. Considering that the bill was opposed to English ideas of liberty, Head was inclined to refuse assent, but his government would not give the desired advice and he shrank from the odium that would follow. He urged the Colonial Office to exercise the power of disallowance.

But Downing Street, by this time wise to the risks of pulling colonial chestnuts out of the fire, refused to interfere.[44]

It quickly became evident in 1853 that the sophisticated, who declared that the act could not be operated, had been right. The lawyers in the house, it was bitterly alleged by the temperance men, had seen the flaws in the act and had slyly let them slip through. The judges of the Supreme Court found it inconvenient to deal with appeals from the lower courts. In Saint John, the mayor, considering authority of the city's charter to be supreme, serenely continued to grant licences for the sale of liquors so that the city became a resort for all who wanted to drink freely. In those parts of the country where magistrates discontinued the sale of licences, taverns closed; but illegal replacements quickly appeared. At the Bend of Petitcodiac the number of taverns suddenly increased from three to thirty-seven. During the winter months liquor was dispensed from sleighs. Not even the Sons of Temperance long enjoyed the role of informers, for "they had to depend upon the community for a living".[45] Opponents of the act took heart at the pronouncement from the judicial seat of Lemuel Allen Wilmot that "the law was conceived in tyranny and ended in fanaticism and violence".

In a year in which the financial obligations of the province had been vastly increased by the acts to facilitate railway construction, the legislature had agreed to sacrifice one-sixth of the revenue and to accept unascertained charges for the prevention of smuggling. But within months public opinion turned positively against the prohibition act. In 1854 it was quietly repealed. The experiment had been a great failure, but in June of that year Samuel Leonard Tilley became Most Worthy Patriarch for the Sons of Temperance for all of North America. In his own province he had behind him a piece of political machinery redoubtable for its moral power at election time and an agency for propaganda that in the future would stand him in good stead.[46]

Possibly something of the truculence and disunion of the white inhabitants of New Brunswick was in these years imparted to the aborigines. Peter Basket was a renegade Malecite who in his youth had gone off to the Miramichi and taught basket-weaving to the Micmacs. Clever and expressive, he had been made their chief. Parchments commanding obedience of the Indians to their chieftains had become a notorious cause for grief, and Head had refused to continue issuing them. It was with anger that he read in an edition of the London *Mail* of January 1852 that Basket, dressed in European costume but wearing a scarlet sash from which was suspended a long constable's staff, and decked in a row of medals, had appeared before the Lord Chancellor in Lincoln's Inn and applied for a writ of *quo warranto*. It was irritating to be informed by the popular prints that London laughed at New Brunswick's eccentricities.

CHAPTER 14

The Rule of the Smashers

1854-1864

The year of the Reciprocity Treaty was remarkable for other novelties as well. Succeeding Sir Edmund Head as lieutenant-governor came John Henry Thomas Manners-Sutton. A young man of thirty-nine, trained in the law but never called to the bar, educated at Eton and Cambridge, he had been selected by reason of a promising ability that had been displayed in an under-secretaryship of the Home Office. His family had important connections with the Church, and his father was a renowned Speaker of the House of Commons. He himself had served in the House of Commons, though at his first election he had been unseated for bribery. He came to New Brunswick clearly under the conviction that even in the days of responsible government the office of lieutenant-governor retained a large area of responsibility.

Novelties were the rule, for in October of this year a new house of assembly gathered to meet Manners-Sutton for the purpose of ratifying the treaty with the United States. It was in a humour rather proud, since "the commons" of New Brunswick (as they now called themselves) for the first time exercised the right of giving formal and necessary approval to a treaty with a foreign state. The result could be foreseen. The failure of the British government to secure the registration of New Brunswick vessels for the coasting trade of the United States, it was argued, had inflicted an injustice upon the province. But it was generally agreed that this injustice could be endured in return for the great possibilities that lay ahead. Money-wise men were saying that within a few years the historic balance of payments would be reversed and the Americans would be paying the province in specie for fish and lumber instead of draining away all the hard currency that could be mustered.

There was another and more immediate cause for excitement. The election in the spring had returned sixteen new members to the house of assembly. The government professed to be unworried, and there was a certain amount of patronizing talk of the necessity of educating youthful and inexperienced politicians. Three members of the administration from Saint John, Partelow, Wilmot, and Gray, had headed the poll in the county vote, and Street had won resoundingly on the Miramichi. It was loudly asserted that the people had given ample proof of confidence in their rulers. Yet when the meeting of youth and age took place at Fredericton, rumours began to dispel the confidence of the régime that had, under the leadership of Chandler and Hazen, been in power for so long. Charles Fisher, out of the legislature for four years, had been returned for York and was preparing the evidence to show that, in the crisis of 1851 concerning the appointment of the Chief Justice, the government had "kow-towed to the dictatorship of Sir Edmund Head". Old members returned with new griefs on the failure to win municipal incorporation, the leasing of Crown lands to large capitalists at the expense of small business men, the refusal to incorporate the Grand Orange Lodge, and the distribution of patronage to official favourites. "It was the prevailing opinion in the north that if a man was defeated in an election it immediately qualified him to office." In the election the government had avoided issues of principle. John Cutler of Kent made this remarkable announcement: "When I went to the hustings in June last and met the electors of Kent no question concerning the government came up that I remember." But a host of local causes were accumulating to defeat it. The old tribune of Gloucester, William End, who had been called back from the United States by telegraph to fight the election, declared that the government's election bill of the year before had been designed to exclude him from the legislature. Against the opposition of Ferguson, Rankin, and Company, and the other merchants of the constituency who had intimidated the French voters by threatening refusal to purchase the socks and mittens knitted by their wives, he had triumphed. Armand Landry of Westmorland, though speaking English imperfectly, was plain enough in his remarks to make it certain that he had been sent by his constituents to turn out the government.[1]

What the traditionally-minded found novel and sinister was a succession of caucuses followed by reports of the circulation of a document by which members pledged themselves to vote against the government in the debate on the Speech from the Throne. Charles Fisher was imparting a new intensity to the organization of the house of assembly, welding together a political party from the rump of the former opposition and the new members who had appeared on the scene. Labels that suggested abstraction or enlightenment had never been popular in New Brunswick, but an extraordinary number of the new members were speaking of liberalism and liberal principles. New Brunswick had heard of liberalism before, but in the confusion of 1847-8 the discipline and unity essential for the formation of a liberal party had failed to appear. The fragmentation of opinion in sectional rivalries among those who favoured reform prevented reform from making any real headway.

With the knowledge of certain victory before him, Fisher on October 20 introduced an amendment to the fifth paragraph of the Address in Reply, declaring a want of confidence in the government. Like so many other speeches of the period in New Brunswick politics, it contained innumerable references to the grievances of the past, concentrating on the circumstances of his resignation in 1851. Awkward in his appearance and mannerisms, but highly logical in his reasoning, he gave most of his effort to showing that the government in that year had "quailed" before Sir Edmund Head, and that responsible government had not really come in 1848, but that it now shone luminously on the horizon. Something more than a mild note of challenge to the new lieutenant-governor, a defiance of all future custodians of the royal prerogative, was contained in the words: "If, as some supposed, Sir Edmund had met him in Boston, and informed him how he could rule his Council, and through them the country; that the Bluenoses had no pluck, that the new members were divided and could be beaten in detail . . .".

The burden of defending the government fell principally on the shoulders of John Ambrose Street. By reason of his zealous championship of the office-holders whose independence was safeguarded by the Civil List, he was a principal target for the politicians who had acquired popularity by attacking privilege.

His resourcefulness and pugnacity were of no avail. He complained that the government had been prejudged, that it was a victim of a "Barker House Conspiracy", that nothing like the taking of pledges from members to oppose a government was known in all parliamentary history, not even in the political bible of the mover of the amendment, the Durham Report. By October 27 he good-humouredly agreed that the success of the allied army at Sebastopol was as certain as the defeat of the government. On the following day the anticipated result occurred when the division was twenty-seven to twelve against him.

Shortly after, for the first time in New Brunswick history, a government resigned because of an adverse vote in the house of assembly. Even the "liberals" were at last certain that responsible government had come.

Appointing Fisher, the recognized leader of the opposition, as attorney-general, Manners-Sutton called upon him to form a new administration. The other leaders in this political revolution, as it was jubilantly called, were men whose social philosophies, interests, and ambitions had brought them together against the long established "compact" government. Leonard Tilley, not the most eloquent but generally the most respected, had been born at Gagetown, the son of a Loyalist. He had become an apprentice to an apothecary in Saint John, had taken part in the debates of the Mechanics' Institute and the Sons of Temperance. His advertisements for patent medicines and pills had been featured regularly in the issues of the Saint John press, and, over the years, he had acquired a reputation as a man of wealth, estimated by Manners-Sutton at £10,000-£15,000 – a great sum for New Brunswick at this time.[2] Learning how to conduct public business at the frequent meetings of the Sons of Temperance, he had made of that organization a political engine that rested at his disposal. Added to the prestige this power gave him in the legislature was a wondrous capacity for figures and statistics of trade. Economy had been his watchword. In Fisher's new government he assumed the office of provincial secretary.

Also from Saint John was William J. Ritchie, the Liberal purist who had violently resented the entrance of Fisher and Wilmot into the coalition government of 1848. He was peculiarly identified with the local interests of Saint John, having more than once headed movements for the establishment of the capital in that city. As legal counsel for the European and North American Railway, he was bound to the idea of what was beginning to be called "western extension" – the connection of Saint John by railway with the United States – having opposed with all his influence the intercolonial project of Joseph Howe. "That gentleman had misled the people by visions of bags of gold which never had any existence but in his own fevered imagination."[3] Other lawyers taking places in the new government were John Mercer Johnson, the solicitor-general, who represented the less gentlemanly and more robust qualities of the Miramichi, and Albert J. Smith of Westmorland. In opposition, both had been notable for the violence of their views upon "the privileges" of the compact government and its friends. James Brown, an immigrant from Forfarshire who farmed in Charlotte County, was the new surveyor-general. A Universalist by faith, self-educated, the author of a widely-acclaimed literary production, *The Deil's Reply to Robbie Burns*, he had pursued a political career remarkably independent. He had no appetite for constitutional subtleties but was noted for the honesty and practicality of his opinions. The government of seven was completed by William Henry Steeves, a lumberman of Albert.[4]

The change had social as well as political implications. No member of the new government was of the historic families that had ruled in the earlier days of the province. It was not surprising that there should be murmurings to the effect that the decorous days of the legislature were gone. The change had been gradual, but its full meaning came suddenly in 1854. Patrician attitudes were no longer in fashion. The way was cleared for a new and young government, none of whose members was over fifty, to give full play to the progressive impulses known as Liberalism. The "compact" had been the heirs of the close dependence upon Great Britain of earlier times. They had made changes slowly. Their character as a "compact", especially as a "family compact", had been grossly oversimplified by their opponents. In assessing the course of past New Brunswick politics, Manners-Sutton honestly doubted if a compact had ever existed.[5] But there was no doubt in his mind about the nature of the change that occurred at the outset of his régime. "The existing government was formed upon the principle that the direction of public affairs had been too long in the hands of men of property and liberal education."[6]

II

Manners-Sutton did not like his new advisers. The Liberals, as they called themselves in moments more pontifical, had inherited the benefits of prevailing currents of thought both in Britain and in British North America. All had preached the necessity of reform. Their extremists, in the turmoil of elections, had not hesitated to tell the people that an alien governor from across the water was trifling with their liberties. Charles Connell and John Mercer Johnson had urged the feasibility of electing governors. Head had suffered from their innuendoes, and Manners-Sutton quickly came to the opinion that Fisher and his following were opposed to the imperial connection and what remained of the lieutenant-governor's authority.

It was only upon occasions when responsible government functioned imperfectly that a lieutenant-governor could exert real influence, but these were to be frequent in Manners-Sutton's time. When a government evaded responsibility or was divided upon matters of fundamental importance, the royal prerogative could still be used with devastating effect. In 1855 the lieutenant-governor scented an opportunity for getting rid of the executive council, whose habits of thought and political policies he found so distasteful. In the legislative session of that year, Tilley, inaugurating a second crusade against intoxicating liquors, introduced a prohibitory bill. It was carried in the house by twenty-one to eighteen and twenty-one to seventeen, with the members of the government dividing evenly in the voting. Rather surprisingly, it passed the legislative council by ten to seven. When Manners-Sutton asked his council whether or not he should give his assent to the bill, he was told that he should do so. If Ritchie alone, he said, had failed to give him such advice, he would have refused assent.[7]

At the time, the Sons of Temperance were making a concerted effort throughout British North America. The Canadian and Nova Scotian legislatures were considering prohibitory bills that seemed likely to pass into law, and the efficiency and zeal of the "temperance men" were so great that the most experienced and hardened of politicians feared to place obstacles in their way. Yet throughout the province the sensibilities of the public at large were in great trepidation as the date for enforcement, January 1, 1856, was awaited. Though the act was far more stringent than its predecessor of 1853, some refused to take the prospect seriously, since the enforcement of the former law had been farcical. Others hoped that Manners-Sutton would refuse assent, though he could not do so constitutionally. The last hope of the rather inarticulate opponents of the act was that the British government would disallow it. In spite of responsible government, several petitions liberally signed by magistrates and other leading persons went to the Colonial Office, where long experience had taught well-informed under-secretaries that nothing was to be gained by attempts to solve colonial dilemmas. Most pointedly, Manners-Sutton exhorted Lord John Russell to advise the Queen to disallow the act. Lord John Russell could find no excuse for doing so.[8]

When the act went into effect, a cry of outrage swept over the province. The breweries at Saint John and St. Andrews closed down. Enforcement was general and effective enough to hurt a great many people, and it told upon the poor with especial rigour. "The land was filled with spies, pimps and informers. . . . The country was almost in a state of civil war."[9] The Sons of Temperance were rampantly on the offensive, spurring on the magistrates with information, prowling about the public places of Saint John in search of evidence. Early in the winter, upon the meeting of the legislature, members arrived in the expectation that, in deference to the general feeling throughout the country, the government would move to repeal the act. Tales of hardship had become frequent. On the lips of a great many was the story of the poor man of Kent who, as he was emerging from the woods near his house, was taken by the officers of the law, sent to Saint John for trial, released by writ of habeas corpus, and discharged into the streets a pauper without the means of returning to his wife and family.

Glumly the legislature waited for action, but nothing happened. Neither the government nor any substantial group of private members was prepared to sponsor repeal for which, it was generally agreed, the country was eagerly waiting. Then Manners-Sutton made his move. On May 6, shortly after the session had broken up, he addressed to the government a memorandum declaring that habits of lawlessness were being engendered among the people, that the prohibitory act must be either enforced or repealed. If they should refuse to do either, he warned, a dissolution of the house of assembly would become necessary. On May 17 the government replied that the act was not "wholly inoperative", and that the true state of public opinion upon it could not be ascertained at the time. On the 19th Manners-Sutton expressed himself as disappointed that the tendering of such advice had not been accompanied by a resignation, avowing his belief that a dissolution of the house of assembly was the remedy for the difficulty. Would the government take responsibility for that? Tartly the government replied that the lieutenant-governor had not yet done anything to render such a course necessary; and on the 21st Manners-Sutton, pressing his case to the extremity, directed that the dissolution should be proclaimed. The executive council refused to do so, and the instruction was redirected to Tilley, the provincial secretary, who complied. On the same day, the government resigned and Manners-Sutton at once indicated that he had found advisers who were willing to take responsibility for the course he had urged.

Headed by Chandler and Hazen, "the compact party" returned to office. John H. Gray became attorney-general and Robert Duncan Wilmot, provincial secretary. Novices to executive power were John Campbell Allen of York and Francis McPhelim of Kent. The latter appointment could be taken as evidence that no government could now be formed in New Brunswick without at least one Roman Catholic member.[10]

Taking advantage of the prevailing excitement concerning the liquor act and losing no time while opinion was on his side, Manners-Sutton called for new elections, which took place in June. A political crisis had been added to the moral one. The power of dissolution, exercised in such a way as this, was faintly reminiscent of Charles I. There was consternation at the Colonial Office when it was realized that, in a colony where responsible government was the rule, the lieutenant-governor had used his authority to the very limit and had forced his advisers to resign. The gamble had been a bold one, and Herman Merivale, the under-secretary, suggested an expression of disapproval preliminary to a possible recall.[11] Manners-Sutton knew full well the risk he had taken. He had pledged his whole repute in New Brunswick and that of the royal prerogative as well.

In the hasty contest that followed, Fisher and his party were at a great disadvantage. They did their best to disavow responsibility for the prohibitory act, endeavouring to concentrate attention on the circumstances of the dissolution. A canvass against the lieutenant-governor had been made inevitable, and the Liberal cry, divested of its refinements, was that Manners-

Sutton had come out from England to trample upon the people. As John Mercer Johnson somewhat ruefully said later in the legislature, "It was unparliamentary to attribute improper conduct to the governor, but if any other man had done it, it would have been called a trick."[12] Seconding the constitutional issue raised by the Liberals came the strenuous canvass of the Sons of Temperance, behind whom the forces of evangelical Protestantism were largely ranged. "Preachers had gone through the country to cry that the dissolution was an attempt to put down dissenters."[13] The *Religious Intelligencer* viewed the contest as one between a polluted, Puseyite Protestantism and Romanism on the one side and pure Protestantism on the other, a conspiracy on the part of aristocracy and Romanism to deprive the people of the right to self-government.

Still wasting no time, Manners-Sutton convened the newly elected house of assembly on July 17. A remarkable number of the old house had survived an interlude of almost unprecedented political confusion, but sufficient change had taken place to bring about a realignment that would be favourable to the new government. Those who had gone to the people with the two appeals of doing away with the prohibitory act and supporting the governor were clearly in the majority. Several who had voted for prohibition in the previous session had changed their minds during the campaign. Tilley, in company with other champions of the prohibitory principle, lost his seat. Again the debate on the Speech from the Throne was the testing time for a government. Deliberately Manners-Sutton invited discussion of the dissolution, and he was triumphantly vindicated. By twenty-three to sixteen and twenty-four to fifteen "the faithful commons" of New Brunswick acknowledged with satisfaction the propriety of his reference to the people and declared that "so judicious an exercise of the power entrusted to Your Excellency by the Constitution" would be followed by beneficial results. The most appropriate comment was probably that of John H. Gray, that the dissolution had been justified by electoral success.

The repeal of the prohibitory act by thirty-eight to two was a mere formality of the nine-day summer session. In less than two months Manners-Sutton had not only rid himself of advisers whom he disliked but had rid the country of a measure that was alien and unpopular. That future historian of New Brunswick, Joseph W. Lawrence, speaking for the first time in

the house as "a progressive conservative", hailed the lieutenant-
governor as a saviour and hoped that the great fame of Mr.
Speaker Manners-Sutton would be exceeded by that of his son.[14]

The hard, swift election campaign had produced a new political nomenclature. The supporters of Manners-Sutton and his
new government were called "Rummies". In retort they called
Fisher and the Liberals – allegedly the destroyers of the good
old way of doing public business and the apostles of radical
change – the "Smashers". The latter expression lasted through
the ascendancy that Fisher and his colleagues were presently
able to restore.

III

The triumph of "the gentlemen", so manifestly a triumph for
Manners-Sutton, could not last long. No sooner had the night-
mare of the prohibitory act passed from the scene than the
forces that really dominated the politics of the colony regained
control. The traditionalists could not survive the novelty of the
party spirit Fisher had engendered. The house of 1857 met amid
the same kind of uncertainty as the house of 1854. In vain the
government complained of the curse of party spirit, made accu-
sations of bribery, and spoke of the sinister influence of Barker
House plots. In a scene somewhat akin to that of the twilight
of the gods they won their first important division on February
23 when the Speaker, the aged Charles Simonds, cast his decid-
ing vote in their favour, denouncing responsible government as
an abominable system in which members of the house of assembly merely warred for office. The quotation from Montes-
quieu, that "when the legislative and executive powers are
united there is no liberty", fell heavily upon all, but especially
enraged Fisher and his supporters. To the reformer of 1837, the
man who had taken the leading part in the winning of the
Crown lands, it still seemed essential that the heads of public
departments should be the servants of the people and not their
rulers.[15]

Faced with an even balance in the house, the government
could do nothing of importance, and the end came before the
session closed. When Hugh McMonagle, a member for Kings,
announced his defection, Gray quickly declared that a dissolution was impending. A vote on Albert Smith's want-of-con-
fidence motion was forestalled by the arrival of the lieutenant-
governor with his speech of dismissal. The results of the election

in May were so certain that the government resigned and the Smashers returned to power.

Their dilemmas were the familiar ones of reformers in many parts of the world at the time. They talked of uplifting the toiling masses and of the new era of progress that would come in the wake of enlightened legislation, but in practice they moved from one gentle expediency to another. Fisher feared "unbridled democracy" and detested universal manhood suffrage. The franchise bill of 1857, passed after meeting a host of objections and amendments from both within and without the fold, is probably the best stick by which the Smashers can be measured. It extended the vote to all who earned £100 a year, supplementing the historic qualification of real estate worth £25. This was legislation for the middle classes of the more urban areas, "the most disinterested, the most independent and the most unprejudiced of all".[16] With it came the secret ballot, regarded by the traditionalists as sinister and dangerous, out of keeping with the British way of doing things.

The Smasher period of ascendancy, extending over thirteen years to the time of Confederation, was one of almost unbroken economic prosperity, not conducive to political and social reform. Fisher and his party freely allowed themselves the designation of reformers, but their record scarcely warrants it. More and more they gloried in the memories of the past, identifying themselves as the heirs of Durham and the allies of the liberalizing tendencies that were dominant in British life. When they came to power in 1854, it seemed certain that they would remove the important remaining fragment of the old colonial system of government, the appointed legislative council. The way had been prepared for an elected second chamber by a resolution of the house of assembly in 1850. In Canada and Nova Scotia there had been similar assertions of faith in the sovereign will of the people, and both of these colonies acquired elected councils in 1856. The British government had agreed to the general principle, merely expressing a preference that the change should be made simultaneously in all colonies.

Yet, even under the Smashers, New Brunswick contemplated the reform reluctantly. The feeling grew that the people could be adequately represented in a second chamber if appointments were more widely diffused, so that all counties, religious denominations, and commercial interests should have spokesmen. This was the principle that was followed. Steadily the legislative council grew in numbers, assuming a quasi-representative character. The Colonial Office, holding that members of a second chamber should represent the province as a whole rather than particular groups, regularly protested in principle but submitted in detail.[17] Responsible government had made appointments to the legislative council the patronage of the government. Year by year its members became less independent and more compliant to the party in power, seldom exposing themselves to the acrimonies of public debate. Frequently, high-spirited councillors, yearning for a more effective voice in public affairs, resigned in order to contest seats in the house of assembly. Fisher's government reduced the legislative council's stature and capacity to interfere with its programme by enacting that the president of that body should be a member of the executive council.[18]

Financial reform came in response to practical necessity rather than in accordance with the profession of ideologies. The start of railway construction compelled large-scale borrowings in the money markets of London and New York. A province whose finances were regulated by committees of the house of assembly and made subject to the casual and prodigal demands for parochial expenditures could not inspire confidence in such quarters. Largely in response to suspicious queries from the outside, politicians were moved to accept the inevitable – a greater degree of control and responsibility to the government. The policy inaugurated by Sir Edmund Head of filling up the departmental offices with members of the government was gradually extended. In consequence of legislation passed in 1855, William Henry Steeves became the first chairman of a board of works with power to supervise the details of construction. Shortly after, the Post Office was made a separate department in charge of a member of the government.

While in opposition, the leading Smashers had always contended that the initiation of money grants by the government was a necessary corollary to responsible government. Fisher, in the debates prior to 1848, had been more active than any other member of the house of assembly in insisting on its relevancy and its efficiency. But in office it was necessary to move most hesitantly and indirectly to bring about this necessary centralization and control. The susceptibilities of "the country members" – like John Earle of Kings County, who insisted on his "rights" to dictate public expenditure in his constituency –

compelled respect. Yet a government without the power to introduce a budget to the house of assembly could not do important business outside the province. For twenty years the Colonial Office, a succession of lieutenant-governors, a cluster of the abler journalists such as Fenety, and the more prescient members of the house of assembly, had been attempting to break down resistance. Added to the other pressures came a tempting offer from Downing Street. The surplus of the Civil List fund had, since 1837, accumulated to the sum of £25,000. The lieutenant-governor was now authorized to open a negotiation for its surrender provided that the house of assembly should adopt the British parliamentary system of financial appropriation.

By a resolution of 1856, characteristically introduced by a private member, George L. Hatheway, the house of assembly agreed to abandon the whole control over financial initiation to the government.[19] It was carried by twenty to eighteen, the negative vote being a testimony to the weight of tradition and self-interest of the members. Manners-Sutton regarded the resolution as of no value until the following year when it was acted upon and received the force of precedent, if not of statute.[20] The hoary and highly individualistic system by which hard-bargaining assemblymen came to Fredericton to answer in the most direct manner possible the extremely practical demands of their constituents fell into disuse in 1857.

Tilting with schemes of reform was, for the Smashers, flirting with defeat in the legislature. Their School Act, heralded as a measure to lift New Brunswick into the forefront of progress, proved to be little more than a definition of existing practice. Bold spirits had suggested compulsory assessment of local rates for the support of parish schools and the creation of local boards of trustees for their administration. But the act of 1858, like its ill-fated predecessor, the Municipalities Act, proved to be permissive only. The cry that the poor man could not stand a direct tax had an authoritative ring, and the Smashers shrank from the prospect of compelling parishes to pay even a portion of their school costs. Relying strongly on the principle of teacher training, the Board of Education worked hard to improve conditions in schools and to raise standards. But the apathy of the public in the parishes drove its inspectors almost to despair. Local assessment made very little progress.

The Parish School Act of 1858 reflected important divisions in public opinion in New Brunswick. In the early days of the province, schools of any kind, whether they were supported by religious denominations or not, had been given help by the legislature. Schoolmasters had cheerfully complied with local demands that they give each child the form of religious instruction prescribed by the faith of his parents. But it was now commonplace for members of the house of assembly to declare in round terms that public money should no longer be expended upon schools that were denominationally controlled. Protestant Anglo-Saxondom resented the rapid increase of the Roman Catholic population and the development of a school system that employed priests and nuns as teachers and made religious instruction a central portion of its work. In the session of 1858, the character of religious instruction in the schools became a subject that seriously concerned the attention of members. Church of England education, as well as Roman Catholic, came under fire. For placing a very liberal interpretation upon the meaning of religious instruction and introducing a gentle amendment to the school bill, John Hamilton Gray was designated by Albert Smith as Archbishop Gray who, by a stroke of the pen, would turn 600 men and 200 women into preachers.[21]

Upholding their faith in pure democracy, the Smashers believed that one public education should be imparted to all. This principle had triumphed in the states of the American Union and was making rapid progress in determining the educational policies of the provinces of British North America. In Prince Edward Island the fervour to prevent public money from being expended upon religiously controlled schools had resulted in a prohibition of Bible reading during classroom hours. Tilley was strongly secular in his views upon school policy, but he could not abide so drastic an expediency. He would uphold the Bible even if it should sink the government.

This breach in the front of those who favoured a completely secular school system supported by public funds provided the opportunity Roman Catholics were seeking. To the careful requirement that each day in school a chapter of Holy Scripture should be read without note or comment, Francis McPhelim introduced an amendment that, for Catholic children, the Douay version of the Bible should be read. Having accepted this mild but important proposal, the house of assembly provided Roman Catholics with the basis for their later claim that separate schools had been given the sanction of the province's laws.

French-speaking people at this time made up nearly twenty-five per cent of New Brunswick's population. The Irish and other Roman Catholic minorities, added to this, made up a most significant part of the total. Anti-Catholic crusades, conducted on the broad scale of Joseph Howe's in Nova Scotia, were politically unfeasible. Yet the Smashers were not disposed to truckle to minorities. In 1858 the publication of the synoptic debates of the house of assembly in French was opposed by Fisher, who argued that his own Welsh constituents in Cardigan had the right to the same privilege. Tilley spoke on behalf of his Germans, and there was no want of partisans for the Gaelic.[22] Like the Clear Grits of Canada, the Smashers of New Brunswick rejoiced in the idea that progress could be reconciled solely with the English language and the Protestant faith.

IV

What gave the Smashers cohesion more than anything else was the role they played as the champions of self-government. They were a party that might be described as of the native-born, now the vast majority of the population, representing the provincial *amour-propre* against affectations of superiority from the outside. Politically they found it highly advantageous to adopt a belligerent attitude towards any suggestion of imperial interference in the domestic affairs of the province. There were still sufficient remnants of imperial control to make a case for them, and, especially at election time, they continued to preach from the literature of emancipation and to exalt the tradition of reform. Their opponents, led in the legislature by John Hamilton Gray, could never overcome the Smashers' conviction that they were the party of the people.

One of the minor forms of continuing imperial dictation from which the Smashers drew great capital was the surplus of the Civil List fund. At the Colonial Office Earl Grey had frankly used his veto upon expenditures from the fund as an instrument to compel the province to adopt financial reform, especially the surrender of the initiative to the executive and the adoption of municipal corporations. A succession of colonial secretaries found this control an almost intolerable nuisance. Time and again the house of assembly made recommendations that payments they were unwilling to make from their own revenues should be made from this surplus, which was accumulating with the years. Occasionally, to the anger of the house of assembly, the lieutenant-governor, securing the permission of the colonial secretary, made payments that the house had rejected. The fund was a small but significant remainder of the independence of the prerogative that had survived the coming of responsible government. The house frequently invoked the constitutional argument of the American Revolution, that money had been taken from the people and expended without their consent. The Colonial Office felt the sting of the consequent unpopularity. "We retain it [the fund] as a bribe to the local legislature," wrote Herman Merivale bitterly, "by which we may induce them to accept a very sound principle of administration which they do not sufficiently appreciate."[23]

The inevitable imperial surrender was accompanied by complications. Immediately before leaving the province in 1854, Sir Edmund Head had made a recommendation that a payment of £1,592 should be made to the descendants of the illegitimate family of Colonel DesBarres, "not in right but in conscience". This was a heritage of the confusion of thirty years earlier, when the great bulk of the estate at Memramcook had been escheated without any great regard for the niceties of the situation. The British government accepted the recommendation but would not authorize the payment without the consent of the government of New Brunswick. Fearing unpopularity in the legislature, the governments of both Fisher and Chandler, from 1855 to 1857, declined to advise Manners-Sutton to concur in the arrangement. Other old accounts against the province, notably a bill for £912 for expenses of the Halifax-Quebec survey of 1847, were raked up by the British treasury. Not until late in 1857, when political uncertainty was ended by the Smashers' triumph in the elections, did the government agree to accept the windfall of £25,000 that was offered, promising in return to pay the specified bills and to secure the initiation of money grants from the house of assembly.[24]

The powerful animus that seemed to drive the Smashers, of cutting connections with the past and making their party the symbol of a brave new age of freedom, compelled them to embarrass the Church of England in the possession of its last tatters of privilege. Suggestions of the foibles of an earlier era, such as the exclusive right to ferry passengers across the St. Croix – held by the corporation of Christchurch, St. Stephen – which quickly came under public review when the Lower St. Stephen's Bridge Company was formed in 1855, were ruthlessly swept away.[25] More fundamental was Bishop Medley's right to his seat

on the legislative council. This had survived an act of the legislature of 1852 designed to unseat him, disallowed by the British
government on constitutional grounds. In 1856, when the
Smashers went temporarily into opposition, Manners-Sutton,
anticipating a new attack that would severely embarrass his
favourites in office, took prompt action to arrange for the acceptance of Medley's resignation.[26] This may be taken as the
formal conclusion of the Church of England establishment, long
under hostile criticism.

Following the publication of the Dawson Report in 1855, a
fresh attack on King's College lay in the logical order of events.
During the political turmoil of 1856-7, its affairs had largely
been in abeyance, though in a debate of 1856 Albert Smith, the
fiery Smasher of Westmorland, the man of mark who was making his way by a ceaseless attack on "privilege", was roundly
cuffed on the ear by John Ambrose Street, and the house of
assembly had spent the remainder of the day in a discussion of
duelling.[27] Politically King's College could arouse prejudices
that no government, unless it had a certain command of the
house, a condition of things unknown, could dare to engage. In
1858 stability had returned to politics, but neither the Fisher
government nor the college council could produce a plan from
the recommendations of the Dawson Report that could safely
be introduced to the legislature. The situation at the opening
of the session presented an opportunity for the firebrands who
supported the government, a challenge that would enable ambitious Smashers to earn their spurs. Without debate the house
passed a bill to establish a degree-conferring institution at
Mount Allison in Sackville, where for fifteen years the Methodists had conducted a seminary. A few days later, on February
16, Charles Connell of Carleton, one of the Smashers who for
many years had headed the assault on privilege, introduced a
bill to discontinue the grant to King's. Friends of the college
could see in these two measures an iniquitous conspiracy by
which Smith, the sponsor of the Mount Allison bill, was attempting to bring the whole provincial grant for higher education to Westmorland County, and Connell was trying to win it
for the Methodist denomination. Against the wishes of Fisher,
whose salary of £100 as registrar of the college had fallen upon
the block, Connell pressed his point.[28]

The subsequent debate showed that the majority of the house
of assembly were in favour of a provincial institution of higher

learning, but King's was prejudged by years of failure to adjust itself to contemporary requirements. Principal Jacob was an object of general detestation. "The greatest curse of the College was the head of it."[29] It was in vain that Connell's opponents counselled further delay in preparation for the establishment of a University of New Brunswick that should be refashioned from King's. Fisher spoke of Connell's bill as Gothic and barbaric. John Hamilton Gray voiced the great vision of the age – a provincial university beyond denominational control that should be open to all on equal terms. Tilley echoed the same sentiment, but he wanted the new university in Saint John.[30] The vote in favour of Connell of twenty-seven to twelve on March 10 represented a determination to destroy the existing establishment before passing on to a consideration of what should take its place.

It was at this point that Manners-Sutton intervened. He did not dare refuse assent to the bill, for, amidst the violent state of public feeling upon the college, a ministerial crisis would quickly have developed. But, taking advantage of the contrary opinions that divided members of the government, he won them over to the point of view that a royal disallowance would be relevant to the circumstances of the case. Good constitutional grounds were readily available for such a course. King's College had originally been endowed by a grant of £1,000 sterling from the Casual and Territorial revenues of the Crown. In assuming control of the Crown lands in 1837 the legislature had agreed to continue the endowment by the Civil List Act. An additional £1,100 currency per annum from ordinary revenues, granted in 1823, had acquired the sanction of what was called a permanent law. So far as the first sum was concerned, the British government would be clearly within its rights in exercising the power of disallowance. After constraining the government to the acceptance of this easy way out of an embarrassing difficulty, Manners-Sutton was able to tell the colonial secretary that no public inconvenience could result if the act were disallowed. Fisher would be compelled to moderate the impetuosities of his followers. Almost to a man, the opposition in the house of assembly had been against the bill, considering that it dealt harshly with the principal and the professors, who, if it should go into effect, would suddenly find themselves without income.[31]

Compromised by this decision that would reverse the wishes of the house of assembly, Fisher moved quickly to avert trouble.

Connell, "the arch enemy of the College", was made a member of the government and given the office of postmaster-general with a salary of £600. The salary, mused Manners-Sutton, was "very enticing".[32] Radicalism could pave the way to fame, but responsibility in office was more remunerative. Connell, as a member of a government committed to sustain the college, could no longer lead the legislative attack to destroy it.

In the session of 1859, the government introduced the University of New Brunswick Bill, which transformed King's College into a provincial university, governed by a senate of eight laymen and completely secularized. Drafted by Lemuel Allen Wilmot and fortified by a simple prayer for university exercises that would presumably be acceptable to all religious denominations, it passed without important opposition. Wishing to stop controversy as soon as possible, Manners-Sutton procured immediate confirmation at the Colonial Office.

A prime cause of political agitation that had lasted for thirty years had been removed, but painful consequences developed within the academic community. Edwin Jacob, the aged principal of King's, could not permit himself to believe that an act of the provincial legislature could supplant a royal charter, that the chair of theology could legally be abolished, and that the faith of the Crown, pledged to him thirty years before by Sir Howard Douglas, could be so easily set aside. When he was reduced to the position of professor of classical and moral philosophy and ordered to vacate the commodious premises he had occupied within the college for so long, he refused to recognize the propriety or the legality of the transformation. The new president of the university, Joseph R. Hea, ordered the opening of the fall term for 1860 to be postponed until the second Tuesday in September owing to repairs to the building. On the first Tuesday, according to his own custom, Jacob rang a bell in the hall of the college to signify that the term had opened and conducted a service in the chapel that was attended by but one other person, his daughter. His letters to Hea were addressed to "Joseph R. Hea, calling himself President of the University of New Brunswick". When Hea ordered him to use American textbooks and interfered with the regimen of his lectures, which he conducted in his private room, Jacob declared that the exercises submitted by his students consisted of "utter nonsense and absurdity".[33] For refusal to accept the new order of things he was pensioned off in 1861, being evicted from the premises he occupied, according to a pathetic letter from his daughter, by the use of skeleton keys.[34] He was probably the only public functionary in the province upon whom the political changes of the passing years had made utterly no impression. Almost every lieutenant-governor under whom he served had considered him, for one reason or another, unfitted for his duties.

V

Pressing uncompromisingly for complete self-government in domestic affairs, the Smashers, following the Nova Scotian example, demanded the right to supervise the drafting of confidential dispatches sent by Manners-Sutton to London.[35] From the days of his youth Fisher had brooded on what he called "backstairs influence". It was intolerable that the Colonial Office should make decisions upon provincial affairs on advice or information offered by persons who were not within the government. The certain knowledge that Manners-Sutton was conveying his personal opinions to the fount of ultimate authority, that the government could be circumvented by dispatches that might never be published, inspired a fresh cry that responsible government was not fully in effect.

The Colonial Office supported Manners-Sutton in his right to give confidential and private advice, but the persistent pressure of the Smashers compelled him to be careful. Forced by popular choice to work with advisers who were nearly always opposed to him in substantial detail, if not in principle, he was never able, after his bold venture of 1856, to exercise very much influence on affairs of domestic concern. Though Fisher could not make his principal point, successive victories in detail steadily reduced the practical power of the lieutenant-governor. When, during the King's College crisis, reports came to Fredericton that not only Sir Howard Douglas but Bishop Medley and Edward Barron Chandler had called at the Colonial Office to make representations, the New Brunswick government successfully demanded that copies of the documents should be made available for rebuttal.[36]

Many New Brunswickers did not see, or did not wish to see, the full refinements of responsible government. The Colonial Office was frequently compelled to set aside the appeals of disgruntled groups and individuals who wished to exercise the historic right of subjects to address themselves directly to the foot of the Throne. Requests from the descendants of Loyalists for compensation, or from New Brunswickers who sought imperial office or patronage, had to be returned to the provincial government. Self-government for the colonies was almost as popular in Downing Street as in Fredericton. Old loyalties lost much of their meaning as Fisher and his colleagues persistently thinned the strand of dependence upon Britain. The idea of self-government was so strongly in the ascendancy that even its original proponents at times seemed laggard. Owing to pressure in the house of assembly, Fisher was compelled to sustain the attack upon Manners-Sutton's private correspondence. James Steadman, member for Westmorland, made such a nuisance of himself by arguing that the government was responsible for all the opinions of the lieutenant-governor, even those contained in his private letters to England, that the only way to keep him quiet was to bring him into the government.[37] The opportunity came in the spring of 1860 when Charles Connell resigned from the postmaster-generalship following the unaccountable act of printing a postage stamp that bore his own portrait. "When he lost regard for his Queen and put his own beautiful face upon the Postage Stamps instead of hers, the people regarded it as an insult to their sovereign and to themselves, and there rose such a torrent of ridicule throughout the country, that the government would have been hurled from power had they not got rid of him."[38] Fisher's method of dealing with those who played his own game a little too lustily was to thrust responsibility upon them.

Gradually but surely, the role of the lieutenant-governor was being reduced to a position approximating that of the Queen in Britain. But a new set of difficulties was in the making. The line between internal and imperial affairs was blurred and irregular. In a world of expanding and highly competitive trade, one of the most precious of freedoms was that of negotiating with foreign states for the entrance of provincial products to their markets and of adjusting provincial tariffs by regulations that were advantageous to provincial interests. Yet the provinces of British North America had no power to negotiate with foreign states, and their tariff policies were very much under the control of the Board of Trade in London. British free trade and the whole succession of British injunctions to the colonies on the necessity of keeping tariffs low had not been received with the reverence so freely accorded them in the British Isles. In the colonies it became customary, rather, to regard free trade as a hypocritical contraption to bring British manufactured products to colonial markets on the best possible terms. Under the Smashers there emerged in New Brunswick, coincident with Alexander Galt's bold stand in Canada, a clear tendency to balk at British control over the international trade of the colony.

After 1854, when railway construction began to make heavy demands on the revenues, tariffs had been adjusted sharply upwards. On general principles the British had found this objectionable but had made no complaint so long as the inviolable rule of "no differential duties" was observed. Yet, as tariffs became higher and more flexible, this precept of enlightenment seemed increasingly an imposition. Rather daringly the legislature of 1859 passed an act authorizing the lieutenant-governor to make changes, by proclamation, in the rates on goods from the British provinces and the United States. Manners-Sutton felt that there was a clear possibility that it would be employed to the detriment of British manufacturing, contrary to the royal instructions issued by Lord John Russell in 1855.[39] In 1860, when the government prepared to unite with Canada and Nova Scotia in an effort to gain free admission for timber to the French empire, there were spasms of alarm at the Colonial Office.[40] Later in the same year the disposition to initiate trade agreements with foreign powers took more pointed form when William Lindsay, member for Carleton, and John Robertson of the Saint John Chamber of Commerce went to Washington to secure the removal of restrictions on New Brunswick shipping, an aspiration that proved to be as vain as it had been in 1854.[41]

VI

This incipient colonial nationalism, rapidly developing through the 1850s when, owing to the prosperity in Britain, immigration declined and the proportion of the native-born sharply rose, took many forms of self-assertion. In anger, the legislature had in 1851 suspended the financial sections of the militia act, putting an end to the midsummer drills and frolics that for so long had disturbed the labour market and irritated the commercial classes. In 1856 Fisher renewed the suspending act, ensuring that for another five years the province would not support a militia system. The Smasher point of view was that the Empire existed for trade, and that, since trading privileges in Britain had been denied to the colonies, Britain should accept the entire burden of imperial defence. Exemption from taxation for military purposes was a compensation for colonial status. They reinforced this precept with the more stringent argument that, since appointments in the militia rested with the Crown, the wherewithal should come from the same source. Fisher refused to contribute provincial funds for the fortification of Partridge Island in Saint John harbour, though military men generally agreed that two or three hostile cruisers could quickly occupy the city and nullify the province as an element of any account in war. In 1860 the most influential of Smasher journals, the *Globe* of Saint John, reviewing the report of the defence committee of the imperial parliament and Gladstone's recent remark that the colonies were an encumbrance, struck a note that was providential. New Brunswick, it declared, had no wars of her own, and if she were to contribute to defence she should have a voice in the councils of the Empire. Manners-Sutton vouched for the reliability of the article as a reflection of the thinking of leading persons in the colony.[42]

Yet the apathy of the politicians to the militia, and the open hostility of a minority of them, presented the superficial rather than the elemental feelings of the population. The rapidly fading "aristocracy", who prided themselves upon ancestral loyalties to the Crown and whose daughters married officers of the British garrisons, stood for a point of view that was general rather than particular. When, during the Crimean War, the garrisons at Saint John and Fredericton were cut to a company of infantry at each place, Manners-Sutton bemoaned the weakening of a social factor that was significant in sustaining the imperial connection.[43] When the British government gazetted four young New Brunswickers to commissions in the armed forces without the necessity of purchase, a ripple of enthusiasm circulated through the province, and many more educated young men – of whom there was a superfluity that could not be absorbed by the learned professions of law and medicine – applied for the same privilege. Yet, in spite of patriotic pride engendered by the fall of Sebastopol and the crushing of the Indian Mutiny, Manners-Sutton could do nothing to persuade the government to expend money on the militia establishment. Tilley, the only member for whom the lieutenant-governor held real respect, confided that it would be idle and hopeless to consider the introduction of a programme to the house of assembly.[44]

Urged on by the British government to improve the defences

of the province, Manners-Sutton could do nothing until circumstances came to his assistance. The French declaration of war
against Austria in 1859, the possibility of British intervention,
and the fears of the havoc that could be wrought by a French
fleet in the Gulf of St. Lawrence where the dispute concerning
the rights of French fishermen off Newfoundland had created
tension, invoked some of the former martial ardour of the people
of New Brunswick. All that he could suggest was the formation
of militia companies at particular points where danger especially
threatened, the men to serve without pay and to provide their
own uniforms and accoutrements. To pay for administrative
expenses he had £200, guaranteed for contingencies by the Civil
List Act. The movement was surprisingly successful. It began
with the formation of a company of artillery at Saint John. The
appearance of Sir Fenwick Williams, the Nova Scotian hero of
Kars, was in the nature of a fillip, and the British government's
promise of 3,000 new Enfield rifles gave it an even greater boost.
By the end of the year there were four companies of artillery at
Saint John. When the Prince of Wales paid his visit to the province in August 1860, over 3,000 men were enrolled in twenty-
three companies of infantry and artillery and two troops of
cavalry.[45] The third John Saunders of New Brunswick revived
memories of the first – whose Saunders' Horse had terrorized the
southern rebels in the initial stages of the Revolutionary War
– when his company of cavalry clustered about his residence at
Fox Hill in Kings County. For lack of funds, no uniformity
could be enforced in terms of enlistment. Manners-Sutton had
to meet a certain amount of feeling that officers should be
elected rather than appointed. But the force, organized by
Lieutenant-Colonel Hayne who had come to the province many
years before as an agent for the New Brunswick and Nova
Scotia Land Company, produced at least the shell of a defence.
Though he could refer to the loyalty of the people as "stainless",
Manners-Sutton was fearful that the legislature would interfere
to destroy his work. Yet, surprisingly enough, the legislature of
1860, influenced by the new temper that had arisen, produced
£300 to pay for the services of twelve drill-sergeants sent out
by the British government – "the twelve apostles".

The most sacrosanct of loyalties could not be safeguarded
from political pressures. Mixed feelings were aroused on the
floor of the house of assembly on March 19, 1860, when Fisher
moved for an address to invite the Prince of Wales to visit the

province. His remarks rang with loyalty and were couched in terms of great emotion, but their effect was negative. James Brown, the surveyor-general, declared that since the province was in debt no public money could be expended. Albert Smith, who for a long time had been trying to force Fisher's resignation, supported the argument. Led by two members of the government, the majority of the assembly decided that no invitation should be given. There were objections to the expenditure of public money in Fredericton and Saint John, and to the Canadian initiative of the invitation to the Prince of Wales to visit North America. McPhelim of Kent declared that the visit would do his county no good whatever since none of his constituents would see the Prince. Generally it was felt that a few would receive the greater glory. John Chandler of Charlotte visualized the prostration of Fisher before the Prince and the pronouncement of the words, "Rise, Sir Charles!"

On the following day, overpowered by a sense of shame for the province before the bar of posterity, Robert Duncan Wilmot moved that these proceedings of March 19 should be expunged from the journals of the house and that Fisher's address should be carried. Having been exposed to the rancour and ridicule of Fredericton the night before, the house reversed its decision, though not unanimously.[46]

New Brunswick reflected North American standards of social decorum that glorified the equality of all and eschewed distinction. The Smashers, however, placed a high value upon precedence, a factor that contributed greatly to the personal jealousies that abounded among them. In 1851 Fisher had been one of the first New Brunswick politicians to request the permanent designation of "honourable" upon retirement from the executive council, badgering the Colonial Office for a fixed rule upon a subject of considerable delicacy. The question became mildly explosive in 1860 upon the visit of the Prince of Wales when the Roman Catholic bishop of Saint John exercised his right to official precedence before the Chief Justice and the members of the government. The Smashers, putting forward the point of view of what Manners-Sutton called the Puritan party – Baptists, Wesleyans, and Free Presbyterians – demanded that the rule should be rescinded. A memorandum, signed by all the members of the government with the exception of the one Roman Catholic, Charles Watters, asked that ecclesiastical precedence should be abolished, arguing, in effect, that the precedence of the Church of England bishop would not be injured.[47] This the Colonial Office refused to do, declaring that no complaints had been received from other colonies. In parts of the province where Protestant susceptibilities were acute, ambitious politicians were always prepared to create embarrassment by taking the lead in anti-Catholic crusades. The influence of Howe in Nova Scotia had overlapped the boundaries of his own province. Manners-Sutton considered him to be "a pernicious individual" who, if he had his way, would have the Roman Catholics and Protestants of New Brunswick and Prince Edward Island in arms against one another.[48]

Within their own enclaves Irish Roman Catholics were organizing to make their presence felt in the politics of the province. In July 1849, just before the fearsome riot on the 12th, the belligerent Timothy Warren Anglin arrived in Saint John. A schoolmaster of County Cork and a rebel of 1848, he was, according to tradition, on his way to join his friend Thomas D'Arcy McGee in Canada. What he saw in Saint John was sufficient to give him pause; he remained to found a newspaper. The politics of the *Freeman* quickly became an element of importance in the city and the county, and from there extended to the Irish all through the province. It soon became an accepted convention that the reform ticket in Saint John elections should include a Roman Catholic. Robert Duncan Wilmot, in speaking of the election of 1854, said that of 500 Roman Catholic votes in Saint John County, he had received only five and his opponent, Ritchie, had received every other one.[49] With memories of persecution in Ireland, Anglin cheerfully adopted the course of ensuring that the Irish Roman Catholics of New Brunswick should acquire rights equivalent to those of their Protestant fellow-subjects. Like McGee in Canada he discarded the methods of revolution for those of constitutional progress.

Amid a society that was so devoted to the practice of equalitarian principles, knighthood surprisingly flowered. Early in 1859 the British government, seeking a means of enlarging imperial affinities in the province, suggested the award of knighthood along with other lesser honours to eminent citizens. Not daring to seek the advice of his government, Manners-Sutton replied that he could recommend only one man for knighthood but that the conferring of such an honour would be politically adverse and would not achieve the effect intended. The one man was James Carter, the young Englishman who had arrived in 1835 as a judge and whose appointment as Chief Justice in 1851 had been almost equally unpopular. No member of the government, Manners-Sutton declared, possessed the character or the liberal education worthy of such notice from the Queen.[50] Yet very quickly the whole position changed. When word came in June that the Chief Justice of Nova Scotia had been knighted, prejudices were suddenly nullified. Carter became the first resident of the province to accept the honour.

VII

Cheered by the conviction that the Reciprocity Treaty would bring a completely new kind of prosperity to New Brunswick, the Smashers approached problems of finance with a high degree of optimism. At the outset they faced a severe setback when, in the spring of 1855, railway construction failed to recommence. During the inflation of the Crimean War, costs mounted and the contractors, though they had started the work with a large outlay of capital and material, were prepared to make sacrifices in order to evade their commitments. Largely owing to the widespread scandals that attended railway construction in the United States, the public refused to purchase the provincial bonds that made up a large portion of their assets. The European and North American Railway Company, with most of its capital fictitious, failed to provide land and other facilities. In July, Messrs. Peto, Brassey, Betts, and Jackson auctioned off the horses employed on construction, a plain indication that they proposed to do nothing further. Nothing daunted, Fisher and his colleagues, rather than permit the hopes of Saint John to flicker out, prepared to accept the onus of public responsibility.[51]

Following a legal reconnaissance by Ritchie, who was counsel for the European and North American as well as a member of the government, John Robertson, representing the company, and Fisher, acting on behalf of the government, left for England in November. A year of inactivity on the railway compelled speed, for weathering threatened to undo completely the construction of 1854. Ignoring the complaints of the opposition, who insisted that the contractors should be held rigidly to the terms of their agreement, and the resistance of Manners-Sutton, who believed that the resources of the province could not be developed quickly enough to pay for a programme of railway construction, Fisher pressed his case to a triumphant conclu-

sion. For a total payment of £90,000, including the provincial
debentures already given to the contractors,[52] he bought up the
construction that had been completed, the materials brought by
the contractors into the province, and the plans and specifications, all valued at approximately £150,000. Rejected in his
application for a loan by the British government, he turned to
Baring Brothers and with little difficulty secured £800,000.

Going into debt was the palpable solution for meeting the
sanguine expectations of the people of New Brunswick. Recognizing the necessity for reform of the provincial finances, to
secure the initiative of money grants to the government, the
Smashers bravely contemplated a railway debt of £2,000,000,
to be redeemed over a ten-year period. The house of assembly
grumbled over a railway impost of two and a half per cent on
the importation of all goods except those exempted by the
Reciprocity Treaty and the act establishing intercolonial free
trade on natural produce, but accepted Fisher's legislation of
1856 without notable reluctance. Sectional prejudices were overpowered by the provision for the extension of the Saint John-
Shediac Railway to Woodstock, the Miramichi, and Calais. A
board of five railway commissioners with control over the details
of construction and expenditure was established.

Proceeding by piece-work and calling for tenders from local
contractors, the commissioners pushed forward the work on the
European and North American for the next four years, not with
the speed anticipated but with a fair degree of continuity. The
first section from Pointe du Chêne to Moncton was opened in
August 1857, the second from Saint John to Rothesay in June
1858. The project was completed in August 1860, when the first
train ran from Saint John to Shediac. Costs considerably exceeded the estimates, and as completion neared it became
apparent that earning capacity, too, had been considerably
over-estimated. Fish in vast quantities did not come from the
Gulf to Saint John. Though there was general satisfaction that
the railway was bringing the two sections of the province more
closely together, it was plain from the beginning that the
European and North American would pay for no more than
wear and tear. Fisher had to fend off demands for fresh construction from Fredericton, Woodstock, and St. Stephen, all
envious of the vast expenditure of public money at Saint John
and Moncton – the name of the new city that was growing up
at the Bend of Petitcodiac. The tranquillizing observation that

became familiar was that the province could afford no new railway construction. In Charlotte County the private enterprise of the reorganized St. Andrews and Quebec Company, the New Brunswick and Canada Railway and Land Company, produced results even less spectacular. On October 1, 1857, the first stretch of thirty-four miles was opened to the public when a train, consisting of two engines, two brake-vans, one passenger car, and twenty-two flatcars fitted with seats, carried 600 exuberant passengers on an excursion. A year later the line reached Canterbury, sixty-four miles from St. Andrews, and by 1862 it was carried to Richmond Corners. This performance was vitiated in 1863 when the company defaulted on its bonds and the line passed into receivership. It continued to be operated in the interests of the creditors.

The conviction that the province had gone as far as it judiciously could in the financing of railway construction destroyed the unbridled speculation that had reigned five years before, and impelled a high degree of sobriety in dealing with overtures that continued to come from outside. From the American promoters who had prompted the grand idea of the European and North American at the Portland Convention in 1850 there was no embarrassment. Not a rail had they laid from Bangor in the direction of New Brunswick. But suggestions for intercolonial co-operation continued to come from Nova Scotia and Canada. Nova Scotia was pushing its line from Halifax to Truro, its avowed policy being to continue to the New Brunswick border. Yet the government at Halifax could acquire no satisfaction concerning New Brunswick's intention about the twenty-two miles from Shediac to the boundary. Could Nova Scotia build a railway to the border in confidence that her sister province would meet her there, or should she direct her energies to the construction of a line from Truro to Pictou?[53] A quick answer was requested, but a non-committal one was given. The Saint John interests that dominated railway policy had no intention of linking their line with Halifax. On the floor of the house of assembly Fisher's government was attacked for failure to co-operate with Nova Scotia, and the retort was given that, since Nova Scotia would derive the entire benefit, she should pay for a line from Shediac to the border.[54]

Intercolonial co-operation became more plausible as the Grand Trunk moved along the south bank of the St. Lawrence to Rivière du Loup, where it finally came to a halt in 1860.

Though opponents heatedly argued that increasing Canadian interest in connection with the lower provinces betokened Montreal's commercial dominance in the upper St. John Valley, the New Brunswick legislature in 1857 pressed for an inquiry into Canadian intentions. Yet such speculation had to be governed by consideration of cost and the possibility of a British guarantee of a loan to meet it. Nova Scotian initiative in 1857 promoted a new series of conversations on the old idea of an intercolonial line, but in the following year the British government, faced with the expenditures of the Indian Mutiny, was in no humour to co-operate.

Still the priority of Saint John and the St. John Valley was the reigning consideration in all matters concerning railways. All consideration of an intercolonial line blandly ignored the stipulation that would be a condition of British assistance – the selection of a North Shore route. Manners-Sutton wrote that Saint John interests would throw every possible obstruction in the way of a North Shore line that, by-passing their city, would bring Canadian goods through to the Atlantic at Halifax.[55] New Brunswick politicians had by this time been well schooled to turn a blind eye to the more specific features of the intercolonial scheme. At times when the grand idea came into favour, when cheap money seemed likely, it was studiously assumed that Saint John and its railway to Shediac would be taken into the system.

Two British refusals of 1858 were based on excuses of temporary financial embarrassment, but confidential reports from the colonies gave the Colonial Office confidence in sending the British North Americans home empty-handed. While Fisher and Smith were on the way to England in September, Manners-Sutton reported that he had no faith in the prudence of his legislature or his government, that he feared they would enter upon financial engagements that could lead to repudiation of contracts and grave consequences for the Empire. The benefits of an intercolonial railway, he maintained, could be purchased too dearly. This was the opinion the Colonial Office wanted to hear, and it was promptly dispatched to the Exchequer.[56]

Smasher ideas of easy money reflected the expansive world economy of the 1850s. In the execution of their confident policy of railway financing they suffered no misfortune, though the Board of Railway Commissioners was assailed by the opposition for all kinds of carelessness in detail and for gross favouritism in the granting of patronage. Privately, Manners-Sutton deprecated the rashness of the Smashers. Publicly, he was compelled to applaud their good judgment. The Speech from the Throne of 1859 referred to the high price of provincial bonds on the London money market. The next three years yielded unprecedented revenues. The demand for timber remained strong, and the Reciprocity Treaty had unquestionably instilled new vigour into the fisheries. The sole impediment to still more rapid progress was the scarcity of labour.

The general prosperity of the era of railway construction received additional accent from the development of New Brunswick's mineral resources. For twenty years the most optimistic forecasts had been made concerning the coal of Grand Lake. North American Newcastles had been freely predicted. But the lessees of mines and mineral privileges had been consistently blocked in their endeavours by the proprietors of the soil. Land grants reserved minerals to the Crown. Nevertheless, the courts, notably in a Queens County case, that of M'Mahon vs. Berton and Francis in 1852, had asserted the right of the proprietors to resist the entry of mining speculators. By incorporating the Albert Mining Company in 1852, the legislature insisted on the right of lessees to enter, subject to the payment of fair compensation for damage, but the whole position was still clogged with uncertainty.[57] Even after considerable capital had been expended, and while the mines at Grand Lake were being worked, nervousness over what the ultimate decision might be hindered progress. Throughout Westmorland, Albert, and Queens, where there was great optimism concerning the wealth of mineral deposits, communities were fiercely divided on the legality of the privileges issued to mining promoters by the government at Fredericton. In 1855 the more conservative and landed interests triumphed in the legislature, and an act was passed giving to proprietors of the soil the exclusive right to dig for minerals. Compensation of £1,000 was granted to lessees compelled to abandon their operations.[58] This brought all activity in the search for minerals virtually to a standstill.

Yet over the next five years the demand for coal was strong enough to overpower even an obstacle as great as this. Coal-mining entrepreneurs were able to identify their interests with those of the proprietors of the soil. Not only was the coal of Grand Lake capable of satisfying a large portion of the requirements of the domestic market: between 1854 and 1859 the value of exports rose from £565 to £33,598. Importation of oil to the province ceased, and oil extracted from the coal of Grand Lake was exported to the value of over £10,000 in 1859.[59]

VIII

The Smashers, after being outfoxed in the prohibition crisis of 1856, never came close to losing their ascendancy in politics. The cause for which they stood had been vindicated by the British Liberals, by the Canadian and Nova Scotian reformers, and by what they themselves called, a little hazily and mystically, the spirit of the times. So far as their basic beliefs were concerned – those of complete self-government – there could be no turning back. For the sake of at least a show of consistency and of moral force they were compelled to work to the very limit what had become the prepossession of the age.

In the advance towards a new concept of what the imperial connection could mean, Fisher was the only really articulate spokesman of the Smashers. Like other reformers before him, he had made his grand pronouncements when out of office, but once in power he was compelled to abstain from statements of principle and concentrate upon the more parochial business of holding his party together and sustaining his majority in the legislature. He could capitalize on the self-assertiveness of New Brunswickers in the face of the Colonial Office, the Americans, or the Canadians, and he could rejoice in his memories of the early defeats of the victorious cause he had led. But he could not swiftly move the province to the new social and political order. Having achieved power, he did not wish to do so.

His great contribution to New Brunswick's development was the translation of the theory of responsible government into a more precise practice than had obtained under Sir Edmund Head. It was Fisher who introduced the savage party warfare of Westminster to the province. The Barker House conspiracy of 1854 was nothing more than a normal feature of parliamentary life in British countries. Responsible government had come in 1848, but its operation had depended upon the manipulations of a lieutenant-governor who was an adroit trimmer. Head had introduced responsible government gently and easily, but the Barker House conspiracy indicated that the period of education was over, or almost over. Responsible government required disciplined political parties for its proper functioning. Fisher's Liberal party of 1854 represented a conscious attempt to bring to New Brunswick something more of the drill and rigour that made the British constitutional process so admirable.

The lofty professions of liberalism and high-mindedness that characterized the reformers of British North America were accompanied by a novel and practical concept of the utility of public patronage. Office-holders who opposed the Smashers at election time were ruthlessly stripped of their places. Friends of the Smashers stepped into them. To those who still entertained the older and more gentlemanly notion that a public office was a piece of private property that could not be removed except for grave misdemeanour, this manifestation of Smasher philosophy was frightening. Edward Barron Chandler, who in his youth had carried the reform banner, lost the lesser public offices he had held in Westmorland for twenty years. Moses H. Perley, long a favourite of government, who had performed invaluable services, lost his post as immigration agent. A few years later, serving as fisheries commissioner for the British government under the Reciprocity Treaty, he died off the coast of Labrador, still fearful of measures his political enemies might employ against him.[60] Sheriff Winslow, who had held his office in Carleton for twenty-nine years after his discharge from the 41st Regiment, was summarily released from his post.[61] Marshall d'Avray was removed from his office as chief superintendent of education and replaced by Henry Fisher, a brother of the attorney-general. Admittedly, some of these and virtually all of the lesser fry whom Fisher let out of office were avowedly opposed to the régime. But the new rule that office-holders took part in politics at their peril produced a terrorizing effect. The lowly were being raised up at a somewhat frightening rate, very much at the expense of those who had long been accustomed to affluence. With Frederick Phillips Robinson, the auditor-general and bearer of another name that had long been honoured, the Smashers were more gentle. They bought him out for £350, a curious deference to the usages of the past. Still more curiously, they awarded the office to Partelow – an opponent from 1848 to 1854, but in still earlier times one of the pillars of reform and the great trimmer in all matters financial – later increasing the salary by a substantial margin.[62]

Fortified by their philosophy of the worth of the common man and by a new appreciation for the efficacy of the pork-barrel, the Smashers rode rough-shod over their opposition, but as long as Fisher was their leader a dangerous element of instability was present in their counsels: constantly the government seemed on the verge of breaking up, owing to the presence at the top of the very man who had led them to power in 1854. Yet the Smashers were so strong that they could afford internal dissension. In 1858 Ritchie and Smith, two of Fisher's abler colleagues, and his bitter rivals, attempted to force his resignation by opening the "seat-of-government" question. The construction of the railway was making the comparative inaccessibility of Fredericton considerably more obvious and, though the people of Saint John were divided upon the desirability of the measure, those of the eastern counties were vociferously in favour of moving the capital to that city. As a loyal York County man, Fisher was bound to resist, and he was mercifully delivered from hostile pressures when the house of assembly accepted, by a vote of twenty to nineteen, an amendment to the motion that would set up a commission to ascertain the costs of removal.[63] The leader of the government could readily deal with his opponents in the legislature, but many of his colleagues and supporters missed no opportunity to embarrass him personally and to make his position difficult. The removal of Ritchie to a judgeship did not weaken the undercurrents at work against him.

Ultimately, in 1861, Fisher's enemies secured their big chance when whisperings of irregularities in the administration of the Crown Lands Office were given publicity by the *Colonial Empire* of Saint John, an opposition journal owned in part by Moses H. Perley. The stipulation in the act governing purchases of Crown lands, that an individual might purchase but 100 acres for the purposes of permanent settlement, had for years been by-passed by fictions and evasions of one kind or another. The prosperity of the timber trade had impelled the larger operators to gain control, either by lease or purchase, of large tracts of land. The construction of the railway from Saint John to Shediac promoted a keen speculation in properties along its route. In the interests of the public, the Crown Lands Office had promulgated a regulation that nobody connected with the government should be permitted to purchase public land. Official persons were closely under scrutiny, and in 1858 Tilley was compelled indignantly to deny a charge in the *Freeman* that he was engaging in activity of this kind.[64]

Following the *Empire*'s allegations that officials were purchasing land under cover of fictitious names, James Tibbits, supported by Albert Smith, moved in the house of assembly for the appointment of a select committee to investigate.[65] At the opening of the inquiry that immediately took place, Andrew Inches, chief clerk of the Crown Lands Office, testified that he had been importuned by Fisher to refuse evidence. The attorney-general had advised him, he said, that for refusal he could be committed to prison only for the duration of the session, and that it would be well for him to keep a closed mouth upon the alleged irregularities. But he decided to make "a clean breast" of it, and proceeded to tell the committee of how he himself had purchased a half interest in 26,408 acres in Westmorland, Albert, and Kings, of purchases made by members of the legislature within the past twenty years, of the systematic use of the names of women and infants, and of the non-enforcement of instalment paying. He gave the details of several purchases by Fisher. Tilley, he said, knew what was going on, but James Brown, the surveyor-general, who was directly responsible, did not.[66]

Fisher immediately became the sacrificial goat. A memorandum of the executive council to Manners-Sutton offered their resignations and affirmed their refusal to serve in the government with him on the grounds that he had purchased Crown lands contrary to the regulations. On March 18 the attorney-general declared in the legislature that, like a good captain, he would be the last to leave the ship, that he had committed no moral wrong.[67] He professed an ability to reorganize the government and retain control of the house of assembly, but Manners-Sutton, immensely enjoying Fisher's discomfiture, turned to Tilley. The government was reconstructed with Tilley at its head and Fisher excluded. Manners-Sutton preferred the loss of one executive councillor to the loss of seven.

The affair had a curious epilogue, dismaying to those who liked to recall the part Fisher had played in the movement for responsible government. Manners-Sutton could remove Fisher from the executive council but not from the attorney-generalship, which was held under the Royal Sign Manual. This had been the refuge and strength of many office-holders before 1848, but Fisher had no qualms about resorting to its legal and historical authority, though he had so clearly lost the confidence of his colleagues in the government and the legislature. After a month of waiting for him to resign, Tilley advised the lieutenant-governor to exercise the powers conveyed to him in

the royal instructions of suspending the attorney-general. Only
after this was done did Fisher, whose behaviour was rather
reminiscent of that of the privileged opponents of his youth,
yield to the great weight of opinion against him. His bad reputation, deserved or not, had gone beyond New Brunswick. The
Duke of Newcastle, the colonial secretary, had met him both in
London and in Fredericton. On the back of Manners-Sutton's
dispatch announcing the constitutional crisis was the Duke's
minute: "I am not ignorant that Mr. Fisher is one of the worst
public men in the British North American provinces and his
riddance is a great gain to the cause of good government in
New Brunswick." As an afterthought came the equally firm
conclusion: "Mr. Tilley is a respectable man."[68]

From this chastening the Smashers emerged the stronger. In
the house of assembly the opposition declared that the government had sacrificed one of its members in order to escape responsibility for the scandal. It was argued that by implication
Tilley was involved as well as Fisher, but around Tilley the
Smashers clustered the more closely together. The election that
quickly followed the reorganization of the government confirmed the ascendancy of the new leader as a man of consummate business ability. If compensation for his mild manners
were required, the new attorney-general, Albert Smith, was well
known as an adequate bully-boy. Shortly after his elevation
and on the occasion of a bitter debate in the house of assembly,
Smith was followed into the Speaker's room by Lestock Des-
Brisay, member for Kent, who "deliberately wrung his nose".
As Smith was about to seize a fire-iron, the affair was halted by
other members, though another account declared that Smith
was kicked as well.[69] "We live in peace with no other danger of
war than what may arise from the stealing of our lands by the
immaculate Smashers or the pulling of Bully Albert Smith's
nose by an outraged Senator."[70]

CHAPTER 15

Confederation: the Prelude

1858-1864

New Brunswick's destiny was not inevitably linked with Canada's. By 1860 the larger colony was acquiring the character of a continental country whose dominion extended almost halfway to the Pacific. New Brunswick, looking eastward and southward over the Atlantic for her means of livelihood, was still isolated from the continent by vast forest barriers. Only three to four per cent of her trade was with Canada. Like the other Maritime Provinces, she had but a casual, rather regretful interest in the westward expansion that was the dominating feature of North American life at the time. Purely natural and material factors suggested that, if mergers should become desirable, a union should come with Nova Scotia and Prince Edward Island, or, if drastic expedients should become necessary, the province should gravitate to the United States rather than to Canada.

To Sir John Harvey and the New Brunswick delegation that had visited Durham at Quebec in 1838, the idea of a British North American union had seemed mildly preposterous. Schemes of federalism had been given the cold shoulder. In that heyday of the timber trade and of greatly increased local autonomy, the suggestion of new departures had been a signal of danger. The railway on which Lord Durham had based his premises had still not been constructed. Knowledgeable men declared that, even if it were constructed, it could never pay. But the traditional faith in the destiny of an autonomous province of the British Empire, enjoying local liberties and privileges of trade in British markets, had suffered rude shocks. Together, New

Brunswick and Canada had been thrust from the exclusive
British trading ring, and together they had considered their
complaints. It was reasonable that public men of the smaller
colony should look to those of the larger for an example.
Canadian excitability and truculence in 1848-9 stimulated similar manifestations in New Brunswick. In the strange new world
of the mid-century, when the colonies were trading without
privileges anywhere, Canada became the leader of the smaller
provinces, though a leader whose intentions were frequently
suspect.

Good humour had returned with the good times of 1851-2,
but the old colonialism, fashionable and profitable in the earlier
part of the century, was gone forever. The British tradition was
tenacious, but the British connection had become an open question. Annexation to the United States, an expediency that could
be considered only under the direst straits, became a clear possibility for extremists. The mere fact that it became a topic for
discussion in the broad light of day impelled reflection upon
alternatives. The colonies were independent of the United States
and of each other, and very nearly independent of Britain, but
individually they were beyond their depths in the wake of the
great nation to the south. The common predicament was the
basis for union.

In June 1855, when Lieutenant-Governor Manners-Sutton
paid a visit to St. Stephen, a town whose inhabitants owned
mills on the other side of the river at Calais and where there
was nothing to distinguish the mannerisms of the two peoples
of the border from one another, he was flabbergasted by what
he called a remarkable address. Leading citizens set forth "the
want" of a union of the North American colonies, stipulating
that a railway must first be constructed to the St. Lawrence.
Manners-Sutton made a hasty and inconsequential reply, saying that he would do all he could to stimulate trade with
Canada, but the address made a great impression upon him
because it made a public issue of what men had long been
saying in private. The people of New Brunswick were not prepared for such a union, he declared, but the advocates of it
commanded great respect.[1] In the legislative council, where
politicians could speak their minds freely, without fear of electoral consequences, discussion for several years back had frequently turned to consideration of the union of the British
North American provinces.

In Canada, where the political situation was steadily deteriorating and where the future of the union was becoming increasingly uncertain, a possible reorganization of British North America was regarded with a sense of urgency. No such factor was present in New Brunswick. Commercial prosperity brightened the skies. Only a changed and adverse set of circumstances could convert the intellectual conviction of the more thoughtful on the desirability of union into a movement that could lead to a definite goal. In August 1858, when the Speech from the Throne in the Canadian parliament proposed discussions among the provinces on union and when, shortly afterwards, a Canadian memorandum came to Fredericton, the New Brunswick government turned coldly away. The official reply was that the people were envied by those of the neighbouring republic, that prosperity was general and that, if the colonial secretary should authorize discussions in consequence of the Canadian suggestion, New Brunswick would not consider a legislative union in which her identity would be lost.[2]

There was considerable irritation because the Canadian government, urged on by Alexander Galt, had ventured to ask the Colonial Office for a conference on union without asking the other colonies first. There were fears that Governor General Sir Edmund Head had already secured the approval of the British government for such a conference, and that a union, overwhelmingly dominated by Canada, would be imposed on the other colonies. The question of union had never been considered in the New Brunswick house of assembly, and the government, completely unprepared for the proposal, refused to consider the possibility of action in a favourable light.

Fisher and the Smashers, enjoying the sunshine of rapid commercial development and of certain popular favour, were not disposed to view with approval a vast alteration in the status of New Brunswick merely in order to help relieve Canadians of their internal difficulties. The answer to the Canadian overture – "not cordial", as it was described at the Colonial Office – was heartily endorsed by Manners-Sutton. The lieutenant-governor considered the prospect of union with Canada from the lofty perspective of the long-term interests of the Empire. A legislative union in which the provincial governments would disappear, he reasoned, could not be productive of good, but a federal union would be infinitely worse. A central government for British North America, presiding over a union of provinces whose local powers would still be great, would have little to do except invade imperial control over foreign trade and collide with the British government. Even if the lesser evil, a legislative union, were to be accepted, the lower provinces, he prophesied, would become discontented with their loss of autonomy and look to the northern states of the American union for relief. Reminding the Colonial Office that in the colonies constitutional talk was always dangerous, Manners-Sutton could foresee the complete disappearance of the connection with the Crown. In this he entirely disagreed with the Governor General, who, in order to resolve the imbroglios of Canadian politics, was disposed to hazard the whole future of British North America in a new melting-pot.

To the idea of a general union of the colonies Manners-Sutton had a ready alternative that was "practical as well as politic", one that he hoped would be an immediate distraction from the larger and more remote project. This was a union of New Brunswick with Nova Scotia and Prince Edward Island in a more local merger of provinces whose peoples were traditionally homogeneous as well as geographically contiguous. Like Colebrooke and Head before him, he disdained the enormous volume of parochial business that was done in the provincial legislature. The annihilation of such a legislature and of the huckstering politicians who filled its seats could be accomplished by the creation of a united parliament for the lower provinces in which larger constituencies would be represented by men with larger minds. The seat-of-government question, which was plaguing Canada at this time, could cause trouble, but he was certain that the union was desirable even if a migratory government should become necessary. To Manners-Sutton it seemed that the Chignecto region was the logical one for the establishment of a capital, and he mentioned Amherst and Sackville as possible sites.[3]

The lieutenant-governor was not alone in urging that the low level of public life in New Brunswick was a sufficient reason for leading the province into a union in which its identity would be obliterated. A considerable core of educated persons, regretting the departure of the good days when government had been the prerogative of the educated, could see only degradation in the provincial legislature. In 1858 Robert Duncan Wilmot, speaking his mind on the seat-of-government question, sighed for a union of the colonies that would dissolve their petty legislatures.[4] To men engaged in large commercial ventures beyond the seas, who were winning for the province a considerable place in international trade, the annual gatherings of the legislature at Fredericton seemed not merely contemptible but mildly comic as well. Business was often small and motives narrow.

Yet it would require a powerful combination of circumstances to convert these loosely held opinions into a movement for union with Canada. Suspicion that Galt was merely attempting to create a new balance of power within the Canadian union by adding the lower provinces, to enlarge the area within which the manufacturing industries of Canada would enjoy monopolistic privileges, prevailed over professions of faith. For the time being, favour swung to the smaller union with the other Maritime Provinces. In September 1859 Manners-Sutton reported his belief that action would soon be taken by leading public men in Nova Scotia and New Brunswick. A higher status among the colonies would be the object sought.[5] But nothing happened. Action leading to union, urged in Nova Scotia by Lord Mulgrave, did not develop.

The Colonial Office was converted to the desirability of both large ideas but feared premature discussions promoted by some, not all, of the provinces. In January 1860 the Duke of Newcastle forbade the holding of a conference on union without his own previous knowledge and consent. The requirement for such a conference "at Quebec or elsewhere" was to be a clear initiative from the government of every province concerned.

Until such a common initiative could develop, the situation was to lie at rest. In New Brunswick, following this reconnaissance into the feasibility of intercolonial union, attended by results so negative, the principal performers changed. Fisher was replaced by Tilley as chief minister, and Manners-Sutton was succeeded late in 1861 by Arthur Hamilton Gordon, a young man of thirty-three and a younger son of Lord Aberdeen, former prime minister of Britain. As a private secretary to William Gladstone he had procured an intimate knowledge of the intricacies of public business and great confidence in the Whiggish principle that education and enlightenment could correct the ills of public affairs. A lover of nature, he was to devote his leisure time in New Brunswick to traversing the great forests and rivers. "Few things are more delightful than to drop down some great river, where every frequent turn presents, notwith-

standing the monotony of continual forest, some new view; and
where, as you smoothly glide on, a perpetual succession of
fresh pictures is presented to the eye."[6] As an exponent of the
new Oxford Movement within the Church of England, he frequently found solace from his official duties in Fredericton
beneath the arches of Medley's Gothic cathedral, a reminder of
the life and civilization of old Europe in remarkable contrast to
the wilderness that stretched in almost every direction from the
hills by which the town was surrounded.

II

The prosperous, expansive state of the economy, now at the
zenith of the great age of wood, wind, and water, provided no
basis for the contemplation of new schemes of empire or argument for mergers. Deeply involved as they were in the system
of patronage, Smasher politicians had no appetite for hazards
that could not be calculated. The climate of opinion in New
Brunswick in the early sixties was almost entirely self-congratu-
latory. As a self-governing colony with a flourishing trade, the
province was content to pursue its course. The great impulses
leading to confederation came not from within but from
without.

The outbreak of the American Civil War in 1861 introduced
a new and unfortunate era in Anglo-American relations that
compelled the people of the North American colonies critically
to review their status. What was probably of greater importance
was that it compelled the British government to appraise its
own responsibilities and to persuade the colonies to seek their
salvation in union. Yet, so far as the people of New Brunswick
were concerned, there was nothing very direct or palpable in
these consequences. As spectators they watched the great conflict develop, rejoicing in the traditional belief handed down to
them by their fathers, that the American union could never be
held together. Their puritanic morals had been outraged by the
Fugitive Slave Law. An elemental sympathy for the North at
the outset, never dominant and always critical, receded with
the initial Southern victories and with the gradual realization
that the Union's calamity could produce nothing but gain for
New Brunswick. The predominant sentiment in the press of the
province became one of sympathy for the South. Alone among
the newspapers of the province, the *Globe* of Saint John acquired
the reputation of being a strong Northern partisan; the offices

of the *Telegraph* became a meeting-place for Southerners far from home, and their local supporters. In Maine it was seriously advocated that New Brunswick newspapers should be banned for circulating treason. Not until Atlanta fell, late in 1864, did the majority of the press abandon the hopeful attitude that the long-promised but highly elusive Southern victory was soon to be achieved.

It was not entirely as spectators that the people of the province regarded the war, for the temptations to participate were great. Merchants immediately experienced the benefit of a quickened demand for raw materials of all kinds. Shippers could not resist the opportunity of cashing in on the lush rewards for running the blockade, at first so slack, established by the North over Southern ports. Gordon adopted strenuous measures for the preservation of a proper neutrality, posting proclamations to forbid the enlistment of British subjects in the forces of either side, and taking special precautions to obstruct the efforts of Northern agents to seduce across the border soldiers of the British garrisons and members of the militia, who were promised high pay and quick promotion. Maine was an armed camp. By the end of 1861 it had dispatched fourteen regiments to the front, and four others were in process of formation. Rather brashly the St. Croix *Herald*, published in St. Stephen, carried advertisements of the opportunities for adventure with "the flying artillery". A new American consul appeared at Saint John, propagandizing for his government and determined to contest any disposition to establish friendly relations, public or private, with the Confederacy.

Scarcely had these irritating restrictions upon the more adventurous made their impact when the affair of Mason and Slidell inflamed Anglo-American relations. Consequent on the stopping of the *Trent* on the high seas and the seizure of the two Confederate agents, war seemed immediately at hand for four weeks. All through the province there were martial manifestations. In Maine the movement of troops to the theatre of war came to a halt, and on both sides of the border attention was concentrated on the great military road from Bangor to the Aroostook Valley. Whether or not to defend Woodstock became a cardinal problem for Gordon and General Sir Hastings Doyle, commander of the British troops in the Atlantic provinces. From London came a special dispatch announcing that the Queen was determined to defend New Brunswick, followed by the news that British troops were already on the water.

By the time they were landing at Saint John early in 1862 the emergency was over, but its repercussions were very much in evidence in New Brunswick. The ports of the St. Lawrence being closed, the province became an avenue for the transportation of 7,000 troops to Canada. As the ships docked amid cold weather and heavy storms, the volunteer militia turned out to perform rigorous guard duty. Working by torchlight, parties of citizens transformed schools and churches into barracks. The ladies of the city patriotically served the cold and weary soldiers with hot dinner. Gordon had proceeded to Saint John to ensure the co-ordination of arrangements for the reception and movement northward of the troops, but found that the co-operation of all made his efforts unnecessary. It was boasted in the legislature that the British troops received a better welcome in Saint John than on their home-coming from the Crimea.[7] Farmers broke the road through the snow, and daily detachments of 200 men moved up the river through Fredericton and on to Rivière du Loup, where they could be accommodated by the Grand Trunk Railway. Some were moved as far north as Richmond by the St. Andrews Railway, and others by the European and North American to Shediac where they proceeded by Gulf steamers to Rivière du Loup. Assistance of the population, said Gordon sardonically, was always willing and sometimes efficient.[8]

Casualties were few. Two men died of pneumonia and two of excessive drinking. One soldier lost both hands from frost-bite, but this was owing to alcoholism. Desertion presented a minor problem. Gordon successfully opposed Doyle, who wanted to establish a force of 500 cavalrymen along the border where the activity of American "crimps" was especially notorious. Nobody in New Brunswick, he argued, could ride on horseback between December and April: it was too cold.[9] Provincial derision was excited in the spring when an article in the *Illustrated London News* depicted the hardships of the Guards Battalion as they "marched" over the mountainous, unrouted terrain of New Brunswick. A large coloured print showed bearskinned officers anxiously consulting with Indian guides concerning the route to be followed. In actuality, not a single soldier had marched a yard of the way. Sleighs had provided carriage. The route along the highway to Rivière du Loup was well marked by a line of telegraph wires all the way from Fredericton.[10]

The affair of the *Trent* and the excitement that followed brought to a halt the tendencies that had been at work for so many years to bring New Brunswick to a position of lesser dependence upon Great Britain. The argument of those who pressed for a still greater degree of self-government, claiming that Britain would not stir herself to protect the colonies from the aggressions of the United States, that she placed no value upon the connections that remained with them, had been dramatically discredited. The historic Loyalist prejudice, chilled by seeming British indifference for the past twenty years, was sparked into considerable revival. What Gordon called "a strong English feeling" became apparent. Everywhere he went he received addresses announcing a willingness to fight if Britain and the United States should go to war.

III

Following the *Trent* incident, American relations improved with Britain but not with the British colonies. In New Brunswick the animus against the North was constantly nourished by the undisguised hostility prevailing across the border and by a succession of incidents arising from the maritime and commercial opportunities that presented themselves to the shippers of the province. Materially the province had everything to gain from successful Southern resistance. The South had no shipping of its own, but New Brunswick and Nova Scotia could supply it. Entrance to the rich American coasting trade, denied by the Reciprocity Treaty, was now in part feasible. The carriage of the scarce cotton and tobacco, tar and turpentine, not only to Britain and Europe but even to the ports of the embattled North, represented a latter-day renewal of the challenging conditions by which the commerce of the province had risen to affluence during the War of 1812.

Saint John flourished as Northern commerce, harassed by Southern cruisers, entered upon lean years. Shipowners of Boston and New York sent their vessels to colonial ports for British registry. Frequent cases in which blockade-runners were subjected to Northern reprisals excited wide animosity. Great indignation arose at Saint John when word came that the locally-owned schooner *Adelso*, having sailed from North Carolina with naval stores for Great Britain without interference from the Northern blockaders, who never came in sight, was arrested at Newport, Rhode Island, where she had taken refuge

from heavy weather.[11] Fearing that goods cleared from Northern
ports to New Brunswick and Nova Scotia would ultimately be
carried through the blockade to the Confederacy, the American
government insisted on taking bonds from the shippers, guaranteed by persons who held real estate in the United States.[12]
This had the effect of restricting a great deal of legitimate trade
and increased the conviction that the North was the enemy. On
a small island between Eastport and Campobello appeared a
battery of five guns, erected during electioneering excitement
in Maine and menacing Welshpool. On the border a general
uneasiness prevailed. British troops guarded St. Andrews and
Woodstock. St. Stephen saw scenes of violence produced by the
supporters of the two causes. The editor of the St. Croix *Herald*,
having violently disagreed with pro-Southern journals in Saint
John, had his office invaded by a mob and his type scattered in
the streets.[13] Some fifty draft-dodgers from Maine crossed the
border and settled Skedaddle Ridge behind St. Stephen. The
maintenance of a proper neutrality became more difficult as the
war proceeded.

The most spectacular of all such incidents, illustrative of the
enticements to abandon neutrality, occurred in December 1863
when Saint John was electrified by the arrival of the steamship
Chesapeake, allegedly the captive of the navy of the Confederate States of America. On December 5 she had sailed from
New York for Portland, Maine, and at night, when about
twenty miles north of Cape Cod, fifteen of her "passengers" had
forcibly taken possession of her. The second engineer had been
shot and killed as he rushed up the companion-way to make
resistance. Colonel Braine of the Confederate Army had taken
command "in the name of Jefferson Davis". As tidings of the
incident flooded over the continent, the New York *Herald*
declared that no true Southerner had been involved, that all
fifteen of the captors were Bluenoses "whose blood is as cold
and whose circulation is as feeble as that of reptiles".

The *Chesapeake* merely discharged the legitimate passengers
and crew at Saint John and slipped away in search of coal to
replenish her half-empty bunkers. Hounded by Northern cruisers, she was finally seized – rather illegally – at Sambro, Nova
Scotia, by the warship *Ella and Annie*, and taken into Halifax
where she became the subject of complex and involved negotiation between Britain and the United States.[14] All of her captors
escaped, but a few days later Colonel Braine was identified on

the streets of Saint John by Northern agents and arrested on a warrant issued by the American consul, for piracy and murder. The legal question that emerged concerned the status of Braine and his comrades – whether they were criminals guilty of the alleged offences, or true belligerents in the service of the Confederate States. Whatever their status, Gordon could safely proceed against them under the Foreign Enlistment Act, which forbade British subjects to serve in foreign armies. Three others were apprehended: David Collins of Loch Lomond, James McKinley of Spruce Cove, and Linus Seeley of Saint John.

On a warrant of extradition for trial for murder and piracy, issued by the American consul, these three faced Magistrate Gilbert in Saint John in January. Braine avoided proceedings of this kind by what was termed "a clever legal subterfuge". The magistrate granted the required order and was, according to the *Telegraph*, "worthy of the concentrated indignation of thirty thousand people". The sympathy of the Saint John populace welled up in favour of the prisoners and a strong organization was created for their protection. John Hamilton Gray, whose brother had been killed on a Southern battlefield while fighting for the Confederacy, was retained as their counsel, and, when an appeal was brought before Judge Ritchie, Gilbert's judgment was reversed. During the proceedings the three produced written orders, from the government of the Confederate States, for the taking of the *Chesapeake*. Their belligerency having been established, they were acquitted, to the intense mortification of the American consul.

Acting on orders from the Colonial Office, Gordon had given instructions that, should the prisoners be acquitted under the proceedings for extradition, they should be rearrested for violation of the Foreign Enlistment Act. To his disgust, but not really to his surprise, the instructions were not carried out. The necessary interval of freedom was allowed, and the prisoners, fearful desperadoes to the American government but heroes to a considerable section of the Saint John populace, disappeared. The attorney-general, John Mercer Johnson, would give Gordon no explanation of why the order for rearrest was not executed. All of the proceedings, in Gordon's opinion, had been questionable, and even among the judges there had been dissimulation. It had been impossible to find the commission under the Great Seal setting up the High Court of Piracy. The city buzzed with rumours of nefarious activities of agents of the Northern government. Statements were openly made that the entire affair of the *Chesapeake* had been engineered by persons who had been ruined because of seizures of their ships and cargoes off the Northern coasts.[15] At the Colonial Office there were ministerial mutterings about the anomalous situation. New Brunswick was a part of the Empire, but in granting responsible government Britain had surrendered the power of compelling New Brunswick to behave in a neutral way.[16]

St. Stephen remained a hotbed of partisanship and a base for a small band of Confederate sympathizers of British birth. There Gordon was compelled to restrain those who wished to encourage hostilities with the Republic.[17] For a long time the town had been under a peculiar handicap. The provincial tax on the exportation of New Brunswick timber, in effect since 1845, had made it profitable for all the lumbering interests on the St. Croix to employ the port of Calais for the carriage of their produce to the United States. When the disability was removed in 1863, prosperity mounted on the New Brunswick side of the border. But the excitement of the war lasted until the end came. Calais was alarmed by accounts of the efforts made in St. Stephen to arouse the Passamaquoddy Indians against the North. In the summer of 1864 four Confederate partisans, headed by William Collins, brother of David Collins of *Chesapeake* fame, walked into a trap and were arrested, carrying a Confederate flag, while attempting to rob a Calais bank.

The proud attitude of being independent of all the world, fostered by the Smashers during their prosperous years, lost much of its strength as the implications of the American Civil War acquired meaning for the people of New Brunswick. Independence for such a small colony could have but little appeal on a continent given over to martial alarms and tensions. Half-instinctively the people looked back upon the Mother Country for reassurance and were gratified by the degree of support extended. Under the circumstances Gordon had little difficulty in rapidly advancing the efficiency of the unpaid militia companies organized by Manners-Sutton. Following the excitement over the *Trent* affair, the legislature, making a break with the past, voted the sum of $3,000, which was chiefly employed to pay the twelve drill-sergeants sent out from Britain – all of whom had gained the good graces of the citizens of Fredericton shortly after their arrival by joining a temperance association.

The cluster of companies, scattered throughout the country and uniformed in all kinds of clothing, were gradually shaped into a system, though Gordon found the independence of commanding officers rather distasteful. The employment of the new Enfield rifle for sport in the backwoods of the province aroused the ire of professional soldiers. The presence of an Orange company in Saint John, side by side with an Irish Catholic company clad in green, excited misgivings about the dire potentialities of this remarkable weapon if the religious riots that had formerly disgraced the city should be renewed.[18] In 1863 the legislature, in spite of serious opposition, raised the militia grant to $10,000, and inspecting field officers arrived from England. Tilley promised increased support for the movement if efficiency was increased and public support was shown.

The refusal to enter Confederation early in 1865 thrust responsibility for defence more squarely upon the province. If New Brunswick should refuse to join the other provinces in a union, Cardwell, the colonial secretary, argued, she must accept responsibility for her security. The anti-Confederate legislature of that year vigorously sustained the idea of independence by raising the defence budget to $30,000. This enabled Gordon and his military advisers to inaugurate a new system. A great military camp of 950 men, clad in scarlet tunics and blue flannel caps without peaks, was conducted at the new Exhibition Hall in Fredericton. Its success, featured by the complete absence of drunkenness and insubordination, went a long way towards disarming the opponents of military training. Gordon could now look forward to the intensive training of half the volunteer militia for twenty-eight days in each year. Rifle-shooting under military conditions and discipline became a regular pastime for the adventurous young men of the country. Though the volunteer movement lost impetus in the more rural areas, it continued to gain adherents in Saint John and the towns of the province.

The end of the Civil War produced an apparent American determination to gain vengeance on the British provinces which had so often appeared to give aid and comfort to the defeated Confederacy. Thousands of victorious, battle-hardened troops appeared poised for a turn to the north. Because of American susceptibilities, the Canadian government was obliged to line its frontier with militia in order to guarantee the correct neutrality demanded by the government at Washington. Some of the St. Alban's raiders, the notorious Confederate partisans who had crossed the Canadian border and invaded Vermont, appeared in New Brunswick, but, knowing no names, the government could not legally issue warrants against them, an embarrassment that aroused fury in American official circles.[19] Seward, the American Secretary of State, who was trying to secure recognition in New Brunswick for an increasing number of American consuls, learned of a band of Confederate sympathizers in the province who planned to commit depredations in Maine, then to join another band in that state for a march through to Kentucky.[20] In attempting to persuade the British government that New Brunswick was not deliberately harbouring Confederate sympathizers, Gordon had testy exchanges not only with the Colonial Office but with Lord Lyons, the ambassador at Washington.

IV

In spite of the clouds in the south, a feeling of well-being and self-importance prevailed as the province entered the 1860s. The American Civil War initially damaged commerce, and in 1861 provincial revenues from imports notably diminished. Following this temporary set-back, however, trade uniformly prospered. The achievements of provincial shipbuilders continued to arouse pride. In New England the war accelerated the shift to the construction of iron ships, but in the British provinces there seemed to be no limit to what wooden ships could still do. At Saint John, James Nevins, the Olive brothers, John S. Parker, and others were annually building great ships of the most modern design, which acquired a reputation for speed and seaworthiness on the England-Australia run. St. Martin's saw its palmy days as a shipbuilding centre. Up the creeks of Richibucto, Dorchester, Moncton, Sackville, and the Miramichi, in almost any small town or village adjacent to tide-water, shipbuilders' yards echoed with activity. Many of the vessels were sold abroad. In 1865 the sale of ships was reckoned as being worth $800,000 in invisible exports.[21] Many were owned in shares of sixty-fourths by firms and individuals, the returns making many families well-to-do. Ambitious young men went to sea, knowing full well that a ship's command would be the reward of faithful service. Aboard Bluenose ships efficiency and cleanliness were proverbial. Discipline was stern; "no brass buttons and ease" as aboard "the limejuicer windwagons" from which they were distinguished the world over.[22] The shipping of the Maritime Provinces had become a power in the commercial world.

All the timber New Brunswick could produce was readily sold. In 1860 one-fifth of British imports came from the province. Markets constituted no problem, the principal complaint being that bad management of the Crown lands severely limited output. Legislation could not deprive the larger operators of the virtual monopoly they possessed over the cutting and exporting of timber. Almost annually the legislature considered ways and means of opening the forests to the enterprise of a larger number of entrepreneurs, but no satisfying solution could be found. The millions of acres of land still within the public domain yielded little or no revenue for roads and schools. "Legislate as you will, the larger operators will monopolize the trade." Men of large ambitions but small resources who attempted to break into the circle of those who secured timber concessions from the government by one means or another were forced to become dependent on the well-established few. One method of eliminating competition was described in a speech in the legislative council in 1862. As the crowd of eager buyers waited in the office of the commissioner for the auctioning of timber berths, "a very repulsive looking person" would appear upon the scene. Somebody would cry, "He is from the lazaretto at Tracadie"; and "the uninitiated" would immediately take to flight.[23]

Keen enterprise and ruthless competition prevailed in business, but opinion from the outside world upon the two provinces, New Brunswick and Nova Scotia, was almost always disparaging. One visitor was amazed by the low standard of public men, whose principal art was that of "stooping to conquer". Demagogues kept gentlemen out of politics, and pork-barrel ethics were general. Politicians modelled themselves on Joseph Howe, whose phase of constitutional uplift was now past, and whose crusade of Protestant and Saxon against Catholic and Celt, couched in coarse, insulting language, fostered religious bigotry and a war of sects.[24] Gordon himself blamed the poor quality of political leadership in New Brunswick for the absence of a higher degree of progress. Colebrooke, Head, and Manners-Sutton had expressed the same sentiments, but Gordon entertained them more arrogantly and expressed them more succinctly. Keepers of grog-shops and petty attorneys who filled up the legislature, and concerned themselves primarily with their pay and with the purely local wants of their constituents, said Gordon, could not give the province the leadership and strength it needed to keep up with the progress that was so apparent elsewhere in North America. The priceless boon of self-government had been granted, and the British government had done well to grant it merely to escape responsibility for what was happening in New Brunswick.

Compared to Canada, New Brunswick was, according to Gordon, "poverty-stricken, stagnant and decaying". A house or public building of stone stood as a certain mark of an earlier generation. Everywhere was "the bare, sad desolation of cleared land, once farmed but now abandoned". Everywhere except Saint John "the truck system" prevailed. The theory that employers would sell to employees at just prices was plausible, but in actual practice the temptation to sell at high prices was too great. In some places workmen never saw cash at all. "The apathetic listlessness of the people" contrasted strangely with general impressions of the North American character.[25] Gordon loved what Nature had done in New Brunswick, but he had no praise for institutions and men. His quick, sensitive mind, always sure of itself, could see remarkable paradoxes. The lazaretto at Tracadie, where nothing whatever was done for the minds and bodies of the lepers, was dreary and unpleasing. But he was surprised and rather pleased to find low skew windows similar to those in the chancels of ancient churches. "In a remote corner of North America in a rude wooden building of modern date erected by men who never saw a mediaeval church or possess the least acquaintance with Gothic architecture, convenience has suggested an arrangement precisely similar to one which has long puzzled the antiquaries and architects of Europe."[26]

The elections of 1861, when the remarkable New Brunswick ballot, printed for each candidate or slate of candidates and circulated to their supporters, appeared, emphasized the strong trend towards democratization that had been in progress for forty years. The older members – such as John Ambrose Street, John Hamilton Gray, and Robert Duncan Wilmot – who professed to remember the old times as the good times, were mostly defeated. The ballot did not forestall bribery, for accounts of the expenditure of large sums of money were confidently and publicly reported. In entertaining the victorious members at his table, Gordon listened to boastful comparisons of the costs of votes in the constituencies, one member of the government declaring that he had paid a guinea apiece, though some of his less generous colleagues had got off with three shillings and sixpence. Fisher led the poll in York County, the electorate taking an enlightened view of his unpleasant predicament and forced resignation of the year before, since it was generally considered that he had been only one of many public men using their positions to speculate in the purchase of public lands. According to Gordon the new house had only two or three "gentlemen of education and position". Debate consisted of "the raking up of old history, bare assertions and flat contradictions, disparaging innuendoes. . . . An honourable member speaking from his place stated that he considered he was sent to Parliament to look after the interests of his own county, not those of the province, that when a measure was before the House he always asked himself how it would affect the interests of the county he represented; that if it appeared likely to benefit the province but not his county he voted against it."[27] Presiding over the assembly at first was John Mercer Johnson of the Miramichi, allowed even by Gordon to be able, but incapable of the judicial role required of the Speaker. Sofa cushions were pitched about the scene of deliberation, "the grave, deaf old clerk, the relic of a more decorous age, attired in gown and bands" successfully managing to evade them. As a partisan Johnson could always excite reprisal. Timothy Warren Anglin, his fighting Irish always up, once called him "a pothouse brawler and swaggerer". When Anglin wrote in the *Freeman* that Johnson had referred to the government supporters in the house as sheep, the member for Northumberland replied that he was expressing solicitation for the agricultural interests of the province. Anglin's further retort was that Johnson was "a low, worthless blackguard" who could say what he pleased about anybody without exciting any feeling of resentment or sense of insult.[28]

To those schooled in the formal and constitutional restraints of British politics, contempt for government seemed to be the rule in New Brunswick. The democracy that had arisen from the wilderness appeared to be raw and unrefined, incapable of assessing its truer and larger interests, grossly contaminated by the brash, frontier influences from across the border where, in Maine, the "Know Nothing" party was a power to be reckoned with. Administration seemed shiftless and corrupt. In April 1862 treasury bills to the value of £10,000 were abstracted from the mails on the route from Sackville to Saint John. The post-

master was indisposed to press investigation because his deputies were all fervent political supporters.[29] The government was
timid in enforcing its authority upon a people who were
accustomed freely to roam great spaces and do what they
pleased in ignorance or defiance of the law. Contrary to regulations, the netting and spearing of salmon in the narrow headwaters were practised with deadly effect, the extinction of this
part of the fishery being freely forecast. Necessity compelled a
general admission of willingness to obey the regulations if uniformly enforced, but for a long time the legislature refused to
act. When finally, in consequence of a recommendation instituted by Gordon, the policy of renting fishing stations was
adopted, the first yield of a concession sold by auction was a
bonanza of £770.[30] Only when public opinion manifested itself in
a most certain way could government declare its authority.
Government was tame, but the people were not. In November
1862, 400 labourers working on the St. Andrews and Quebec
Railway in the vicinity of Richmond tore up the tracks and
commandeered three locomotives because they had not been
paid by the contractors. Local farmers who likewise had not
been paid for their services aided and abetted them. The sheriff
of Carleton called for military assistance, and Gordon, not daring to trust the militia, had to send 100 men of the 15th
Regiment.[31]

On the Fredericton scene individuality and eccentricity were
rife, but Tilley's place remained unchallenged. His rosy cheeks
and half-smile, sharp features, and encyclopaedic command of
statistics, and the respect in which he was held throughout the
New Brunswick community, imparted to government a stability
that otherwise would have been absent. He did not have very
much assistance. Many members of the administration were
habitually absent from Fredericton. Concerning their quality,
there are not only the strictures of Gordon but the opinion of
the independent *Telegraph* of Saint John, which declared them
to be "utterly incapable and inefficient".

V

Under political direction such as this New Brunswick did not
look out upon the world; rather, the world was crowding in
upon New Brunswick. The dubious future of the province was
coming more clearly into relief. A small community of fewer
than 300,000 people could scarcely aspire to independence in an

era when great spaces were being conquered and ideas were oriented to political mergers and the creation of new empires. A few thinkers could see the necessity of facing alternatives and for years had considered the feasibility of union with Canada. Yet talk of this was unpolitical and, to the great mass of the people, mildly metaphysical.

On the other hand, the subject of railway communication with Canada was of intense political interest. Even the barely literate could take seriously the view that the progress of the province and the welfare of the people depended on the connection of the government-owned European and North American Railway with the railway systems of Canada and the United States. Popular sentiment demanded action to bring the province into closer relations with countries whose progress was more notable than New Brunswick's. With some people considerations other than material could arouse enthusiasm. In 1861, sitting in "a plain little room" in Fredericton, Edward Watkin, the president of the Grand Trunk Railway, and Tilley had exchanged "vows" upon a particular project with respect to "an Anglo-American" empire. Neither would die, if he could help it, "until we had looked upon the waters of the Pacific from the windows of a British railway carriage."[32]

The tensions of 1862 between Britain and the United States helped to produce in London a climate of opinion favourable to the revival of the Intercolonial project. At Quebec, in the autumn of 1861, a meeting of the three governments concerned renewed the 1858 request for British financial assistance, offering as an additional inducement a willingness to accept the decision of the British government upon the route the railway should follow. In November, Tilley left for England in company with Howe and Philip Van Koughnet of Canada. While they were there, the affair of the *Trent* and the transportation of thousands of British troops across New Brunswick under conditions described as half-primitive dramatically demonstrated the military necessity of a railway linking the lower provinces with the St. Lawrence. Yet the Duke of Newcastle was not sufficiently impressed. All that the British government would do would be to guarantee a loan of £3,000,000 sterling.

In September 1862, a second conference at Quebec worked out the details by which the three provinces should finance the great enterprise. Canada agreed to assume five-twelfths of the total liability, the remaining seven-twelfths to be divided equally between Nova Scotia and New Brunswick. Immediately the agreement was reached, the railway question attracted the excitement always associated with it at times when great decisions were to be made. With an annual revenue of £120,000, New Brunswick was already a million in debt for railway construction. In the spring of 1862 the house of assembly had asked for and received guarantees that no fresh railway construction would be undertaken. Financial scruples made Tilley waver, but, when he finally made up his mind to endorse the plan – a decision Gordon credited to his own influence – he did so wholeheartedly.

Sectional hostilities again came to the fore. The northern counties, taxed for years to pay the interest on the debt for the European and North American without drawing any benefit from it, were unreservedly behind the plan. Considering that Tilley would certainly support a central route that would detour from Boiestown to link up with the St. Andrews-Quebec and the European and North American, they did not really trust him, but they were completely convinced that the British government would insist upon the North Shore line. Peter Mitchell volubly sustained this point of view. The North Shore already traded with Canada to some extent, and it relished the prospect of an increasing volume of intercourse with the St. Lawrence. There were many doubts and hesitations, but at the end of 1862 it was certain that Tilley would have behind him the vast majority of the legislature and the public. A great preoccupation, shared by almost everybody, was that vast amounts of cash would come into circulation following renewed railway construction.

Gloomy financial prophets were not popular, but Albert James Smith, the Smasher attorney-general who had succeeded Fisher the year before, accepted the role with aplomb. This popular prototype of New Brunswick politician, whose conduct invariably caused the lips of the well-bred to curl with contempt and fury, who trumpeted the literature of revolt from the hustings of Westmorland and told the people that their rights were trampled in the dust by family compacts and dictatorial governors, had fallen under a cloud. In the last days of the session of 1862 he had piloted through the legislature an act explaining the boundary agreement with Nova Scotia. The original act of 1858 had not been precise upon the source of the Missiquash, and certain parties of Westmorland County, constructing a dam, discovered that they were labouring, not in Nova Scotia as they had thought, but in New Brunswick. Other parties, seeking an injunction restraining them from constructing the dam, had employed Smith as counsel. The courts, by the authority of the revised act, had no difficulty in establishing the right of Smith's clients, but it appeared almost certain that Smith had employed his public position to win their case. Gordon took him severely to task, and Smith's reply was to the effect that it was none of Gordon's business. The Duke of Newcastle, although surprised by Smith's conduct, would not disallow the act. He later concurred in the granting of the award of Queen's Counsel to the attorney-general, his conduct having been "not sufficiently discreditable" for refusal.[33]

The hot temper that was displayed in this, as in many another of Smith's private quarrels, was combined with a cautious conservatism so far as the general problems of politics were concerned. The violent radicalism that had distinguished Smith's career stopped short at the provincial balance-sheet. The European and North American was paying no interest on its debentures. The Intercolonial would rush the province into an incalculable morass of further debt.

His dramatic resignation, implying a hard line of caution, made little impact on the general state of opinion concerning railways. Tilley again proceeded to London at the end of the year on a mission which, it was supposed, would result in a firm agreement with the British government and the other colonies to construct the Intercolonial. But unfavourable breezes were blowing from the direction of Canada. There the government had changed, and it was well known that the coalition of Grits and Rouges was far more interested in the Red River country than in a railway to the lower provinces. In Quebec the Rouge press had been filled with remarks derogatory to the venture. Canada was attempting to persuade the British government that a financial grant for the Intercolonial could be accepted as a contribution to defence, but the Duke of Newcastle could not see it as any substitute for soldiers.[34] Suspicions against Canada seemed to be confirmed when the conference broke up. Tilley and Howe returned to their provinces, prepared to believe that the September agreement at Quebec had been made hard and fast, while the two Canadian delegates, Howland and Sicotte, went off on a junket to Paris. The news that Canada was hedging on one specific feature of the plan, the creation of a sinking

fund to redeem Intercolonial debentures, came as a shock,
though not entirely unexpected. Albert Smith's uninhibited remarks about "oily Canadian politicians" appeared to have
precise meaning.

VI

On the subject of the Intercolonial, Canada balked but was
determined not to lose face. The government at Quebec announced that, though the agreement had not been completed, it
was prepared to proceed with a survey for the route. Tilley's
government, encouraged by the result of a by-election in Saint
John, where John Hamilton Gray was elected by a two-to-one
majority as a supporter of the Intercolonial, hastened to retrieve
what it could from the rapidly deteriorating position. The legislation necessary for participation in the scheme was passed.
Cheerfully the government agreed to co-operate with Canada in
the survey. A dour determination to hold Canada to account
sustained flickering hopes in the Intercolonial. Bad news, however, came from Nova Scotia. Howe was on his way out of
politics, and, in the uncertain state of party and personal rivalries in that colony, nothing could be done to enact the legislation
necessary to guarantee Nova Scotian participation. Of the three
parties to the Quebec and London agreements, New Brunswick
was the only one that sustained the provisions of the Intercolonial scheme with sureties of firm intention.

Later in 1863, as the Canadian government revealed its intentions in statements at the Quebec parliament, and Canada
assumed the right to repudiate the London agreement if it should
choose to do so, hopes died, though New Brunswick insisted,
contrary to the Canadian position, that the agreement had
merely gone into a state of suspension. To the anger of the
Colonial Office, Gordon, in a public dispatch, assailed the Canadian government for a breach of faith and a blow at the unity
and loyalty of all British North America. Confidentially he
declared that he was trying to strengthen the opposition party
in Canada, which believed, much more than the Grit-Rouge
coalition in power, in the value of railway connection with the
Maritime Provinces. The young lieutenant-governor of New
Brunswick was not the kind of man who could confine himself
to a provincial stage, and his relations with Lord Monck, the
Governor General, suffered accordingly. Relations with Canada
were not improved by comments in the Saint John press. The

Telegraph, usually considered a cut or two above the other journals, called Antoine Dorion, the Rouge leader, a liar and declared the Canadian government to be "bankrupt in truth". Thomas D'Arcy McGee, who made himself a champion of the idea of railway communication with New Brunswick in the Canadian parliament, became something of a provincial hero.

By November the projected iron link to unite the colonies, which some considered the indispensable preliminary to political union, became a subject for recrimination and abuse. At this time of supreme disappointment an alternative scheme, considered by Gordon to be sinister, came from across the border. Agitation for a railway to link New Brunswick and Maine replaced the Intercolonial as the grand object for speculation. Lustily supported by Saint John merchants, John A. Poor, "the old friend" of the European and North American from the time of the Portland convention in 1850, wrote to Tilley asking for a review of the railway policy of the New Brunswick government. He had talked with Tupper and Dickey of Nova Scotia and had received sympathy. He presented a plan to link Halifax and Saint John with Bangor by rail. Nova Scotia and New Brunswick, he declared, could take stock in the new company he was forming if they wished to do so, but, if not, it would all be taken up by capitalists of Maine who wanted to develop their own public lands. Echoing the business sentiment that clearly existed in Saint John, he argued that the collapse of the Intercolonial negotiations represented "a matter that has too long kept men's minds in doubt as to the true intentions of the British Government".[35]

The strength of the reaction in favour of this other old idea, now called in Saint John by the name of Western Extension, appalled Gordon. Almost daily, in various sections of the province, meetings were being called to applaud it at the expense of the Intercolonial. If the idea should take shape and Western Extension go into construction, much of the justification for the Intercolonial would be removed and it would be condemned to almost certain financial failure. Ostensibly, Western Extension was a far cheaper proposition for New Brunswick than the Intercolonial was. If, its apologists warned, Saint John should not become the focal point of an international railway linking it with Bangor, the Maine capitalists would move their line across the border farther north, appropriating for themselves the whole trade of the upper Saint John. Those who could see railways as instruments of things other than the mere commercial thought they were seeing the beginnings of the process by which New Brunswick would become a ragtag extremity of the United States. "The New Brunswickers," remarked the Halifax *Citizen*, "in laying down the rails to the boundaries, would be forging link after link of a chain which would bind them inevitably to the chariot wheels of the North, commercially and socially at first, and probably politically afterwards."[36] As the imperial idea withered almost to death, Saint John and the communities of Charlotte County exhibited what appeared to be a desperate determination to hurl themselves into the arms of American capitalists. At the Colonial Office the Duke of Newcastle anxiously consulted with Edward W. Watkin upon "this embarrassing desire". Edward R. Burpee, a civil engineer and a New Brunswick agent for Poor, presented to the government a sanguine prospectus upon the details of the plan. Distaste for Canada and Canadians was expressed by all the Smasher papers of Saint John. The *Globe*, the leading government organ, declared that Canada had more need of the seaboard facilities of the Atlantic provinces than the latter had of anything Canada had to offer. "The Lower Provinces have all the elements of social, commercial and political prosperity and greatness without respect to Canada."[37] The blandishments of the United States seemed infinitely more attractive. In this boom time of Western Extension it was commonly asserted that Watkin and the Grand Trunk were trying to get the publicly-owned New Brunswick railway system under their control.

Uncertainty dominated the legislature of 1864 as all the bewildering ramifications of numerous schemes for railway construction seemed to burst upon it simultaneously. Tilley's government held to the line it had taken with respect to Canada, that the Intercolonial idea was not dead. The breath of life was still there. Sandford Fleming and a party of engineers from Canada were surveying three proposed routes, and New Brunswick approved, though refusing to be bound by any decision he might make.[38] Yet Tilley was also compelled to face up to pressure from the southern counties for action that would facilitate Western Extension. John W. Cudlip, a liquor salesman from Saint John with a seat in the house of assembly, took the lead in a movement designed to force the government to action, declaring that in the house a new basis for party division should be established, and that if the government would not co-operate with the interests supporting Western Extension it should be replaced.

Early in March, Cudlip introduced a motion to declare a clear preference for Western Extension over the Intercolonial. Charles Fisher, acting for the government, introduced an amendment to deprive the resolution of its force. As the debate continued heatedly, news came from Nova Scotia that the legislature of that province had given quietus to the whole Intercolonial plan by again failing to take action. In contrast with the apathy of the Nova Scotians was the political turnover in Canada. One of the very first acts of the new Macdonald-Brown coalition was the dispatch of a telegram to Fredericton and Halifax offering to fulfil the pledges made at Quebec in 1862.

Since there was no clarity, the legislature could offer only a general solution attempting simultaneously to reassure the public in all sections of the province of its good intentions. In passing the Facility Act it offered financial aid to railway companies that would extend the existing European and North American in a variety of directions, northward to Fredericton and the Miramichi, southward into Albert County, and westward to Maine. Subsidies of $10,000 a mile would be granted to any parties taking up the offer. In addition a grant of $20,000 was provided for any company that would link New Brunswick with Canada. The province had limited resources. Sectional rivalries forbade the concentration of resources in any one area. In this, as in so many other things, dispersal was the rule of life in New Brunswick. Peter Mitchell incisively fought the battle of the Intercolonial and of the northern counties, which were sufficiently powerful in the legislature to prevent Saint John from acquiring for its own projects the total resources available. Only public money could answer Saint John's problems. The two companies organized to forward Western Extension had sold shares but collected no cash.

The facility bills of 1864 were referred to as "the Lobster Act" because they provided for the construction of railways in as many directions as a lobster extends its claws. They pointed up the essential fact that the province could do little to continue railway construction unless aid should come from the outside. They were reminders too, of the absence of decision on great political projects to which railways were only ancillary.

CHAPTER 16

Confederation:
the Achievement

1864-1867

No real initiative to union came from the people and legislature of New Brunswick. Only one eminent individual in the province, the lieutenant-governor, was so profoundly dissatisfied with the state of things that he was prepared to set in motion ideas that could lead to practical action. Arthur Hamilton Gordon stood on a plane that enabled him to contemplate the progress of New Brunswick not from material but from moral grounds. Contemptuous of the men who gave him advice and who enacted laws in the legislature, he made his principal preoccupation the reduction of the total number of politicians and the creation of a new area of administration of which the province should be merely a part. Gordon was not one of the more popular representatives of the Crown in New Brunswick, but as a catalyst working at the higher level to bring about change he was exceedingly influential. Taking advantage of the permission given by the Duke of Newcastle for the calling of a conference of the colonies to consider union, he drafted a series of dispatches to Downing Street that graphically described the imperfections of responsible government in New Brunswick, inevitably reinforcing the conviction, already established there, that change was highly desirable.

Early in 1863 Gordon had eagerly revived Manners-Sutton's idea of Maritime union. The idea was an old one, but the time was perhaps more propitious than ever before. The tensions of the American Civil War had the effect of preparing the public mind for new departures. The idea of the larger union that

414

would include Canada was adversely prejudiced by the alleged sabotage of the scheme for the Intercolonial Railway. Tilley, the only member of the New Brunswick government in whom Gordon had confidence, was steadily won to the acceptance of the idea that the three lower provinces could together form a prosperous, united province of the British Empire. No evidence exists to contradict the impression given in Gordon's dispatches, that he and Tilley worked almost conspiratorially through 1863 to bring the members of the government to agreement upon this aim. The departure from Nova Scotia of Lord Mulgrave, long a supporter of the same project, made Gordon the foremost exponent of the course that logic and morality seemed to dictate. During the summer he visited Prince Edward Island. Among the leaders of both government and opposition his ideas met with a favourable reception, though it is reasonable to suppose that some of the opinions were rather studiously polite.

In September, Charles Tupper, volubly articulate, the rising star in the politics of Nova Scotia, visited Saint John to reveal himself a warm advocate of Maritime union. In an interview with Gordon and Tilley, detailed schemes were made. Tilley declared the tactics by which he hoped to disarm the opposition of members of the house of assembly in New Brunswick who, he believed, would not be so much against the design as fearful of a quick dissolution of the legislature and the consequent loss of their pay. A complete legislative and administrative union would be the objective. The first parliament of the united province would consist of members of the three existing legislatures who should decide the basis of representation and the fundamental laws of a new constitution. Prince Edward Island, since its debt was considerably lighter than those of the other two provinces, would be exempted from taxation for railways, of which she had none. Opposition in that province could be overcome by an offer to purchase the lands of the absentee proprietors by the other two provinces. The choice of a capital was to be reserved for the Queen. Gordon, according to his own account, persuaded Tupper to commence the formal motions leading to Maritime union by addresses to the Crown from the provincial legislatures rather than by simple resolutions. With a nice sense of history and respect for Nova Scotian pride, New Brunswickers were willing to defer to the seniority of the older province.

The project continued to enjoy official favour as the year

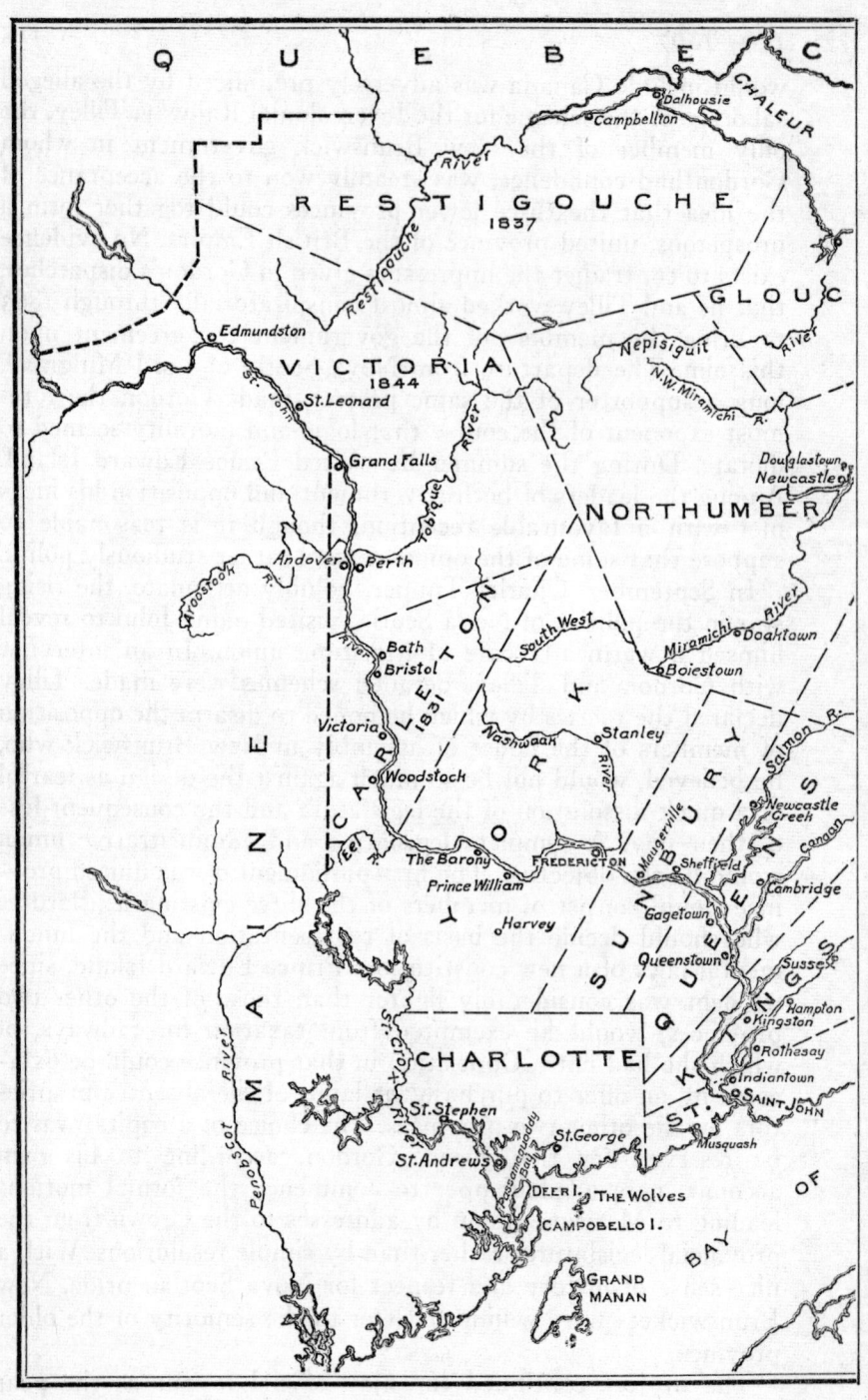

BAY

Miscou I.

SHIPPEGAN I.

Caraquet

Bathurst

ESTER
1826

Tracadie

MIRAMICHI BAY

Chatham

LAND

KENT
1826

Richibucto

Rexton

NORTHUMBERLAND STRAIT

P. E. I.

Shediac

WESTMORLAND

Moncton

Petitcodiac

BAIE VERTE

Hopewell

Sackville

Dorchester

ALBERT
1845
Albert

Kennebecasis

Mechanics
Settlement

NOVA

JOHN

CHIGNECTO BAY

FUNDY

MINAS CHANNEL

SCOTIA

NEW BRUNSWICK
AT
CONFEDERATION

came to a close. In the meetings of the executive council Tilley encountered some difficulties, but only on details.[1] By October the idea was being discussed in the newspapers of the three provinces, receiving notably strong support in Nova Scotia. In New Brunswick, though there was no downright opposition, there was little enthusiastic support. At the Colonial Office in London, interest and approval were warm but optimism was moderate. The Duke of Newcastle preferred to see the construction of the Intercolonial as a necessary prelude to any kind of political union.

The results of the propaganda so industriously circulated by the lieutenant-governor of New Brunswick had been mildly spectacular. Maritime union was in the air, though very much overshadowed by the tensions that came to the three provinces in consequence of the *Chesapeake* affair. Yet Gordon was made painfully aware of a certain superficiality in the proceedings. It was difficult to persuade the politicians, not only of his own province but of the other two as well, to settle the simple but serious business of agreeing on a time and place for the important conference at which union should be discussed. Obediently the legislatures of the three provinces in their sessions of 1864 passed resolutions in favour of such a conference. But a curious immobility ensued. Nova Scotia had resolved that the conference should be "for the purpose of arranging a preliminary plan for the Union". New Brunswick had decided less pointedly to send delegates to a conference "for the purpose of considering the subject of the Union". All that could be said of the politicians at Fredericton was that they were willing to listen: they had no positive volition to act. Maritime union seemed a sovereign solution. But was there a problem? From Prince Edward Island came suggestions of a strong intransigence that belied the easy assurances of W. H. Pope, the secretary of that province, who a year before had told the Colonial Office that there would be no resistance of any account to Maritime union. What was most certain was that the Islanders would not leave the Island. When Gordon left for England in May, no arrangements had been made and nobody of consequence was becoming angry at the failure to push through to a conclusion the impulses that he had in large part originated.

II

By the first days of summer it was altogether probable that the vast majority of Maritime politicians would cheerfully have permitted the idea of union to slip into oblivion. That they were not permitted to do so was due to a powerful impetus that had arisen elsewhere. In Canada the Macdonald-Brown coalition had been formed on a programme for the reorganization of British North America. Brown's project for a simple Canadian federation had been by-passed for a more ambitious scheme.

On July 9 Richard Graves MacDonnell, the new lieutenant-governor of Nova Scotia, was surprised to receive from Quebec a dispatch from Lord Monck expressing interest in the meeting about to be held in the Maritime Provinces and asking that Canada should be permitted to send delegates. As the head of the senior government concerned, he was forced into an initiative that resulted in the calling of a conference at Charlottetown on September 1. There was no time for quibbling about place and date. Lieutenant-Colonel Cole, the administrator of New Brunswick in Gordon's absence, accepted the invitation without reserve. But the pace of arrangements was lethargic. On August 6, when Gordon returned to Fredericton, no delegates had been appointed.

Governments did not act rapidly, but feeling was nevertheless excited. Fredericton and Saint John were murmuring about the rhetoric of Thomas D'Arcy McGee and a large party of Canadian members of parliament who had been taking a pleasure excursion through the province. On the evening of Gordon's return the capital was buzzing with talk of a coming union. At a banquet in the chamber of the legislative council, Tilley, upon concluding his speech of welcome and brotherly sentiment to the Canadians, theatrically clasped hands with Ferguson of Canada and Weir of Nova Scotia. Gordon's immediate aim of a legislative union of the Maritime Provinces was being cast in the shadow of greater things. But at his levee on the following afternoon he declared his hope that the visit of the Canadians would accelerate the day when all citizens of British North America should become members of one mighty state. Promptly he appointed as delegates to Charlottetown Tilley, Steeves, Johnson, Gray, and Chandler, the last two being the leaders of the opposition in the two houses of the legislature.

From Gordon's particular point of view almost everything went wrong at Charlottetown. Hovering on the fringes of the conference, he could see Maritime union and the moral uplift it represented almost completely thrust aside. The intensely local prejudices of the Prince Edward Island delegation were quite sufficient to dispel all possibility that a legislative union of the three provinces could come about. Amidst the clear possibility of a more general and federal union, dramatically described and rationally presented by Macdonald and his colleagues, the very lukewarm interest of the New Brunswick delegation in the smaller scheme disappeared.

To the conservative, entrenched political interests of the province, federal union was a much less radical project than that for which the Charlottetown conference was convened. It offered fewer sacrifices and far greater advantages. No vested interest of a commercial kind stood behind Maritime union. Tilley and the intensely business-like members of the New Brunswick delegation were interested in political union primarily for the economic benefits it could bring. To men of large ambitions brought up in small provinces, the proximity of the enormous, expanding, closed market of the United States had been a source of burning envy. Like other public figures of the age they had been caught up in admiration for the progress of the German states within their exclusive *Zollverein*, which represented a kind of political desideratum appealing to commercial men. Now there was painted at Charlottetown the picture of a market comparable to that of the United States, bound together by a federal union and extending from sea to sea, to which New Brunswick could be joined by the Intercolonial Railway promised by the Canadians. Compared with this, Maritime union could offer nothing solid and tangible.

The opening meeting of the delegates of the three provinces produced only the invitation to the Canadians to state their case. Cartier's promise that the building of a great nation could be reconciled with the retention of provincial rights and identities, Brown's stress upon the Maritime Provinces as one of the three great regions within the nation, Macdonald's depiction of a strong central government that could protect the interests of all British North Americans, and the financial acumen of Galt, whose mastery of figures overshadowed even Tilley's and who showed that within the federation the three provinces would not really lose revenue, accomplished their desired effect. By the second day of the conference it was the mechanism of the proposed federation that engrossed the attention of the Maritimers. The communication of views was entirely unofficial, but the delegations of the three provinces surrendered to the blandishments of the Canadians and to the deep conviction that any arrangement by which their own legislatures should be obliterated would be highly unpopular. They made contributions of their own to the large point of view that the federation should be strong, that no replica of the American union, in which the rights of the states should take precedence over those of the general government, should be created. Edward Barron Chandler made a strong speech, seconded by Tilley, urging that provincial governments should not be permitted to make appointments to the Bench, for fear that it would be filled with obscure and incompetent men. Yet there seems little doubt, from what emerged from the unrecorded and semi-secret Charlottetown conference, that the Canadians were the mentors and the Maritimers the pupils.

The conference laid down the broad principles on which a British North American union could be promoted, and as it became clear, as the conference moved to Halifax, Saint John, and Fredericton, that the original aim was to be ignored, Gordon's displeasure turned to dread and anger. To the lieutenant-governor and to a small group of persons at Fredericton and Saint John who believed in a union for intellectual, moral, and patriotic reasons, it seemed unbelievable that the wretched legislatures of the lower provinces should be permitted to remain "for the maintenance of provincial independence, that is to say facilities for local jobbing".[2] He gained some comfort from his talks with Galt and Brown, who were guests at his mansion in Fredericton. They believed that, though the provinces must be allowed a considerable degree of power at the outset, ultimately they should sink to the level of municipalities. He ascribed the behaviour of the Maritime delegations at Charlottetown, especially those from New Brunswick and Prince Edward Island, to "a miserable and cowardly dread of their constituents". The continued expression of such disdainful sentiments represented for Gordon a great dilemma. To advocate Maritime union implied hostility to the federal plan towards which six colonies were now moving.

For the conference at Quebec, which was to work out the federal settlement in detail, Gordon added Peter Mitchell and Charles Fisher to the New Brunswick delegation, an even distribution of weight for the North Shore and the Valley railway interests. Sick at heart, as the great principle of central su-

premacy he advocated appeared to be abandoned, he contemplated the apparent apathy of the New Brunswick population,
quite convinced that Tilley and his associates would easily win
acquiescence in the federal plan of union. The thinking portion
of the people, he declared, wanted the more national and
patriotic legislative union. The recent publication of *The Northern Kingdom* in Montreal had received widespread approval
in New Brunswick. The existing province, he argued, had no
real unity of interest. Westmorland had close ties with Cumberland in Nova Scotia. Gloucester and Victoria looked to
Quebec. The Miramichi had separate interests all its own.
Although in the Maritime Provinces there were no provincial
jealousies, there were numerous sectional jealousies. A powerful
central government was needed to reduce them to discipline.
There was no more need for three legislatures in the Maritime
Provinces than in Wales or Cornwall, and in either of these
there was more human material fit for the formation of legislative bodies. He was horrified to sense in certain quarters a
feeling that the federal plan was welcomed on the grounds that
most of those enjoying positions of authority in New Brunswick
would be transferred to the federal scene, making way for a new
and still more inferior set of men who would descend upon
Fredericton. The British North American movement seemed
likely to produce a multiplication of politicians rather than a
reduction.[3]

At Quebec, Tilley and his fellow delegates were helping to
draft the celebrated resolutions that presently were to become
known as "the Quebec plan", banking almost everything on an
attempt to secure in the upper house of the proposed federation
a quota of representatives that could adequately secure the
rights and interests of the Maritime Provinces. Representation
in the lower house on a basis of population would give the four
– now including Newfoundland – forty-six seats in a house of
200. This, in the estimation of the Maritimers, could be somewhat counterbalanced by the control of one-third or more of
the seats in the second chamber. In the division of powers
between the general government and the provinces, Edward
Barron Chandler fought a strong rear-guard action for a greater
area of responsibility for the provinces, but was overpowered
by the managerial capacities of Macdonald.[4] To Tilley the
arrangement at Quebec was business-like and satisfactory. In
effect, only the Post Office, he later told his electorate, would

leave New Brunswick. The province, while sharing in a great national union, could emerge from an implementation of the Quebec plan substantially intact. To this more optimistic view that the preservation of provincial identity was sacrosanct he would seem to have surrendered steadily as negotiations at Charlottetown and Quebec proceeded.

There was little if any unity among the three Maritime delegations at Quebec, New Brunswick and Nova Scotia generally refusing to support the importunities of Prince Edward Island. *En route* to Niagara Falls, on a circuitous journey homeward, they met at the Queen's Hotel in Toronto on November 3 and buried Maritime union, not very decently, with another postponement.[5] Not as one but as three would the provinces enter the federation.

III

The New Brunswick delegates to Quebec arrived in Saint John by boat from Portland on November 7, and in a few days the veil of secrecy that had surrounded the conference was lifted by the publication of the Seventy-two Resolutions. Tilley immediately became aware that he had stepped into a hornet's nest. His first meeting with the executive council indicated a clear absence of unanimity, George L. Hatheway, the large-bodied lumberman of York, displaying the independence and eccentricities that had always made stable party government so difficult to achieve in New Brunswick. Tilley's prospect, of facing his Smashers in the house of assembly, was entirely different from Macdonald's prospect in Canada. The Macdonald-Brown majority had been organized for the clear purpose of putting union through. The New Brunswick majority was organized on the simple premise that Tilley was the one politician who universally commanded respect. Great questions such as that of union, which now burst so suddenly on the immediate horizon, had seldom intruded upon the workaday scene in the New Brunswick house of assembly. Still less frequently had great questions been permitted to determine the fate of the government. More than anything else the Smasher majority wanted to serve out its time until June and earn its pay.

Beyond the circle of Tilley's immediate following, opposition developed at whirlwind speed, anticipating by a full two months the storm Howe was about to raise in Nova Scotia. On Novem-

ber 15 Anglin's *Freeman* attacked the whole basis of authority of
the Quebec conference, declaring that a statute of the British
Parliament, proposed as the ultimate legal measure to inaugurate
Confederation, would undo all the work of responsible government. Everything, said the editorial, would be surrendered to
Canada, whose leaders wanted to spend millions in opening up
the West. "The glorious privilege of direct taxation" would
come. Friends and sympathizers of union were attacking the
Quebec Resolutions, urging that they represented a mere
mockery of the kind of union to which all good British North
Americans should aspire.

To give leadership to the opposition of all kinds, open and
covert, Albert J. Smith entered the arena. His *Letter to the
Electors of Westmorland*, published before the end of November, declared that if union of the Quebec pattern should go
through the only relief would lie in rebellion. Accusing Tilley of
being privy to a conspiracy with the Canadians that had originated in the spring of the year, he wrote of tyranny and
oppression. The ministry was the creation of the people and had
exceeded its legitimate authority. George Brown had consented
to the construction of the Intercolonial at Quebec only on condition that the canal system of Upper Canada should be developed. How many millions would go towards this project
from the Maritime Provinces? There was no single party opposed
to the Quebec plan in New Brunswick, but of the numerous
opposition that clustered together from all quarters Albert
Smith quickly became "the heart and soul".

Tilley recoiled before the tempest that arose. His campaign
of education and propaganda rapidly turned into a violently
partisan affair. On November 17 he and Gray addressed a large
meeting in Saint John. Fortified by an armful of books, he
roundly declared that forty-seven members from the Maritime
Provinces would take care of any attempt to raise the tariffs of
the proposed union. He was certain that taxes of any kind
would go no higher. On November 28 they again faced the
same audience, this time, according to the *Telegraph*, in much
better form. But there were questions from the floor: Does the
Confederation movement come from the British government?
Does the British government desire separation? A considerable
section of the public had become obsessed with the idea that a
union with Canada was to be the prelude to separation from
Britain. The visit of Lieutenant-Colonel Jervois the year

before and the views he had expressed on the subject of colonial defence had aroused fears that Britain, in attempting to persuade the colonies to pay for their own defence, was merely seeking a reason for casting them off. Gladstone's widely quoted remark that the colonies were encumbrances, and frequent anti-colonial outbursts of other members of the British cabinet, created a new sensitivity of the kind that had been so prevalent in 1849. If separation from Britain were to come, many thought it reasonable to look to the United States for union rather than to Canada. At a meeting a few weeks later Gray coldly calculated the financial advantages, in terms of lower taxation, of being in a union with Canada over the possibility of annexation to the American union.

Eighty-seven manufacturers of Saint John, declared Gray, wanted Confederation because railway communication with Canada would give them larger markets and enable them to compete at lower prices. Yet the question from the floor as to where he got his authority for saying that the terminal of the railway would be at Saint John could not be answered in precise terms. The proponents of Western Extension had caught alarm. Confederation seemed simply a more elaborate red herring than the broken promises of the perfidious Canadians in 1862. New Brunswickers, said Gordon at this stage, regarded the whole Confederation programme as a political manoeuvre. Western Extension seemed a solid reality for the prospects of Saint John. Tilley and Gray could not answer the question with any assurance, could not demonstrate with any authority that if the Intercolonial were constructed it would bear the produce of Canada in the winter season to the wharves and ships of their own port.

Forced to the defensive, Tilley announced on November 30, only twenty-two days after his return from Quebec, that he would not present resolutions favouring Confederation to the existing house of assembly, whose legal term would expire in June. More than anything else he needed time to relieve the people of New Brunswick of deeply conceived suspicions. At the beginning of 1865 he was inexorably campaigning through the southern part of the province, making a reconnaissance in force into Smith's home territory in Westmorland in company with his postmaster-general, Steadman. On January 19 he was back in Fredericton to address another great meeting and to discuss tactics with the executive council. He had in his pocket a letter from Gordon that forced upon him a decision of momentous importance. The lieutenant-governor had abruptly inserted his initiative into the business. If, he argued, the government should face the legislature without introducing resolutions favouring Confederation, the opposition might bring down a motion of censure. He might be compelled to record his own opinion on the minutes of the executive council, an opinion that could be different from that of his advisers. What he demanded was a quick dissolution of the legislature and an appeal to the people, precisely what Tilley did not want and what was abhorred by John A. Macdonald in Canada as "an obvious absurdity".

As Gordon saw the situation, haste was essential. The Canadian parliament was about to debate the Seventy-two Resolutions. Hesitation in New Brunswick would give impetus to the powerful opposition to Confederation that Howe was raising in Nova Scotia. In Britain the political situation was uncertain, and it was important to get the imperial statute, necessary for the establishment of the new federation, through the existing parliament. If the whole Confederation scheme should fall through, he argued, New Brunswick might be held to blame for want of bold action. To Tilley the implication was obvious. In advancing a dissolution of the legislature, Gordon would be prepared to seek the counsels of other advisers. Manners-Sutton had dismissed a ministry and had been sustained by public opinion. Removed from the rough-and-tumble of practical politics, Gordon was rather airily able to convince himself that Tilley or any good substitute could persuade the people of New Brunswick to vote for Confederation at the polls. In seeking simplicity from a situation that was rapidly becoming complex, he was prepared to take the hazard that Manners-Sutton had surmounted.

The reasons for this sudden interruption of Tilley's leisurely plans have been discussed by historians greatly to Gordon's disadvantage. A dispatch from Cardwell, the colonial secretary, had rebuked him for his outspoken hostility to the details of the Quebec plan and for his dearly conceived notion that Maritime union should take precedence over all other designs. Pique and ruffled vanity due to the derailment of his own darling project, even a guileful and Machiavellian intention of wrecking Confederation under the pretext of advancing it, have been ascribed to the confident young man.[6] It might be difficult to deny that Gordon was a snob, but that he was a rogue has

never been proved. His abrupt dealings with Tilley can be justified by honest motives if not by the anticipated results. Under
all the circumstances of January 1865, haste seemed to be
required. Bold and successful action in New Brunswick could
produce repercussions favourable to the Quebec plan through
all the colonies. A confidential dispatch from Cardwell on February 4 urging Gordon to avoid delay proved to be entirely
unnecessary. A decision was already being sought in New Brunswick, and in a hurry. It is just as easy to argue that Gordon, in
forcing Tilley to premature action, was seeking a role of glory
in the pursuit of the Quebec plan rather than the coldly calculated part of wrecker and destroyer.

IV

On January 30, Tilley, after experiencing great dissension in
his government, made the hard choice and decided for immediate dissolution. In protest Hatheway resigned – not a loss
that weakened the government, Gordon declared. Tilley did not
share Gordon's opinion that he could win the election no matter
what the issue might be. Gordon was contemptuous of public
opinion in New Brunswick, professing to believe that the election would be won on personalities and local patronage, but
already a lively public opinion on – and mostly against – Confederation was manifesting itself in York and Westmorland, as
well as in Saint John. New edge was being given to the formidable forces against Tilley. It was not idly said that Anglin,
through the columns of the *Freeman*, commanded the political
conscience of the Catholic Irish of the province. He appeared
as an anti-Confederate candidate in Saint John, one of a
strangely assorted team of four that included Joseph Coram,
whose great claim to fame was that he had acted the part of
King William in the July 12 riot of 1849. A vague sensibility
was circulating among the Catholic Irish, a feeling that New
Brunswick's union with Canada would be as bad an omen as
Ireland's union with Great Britain, a notion that all that Irish-
men had gained for themselves by their labours would be lost if
Confederation with Canada should come. Out of fear of the
influence of Protestant Upper Canada, Bishop Sweeney of Saint
John addressed circulars to his people, calling on them to oppose
Confederation. The *Globe*, the leading Smasher newspaper, followed by the *Telegraph*, probably the most influential of all
journals, turned against Tilley, taking the line generally followed

that the Quebec plan had been worked out for the convenience
of Canadian politicians and that New Brunswick could be
sacrificed to their ambitious caprices. The haste that Gordon
had demanded and Tilley had nervously accepted was roundly
condemned. "If Confederation comes," said the *Telegraph*, "it
will be a six months' conception and a sickly child."[7]

Forced to explain his precipitate course, Tilley argued that
the British government was pushing the colonies into union.
His way was a hard one. On January 31 he was shouted down
at a most disorderly meeting in Saint John, though Smith
begged the audience to give him a hearing. Stumping the North
Shore as well as the southern counties, Smith retorted that it
was the extremity of the Canadian government, not the British,
that New Brunswick was expected to relieve. He challenged
the publication of any dispatch wherein England threatened to
throw the colonies off. "Who says something must be done?"

On both sides there was a degree of romanticizing. Thomas
D'Arcy McGee's speech in which he visualized the sailors of the
Maritimes defending Canada on the lakes was widely employed
by the Confederates. On the circuit of the Supreme Court in
Sunbury Lemuel Allen Wilmot, never really out of politics,
abandoned his judicial role to harangue his audience on the
prospect of a great nation from sea to sea. The personal attacks
so familiar to New Brunswick elections could not be dispensed
with. The anti-Confederates liked to speculate on the creation
of a House of Lords under the proposed federal constitution and
on some of their opponents who would like to become members.
The speed of events was disconcerting. Without condemning
union in principle, Smith could score points by condemning
features of the Quebec plan, urging that the whole programme
should be postponed for a year.

Many were unstirred by the conception of a great national
union and confined their speculations to what appeared to be
the most material feature of the Quebec plan, the promise to
construct an intercolonial railway contained in the sixty-eighth
resolution. Tilley's opponents took merciless advantage of his
failure to be precise concerning its route. Hatheway was certain
that the North Shore route would be chosen. He could readily
forecast the ruin of Saint John and the neglect of the populous
valley:

> Mr. Tilley will you stop your puffing and blowing
> And tell us which way the railway is going.[8]

All Nova Scotia and Canada plus one-half of New Brunswick, said the anti-Confederates, favoured the North Shore route, so it was certain that the central or valley route, favoured but not promised by Tilley, would be set aside. Tilley could give no guarantee that Western Extension, regarded as the salvation of Saint John, would be facilitated if Confederation should come. In the north, John Mercer Johnson and Peter Mitchell, both opponents of Western Extension, escaped unscathed from this feature of the opposition's attack. But Tilley and Fisher, who led the Confederate battle along the St. John, had aroused against them the leading commercial interests of the south where railway connection with the United States was pretty generally regarded as a prime objective. Saint John bankers, fearing competition from the Canadians in their own field, were taking a strong stand against Confederation and using their immense influence to bring about its defeat. Smith, who all through his career had been an opponent of railways, made himself a champion of both the Intercolonial and Western Extension. Irresponsibility out of office enabled him to offer all things to all men.

Just how important the railway issue could be was strikingly revealed when Macdonald, unwittingly and out of a passion for being too precise, answered a question in the Canadian parliament by saying that the promise of the Intercolonial Railway would not be written into the new constitution. The *Globe* quickly exploited the statement as a straw in the wind that indicated a great betrayal: the faithless Canadians would fail to honour a most solemn promise, just as they had done in 1862. New Brunswickers were convinced that the most solid of guarantees should be demanded for the construction of the railway. The Confederates had been asserting that such a stipulation should be contained in the British act by which federation should be established. Desperately, Tilley, two weeks before the polls were to open, sought to remove the doubt that had so unnecessarily been raised. "Now I can assure you," he wrote to Macdonald, "that no Delegate from this province will consent to Union unless we have this guarantee. And we will entirely fail in all our elections unless I have word from you, and to be in time must be by telegraph, saying that this security will be given us. All will be lost without this." Macdonald telegraphed back: "My remark was that an agreement to build a railway could not be a portion of the Constitution.

In our case it was one of the conditions on which Constitution was adopted. Such condition will of course be inserted in the Imperial Act."⁹

The incident was only one of many that kept Tilley on the defensive and emphasized the quandary in which the railway issue placed him. His declarations of honest intentions, the rarefied eloquence of John H. Gray, and the practical, down-to-earth appeals of Fisher were of no avail. They were not allowed the time that was necessary to dispel the feeling that united all of those opposed to Confederation for one reason or another, that the province was needlessly being precipitated into a fundamental course of action. As that durable conservative by temperament, Robert L. Hazen, said later, New Brunswick did not wish "to fall into the maw of Canada on her own terms".¹⁰ In York the anti-Confederate, William H. Needham, conducted a lusty and effective campaign, ridiculing the manufacturers of New Brunswick who thought they could flood Canada with their goods, prophesying that they themselves would be flooded with the produce of the highly protected factories of Montreal.

From the returns that commenced with those of Kent County on February 28 it became perfectly certain that Confederation had failed to attract the people of New Brunswick. An overwhelming defeat in York on March 2 powerfully contributed to a defeat in Saint John on March 3. The vote of the French in Dorchester and Shediac lost Westmorland. Every delegate to Quebec who was a member of the house of assembly lost his seat. The supporters of Tilley in the new house were variously estimated at from nine to thirteen. Albert County showed a sharp reversal of the trend by voting for Confederation by four to one. In Saint John, according to the *Telegraph*, free speech was denied on Declaration Day and Tilley and Gray were insulted in the streets. The Catholic vote had lost Saint John for Confederation by a narrow margin. "Pope Anglin and King Coram" were in the saddle. Two sleds, each drawn by six grey horses, one carrying a brass band and the second the victorious anti-Confederate candidates, drove through the city.¹¹

Western Extension and, it was commonly alleged, the money of American capitalists had triumphed. The great defeat transcended local causes. In Quebec City, on the evening of March 4, the Grits and Rouges of Canada opposing Confederation, chastened by the power of the Macdonald-Cartier-Brown coalition, finally had something to cheer about. Excitedly they gathered in the halls of the legislative building as the telegraph wires from New Brunswick brought news of their triumph in a distant field. In Halifax the tribune of Nova Scotia had blown his trumpet, but it seemed certain that he would not have to go forth to battle. Superficially at any rate, New Brunswick had killed Confederation. The British government had made it absolutely clear that it would entertain no scheme for union unless initiative should come from all the provinces concerned. The defection of Newfoundland and Prince Edward Island had been not much more than regrettable. New Brunswick's decision appeared to destroy all reasonable basis for continued consideration of the plans that had been worked out at Quebec.

Nonchalantly and unapologetically, Gordon explained to the Colonial Office why the strategy he had forced upon Tilley had brought seeming ruin to the exertions of the leaders of British North America. He listed the unpopularity of the Quebec scheme among those who believed in union, its rejection in Prince Edward Island and Newfoundland, along with the certain defeat that appeared to await it in Nova Scotia, and the ten-year period in office of the Smasher government which, by reason of the dubious public morals and competence of its members, had prejudiced Confederation in the public eye.

Tilley had not lost heart. Even before the election returns were completed he prophesied, with remarkable accuracy, that within fifteen months the people of New Brunswick would be compelled to change their opinion. The intelligent voters, he was convinced, favoured Confederation. In the meantime he worried about the effects of the election on provincial credit abroad. Would New Brunswick debentures fall still lower on the London market? Would his friend William Parks, then in England attempting to raise money for new railway construction, succeed in his purpose? Would the province be left out in the cold during the important conversations the Canadians were about to open with the British government on union, defence, and the abrogation of the Reciprocity Treaty?[12]

V

"A queer mixture of Tories and Liberals," said the *Telegraph* in describing the new administration which was to become known as the anti-Confederate government of New Brunswick.[13] Gordon first offered the honour of forming it to George L. Hatheway who, as expected, declined. Albert Smith and Robert

Duncan Wilmot, who represented the two principal schools of
thought composing the victorious anti's – those who wanted
more powers of government reserved for the province and those
who wanted the province virtually legislated out of existence –
accepted the duty. Largely owing to the personal unpopularity
of his colleague, it was Smith who acquired the prestige of
de facto leader. "The Lion of Westmorland", "The Douglas of
Dorchester", had a capacity to fight more furiously at the hustings and a depth of conviction considerably more pronounced
than most of his associates. A lumberman of Charlotte, A. H.
Gillmore, became provincial secretary, Bliss Botsford of Westmorland became surveyor-general, and Hatheway became postmaster-general. Anglin, intent on forwarding Western Extension,
entered without office. The attorney-general was John Campbell Allen, a confidant of Gordon, who described him as one of
the few trustworthy politicians of the province. During the
election campaign the lieutenant-governor had endeavoured to
persuade Allen to reverse his position and accept the Quebec
plan, but Allen had persisted in regarding it as "a flimsy substitute for legislative union".[14] The government was later filled up
by William H. Odell, who had inherited the landed wealth
of his father in the vicinity of Fredericton, and Richard
Hutchinson, a member of the firm of Gilmour, Rankin and
Company who still dominated lumbering operations on the
Miramichi.

Altogether, Gordon said rather surprisedly, it was a "most
respectable government". Compared with the outgoing Tilley
administration, it was definitely superior. Though it contained
nobody of the natural abilities of Tilley himself, the general level
was much higher. It was a change, he added, not only of men
but of the class of men. "Whether or not the rule of educated
gentlemen will be long endured remains to be seen."[15]

The percentage of patricians was high, but the Smith government was ultimately to reveal a high degree of human frailty
as well. Yet as long as the legislature of 1865 was in session its
course seemed reasonably consistent. No longer now, informed
sources said in the spring of 1865, would any New Brunswick
politician dare to express approval for the Seventy-two Resolutions in full. Centrifugal forces appeared to be in the ascendancy.
New Brunswick had declared for independence of Canada, a
brave gesture that was sustained by the unprecedentedly high
budget for provincial defence that was brought down to antici-

pate the strictures of the British government and the cavilling comments of Canadian newspapers. The province had proclaimed a destiny of her own and was in the mood to pay for it. John W. Cudlip, the most forthright of the supporters of Western Extension from Saint John and a politician whose political bearings were subject to grave suspicion, introduced resolutions asking the government to send a delegation to England in order to remove any doubt in the Colonial Office concerning New Brunswick's stand on Confederation.[16] These were carried by twenty-seven to ten. Propped up by the generous subsidies under the Railway Facility Act of the year before, a revived Western Extension company headed by William Parks went into action. The new government and the City of Saint John compromised their financial stability by taking up substantial blocks of stock. Hovering in the background was John A. Poor, still working on behalf of his American interests and continuing to make attractive offers to government and company. If accepted, warned the Confederates, these deals would bring the whole railway traffic of the Maritime Provinces under American control. Amid great rejoicing, the first sod of Western Extension leading to Bangor was turned at Saint John on November 10.

If there was a desperate determination on the part of any set of public men to keep the province out of union, fate was against them. Smith, who might be described as a conservative kind of radical, was a man of few positive impulses. His radicalism had brought him to the forefront of politics. His conservatism, manifesting itself in opposition to Confederation, could produce no attractive alternative. Having achieved power, he made it his ambition to keep it, and had he been allowed to cope with the merely provincial elements in opposition to him he might have succeeded. Had the forces working for Confederation from the outside become quiescent in consequence of the shattering New Brunswick defeat, Smith might have continued to govern according to the traditional methods of trimming and appeasing local interests.

This was not to be. Macdonald and the Canadians, after recovering from the shock of the New Brunswick elections, determined to persevere. A mission to London in May and June stiffened the British prejudice in favour of the Quebec Resolutions. The Colonial Office was generally convinced that only "selfish interests of small men in small provinces" were holding up Confederation. On June 24 Cardwell wrote to Gordon a dispatch that could leave no doubt concerning the eagerness entertained by the British government for the execution of the Quebec plan, and enjoined him to do all in his power to push it through to a conclusion. Privately, there came another communication informing him that the British government was in deadly earnest.

Gordon forthwith published the dispatch of June 24 in the *Royal Gazette*, together with other correspondence between the Colonial Office and Lord Monck, the Governor General. Those who had argued that Confederation meant cutting the link with Britain, that the Quebec plan owed its entire origins to the machinations of the Canadians, were now silenced. Upon the deliberations of the government, at this stage enjoying a phase of tranquillity, this Canadian-British intrusion came as a rude and unexpected shock. While Smith was absent in England the fiery Anglin was in control of proceedings. A minute of council reaffirmed the anti-Confederate stand, declaiming upon the ignorance of the British government and British public, who should surely by this time realize that Confederation was a lost cause.[17] Provincial gorge had risen at the publication of uninformed articles in *The Times* on the situation in British North America. Statements had been made in the House of Commons and elsewhere that the people of New Brunswick, having turned their backs upon Confederation, were disloyal. Smith, closeted in London with the colonial secretary, rebuffed in his attempt to find British money for the building of railways, and informed that the British government would not allow Tupper's revived plan for Maritime union to stand in the way of Confederation, told Cardwell that he was proud of his fellow ministers in New Brunswick for their stout stand.[18] Truculence and independence marked the conduct of the anti-Confederate government at this stage. Yet its leaders had become aware of the great forces ranged against them and could sense an ultimate necessity of trimming their course. After interviewing the New Brunswick and Nova Scotian visitors, Cardwell reported a great jealousy of Canadian influence but an apparent readiness to submit to imperial suggestion.

From quarters all around them the anti-Confederate leaders were beginning to realize that the fight against Confederation had only just begun. In Nova Scotia Tupper was nourishing his dormant hopes. Macdonald in Canada was cockily declaring that sooner or later Confederation would come. In spite of New

Brunswick's stand, British ministers continued to regard Confederation as an open question. And there was a redoubtable enemy within the gate. Gordon, with his large ideas of the constitutional role of a colonial governor, was preparing to execute literally his instructions to do all he could to bring about a reversal of New Brunswick opinion.

As early as May he held a highly confidential conversation with Tilley concerning the means by which the change could be brought about. The fallen chief minister spoke confidently of renewing the agitation for union, of employing the influence of the temperance societies that had always constituted such a strong basis for his support. He would wait until November when he would convene meetings, submit petitions, and demand a dissolution of the house of assembly and a fresh appeal to the people.[19] But Tilley was only one string to Gordon's bow. The lieutenant-governor felt entirely confident that the divisions within the Smith government could be exploited to such a degree that it could be compelled to a decision almost completely opposite to that on which it had attained power. Failing this it could be broken up by a succession of urgencies, and a new coalition government created from elements of its own and Tilley's following.

Gordon's ambitions for usefulness in a gubernatorial role had irritated the friends of union in New Brunswick and beyond. Yet his ability at this stage to plot an alternative course by which the adherence of New Brunswick to the Quebec plan could be secured was to be one of the great factors by which the impasse could be removed and Confederation hastened. Bold initiative would be required to capitalize upon the favouring influences at work. The second half of 1865 witnessed a rapid transformation in the climate of opinion. The publication of the instructions of June 24 was removing a great misapprehension by which the people of New Brunswick had largely been bound. A man so close to the people as James Brown was certain of what was happening. Writing in October he declared: "The case is no doubt materially changed since the last election. . . . There was not at that time anything at all to show that the Imperial Government was at all desirous of its [Confederation's] immediate adoption. . . . But the whole correspondence set forth in the various despatches proves beyond a doubt that the Imperial authorities are in favour of the Union. There is no appearance of coercion and there will be no need of any, for, if the people are assured that such is Her Majesty's desire, they will agree to it."[20]

VI

Faced with continuing opposition of the most formidable kind from London and Quebec City, Smith and his government were more and more compelled to depend upon what was, in the nature of things, the fundamental premise of the anti-Confederate stand – the development of railway and commercial connections with the United States. Yet in this direction, too, there was gall and wormwood. As the promoters of Western Extension made preparations for the construction of their line, they were heading for an obstacle they preferred not to see: the determination of Washington to bring to an end the period of happy and harmonious trading relations with British North America. Convinced of British enmity to their victorious cause, the Americans in the spring of 1865 gave formal notice of the abrogation of the Reciprocity Treaty. No clouds of gloom settled over the thriving New Brunswick economy, but, following this statement of the American position, its implications began to settle more deeply in the public mind. The denial of the free entrance of natural products to American markets made a union of British North America more plausible and attractive. Even as he looked southward Smith realized he was beating against the wind.

Going it alone became an increasingly difficult and bitter business. Dissensions gnawed at the vitals of the anti-Confederate administration, increasing the difficulty of sustaining the cause for which it had been elected. Anglin, a supporter of public control of railways, resigned from the government in November because the Western Extension contract was awarded to a private corporation. In September Robert Duncan Wilmot had gone to Quebec to discuss with the Canadian government the measures necessary to face the emergency of the repeal of the Reciprocity Treaty. There he had succumbed to the witchery of the Canadians, returning to Fredericton as a pro-Confederate. "Let us alone for a time and the strong attachment we have for Britain will soon effect the object desired."[21] His conversion was not considered to be sufficient reason for resignation from the government. From Gordon's point of view it was far better to keep him within the government as an instrument of division.

But keeping Wilmot in office proved to be too difficult, not for reasons connected with the great cause of Confederation but for more parochial considerations. Great changes were occurring within the judiciary. Sir James Carter, the quiet and erudite jurist, who for years had played the organ in St. Anne's Church, had decided to retire. He was succeeded by Justice Robert Parker, a worthy of the old aristocracy who said he would rather vote for a hedgehog than for a supporter of Confederation, and who died after enjoying his preferment but a few weeks. Of the remaining judiciary Lemuel Allen Wilmot was easily the senior and felt he had a firm claim to the promotion. "Wilmot expected to be Chief Justice fifteen years ago."[22] But Smith turned his favour to William J. Ritchie, who in 1848 had held hard to the gospel of reform when Wilmot had seemingly deserted it. By reason of the slight to his cousin, Robert Duncan Wilmot felt aggrieved and neglected. When another slight occurred in February 1866 – his omission from the delegation to Washington – he finally quit the government, very much to the regret of Gordon who wished to make appropriate use of him when the time for Smith's removal should come. On a basis equal to that of Smith, Wilmot had been asked to form the administration. If the circumstances had been more propitious and certain at this particular time Gordon would have had no qualms in asking Smith to resign and Wilmot to form a new ministry.

As a harbinger of the denouement came the York by-election in November when auspices were offered to those who pretended to foresee events. John Campbell Allen, the attorney-general, had been appointed to fill the vacancy on the Bench. According to Gordon, he was the most respected of all the members of the government and the appointment gave universal satisfaction. Under this strangely genteel anti-Confederate government many things were going to the lieutenant-governor's liking, not the least of which was the selection of persons to occupy judicial seats. He contemplated with approval the promotion of Ritchie and the elevation of Allen and of John Wesley Weldon, shuddering to reflect upon the manner in which the vacancies might have been filled had Tilley and his rude, intemperate attorney-general, John Mercer Johnson, remained in power. The removal of Allen from politics prepared the way for a spectacular trial of strength in Fredericton and the surrounding countryside, always fighting ground where nothing was assured and where Charles Fisher faced John Pickard, the government candidate.

In this combat, on which the eyes of all British North America were fixed, one of the cardinal rules of the less admirable type of politician was generally observed, that of avoiding issues in principle. Though he had lost his election early in the year on the Confederation platform, Fisher did not on this occasion freely avow himself as a supporter of union with Canada. On the hustings, local and personal issues were allowed to transcend the great cause. Fisher spoke glibly and confidently of the Intercolonial Railway. He was certain that Sandford Fleming would advocate the central route down the St. John Valley. Surrendering the votes of the 600 Catholics of York County to Pickard, he found it profitable to fight a bitter anti-Catholic campaign.[23] The Orange vote was mobilized and elemental Loyalist emotions stirred. Evangelical Protestantism rose to his support. "The Protestant faith and the open Bible are in danger," declared the *Religious Intelligencer*. It took more than this to win an election in York. Eight or ten thousand dollars, Tilley wrote to Macdonald, would be needed to make Fisher's victory certain. Could the Canadians provide half, not to exceed five thousand? The Canadians obliged.[24]

Fisher's majority was over 700. "The most important thing that has happened since the Quebec conference," Lord Monck wrote to Macdonald. In New Brunswick there was some uncertainty concerning the precise meaning of the result in York, but there was none in Canada.

By December Smith was wobbling from his anti-Confederate stand. Under all the heavy pressures set in motion against him it had been incumbent upon him to produce a policy. But, wherever he had turned, he had found nothing that was positive and attractive. For reasons that were entirely unconnected with the question of Confederation, his government was acquiring unpopularity. Curiously enough, his rule had introduced more gentlemanly standards in the dispensation of patronage and his close supporters were becoming estranged. George Brown, who was spying out the land for the Canadian government during the month of November, reported that in all probability the Smith government would accept Confederation "if it could save face".

In a series of closely guarded interviews with Gordon, in which he refused to commit anything to paper, Smith made it known that he might declare for union, and discussed the details by which it might be brought about. He could say, in justice to himself, that he had never opposed the general concept of British North American union, and that his opposition had been confined to the greatly reduced status of the provinces contemplated in the Quebec plan. Alterations favourable to the provinces in the Quebec plan could relieve him of charges of inconsistency. His government, he declared, would for the most part follow him. To such an extent was public opinion swinging in favour of Confederation, sensing that it must come "sooner or later", that a swing of the government along with it might seem in the order of events.[25]

At the end of 1865 Gordon was sure that the passage of resolutions through the house of assembly in favour of the Quebec plan could be managed under the leadership of Smith's government. Over the scene the instructions of June 24 hung like a sword of Damocles. By virtue of them Gordon was prepared to use the power of dissolution to gain a new house of assembly if the existing legislature should obstruct the necessary resolutions. Smith was well aware of Gordon's willingness to employ this drastic recourse. But dissolution, it seemed, would be unnecessary.

The two men had been enemies for five years. Smith's political capital of early days had largely been built up on a capacity to bait lieutenant-governors and to arouse proletarian animosities against them. There had been the stormy interlude of his resignation in 1862, his allegations of persecution by Gordon in the affair of the Westmorland dam. More recently he had taken the lead in the legislature in forcing the lieutenant-governor to return to the public treasury the profits on his salary payments resulting from the decline of colonial currencies in relation to sterling. The issue of this mortifying agitation had been enigmatic. Gordon continued to take the profits as his by right but made repayments in order to keep the legislature quiet. In effect, Smith had won. In spite of this background of private acrimonies, the two, at the opening of 1866, seemed very likely to become partners in a transaction that could lead New Brunswick into Confederation.

VII

While Gordon was preparing to administer the *coup de grâce* that would force the issue to the limit, the tensions that enveloped New Brunswick were sharpened by the intrusion of a new and alien influence. In mid-December the managers of banks in Saint John received warnings of an impending attack upon the city by gangs of Irish Fenians, recently demobilized from the Union army, who, in search of new excitement, wished to strike a blow for the freedom of Ireland in North America. Sustained by continuing American hostility to Great Britain, the Fenian movement, though it was hardly competent to organize a full-scale invasion, could launch piratical raids on exposed communities. The destruction of property was part of their stock-in-trade and banks their avowed objectives. Two of their leaders, Sweeney and Roberts, were calling for a bold stroke on St. Patrick's Day and an invasion of British North America.

In Saint John the principal banks were close to the waterfront, and it was not inconceivable that a band of half-sane desperadoes, landing by surprise, could in a short time do an immense amount of damage and readily escape. A man-of-war in the harbour could render such an incursion impossible, and Gordon promptly secured the dispatch of H.M.S. *Pylades* from Halifax. Along the border, at St. Andrews, St. Stephen, and Woodstock, there were similar fears. Visiting all these places in December and stiffening up the home guards that were called into being, Gordon reported that an excellent spirit prevailed. At Calais the mayor of the town agreed to co-operate by sending intelligence of Fenian movements. In the face of what might be a serious emergency, nervousness developed in Saint John when mischievous members of the Protestant majority attempted to arouse anti-Irish and anti-Catholic manifestations. Such activity, reminiscent of the troubles of twenty years before, resulted in nothing but discredit to the perpetrators. A letter from the Reverend Dr. Connolly, Archbishop of Halifax, addressed to Gordon and published in the *Globe*, did a great deal to allay mischief. While travelling in the United States the archbishop had encountered many Irish, "knaves and fools", who had flippantly spoken of taking over British North America. Comparing the position of the Irish in the United States with that of the Irish in the British provinces, where they received honours and awards according to their numbers, he fervently urged his spiritual following to give no encouragement to Fenian attempts at violence.[26]

The braggadocio threats from across the border, supported by enough evidence to show that the Fenians meant real mischief, accelerated speculation on the future of British North America and demonstrated the necessity for common action. All the talk about imperial defence of the past five years, often considered to have been on a purely theoretical plane, acquired pertinence. The unhallowed isolation offered to New Brunswick by the anti-Confederates seemed considerably less attractive when urgencies of this kind could so suddenly arise. An inevitable drift into the arms of the neighbouring republic, the source of the present distasteful alarms, seemed the more likely if the policy of isolation should be pursued.

The Fenian peril added itself to all the other external forces that were combining to compel Smith to capitulate to the Confederate cause. In Nova Scotia, Tupper was waiting for a favourable decision in New Brunswick before submitting his resolutions on the Quebec plan to his nervous majority in the house of assembly, whose legal lifetime would expire in the following year. Canadian leaders were fretting about the delay, inclining more to the alternative plan that was still popular, a federal union of the Canadas alone. Yet all of the impatient queries were wasted upon Smith. In spite of his spoken but unwritten assurances to Gordon, he was impervious to the pressures from outside, waiting for a new stroke of fortune to help him in the lonely game he was playing. His last hope for a turn of luck expired in February when he went to Washington in company with delegates from the other provinces and shared their common insult. In return for the right to the in-shore fisheries of New Brunswick, the Committee on Ways and Means of the House of Representatives would offer virtually nothing.[27] The American tariff on fish, he was informed, would be almost as high as before the Reciprocity Treaty went into effect in 1855. Even here the pressures from the outside were at his elbow in the person of Alexander Galt, who did his best to convert Smith to Confederation.[28] If keeping Smith at Washington to persuade the Americans to open their markets to New Brunswick would help the cause of Confederation in Fredericton, Galt was willing to do his best. Returning to New Brunswick empty-handed, Smith found Saint John enveloped in disappointment so far as trade with the United States was concerned. The few workmen who had been employed on the railway to the American frontier did not return to their labours when the spring season came. With the execution of the American threat to abrogate the

Reciprocity Treaty, Western Extension declined.

While Smith was in Washington, Gordon, impatient of procrastination, began to doubt his reliability. A ministerial crisis
and a dissolution of the house of assembly might become necessary to bring Confederation to the fore. He considered schemes
of coalition, and years later Peter Mitchell, the only minister of
Tilley who enjoyed official place by virtue of his seat in the
legislative council, was to write in his *Secret History* of how he
drove 105 miles over winter roads from Newcastle to Fredericton to consider with Gordon the possibility of forming a new
ministry with Robert Duncan Wilmot, and of how he rejected
the device because he doubted the honesty of Wilmot's conversion.[29] For Gordon, dissolution was the ultimate weapon, but
it could be dangerous. A second electoral defeat in New Brunswick could postpone Confederation for many years to come.
Within reason, delay was efficacious. Every day of delay, he told
Cardwell, helped the cause of Confederation in New Brunswick,
though it had an adverse effect on the situation in the other
provinces where the New Brunswick decision could be almost as
critical as it was at home.

Something like certainty seemed to come after Smith returned
from Washington. On February 15, in the course of a long interview, he informed Gordon that he and his fellow ministers
"were not indisposed to acquiesce in a recommendation for
union" but were uncertain about the best method of making
their opinion known. Could the British instruction of June 24
be submitted to a committee of both houses on the understanding that it should recommend in favour of union? Gordon
replied that he had no objection if such a course would make
things easier for the government. Enjoining the lieutenant-
governor to the strictest secrecy, Smith took his leave, asking
for a week of consultation with his friends and supporters in
the country. He had avowed a favourable opinion of the Quebec plan, but Gordon felt certain that his private opinion would
not determine his public behaviour.[30] Smith was still at liberty
to oppose Confederation. The instruction of June 24 might be
handed to a legislative committee, but the government could
move one way or another according to the caprices of the hour.

Yet when Smith returned to Fredericton a week later he
brought the somewhat surprising news that his party supporters
were willing to adopt a Confederate course. The government
would agree to the insertion in the Speech from the Throne of

a paragraph advocating union and the appointment of a joint legislative committee to consider it, though reserving the right to mention objections in detail to the Quebec plan. It had come perhaps a little too easily, but Gordon felt relieved. He wrote a confidential dispatch to Cardwell, congratulating Her Majesty's Government on the success of the movement for union. It was certain to come in a few weeks, he said, though he did not know what would happen to Smith and his government.

VIII

Early in March 1866, as the legislature assembled, a curious hush descended upon Fredericton. No public meetings to forward Confederation were being held. Not a single petition asking for dissolution of the house of assembly had come to Gordon. It was only with reluctance that the majority of the New Brunswick population were turning to accept Confederation. Resignation prevailed. Even among those who had come to regard it as the only possible expedient there was a distaste for details. Union with Canada appeared to be the only prospect open; there was no exhilaration.

The quiet that reigned in the capital was largely due to excitement elsewhere. The Fenian menace, based only on uncertain intelligence of the year before, was assuming solid form. In Canada, Macdonald was calling out 10,000 militiamen to man the frontier. Back of Eastport and Calais Fenians were mustering in considerable numbers. St. Stephen and Woodstock seemed possible objectives, St. Andrews and Campobello much more likely. At an iron foundry in the outskirts of Calais they were preparing armaments and converting old cannon to their purposes. On St. Patrick's night, as evidence of warlike intentions, they fired three heavy guns from Lubec, and a rocket flared over the border. They appeared strong enough to try a descent upon Saint John, and Gordon, taking charge of its defences, lined the ridge behind Carleton with a strong guard of militiamen. Having conducted a searching investigation into the sympathies of the Irish population of the city, he came to the conclusion that possibly but two or three persons were conducting a correspondence with the Fenians. Though many would contemplate an uprising in Ireland without displeasure, they had no affection for an enterprise that could result in damage to their property. There was no "Fenian Circle" in Saint John.[31]

The house of assembly made financial provision for calling

out the militia, and Gordon was embarrassed by the want of necessity for calling out all. Every commanding officer offered the force at his disposal, but he mobilized for active service only the battalion of Saint John Volunteers, the New Brunswick Regiment of Artillery, consisting of four batteries, and portions of the four Charlotte County battalions. The companies were in fine fettle, many of the men being much more familiar with pick-pole and peavy than with rifle and bayonet. Halifax sent warships and prepared to move troops. Gordon conducted a spirited and successful controversy with General Hastings Doyle, the commander of the regular troops at Halifax, who wanted to permit the Fenians to take St. Stephen and St. Andrews, then to land in their rear in order to surround them. It would be morally wrong, Gordon argued, to permit such an unprincipled enemy to walk through two of the most important towns in the province, "one of which is perhaps the most thriving and progressive place in its borders".[32] Between mid-March and mid-April, as he moved from one threatened community to another waiting for the Fenians to make a compromising move, the province seethed with alarms of invasion. But the lieutenant-governor felt that the Fenians could be managed. What he was waiting for with considerably more impatience was positive action on the part of the Smith government to introduce to the legislature resolutions in favour of Confederation.

As it had been arranged, so unofficially and so secretly, the Speech from the Throne on March 8 contained a paragraph concerning the deliberate opinion of the British government that a union of the North American colonies was desirable; the crowd outside the bar of the house of assembly raised a great cheer when it was read. The debate on the Address in Reply commenced on March 12, Charles Fisher challenging the government by an amendment censuring it for failure to take sufficient precaution in dealing with the Fenian danger. This was a flank attack, a mark of the disinclination on both sides of the house to make any haste in coming to grips with the problem of union. Both sides rejoiced in playing a waiting game. The *Telegraph* explained the uncertain proceedings by declaring that the conflict was between the advocates of the Quebec plan and those of the Dorchester plan, the chief cause of quarrel being whether Smith's adherents rather than Tilley's should go to Ottawa, where the capital of Canada had recently been moved.[33] Fisher, the only articulate spokesman of the pro-

Confederates, was experienced and useful in a diversion of this kind. While he fought his battle behind a smoke-screen nobody quite trusted him; Macdonald, waiting anxiously in Canada for a decision in principle upon Confederation, suspected him of playing politics.

Smith had the majority of the house behind him and at any time could have brought closure to the debate, but he, too, was in no hurry to bring the legislature to action. The arrival of his following in Fredericton from the four corners of the province lessened any intention he possessed of publicly giving an opinion on the Quebec plan. Like other leaders of governments before him he had to feel his way, following opinion in the house of assembly rather than leading it. From Nova Scotia came powerful encouragement for the anti-Confederate course – "trusting that there may be no change in the political condition of these two provinces for many a day to come". William Annand wanted concert in resistance to the Quebec plan. While New Brunswick held against the Confederate tide Nova Scotia was safe. He declared himself in agreement with Smith, opposed to any kind of union with Canada. But if, through British pressure or "want of pluck" on the part of the people of the seaboard provinces, union should become necessary, he preferred to be in the best possible position to make an advantageous bargain.[34]

From the opening of the debate on the Address in Reply, five weeks passed and still the end was not in sight. For Smith the rule of life was vacillation between the course to which he had unofficially committed himself in his conversations with Gordon and the one on which he had stood in 1865. It was generally known that the government was leaning strongly towards union. It was equally well understood that Smith and his friends were not publicly compromised and might still oppose Confederation with all the vehemence they had mustered the year before. From Halifax there came rumours and suggestions of an understanding between the anti's of the two provinces, fostered by William Annand and Smith's other friends of that city, to promote another great conference on the details of union that would organize the premeditated scuppering of the entire scheme. For Gordon action was becoming imperative. While honourable members exchanged old-time reminiscences and angry recriminations, addressing one another rather than the Speaker, and while the spectators of Fredericton cheered and applauded, pleas for an end to the delay came from London, Ottawa, and Halifax. It was necessary to find an opportunity for provoking a crisis, and Gordon presently found one. It was not the best, but it would do.

Returning from the border late in March, Gordon came to the conviction that it was now better to depend on the opponents of the Smith government. Though a minority in the house of assembly, they were in control of the legislative council. By careful pre-arrangement he was pleased to receive on April 7 an address to the Queen from that body, praying for a measure to unite the colonies. The upper house would consent to "any measure", but the Quebec Resolutions were specified as a plan that would be approved. From the minority came a protest, couched in archaic language, citing the results of the election of the year before, complaining against "a policy totally at variance with that benign rule heretofore enjoyed" and "the subversion of the rights of the subject".

IX

The question that now assumed overwhelming importance was whether or not Gordon should return a favourable answer to the address of the legislative council. Should he reject the opinion of his ministry, take a course contrary to their advice, and find advisers willing to take responsibility for his action? Should he face the hazard accepted by Manners-Sutton in 1856 when the lieutenant-governor had forced Fisher's administration from power by refusing to accept its advice on the temperance question? In following the bold example of his predecessor, Gordon was fearful that the address of the legislative council might be his last opportunity to force a decision on the question of Confederation. If the debate on the Address in Reply in the house of assembly finished with a vote of confidence for Smith, it would imply approval for the long course of procrastination he was pursuing. Gordon now refused to believe that Smith's professions of sympathy for union carried any guarantee of action.

Called on for advice at rather short notice on the morning of April 7, Smith deprecated the address of the legislative council and suggested that Gordon should simply transmit it to the Colonial Office. Gordon replied that he would consider the suggestion, but the consideration did not last for long. At noon he again sent for Smith, but, for some unexplained reason, the message did not arrive until three o'clock. Gossip among Smith's opponents averred that he had gone into hiding. When he finally did arrive at Government House he found Gordon again closeted with the delegation from the legislative council, giving gracious reception and fair words to the sentiments of the Address in favour of union. When Smith protested, he was answered by the suggestion that he resign. Amid bitter recriminations he refused to do so. Three days later this hot-tempered decision was reversed, and the anti-Confederate government resigned in a body.

The royal prerogative had been used with devastating effect. Collusion between Gordon and leading members of the opposition instantly became the cry of the departing ministerial party. As the lieutenant-governor prepared to form a new ministry, the confused reaction of Smith and his supporters, smoked out of office by what they considered to be an unfair stratagem and the tyrannic employment of the prerogative, was to relapse into the outspoken hostility to Confederation that had brought them victory the year before. In the light of statements made by Smith long after the affair was terminated, it is highly probable that his willingness to adopt a Confederate course, stated in his secret interviews with Gordon, was based on a determination to delay and improvise.

To form a new government Gordon called upon Peter Mitchell, the leading protagonist of the Confederate party in the legislative council, in partnership with whom Gordon had arranged the highly provoking address that had brought about the ministerial crisis. Carrying a talent for dash and drama in the good tradition of the Miramichi, utterly relentless in the pursuit of an opponent, Mitchell was to gain the appellation of "Bismarck" for his part in the highly controversial events of 1866.[35] An anecdote testifying to his rigour is that when his wife, thumbing over the pages of the Bible during a temperance meeting, asked the question: "And what did Peter say?", a voice from the rear of the hall replied: "He says we must have Confederation at all costs."[36] Tilley, "the real leader" of the Confederates, who, with his good Smasher background, was disconcerted by the method taken to provoke the crisis, took his former post as provincial secretary. Robert Duncan Wilmot, whose wavering course had damaged the Smith government, Fisher, Edward Williston of Chatham, Abner MacLellan of Albert, John MacMillan of Restigouche, and Charles Connell

made up the new administration whose business it was to lead
New Brunswick into Confederation.

Yet for Confederation the position as Mitchell's government
was sworn into office was more than a little forbidding. Public
opinion had changed, but would all the consequences of a year
of steady conversion now be lost owing to the manner in which
Gordon staged his political revolution? Even in Downing Street
eyebrows were raised as the details of the *fait accompli* became
understood. Mr. Under-Secretary Blackwood acknowledged that
there was some force in the complaints of Smith and his colleagues. In the whole history of Great Britain never had the
House of Lords addressed the Throne asking that a certain
measure should be brought about.

Under duress from New Brunswick's replica of the House of
Lords, Gordon had forced the resignation of a ministry. His
conduct, said the memorandum of the retiring executive council,
was "insulting to the power and majesty of the people".[37] "The
Lion of Westmorland" was back on the "Governor cry", the
appeal he had addressed to his public in his youth. The "Governor cry" had a familiar ring, a trenchant quality that could
readily be put to work upon a people educated to believe that
their struggle was against privilege. The unconstitutionality of
Gordon's choice of new advisers from the ranks of the opposition became the theme of the vengeful anti-Confederates. Tilley
and his friends were frankly fearful of it. Still to be reckoned
with was the unanimity of the Irish in opposition to Confederation. It was clear that the various elements Smith had
gathered about him to form a party were strongly buttressed by
this formidable ingredient of the New Brunswick population.
Racial and religious antagonisms were fundamental political
premises taken into account by the knowledgeable, and com-
plicating a picture that was superficially simple. To the Irish,
said Edward Barron Chandler in the legislative council, union
was a talismanic word suggestive of all the wrongs endured in
the union of Ireland with Great Britain.[38] "Smith has gone to
your citadel," wrote a supporter to Tilley. "Can he make any
impression on the Protestants?"[39]

The removal of one government and the substitution of another by methods that were highly irregular aroused feelings
more personal and more vindictive than anything that had been
seen the year before. Smith was in no humour to consider an
adjournment of the legislature to give the new ministers the

opportunity, required by law, to appeal to their constituents. He prepared resolutions alleging that Gordon had encouraged unconstitutional conduct in the legislative council and appealing to the British government for his recall. Tilley and most of the new ministers found it more than mildly embarrassing to defend a lieutenant-governor for conduct for the like of which they had condemned Manners-Sutton in 1856. A call to the border that came in mid-April must have given Gordon a sensation of considerable relief.

There the Fenians, after a month of noisy preparation, at last appeared poised for the effort to invade New Brunswick. Between two and three thousand of them, many dressed in flashy uniforms and armed with knives and revolvers, were dispersed along the frontier from Machias to Calais under the command of their general, Bernard Doran Killian. Gordon suddenly realized that fourteen militia companies, extending from St. Andrews to above St. Stephen, could no longer deal with this formidable threat. Appeals to Halifax produced three British men-of-war in the estuary of the St. Croix and the 17th Regiment, supported by artillery and engineers. On board H.M.S. *Rosario* Gordon sailed up the river on April 19 in company with General Doyle and was exuberantly received by the populace of St. Stephen.

The bonfires of the Fenians at night, the random firing that occurred, and the numerous rumours of crossings of the river by small parties of Fenians, created considerable alarm. On the night of April 21 the customs house at Indian Island was destroyed by fire, the only noteworthy incident of "the Fenian raid" that caused damage. The citizens of the little town of St. George turned out in the streets at midnight in their nightclothes when H.M.S. *Cordelia* turned out her crew for gun drill.[40] A New Brunswick schooner, carrying plaster down the bay, was seized by a party of Fenians and put to their rather aimless purposes, but the captain and crew were treated kindly and released with their ship at New York.[41] The dispatch from Washington of General Meade, the victor of Gettysburg, to keep order on the American side, virtually brought the affair to a close. Early in May it was certain that only "the scum" of the Fenians who had no money to take themselves back to New York remained on the border. On the St. Croix, business had been at a standstill for two months.

Active service on the banks of the St. Croix put new life into

the militia movement. The contempt entertained for it by many
politicians for years back was discredited by the real use to
which it had been put. At Woodstock throughout the emergency
a battalion of 400 volunteers, uniformed in rough scarlet cloth
of their own purchasing and capable of performing the most
intricate drills, had been in constant readiness for action.[42] But
the effect of the Fenian threats was of far greater consequence
than this. It gave some meaning and colour to the propaganda
of the more extreme pro-Confederates, such as Fisher, who were
working their way to the point of view that everything New
Brunswickers had valued in the past, the British connection and
the Protestant faith, could now be safely guarded only by union
with Canada. Along the Canadian border the Fenians were organized for invasion. The need for common defence of the
colonies was an immediate spur to political union. In a speech
at Calais, Killian, the Fenian leader, had declared his purpose
to be the obstruction of Confederation in the British colonies.
The anti-Confederates of New Brunswick had gained an ally
whose intrusion into the affairs of British North America they
could heartily deprecate. Their cause could, with a degree of
conviction, be associated with the boastful talk and reckless
conduct of those south of the border who were working for
Manifest Destiny.

Returning to Fredericton, Gordon found that the alarms of
the capital had not subsided. Awaiting the house of assembly
was a protest from twenty-two members, in the form of an
address to the Queen asking for his recall. Unsure that his new
government could gain the confidence of the house of assembly,
he decided upon dissolution as "the most discreet measure".
Again he would hazard his own decision at the polls. For the
second time in two years he would force the reluctant politicians
and people of New Brunswick to come to a decision upon the
question of Confederation.

X

The initial fire in Smith's fierce counter-attack could not last as
the quick election campaign of 1866 moved into the second of
its three weeks. The "Governor cry" recoiled upon him as the
inexorable hostile forces made their weight felt. He could com-
pare Gordon with Charles I and charge that the power of the
Crown had been prostituted. He could speak of high birth,
cocked hats, and gold lace compared with the humble position

from which he himself had risen in life; he could speak of how Gordon's lofty authority had been meanly and ungenerously used against him. Yet his meetings were poorly attended. He had nothing to offer. Looking southward had drawn nothing but rebuffs. Western Extension appeared a mirage.

For his own protection against the sweeping charges levelled against him, Gordon published in the *Royal Gazette* accounts of his interviews with Smith in December and January. Altogether apart from these, it was widely known that Smith had gone a long way in the direction of union. Yet, dominated by the necessity of preserving his own authority, he was now attacking union in a most precipitate manner. Altogether, as the fire smouldered, he could not escape the charges of inconsistency to which he was prone or master the conviction necessary to refute them. The instructions of June 24, widely published by the pro-Confederates, made it clear that he was opposing the wishes of the British government. Forced into a corner from which he could emerge only for fitful sallies and personal attacks upon the lieutenant-governor, he had no programme that appeared to be acceptable either in New Brunswick or beyond.

The weight of prejudice as well as of reason fell hard upon Smith and his party. Since the cause of Confederation was so rapidly becoming synonymous with loyalty to Britain, they became known as "the annexation antis". Religious as well as national prejudices were on Tilley's side. According to the *Christian Visitor*, not only those who wanted annexation and the dismemberment of the British Empire were against Confederation, but also "the whole Fenian fraternity and nearly all Irish and French Roman Catholics". On the side of those in favour were the Queen, the British government, seven-eighths of all Protestant ministers, and the editors of all great religious papers.[43] Such strong opinions had been given credibility by the Fenian affair, and before the campaign was over Smith's party was saying that the raiders had been brought to the borders of New Brunswick in order to frighten the people into Confederation.

Suddenly one of the chief props of Smith's support fell to the ground. On the Miramichi, where the Irish proportionately were perhaps as numerous as in Saint John, Edward Williston, a member of the Mitchell-Tilley government, openly solicited in the press the support of Bishop Rogers of Chatham. The bishop just as openly replied that it was the duty of the people of New

Brunswick to acquiesce in the wishes of the British government. John Mercer Johnson followed up this startling success by eliciting from the bishop an opinion on "the unbecoming censure of the Governor in the St. John *Freeman*". The reply paid a personal tribute to Anglin, who was pursuing his isolationist views with vigour, but announced disapproval of his policy. No longer could the anti-Confederates depend on a solid Irish Catholic vote. On the Miramichi as elsewhere, motives were mixed. The *Northern Post* reflected a sense of anticipation in the building of a new nationality, coupling this remark with the firm assertion that Sandford Fleming had declared in favour of the North Shore route for the Intercolonial. "If the people want cash payments they must have public works."[44]

As Gordon confidently prophesied, there was no doubt about the outcome, though at the beginning of the campaign there were fearful shakings of heads among the friends of Confederation, both in New Brunswick and elsewhere. It seemed quite possible that the lieutenant-governor, by his arbitrary employment of the power of dissolution, had fouled up a fair situation. With his temperance clubs well organized behind him and with a high sense of patriotic and moral purpose, Tilley had experience enough to know that something more than a sound case and professions of good faith were required to win a New Brunswick, or any other, provincial election. Money had helped to win the election of 1865 for his opponents. Forty or fifty thousand of "the needful" would be required to do the work in all the counties, he told Macdonald. This was nothing new to Macdonald, and, manfully as always, he rose to the emergency. Tilley's cause in New Brunswick was his own cause. An emissary from New Brunswick travelled to Portland by boat to pick up the funds from a Canadian who came by rail from Montreal, care being taken that names should not be mentioned and that no details of this methodical and highly important transaction should reach the public prints.[45]

From May 25 until June 12, as the counties made their returns, it was clear that Confederation was winning an overwhelming victory. In York two of the anti-Confederate candidates, one of whom was George L. Hatheway, withdrew from the contest. In Saint John the able lawyer A. R. Wetmore, who the year before had been one of the winning anti-Confederate members, won again, but this time as Tilley's colleague. Anti-Confederacy had really lost its heart well before the polls opened. For a house of forty-one members, only eight anti-Confederates were returned. Majorities in favour of Confederation almost everywhere were very high.

The jubilation that followed was Protestant and British rather than a paean of praise for the new nation that was to come into being. On many an occasion in later years Smith declared that it was a racial and religious cry that had defeated him. Edward Barron Chandler had assured the people that in the new union the Maritime Provinces could hold a decisive balance of power between Upper and Lower Canada. Tilley had satisfied them that they would endure no increase in taxes. But of the rhetoric and prophecy that frequently accompany the birth of new nations there was little in New Brunswick, especially during the excitement of elections.

What caused most comment in the results was the stand of the three counties in opposition – Westmorland, Kent, and Gloucester. Analysis convincingly showed that it was the almost solid vote of the French that had been responsible for the return of anti-Confederate candidates. Not a single anti-Confederate would have been returned, said the *Telegraph*, had it not been for "the ignorant and illiterate" French population.[46] There were other equally contemptuous remarks, one on "the half-savages of Tracadie". These overbearing comments were accompanied by the uncomfortable reflection that the French of New Brunswick were on their way to better things, capable of making themselves felt as a new political force. There were now over 60,000 of them, nearly one-quarter of the population. Many of them had become literate, reading Quebec newspapers, and a large percentage were bilingual. Their poverty and unprogressiveness had long been proverbial, but in a debate of 1862 Fisher had declared that they were no longer "in a kind of primitive state".[47]

For years those of Westmorland had been nourished on the speeches of politicians such as Smith and Steadman, who reminded them of the deeds of their forefathers on the Plains of Abraham and encouraged them to seek rights of their own. The memory of their exile, reinforced by the invented and distorted history but popular poetry of *Evangeline*, had attracted many professions of sympathy and assistance. For a long time Armand Landry had held a seat in the house of assembly, a persistent though not very articulate tribune, invariably voting for what he thought to be in the interests of his race, working in concert

with Smith, who had always drawn heavily on the French vote.
In 1864 Father Camille Lefevre arrived in Memramcook with a
working capital of eight dollars in his pocket. His purpose was
to found a college that would provide the priests, jurists, and
savants who could give leadership and instruction to the Acadians of New Brunswick. A few years before, a French-Canadian
writer had declared: "Providence has willed that the Acadians
must disappear." But with the founding of St. Joseph's the idea
of *la survivance* took some meaning. What was generated at
Memramcook was a spirit not merely racial and religious but
national as well. The idea of the distinctiveness of the Acadian
race in the face of not merely the English-speaking majority
but of French-Canadians as well, was sustained and encouraged.

At the opening of the second session of 1866, the members
from Westmorland, Kent, and Gloucester were heralded as "the
French brigade". They could do nothing to delay union, but the
appellation, derisively given, was suggestive of a new awareness
that something like a state within a state was coming into
existence.

XI

Little but formality remained to conclude the history of the
province of New Brunswick as a separate entity within the
British Empire. A few leaders of imagination and daring had
made themselves the instruments of the grand idea that was
British North America's response to the problem of the time, to
the urge for mergers and the manufacturing of great states.
Compared with the plight of the defeated states of the Southern
Confederacy, of the German principalities taken captive by
Bismarck in 1866, New Brunswick stood in a position that was
proud and free. But like these she bowed to the will of those
from without. Tilley, Mitchell, Fisher, were servants of a
Canadian initiative. Behind the adroit persuasions of Macdonald and his colleagues in Canada lay the authority of the
British government, not forced but nevertheless strongly asserted, working for the composite solution British world interests required. The problem had not been of New Brunswick's
making, but she was compelled to recognize its existence. Her
elemental loyalties powerfully invoked, exposed to the appeal of
building a new and great nation whose promise hung upon
imponderables, pressed by the impact of immediate events,
cajoled by rather flimsy assurances of commercial prosperity,

and somewhat bribed, the province entered Confederation with very little grace and no gratitude. There was mourning for the freedom of the past. Many of the oldest families of the province, whose respectability was founded upon their record of service – Hazens, Odells, Allens, Parkers, Botsfords – found virtue in opposing union.

A short session of eighteen days in June and July was all that was needed to secure the passing of the necessary resolutions through the legislature. It was Fisher, whose career in the past six years had witnessed several notable changes of fortune, who moved their adoption. Smith made his last stand. His amendment in large part reflected the ideas of American federalism. He demanded an equality of representation in the upper chamber of the new union for each province, a limitation on the number of the representatives of the larger provinces in the lower house, the establishment of a court to decide upon cases of disputed jurisdiction between central government and provinces, and a guarantee of one cabinet member for each of the Maritime Provinces. He had always been suspicious of George Brown and the Clear Grit determination to open up the West, and he insisted upon an exemption from taxation of New Brunswick for the measures that would develop the system of Canadian canals. He voiced a feeling shared by most New Brunswickers, that the new Intercolonial Railway should actually be started before taxes should be increased for the purpose of building it. But the excitement was over. Smith was speaking to a bored and listless house of assembly that reflected the complete apathy that had overcome the people of the province on the whole question of Confederation.

Having been given authority to complete the business, Tilley lost no time in securing the appointment of a delegation to London for the preparation of an act of the British Parliament to unite the three colonies. For this final stage in the proceedings he took with him Mitchell, Fisher, Wilmot, and Johnson. Haste seemed necessary as, in company with the Nova Scotians, they sailed on July 21. British politics were shrouded in instability and uncertainty. It would be well to get the British North America bill passed before the Conservative government should fall and a general election impose months of delay. There was, furthermore, the urgent consideration that in 1867 a general election would be held by law in Nova Scotia. Public opinion in that province was so clearly opposed to Confederation that a new legislature would certainly reverse the decision imposed by Tupper's majority who, in passing resolution for union, defied the ascendant isolationist sentiments ranged against them. In taking the decision to cross the water so quickly they ignored the injunctions of Macdonald, who was certain that haste was unnecessary. From August until November the Maritime delegates kicked their heels and cooled their tempers in London until the Canadians, in their magnanimity, were prepared to do business. Macdonald was sure that the bill to be drafted could handily be worked through Parliament in the new year. A new threat of a Fenian raid and other press of public business kept him in Canada until, in his own good time, he was ready to consummate the work of union. Moralists were already complaining that the Maritimers were being treated like poor relations. Tilley threatened to come home, but Macdonald knew that he was far too deeply committed to Confederation to create obstruction or delay.[48]

Opening on December 4, the London Conference went to work on the Seventy-two Resolutions of Quebec and brought them to the form of a bill that was soon to become law. It was the last opportunity for the Maritimers to win constitutional adjustments that would improve their position within union, but only gestures of this kind were possible. The Canadians had come to London with authority from their legislature to adhere to the Quebec plan only. The legislatures of New Brunswick and Nova Scotia, on the other hand, had resolved in favour of union but not necessarily along the lines of the grand design of 1864. When their delegates quibbled on details, the Canadians were compelled to be adamant. Objections to the Quebec plan heard in the two legislatures of 1866 were politely considered, but no action was taken. New Brunswick confirmed its right, established at Quebec, to collect export duties on timber, which told severely on American operators using the St. John River. Since timber cut on privately owned lands was seldom exported, the measure, dating back to 1844, had given satisfaction to all except the Americans.

In achieving complete harmony Macdonald had little trouble. Tilley and Tupper were generally in agreement, but their colleagues frequently disagreed with one another on details. The Canadians went to London as a disciplined team, the Maritimers as purveyors of particular and rather inconsequential complaints. To judge from the few records available, delegates appeared willing to mention objections but not to support them by sustained controversy. Politically they could not afford to do so, so completely captive were they to the union that was now so near, so personally bound in their future fortunes to the overpowering Canadian initiative. Fisher could recall forty objections to the Quebec plan he had heard in the legislature of New Brunswick. When forced to make a decision he felt compelled to stand by the principles that had been adopted two years before.[49]

In considerable disunion and with some humility, New Brunswick entered Confederation. Nova Scotia was still resisting and a hard road lay ahead for Tupper. It was at London that a delegate from the Maritime Provinces made the formal proposal that the new confederation of provinces should be called Canada, a mark of deference to the preponderance of Canadian enterprise and authority.[50] Moralists in opposition to Confederation might well have interpreted this gracious gesture as the outward and visible sign that everything that had happened since 1864 was a simple act of annexation elaborately concealed. After British concern for American sensibilities resulted in the discarding of Macdonald's favourite designation of "Kingdom", it was Tilley who, according to his eulogists, produced the nomenclature of "Dominion". In the midst of the perplexity caused by British faint-heartedness he came, while reading his Bible on a Sunday morning, upon the passage of the Psalmist: "And his Dominion shall stretch from sea to sea and from the river to the ends of the earth."[51] Out of the hard school of New Brunswick politics that abominated all but the immediate and the parochial came the title of a nation. Tilley's canny realism was generously tinctured by religious and patriotic emotion. His complete mastery of New Brunswick politics over a great many years had allowed him the leisure and the perspective to indulge his imagination upon great prospects for British North America. Not so prosy as Howe or McGee, he was of the same strain as Macdonald, best when in action over the conference table or in the hard details of debate. His fresh complexion, ascribed by his contemporaries to his habits of total abstinence, suggested an abundance of confidence and energy.

As Gordon had fearfully predicted, a mass migration of New Brunswick politicians to Ottawa was set in motion, leaving a vacuum at Fredericton into which lesser-known men were to move. The pre-eminence of Tilley among provincial leaders was the principal fact of life as the London Conference broke up and as the public listlessly waited for the day when they should become citizens of the new Dominion. When Lord Monck informed Macdonald that he was to head the first ministry of Confederated Canada, it was to Tilley that Macdonald turned. He was not only invited to assume a cabinet post but given the onus of nominating a colleague from New Brunswick. Later in his disappointed life, Peter Mitchell complained bitterly about this unhesitating decision of Macdonald. For two or three crucial weeks in April 1866 he had been the star pro-Confederate performer. He had accepted the task of forming a new ministry at a time when Gordon's constitutional heterodoxy had apparently befouled the whole issue of union, when Smith and his friends had seemed to enjoy a fair prospect of making the "Governor cry" the prime subject of contention in the election that was to follow. Mitchell's leading qualities were energy, certainty, and forthrightness. Tilley was more politic and manageable in his methods, more capable of subordinating a private cause, no matter how demanding, to the larger exigencies upon the scene. Macdonald, who had had a great deal of experience with politicians of all varieties, did not really admit a choice between the two.

Faced with the task of designating a cabinet colleague from New Brunswick, Tilley was inclined to select Fisher, but personal preference could not prevail. Confederation was primarily a business proposition. The largest element in practical consideration was the construction of the Intercolonial Railway, and at London the New Brunswick delegation had, at the very outset of proceedings, insisted on a firm declaration to this effect. It would be politically injudicious to send two St. John River men to Ottawa to represent the province in the Dominion cabinet.[52] Therefore it was Mitchell who received the post of minister of Marine and Fisheries, accompanying Tilley who took the portfolio of Customs and Excise. Twelve members of the legislative council, according to the terms of the Quebec and London agreements, were to make the journey to Ottawa that was to become so familiar, to the incipient capital of a nation that as yet did not seem quite real, in the backwoods of Canada. There they would become members of the second legislative body, to be known as the Senate. In the calculations of the times they were to be the watch-dogs of provincial and regional rights. The only member of note who refused the honour was

Edward Barron Chandler, perhaps a little too old to contemplate new adventures in nation-building.

Rewards fell lightly into the hands of all who had taken leading parts in the struggle for Confederation. The new House of Commons at Ottawa was to witness the appearance of many old partisans of the New Brunswick house of assembly. Making something of a break with the past, five anti-Confederates were to win seats in the Dominion election of 1867. Among them was Smith, who could still put his personal popularity in Westmorland to good service. He persisted in believing that the Quebec plan was not perfect, but as a man of the people he was still willing to protect their rights. With the removal of so many doughty performers from the field, the political situation at Fredericton lay in chaos. Democratically, the legislature, in its second session of 1866, had decided that dual representation would not be permitted, that no individual could hold seats in the legislative bodies at Fredericton and at Ottawa, a decision Fisher objected to on the ground that it was "a kind of American measure". A host of new men appearing from the general election of 1867 were to acquiesce in the choice of A. R. Wetmore as the first premier of New Brunswick in Confederation. During the turmoil of 1865-6 he had been a thorn in the flesh, first to Tilley and later to Smith.

Except for the politicians who could contemplate new vistas and new affluence, the mood was one of uncheerful resignation as Confederation came on July 1, 1867. The loyal old colony of Thomas Carleton and his contemporaries, the proud, self-governing province of the Smashers, had become enveloped in an enterprise that was to outgrow rapidly the careful calculations of Tilley and the pro-Confederates. In over eighty years of separate development New Brunswick had failed to attain the realization of many expectations confidently entertained. The Loyalist founders, who had aspired to the decently graded society of Old England and to the enormous estates reminiscent of the large land-holders of Virginia and New York, had been defeated by the hard environment. The commercial democracy which had gained ascendancy in 1837 had in some ways failed just as completely because its own ingredients were too tough and too undisciplined. Heroic figures had come and gone, but the stage had never been much more than miniature. The fierce, unyielding spirit of local independence and self-sufficiency, brought to the country by the Americans in the eighteenth cen-

tury and by the inhabitants of the British Isles in the nineteenth, was channelled off in a dozen directions. If the spectacular
and the grand were possible in New Brunswick, it was the
violent spirit of sectionalism, so clearly apparent in all political,
social, and economic activity, that denied them free expression.
The rural democracy that confronted Carleton became the more
firmly entrenched as the authoritarian perspectives of Thomas
Baillie and those like him gave way to responsible government.
Canada had its St. Lawrence as a great unifying influence by
which local eccentricities had been conquered. A community of
interest based upon a single economic impulse was denied to
New Brunswick because there were so many ways to the outside
world. Mercantile capitalism as well as government had failed
to impart a spirit of unity.

It may be difficult to allow very much praise for the politicians, but the grandeur of New Brunswick lay in the response
of tens of thousands of forgotten men and women to the rigours
of their surroundings and to the business of earning a living. The
tough economic life of the province was in sharpest contrast
with the pettifogging crafts and guiles of the legislators at
Fredericton. As the great ships of the Miramichi were launched
into the river to the cries of "shipyard down", as Saint John
amid great expectations sent its vessels to the waters of the
world, as Main John Glasier and hundreds of other adventurers
scoured the forests of Madawaska for big trees, politics may
have seemed trivial and irrelevant. None of the provinces of
British North America enjoyed government that could be called
progressive, but the temper of the times did not ask very much
of government. The progress of Canada came largely from the
activities of great capitalists who were able to harness the
energies of the country and dictate political policies. Confederation came about because the policies of Macdonald promised
an expansion of their markets, and this great commercial impulse looked westward as well as eastward. In New Brunswick
the capitalists, like the politicians, neutralized one another so
effectively that no group could effectively dominate and direct.

The strength of New Brunswick was a stunted strength.[53] Men
were virile but institutions were puny. Such a country, not so
blessed by nature as other parts of British North America, required art and strong management, but, in the nature of things,
these were denied. Even before union, Canadians had learned
to look down their noses at the backward Maritimers who had

failed to face up to one of the great necessities of modern progress, the direct tax for local improvement. For a long time to come, the consequences of Confederation would appear baneful to all but the most optimistic. The first session of the Dominion Parliament found Albert Smith arguing that his predictions had been correct. Ontario would dominate, and untold sums of money extracted from the Maritime Provinces would be expended in developing the West. The tariff of 1868 seemed to belie Tilley's fair promises; the Canadian coils were being firmly fastened about the captive provinces. Hopeful citizens journeying to Ottawa in search of office and patronage came home unrewarded, and already the cry was raised that their representatives had no influence in this far-removed capital. There was little grace in the retorts made to these complaints. Joseph Cauchon, the Speaker of the Senate, wrote in his newspaper: "What has New Brunswick given, or what will she give for that which she receives or will shortly receive? For the sake of seeing the sea, we are like the proprietor who, wanting a few more feet of land at the end of his property, pays a most exorbitant price for his fancy."[54] What was to be given and received was to be the subject for many fretful negotiations in the future, but it was to be far more than the men of 1867 dared to dream.

Notes

ABBREVIATIONS USED IN THE NOTES

A.O. – American Office

B.M. – British Museum, London

B.T. – Board of Trade

C.O. – Colonial Office

H.M.C. – Reports of the Historical Manuscripts Commission of the United Kingdom

N.B.Leg.Lib. – New Brunswick Legislative Library, Fredericton

N.B.Hist.Soc.Coll. – New Brunswick Historical Society Collections

N.B.Mus. – New Brunswick Museum, Saint John

P.A.C. – Public Archives of Canada, Ottawa

P.A.N.S. – Public Archives of Nova Scotia, Halifax

P.R.O. – Public Records Office, London

U.N.B.Arch. – University of New Brunswick Archives, Fredericton

W.O. – War Office

CHAPTER 1

1. For a description in detail of the organization of Maugerville see James Hannay's article in N.B.Hist.Soc.Coll., vol. 1.
2. *Acadiensis*, January 1907, G.O.Bent, 'Seth Noble'.
3. N.B.Hist.Soc.Coll., vol. 2, W.O.Raymond, *Old Townships on the St. John River*.
4. *Acadiensis*, April 1907, W.F.Ganong, 'History of Caraquet'.
5. P.A.C.Report, 1888, Gaspé Papers.
6. For an explanation of Allan's career the best work is F. Kidder's *Military Operations in Eastern Maine and Nova Scotia*, Boston, 1867.
7. The details of transactions between Goold and the inhabitants of Maugerville are to be found in P.A.N.S., St. John River Papers, vol. 409.
8. James Hannay's article on Maugerville, N.B.Hist.Soc.Coll., vol. 1.
9. For interesting information on this first phase of the timber trade see James White Papers (ed. W.O.Raymond), N.B.Hist.Soc.Coll., vol. 4.
10. N.B.Mus., White Papers, Sir A.Hamond to Hazen and White, December 25, 1782.
11. P.A.C.Report, 1891.
12. Knox's own account of the part he played in the war and in the direction of American affairs is found in his own *Semi-Official State Papers*, London, 1789.
13. B.M., Add. MSS. 34,420, Knox to Wm. Eden, December 11, 1785.

14. These ideas are elaborated in Knox's Plan for New Ireland, set forth in *Semi-Official State Papers*.
15. E.C.Burnett, *Letters of Members of the Continental Congress*, Washington, 1928, vol. 4, p. 103.
16. F.Wharton, *Diplomatic Correspondence of the American Revolution*, Washington, 1889, vol. 3, pp. 274, 295, 302.
17. *Ibid.*, vol. 5, p. 571.
18. Sir John Fortescue, *Correspondence of King George III*, vol. 6, p. 143.
19. B.M., Add. MSS. 42,415, De la Luzerne to Vergennes, August 8, 1783.

CHAPTER 2

1. H.M.C., Stopford-Sackville MSS., Benjamin Thompson to Germaine, August 6, 1782.
2. P.R.O., C.O. 5/108, Carleton to Washington, December 11, 1782.
3. P.A.C., Raymond Coll., vol. 2, Geyer to Chipman, February 5, 1783.
4. P.R.O., C.O. 5/107, Carleton to Shelburne, August 17, 1782.
5. P.R.O., C.O. 5/109, Carleton to Townshend, April 13, 1783.
6. P.R.O., C.O. 5/107, Carleton to Townshend, November 16, 1782.
7. *Ibid.*, Carleton to Shelburne, August 17, 1782.
8. P.R.O., C.O. 5/109, Townshend to Carleton, February 16, 1783.
9. P.R.O., C.O. 5/110, Carleton to North, August 29, 1783.
10. E.C.Burnett, *Letters to Members of the Continental Congress*, Washington, 1928, vol. 8, p. 277. Arthur Lee to James Munro, August 23, 1783.
11. *Ibid.*, Virginia delegation to the Governor, September 8, 1783.
12. B.M., Add. MSS. 42,422, De la Luzerne to Vergennes, November 2, 1783.
13. P.R.O., C.O. 5/108, Carleton to Townshend, April 11, 1783. C.O. 5/110, Memorial of Morgan (Carleton's secretary), undated. C.O. 5/111, Carleton to North, October 5, 1783.
14. P.R.O., C.O. 5/108, Carleton to Townshend, April 11, 1783. C.O. 5/110, Carleton to North, August 26, 1783.
15. P.R.O., C.O. 5/111, Carleton to North, October 26, 1783. Carleton to Parr, October 23, 1783. Carleton to North, November 8, 1783.
16. Sir G.O.Trevelyan, *The American Revolution* (7 vols.), London, 1899-1914.
17. H.M.C., Stopford-Sackville MSS., Thompson to Sackville, August 6, 1782.
18. Odell's address is to be found in N.B.Mus., Odell Coll., Packet 16.
19. George E. Ellis, *Memoir of Sir Benjamin Thompson, Count Rumford*, Boston, 1870, vol. 1, p. 133.
20. Winslow Papers (ed. W.O.Raymond), Saint John, 1901, p. 121.
21. H.M.C., Stopford-Sackville MSS., Thompson to Sackville, January 11, 1782.
22. J.H. Stark, *History of the Loyalists of Massachusetts*, Boston, 1910.
23. B.M., Add. MSS. 42,426, Parr to Shelburne, April 22, 1784.
24. B.M., Add. MSS. 42,427, Parr to Shelburne, July 26, 1784.
25. Winslow Papers, Thos. Knox to Winslow, July 25, 1784, p. 215.
26. H.M.C., American MSS., Haldimand correspondence.
27. P.R.O., C.O. 5/109, Carleton to Parr, April 26, 1783.
28. Lord Ilchester, *Henry Fox, First Lord Holland*, London, 1920, vol. 2, p. 352.
29. B.M., Add. MSS. 42,418, Carleton to Parr, September 5, 1783.
30. Winslow Papers.
31. B.M., Add. MSS. 42,419, Fox to Carleton, September 16, 1783.
32. *Ibid.*, 42,420, Fox to Carleton, October 3, 1783.
33. *Acadiensis*, January 1907, article by D. R. Jack.
34. B.M., Add. MSS. 42,419, Carleton to deputy inspector-general, September 12, 1783.
35. *Ibid.*, Parr to North, October 25, 1783.
36. The manner in which land was allotted to units is described in one of Winslow's

letters to Brook Watson, P.R.O., 217/56, January 10, 1784.
37. P.R.O., C.O. 5/110, Carleton to North, June 17, 1783.
38. *Acadiensis*, April-July 1905, G.O.Bent, 'The Loyalist Willards'.
39. The two points of view in the controversy are presented by *Vindication of Governor Parr and His Council*, by a Gentleman of Halifax, London, 1784, and *Reply to Remarks in a Late Pamphlet*, by J. Viator, London, 1784.
40. P.R.O., C.O. 217/56, Parr to North, March 4, 1784.
41. B.M., Add. MSS. 42,427, Parr to Shelburne, June 16, 1784.
42. Winslow Papers, p. 185.
43. Documents explaining this situation are to be found in the Winslow Papers, pp. 180-7.
44. P.R.O., 217/56, Parr to Carleton, December 31, 1783, with enclosure.
45. It is convenient to write of the firm as if it were still in existence, though at this time a disruption had taken place between James Simonds and his partners. It was still a single vested interest, for their assets were not completely liquidated until many years later.
46. N.B.Hist.Soc.Coll., vol. 2, Simonds Papers.
47. B.M., Add. MSS. 42,426, Parr to Shelburne, January 1784.
48. P.R.O., 217/56, memorial of Morris, May 4, 1783.
49. *Ibid.*, Parr to North, February 2, March 4, 1783.
50. B.M., Add. MSS. 42,426, Parr to Shelburne, May 1, 1784.
51. P.A.C., Raymond Coll., vol. 10, Winslow to Chipman, June 8, 1784.
52. The petition of the Loyalist agents to Parr, undated, reprinted in the *Royal Gazette*, December 6, 1785.
53. Winslow Papers, p. 186.
54. B.M., Add. MSS. 42,427, Parr to Shelburne, June 16, 1784.
55. H.M.C., Kenyon MSS. Coll., Pemberton to Sir Lloyd Kenyon, December 13, 1785.
56. P.A.N.S., Wentworth Letters, John Cochran to Sir John Wentworth, undated.
57. B.M., Add. MSS. 42,421, John Curry to Studholm, October 14, 1783. 42,419, Curry to Studholm, September 25, 1783. Parr to Carleton, September 20, 1783. P.R.O., C.O. 5/111, Carleton to North, with enclosures, September 6, 1783.
58. For papers concerning this group see P.A.C.Report, 1891.
59. F.C.Murray, *Memoir of LeBaron Botsford, M.D.*, Saint John, 1891.
60. The Loyalist ingredient in the population of New Brunswick has been so accurately analysed elsewhere that there is no need to expand upon this evidence for these conclusions. (See Esther Clark Wright, *The Loyalists of New Brunswick*, Fredericton, 1955; and A.C.Flick, *Loyalism in New York during the American Revolution*, New York, 1902.)

CHAPTER 3

1. Certain authors, notably Professor Chester Martin of the University of Toronto, have taken the point of view that the partition of Nova Scotia came about because of the British government's closely calculated policy of 'divide and rule'. (See C.B.Martin, *Empire and Commonwealth*; also Marion Gilroy, 'The Partition of Nova Scotia', *Canadian Historical Review*, vol. 14.) The author has been unable to find evidence to substantiate this position.
2. P.R.O., C.O. 188/12, Carleton to Hobart, May 6, 1803.
3. B.M., Add. MSS. 42,421, Carleton to Parr, October 23, 1783.
4. B.M., Add. MSS. 42,424, Benj. Vaughan to Shelburne, December 14, 1783.
5. P.A.C., Raymond Coll., vol. 6, Winslow to Chipman, January 7, 1784.
6. B.M., Add. MSS. 42,427, Parr to Shelburne, July 26, 1784.
7. P.R.O., C.O. 5/111, North to Carleton, December 5, 1783, most secret and confidential.
8. B.M., Add. MSS. 38,388, minutes of the Board of Trade, March 16, 1784.
9. Queen's Archives, Windsor, No. 5827.

10. P.R.O., C.O. 5/32, acts of the Privy Council.
11. William Knox, *Semi-Official State Papers*, London, 1789.
12. P.R.O., C.O. 217/56.
13. William Knox, *Semi-Official State Papers*.
14. B.M., Add. MSS. 38,388, minutes of the Board of Trade, March 16, 1784.
15. P.R.O., C.O. 188/3, Carleton to Nepean, April 20, 1784.
16. N.B.Mus., Chipman Papers, Mather Byles to Chipman, January 8, 1788.
17. P.R.O., W.O. 4/275, Yonge to Carleton, August 20, 1784.
18. P.R.O., A.O. 12/6, memorial of Odell to the Loyalist commission, March 23, 1784.
19. N.B.Mus., Odell Papers, packet 1.
20. P.R.O., A.O., 12/19, memorial of Ludlow.
21. T.Jones, *History of New York*, New York, 1889, vol. 2, p. 12.
22. H.M.C., Stopford-Sackville MSS., Thompson to Sackville, August 6, 1782.
23. St. John's *Royal Gazette*, January 29, 1784.
24. P.A.N.S., council minutes, July 29, August 3, 1784.
25. The letters clearly revealing Parr's change of attitude are private and are written to Lord Shelburne. They are to be found in transcript in the British Museum, Add. MSS. 42,426-7.
26. P.R.O., C.O. 217/56, Parr to Sydney, September 3, 1784. Sydney to Parr, October 5, 1784.
27. N.B.Leg.Lib., sessional papers, 1786.
28. P.R.O., C.O. 188/3, Carleton to Sydney, with enclosure, December 15, 1784.
29. P.R.O., C.O. 188/3, Carleton to Nepean, October 30, 1784.
30. P.R.O., C.O. 188/3, Carleton to Yonge, June 15, 1785.
31. P.R.O., B.T. 6/81, minutes, March 14, 1785.
32. P.R.O., C.O. 188/3, Carleton to Sydney, June 25, 1785.
33. *Ibid.*, Sydney to Carleton, October 5, 1785. Carleton to Sydney, May 13, 1786.
34. *Ibid.*, Carleton to Sydney, October 25, 1785.
35. *Ibid.*, Carleton to Sydney, November 20, 1785.
36. *Royal Gazette*, November 29, 1785, letter by 'Y'.
37. N.B.Hist.Soc.Coll., vol. 6, W.O.Raymond's paper on Carleton.
38. *Royal Gazette*, February 21, 1786.
39. *Ibid.*, November 22, 1785.
40. P.A.C., Raymond Coll., vol. 6.

CHAPTER 4

1. *Royal Gazette*, August 22, 1786.
2. N.B.Mus., White Papers, vol. 22, Henry Newton to Jas. White, January 14, 1785.
3. P.A.N.S., Wentworth Letters, vol. 44, Paine to Wentworth, January 17, 1787.
4. N.B.Leg.Lib., sessional papers, 1786.
5. N.B.Mus., Chipman Coll., Lieut. Milledge to Chipman, January 23, 1788.
6. P.A.C., Raymond Coll., vol. 6, Kemble to Chipman, July 20, 1797.
7. *Ibid.*, March 3, 1790.
8. N.B.Mus., Chipman Coll., Winslow to Chipman, March 24, 1789.
9. *Ibid.*, Chipman to H.Appleton, November 7, 1789.
10. P.R.O., B.T. 6/20, Board of Trade Papers, February 24, 1790, with enclosure. Grenville to the Lord President, February 20, 1790.
11. P.R.O., A.O. 12/54, memorial of Saunders.
12. P.R.O., C.O. 188/3, memorial of Finucane enclosed in letter of Sydney to Carleton, February 20, 1789.
13. P.R.O., C.O. 188/4, Glenie to Finucane, November 30, 1789, January 1, 1790.
14. N.B.Leg.Lib., papers referring to land grants.
15. P.R.O., C.O. 188/6, Carleton to Portland, with enclosures, September 10, 1795. C.O. 188/9, Carleton to Portland, May 1, 1798. C.O. 188/10, Spry to Portland, March 17, 1800.

16. P.A.N.S., Wentworth Letters, vol. 44, Paine to Wentworth, July 1, 1786. All of the correspondence between Paine and Wentworth is found in this volume. Paine, a son of Timothy Paine, the mandamus councillor of Worcester, Massachusetts, might reasonably be suspected of impulsiveness. As a student of medicine in England he had been presented to the King and Queen wearing the court dress prescribed for medical men: a grey cloth coat with silver buttons, satin small clothes, silk hose, a fall of lace from the collar and lace in the sleeves, a sword by his side. In 1778 he wrote to his friends in Worcester, 'The colonists had better lay down their arms at once for we are coming over with an overwhelming force to destroy them.' A good story is told of this sprightly young man whose letters nearly always abound with certain opinions. During the unsure course of events following Lexington when men's loyalties were being determined, he entertained John Adams at dinner and, following its conclusion, he rose and proposed a toast to His Majesty the King. A hush descended upon the cheerful assemblage and there was a slight murmur of surprise as Adams, with darkened brow, rose to honour it. The relief lasted only for a moment, for Adams lost no time in proposing a toast to His Satanic Majesty. Paine was about to become unpleasant but was restrained by his clever wife who said, 'Do, my dear, permit the gentleman to do honour to his friends.' In 1787 Paine, able to earn but a precarious living, left New Brunswick for the purpose of 'gathering up a little property in New England'. He never returned, ultimately inheriting his father's large estate in Worcester.

17. *Ibid.*, vol. 51, Wentworth to the Commissioners and Principal Officers of His Majesty's Navy, January 10, 1794.

18. P.R.O., C.O. 188/4, Carleton to Grenville, July 15, 1791. Dundas to Carleton, June 7, 1792.

19. P.R.O., C.O. 188/5, Carleton to Dundas, November 20, 1792.

20. P.A.C., Raymond Coll., vol. 2, Winslow to Chipman, May 26, 1786. This affair, the occasion of the first Supreme Court trial in Fredericton, came about when two settlers, David Nelson and William Harboard, shot and killed an Indian whose dog they suspected of killing their hogs, in the parish of Queensbury. Nelson was convicted of murder and executed, Harboard convicted but reprieved.

21. P.A.C., Raymond Coll., vol. 20, Report of New England Company. Report of the Reverend John West following his visit in 1826.

22. *Ibid.*, vol. 21, memorial of the French settlers, June 28, 1786. The petition of the Acadian inhabitants of Kings County, December 24, 1789.

23. *Ibid.*, Odell to Sprague, July 14, 1787.

24. *Ibid.*, memorial of sundry Canadians for lands at Richibucto, October 7, 1791.

25. P.R.O., C.O. 188/8, Dorchester to Carleton, August 6, 1787.

26. P.R.O., C.O. 188/4, Carleton to Grenville, October 9, 1790.

27. *Ibid.*, Carleton to Dorchester, October 1, 1790.

28. P.A.C., Raymond Coll., vol. 22, Costin to Odell, March 24, 1791.

29. P.R.O., C.O. 188/4, Dundas to Carleton, December 10, 1792. C.O. 188/5, Carleton to Dundas, March 27, 1793.

30. P.A.C., Raymond Coll., vol. 12, Chipman to Blowers, December 15, 1799. Blowers to Chipman, January 7, 1800. Undated letter of April 1800.

31. J.W.Lawrence, *Foot-Prints*, Saint John, 1883, pp. 57-8.

32. P.R.O., C.O. 188/4, Grenville to Carleton, August 6, 1791. Carleton to Grenville, December 13, 1791, March 2, 1792.

33. *Ibid.*, Carleton to Grenville, July 15, 1791.

34. C.L.Hathaway, *History of New Brunswick*, 1846.

35. P.A.N.S., Wentworth Letters, Winslow to Wentworth, February 5, 1786.

36. P.A.C., Raymond Coll., vol. 7.

37. Appleton's American Dictionary, article on Coffin.

38. P.R.O., W.O. 1/1051, charges laid by Cobbett.

39. *Acadiensis*, April 1905, S.D.Scott, 'Cobbett's Writing on New Brunswick'.

40. B.M., Add. MSS. 38, 348, memorial of Arnold to Jenkinson.

41. C.C.Sellers, *Benedict Arnold, The Proud Warrior*, New York, 1930, pp. 271-6.
42. N.B.Leg.Lib., petitions, 1792.
43. B.M., Add. MSS. 38,219, 'For Promoting Religion and Literature in the Colonies'.
44. D.R.Jack, *Saint Andrew's Church*, Saint John, 1913, p. 43.
45. P.A.C., Raymond Coll., vol. 22, memorial of the Protestant dissenters of Mauger-ville, May 22, 1792. Memorial of Hugh Johnston and Israel Perley, April 10, 1792. T. Watson Smith's *History of the Methodist Church*, Halifax, 1877, vol. 1, gives first-rate evidence of the religious and emotional tumults that raged among the remnants of those in the Maritime Provinces who had been converted to the New Light enthusiasms of Henry Alline. Probably no place was more notable than Maugerville in this respect. The chief element of religious doctrine that appears to have prevailed was Antinomianism, a belief that those who had once received the grace of Christ were not bound by the moral law and could, though sinning without compunction, be raised up at the Last Day. Smith quotes McColl (p. 262) to say that the eccentricities of these people caused them a few years later to sell their good farms at Maugerville and move up the river.
46. For a full and very readable account of Black's work see T.W. Smith, *A History of the Methodist Church*, Halifax, 1877.
47. P.A.C., Raymond Coll., vol. 21, sundry documents.
48. P.R.O., B.T. 6/56, Inglis's remarks on the New Brunswick law.
49. R.V.Harris, *Charles Inglis, Missionary, Loyalist Bishop*, Toronto, 1937. The Bishop's correspondence in the Public Archives of Canada explains this incident and throws some rather unfavourable illumination on the early religious rivalries of Saint John. William Caleff, an enthusiast of Lady Huntington's persuasion, had unsuccessfully attempted to persuade Inglis to ordain Methodist missionaries and to allow them the use of the newly constructed church. 'To this Caleff a common prostitute applied recently to be cured of a disorder which she had contracted by her commerce with a seaman, and Caleff repeatedly teased her and urged her to declare upon oath that she had a criminal connection with me when I was in Saint John last summer.' (Inglis to Archbishop of Canterbury, January 28, 1789.)

CHAPTER 5

1. P.R.O., C.O. 188/5, Carleton to Clarke, November 20, 1792.
2. N.B.Leg.Lib., Committee of Correspondence to Watson, July 12, 1787.
3. *Ibid.*, Watson to Committee of Correspondence, March 3, 1788.
4. P.R.O., C.O. 5/32, acts of the Privy Council, August 27, 1784. The same instruction was sent to the Governor of Nova Scotia.
5. N.B.Leg.Lib., Committee of Correspondence to Knox, August 20, 1794.
6. P.R.O., 188/6, Daniel Lyman to John King, April 15, 1795.
7. P.R.O., C.O. 188/4, Bliss to Nepean, November 23, 1791.
8. P.A.N.S., Wentworth Letters, Winslow to Wentworth, May 3, 1786.
9. N.B.Leg.Lib., legislative papers, 1795.
10. A great deal of valuable research from the Haldimand Papers contributory to this section was done by Prof. G.F.G.Stanley of the Royal Military College. (See N.S.Hist.Soc.Coll., 1941.)
11. P.A.N.S., Wentworth Letters, vol. 44. Glenie to John N.Flieger, December 16, 1791.
12. P.R.O., C.O. 188/4, Glenie to Finucane, November 30, 1789.
13. P.R.O., C.O. 188/5, Glenie to Dundas, June 12, 1793.
14. Three of Glenie's letters in which these points of view are expressed are to be found in P.R.O., C.O. 188/4 and 5.
15. P.A.N.S., Wentworth Letters, vol. 51, Wentworth to Commissioners of the Navy, January 24, 1795.
16. *Ibid.*, vol. 44, Glenie to John N.Flieger, December 16, 1791.
17. *Ibid.*, vol. 51, Wentworth to the Commissioners, November 8, 1795.

18. P.R.O., C.O. 188/6, Daniel Lyman to John King, April 15, 1795.
19. Assembly Journals, February 13, 1795. N.B.Leg.Lib., sessional papers, 1795, petitions.
20. P.R.O., C.O. 188/14, G.F.Street to Cooke, November 29, 1808.
21. Council minutes, March 8, 1793.
22. P.R.O., C.O. 188/6, Carleton to Portland, with enclosures, March 12, 1795.
23. Winslow Papers, p. 710, Winslow to Sewell, January 14, 1795.
24. P.R.O., C.O. 188/6, Daniel Lyman to John King, April 15, 1795.
25. N.B.Leg.Lib., correspondence with the Agent-General for the colony, Knox to Committee, August 4, 1796.
26. N.B.Leg.Lib., sessional papers, 1796, petitions.
27. *A Fair and Candid View of the Proceedings of the House of Assembly*, printed for the author, Saint John, 1802.
28. P.A.N.S., Wentworth Letters, vol. 52, Wentworth to Glenie, April 12, 1797.
29. P.R.O., C.O. 188/6, Portland to Carleton, May 30, 1795.
30. P.R.O., C.O. 188/9, Portland to Carleton, June 6, 1798.
31. N.B.Leg.Lib., assembly address, February 22, 1797.
32. *Ibid.*, Knox to Botsford, June 7, 1797, May 12, 1798. Knox lost his position as agent for the assembly because the assembly derived the impression that both he and Carleton had concealed the real meaning of Portland's dispatches. Thomas Street, brother to Samuel Denny and an emissary of the assembly to the Colonial Office, had an interview upon the subject with John King, the clerk of the privy Council, late in 1798. According to King, the lieutenant-governor of the province was not bound by precedents to reveal the dispatches of the secretary of state to the colonial legislature, though it was customary for the agent-general to be acquainted with their contents. (N.B.Leg.Lib., sessional papers, 1799, Thos.Street to Botsford, November 9, 1798.)
33. Wm.L.Clements Library, Ann Arbor, Michigan, Knox MSS., Leonard to Knox, June 23, 1789. The grant was made in the parish of Norton, Kings County, and was later occupied by one of Knox's sons, Wills Frederick Knox, who was a justice of the peace and churchwarden in Norton and who left descendants in New Brunswick.
34. N.B.Leg.Lib., sessional papers, 1798.
35. Wm.L.Clements Library, Ann Arbor, Michigan, Knox MSS., Leonard to Knox, June 23, 1798.
36. N.B.Mus., Chipman Papers, Leonard to Chipman, November 13, 1794.
37. *Ibid.*, Hazen to Chipman, March 12, 1800.
38. N.B.Mus., Chipman Papers, T. Coffin to Chipman, March 6, 1799.
39. *Ibid.*, Odell to Chipman, August 21, 1800. The appointee at Quebec was Sir Robert Milnes, first cousin to the Duke of Portland. No other explanation need be sought for Carleton's continuance in office at Fredericton. The failure of the British Government to honour the understanding made in 1784, that he should be promoted to the lieutenant-governorship in Canada, would seem to have been compensated for by his succession of military promotions to the rank of full general.
40. There is no documentation for this, but it has been mentioned by several early writers on New Brunswick history. For the fullest account see D. R. Jack, 'An Affair of Honour', *Acadiensis*, April 1905.
41. *A Fair and Candid Review of the Proceedings of the House of Assembly*, printed for the author, Saint John, 1802.
42. *A Statement of Facts Relative to the Standfasts and the Runaways. Or Sammy Creon's Pamphlet Turn'd Right Side Outwards*, 'Published for Fun'. Saint John, 1802.
43. P.A.C., Raymond Coll., vol. 12, Odell to Chipman, undated.
44. N.B.Leg.Lib., sessional papers, 1803, testimony of Xenophon Jouett.
45. Council minutes, March 4, 1802, testimony of Israel Perley.
46. P.R.O., C.O. 188/11, anonymous letter from Saint John, March 23, 1802.

47. P.A.C., Raymond Coll., vol. 13, Chipman to Odell, March 10, May 17, 1802.
48. P.R.O., C.O. 188/11, Carleton to Hobart, April 11, 1802.
49. For an account of the later years of Glenie's life see G.F.G.Stanley's paper in N.S.Hist.Soc.Coll., 1941.

CHAPTER 6

1. P.A.C., Raymond MSS., vol. 18, Chipman to Kemble, October 25, 1792.
2. *Acadiensis*, April 1907, G.O.Bent, 'New Brunswick in 1802'.
3. P.R.O., C.O. 188/9, Carleton to Portland, June 6, 1798. C.O. 188/10, Carleton to Portland, June 24, 1800.
4. N.B.Leg.Lib., sessional papers, 1802.
5. P.R.O., C.O. 188/10, Leonard to King, March 29, 1799.
6. P.R.O., C.O. 188/9, Carleton to Portland, June 6, 1798.
7. P.R.O., C.O. 188/10, Knox to Portland, November 7, 1799.
8. P.R.O., C.O. 188/11, council minute, January 31, 1800, with enclosures.
9. *Ibid.*, Hobart to Carleton, September 4, 1802.
10. *Ibid.*, Carleton to Hobart, November 6, 1802.
11. P.R.O., C.O. 188/12 memorial of Carleton, May 16, 1805.
12. P.R.O., C.O. 188/14, Fawkener to Shee, February 13, 1807.
13. *Ibid.*, Carleton to Fawkener, January 18, 1807.
14. H.M.C., Dropmore MSS., vol. 8, pp. 123, 142, 211.
15. Wm.L.Clements Lib., Ann Arbor, Michigan, Knox MSS., Leonard to Knox, November 21, 1802.
16. P.R.O., C.O. 188/8, A Well-Wisher to Great Britain to Portland, December 5, 1796.
17. *Ibid.*
18. *Ibid.*, Chalmers to King, January 29, 1797. Brown to King, July 19, 1797.
19. P.R.O., C.O. 188/10, Carleton to Portland, December 1, 1798, with enclosure.
20. P.R.O., C.O. 188/11, Hobart to Carleton, March 3, 1803, with enclosures.
21. P.R.O., C.O. 188/12, Carleton to Hobart, May 6, 1803.
22. N. Atcheson, *American Encroachments on British Rights*, London, 1808. With respect to the paucity of official documents in the years following 1800 it should be noted that New Brunswick was not in a peculiar situation. Following the transfer of colonial business from the Home Office to the War Office at this time, the British government appears to have had no leisure whatever to consider in detail the civil affairs of any of the colonies.
23. *Royal Gazette*, August 26, 1800.
24. P.R.O., C.O. 188/12, correspondence, 1804, with opinions of law officers.
25. N.B.Leg.Lib., petitions, 1799.
26. *Ibid.*, petition of Sunbury settlers, 1810.
27. N.B.Leg.Lib., correspondence with the Agent-General, Knox to committee, April 6, 1808.
28. P.R.O., C.O. 188/13, Castlereagh to Ludlow, September 5, 1807.
29. *Ibid.*, Ludlow to Castlereagh, October 30, 1807.
30. *Ibid.*, Carleton to Castlereagh, August 27, 1807. The letters of James Chalmers to his son-in-law, John Saunders, in U.N.B.Archives strongly indicate that Carleton never really intended to return to the province, that his ambition was to obtain a military command in Britain. It was his fashion to deny all possibility of securing favours, either for himself or his friends in New Brunswick, so long as Lord Castlereagh remained in power.
31. P.R.O., C.O. 188/15, Hunter to Castlereagh, November 16, 1808.
32. N.B.Mus., Chipman Papers, Odell to Chipman, August 17, 1808.
33. P.R.O., C.O. 188/14, Bliss to Castlereagh, November 18, 1808. C.O. 188/15, miscellaneous papers.
34. N.B.Mus., Chipman Papers, Chipman to Hazen, June 3, 1809.
35. P.R.O., C.O. 188/21, Smyth to Bathurst, July 14, 1815, with memorial of Miss Upham.

36. P.R.O., C.O. 188/13, Winslow to Lutwyche, October 12, 1806.
37. N.B.Mus., from *Glenie's Creed*, published 1800. This was a lampoon on Glenie.
38. P.R.O., C.O. 188/15, Hunter to Castlereagh, with enclosure, September 13, 1808.
39. P.R.O., C.O. 188/17, Liverpool to Hunter, December 5, 1811.
40. P.R.O., C.O. 188/12, Ludlow to Hobart, May 16, 1804, with enclosure.
41. *Report of the Committee of the House of Commons on the State of the West Indies*, 1808, evidence of Venner.
42. N.B.Leg.Lib., sessional papers, 1807, petition of Robert Wood.
43. P.R.O., C.O. 188/9, Leonard to Portland, September 10, 1798.
44. Owen's letters and memorials are generously spread through the miscellaneous sections of the C.O. 188 series from 1785 until 1829 when he died.
45. P.R.O., C.O. 188/19, miscellaneous papers, memorial of Owen.
46. N.Atcheson, *American Encroachments on British Rights*, London, 1808.
47. P.R.O., C.O. 188/9, anonymous letter to Portland, November 8, 1798.
48. P.R.O., C.O. 188/12, Leonard to Sullivan, December 14, 1803.
49. *The Question Relating to the Right of the United States of America to the Islands in Passamaquoddy Bay*, printed by J.Ryan, October 1805. This was a pamphlet written by Chipman, containing a statement of the judgment. Enclosed in P.R.O., C.O. 188/13, Leonard to Portland, February 4, 1806. There are references to it in the Winslow Papers.
50. P.R.O., C.O. 188/13, Merry to Windham, January 22, 1808.
51. P.R.O., C.O. 188/14, Wanton to Castlereagh, June 3, 1808.
52. N.B.Leg.Lib., sessional papers, 1807.
53. N.B.Mus., Ward Coll., packet 34, John Ward to Caleb Ward, August 25, 1810.
54. Figures are taken from the statistical appendices to R.G.Albion, *Forests and Seapower*, Cambridge, 1926.
55. P.A.N.S., Wentworth Letters, vol. 53, Wentworth to Glenie, January 25, March 25, May 2, 1801; to Chipman, October 18, 1801.
56. *Ibid.*

CHAPTER 7

1. P.R.O., C.O. 188/13, Knox to Clerk of Council, July 12, 1806.
2. N.B.Leg.Lib., sessional papers, 1808. Knox to Castlereagh, October 15, 1807.
3. P.R.O., B.T. 5/16, minutes, April 28, 1806. Winslow Papers, p. 569.
4. See Gerald S. Graham, 'The Origins of Free Ports in British North America', *Canadian Historical Review*, 1941.
5. N.B.Leg.Lib., sessional papers, 1810. The petition of William Campbell.
6. W.H.Kilby, *Eastport and Passamaquoddy*, Eastport, 1883, p. 143.
7. Winslow Papers, pp. 621-3.
8. Wm.L.Clements Library, Ann Arbor, Michigan, Knox MSS., Knox to Committee of Correspondence, September 7, 1808.
9. *Ibid.*, Leonard to Knox, February 23, 1809.
10. Letter in London *Morning Post* reprinted in *Royal Gazette*, December 16, 1811.
11. R.G.Albion, *Forests and Seapower*, Cambridge, 1926, statistical appendix.
12. N.B.Leg.Lib., sessional papers (miscellaneous), 1816, Nathan Frink to John Saunders, June 25, 1814.
13. *Royal Gazette*, February 18, 1811.
14. N.B.Leg.Lib., sessional papers, 1810, petition of the merchants of Saint John. See also *Royal Gazette*, November 12, 1810.
15. Winslow Papers, Hatch to Winslow, April 23, 1809.
16. N.B.Leg.Lib., sessional papers, 1808, memorandum on pine by R.Anderson.
17. P.R.O., C.O. 188/16, Hunter to Liverpool, November 3, 1810.
18. N.B.Leg.Lib., Mann Papers, Mann to Wentworth, January 26, 1809.
19. P.R.O., C.O. 188/18, Hunter to Liverpool, June 27, 1812.
20. N.B.Leg.Lib., military papers, Smyth to Leonard, July 3, 1812.
21. N.B.Mus., Chipman Papers, Odell to Chipman, March 6, 1813.

22. For a full account see H.A.Davis, *An International Community on the St. Croix*, University of Maine Studies (Second Series, No. 64).
23. P.R.O., C.O. 188/18, Liverpool to Smyth, September 30, October 3, 1812.
24. P.A.C., Raymond Coll., vol. 14, Chipman to Odell, May 16, 1814.
25. Most of the material for this description is drawn from the account of Captain John Le Couteur, printed in the *Albion* of November 1831, and reprinted in *Canadian Defence Quarterly*, July 1930. For an authoritative account based on War Office documents, see the article on the 104th Regiment by W. A. Squires in *The Atlantic Advocate*, February 1961.
26. P.R.O., C.O. 188/145, Gordon to Cardwell, with memorial of Rainsford and other enclosures, June 18, 1866.
27. P.R.O., C.O. 188/20, Owen to Goulburn, August 13, 1814.

CHAPTER 8

1. G. G. Little, *The Littles of Galloway and County Kent*, 1955, U.N.B.Arch.
2. P.R.O., C.O. 188/23, Smyth to Bathurst, April 8, 1818.
3. P.R.O., C.O. 188/26, Smyth to Bathurst, with enclosure, February 25, 1820.
4. B.M., Add. MSS. 38,747, Huskisson Papers, J.E.Dennison to Canning.
5. P.R.O., C.O. 188/25, anonymous letter from N.B., April 20, 1819.
6. P.R.O., C.O. 188/23, Smyth to Bathurst, September 24, 1818.
7. P.R.O., C.O. 188/28, Smyth to Bathurst with enclosure, August 21, 1821.
8. *Ibid.*, Smyth to Bathurst, April 27, 1822.
9. I.E.Bill, *Fifty Years with the Baptists*, Saint John, 1880, p. 23.
10. *Ibid.*, pp. 208-9.
11. *New Brunswick Magazine*, October 1898, 'The Babcock Tragedy' by Roslynde. This account, written under a *nom de plume*, is well documented.
12. P.A.C., Raymond Coll., vol. 21, Bates MSS.
13. I.E.Bill, *Fifty Years with the Baptists*, p. 130.
14. A history of the DesBarres case is to be found in the dispatches of Sir Edmund Head, who was asked to report many years later. Head declared that the grant was not registered in the New Brunswick courts in 1786 because the land was then in the hands of DesBarres' creditors. (See P.R.O., C.O. 188/122, Head to Sir George Grey, August 2, August 26, 1854; also P.A.C., Series A, Black to Goderich, May 10, 1831.) DesBarres' own account of his contest with his daughters, written shortly before he died, is to be found in his memorial in P.R.O., C.O. 188/30. There are papers concerning the DesBarres estate in P.A.C., Raymond Coll., vol. 12. (See also J.C.Webster, *The Life of J.F.W. DesBarres*, Shediac, 1933.) In addition to all the evidence of the remarkable virility of Colonel DesBarres there is the account that on his hundredth birthday he danced a jig on a table at an officers' mess in Halifax.
15. Joshua Marsden, *The Narrative of a Mission to Nova Scotia, New Brunswick and the Somers Islands*, London, 1816.
16. N.B.Leg.Lib., sessional papers, 1816.
17. P.R.O., C.O. 188/25, Smyth to Bathurst, with enclosure, October 11, 1819.
18. P.A.C., Raymond Coll., vol. 21, Bates MSS.
19. *The Colonial Policy of Great Britain Considered with Relation to Her North American Provinces and West Indian Possessions*, by a British Traveller, Philadelphia, 1816, pp. 78-9.
20. P.R.O., C.O. 188/20, Smyth to Bathurst, May 15, 1814.
21. N.B.Leg.Lib., sessional papers, 1810, petition of Gerrish.
22. P.A.C., Raymond Coll., vol. 4, Sabattis to Chipman, August 31, 1809.
23. For more detailed treatment see G.S. Graham, 'The Gypsum Trade in the Maritime Provinces: Its Relation to American Diplomacy in the Early Nineteenth Century', *Agricultural History*, July 1938.
24. Reprinted in *Royal Gazette*, May 23, 1820.
25. *Royal Gazette*, May 30, 1820.

26. P.R.O., C.O. 188/28, Owen to Bathurst, August 2, 1822.

27. N.B.Mus., Odell Coll., packet 20, Bainbridge and Brown to Jonathan Bliss, April 12, 1822.

28. P.R.O., C.O. 188/28, Smyth to Bathurst, with enclosure, March 25, 1822.

29. P.R.O., C.O. 188/23, Bonnar to Bathurst, with enclosure, October 20, 1817. C.O. 188/24, Smyth to Bathurst, with enclosure, August 28, 1818.

30. P.R.O., C.O. 188/24, Coffin to Bathurst, March 23, 1818.

31. *Royal Gazette*, March 28, 1820.

32. P.R.O., 188/28, Nathaniel Atcheson to Bathurst, with enclosure, March 10, 1821.

33. See evidence given by Gilmour to the Select Committee on Timber Duties of the House of Commons, 1835.

34. N.B.Mus., Chipman Papers, petition of the magistrates and inhabitants of Miramichi, August 15, 1823.

35. *Royal Gazette*, April 6, 1824.

36. P.R.O., C.O. 188/22, Smyth to Bathurst, January 31, 1816.

37. *Ibid.*, Lushington to Goulburn, September 18, 1816.

38. P.R.O., C.O. 188/25, Smyth to Bathurst, March 31, 1819.

39. Fees for a grant of 200 acres cost £11.15.0, for a grant of 500 acres £13.8.0. They were payable to the lieutenant-governor, the provincial secretary, the attorney-general, the surveyor-general, and the receiver-general. In defence of such high fees Smyth asserted several times that in cases of penurious grantees they were imposed only in part or not at all.

40. P.R.O., C.O. 188/26, Smyth to Bathurst, with enclosure, March 4, 1820.

41. P.R.O., C.O. 188/27, Wallace to Bathurst, August 16, 1820.

42. P.R.O., C.O. 188/23, Smyth to Bathurst, June 29, 1817.

43. *Ibid.*, July 30, 1817.

44. P.R.O., C.O. 188/29, Chipman to Bathurst, May 15, 1823.

45. The two families of the name of Bliss that were prominent in the public life of New Brunswick at this time were quite distinct from each other. Jonathan Bliss came to the province as attorney-general in 1785 and died as chief justice in 1822. All of his surviving sons removed from the province. Henry Bliss, his youngest son, after reinstatement to the office of clerk of the Supreme Court, left for London, where he eventually became agent for the province and a persistent advocate of the interests of the timber trade in British North America, working closely in accord with the British North America Merchants' Association. His last months in the province were not happy. Fredericton was 'the worst hole in the worst province in the worst corner of the worst quarter of the globe. . . . The Yahoo society is infinitely worse than ever.' (To J.S. Saunders, December 28, 1824, Saunders Coll., U.N.B.Arch.) John Murray Bliss was a son of Daniel Bliss, a member of the council of New Brunswick in its early years.

46. N.B.Mus., Odell Coll., packet 20, Bliss to Bainbridge and Brown, February 27, 1822.

47. P.R.O., C.O. 188/29, Chipman, Jr., to Bathurst, April 25, 1823.

48. P.R.O., C.O. 188/28, Smyth to Bathurst, August 1, 1822. Legislative council journals, March 22, 1822.

49. P.R.O., C.O. 188/23, Smyth to Bathurst, March 25, 1818.

50. P.R.O., C.O. 188/28, Bathurst to Smyth, June 12, 1822.

51. Assembly journals, 1822.

52. P.R.O., C.O. 188/28, Owen to Wilmot Horton, October 30, 1822.

53. P.R.O., C.O. 188/30, memorial of Henry Bliss. There was a general acceptance of the idea that the office of clerk of the Crown in the Supreme Court was the gift of the chief justice. In appointing his son to the office in 1819 Jonathan Bliss expelled the previous holder, William F. Odell. (See N.B.Mus., Chipman Coll., Odell to Smyth, April 16, 1819.)

54. P.R.O., C.O. 188/29, Chipman to Bathurst, June 6, 1823.

55. See an unpublished thesis on the life of Ward Chipman, written by Miss Patricia Ryder for the M.A. degree, U.N.B.Archives.
56. Council minutes, February 16, 1824.
57. P.R.O., C.O. 188/30, Douglas to Bathurst, September 30, 1824.

CHAPTER 9

1. J. S. Buckingham, *Canada, Nova Scotia and New Brunswick*, London, 1843, p. 415.
2. P.A.C., N.B.Series A, Douglas to Bathurst, October 20, 1824.
3. *Ibid.*, Douglas to Herries, February 1, 1827.
4. U.N.B.Library, Douglas letter-books, Douglas to Bliss, November 18, 1824.
5. P.A.C., Series A, Douglas to Bathurst, April 22, 1825. Series B, Bathurst to Douglas, March 1, 1826.
6. P.R.O., C.O. 323/54, Douglas to Hay, April 7, 1828.
7. P.A.C., Series B, Bathurst to Douglas, October 26, 1825. In spite of the strong feelings in the colonies against a pension for Bishop Stanser from the casual revenues of the colonies, Earl Bathurst considered it necessary to make an award, £350 from Nova Scotia and £250 from New Brunswick. Defending this decision in the House of Lords, he pointed out how the Bishop, in failing health, had suffered severe injury while fighting a fire in Halifax. 'I do not think that this was an extravagant sum. What could I do, my Lords? I had no power to require his resignation, no authority to demand it. If I had had authority I should never have enforced it. (Cheers.) Could I have said to him, my Lords, go back to Halifax and die, or stay in this country and starve? (Loud cheers.)' (Proceedings in the House of Lords, March 14, 1828.)
8. P.A.C., Series B, Bathurst to Douglas, May 31, 1825. Series A, Douglas to Bathurst, August 30, 1825.
9. P.R.O., C.O. 324/97, Wilmot Horton to Kempt, January 16, 1827.
10. The total cost of the building was £13,000 and the builder was John Murray, master mason. It was designed by A.Woolforde, a British military engineer. The legislature in all voted £7,300, far more than had originally been intended. This may be taken as another indication of the masterful manner in which Douglas dealt with the politicians of the province.
11. P.A.C., Inglis correspondence, Inglis to Douglas, April 18, 1825.
12. P.R.O., C.O. 324/95, Wilmot Horton to Archbishop of Canterbury, November 23, 1825.
13. U.N.B.Library, diary of Mrs.L.W.Bailey.
14. *Royal Gazette*, February 11, 1825.
15. P.A.C., Series A, Douglas to Bathurst, with enclosure, September 6, 1825; to Wilmot Horton, November 10, 1825; to Hill, October 27, 1827; to Huskisson, October 29, 1827. It is worth noting that the Colonial Office, in moving towards the withdrawal of the Parliamentary grant, was largely inspired by the economizing policies of the Lords of the Treasury. Lord Bathurst was personally opposed to the withdrawal of the grant and was probably responsible for much of the delay in putting the withdrawal into effect.
16. P.R.O., C.O. 323/54, Douglas to Hay, October 14, 1828. It is necessary to remark that the real authorship of the idea of sale of colonial lands cannot be attached to the name of a particular individual or even to a particular period. The idea certainly goes back as far as Pitt's policy of 1789. Huskisson favoured it while he was at the Colonial Office. The policy was initiated at this stage by Bathurst, but the degree of his enthusiasm is of some doubt.
17. *Ibid.*, July 23, 1828.
18. P.A.C., private papers of Thomas Baillie, Douglas to G.Baillie, March 23, 1825.
19. N.B.Mus., Odell Coll., packet 20, A.Mountain to W.F.Odell, January 31, 1822.
20. *Ibid.*, Colin Campbell to W.F.Odell, July 29, 1843.
21. *American State Papers*, vol. 5, p. 526. This view has been reiterated by the

Canadian scholar who has conducted the most searching investigation into the boundary dispute. 'Chipman did indulge in sophistries, but it was that or nothing. He was an advocate with a very weak case to defend.' (See W.F.Ganong, 'Boundaries of New Brunswick', *Proceedings of Royal Society of Canada*, 1901-2, p. 330.) Yet this follows from an extremely legalistic interpretation of the wording of the Treaty of Versailles. It is still possible to argue with great reason, as Chipman did, that the intention of the treaty-makers was not to bring the American frontier within a few miles of the St. Lawrence.

22. *Ibid.*
23. P.R.O., C.O. 323/54, Douglas to Hay, July 23, 1828.
24. *Hansard's Parliamentary Debates*, LXVII, pp. 1273-4.
25. P.A.C., Series A, Black to Vaughan, with enclosure, May 11, 1829.
26. *Letters from Nova Scotia and New Brunswick* (anon.), Edinburgh, 1829, p. 128.
27. *Ibid.*, p. 35.
28. *Ibid.*
29. N.B.Mus., Ward Coll., packet 21, John Bainbridge to John Ward, May 19, 1828.
30. *Letters, op. cit.*, No. 26.
31. P.A.C., Series A, Black to Lieutenant-Colonel Norcott, October 28, 1829.
32. P.R.O., C.O. 188/118, letter of Mrs.Donald, 1852.
33. P.A.C., Series A, Douglas to Bathurst, December 6, 1826.
34. Details of the contest between Munro and End can be found in P.A.C., Series A, Goderich to Black, with enclosures, July 1, 1831; Proceedings in Council, with enclosures; March 8, 28, with enclosures.
35. P.A.C., Series A, Goderich to Black, July 1, 1831.
36. *Courier*, March 5, 1831. Report of debate in house of assembly of February 25.
37 P.A.C., Series A, Huskisson to Douglas, October 30, 1827.
38. P.A.C., Series A, Douglas to Goderich, with enclosures, September 14, 1827.
39. P.A.C., Series A, report of Capt.Hurd, surveyor-general, to the Committee of the House of Commons on Emigration, Nov. 11, 1826, with attached Report of the Committee of the Saint John Agricultural and Emigrant Society.
40. P.A.C., Series A, Rt.Hon.R.Gordon to Douglas, July 22, and Douglas to Gordon, September 24, 1828.
41. S.W.Fullom, *The Life of General Sir Howard Douglas, Bart.*, London, 1863, p. 297. The truth of this spirited account may be called in question since Douglas's term had virtually expired and it was not the policy of the Colonial Office to appoint for second terms.
42. *Courier*, April 30, 1831.
43. P.A.C., Raymond Coll., vol. 6, Henry Bliss to Chipman, July 19, 1828.
44. *Ibid.*
45. *Summary of the Case of Mr. Thomas Baillie*, London, undated, p. 16.
46. P.A.C., Series A, Black to Murray, December 5, 1829, with memorial of Baillie enclosed.
47. P.A.C., Series A, Murray to Black, April 2, 1830.
48. N.B.Mus., Chipman Coll., Odell to Chipman, August 20, 1808.
49. P.A.C., enclosures to council minutes, 1831, Peters to Black, December 29.

CHAPTER 10

1. P.A.C., Series A, Goderich to Black, December 7, 1830.
2. *Ibid.*, Goderich to Campbell, with enclosures, May 26, 1831. The resignations were not accepted until several months later.
3. N.B.Mus., Ward Coll., John Ward to Charles Ward, February 17, 1832.
4. P.A.C., Series A, Campbell to Goderich, February 14, June 9, 1832.
5. P.A.C., Series A, Goderich to Campbell, with enclosures, October 3, 1831.
6. P.A.C., council minutes, with enclosed letters from Alexander Rankin, August 25, 1833.

7. P.A.C., Series A, Campbell to Goderich, June 5, 1832.

8. P.A.C., Inglis correspondence, Inglis to Stanley, February 25, November 14, 1833. Series A, Campbell to Inglis, April 16, 1833.

9. P.A.C., Series A, Campbell to Goderich, January 16, 1832, confidential.

10. P.A.C., enclosures to council minutes, 1831. Petitions of lumbermen of Gloucester, September 14, and of Northumberland, October 1.

11. *Ibid.*, 1833, memorial of Munro, December 17, 1832.

12. P.A.C., Series A, Campbell to Goderich, January 16, 1832.

13. Gowan came to Fredericton in 1820 and later became hospital sergeant of his regiment. After being one of the founders of the Central Bank he accepted a clerkship in the Crown Lands Office and held it until his death in 1870. 'He wielded a facile and sprightly pen; and his "Johnny Gape" letters to the St. John Courier created a wider interest in the Province than any letters before or since. They made the pathway smooth for those who were then working for Reform and Responsible Government. With what keen satire he discussed the management of the Crown Lands Office and described the treatment of the people who sought to do business with it! What old resident of New Brunswick has forgotten these famous letters?' (See P.A.C., Lawrence Scrap-books, No. 21, obituaries of Robert Gowan.)

14. Legislative debates, March 15, 1833, reported in the *Weekly Observer*. The debates of 1833 were comprehensively reported for the *Observer* and the *Courier* by John Blatch after a public subscription was taken for the purpose.

15. From Pictou *Colonial Patriot*, reprinted in the *Courier*, November 9, 1833.

16. *Observer*, February 7, 1833, Henry Gilbert's speech.

17. It was published in the *Courier* in three parts commencing February 23, 1833, and was signed O.P., another *nom de plume* for Gowan. Apart from all the internal evidence suggesting that his was the authorship, there is the considered opinion of one of the enraged opposite faction: 'The coarse vulgarity and hatred of O.P. must work its own cure; every sensible man must perceive what a menace the public press of a country will become if such licentiousness is tolerated. . . . Are you aware that the author of O.P. is John Gape? Pray read attentively O.P.'s Intrigue in this day's paper. I have no idea of law if you, Mr. Odell, Cunard, Scott and Crum cannot each bring an action against the base ruffian.' (P.A.C., C.O. 193/3, private papers of Thomas Baillie, Luddy to Baillie, March 1, 1833.) A more complimentary opinion of Gape was 'The Song of Thousands' by William L.Leggett, printed in the *Courier* of September 28:

> Here's to John Gape – let his name
> Be the name for me – nobody more.
> Here's to John Gape – whilst the light of his fame
> Dispels the dark mist from our shore.
> I have listened with feeling profound
> To the voice that holds tyrants in thrall –
> I have listened with pride, whilst the multitude found
> There was one who dared speak for us all.

18. P.A.C., C.O. 193/3, Luddy to Baillie, March 9, 1833.

19. *Ibid.*, March 14, 1833.

20. *Ibid.*, March 9, 1833.

21. P.A.C., Series B, Stanley to Campbell, September 5, 1833.

22. P.A.C., C.O. 193/3, Baillie to Stanley, August 29, 1833.

23. P.A.C., Series B, Stanley to Campbell, June 1, 1833.

24. *Ibid.*, July 31, 1833.

25. This requirement aroused old prejudices. Protests from Saint John against the former pretensions of Simonds, White and Hazen appeared. (P.A.C., Series A, Campbell to Stanley, with enclosure, March 12, 1834.) Peters, the attorney-general, was compelled to report that it was impossible to devise a bill by which

both public and private interests could be protected. Stanley accepted this opinion.

26. Prior to the receipt of the instruction, Cunard had bowed to public opinion and had given up the reserves.
27. P.A.C., Series A, Campbell to Stanley, March 22, 1834.
28. *Ibid.*, May 3, 1834.
29. P.A.C., Series B, Stanley to Campbell, December 26, 1834.
30. *Courier*, September 5, 1835.
31. P.A.C., Series A, Campbell to Stanley, September 14, 1835.
32. P.A.C., council minutes, February 13, 25, with enclosures from Perley.
33. *Courier*, March 8, 1834, speech of Jedidiah Slason.
34. P.A.C., Series B, Glenelg to Campbell, May 26, 1835.
35. P.A.C., council minutes, January 21 and following, 1836, with enclosures.
36. P.A.C., Series A, Glenelg to Campbell, March 31, 1836, with enclosure.
37. *Courier*, report of proceedings in house of assembly, March 7, 1836.
38. N.B.Mus., Odell Coll., packet 20, Sir A.Campbell to W.F.Odell, October 3, 1837. This letter was written nearly a year after the events described, but it may be taken as a revelation of Campbell's opinions and intentions.
39. Assembly journals, February 6, 1837. Pierce was imprisoned in the county jail at Fredericton for the remainder of the session, receiving an uproarious welcome from his numerous friends on the Miramichi upon his release. This was one of the occasions when the house of assembly of New Brunswick exerted its privilege of Parliament in this way. In the first session of 1786, an individual, George Handyside, was brought to the discipline of the house for his public expression of contempt for its proceedings. The custom, which told most heavily upon journalists, was based upon a great number of precedents, both British and colonial, the case of Sir Francis Burdett in 1811 being one of the most familiar. In New Brunswick the exercise of the privilege was finally quashed in 1844 in the famous case of Robert Doak and Thomas Hill, the editors of the *Loyalist*. Lemuel Allen Wilmot was again the victim of a journalistic attack and again the house of assembly imprisoned the alleged offenders. They applied for a writ of habeas corpus and were released by order of Justice Carter. (See Fenety, pp. 96-100; also assembly journals of 1844, p. 231 and appendix.) James Brown was one member of the assembly who was not certain of its privileges, wanting a ruling from the courts. 'Hill having libelled us most grossly in the Loyalist newspaper of which he and Doak are publishers, we in accordance with our old custom cast them both into prison.' (Brown to A.Bustin, February 29, 1844, Maxwell Coll., U.N.B.Arch.)
40. *New Brunswick Magazine*, January 1899, W.K. Reynolds, 'The Fire of Thirty-Seven'. Owing to the amount of thieving they were alleged to have done during the fire, the dwellers of the west side of the harbour were compared to the pirates of Algiers. For many years after, the people of Carleton were nicknamed 'Algerines'.
41. Sir Francis B. Head, *A Narrative*, London, 1839, pp. 157-65.
42. The documents revealing the character of Street's mission to London are printed in the appendix to the legislative journals of the summer session of 1837.
43. P.A.C., Series B, Glenelg to Harvey, April 6, 1837.

CHAPTER 11

1. *Creevey Papers*, London, 1904, vol. 1, p. 328.
2. *Conservative and Loyalist*, December 23, 1847.
3. P.A.C., letter-book of Sir John Harvey, Campbell to Harvey, May 17, 1837.
4. P.A.C., Series A, Harvey to Glenelg, June 1, 1837.
5. P.A.C., council minutes, August 19, 1837.
6. N.B.Mus., Odell Coll., packet 20, Sir A.Campbell to W.F.Odell, October 3, 1837.
7. Durham Report, London, 1839, p. 69.

8. P.A.C., Durham Papers, sec. 7, vol. 1. Confidential minute on the state of affairs in Lower Canada, November, 1836. At this stage the British government appeared to be seeking inspiration for the resolution of Lower Canadian troubles in the New Brunswick conversations with Crane and Wilmot of a few weeks earlier.

9. Letter to *Chronicle*, August 14, 1840.

10. J.W. Lawrence, *The Judges of New Brunswick and Their Times*, p. 501.

11. Quoted in *Courier*, August 19, 1837.

12. *Courier*, February 17, 1838.

13. *Ibid.*, March 24, 1838.

14. *Chronicle*, February 28, 1840. 'Another New and Improved Constitution'.

15. P.A.C., Durham Papers, sec. 3, vol. 2, Harvey to Durham, August 7, 1839.

16. *Chronicle*, February 28, 1840.

17. *Ibid.*, March 9, 1840.

18. For the outcome of the case against Baillie see chapters 12 and 13.

19. P.A.C., Sir John Harvey's letter-book, Harvey to Odell with memorandum, July 6, 1840.

20. This incident is referred to on several occasions in communications to the *Chronicle* in 1840. The horse-whipping is alleged to have been administered by James Wetmore. It was further alleged that Wilmot, in order to protect himself against additional attacks, carried a cane about the streets of Fredericton.

21. *Chronicle*, October 23, 1840.

22. P.A.C., Series A, Harvey to Russell, November 26, 1840.

23. P.A.C., Series A, Harvey to Normanby, April 25, 1839. Normanby to Harvey, with enclosure, June 6, 1839.

24. P.A.C., Series A, Harvey to Normanby, August 3, 1839.

25. P.A.C., Series A, Harvey to Glenelg, September 11, 16, October 1, 9, 13, 1838.

26. David Lowenthal, 'The Maine Press and the Aroostook War', *Canadian Historical Review*, December 1951.

27. P.A.C., Series A, Normanby to Harvey, August 16, 1839.

28. P.A.C., Series A, Harvey to Normanby, October 7, 17, 1839.

29. *Ibid.*, May 15, 1839.

30. P.A.C., Series G7, vols. 4 and 5, Harvey to Sydenham, with enclosures, December 12, 1840.

31. P.A.C., Series G12, vol. 27, Sydenham to Russell, with enclosures, January 27, 1841.

32. P.A.C., Series A, Russell to Harvey, March 18, 1841.

33. P.A.C., Series A, Harvey to Russell, March 15, 1841.

34. *Chronicle*, January 23, 1837.

35. P.A.C., Series A, Campbell to Stanley, April 24, 1834.

36. For a vivid account of Cunard see Esther Clark Wright, *The Miramichi*, Sackville, 1944.

37. P.A.C., Series A, Harvey to Glenelg, private and confidential, April 12, 1839.

38. 'For he has been much more the Dictator of this location than Sir John Harvey has been or is the Governor of the province – and to such an extent that for years I have called him the Emperor of Grand Manan.' (Lauchlan Donald to Simonds, September 13, 1840.) For papers relative to this affair see P.A.C., enclosures to council minutes, October 2, 1840.

CHAPTER 12

1. P.A.C., Series A, memorial of Marcus Gunn, August 14, 1835.

2. J.F.W.Johnston, *Report on the Agricultural Capabilities of the Province of New Brunswick*, Fredericton, 1850, p. 8.

3. P.A.C., Inglis correspondence, Inglis to Hamilton, April 9, 1827.

4. Mrs.F.Beavan, *Life in the Backwoods of New Brunswick*, London, 1845, p. 2.

5. Rev.M.C.Atkinson, *Historical and Statistical Account of New Brunswick*, Edinburgh, 1844.
6. P.A.C., council minutes, with enclosures, February 28, March 21, 1841.
7. J.S.Buckingham, *Canada, Nova Scotia and New Brunswick*, London, 1843, p. 419.
8. *Loyalist*, December 23, 1847.
9. P.A.C., Series A, Stanley to Colebrooke, August 11, 1842.
10. *Ibid.*, Colebrooke to Stanley, September 27, 1842.
11. Assembly journals, February 9, 1842.
12. *Ibid.*, January 31, 1843.
13. P.A.C., Series A, Colebrooke to Stanley, March 25, 1843.
14. *Ibid.*
15. *Ibid.*, Stanley to Colebrooke, with enclosures, July 11, 1843.
16. Colebrooke's own account of interviews with members of his council are most complete and recapitulary. They are to be found in P.A.C., Series A, Colebrooke to Stanley, February 25, 27, March 26, April 26, 27, May 12, 29, 1845.
17. Assembly journals, February 20, 1845.
18. *Loyalist*, December 23, 1847.
19. P.A.C., Series A, Colebrooke to Stanley, May 12, 1845.
20. P.A.C., Howe Papers, Fisher to Howe, August 25, 1847.
21. P.A.C., Series A, Colebrooke to Gladstone, April 28, 1846. Gladstone to Colebrooke, June 20, 1846.
22. G.E.Fenety, *Political Notes*, pp. 254-5.
23. N.B.*Courier*, February 20, 1847. These two designations, of comparatively recent origin in Britain, had been casually employed for the purposes of simplicity for some years past, but not with any consistency. George E. Fenety's *Political Notes*, published in 1867, a commentary upon the legislative debates of the period, conveys the impression of a two-party warfare dominating politics from 1842 into the years following, yet the dispatches of the lieutenant-governor and other official documents, as well as the newspapers of the province, make no recognition of the existence of two political parties that were divided upon the issue of responsible government. It is possible to show that for many years after Confederation, owing to the large number of what were called 'loose fish' in the legislature, the two-party system in New Brunswick was not firmly established.
24. N.B.*Courier*, March 20, 1847, debate on parish schools.
25. Assembly journals, April 13, 1847.
26. N.B.*Courier*, January 1, 1848, future prospects of the province.
27. Assembly journals, March 18, 20, 1848.
28. N.B.*Courier*, February 19, 1848.
29. *Ibid.*, January 29, 1848.
30. P.A.C., Series A, Colebrooke to Grey, February 8, March 25, 1848. Grey to Colebrooke, March 4, 1848.
31. *Loyalist*, December 23, 1847.
32. P.A.C., Series A, Colebrooke to Stanley, April 23, 1844.
33. John Wilson of St. Andrews, who convened a public meeting for the purpose as early as 1828, is allowed the credit for initiating the St. Andrews-Quebec project. The idea gained further publicity from an article by Henry Fairbairn in the *United Services Journal* in 1832. Wilson also called the first mee ing that resulted in action in 1835. (Sandford Fleming, *The Intercolonial Railway*, Montreal, 1876, p. 6.)
34. P.A.C., Series A, Gladstone to Colebrooke, confidential, February 3, 1846.
35. Fenety, pp. 267-8.
36. P.A.C., Series A, Gladstone to Colebrooke, March 16, 1846.
37. *Ibid.*, Colebrooke to Grey, March 29, 1847.
38. Council minutes, with enclosures, May 4, 1842. Petition of the inhabitants of Nashwaaksis.
39. P.A.C., Series A, Colebrooke to Stanley, October 25, 1845.

40. P.R.O., C.O. 188/106, Head to Grey, August 17, 1848, with Perley's report enclosed.
41. P.A.C., Series A, Colebrooke to Grey, July 30, 1847.
42. *Ibid.*, Stanley to Grey, with enclosures, September 26, 1846.
43. *Ibid.*, Gladstone to Colebrooke, with enclosures, July 26, 28, 1846.
44. P.A.C., Series A, Colebrooke to Stanley, August 10, 1841.
45. One of the best examples of the constant attacks waged upon the Church of England establishment was that of the missionary on the Miramichi who taught in one of the parish schools. The School Act required that the Creed, the Lord's Prayer, and the Ten Commandments should be taught, but the local school board, headed by a Presbyterian minister, would not pay his salary unless he should teach the Shorter Catechism as well. (P.A.C., Inglis correspondence, Inglis to Douglas, October 30, 1826.)
46. Fenety, p. 139.
47. P.A.C., Series A, Colebrooke to Stanley, October 30, 1846.
48. P.A.C., Inglis correspondence, Inglis to Canterbury, September 30, 1841. Chipman to Canterbury, July 31, December 19, 1842.
49. P.A.C., Series A, Stanley to Colebrooke, June 3, 1843. Colebrooke to Stanley, June 27, 1843.
50. Fenety, p. 142.
51. C.H.Mockridge, *The Bishops of the Church of England in Canada*, Toronto, 1896, p. 119.
52. T.Hodgins, *British and American Diplomacy Affecting Canada*, 1782-1899, Toronto, 1900.
53. Greville's *Memoirs of the Reign of Queen Victoria*, part 2, vol. 1, London, 1896, p. 469.
54. N.B.Mus., Odell Papers, packet 20, Campbell to Odell, July 21, 1843.
55. This method of raising revenue from American timber, as well as from New Brunswick timber cut for export, continued until 1855 when it lapsed following the Reciprocity Treaty with the U.S. It was revived in 1866 and at the entrance of New Brunswick to Confederation it was further legalized by the British North America Act. Following American protests at the Treaty of Washington it was finally abandoned in 1871.
56. P.A.C., Series A, Stanley to Colebrooke, July 31, 1844.

CHAPTER 13

1. P.A.C., Raymond Coll., vol. 21. Thomas Hill was probably the most brilliant and versatile of New Brunswick editors at this period. There is no record of his origins, but he was supposed by his own generation to have been a deserter from the American army. In the *Conservative and Loyalist* he opposed political change of almost every kind. After a life of dissipation he died in poverty in 1860. (See W.G.MacFarlane, *New Brunswick Bibliography*, Saint John, 1895.) This song was first heard at a dinner in Hibernia Hall, July 12, 1844.
2. The career of Saunders in public office is illustrative of the political changes that were at work. In 1845 he became the first provincial secretary holding office 'during pleasure', on a political basis according to the terms of Lord John Russell's dispatch of 1839. In 1848 he resigned the office because he was unwilling to stand for a seat in the house of assembly and fight the battles of the government. Educated at the Inns of Court in London, Saunders was the author of widely read legal texts and commentaries. According to contemporary opinion he was too gentlemanly and scholarly to take an active part in public affairs.
3. P.A.C., Sir Edmund Head's letter-books, vol. 1, Head to Chandler, May 11, 16, 1848; to Hazen, May 13, 1848.
4. P.R.O., C.O. 188/105, Head to Grey, May 20, 1848.
5. *Ibid.*, January 6, 1849.

6. *Ibid.*, May 20, 1848, confidential.
7. *Ibid.*, January 15, May 30, 1848, with enclosures.
8. Louise Manny, *Ships of Miramichi*, Saint John, 1960, p. 24.
9. P.R.O., C.O. 188/105, Head to Grey, June 19, 1849, with enclosure. Grey to Head, February 8, 1849.
10. P.R.O., C.O. 188/108, Head to Grey, January 8, 1849, with enclosure. Grey to Head, February 8, 1849.
11. W.R. Manning, *Diplomatic Correspondence of the United States, Canadian Relations*, Washington, 1940, vol. 4, pp. 293-4, Andrews to Clayton, August 1, 1849.
12. P.R.O., C.O. 188/110, Grey to Head, August 2, 1849, with enclosures.
13. *Ibid.*, Head to Grey, September 15, 1849, with enclosures.
14. Assembly journals, April 6, 1850.
15. P.R.O., C.O. 188/108, Head to Grey, March 6, 1849, with address of house of assembly enclosed.
16. P.R.O., C.O. 188/107, Head to Grey, January 1, 1849, with enclosure.
17. P.R.O., C.O. 188/108, Head to Grey, January 6, 1849, with enclosure.
18. P.R.O., C.O. 188/113, Head to Elgin, November 20, 1850.
19. P.R.O., C.O. 188/117, Head to Pakenham, October 4, 1852.
20. P.R.O., C.O. 188/115, Seymour to Merivale, January 30, 1851.
21. P.R.O., C.O. 188/117, Murray to Pakenham, July 1, 1852.
22. Conspicuous among the New Brunswick politicians accepting cash payments from Andrews, whose funds were derived from Canadian as well as American sources, was William H. Needham. These need not be interpreted in a sinister light. Reciprocity was generally in favour, and politicians could consistently accept reward of this kind for doing the missionary work of persuasion in quarters where there were pockets of resistance. Andrews refers to Hazen and Chandler as men of 'high character' who could not be bought. (See Manning, *Diplomatic Correspondence of the United States, Canadian Relations*, Washington, 1940, vol. 4, p. 571.)
23. P.R.O., C.O. 188/117, Head to Pakenham, December 16, 1852, with enclosure.
24. W.C.Milner, *Early History of Dorchester*, Sackville, 1932.
25. P.R.O., C.O. 188/122, Head to Grey, September 5, 1854.
26. Laura E.Poor, *Life and Writings of John Alfred Poor*, New York, 1892, pp. 28-9.
27. For the best account of this elaborate misunderstanding see W.M.Whitelaw, *The Maritimes and Canada before Confederation*, Toronto, 1934, pp. 94-5.
28. *Morning News*, July 15, 1850.
29. P.R.O., C.O. 188/121, Head to Newcastle, January 14, 1854.
30. P.R.O., C.O. 188/112, Head to Grey, May 2, 1850.
31. *Ibid.*, confidential.
32. P.R.O., C.O. 188/113, Head to Grey, November 6, 1850.
33. P.R.O., C.O. 188/114, Head to Grey, with enclosures, January 10, February 15, 1852.
34. P.A.C., Series A, Colebrooke to Gladstone, February 26, 1846.
35. This marks the disappearance of Baillie from the New Brunswick scene. He retired to England but continued to press his claims upon the British government consequent to the obligations made to him by Lord Bathurst in 1823-4. In 1856 the Colonial Office supplemented his New Brunswick pension of £500 by £250. His last known address was 10, St. Germain's Terrace, Blackheath. (See *Summary of the Case of Mr. Thomas Baillie*, London, undated, printed by G.Prince, Strand. A copy of this pamphlet is to be found in the Colonial Office Library. A summary of his case in 1854 is in P.R.O., C.O. 188/123.)
36. *Miramichi Gleaner*, March 15, May 3, 10, June 7, 1852, January 10, 1853.
37. House of assembly synoptic debates, March 1, 1854.
38. P.R.O., C.O. 188/118, Head to Pakenham, December 16, 1852, separate and confidential.

39. J.F.W. Johnston, *Notes on North America*, vol. 1, London, 1851, p. 55.
40. P.R.O., C.O. 188/110, Head to Grey, with enclosures, September 7, 1849.
41. *Ibid.*, Head to Grey, July 15, 1849.
42. House of assembly synoptic debates, speech of J.M. Johnson, April 5, 1854.
43. House of assembly synoptic debates, April 5, 1854.
44. P.R.O., C.O. 188/116, Head to Pakenham, April 8, 1852.
45. House of assembly synoptic debates, April 10, 1854.
46. For an exhaustive account of the relationship between the temperance movements in Maine and New Brunswick see J.K.Chapman, 'The Mid-Nineteenth Century Temperance Movements in New Brunswick and Maine', *Canadian Historical Review*, March, 1954.

CHAPTER 14

1. *Debate in the House of Assembly on Mr. Fisher's Amendment to the 5th Paragraph of the Address in Reply to the Speech from the Throne*, T. Hill, Fredericton, 1854.
2. P.R.O., C.O. 188/124, Manners-Sutton to Grey, June 8, 1855.
3. *Debate in the House . . .*, p. 45.
4. In November 1855 the government was increased to nine members by the addition of David Wark of Richibucto and Charles Watters, a barrister of Saint John.
5. P.R.O., C.O. 188/124, Manners-Sutton to Russell, May 14, 1855.
6. P.R.O., C.O. 188/132, Manners-Sutton to Lytton, March 3, 1859.
7. P.R.O., C.O. 188/125, Manners-Sutton to Russell, July 4, 1855.
8. P.R.O., C.O. 188/124, Russell to Manners-Sutton, November 28, 1855.
9. Synoptic debates, 1856 (extra session), speeches of John Boyd, July 19, and Hugh McMonagle, July 21.
10. P.R.O., C.O. 188/126, Manners-Sutton to Labouchere, May 31, 1856, and June 13, 1856, private with enclosures.
11. Minute of Manners-Sutton to Labouchere, May 31, 1856.
12. Synoptic debates, July 19, 1856.
13. *Ibid.*, speech by Chas. Hatheway.
14. *Ibid.*, July 21, 1856.
15. *Ibid.*, February 23, 24, 1857.
16. *Ibid.*, February 24, 1855, Fisher's address.
17. P.R.O., C.O. 188/124, Manners-Sutton to Grey, February 24, 1855; and 188/125, Manners-Sutton to Russell, with enclosures, October 16, 1855.
18. P.R.O., C.O. 188/124, Manners-Sutton to Grey, with enclosures, January 19, 1855.
19. See house of assembly journals, April 2, 1856.
20. P.R.O., C.O. 188/126, Manners-Sutton to Labouchere, November 24, 1856.
21. Synoptic debates, March 22, 1858.
22. *Ibid.*, February 12, 1858.
23. P.R.O., C.O. 188/125, Minute of Manners-Sutton to Russell, October 30, 1856.
24. *Ibid.*, Manners-Sutton to Labouchere, November 24, 1856; and 188/127. March 3, August 24, 1857, with enclosures.
25. *Ibid.*, Manners-Sutton to Russell, with enclosure, June 27, 1855.
26. P.R.O., C.O. 188/126, Manners-Sutton to Labouchere, with enclosures, September 30, 1856.
27. Saint John *Morning News*, April 25, 1856.
28. Synoptic debates, February 27, 1858.
29. *Ibid.*, remarks of the Speaker, March 9, 1858.
30. *Ibid.*, March 5, 9, 1858.
31. P.R.O., C.O. 188/131, Manners-Sutton to Stanley, July 28, 1858, private and confidential.
32. *Ibid.*, Manners-Sutton to Blackwood, October 30, 1858, private.
33. P.R.O., C.O. 188/133, Manners-Sutton to Newcastle, October 13, 1860; and 188/134, April 24, 1861, with minutes of the senate of the university and other enclosures.

34. P.R.O., C.O. 188/139, Miss Jacob to Newcastle, December 21, 1863. According to this letter all of Jacob's property was in the hands of the sheriff. A minute of Frederic Rogers to an earlier letter of January 6 declares there was every evidence that Jacob was 'an obstinate, inefficient person'.
35. P.R.O., C.O. 188/131, Manners-Sutton to Stanley, April 17, 1858.
36. P.R.O., C.O. 188/132, Manners-Sutton to Lytton, with minutes, March 1, 1858.
37. P.R.O., C.O. 188/133, Manners-Sutton to Newcastle, with enclosures, May 28, 1860.
38. Synoptic debates, March 19, 1861, speech of solicitor-general.
39. P.R.O., C.O. 188/133, Manners-Sutton to Newcastle, November 22, 1859.
40. *Ibid.*, Manners-Sutton to Newcastle, with C.O. minutes, March 5, 1860.
41. *Ibid.*, Manners-Sutton to Newcastle, September 19, 1860.
42. *Ibid.*, Manners-Sutton to Newcastle, October 24, 1860 with enclosure.
43. P.R.O., C.O. 188/125, Manners-Sutton to Russell, July 14, 1855.
44. P.R.O., C.O. 188/132, Manners-Sutton to Lytton, June 25, 1859.
45. P.R.O., C.O. 188/132, Manners-Sutton to Stanley, December 1, 1859; and 188/133 Manners-Sutton to Newcastle, January 20, 23, August 20, 1860, all with enclosures.
46. Synoptic debates, March 19, 20, 1860. Knighthood was very much in the wind in 1860. 'Our members have scattered all over creation, three of them gone to Canada after the Prince of Wales, sure, no doubt, in the hope of being knighted. I wish the Prince could make honest men of them all, but that, I fear, is more than he can do.' (Surveyor-General James Brown to his son, August 26, 1860, U.N.B. Arch., Maxwell Coll.)
47. P.R.O., C.O. 188/133, Manners-Sutton to Newcastle, with enclosures, December 24, 1860.
48. P.R.O., C.O. 188/131, Manners-Sutton to Blackwood, October 30, 1858, private.
49. *Debate in the House of Assembly on Mr. Fisher's Amendment*, p. 76.
50. P.R.O., C.O. 188/132, Manners-Sutton to Lytton, March 3, April 2, 1859. In several opinions that were not acted upon, Manners-Sutton recommended Edward Barron Chandler, the most influential politician in opposition to the government, and William Black, who had administered the province in 1831-2. In his early days Black was a leader in the commercial community of Saint John, but he had lost his fortune in the timber trade. In 1859 he was in his eighty-fifth year and had for a long time been president of the legislative council.
51. The pros and cons for the government's decision are to be found in P.R.O., C.O. 188/125, Manners-Sutton to Grey, with minutes of council and Manners-Sutton's memoranda attached.
52. These were for £43,200. The balance of £46,800 was to be provided in thirty-year debentures of the province at six per cent.
53. P.R.O., C.O. 188/130, Manners-Sutton to Lytton, December 28, 1857, with Tupper's letter attached.
54. Synoptic debates, 1858, speeches of L.DesBrisay, March 17, and Jas.Tibbits, March 19.
55. P.R.O., C.O. 188/130, Manners-Sutton to Labouchere, August 10, 1857.
56. *Ibid.*, Manners-Sutton to Stanley, with C.O. minutes, September 29, 1858, private and confidential.
57. P.R.O., C.O. 188/116, Head to Pakington, April 26, May 6, 1852. Pakington to Head, with enclosures, September 25, 1852.
58. P.R.O., C.O. 188/124, Manners-Sutton to Russell, June 27, 1855.
59. P.R.O., C.O. 188/133, Manners-Sutton to Newcastle on transmitting the Blue Book, December 31, 1860.
60. P.R.O., C.O. 188/137, Captain Thrupp to Milne, May 22, 1862.
61. P.R.O., C.O. 188/131, Stanley to Manners-Sutton to Russell, with enclosures, May 14, 1855.
62. P.R.O., C.O. 188/124, Manners-Sutton to Russell, with enclosures, May 14, 1855.
63. House of assembly journals, March 26, 1858. C.O. 188/131, Manners-Sutton to

Stanley, September 28, 1858, two dispatches – one private and confidential.

64. Synoptic debates, March 8, 1858.
65. *Ibid.*, February 26, 1861.
66. Appendix to legislative journals of 1861, evidence taken before the select committee.
67. Synoptic debates, March 18, 1861.
68. P.R.O., C.O. 188/134, Manners-Sutton to Newcastle, March 19, April 27, 1861, with enclosures.
69. *Freeman*, April 16, 1861.
70. N.B.Mus., R.P.Starr to W.M.Jarvis, April 15, 1861.

CHAPTER 15

1. P.R.O., C.O. 188/124, Manners-Sutton to Russell, with enclosures, June 12, 1855.
2. P.R.O., C.O. 188/131, Manners-Sutton to Stanley, with enclosures, September 29, 1858.
3. These very speculative points of view, on the highest political level, are set forth in P.R.O., C.O. 188/131, Manners-Sutton to Stanley, September 29, October 2, confidential; and to Lytton, October 11, 1858, confidential. One eminent authority has implied that Manners-Sutton was so warm and vigorous in his views upon Maritime union that he succeeded in imposing them upon members of his government. (See W.M.Whitelaw, *The Maritimes and Canada before Confederation*, Toronto, 1934, p. 129.) Considering the history of almost chronic disagreement between Manners-Sutton and the Smashers, the implication might seem to be too strongly stated.
4. Synoptic debates, March 26, 1858.
5. P.R.O., C.O. 188/132, Manners-Sutton to Newcastle, September 29, 1859.
6. A.H.Gordon, *Wilderness Journeys in New Brunswick*, Saint John, 1864, p. 5.
7. Synoptic debates, legislative council, April 16, 1862.
8. P.R.O., C.O. 188/136, Gordon to Newcastle, February 15, 1862.
9. *Ibid.*
10. Gordon, *op. cit.*, pp. 42-3.
11. P.R.O., C.O. 188/136, Gordon to Newcastle, March 31, 1862.
12. P.R.O., C.O. 188/140, Gordon to Newcastle, March 14, 1864.
13. H.M.Davis, *An International Community on the St. Croix*, pp. 191-2.
14. For a fairly full account of the *Chesapeake* adventure see N.S.Hist.Soc.Coll., 1951, Dr. George Cox, *Sidelights on the Chesapeake Affair.*
15. P.R.O., C.O. 188/140, Gordon to Newcastle, with report of Wetmore, March 29, 1864.
16. *Ibid.*, Gordon to Newcastle, with minutes, March 28, 1864.
17. P.R.O., C.O. 188/138, Gordon to Newcastle, July 20, 1863.
18. P.R.O., C.O. 188/141, Gordon to Cardwell, November 21, 1864.
19. P.R.O., C.O. 188/143, Gordon to Newcastle, January 2, February 8, 27, 1865.
20. P.R.O., C.O. 188/141, Cole to Cardwell, August 1, 1864 with enclosures.
21. P.R.O., C.O. 188/144, Gordon to Cardwell, December 31, 1865.
22. For a full account see F. W. Wallace, *Wooden Ships and Iron Men*, London, 1924; and Louise Manny, *Ships of the Miramichi*, Saint John, 1961.
23. Synoptic debates, legislative council, March 27, April 5, 1862, debate on the Lumber Facility Bill.
24. H.Reid, *The American Crisis*, London, 1861.
25. These pronounced and unfavourable views are to be found in P.R.O., C.O. 188/137, Gordon to Newcastle, December 31, 1862.
26. P.R.O., C.O. 188/138, Gordon to Newcastle, April 13, 1862.
27. P.R.O., C.O. 188/137, Gordon to Newcastle, December 31, 1862.
28. *Freeman*, March 8, 1864.
29. P.R.O., C.O. 188/136, Gordon to Newcastle, April 14, 1862, two dispatches – one confidential.
30. P.R.O., C.O. 188/138, Gordon to Newcastle, April 13, June 23, 1863.

31. P.R.O., C.O. 188/137, Gordon to Newcastle, November 10, 1862. Ultimately the men were paid. The reason for delay of payment was that the only available asset of the contractors consisted of bonds of the railway company. Since the contractors were hoping that these would appreciate they did not wish to liquidate them at this time.
32. E.W.Watkin, *Canada and the States*, London, 1887, p. 3.
33. P.R.O., C.O. 188/137, Gordon to Newcastle, August 18, September 1; Newcastle to Gordon, September 22, 1862, with enclosures and minutes.
34. P.R.O., C.O. 188/139, Gordon to Newcastle, November 9, 1863, confidential, with a report of a conversation between Tilley and John Sandfield Macdonald.
35. *Ibid.*, Gordon to Newcastle, with enclosure, November 23, 1863.
36. Quoted in A.G.Bailey, 'Railways and the Confederation Issue in New Brunswick', *Canadian Historical Review*, December 1940. This article, which stresses the importance of Western Extension as a factor in the making of opinion on Confederation, gives a fuller account of the railway tensions at work in the province.
37. P.R.O., C.O. 188/140, Gordon to Newcastle, February 1, 1864, with newspaper clippings.
38. *Ibid.*, Gordon to Newcastle, with enclosures, March 1, 1864.

CHAPTER 16

1. Gordon's account of the development of the idea of Maritime union is to be found in his dispatches of December 31, 1862, July 6, August 29, September 28, December 7, 1863 (P.R.O., 188/137-9). For an exhaustive treatment of the negotiations in which all three provinces were concerned see W.M. Whitelaw, *The Maritimes and Canada before Confederation*, Toronto, 1934.
2. P.R.O., C.O. 188/141, Gordon to Cardwell, September 12, 1864.
3. *Ibid.*, Gordon to Cardwell, October 11, November 7, 1864.
4. The story of the Quebec Conference is told in great detail in Whitelaw, Chapter 11; and D.G. Creighton, *John A. Macdonald, the Young Politician*, Chapter 13.
5. P.R.O., C.O. 188/143, Gordon to Cardwell, January 30, 1865, with report of the final meeting. Later attempts to resurrect Maritime union, by Tupper and Howe of Nova Scotia, made no progress.
6. Hannay hints at this darkly. Creighton makes the suggestion in the form of a rhetorical question. At the Colonial Office Mr. Secretary Cardwell acquired suspicions concerning Gordon's motives because the lieutenant-governor made no secret of his distaste for the details of the Quebec plan. Gordon was reproved for his forthright statement of views, but after the British government made known its intention to support the Quebec plan whole-heartedly there was little reason to complain about the manner in which he put his instructions into effect. (For a full account see J.K.Chapman, 'Arthur Gordon and Confederation', *Canadian Historical Review*, June 1956.)
7. P.R.O., C.O. 188/143, Gordon to Cardwell, with newspaper clippings, February 9, 1865. Great division existed in the cabinet on the issue of the dissolution forced by Gordon. Hatheway declared in his nomination speech of February 24 that if he had not resigned Tilley would not have dissolved. (Fredericton *Headquarters*, March 1, 1865.) Another view was that the majority of the cabinet supported Gordon, that the vote was 5-4 in favour, Tilley being in the minority. (*Globe*, October 10, 1865, letter signed by 'Ivan'.)
8. Fredericton *Headquarters*, February 1, 1865, quoted in A.G.Bailey, 'The Basis and Persistence of Opposition to Confederation in New Brunswick', *Canadian Historical Review*, December 1942.
9. Creighton, pp. 404-5.
10. Legislative council debates, May 17, 1865.
11. *Telegraph*, March 6, 1865.
12. Tilley to William Parks, March 15, 1865, a letter in possession of L.M.Bell, Saint John.

13. *Telegraph*, April 5, 1865.
14. P.R.O., C.O. 188/143, Gordon to Cardwell, February 9, 1865.
15. *Ibid.*, Gordon to Cardwell, May 8, 1865, confidential.
16. It may be fair at this stage to call Cudlip an annexationist. In 1868 he was the author of annexationist resolutions in the house of assembly. (See Hannay, vol. 2, p. 286.)
17. P.R.O., C.O. 188/143, Gordon to Cardwell, with enclosure, July 15, 1865.
18. See Chapman, *op. cit.*
19. P.R.O., C.O. 188/143, Gordon to Cardwell, May 22, 1865, confidential.
20. U.N.B.Arch., Maxwell Coll., Jas.Brown to A.H.Gillmore, October 1, 1865.
21. *Telegraph*, October 3, 1865.
22. Jas.Brown, *op. cit.*
23. This contest is described in some detail in Bailey, 'Basis and Persistence of Opposition', *op. cit.*
24. Creighton, p. 424.
25. P.R.O., C.O. 188/144, Gordon to Cardwell, December 4, 1865, confidential.
26. P.R.O., C.O. 188/145, Gordon to Cardwell, with enclosure, January 15, 1866.
27. *Ibid.*, Gordon to Cardwell, with Smith's report, February 21, 1866.
28. *Daily Evening Globe*, January 2, 1868, speech delivered by Smith at Saint John. While in Washington Smith created the general impression that he would oppose Confederation.
29. E.H. Greaves, 'Peter Mitchell', an unpublished thesis for the Master's degree at the University of New Brunswick, 1958.
30. P.R.O., C.O. 188/145, Gordon to Cardwell, February 21, 1866.
31. *Ibid.*, Gordon to Cardwell, March 25, 1866.
32. *Ibid.*, Gordon to Cardwell, with enclosures, April 18, 1866.
33. *Ibid.*, Gordon to Cardwell, with newspaper enclosures, March 25, 1866.
34. Annand to Smith, March 20, 1866, printed in Halifax *Morning Chronicle*, March 2, 1869 (by courtesy of Prof. P. B. Waite).
35. George Stewart, *Canada under the Administration of Lord Dufferin*, Toronto, 1879, pp. 240-1.
36. Greaves, *op. cit.* This anecdote is credited to Senator G.P.Burchill of South Nelson.
37. P.R.O., C.O. 188/145, Gordon to Cardwell, April 15, 1866, with C.O. minutes.
38. *Ibid.*, with enclosures.
39. N.B.Mus., Tilley Papers, box 4, R.L.Hanington to Tilley, April 19, 1866.
40. Thomas McKenzie, *My Life as a Soldier*, Saint John, 1898, p. 149.
41. P.R.O., C.O. 188/145, Gordon to Cardwell, with enclosures, June 4, 1866.
42. P.R.O., C.O. 188/146, Gordon to Cardwell, July 2, 1866.
43. Quoted in *Telegraph*, March 3, 1866.
44. P.R.O., C.O. 188/145, Gordon to Cardwell, June 4, 1866, with newspaper enclosures.
45. Creighton, pp. 434-5. See also G.E.Wilson, 'New Brunswick's Entrance into Confederation', *Canadian Historical Review*, March 1928.
46. *Telegraph*, June 4, 1866.
47. House of assembly debates, March 7, 1862.
48. Creighton, pp. 444-50.
49. Joseph Pope, *Confederation Documents*, Toronto, 1895, p. 121.
50. This important question of nomenclature has been given remarkably little attention. From 1864 to 1866 it was not completely taken for granted that the new Dominion would be called Canada. (See Creighton, p. 459.)
51. Tilley's authorship of the title, credited to him by his admirers in Saint John, has not, to the knowledge of the author, been denied.
52. Creighton, p. 472.
53. Corroboration of this opinion may be obtained from the work of a contemporary poet. (See Fred Cogswell, *The Stunted Strong*, Fredericton, 1954.)
54. From *Journal de Québec*, quoted in *Telegraph*, February 11, 1868.

Bibliographic Note

Manuscript sources for the history of the colonial period in New Brunswick are far better than might be supposed. The official correspondence, housed in the Public Record Office and the Public Archives of Canada, for the most part supplies an adequate basis from which to work. Only during the period from 1801 to 1810, when the colonies were ruled by the War Office, does continuity fail. Unfortunately there are few private collections available to help fill the gap.

Though there are no provincial archives, there are three institutions actively engaged in archival work. The Legislative Library at Fredericton keeps in good order a great many legislative papers, chiefly reports of committees and estimates of public accounts. The New Brunswick Museum at Saint John contains several fine collections, notably the Odell, Ward, and Chipman, that were most helpful for this work. The University of New Brunswick Library, the home of the Winslow Collection, contains a great variety of manuscript source materials. Following the completion of this history, the Saunders Collection was brought to this library. From it several additions were made to the book, but not all of them are footnoted.

The historian of New Brunswick must ever be grateful to the small group of citizens of Saint John who made up the nucleus of membership in the New Brunswick Historical Society during the first ten years of the present century. They not only collected and preserved original documents but wrote copiously as well. In addition to their reports they produced the *Winslow Papers* (ed. W. O. Raymond, 1901), *Acadiensis* (1901-8), and the *New Brunswick Magazine* (1898-1900). All of these, as well as the works of Dr. W. F. Ganong, have made the first three chapters of the book as much a task of careful selection as a search for new material.

No attempt is made to list the immense number of books, articles and other printed material from which this book is in part derived.

Particularly in cases of novel or controversial points the author has cited his authorities in the notes. It is proper, however, to designate the works on which he has depended a great deal:

Burrage, H. S.: *Maine in the Northeastern Boundary Controversy.* Printed for the State, Portland, 1919.

Campbell, P.: *Travels in the Interior, Inhabited Parts of British North America in the Years 1790 and 1792.* Reprinted for the Champlain Society, Toronto, 1937.

Creighton, D. G.: *John A. Macdonald, the Young Politician.* Macmillan Company of Canada, Toronto, 1952.

Davis, H. A.: *An International Community on the St. Croix.* University of Maine Press, Orono, 1950.

Fenety, G. E.: *Political Notes.* S. R. Miller, Fredericton, 1867.

Hannay, J.: *History of New Brunswick* (2 vols.). Bowes, Saint John, 1909.

Harper, J. R.: *Historical Dictionary of New Brunswick Newspapers and Periodicals.* University of New Brunswick, Fredericton, 1961.

Kerr, D. G. G.: *Sir Edmund Head, a Scholarly Governor.* University of Toronto Press, Toronto, 1954.

Lawrence, J. W.: *Footprints or Incidents in the Early History of New Brunswick.* J. and A. MacMillan, Saint John, 1883.
   The Judges of New Brunswick and Their Times (ed. A. A. Stockton). *Acadiensis*, Saint John, 1907.

MacFarlane, W. G.: *New Brunswick Bibliography, the Books and Writers of the Province.* Sun Printing Company, Saint John, 1895.

MacNaughton, K. F. C.: *The Development of the Theory and Practice of Education in New Brunswick, 1784-1900.* University of New Brunswick, Fredericton, 1947.

Whitelaw, W. M.: *The Maritimes and Canada before Confederation.* Oxford, Toronto, 1934.

Wright, E. C.: *The Loyalists of New Brunswick.* Published by the author, Fredericton, 1955.

Index

Date